MW01479816

PROFESSING ENGLISH
A Life of Roy Daniells

Professing English

A Life of Roy Daniells

SANDRA DJWA

UNIVERSITY OF TORONTO PRESS
Toronto Buffalo London

© University of Toronto Press Incorporated 2002
Toronto Buffalo London
Printed in Canada

ISBN 0-8020-4770-X

Printed on acid-free paper

National Library of Canada Cataloguing in Publication Data

Djwa, Sandra, 1939–
    Professing English : a life of Roy Daniells

    Includes bibliographical references and index.
    ISBN 0-8020-4770-X

    1. Daniells, Roy   2. English teachers – British Columbia –
    Vancouver – Biography.   3. University of British Columbia.
    Faculty – Biography.   4. English literature – Study and teaching
    (Higher) – British Columbia – Vancouver – History.   I. Title.

    PR55.D35D58 2001   810.9   C2001-902226-3

The lines from T.S. Eliot's 'Ash-Wednesday' and 'La Figlia che Piange' are
reprinted with the permission of Faber and Faber and Harcourt, Inc.

University of Toronto Press acknowledges the financial assistance to its
publishing program of the Canada Council for the Arts and the Ontario
Arts Council.

This book has been published with the help of a grant from the Humanities
and Social Sciences Federation of Canada, using funds provided by the
Social Sciences and Humanities Research Council of Canada.

University of Toronto Press acknowledges the financial support for its
publishing activities of the Government of Canada through the Book
Publishing Industry Development Program (BPIDP).

To my husband, Lalit Srivastava

Contents

University of British Columbia: 1960–1970

Vancouver: 1970–1979

Illustrations follow page 220

Acknowledgments

This biography could not have been written without the help of many individuals, especially Laurenda Daniells, widow of Roy Daniells and University Archivist Emerita at University of British Columbia, who archived her husband's papers, participated in interviews, and provided generous and thoughtful assistance throughout the last eight years. I am indebted to Joan Givner, for her vision and good advice, to W.J. Keith, for his astute reading of the near final manuscript, and to Margery Fee, Elliott and Kathy Gose, and F.W. Watt for help of various kinds. My thanks, as always, to my husband, Lalit Srivastava, for his continued help and encouragement. Financial support for this book was provided by the Social Sciences and Humanities Research Council of Canada, by the Simon Fraser University President's Research Grant Fund, and by the Simon Fraser Dean of Arts Fund.

Colleagues of Roy Daniells at the University of British Columbia, and his friends and acquaintances across the country, have taken part in interviews, read drafts of the manuscript in part or in whole, or answered questions regarding individuals and conditions at four universities: for this and other assistance, I would like to thank Alan Adamson, Robert and Ruth apRoberts, Margaret Avison, R.G. and Frances Baker, Roger Bishop, Claude Bissell, Michael Booth, Mrs E.K. Brown, Frank Davey, Jan de Bruyn, Gwladys Downes, Daryl Duke, Chester Duncan, Robert Finch, Fred Flahiff, George and Patricia Ford, William Fredeman, Janet Friskney, Carole Gerson, Mary Ann Gillies, Janet Giltrow, Barbara Godard, Sherrill Grace, Mildred (Shanas) Gutkin, A.C. Hamilton, Peter Howarth, John Hulcoop, Robert Jordan, Hugh MacCallum, Ingrid and Manfred Mackauer, Murdo MacKinnon, Jean Mallinson, Kay Mark,

Ruth McConnell, Patricia Merivale, Craig Miller, Edward Morrison, W.H. and Margaret New, Philip Pinkus, Grosvenor Powell, Allan Pritchard, Laurie Ricou, William Robbins, Ian Ross, Malcolm Ross, Jane Rule, Jack Shadbolt, Ernest Sirluck, Helen Sontoff, Paul Stanwood, M.W. Steinberg, D.G. Stephens, Fred Stockholder, David Stouck, Basil Stuart-Stubbs, Walter Sudmant, Walter Swayze, Ellen Tallman, Hilda Thomas, Ogden Turner, George Volkoff, Ruth (Schlass)Waldfogel, Sheila and Wilfred Watson, Phyllis Webb, Eve Whittaker, and George Woodcock. Interviews conducted prior to the start of this project with Roy Daniells, Earle Birney, Northrop Frye, and Carl F. Klinck have also been incorporated into the text.

The staff of the University of British Columbia Library Special Collections Division have been exceptionally helpful, especially Anne Yandle, the former Head, Chris Hives, Archivist, George Brandak, Manuscripts Curator, Joan Selby, former Colbeck Librarian, and Frances Woodward, Map Librarian. At Simon Fraser University, I have especially appreciated the help of Heather-Ann Tingley, Head of the Woodsworth Collection, and Jack Corse, Reference Librarian; at the Fisher Rare Book Room, University of Toronto, I am indebted to the Chief Librarian, Richard Landon, and staff members Edna Hajnal and Albert Masters, who have been very helpful in tracking references and individuals; and at the Victoria University Library, I would like to thank Robert Brandeis, Chief Librarian, Lisa Sherlock, Head of Reader Services, and former Librarian, Lila Laakso. I owe special thanks also to John H. Lutman, Head of the James Alexander and Ellen Rea Benson Special Collections at the University of Western Ontario, who helped search for correspondence of Carl F. Klinck; as well as to Anne Goddard, Achivist with the Canadian Archives Branch, and Michael McDonald of the Researcher Services Division of the National Archives of Canada for similar assistance.

Many individuals have been involved in the gathering of information for this book and the task of putting it together. Perry L. Millar, now with the University of Saskatoon, saw the book almost to completion; her research and indexing skills helped establish the initial structure of this biography. Undergraduate SFU students Chris Turnbull and Jason Le Heup were largely responsible for transcribing documents and the computer entry of letters, diaries, and interviews; Monica Meyer and Brian Saunders assisted with occasional library research and computer entry, as did graduates Rachel Friederich, Kerry Griffin, Nadine Nickull, Helen Takala, and Firouzeh Vaziri. In addition, Yaying Zhang read an early draft of the Preface. Anita Mahoney, of the Dean of

Arts Office, kindly advised on computer entry of the final manuscript. I am grateful to the late Frances Hord, who began the task of transcribing Daniells' diaries, and to Dorothy Chala, whose efficient secretarial skills and unfailing good humour have helped to bring this book to completion. Jean Wilson of University of British Columbia Press provided early advice, and the editorial staff of University of Toronto Press, Gerald Hallowell, Jill McConkey, Siobhan McMenemy, Frances Mundy, and Ken Lewis, have been unfailingly helpful, as has Barbara Schon, who prepared the index.

Above all, I would like to express my gratitude to the more than seventy individuals, many listed previously or in the Notes, who took part in taped interviews, and shared their knowledge, photographs, and anecdotes of Roy Daniells for the purposes of this publication. Acknowledgment for permission to publish from correspondence and books is gratefully made to the following individuals:

Alan H. Adamson
G.P.V. Akrigg
Bob and Ruth apRoberts (for Garnett Sedgewick)
Margaret Avison
Glennis Baker (for Sinclair Ross)
Ron Baker and Frances (Frazer) Baker
Mary Elizabeth Bayer
Esther Birney
Roger Bishop
Michael Booth
Margaret Brown (for E.K. Brown)
John Chant (for Sperrin Chant)
Jane Conway (for Pelham Edgar)
Jan de Bruyn
Gwladys Downes
Elfrieda Duerksen (for David Duerksen)
Chester Duncan
David Easton (for Sylvia Johnstone Easton)
Lady Margaret Elton (Margaret Bjornson)

Ann Falconer and Jane Knowles (for Herbert Davis)
Robert Finch and Colin Friesen (for Robert Finch)
Fred Flahiff (for Sheila Watson)
Patricia Ford (for George Ford)
W.E. Fredeman
William Goodwin (for Irving Layton)
Mildred (Sanas) Gutkin
A.C. Hamilton
Alan Hockin
Peter Howarth
George Johnston
W.J. Keith
David Klinck (for Carl F. Klinck)
Steve Lawson (for Eugenia [Watts] Lawson)
Richard A. Levin
Wailan Low (for Earle Birney)
Marigold Lyall (for Mabel Mackenzie)
Hugh MacCallum (for A.S.P. Woodhouse)
John McDonald

Leith (Ferguson) Macdonald
Jay Macpherson
Corinne McLuhan and Estate
  (for Marshall McLuhan)
Jean Mallinson
Ann Mandel (for Eli Mandel)
Jim Manly
Kay Mark (for Carson Mark)
Rona Maynard (for Fredelle
  Bruser Maynard and Max
  Maynard)
Craig Miller
Edward Morrison
Mary Pacey (for Desmond
  Pacey)
Jack Parnell
J. Max Patrick
Lyall Power
Allan Pritchard
James Reaney
Kay Riddell-Rouillard (for
  Gerald Riddell)

Frances (Aikens) Riley
Peter Robbins (for William
  Robbins)
Malcolm Ross
Jane Rule
Roseann Runte (for Northrop
  Frye Estate)
Doris Saunders
Jack Shadbolt
Paul Stanwood
M.W. Steinberg
Ellen Tallman (for Warren
  Tallman)
Hilda Thomas
William Toye (for A.J.M. Smith)
Ogden Turner
Ruth (Schlass) Waldfogel
F.W. Watt
Phyllis Webb
David Williams
Mary Winspear

PROFESSING ENGLISH

As I walk'd through the wilderness of this world, I lighted on a certain place where was a Den, and I laid me down in that place to sleep; and as I slept I dreamed a Dream. I Dreamed, and behold I saw a man clothed with Rags, standing in a certain place, with his face from his own house, a Book in his hand, and a great Burden upon his back. I looked, and saw him open the Book, and read therein; and as he read, he wept and trembled; and not being able longer to contain, he brake out with a lamentable cry, saying, What shall I do?

I looked then, and saw a Man named Evangelist, coming to him, and asked, Wherefore dost thou cry? He answered, Sir, I perceive by the Book in my hand, that I am condemned to die, and after that come to Judgment.

John Bunyan, *The Pilgrim's Progress*

Prologue

The young man sitting in the sun near the Rothschild tomb in the Cimetière du Père-Lachaise wore a beret like a Parisian, but he was clearly not French – his grey flannels suggested an Englishman, perhaps a colonial, come to see Paris. Thin and broad-shouldered, he had a long bony face with bright blue eyes, just now bent towards long tapering fingers that held a pen and a writing pad. As he wrote, he looked up at the tombs surrounding him, then began to write again: 'Are the majority of these orthodox Jews really now in torment, and as I go home and sit in the Metro, are they still writhing in the eternal flame and gnawed by the undying worm?'

The young man was Roy Daniells. It was summer 1932 and he was writing to his parents in Canada about the Plymouth Brethren belief that all persons who had not accepted Christ as their saviour were condemned to eternal hellfire on the Day of Judgment. This his parents believed and so did he. That is, he had believed this doctrine until now. But away from his friends, 'not in a Protestant country, not in a hot [Plymouth Brethren] Hall ... nor in Toronto, stupefied with work and worry and pains,' he felt suddenly free. He had come to the most important conclusion of his life: 'the Brethren have made a hideous mistake somehow.' This mistake was a doctrine that he felt had eroded his sanity for over twenty years, the belief that all people who were not saved in terms set out by the Brethren were damned, that even at this minute the Jews buried in the Père-Lachaise cemetery were 'turning in torment, crying for water and gnashing their teeth.'[1]

In the past the horrors of this doctrine, which he accepted quite literally, had made it a struggle just to retain his sanity. Like Bunyan's Christian, Daniells carried a large burden on his back – a terror of hellfire and damnation. When still a child, he had been convinced that at the end of a period of time set out in the Bible, the Millennium, God would choose between the saved and the damned. Then he, with all the other unbelievers, would be flung into hell. Although now an adult, and on the Continent to complete his Ph.D. in English, he could not shake off these fears. He recognized: 'I may have to change my whole policy shortly to avoid a break up of some sort.'[2]

Two years later, in Toronto in 1934, the problem was still unresolved. His father was urging him to return to the Plymouth Brethren Assembly, but he knew he could not: 'If I were to deliberately start the prayer-Bible-meetings life I should be in the old pit of horrors in no time.' As he told his parents, it was no longer a matter of choice. 'It's of no use quoting Scripture or telling me to return to "the old paths." We have to deal with simple plain facts here on earth.' Now at the end of his tether, he reminded his parents of his successive mental and emotional breakdowns: 'remember what has happened at Penticton, D'Arcy, Duncan, Genoa Bay, Cook Street, and Chorley Wood – a series of wretched religious manias and fevers. And then tell me WHAT DO YOU WANT ME TO DO?'[3]

What Daniells did – as opposed to what his family wanted him to do – was to reject a religious calling and continue with a literary calling. An acutely sensitive man, he struggled against religious dogma all his life to follow the path leading from the hellfire of the Brethren to the broader (and cooler) avenues of the Anglican *via media* which he found in some of the poetry and prose of the seventeenth century. In his study of Milton, he discovered a context for the extreme beliefs of his family, those of the dissenting Puritans. In later years, his lectures on Milton and English Metaphysical poetry were deepened by his personal understanding of the Protestant search for salvation, now linked with the search for self. Throughout his career as a professor of English, Daniells convinced four generations of students that literature, and the larger truths that it expressed, really mattered. As he once said of one of his own professors, Garnett Sedgewick: 'He gave us the means of grace and the hope of glory, in an intellectual sense. He made us see that learning is difficult and literature, to which it gives access, a ravishing delight.'[4]

Although Daniells' religious background was more extreme than most, a number of individuals associated with the humanities in Canada between the 1920s and the 1960s were either ordained clerics or the children of clerics. Among this group was the poet Charles G.D. Roberts; Lorne Pierce, the chief publisher of Canadian poetry; poets or critics such as Margaret Avison, Northrop Frye, Desmond Pacey, E.J. Pratt, and F.R. Scott; and public figures such as W.A. Irwin, Lester B. Pearson, and J.S. Woodsworth. Others, like Daniells himself and Carl F. Klinck, founding editor of the *Literary History of Canada* (1965), had been expected by their parents to enter some form of the ministry. A.S.P. Woodhouse, for many years Head of the graduate program in English at the University of Toronto, was characterized by Daniells as a 'Christian whose secular avocation is academic.'[5] What this seems to imply is that he, like many of these individuals, brought to the teaching of English some of the same moral passion that had formerly characterized the teaching of religion.

For young men of modest circumstances, training for the clergy was often a means of obtaining an education: these close ties between religion and education reflect the history of the university. The early universities of Paris and Oxford, founded at the start of the thirteenth century by the Bishop of Paris, were monastic institutions of learning from which women were shortly after excluded as masters or students by a papal bull.[6] Subsequently, the seventeenth-century term 'Professor' referred to an individual who professed, or made an open declaration of belief in the Scriptures and faith in Christ. From this definition comes the present-day description of a professor as one who professes or publicly teaches in any branch of learning at a university. In the late nineteenth century, clerics were frequently the primary candidates for professorships in classics and English.

As Gerald Graff reminds us in *Professing Literature: An Institutional History* (1987), religion was secularized in the modernist professing of literature, especially after Matthew Arnold's North American tour in 1883.[7] Arnold's definition of the cultural and moral values of studying literature ('culture, the acquainting ourselves with the best that has been known and said in the world, and thus with the history of the human spirit') strongly influenced the Canadian university.[8] A.B. McKillop has pointed out the importance of Arnoldian idealism in the last quarter of the nineteenth century when evangelical Christianity was challenged by the rise of historical relativism and a liberal ethical education:

> Paralleling this was the remarkable rise of English as a major academic discipline dedicated to the study and criticism of literature and concerned with culture. For some, as will be seen, it became a surrogate religion, fulfilling deep psychological and ideological needs met in the past by Christianity. Exactly when the 'timeless' values of religion were being brought to earth and placed within history rather than beyond it, professors of English emerged as apostles of a new discipline that promised moral transcendence in the form of the universality of literary culture.[9]

As Patricia Jasen had earlier remarked, in a secular system aimed at instructing large numbers of students, Canadian professors of English argued that 'men of culture must assume responsibility for providing the moral guidance and training which clerical authorities had once supplied.' English literature, therefore, had a specific moral and cultural mission.[10]

Both Arnoldian cultural idealism and post–First World War nationalism were significant factors in promoting a Canadian politics, art, and literature; and, by 1920, the desire 'to trace and value those developments of art and literature which are distinctively Canadian' was carried to the country through the *Canadian Forum*.[11] By the mid-thirties, Daniells had become closely associated with the core *Forum* group of Barker Fairley, E.J. Pratt, and Herbert Davis, sharing their nationalist and socialist literary ideals and contributing to the magazine.

Two of the *Forum* supporters, Pratt and Davis, were former candidates for the ministry who had changed their field to literature: as such, they fully understood Daniells' decision in the Paris cemetery. The experience of a loss of faith, followed by the regaining of belief and purpose in life, has been termed as a 'conversion-narrative,' and one of the best-known literary examples is Bunyan's seventeenth-century sequence of *The Pilgrim's Progress* and *Grace Abounding to the Chief of Sinners*.[12] Daniells' own conversion-narrative took place over a long period from 1910 to 1947, and he kept a record of his progress in his journals, letters, and short fiction. Initially, what he lost was his faith in the extreme Puritanism of the Plymouth Brethren, and what he gained was a sense of English as a 'secular scripture,' a vocation worthy of one's best efforts. It is because Daniells was representative of the kind of person who studied English between the wars, because he and

Woodhouse were the two most important persons in developing the Humanities Research Council (the clearing house for all significant academic policy and research in English between the mid-forties and the mid-sixties), and because of his role in the academic study of a Canadian literature, that his story has importance in the history of the development of English in Canada.[13]

Daniells' academic career fits between the era of the great teaching professors whose legacy was their students and the new professional scholars whose legacy is their books and other publications. As a student, Daniells was taught by three fine teachers: Ira Dilworth, Garnett Sedgewick, and A.S.P. Woodhouse. All had studied at Harvard with the famous teacher George Lyman Kittredge, a nineteenth-century philologist who shared some characteristics of the new Arnoldian humanist; and at least two were students of Irving Babbitt, also of Harvard. Babbitt had revolutionized the American curriculum by directing it away from Germanic philology towards a new classicism, which he called New Humanism.[14] Like his mentors, Daniells was an inspiring teacher who considered himself a New Humanist. But in his lectures and critical essays, he also strongly supported the nationalist ideal of a Canadian writing, underlining the connections (links which his own life and creative writing exemplified) between religion, a national literature, and middle-class aspirations to education and class mobility through self-knowledge. In his 1956 introduction to Sinclair Ross's *As for Me and My House* (where Philip Bentley, who aimed to be an artist, entered the ministry to obtain an education), Daniells identified the religious context of the text and added: 'Canadian writing inevitably displays the middle-class desire for self-knowledge as a key to self-development.'[15]

Between 1932 and 1947, Daniells responded to the modernist movement and to secularization. This change began at the University of Toronto during 1931–2 when he began to study Arnold with one of his mentors, E.K. Brown, and was accelerated a year later when Woodhouse became his guide to Milton and opened up the wider vistas of comparative history and religion. At the same time, he was reading the poetry and prose of T.S. Eliot, another route to the modern. By 1934–5, Daniells had been appointed as a lecturer at Victoria College, as it was then known, and was teaching Arnold in the honours course in nineteenth-century thought, a course developed by the first professor of English at Toronto, W.J. Alexander. In 1937, Daniells became Brown's choice as his successor as Head of English at the University of Manitoba, and the honours course was taken over by Northrop Frye, whom Daniells had supported as his own successor at Victoria. Because this small circle of men was closely associated with the development of both English and Canadian literature, I have widened Daniells' personal narrative to show how they interacted, meshing personal and academic concerns.

The cultural application of religion, funnelled through Arnoldian idealism but still linked to older theological concepts, remained strong in the Canadian academy to the end of the First World War. Most Canadian colleges and universities of this period retained a strong denominational basis, reflected at the University of Toronto in the affiliated colleges: Anglican (Trinity), Catholic (St Michael's), and United Church (Victoria) colleges. Even the principal of the non-denominational University College, Malcolm Wallace, was the son of missionaries. One of the most influential University College professors was Herbert Davis, later president of Smith College, who supervised Daniells' Ph.D. on the Baroque and Frye's M.A. on Blake. The denominational focus of the colleges was reinforced by the choice of English faculty and by the moral emphasis in favoured subjects of study (Milton was primary in a pantheon of Spenser, Shakespeare, George Eliot, Matthew Arnold, Thomas Hardy and Henry James); it was apparent, too, in college periodicals. Not surprisingly, there was a modernist backlash. Daniells, when appointed to the Victoria College faculty in 1934, promptly wrote a lampoon of the Methodist worthies; Frye, when he became a student editor of *Acta Victoriana* in 1932, dropped the biographies of Methodist clergymen.

Daniells and Frye, although rebelling mildly, were nonetheless products of an academy structured on the old religious model of a high priest, his peers, and a number of young male acolytes – the future professors. In effect, the university had changed from a priesthood to a professoriate that sometimes displayed a distinct unease with women. Literature had become a new theology in which the professors were priests, where there was a 'laying-on of hands' from one generation to another through the process of guided research, and where there were exclusions from the fraternity on the grounds of theology, gender, and ethnicity.[16] Daniells' life story includes relationships among men in the academy during a period when male bonding was the norm. For this reason, I have shown the process of mentoring through which he gained his place in the academy through professors such as Dilworth, Sedgewick, Wallace, Brown, Davis, Woodhouse, and Pratt.

I have also paused over Daniells' relationship with Earle Birney and Sylvia Johnstone because the rivalry between the two men for Johnstone's affection, characterized by Birney's biographer, Elspeth Cameron, as 'a classic love triangle,'[17] can also be seen as a form of academic power politics in which male bonding and male rivalry are uncomfortably mixed. The professional relationship between Birney and Daniells, which continued over four decades of academic life, is instructive in showing the ways in which struggles for personal power and prestige within academia can function across gender and through sexuality. Similarly, the verbal aggression that surfaces in English department politics, so pronounced in Birney's and Daniells' several jousts at UBC, is not extraordinary but representative. Such vendettas can become a kind of disciplinary spectacle.

Until the 1950s, the representative English professor was male although women students, as Heather Murray reminds us in *Working in English: History, Institution, Resources* (1996), made up half of the Toronto honours program as early as 1889.[18] But women students in English rarely became professors. The message of Genesis, reinforced by the teaching of Milton's *Paradise Lost*, was that Adam's rib had a proclivity for getting man into trouble. Even progressive institutions like the Methodist Victoria College, which encouraged women as undergraduates, discouraged them from graduate work and appointments to faculty. This manifestation of religious and gender ideologies in the disciplinary setting also reflects the wider society in Canada, where women did not become 'persons' until the famous Persons case of 1929.[19]

The occasional 'bluestocking' who did manage to obtain a graduate degree and an introductory position in English – Gladys (Wookey) Davis, Mossie May Kirkwood, and Kathleen Coburn at Toronto, Joyce Hemlow at McGill, Dorothy (Blakey) Smith at UBC – had difficulty in obtaining secure positions in the period between the wars. But with the departure of male students to the front lines in the Second World War, women began to carve out for themselves a larger space within English departments as students and professors, as they had done at the time of First World War. Fredelle (Bruser) Maynard and Mildred (Shanas) Gutkin at Manitoba and Marion Smith, Dorothy Somerset, Mabel Mackenzie, and Sheila Watson at UBC – all students or colleagues of Daniells – undertook graduate work during the forties and fifties.

While researching this biography, I have been conscious of the limited role of women in the academy, often hovering in the background as students, muses, or lovers. Sometimes, like Viola Pratt, Gladys Davis, Helen Frye, and Jeannie Smith, they found their niche as wives who, to a greater or lesser degree, were research helpmates.[20] Occasionally, female graduate students obtained positions as colleagues. Because Daniells' career spanned the change from an almost exclusively male professoriate to an acceptance of women colleagues, I have documented the situations of several women as muse, scholar, and/or creative writer.

Two strands run through Daniells' many papers, articles, letters, class lectures, and radio broadcasts. The first is the personal: his struggle against religious fundamentalism, his developing love of the aesthetic, his search for a wife, and his efforts to maintain emotional equilibrium. The second strand, the scholarly life, is an important part of Canadian cultural history: his association with four Canadian universities over fifty years and his part in the development of English and the emergence of Canadian literature. This is cultural and institutional biography with a human face.

His life impinged on others in curious and revealing ways. Within an extraordinary web of friendships, Daniells functioned as a special kind of interlocutor on issues relating to the academy. Woodhouse wrote him a chaffing verse comparing their respective academic positions; Frye wrote him a series of letters describing why he rejected religion to study English; the poets George Johnston and Robert Finch, and the artists Max Maynard and Jack Shadbolt, also wrote to explain their developing aesthetics. Daniells' friendship with a UBC faculty member, Warren Tallman, caused the latter to change his field from Henry James to contemporary poetry, a shift which strongly affected West Coast poetry. And five decades of students wrote to him to praise what one called Daniells' teaching 'wizardry.'[21]

His own publications include two volumes of poetry, *Deeper into the Forest* (1948) and *The Chequered Shade* (1963), a book of criticism, *Milton, Mannerism and Baroque* (1963), an edition of Thomas Traherne's *A Seri-*

ous and Pathetical Contemplation of the Mercies of God (1941), and a biography, *Alexander Mackenzie and the North West* (1969). As well, he became one of the best-known CBC commentators on literature in the forties and fifties. Daniells helped establish the *Manitoba Arts Review*, established the journal *Canadian Literature*, and invited George Woodcock to become its first editor. He also published articles on Canadian literature and seventeenth-century poetry. He was a founding editor of *The Literary History of Canada* (1965), was elected president of the Royal Society of Canada in 1970, and appointed a Companion of the Order of Canada in 1973.

Daniells' importance as a professor of English is out of proportion to his scholarly books, but not to his teaching, public addresses, articles, and personal influence. His effectiveness in the classroom can be gauged from the fact that in addition to the usual academics, professionals, and administrators, he taught or inspired a large number of playwrights, actors, poets, and novelists. And when president of the Royal Society, he liked to remark that five of his former students were then university presidents. Fictionalized portraits of Daniells appear in a number of memoirs, novels, plays, and poems, including an unpublished poem by Margaret Avison called 'Gregory,' Earle Birney's novel *Down the Long Table* (1955), Patricia Blondal's novel *From Heaven with a Shout* (1962), Fredelle Bruser Maynard's autobiographical *Raisins and Almonds* (1964), and Margaret Laurence's semi-autobiographical novel *The Diviners* (1974). Several artists, including Maynard, Finch, and Barker Fairley, were moved to paint his portrait in an effort to catch what Maynard called Daniells' plastic face: 'a big, sculptural beak, cubistic bone structure and a mouth as varying as the reflection in a river. Altogether, a hell of a face to have to look at continually without painting. Moreover the long entanglements of your figure are just about as intriguing as the face.'[22]

As a biographical subject Daniells is equally difficult to capture. Is he the troubled young fundamentalist of the Père-Lachaise cemetery? Or is he the aesthete of Avison's verse ('He liked the theatre and tea at 4 o'clock, / He liked to lean his head back, and listen to Bach')?[23] Is he primarily a nationalist, the strong supporter of a Canadian literature wanting, as he said, to write 'the great Canadian novel'? Or is he, as

Laurence implies in her mini-portrait in *The Diviners*, just another Englishman standing in the way of a Canadian writing? Is Daniells, as
Birney once said, the 'enemy' of creative writing at UBC?[24] Or is he, as
Frank Davey recalled, the sympathetic head of English who helped get
TISH under way?[25] What held these various selves together, and why,
as he later asked himself, did he not reach the same level of public
accomplishment and recognition as did his friends Birney and Frye?

The following chapters address some of these questions. In the search
for the younger Daniells, I came across letters to his parents that indicated he had suffered several breakdowns. The task of determining
what happened – and why? – has been a detective story in its own right,
leading to a number of written and oral sources, including a dream
diary, assorted biographical notes, short stories about his childhood,
Plymouth Brethren pamphlets, and numerous letters and interviews
with his contemporaries. My aim has been to piece together the pro-
gression of his religious thinking, and, because his trauma is comparable to first-hand accounts in William James's *Varieties of Religious Experience*,
I have documented his progress in his own words.

I wrote *The Politics of the Imagination: A Life of F.R. Scott* (1987) with the
recognition that Scott was a large public figure of general interest.
Increasingly, however, like many biographers, I have become interested
in what Jean Strouse once called 'a twilight zone, a semiprivate realm
occupied by minor poets, lesser dignitaries ... and the friends, relatives,
and disciples of great men and women.'[26] The semiprivate life has the
great advantage of illuminating two aspects of cultural history at once:
the public life of large figures and events, and the hidden drama of
disciplines and ordinary private lives. Roy Daniells lived such a life.
His public life as teacher, scholar, and university administrator illustrates large and continuous changes in the humanities, while his private life illustrates the hidden drama of both individual and discipline.
A multifaceted individual, his life story includes religious biography,
the development of English departments in Canada, and the emergence of a Canadian literature.

In person he was tall and broad-shouldered with a bookish stoop,
and appeared before his classes always dressed conservatively in suit,
waistcoat, and tie. He was an urbane man who loved a good joke, and
his progress at academic gatherings could often be tracked by the
uproarious laughter following in his wake. He could also be sharply
witty when his sense of academic decorum was violated. In the hippie
1960s, in the early days of the Association of the Canadian University

Professors of English, his talk on Alexander Mackenzie followed one given by a young professor who had just changed his topic from *Measure for Measure* to 'Flower Power.' Daniells paused at the podium to write on the blackboard in a small neat hand: 'The mills of the gods grind slow, but they grind exceedingly fine. FLOUR POWER.' Seamlessly, he continued with his talk, and later he introduced a vote of censure.[27]

When attempting to depict such a many-sided personality, it is always tempting to establish an initial psychological profile and to invoke it when explaining his later actions. But such a profile would not do justice to an evolving character. Also, recent biographical theory recognizes the difficulty of living, much less finding, a life of singular identity. This is especially true of the 'Proteus-like' Daniells, as one of his colleagues termed him.[28] Consequently, I have identified the major stages and contexts in his development (familial, social, professional) and shown his various 'doubles': that is, in the words of the biographical theorist James Clifford, the people or situations that in some way compelled Daniells to enter into their world or to play a role for them. This is a helpful biographical strategy for Daniells, whose long poem 'Anthony' (1948) suggests that he saw himself in relation to an alter ego, here clearly Maynard. By looking closely at this relationship in the twenties, and at others with Davis, Frye, and Birney in the thirties, with Margaret Laurence and others in the forties, with Birney and Woodhouse in the fifties and sixties, and with Frye and Finch in the seventies, we can trace aspects of his evolving character and influence as expanded into what Clifford terms a wider political 'network of interpersonal relations.'[29]

The images that recur in Daniells' letters and short fiction – a boy frozen with fear, a youth weeping in a garage 'blotto,' unable to act, a young man gripped by inertia – all suggest a divided personality and paralysis of the will brought on by psychological trauma. In the early forties, Daniells appropriated the persona of Eliot's Prufrock to describe himself at a Winnipeg tea party. Shortly after, he identified himself with the 'cerebrotonic' personality found in a contemporary textbook, a person of high mental intensity who is hypersensitive and needs solitude.[30] This is pre-eminently the scholar or creative artist, the individual at odds with his world such as the suffering narrator of Rilke's *Duino Elegies* or, seen more wryly, the Prufrockian 'sensitive, indecisive guy from Eliot's elegant shelf,' who appears in A.J.M. Smith's 'My Lost Youth.'[31] Today we might prefer terms such as bipolar affective depressive, for although Daniells did not quite fit this category, he did have psychological highs and lows which included periods of sustained wit and animation followed by depression.

———➤●◀———

Professing English: A Life of Roy Daniells is also a personal narrative of the profession that I joined in 1968. Canadian literature had suddenly arrived in 1964 with the simultaneous publication of Margaret Laurence's *The Stone Angel* in London, New York, and Toronto. The academy was now more welcoming to the woman scholar. For my generation, this change was partly because of role models such as Kathleen Coburn, Phyllis Grosskurth, Joyce Hemlow, and Jay Macpherson in the East, and Ruth McConnell, Margaret Prang, Ann Saddlemyer, Doris Saunders, Margaret Stobie, and Sheila Watson in the West. But it was also because a number of established members of English departments, including Daniells, began to mentor women graduates.

Occasionally Daniells would take me to lunch at the UBC faculty club and quiz me about my progress, thesis, hopes. He was immensely curious about Pratt, on whom I had written an honours essay. What was Newfoundland really like? Why had Pratt never succeeded in writing a satisfying long poem? And had I made application to the Canada Council for graduate work? I sensed, without really thinking about it, that Pratt had been kind to Daniells and that he wanted to repay the favour. With two daughters contemplating careers in the professions, he understood the problems that women in the humanities faced and was more sympathetic than he might have been a decade earlier, when he referred in a speech to 'the ideal young man in Canada, whom we are now educating and by whom our debt to the future will ultimately be paid.'[32] He also provided practical help. Many years after his death, I discovered that I, like some dozen or more others, had been the recipient of a 'Daniells Bursary' – support for deserving graduate students given anonymously through the UBC Dean of Arts Scholarship Fund. That he was bemused by the new breed of professor, the married woman academic, is apparent from his diary note of 7 May 1968: 'Lunch with Sandra Djwa, who is in excellent spirits – thesis done, book on the stocks, husband in new business, job for Sept at S[imon] Fraser and baby on the way.'

I have written this biography with mixed feelings of curiosity, admiration, and gratitude – admiration for Daniells, who was the best professor of English I have known, gratitude for his help in entering the profession, and curiosity about the factors that moulded his character and shaped his actions. A month after Daniells died in April 1979, his friend Carl F. Klinck and I stayed up until the small hours of the morning reminiscing – with the tape recorder running – about this remarkable man and his influence. Later, when Daniells' papers were collected by his wife, Laurenda Daniells, then UBC archivist, it became apparent that they documented both a representative professor and the growth of English in Canada. Still later, after I had written on Pratt, Frye, and Klinck, it was clear that in each case there were close ties between religion and the professing of English, some of which are suggested in this text. Admittedly, our biographical topics serve as distant mirrors for the self – I am the product of a Newfoundland denominational school system and had later worked in the United Church.

As an academic, and a former chair of English, writing Daniells' life, I have had the advantage of two decades of acquaintance with the man and access to his large collection of papers in Special Collections at the UBC Library, which includes letters, diaries, and jottings for a possible novel. Throughout the text, I have reproduced passages from his own fiction (in italics) to show his engagement with the creative process. Daniells is very much a transitional figure, a professor of English shaped by the old order but one who became more progressive later in his career. My angle of vision is directed to that point at which English broadens to include Canadian literature and where the academy began to accept the woman scholar. Beyond the English professor, however, this is the biography of a unique individual, a young man whose literary imagination was shaped by the cadences of the King James Bible and *The Pilgrim's Progress*.

To follow Daniells' life is to see how such an individual came to the profession, how English developed from the late 1920s to the 1970s, and how several English departments functioned. Up to the 1950s there was a high degree of idealism involved in the choice of English as a vocation because service to the student, the university, and the community played a large part in the profession. However, after the mid-fifties, there was a new emphasis on professionalism in the sense of advanced degrees, publishing, and the mastery of modes of critical discourse. I have sketched some of these issues and the changing demographics of English departments in the late fifties and early sixties. The story of his academic life, broadening out to the arts in general, becomes a narrative of the consolidation of English as a discipline in Canada by a handful of persons.

This book also introduces some of the personalities and anecdotes that show the developing infrastructures of English and Canadian literature. A dissertation by Kevin Brooks, arguing on the basis of Daniells' essay in Julian Park's *The Culture of Contemporary Canada* (1957) and his work in founding ACUTE, or the Association of Canadian University and College Teachers of English as it is now known, goes as far as to claim that Daniells' literary criticism 'promote[d] the idea of a national identity in scholarship. Much of the contemporary tendency to interpret English studies in Canada as unique and distinct from American practices is the result of Daniells' success in redefining English studies in Canada at mid-century.'[33] Clearly, Roy Daniells is a significant figure in modern Canadian letters and cultural life.

To understand how religion and literature were entangled – in Daniells' own life and in the profession of English in Canada – we need to go back to the start of his story in England, in 1902.

PART ONE

The Beginnings: 1902–1930

Chapter One

Plymouth Brother

Roy Daniells was born a Plymouth Brother. As his mother gave birth on 6 April 1902, his father and grandfather were on their knees in the next room praying. The practice of calling on God to keep a newborn strong in the faith was a common one; Edmund Gosse, in *Father and Son*, tells a similar story about his Plymouth Brethren childhood. Roy, who gave a lusty yell at birth, grew up to be a sickly child and a delicate youth. The prayers and hymns meant to carry life onward and upward filled him, as they did Gosse, only with despair. This was despite the fact that all in the house where he was born, a small semi-detached brick house at 188 Venner Road in south London, Sydenham, were staunch Brethren who termed themselves 'Christians gathered in the name of the Lord.'[1]

The Plymouth Brethren were a fundamentalist Christian sect that originated in Ireland, but they took their name from the fact that one of their largest congregations was in Plymouth, England. Descendants of the seventeenth-century Puritans, the Plymouth Brethren had no prayer book or formal theology – 'nothing but the open Bible, the King James Version, read as the inspired word of God.' Each member was expected to read for him- or herself under the premise that the Holy Spirit would lead each into truth.[2] The group to which the Daniells family belonged, the Open Brethren, were millenarians; they believed that the period set out in the Bible for Christ's Second Coming had been fulfilled. At any minute, the saved would then be gathered at God's right hand and the damned cast down to hell and everlasting torment. Among the damned were all unbelievers – the pagans, Jews, and reprobates who refused to accept Christ as their saviour, as well as the false Christians of the mainstream churches.

The Daniells family lived with the maternal grandparents, also Brethren. The grandfather, James Stevens, a retired bookkeeper from a brick factory, was a small wiry man with a beard, a product of the old evangelical English tradition. His daughter, Constance, tall and large-boned with brown hair and blue eyes, had trained as a kindergarten teacher. In marrying James Daniells, she chose a man who shared her father's name, his physique, and his beliefs. Many Brethren were trades-people, and James Daniells was a carpenter in emulation of Christ.

There was a shadow on their courtship: for over five years, James could not make up his mind to marry, a fact which pained Constance.[3] Yet once married, James Daniells proved to be a fond husband and father. He was sentimental in a Victorian way, liked wordplay, and wrote jokey verses. When his son was born, he clipped verses from the newspaper eulogizing motherhood and small boys. His view of the ideal woman is expressed in a newspaper verse entitled 'Wanted!' that he pasted into the family scrapbook:

Wanted – A wife who can handle a broom,
To brush down the cobwebs and sweep up the room;
To make decent bread that a fellow can eat –
Not the horrible compound you everywhere meet;
Who knows how to broil, to fry, and to roast –
Make a good cup of tea and a platter of toast ...
A sort of good angel and housemaid combined.[4]

Constance Stevens, or Connie, had many of these qualities. If not quite the Victorian angel in the house, she was an intelligent, energetic woman whose heart was in her home. She was always scrubbing and cleaning, and later when the family moved to Canada, baking bread, kalsomining the walls, and digging up the garden. She guided the family, tended to the correspondence, and oversaw Roy's education. She had very deep emotional ties to her father, sharing his religious faith.

Like the Stevens family, James Daniells was a sincere believer. He, too, anticipated the Second Coming at any minute and frequently re-cited the biblical text. 'The Lord Himself shall descend from Heaven with a shout, with the voice of the archangel and the trump of God: and the dead in Christ shall rise first: Then we which are alive and remain shall be caught up together with them in the clouds, to meet the Lord in the air.'[5] What this meant was a specifically Plymouth Brethren version of the Second Coming called 'the rapture,' sometimes 'the secret rapture,' because it meant that living persons could instantly – and without the knowledge of their unsaved family and friends – ascend to be with God in heaven.

For Daniells senior, as for most Brethren, the everyday world was insignificant in relation to the world to come: surprisingly, this faith gave him no peace. Prone to accidents, beset by the daily worries of a builder dependent on unreliable subcontractors, debtors, and banks, he continually walked a narrow path between bankruptcy and upward mobility. To be sure, none of this mattered because each day brought him closer to heaven, providing, of course, that he and his family were among the saved.

The house where Roy was born had two stories, with his parents occupying the lower floor and his maternal grandparents the upper. His bedroom was on his grandparents' floor.[6] His recollections are of 'a crib, painted blue, with bars of wood, – overhung, one Christmas, with all manners of toys and many oranges ... Convalescing from measles and being brought black grapes by Daddy ... My own room with blue-patterned wallpaper ... My desk, a small oak one. Ink pots, which will not spill on falling over – one for black, one for red. The bookcase – "grained" marvellously with steel combs borrowed for the purpose.'[7] The house was surrounded by a small garden with flowers and vegetables; in front was a laurel hedge with a wooden gate.[8] Roy was soon encouraged to grow his own nasturtiums. He recalled guessing games with his grandmother – 'A for aspidistra' – and, when young, sheltering in her thick, dark skirts.[9] He was particularly close to his grandfather. When James Stevens came home from the brick works, Roy would run to meet him – 'Tell me a tale, Grandfather.'[10] At a very early age, he was interested in stories.

The boy was repeating biblical texts before he could read, and by the time he had reached four was attending a nearby private school belonging to Miss Bolton, always dressed in black, where he was drilled in vocabulary, learning to say 'aren't' instead of 'ain't.'[11] During the summers, he and his mother were sent for two weeks' holiday at the seaside, Bournemouth or Boscombe, while his father remained at home to earn 'the brass farthing.' A letter he sent to the seaside suggests that Roy had been sickly: 'give my best love to Mother and get out and enjoy the beautiful fresh air so when you come back you will be strong and well.' His father had high hopes that his son would be a success in life: 'Be a better man than your Daddy by not making the same mistakes that I have made. I would like you also to have a good education that you may grow up a useful man ... [and] follow a different calling.'[12]

The child's memories of Sydenham on a Sunday evening were of suppers in the parlour with people visiting after Plymouth Brethren assembly. 'Coffee. The sofa with horsehair cover. Horsehair seats to chairs – a scratchy yet slippery material, with loose, prickly ends. A balloon jammed between sofa & chair legs, never its old self again. An aspidistra.'[13] For much of his childhood, the even tenor of his life continued without interruption. In later years when attempting an autobiographical novel (which was never completed), he described the child:

So it went on for eight years and the fear had not come. There was scarcely a shadow of it. The speaker with the long gray beard shouted from the curly iron railing of the platform high over one's head. But one didn't know what it was he said ... Open air meetings were more serious: the acetylene lamp (marvel of marvels) and the hymn sheets in huge type on a standard. 'Washed in the blood of the Lamb.' One must be washed in the blood of the lamb. It meant nothing much ... A shining, rippling yellow moon high among the branches of the fir trees as we [were] walking home ... 'Carry me, Daddy.'[14]

When Roy was about seven years old, he became very excited when his father, home at night, took out of his brown leather bag the newest instalment of *The Children's Encyclopaedia*. This happened every second Friday. During the next few days, it would be read, and reread. As there was no radio, and no other entertainment sanctioned by the Brethren, books were Roy's main source of pleasure. He liked to read folk and fairy tales, and the exemplary stories gathered under the heading 'Golden Deeds,' in which acts of kindness were often performed anonymously.[15] Through *The Children's Encyclopaedia*, he discovered science, natural life, the major Bible stories, great art, and the classic books of the Western world, including Bunyan's *The Pilgrim's Progress* and Defoe's *Robinson Crusoe*.

Bunyan was always at hand in the Daniells household, but it was probably in instalments from the *Encyclopaedia* that Roy first learned of Christian, 'a man clothed with rags ... with his face from his own house, a book in his hand, and a great burden on his back.'[16] The family subscribed to the *Encyclopaedia* because they wanted to educate their child, but Roy recognized at once that his parents were distressed by some sections. Roy's father, an intelligent man, would read the *Encyclopaedia* up to the point where some article on the evolution of species contradicted the Bible. Then he would cease to read.[17]

The *Encyclopaedia* introduced the boy to literature, to poetry, and to art. For the small child there was 'One misty, misty morning / When cloudy was the weather.' For the older boy there was Gray's 'Elegy Written in a Country Churchyard,' Keats's 'Ode to Autumn,' Matthew Arnold's *The Forsaken Merman*, and Christina Rossetti's *Goblin Market*. The successive supplements to the *Encyclopaedia* provided coloured reproductions of classic works of art. Although Roy did not remember it, the second volume contained a section on 'Canada, the Empire's Wonderland,' featuring British Columbia, which may have encouraged James Daniells to think of emigration.

In any event, just as the last of Roy's instalments of *The Children's Encyclopaedia* had been bound into six red leather-backed volumes in 1910, the father announced that the family was leaving for Canada. The Chancellor of the Exchequer, Lloyd George, had brought in a budget that made it increasingly difficult to raise risk capital for building, and as a result James Daniells was put out of business. He had two good friends in Victoria, British Columbia, where he had briefly worked as a young man, and they now urged him to return with his family. Canada represented the possibility of a new start, a second chance to fulfil his aspirations as a builder. When the extended Stevens family heard that the Daniells family was leaving, Roy's uncle, Sidney Stevens, drew in the boy's notebook a sketch of his father in a top hat and entitled it 'J.D. Contractor.'[18]

In the fall of 1910, the Daniells family set sail on one of the smallest vessels of the Allan Line, the *Pomeranian*. Their belongings were packed in a big wooden crate, and one of the child's last memories of England was looking down from the rails of the ship to a group of friends, Plymouth Brethren, 'who were calling out their good-byes led by a dignified gentleman named Oldham who was waving an umbrella ... Everyone was full of hope and expectation and good will.' Sidney Stevens had also composed a verse for Roy's notebook:

Before you go and do a bunk
Across the briny ocean.
Take a basin or a bowl,
For when the ship begins to roll
I've got a certain notion,
You'll feel so sick, you'll feel so ill
That basin you are sure to fill.[19]

The voyage was a nightmare, as it was a bad season and the ship was driven far to the north by storms and rolled in rough seas. Roy recalled 'the crockery rolling down the table as the ship stood on its beam ends and a girl calling out "Let's all die together!"'[20]

There were thirteen days of misery before they reached the calm waters of the St Lawrence and the Daniells family finally disembarked at Montreal. They had a short rest in Toronto before beginning the long journey westward by train: 'watching the prairies trail by and counting every leg on every cow.' Then they took the ferry to Vancouver Island. With them all the way was the old wooden packing case containing all their belongings, including *The Children's Encyclopaedia*, and a letter from the Plymouth Brethren introducing the Daniells family to fellow believers in British Columbia.[21]

———»•◦◦«———

Victoria, as viewed from the ferry, was a horizon of low cliffs and curving beaches. The Daniells family first saw the city as masses of green, the gorse on the foreshore, with the outlines of churches, of business blocks, then the steamship offices, the domes of the Parliament buildings, and at last the wharf. Finally, they crossed the gangplank and set foot on Vancouver Island.

To the boy it seemed like an illustrated scene from *The Children's Encyclopaedia*. Victoria was a port city, free and wide and open. Traffic was a combination of horse-drawn drays with the occasional motorized vehicle and in the streets there were English, Scots, Irish, and Americans, with the English predominating. He spotted army men from India and Egypt, missionaries on leave from China, bearded and turbanned Sikhs, Chinese coolies, and Indians with impassive faces selling woven baskets and clams. In this exotic group, the English-born resident seemed to him like a fish among swimmers.[22]

By October 1910 the family had found a niche. His father established himself as a builder, while his mother adapted to the new country; both put a strong emphasis on self-sufficiency. James Daniells eventually found property on which to build a house, and Constance grew her own vegetables and made bread. Gardening and canning took a great deal of time and labour. As an only child who was a reader, but uninterested in sports, Roy spent much of his time with his parents, who were creative and, on the whole, cheerful and happy. But for Plymouth Brethren theology, he later recalled, they might have been content.

At first the family rented a house at 543 Toronto Street, a property with two large mountain ash trees in James Bay, a small peninsula of land surrounded by the sea. It was an old house, and the paint on the slender posts and fretted wooden ornaments had faded yellow; there was coloured glass at the front door, and all around was the wettest and softest and greenest grass the boy had ever seen: 'The bunches of rowan berries were lovely beyond words, hanging heavy, heavy high overhead ...'[23] Roy had a bedroom to himself, with his books on a shelf constructed by his father and his cigarette cards and seashells on a table next to his bed. The big packing case from the voyage had been adapted to make a table, and at the head of the bed he wound a length of tarry, salty-smelling cord that he had carried from the boat on which they had crossed the Atlantic.

He could now walk to school. Just five minutes away from their house was Beacon Hill Park, with its tall trees, wide grasslands, and duck ponds; to the south, a walk of two blocks brought him to open beach with its screaming gulls; four blocks in the other direction would bring him past the Parliament buildings to Victoria's inner harbour, with its busy steamships, passengers, and dockworkers. Then again, if he continued onward and upward several blocks, he could look over the water at Haro Strait on the left and Juan de Fuca Strait to the right from the top of the craggy cliffs of Finlayson Park. He especially loved the sea and the waterfront. The boy knew that he now lived on the fringe of an enormous, untouched territory. As he played on the beaches and climbed over rocks, he sensed that British Columbia was very new and without a history. Whatever history would come, his family and those who followed them would have a hand in making it.

The local school, Kingston Street School, was at first a great adventure, but he soon saw it did not compare with his English school. He knew that he was different from the other boys – the dominant Irish, the sturdy Scots. Unfortunately, his good preparatory education put him in a class where he was one of the youngest – and smallest. As a result, he was bullied by the bigger boys, who mocked his softer English accent, calling him 'Choppy,' short for 'Old Chap.' Being English, so all-important at home, was a handicap at school. A protected child, he had been king of the castle at home (his family joked about the pun on Roy and *Roi*), but now he was isolated and made fun of. In response, he retreated to books and to the world of his imagination.

From 1910 to 1911 he was taught by a Miss Lawson and a Mr Frazer. The former he remembered gratefully as the principal of the lower school, a woman who did her best; the latter, more authoritarian, was resented by the boy. In one of the autobiographical sketches written in later years, Roy described himself as a schoolboy:

> At dinner time Daddy said ... 'Well, what did you learn today, Sonny?' He put the smallest and tenderest carrots he could find, one by one, beside the hot, delicious slices of meat. 'What did you do at school today?' The boy didn't answer. He could remember nothing ... He blushed and went pale again, watching Daddy's hands take a helping of mustard. Then suddenly he burst out without knowing why, 'Old Fuzzy won't let us read out of the new books – he locks them in the cupboard and we're not allowed to read beyond the place for that day – if you read ahead he gets mad and makes you turn the page back.' 'You must do as you are told,' said Mother, 'I expect Mr. Frazer knows best.' Daddy gave thanks and they began dinner.[24]

Devoted to the boy, a sensitive child, the family was nonetheless very obedient to authority.

Around 1914 his father built a house at Cook Street, where Roy attended South Park School. He was there for only a year and during 1915–16 moved to Victoria High School. From the new house, it was a long walk, straight down Cook Street, to the ocean and the beach at Dallas Road. There the hill above Finlayson Point was covered with dark green broom, with bursts of yellow flowers; tangled grass to the cliff edge made a trail as he ran through it; and the approach to the beach was covered with grey and brown stones, a sliver of wave lapping and breaking, the sea, dark, calm to the horizon; finally, mountains with the sun behind them, and a clear purple sky.[25] The raw contrasts of the landscape, the lines of mountains, sea, horizon, trees; the endless stretches –whether beach, or sea, or forest, or mountain – influenced his perceptions for the rest of his life. Nature was always a solace and the land itself offered room for the imagination.

As an adolescent, Roy became interested in geography. In the midst of world geography, rivers, cities, mountains, he saw 'Victoria as the centre of boundlessness.' Although it was a very small, very British capital of a far western province, the city looked into the unknown. To the south was the United States; to the north was a region growing wilder into the Arctic; to the east were the huge coastal mountains of B.C. and then the successive provinces; to the west, most exciting of all, was the huge Pacific with the Orient on the other side.[26] He knew, from listening to his parents' conversations, that the political future of B.C.

was unpredictable, but that, in addition to being part of Canada, it was bound to have a future of its own. As a child and young man, he had no idea what this meant, but somehow the phrase 'this is a new country' was full of significance.[27]

Although he continued to pore over fairy tales in *The Children's Encyclopaedia*, to read Alger, Henty, Ballantyne, and to absorb Victorian manners through texts like *Eric; or, Little by Little*, much of his reading consisted of the Bible and evangelical texts. When still a child, he read all of these books quite literally, surrendering himself, travelling still 'deeper into the forest' of the imagination, a journey later described in his own poem:

'So they went deeper into the forest,' said Jacob Grimm,
And the child sat listening with all his ears,
While the angry queen passed. And in after years
The voice and the fall of words came back to him
(Though the fish and the faithful servant were grown dim,
The aproned witch, the door that disappears,
The lovely maid weeping delicious tears
And the younger brother, with one bright-feathered limb) –
'Deeper into the forest.' [28]

<hr />

The boy's life was one of stark contradiction. In contrast to the freedom of sea and forest was the constrained world of the Plymouth Brethren, where everything was set out in black and white – the black letters of the biblical text on the white page – in a way that often left Roy prey to anxiety and guilt. He was taught that the smallest deviation from right action – say, losing his temper for a moment – was a sin that Christ had to bear on the cross for his salvation. Between the Brethren and nature there was no bridge.

The everyday life of the Daniells family revolved around the religious calendar of the Plymouth Brethren. His parents first attended an assembly that met in a hall on Pandora Street, but then it moved to an old rickety hall on Blanshard Street next to a fine brick synagogue. Both properties were owned by Jews. It was a puzzle to James Daniells that the Jews, who he believed had crucified Christ, were also the pleasant cultivated men to whom he paid the monthly rent. Each Sunday morning, the Brethren met with the chairs arranged in fixed rows below the 'ministering Brethren' on a platform. The usual form of service was a Bible reading and scriptural exegesis interspersed with hymns. Roy, because he had not yet received Christ as his saviour, did not sit at the front with his parents but rather at the back of the hall with the other sinners. To join his father and mother at the front, he had to be 'born again.' Above the door to the hall was a text in sober black and grey, a reminder of the necessity of this salvation for the Second Coming:

'For the Lord Himself shall descend from heaven with a shout with the voice of a trumpet.'[29]

When Roy was still a child in Sunday school, he printed out a passage from Isaiah in halting capitals inscribed 'To my dear Mother (hugs and kisses X 1000) from her loving son Roy':

Fear thou not; for I am with thee;
Be not dismayed; for I am thy God.

The verses were illustrated with a childish drawing of a tree wound round by a serpent, clearly Satan. This suggests that the boy saw even his family in an allegorical way, taking part in an unfolding biblical drama in which his mother, another Eve, was in danger.

His father was 'in the oversight,' which meant that he was a man selected from the congregation to function as an elder: women were not permitted to participate in Assembly. He would sometimes lead discussion of Bible passages during Sunday morning Assembly and was frequently called upon for advice by other members of the group. When there were visitors, ministering Brethren from England or elsewhere, they would often stay with him. For him, the road to salvation was clear. 'When I saw what Christ had done and suffered for me,' he once told his son, 'I came to Him with all my heart.'[30] James Daniells desperately wanted his son to be saved. Even before Roy could read, he was taught to say: 'Suffer the little children to come unto me and forbid them not for such is the kingdom of heaven.'[31]

The father's interpretation of the Bible carried with it the allegorical thinking of Bunyan's The Pilgrim's Progress, where Christian's journey through life is peopled with personifications of Sin, Faith, and Hope. When Roy was about eight, he was given his own copy of the book, which forever conditioned his thinking. Much of the story made sense in terms of what he knew. He associated his father with Christian, who must leave the world behind – even wife and children – to follow the 'narrow path.' He already knew that the path was bordered on one side by a ditch and on the other by a deadly mire, and that Christian must fight the deceiver, Satan. On the road, near the mouth of the burning pit, he would be tempted by wicked ones whispering 'grievous blasphemies.' Salvation could only be accomplished by reading the Bible and by praying on one's knees, like Bunyan's Hopeful, for the Father to reveal his Son. Hopeful knew he had been saved because he saw the Lord look down from heaven and say, 'Believe on the Lord Jesus Christ and Thou shalt be saved.'[32]

The journey to the Promised Land was filled with temptations and dangers. Even Faithful is killed at Vanity Fair, and Christian encounters fearful, bone-rending incarnations of Fiends, Demons, and the Serpent himself. Roy learned there would be suffering, torture, and even death for Christian faith. Yet belief – the key called 'Promise' – would turn the lock on any dungeon, even the iron gate in the prison of Giant Despair. Eternal vigilance was necessary up to the very end of the journey. The deep river with the Shining Spirits on the other side could be crossed only if Christian continued to read Doctrine, hold Faith, and follow the Way.

The final apocalyptic vision of the Day of Judgment was both glorious and fearful. There would be the sound of a trumpet, a man sitting upon a cloud attended by thousands of the heavens, and a voice saying, 'Arise ye dead and come to judgment.' Rocks would be rent apart and graves opened. God would gather the tares, chaff, and stubble and cast them into the bottomless pit, the burning lake, which would yawn open for Sinners. Then the wheat, or the Saved, would be gathered. However, the fearful message that Roy received was that salvation was not for all. The man who wakened from his sleep at the Interpreter's House in *The Pilgrim's Progress* lamented: 'Many were catched up and carried away into the clouds, but I was left behind.'[33]

The accounts that Daniells later gave of his childhood suggest that the boy understood the mechanics of salvation. Christ would appear before him as he had appeared to Hopeful. But when Roy prayed and prayed – but still did not have a vision of God – he knew something was wrong. He searched for an explanation. The reason also came to him from *The Pilgrim's Progress*. There he had found the image of the man in an iron cage who could not be saved because he had denied the Holy Spirit. The boy reasoned that since God had not appeared to him, it must be because he had committed the same sin. This conviction was reinforced by his father's anxiety for his soul and by the preaching of the Brethren.

In the Plymouth Brethren hall on Sundays, ministering Brethren would lean over the lectern that held the open Bible and speak of the danger of sinning against what they called the 'Holy Ghost.' This sin particularly troubled the boy. By some act, perhaps not voluntary, he might offend the Holy Ghost, which would depart from him, never to return. Or perhaps he held a blasphemous thought for a moment. This would be sufficient to seal his fate at the Last Judgment.[34] Hell's mouth continually gaped before him. This fire-and-brimstone theology might not have been so damaging if the boy had believed he was destined for heaven. His problem was that he believed he was damned:

At about nine the horror began to grow on him. One night ... he knelt up in bed with the bedclothes round his shoulders and the red-and-white counterpane over his head and he tried to give himself to God: he tried to accept Christ and be saved; but his form of words was wrong and his heart made a sickening movement of despair, dividing itself from his will. He lay down uneasily, kneeled up again and prayed with the same result but with a sense of receding from the gate of life, then slept thickly until the morning and awoke heavy and pale.[35]

When Roy was about eleven, he began to associate the Second Coming with the Feast of Trumpets, a Jewish festival celebrated in September. Although he did not know it, this was an alternative term for Rosh Hashanah, the Jewish New Year, when Jews are called for judgment and their destiny for the coming year is inscribed in the book of life.[36] The adolescent became convinced that when the apples ripened, the Second Coming would arrive. For more than a decade, this was a recurring terror. As he told his mother in a letter written several decades later: 'Cook Street years were pretty unhappy in many ways ... I can remember so well looking at the apple tree from time to time and thinking that when the apples got red it would be Autumn, the Feast of Trumpets, and perhaps the Lord would come and I be damned.'[37] Now the seasonal changes became a source of anxiety.

This translated into the principal trauma of his childhood and adolescence, the fear that his mother would be carried away in 'the rapture,' gathered up with the Lord, while he would be left behind. As he later recalled: 'I felt myself now to be a sinner who might at any moment be irredeemably lost ... Christ might come at any instant and take the saved, leaving me for judgment ... I have come home from school, opened the kitchen door and found no one in the house, called "Mother! Mother!" No answer. I would search the house and through the garden, full of fear. Nobody there. Then I've reeled against the door post with the conviction, Christ has come; they're all gone; I'm left for judgment.'[38] The boy was living out the experience of the dreamer in Bunyan's Interpreter's House – in effect, all had been saved, 'catched up in the air,' but he had lost Paradise.

When his mother came home, perhaps from visiting a neighbour, she would find him white and terrified. It is curious that neither of his parents recognized how deeply he was troubled. Perhaps he was unable to explain his situation fully. Perhaps they saw but believed that his fear and contrition were the necessary preludes to salvation. In any event, this trauma of separation from his mother – a kind of Oedipal situation in which the boy was threatened with loss of his mother by God, the Father – seems to have been the first manifestation of a religious trauma. As he recognized when an old man: 'From this ultimate terror, this fear of eternal fire and torment, one never recovers.'[39]

In terms of Plymouth Brethren theology, his experience represented the loss of heaven and an eternity of hellfire. What it represented in emotional terms was the devastating loss of his mother, a loss in which the boy felt implicated because he could not, or would not, be 'saved.' The loss of a parent at puberty, even the fear of such loss, appears repeatedly in the literature on depression as a situation likely to create later emotional problems. This is especially true, as the novelist William Styron explains with reference to his own depression, if the young person concerned has been affected by 'incomplete mourning,' has been unable to express his grief and fears, and so carries within himself through later years 'an insufferable burden of which rage and guilt, and not only damned-up sorrow, are a part.'[40]

Normally, during puberty and adolescence, a child separates himself from his mother and establishes himself as an individual. However, if this normal process is interfered with by trauma, it can give way to 'a lasting depressive vulnerability' which tends to trigger depression at times of major change such as adolescence, marriage, and retirement.[41] Terrified of hellfire and of losing his mother, the boy attempted to move even closer to her. It was a vicious circle because his parents, in turn, could not desist from exerting further pressure upon him to be 'saved.'

When Roy was about fourteen, and more capable of the sustained study of his father's approach to the Bible, his fears were given a scriptural framework. He later wrote a short story about a boy, apparently himself, who saved up to buy the *Notes of C.H. Mackintosh* as a Christmas gift for his father. Mackintosh was a Plymouth Brother born in 1820 who had published several authoritative religious texts and edited the journal *Things New and Old*. His notes (the full title was *Genesis to Deuteronomy: Notes on the Pentateuch*) would have been an appropriate gift for James Daniells, who interpreted scripture for Sunday meetings of the Brethren, and who kept large packets of foolscap pages, notes for Sunday addresses, written in tiny script, dealing with minute theological issues.

To the father, Mackintosh represented exact biblical exegesis. To the boy, Mackintosh represented magic, the keys to the promised kingdom:

> *Father's voice ... trembled a little, his eyes shone and he kissed the boy fondly. 'Thank you, Sonny,' he said, and in his grace for meat he prayed God to bless this gift to all of them. That evening the boy ensconced himself in a big chair with Leviticus and later, taking it to bed, read till the first roosters began to crow.*
>
> *The style of C.H. Mackintosh – he had composed these works about 1880 – flowed, copious and uniform, from page to page ... The boy's head was nodding when he reached the chapters on leprosy and the words began to swim a little under the yellow light. 'This leads us to a deeply interesting point in connection with the leper ...'*
>
> *He woke at this, rightly divining a key to his dungeon. He sat up, wrapped the old red-and-white counterpane round his shoulders and began to go over the passage and the following score of papers, word by word. This was it. The key turned in the lock.*[42]

The boy has positioned himself in Bunyan's literary world: he sees himself like Christian and Hopeful, locked in the dungeon of Giant Despair. His vivid imagination, really a literary imagination, was continually constructing a plot in which he was the chief actor.

This section in Mackintosh's actual text of the *Notes* deals with the cleansing of the lepers in Leviticus 13. Reading Mackintosh, the boy saw himself as a leper, seeking grace:

Eternity beckoned through the opening door ... He was the leper, the confessed sinner, admitting his total depravity, his utter helplessness ... He knew he could do nothing, must do nothing, must attempt nothing or all was ruined. He accepted Christ with every fibre of his being. But nothing happened.[43]

We do not know to what extent the boy of the story embodies the young Roy. Yet when he first began to write creatively, he developed a list of events and characters from his own childhood which he correlated with the boy of his stories. All of his fiction that can be checked has proven to be autobiographical. Certainly, in his recollections of childhood, Daniells tells us that he tried desperately to believe but failed to achieve a sense of grace.[44] Despite the fact that he wanted to believe, that he joined a circle with the other Brethren at Johnson and Government Streets distributing tracts ('Are you saved, brother?'), he never felt, as Bunyan's Faithful testified, that God had spoken to him.

The teaching of the Brethren presupposed that once he had given himself to God he would feel different. And because of this assurance – faith – he would indeed have been saved. 'The Holy Ghost, the scriptures said, would enter my heart and fill me with comfort and joy and lead me into all truth. It didn't happen.'[45] His father, given this doctrine, thought simply of Christ and was immediately converted. But it appears that the boy was too intelligent for the wholehearted submission that such salvation required: at the incipient moment of conversion, Hamlet-like, he began a mental soliloquy that erased the possibility of belief. It was a catch twenty-two situation. Roy's Plymouth Brethren view of grace was that he could not receive God's grace because he could not believe. He now thought himself unregenerate and concluded that, like the man in the iron cage, he must have committed the 'unpardonable sin.'

To commit the unpardonable sin would be to place himself beyond the pale, outside the fellowship of believers. Guilt and shame alternated with pride. If a sinner, if condemned, why not the chief of sinners? His fertile imagination began to play with ideas of heresy common to Bunyan; he too had 'whispering fiends' that told him that Christ had a demon, another form of the unpardonable sin. About 1914, he became convinced that not only was he unregenerate, he was also a heretic. In his mind a continuing saga was building, a story in which he, like Bunyan's Christian, might at any moment topple into the abyss.

Chapter Two

Breakdown

Daniells' religious fears were accentuated by the Great War, which existed for him on a personal as well as a metaphoric level. Two cousins had enlisted and gone to France; they returned wounded and shell-shocked, reinforcing the horror of war in the boy's mind. He had been taught that this war was the new Armageddon, a fear intensified by the hellfire preaching of two Plymouth Brethren brothers named Oliver and McClure, who frequently stayed with the family. The boy remembered McClure as a man with false teeth, a white beard, and a shiny bald dome: even in midsummer, he wore long, stinking, woollen underwear. He had baptized James Daniells, who considered him a great man. But he frightened Roy:

> *I was so scared I didn't dare lift my eyes to his face. It was prayers after every meal and Bible reading, his great soft voice ... plugging the irrefutable texts into you like sticks of powder in the soft earth under a stump. He knew that sooner or later the stuff would explode and blow your roots out of the earth and split you in pieces ... He knew it and he thought he was doing the work of God.*[1]

The explosion came at puberty when Roy, aged fifteen, had a breakdown. It is difficult to determine exactly what happened because James and Constance, who made entries in the same diary, were circumspect. Moreover, we cannot be sure whether Roy's later fiction reflects exactly what happened or whether he is rewriting the incident as part fact and part fiction. However, the documented facts do include letters describing a breakdown, thundering preachers named Oliver and McClure, and an attack of hysteria at Penticton at a revival meeting.

Roy had gone to Penticton with his good friend Jimmy Stables, also a Plymouth Brother. James Daniells had a carpentry job in the area, and the two boys had decided to join him. They arrived on 24 July 1917 and were camping, doing some casual farm labour, and attending revival meetings. Something quite serious happened to Roy in the following three weeks because his mother pencilled an entry in his father's diary on 21 August saying that at the weekly prayer meeting in Victoria, 'every brother there prayed for Roy.'[2] It seems that Roy had been seriously ill, so ill that he cut short his visit to the Okanagan, returned home, and could not attend school during the first few weeks of September.

During his illness, Roy wrote to his grandfather in England, James Stevens. His grandfather's reply of 20 September 1917 indicates that Roy had told him what had happened at Penticton. It seems that he attended a Plymouth Brethren meeting, and in response to the evangelist's preaching, had broken down, sobbing uncontrollably, convinced that he was damned. This 'trouble' his grandfather interprets positively:

> God is ordering things for your profit ... You went to the Country ... perhaps only [for] the experience of this life in the world, and while you have been there He has in His Love put you another experience – the experience of you[r] heart and soul – and this experience which you are passing through is the very best experience that God in His Love and grace could have given you.

Stevens thanks God that this trouble has happened to Roy because it is a sign of God's goodness: 'He loves you, and He wants you to be His Servant ... He desires you to know your own nothingness and weakness and then to discover His mighty power and Love.'[3]

The seriousness of Roy's mental upheaval can be gauged from the fact that it persisted through the winter and following spring and caused a hitherto excellent student to leave high school just a few months short of graduation. In a retrospective letter sent to his parents, Daniells referred to the Penticton incident as the first in a series of incapacitating breakdowns which also occurred at D'Arcy, Duncan, Genoa Bay, Cook Street, and Chorley Wood.[4] In fact, the years between 1911 and 1917 appear to have constituted a build-up of spiritual trauma culminating in a 'crash' in 1917, followed by two further breakdowns in 1918 and 1919.

All of his 'crashes' occurred after hearing evangelists preach, and all relate to his fears regarding the Second Coming. In October 1917 his mother's entries in his father's diary record that she and Roy heard a Mr Oliver preach; in March 1919 it was a Mr McClure.[5] Roy later wrote an autobiographical short story in which a young man speaks of 'McClure,' identifying him with Brethren who deceived and then betrayed him: *'I've heard them not once or twice; but scores of times, hundreds of times, up there on the platform, "What God wants is this! What God wants is that!" How do they know what God wants?'*

Roy assigned the blame for his mental breakdowns to *'those damn ministering Brethren.'*[6] And there is no doubt that the Brethren's emphasis on damnation (combined with his father's anxiety for his soul) pushed a sensitive boy over the edge. Were he not also subject to a tendency to depression prevalent in the Stevens family, a strain of melancholia aggravated by stress, he might have shrugged off the matter. Today we would emphasize the psychological component associated with childhood trauma and provide explanations of genetic susceptibility, but in 1916 in Roy's circle, he, his parents, and his grandfather attributed his nervous breakdowns to the struggle of God for his soul.

After he had left school, rested for a time, and recovered his balance, Roy began to look for a job. Among the Brethren was a bank messenger who told the family about an opening for a 'junior' in the Bank of Toronto, then the smallest bank in Victoria. Roy applied for the job on 12 March 1918. The next day he had a medical examination, which suggests that his health was an issue. Dr Wasson, who had seen him when he had had his earlier breakdown in August, must have given him a positive prognosis because the following day Roy began his job at the bank. His duties were routine: he delivered drafts to merchants, carried cheques to the general clearing house, and made up the daily cash book.

As soon as he had been accepted at the bank, his mother bought him a new overcoat and he purchased the requisite grey pinstripe suit. There were four employees: the manager, Mr Boultbee, another teller, and a secretary. Roy, only sixteen, was the youngest of the group. He appears to have remained on an even keel for about a year, despite attending frequent meetings at Victoria Hall two or three times on Sunday and at least twice during the week. He also worked extremely hard. All along his mother carefully monitored his progress. Throughout 1918 she notes in her diary that Roy had been working at the bank until late at night. Often the day's work did not end until 10:30 or 11:00 P.M. In March 1919, he came home early from work 'very poorly' and on several occasions was 'too tired' to engage in planned excursions.

Now seventeen, he became ill again – a combination of nerves, overwork, and religious terrors. On 22 June 1919 he had heard another ministering Brother, C.W. Swan, speak about the 'unpardonable sin.' His mother made a cryptic note in her diary – 'Roy's weight removed' – and there is an arrow circling this comment and flying off the page. Constance believed that Swan's sermon had helped her son and that Roy, like Christian at the end of his journey in *The Pilgrim's Progress*, had been able to put down the burden of his weight of sin. However, three weeks later Roy arrived home from the bank 'very early' and 'very poorly.' He and his mother again saw Dr Wasson. This time the charitable verdict was that Roy was 'worn out,'[7] which Constance interpreted to mean that her son was working too hard.

In fact, the problem was far more complicated. His early terrors regarding the Day of Judgment and the Feast of Trumpets were now linked with the First World War as an omen predicting the Second Coming. He later recalled the war as 'a nightmare unreal, yet terrifying and wholly impinging on the *mind* [in] relation to Biblical prophecy.'[8] The reasoning for this can perhaps be found in a pamphlet printed in 1914 and kept in the family collection of religious tracts. It was entitled *'The Coming of the Lord Draweth Nigh': An Examination of the Scriptures on the Length of the 'Times of the Gentiles.'* The purpose of the tract was to fix the time of Christ's Second Coming.

In September 1914, just before the outbreak of the First World War, Jerusalem was again in danger of invasion. This pamphlet argued that the Second Coming, coincident with the Feast of Trumpets, would soon occur. 'The Lord Himself shall descend from heaven with a shout, with the voice of the archangel AND WITH THE TRUMP OF GOD, and the dead in Christ shall rise first' (1 Thes. 4:16–17).[9] To the boy of twelve, the pamphlet's arguments were convincing: to the boy of seventeen, when seemingly confirmed by current events, they were terrifying.

The British had moved against the Ottoman Empire during the summer of 1917, and the Brethren calculated that as Jerusalem had already been invaded six times, the seventh invasion was imminent. Baghdad had fallen and Field Marshal Allenby was soon to capture Jerusalem from the Turks. In biblical terms this meant that the time of the Gentiles had been fulfilled and the Second Coming was near. Roy therefore concluded that the Millennium was at hand, and he would be thrown into hell. These fears were very probably fanned by the preacher at the revival meeting in Penticton, precipitating his first 'crash' in 1917.

In the summer of 1919, although two years had passed without event, his fear of the Second Coming was still acute. Every summer up to September and the Feast of Trumpets, Roy became agitated. Terrified by visions of eternal damnation, he became ill and was unable to go to work. In July his worried mother contacted a second Victoria doctor but was rebuffed with the comment that it was 'not etiquette' to consult about another doctor's patient.[10] As two weeks passed, the young man felt a little better: he camped out with his friend Jimmy Stables; he walked to Cadboro Bay with his mother, but was utterly tired out after both expeditions. He had all the classic symptoms of depression – weariness, weeping, and inability to function – but his condition was not diagnosed as such.

After three weeks of rest, Roy contacted the Bank of Toronto about returning. On 8 August 1919 he received a letter instructing him to appear before Mr Boultbee, who politely fired him: 'I presented myself but was told that I would have to apply as from the beginning – in other words they didn't want me.'[11] This final rejection, combined with his religious terrors, completely incapacitated him. Roy sat at home unable to work, 'blotto,' sobbing. The family talked it over, prayed, and took counsel from the other elders. It was agreed that Roy should seek a more simple life.

<hr />

On 26 August 1919 Constance Daniells and Roy left for D'Arcy Island, just off the coast of Victoria, where they received a warm welcome from Tom McKee and his wife, Plymouth Brethren who looked after the leper colony on the island. Roy was hired as a handyman and went to D'Arcy on 25 September 'for quietude,' as his mother says, which is the nearest she came to admitting that he had a problem. Admonishing his parents in later years, Roy was much more frank: 'I am afraid you do not understand that when I say "lose my reason" or "go mad" I mean just that, – I can't explain on paper what goes on in my head but you will agree to two things from your own observation: (1) there were times before I went to D'Arcy & while there when I was not far from lunacy ... (2) You will admit also that now I *am* sane.'[12] Anything that returned him to the condition of 1919 was to be avoided at all costs.

His nervous response to religious terrors was aggravated by the isolation of D'Arcy and contact with the lepers. The island was accessible by rowboat in calm seas, but otherwise cut off. The leper colony had been established in the late nineteenth century, but when Roy was hired in 1919 there were only three remaining lepers, all Chinese, who were given as much liberty as possible. Not seriously incapacitated, they lived separately but fished and cultivated gardens together. There was a good-sized house for the McKees. Roy lived separately in a small house behind theirs and each morning delivered food, usually packets of meat and rice, laying them on each leper's verandah carefully, without touching anything. He also worked in the garden, helped with the boats, and chopped firewood.

On Sunday, Roy and any visitors attended the Plymouth Brethren 'breaking of bread.' His memories of this service were pleasant: 'McKee's Irish twang was such that I never knew whether his daily prayer was for "our friends and our enemies" or for "our friends and our animals."' McKee, however, soon became impatient with this awkward town boy. On one occasion, Roy stood up in the rowboat, called the *Mary*, just above projecting rocks and broke a plank in the bottom. 'We may as well take an axe and break up our little Mary boat,' the exasperated McKee said.[13] Nonetheless, there were compensations. The island was situated in Juan de Fuca Strait, the same blue and endless stretch of water Roy had seen in his childhood from James Bay, and during his adolescence on Cook Street. He savoured the familiarity of the scene, its beauty, the coastline, the birds, and the light on the water. Neither Brethren dogma nor leprosy could taint these feelings of enchantment.[14]

But life on D'Arcy was indeed a lonely life. There was a killing monotony in the routine, unrelieved by radio or daily newspapers. And trips to Victoria were infrequent, although his parents visited at Christmas. The only regular visitor was Dr Livesay of William Head Quarantine Station. Every few months, he would inspect the two keepers, the boy, and the lepers, touching them with his bare hands and afterwards washing his hands in coal oil. Roy himself was terrified of catching leprosy. Every night he washed his own hands carefully, no doubt thinking of his early readings in Mackintosh that leprosy was an external badge of internal sin. Living with men with a terminal and disfiguring illness was also extremely depressing. To the highly imaginative seventeen-year-old, the word 'leper' rang with Old Testament connotations of uncleanliness, sin, and removal from God's grace. His old horror of the Day of Judgment rose again. Were he one of the sinful lepers he could never achieve salvation. As thoughts of the physical disease and the biblical disease merged, he became more disturbed, less able to stand the pressure, and unable to do his job. McKee finally lost his temper and Roy left the island, went home for awhile, and then came back to try again. All in vain.[15]

He had failed in high school; he had failed in the bank; he was failing even as a choreboy. There seemed to be nothing he could do well. He could not fulfil people's expectations, least of all his own, and he did not know why. In the early spring of 1920, he was sent home to his parents, where he was completely incapacitated for several months. D'Arcy was the nadir of his emotional life, a time of deep depression when he sat and sobbed uncontrollably, unable to work, convinced that he was good for nothing.[16] His mother nursed him, slowly and patiently bringing him back, and a deep bond formed between them, reinforcing an already overly close connection. Mrs Daniells later told one of his friends, Roger Bishop, 'I blame myself [for his illness].'[17] Presumably, she meant that the boy's early sense of sin and loss was instilled at home and she had not intervened.

As Roy's health gradually improved, he attempted to work with his father as a carpenter, but fortunately for his future life, he proved too clumsy for the trade. Finally, he decided to break with Victoria entirely and travelled up Vancouver Island seeking work.

———————

For the next few years, Roy Daniells remained emotionally and intellectually troubled by his belief in damnation, epitomized by images from Revelations such as 'Armageddon with blood to the horses' bridles.'[18] He worked briefly as a 'hand' on farms on Vancouver Island, picked fruit in Oregon, harvested on the Prairies, worked in a sawmill, milked cows, chopped down trees, and helped to dig wells. He had begun his working life as an itinerant labourer with no apparent hope of escape.

In the latter part of 1920, the fourth year of his 'seven years in the wilderness' as he later viewed it, Roy took the old Island Highway to a farming community called Somenos, near Duncan, to work briefly for a Plymouth Brethren farmer, Cyril Purvey. He was next employed as a farmhand by an ex-army major, Ronald Brett, who was establishing a dairy farm near Maple Bay. Brett, an Englishman, was a proud man with little money, and a wounded arm that might 'go' at any time. Roy milked the cows, separated and poured the cream into a can, loaded it in the buggy, and drove to the main road, where it was picked up for delivery to the creamery.

The drive to the creamery was particularly beautiful: there were perennially green fir trees, maples changing into an assortment of colours, streams rushing in foam to the lakes, and hills partially cleared or thickly forested. Roy sometimes met a member of the Rice family along the way. The Rice family, the general and his son the colonel were, like Major Brett, British colonials and part of the local Plymouth Brethren community. The Brethren meetings, held during the week and twice on Sunday, were often hosted by the aristocratic Colonel Rice at his house at Maple Bay. As Roy drove his horse from the Brett farm down to the Maple Bay road, 'all this would be dimly revolving in my head and how I, filled with a kind of adoring admiration for both the Rices as a family and Brett, his wife and baby ... was incongruous in this whole situation and could not function in it.'[19] As a mere 'hand,' he was outside the social pale: it would never be possible for him to court one of the charming Rice girls. He knew, but was not then able to give words to his emotions, that he had become a hewer of wood and a drawer of water, a Caliban of sorts.

But there was one important difference. Roy was not physically strong enough for the back-breaking labour required to establish Brett's farm from virgin forest. Once again the young man was fired. Fortunately, at Duncan there were other family friends, an older couple, Claude Butcher and his wife, who suggested alternative employment. Seeing that Roy was having a difficult time with Brett, Butcher told him about a job on an older, more established dairy farm nearby started by Peter Flett. The farm was centred around an old white house with a verandah, a wooden barn and milking shed, with long fertile fields which sloped into the distance. When Flett died, his wife had resolved to run the farm herself with her sons and seasonal help.[20] Roy became part of the help on 10 May 1921, working with her oldest son, Wallace, and her younger sons, Ernest and Maurice, helping to mend fences, dig post holes, dig the garden, and sow oats by hand. He soon ordered a sun helmet and wrapped puttees around his ankles, ostensibly to straighten his legs, but more likely in emulation of Major Brett and the other ex-army officers, who wore their old army puttees to protect their legs from the underbrush and Indian topees to shade their eyes from the hot sun.[21]

When he had banked $39, a considerable sum in those days, he enrolled in a Pelman course by correspondence. Pelmanism was touted as beneficial for those recovering from a nervous breakdown and was associated with improving memory. The course offered mental discipline in the persona of a kindly narrator who diagnosed the dangers of an aimless life, suggested goals, and provided a mechanism for change through mental and physical exercises. These opinions combined an early dash of yoga with a Dale Carnegie–like message: 'You are important. You can succeed – all that is needed is a little training.'[22] The young man responded wholeheartedly. When he went to work for Mrs Flett, he began to keep a diary, and over the next year his entries record not only digging and sowing crops, stooking hay, cleaning pig sties, and fetching strayed heifers but also rapid completion of the first, second, and third sections of the Pelman course. He had measured himself against General Rice and Major Brett – the Prospero figures of this island community – and was determined to haul himself up by his bootstraps.

In mid-September 1921, when he was nineteen, Roy returned to Victoria. There, on 25 September, desperately wanting to get on the right road, he made a profession of faith and was baptized and officially brought into membership in the Plymouth Brethren. The baptism, a total immersion, took place in a galvanized iron tank under the platform at Victoria Hall. 'One came up gasping out of the water as the assembly sang with fervor and conviction, "Up from the grave He arose, with a mighty triumph o'er His foes." One was experiencing Christ's triumph over death but unfortunately I felt no sense of triumph; I simply felt wet.' He had decided to take the conscious step of a profession of faith in the hope that grace might follow.

The next day he returned to Duncan by train, where the fall work of preparing ditches, cleaning chimneys, harvesting potatoes, and smoking salmon began. In mid-October, because General Rice was away and his family needed help, Roy moved to the Rice house for a month while helping to harvest the fall crops. In late November, he collected his $28.50 pay from Mrs Flett and returned to Victoria. He began his next job in early December at Genoa Bay, a few miles along the coast from Maple Bay, where he worked for George Seed, sawing and hauling wood, hay, and gravel. Christmas Day was spent, predictably, at a Plymouth Brethren meeting followed by refreshments at the home of General Rice, whose military sons and their children he later recalled as 'handsome, aristocratic in manner, and devoted Christians, as though one had crossed officers out of Kipling with archangels.'[23]

Roy worked for Seed until April 1922, when he returned to work at the Flett dairy farm. He was now doing fairly well as a 'hand,' despite his usual ailments – stomach trouble and neuralgia – for which his mother regularly sent him various nostrums such as 'herb juice.' He enjoyed working at the Fletts. Not only was it an established farm with easier routines, but also he was accepted as part of the family with the three boys. They milked and sowed and harvested the crops together and enjoyed taking tea with Mrs Flett in the hayfield. During this time, he had sufficient leisure to write doggerel verse – rather like his father's – and published one in the 'Farm and Home' pages of a local newspaper:

The Spring is here with power immense.
Inducing buds and grass to sprout
And rousting us poor hayseeds out
   To plough, to disc,
   And get quite brisk
With seeding and with harrowing
And all the toil that comes with Spring ...[24]

The Fletts were not Plymouth Brethren, but Roy continued to attend services at Maple Bay. Butcher participated actively in the Brethren meetings, and Roy was struck by his cheerfulness and kindness, by his acceptance of misfortune and uncertainty as normal. To Butcher he confided his belief that the Second Coming was at hand and that he would be surely damned. In response, Butcher gave him a pamphlet written by a Plymouth Brother named Baker. This pamphlet terrified him further: 'Every summer, the pressure of work being over and the weather hot I nearly fly off the handle and ever since Butcher gave me Baker's theory of the time of the Second Coming, I have had a perfect hell of a time (decreasing the last two or three years) about the end of September.'[25]

Certainly, something extraordinary caused Roy to leave the Flett farm in July 1922. His mother's diary reported that Roy made a 'surprise visit' on 8 July, but entries for the next four weeks are missing. When they resumed on 14 August, Roy was still in Victoria. Given that his parents' diaries covering the period of his 1919 breakdown are also missing and that this is an anniversary date, the time of year when his religious fears reached crisis, it is probable that he experienced another 'crash,' again related to religion. Daniells later told a friend that when he was about nineteen, working near a barn, he had experienced 'a waking nightmare in which a flock of birds descended upon him in a frightening fashion.' This experience he interpreted allegorically as a visitation related to a repudiation of his faith, and probably refers to his time at the Fletts', where a large dairy barn dominates the farm.[26]

Roy appears to have been at home with his family from mid-July until 6 September. Then presumably believing the date of the Feast of Trumpets past, he recovered and worked until mid-October, when he contracted chicken pox and returned to Victoria. Miserably ill, he was confined to home. While he convalesced, he began to enjoy light reading and, in later years, dated the start of his literary life to this period.[27]

Daniells returned to Genoa Bay on 27 November and appears to have stayed until spring 1923. Seed rehired him to haul and stack wood from the sawmill – probably the sawmill at Genoa Bay which extended out over the tide flats. His later fiction suggests this timing, as does his reference to the mill owner, an actual resident of Genoa Bay named Stout:

> The mill was hardly a flourishing concern. It resembled a barnacle who lives at the uppermost level the tide attains ... Twenty odd scarecrows, a mingling of Chinamen, Hindoos, Indians and Whites were induced to spend from nine to twelve hours a day in the yards. Piling lumber, if one piles it slowly, requires little skill ...
>
> After a month at the mill he had become inured to the routine of heavy manual labour. His bones were big and muscles adequate. He was slow and dreamy but got through without arousing comment from the foreman ... There were days when an air of primeval innocence settled over the yard. In the long slow afternoons trucks of sawn lumbers moved slowly down the alleyways, boards poised at a dozen angles in mid air settled steadily into place on their respective piles ...[28]

Daniells could now do physical work satisfactorily – his muscles had hardened and his frame filled out – but he found this occupation solitary. In the little community of Genoa Bay, as in Maple Bay, huge trees cut off light and the vegetation was suffocating. It was now the darkest and gloomiest period of the year, the winter and spring months of heavy, pelting rain and dark afternoons filled with back-breaking, unending toil. He spent much of his time dreaming. But the lack of stimulation, his tendency to depression, and his recognition that he could not spend the rest of his life at a job for which he was ill-fitted, all contributed to a continuing melancholia. This, in turn, reactivated his religious fears.

From Genoa Bay he wrote two letters to a fellow Plymouth Brother, Sidney Burdge, who was farming at Berry Creek, Alberta. He had obviously described his depression, his reliance on scriptural references for the dating of the Second Coming, and his worries that Satan, not God, was speaking to him. In his meticulous search into the meaning of biblical texts, Roy was very much like his father. Burdge replied that he, too, had passed through the same kind of introspection. Indeed he was *'almost worn out* before I was brought to give God the credit of ignoring any inference conveyed to my mind for *which I could not find a reason in His Word.'*[29] Although the Feast of Trumpets might foreshadow the coming of the Lord, Burdge thought that Scripture did not teach this. He comforted Roy by reminding him that Satan could not affect his possession of eternal life and ended by inviting Roy to visit him at Berry Creek.

Roy did, but not immediately. By April, he had left Genoa Bay to work for a German family at Forest Grove, Oregon. There he had been deeply impressed by an old grandmother on a farm where he was picking peaches for a living – her anxious, tremulous accents when she said to him, 'But the children! the children!' The children were there playing in the farmyard, beautiful children of ten or twelve, old enough to have heard the gospel and to be responsible. But they had made no profession of faith and so would be left behind if Jesus came that day.[30] This encounter stayed with Daniells to the end of his life, perhaps because it called up his own situation as a child.

In September he took up Burdge's invitation. Later, describing this journey in a short story, he wrote of the ferry to Vancouver and the train to Hanna, Alberta, followed by a horse and buggy ride to Berry Creek near the Saskatchewan border. He saw this as a journey towards salvation:

> Berry Creek was no more than a store at the cross roads ten miles from a railway ... The sun and wind were that country; the earth seemed less in evidence and water less still. It was all air and fire ... There would be long hours in the fields, still evenings in the farm house: both would be opportunities for him to work through the great plan of salvation, to find exactly where he had missed the path ... In this mood of absolute orientation toward his goal ... he found himself, bag in hand, at Mrs. Burdge's gate.[31]

Sidney Burdge and his wife were an older couple, about sixty. He was often in pain, but uncomplaining; after forty years of Prairie hardship, 'she was withered like a beautiful brown autumn leaf.' By some miracle, the Burdges were harvesting half their crop despite drought.[32]

The boy in Roy's story sought salvation through a Schofield Bible and a number of gospel tracts. To his father, Roy reported similar progress: 'I have been reading the "Gospel & its Ministry" & searching out scriptures in my spare time – as in view of the Lord's coming now so imminent. I wish to be certain I am on no sandy foundation but on the living Rock.' Roy asked James Daniells to pray for him, to ask the Lord to 'reveal himself clearly and remove doubt from my heart. Don't forget this.'[33]

While staying with the Burdges, Daniells wrote to W.E. Vine, editor of *Echoes of Service*, a missionary publication from Bath, England. He had four questions: '1) Who are the people who commit the sin of Esau? And what is the sin? 2) What is it they cannot find though they seek? 3) Is concern or anxiety for the things of God a sure sign that ... they may be found? And 4) does the Word foretell the length of the time of the Gentiles?' Roy, still searching for a reason to explain why he had not yet felt the assurance of salvation, was concerned that he, like Esau, might have given away his spiritual birthright.

Vine was succinct. He reminded the young man that 'Esau sold his birthright simply to gratify his immediate desires.' In response to question two, he set Roy's mind at ease by telling him that the Bible does not speak of believers seeking in vain. Most importantly, he said that he did not know of any scripture that told the length of the time of the Gentiles.[34] This letter provided some relief to Roy. Both Vine and Burdge had emphasized that if the individual earnestly desired salvation, God would be merciful. 'He that believeth in Him i.e., *as The Christ* is not condemned.'[35]

Roy stayed with the Burdges for several months but by December had returned to Victoria. Later, describing this period of his life to his daughter, he summarized it as an escape 'in two stages': 'First ... to the Fletts where everything was older, more established, more cheerful and less demanding. Then, with my parents' backing, the decision: "I think I am well enough to go back to school."'[36]

Chapter Three

Rescue

Victoria in 1923 was a fairly tightly knit little town, an outpost of empire, still dominated by the shipyards and the navy at Esquimalt. The artist Jack Shadbolt, who became Roy's good friend, considered Victoria highly class-conscious and conservative. He recalled the Oak Bay English 'with their beautiful fair-haired daughters and their wonderful complexions and their cultivated accents. Oak Bay High School had a totally different tone to it than Victoria High School had.'[1] He felt that lines were drawn between the Oak Bay and native-born English (which included Scots and Irish), between Oak Bay High School and Victoria High School. There were further social bifurcations between the Anglican Christ Church Cathedral and the Plymouth Brethren Victoria Hall. Between the WASP neighbourhoods of Victoria and the Chinatown ghetto there was an impassable divide.

By dropping out of high school, Roy had also dropped out of Victoria society. At twenty-two, after several years as a manual labourer, his overpowering aim was to rise in the world, perhaps not to the level of the Oak Bay English, but at least to that of the Victoria High group to which he had formerly belonged. In January and February 1924, he studied at the Sprott-Shaw Secretarial School in Victoria, taking shorthand, improving his qualifications as a clerk. He also began to study the academic subjects required to complete grade eleven. By late November, he had studied algebra, geometry, and French in preparation for passing the junior matriculation in June. He added, in his diary, 'D.V.' (*Deo volentei*, God willing) and 'My soul wait thou only upon God.'[2] In January 1925, he enrolled at Rocklands Academy, a private coaching school in the Craigdarroch area of Victoria, and in June successfully completed his junior matriculation. He then began preparing for senior matriculation, or first-year university.

He had done so well in the junior matriculation examinations that the owner of Rocklands, James Beatty, invited him to return to the 'Rock' as a teacher in September 1925. The school was dominated by the ex-principal of Victoria High School, a Mr Smith, and the retired head of a Victoria private school, a Mr Barnacle, who taught chemistry and physics. Intimidated by the other teachers and by his own lack of training, Roy 'worked day and night, hung over every student, pushed even the weakest to do their best ...' At the end of the school year in summer 1926, he anxiously tallied the number of provincial examination passes achieved by his students compared to those of the other two teachers. He had twice as many passes as Smith and Barnacle put together. It was a discovery that changed his life. 'Self-confidence sprang up. I was going to say it returned, but really I had never felt confident before. I was simply mesmerized by the results. If I could do that, I could do anything.'[3]

From September 1925 through to 1927, he taught full-time at Rocklands (and later at Sprott-Shaw Business School after Rocklands amalgamated with it) and took classes towards his senior matriculation at night at Victoria College on Vancouver Island. During the summer of 1925, he took an intensive course in English and in September wrote the senior matriculation exams for English and French. His struggle to get an academic education was unrelenting. He was always seeing student 'x' and marking papers for student 'y,' and running between two institutions. In between, he studied. Every now and then his diary records his fatigue and his sufferings from neuralgia, headaches, and biliousness. But he persevered. By 1927, with the completion of his senior matriculation in sight, he confided to his diary that he was thinking about attending college the following year.[4]

His new Victoria friends had a large part in this decision. He had kept up his connections with the Plymouth Brethren and attended Victoria Hall and Oak Bay Hall regularly. He preached, taught, distributed pamphlets, and took charge of a 'tract band.' As always, his friends came from the congregation, and there he now found Max, the son of the Maynards, central figures at Victoria Hall. Thomas Henry Maynard had recently arrived from India, where he had been a Plymouth Brethren ministering Brother. The family consisted of his seven children and two orphans, Fred and George Brand, taken in by the family. Père Maynard, as Roy liked to call him, was a highly intelligent and emotional man. He looked very much like a goat, with a narrow bony face and a high bald forehead, an effect mitigated by a very impressive presence and a deep voice. His considerable interest in literature was inherited by his son Max.

Max was extraordinary. Shadbolt recalls him as literary from the tip of his toes to the top of his head. Like his father, 'he had this slightly goat-like appearance: a great square jaw, high forehead, pale blue eyes, animal-like mouth.' His most outstanding quality was a strong, rhythmic, somewhat hypnotic voice. Despite the fundamentalist prohibition against 'sins of the flesh,' Max was a true romantic, fascinated by women and fascinating to them:

> He was always breaking into poetry and he could quote it at great length. He was an artist. He was somewhat short but he was athletic and he walked [in] a kind of totally rhythmic way and he moved in a rhythmic way and his voice was in a rhythmic flow. And there was never a break in the rhythm between the way he moved, talked, thought; everything was a consistent kind of [flow].[5]

Whatever it was, both Shadbolt and Daniells were swept into the undertow of Max's personality – although Max later claimed that it was Roy who influenced him.[6] The two had met in 1924 when Roy first came back to Victoria. They were opposites in appearance and character. Roy was constrained, tall, and dark-haired; Max was fluid in speech and movement, short, and quite fair. Roy also walked with a slight stoop and had a somewhat quizzical face – which forecast humour – but he tended to be highly serious in his conversation. When Roy and Max first began to talk at Victoria Hall, it was Roy's concerns that emerged in their discussion about 'the Resurrection of the Lord Jesus Christ.'[7] This discussion took place at the end of July 1924, when Roy's perennial anxieties regarding the Feast of Trumpets recurred. However, as he drew closer to Max and Fred Brand, he discovered that both were sceptical about Plymouth Brethren theology and that Max was beginning to repudiate it. At first, Roy was scandalized and judgmental: 'I went with Max Maynard for a long walk to the Uplands. He is sadly adrift. So is Fred they say. The Lord have pity on them.'[8]

Between 1925 and 1930 he saw a great deal of Max. They had cocoa after Bible class, they took long walks around Victoria, especially by the sea; they played tennis and visited each other's homes. In early June 1928, he went to the birthday party of Edythe Brand, who was twenty-one. The young people played a charade based on the word 'dynamite' – an appropriate noun for the former Edythe Hembroff, who had recently married Fred Brand.[9] An artist, she had studied in Paris, returned to Victoria, and sought out Emily Carr. When Max had met Edythe, she promptly introduced him to Carr.[10] Although Victorians much preferred landscape paintings in the style of Turner and Constable, Carr's art was beginning to make some impact in cultivated circles. Maynard was soon painting in Carr's manner – 'stumps,' Roy reported – and taking Daniells and Shadbolt to meet Emily Carr at tea.

Maynard became a mentor of sorts to Shadbolt, Daniells, and another chum, John McDonald. He instilled in Shadbolt 'the great romantic thought of *being* an artist.' He introduced him to 'aesthetics, to art philosophy, and to the specifics of form ... And it was he who led me to literature.'[11] Max appears to have had the same function for Roy. They talked about literary and artistic matters, exchanged books, and went to lectures and plays together. When Max gave Roy an essay he had written on the poetry of William Butler Yeats,[12] Roy composed a verse in reply. Most importantly, Max took Roy to visit Ira Dilworth, a Victoria teacher, at his regular Thursday evening 'at home.' This was Roy's first important step up the academic ladder.

Just before his breakdown in 1917, he had taken Romantic literature from Dilworth at Victoria High School. While Roy had been working as a labourer, Dilworth had completed his M.A. at Harvard. Dilworth returned to Victoria in 1925, just in time to teach the summer refresher course in English, which Roy attended. When he was appointed principal of Victoria High in 1926, some of the wags among his students were sceptical: 'If a pickle's worth a nickel, what's a dill worth?'[13] Dilworth, as it turned out, was invaluable. As a native of Victoria, he understood what was required by a young man who wanted to make good in the larger world. He belonged to that breed of early twentieth-century teachers who saw the teaching of intelligent young men as his mission in life. He was then in his early thirties, of average height, a little plump, with a mop of fair, almost reddish, hair, and the French habit of gesturing with his hands.[14] He lived with his mother at 570 Simcoe Street in James Bay. Dilworth was full of the newest ideas, and his particular interests were English and French literature and music.

On 13 October 1927 Max took Roy to Dilworth's for an evening get-together. There Roy found a number of other young men, including former Victoria High School students George Brand, Walter Gage, McDonald, William Robbins, and Shadbolt. All except Shadbolt and Maynard, who became artists, were to become academics, most at UBC. Dilworth not only 'placed' his students academically, he educated them in the larger aesthetic sense. He played his beloved Schubert on the piano, and encouraged the group to write verse. One evening, Daniells and Robbins each composed a verse while Maynard brought in a landscape painting he had just finished. On another night, Maynard sang and Dilworth played recordings by Delius and Stravinsky. The attraction of Dilworth's evenings is apparent in one of Daniells' 1928 diary entries, which reports that one night, on arrival, the group found 'MR. D. OUT so we were not able to have our usual good time in the old room by the fire; no coffee and cake; no books.'[15]

Entertainment for young people during this period consisted of attending church on Sundays and hearing visiting lecturers, players, or artists during the week – although the Brethren disapproved of drama. In January 1926, Roy went to Victoria College to hear an individual who was to be important to his future life: Garnett Sedgewick, the first head of the English Department at UBC, who spoke on Thomas Hardy. Rachmaninoff, Pavlova, and Shaw's *Saint Joan* played at the Royal Victoria Theatre; Little Theatre productions and renditions of Shakespeare were given at the Victoria and Oak Bay High Schools. Film was the great leveller: when cinematic sound arrived in 1927 with Al Jolson's *The Jazz Singer*, all social classes went to the Dominion, Victoria's first motion picture theatre. Modern conveniences like the radio, the gramophone, and the telephone arrived slowly. The Daniells family had a telephone installed in July 1924, about the same time the Shadbolts acquired an old Edison funnel that Jack found in a secondhand store, with a great big horn.

The Victoria High group of Daniells, Robbins, McDonald, Maynard, and Shadbolt also met at Terry's, a café on the corner of Fort and Douglas Streets. There Roy stood out. Robbins discovered 'Daniells had a deep-seated and ingrained religious streak that I didn't have and that makes quite a difference. We couldn't sit down at Terry's for an ice cream without his saying grace.' On one occasion, when Roy was teaching at Sprott-Shaw, he came into Terry's looking shaken and told Robbins that he had had the most terrible dream. He had wakened suddenly to see the Devil peering out from the foot of the bed.[16] Daniells was very aware of 'signs.' On another occasion, he told friends of taking the midnight ferry to Victoria and awaking to see a flight of birds descend in a manner he associated with absolution.[17] Robbins, a pragmatist, had no patience with this 'nonsense.'

McDonald was surprised by the exceptional closeness between Roy and his mother. Often, when he had tea in the garden at the Daniellses',

Roy and his mother would chaff and joke with each other, 'almost like sweethearts.'[18] Tea was a ritual in the Daniells home, and the group saw the older couple as a kind of Darby and Joan, who were kind to their son's friends. James Daniells' literary interests (he still wrote verse) and the mother's training kept the tea table witty and amusing. Later, recalling these visits, Shadbolt reminisced: 'Your household and garden were somehow the very image of what my newly awakened poetic spirit (Wordsworth, Shelley, Keats and the rest) had conceived the literary life to be ... At your home I was never made to feel unworthy of not knowing, but only that I might have promise and that the joy of life was significant.'[19] What is startling is the contrast between Shadbolt's view of the Daniells family as creative and permissive, and the young man's sense that the religious views of his family were stifling him.

Shadbolt recognized that Daniells, who had scored the highest mark in Western Canada on an intelligence test given college students by the American military, was the brightest of their group. What amused him was that this prodigy had his failings. Once, around 1927 or 1928, Daniells went into a 'funk,' fearing that he was losing his memory. Shadbolt recalls that Daniells was still studying Pelmanism and that he and Max had gone downtown to meet him at Terry's café. When the three came out, Daniells had forgotten where he had parked his bicycle, and they spent half an hour trying to find it. Ironically, he held in his hand his Pelman certificate, which had just come in the mail.[20]

Daniells had continued the Pelman courses off and on since 1921, when he first went to work at the Flett farm. He must have found its simple message – one could change one's life – both convincing and helpful because he stuck with it for over fifteen years. In fact, the Pelman system was a useful educational device for training literary perception and memory. Lessons taught mnemonic devices for recalling such things as a list of random words: 'dome, a, glass, many, of, white, eternity, life, stains, radiance, of, colored, the, like.'[21] As the Pelman text reminded him, unconnected words are hard to remember, but when united in a line of poetry they are unforgettable:

> Life, like a dome of many-colored glass,
> Stains the white radiance of Eternity

Daniells began to memorize Shelley's 'Adonais' as part of an exercise in mental discipline required for completion of a section of the Pelman handbook.

His Pelman course then moved on to larger topics of classification and definition. It stressed the inherent connections between concepts: analysis was encouraged, and students were asked to write paragraphs and essays. Daniells, although unaware, was engaged in the academic discipline required by university work. He discovered he had a knack for memorizing, and, in later years, he committed much poetry to memory, which gave him a great advantage over other students. Like his friends Robbins and Shadbolt, his horizons were now academic. In 1927 he decided to apply to the University of British Columbia to attend summer school – the next rung on the academic ladder.

On 1 July 1927 he took the overnight ferry to Vancouver. He had made arrangements to stay with the widow of a Plymouth Brother who lived near the university. On Sunday he attended a Plymouth Brethren service, and the following day took the streetcar up 10th Avenue to the UBC campus on the Point Grey peninsula. The university had been on the Point Grey site since the early twenties, and his first impression was of the ordered campus, beautifully green, with the library forming a central axis with the sea in the background.

He met two other students from Victoria, and together they heard a welcoming address from President Leonard Klinck and then registered for courses in geography and English 2. Second-year English was a survey of English literature taught chronologically by the permanent members of the Department of English: the head, Dr Sedgewick, and Professors Thorleif (Tuli) Larsen, W.L. MacDonald, and Frederic (Freddie) Wood. It was a very large class and there he met yet another student from Victoria, Harry Hickman. Early in the term, Dr Sedgewick offered to take an honours group for one hour per week, and both Daniells and Hickman volunteered.

It was Sedgewick's practice, borrowed from his Harvard professor, Kittredge, to bring into the English 2 class framed reproductions of Gainsborough's *The Hon. Mrs. Graeme* and one of Romney's portraits of Lady Hamilton to illustrate the differences between Classicism and Romanticism.[22] He, like Dilworth, also insisted that music and the fine arts were part of the well-rounded education. For Daniells, now taking his first university lectures in English, it must have been apparent that one could not divorce literature from the sister arts of painting and music, an important discovery for his later academic work. During the summer, he applied himself to his texts and passed his courses with distinction.

The new term began at Sprott-Shaw in Victoria on 6 September. Again in the fall of 1927, he taught there during the day and attended Victoria College at night. Christmas 1927 was a happy time: he was home with his family, his health was improving, and he had a new circle of friends. He had also become much more self-reflective. One of his Christmas gifts, a copy of Alexandre Dumas's novel *The Count of Monte Cristo*, crystallized his sense of his own psychological situation. He saw that his seven years between sixteen and twenty-three had been seven years of prison. And, in this book, as earlier in Bunyan, Roy found a figure like himself – Edmond Dantès, who escaped from prison. He read and reread the book, recognizing that he, too, was possessed by one ambition and dominated by one image – that of escape. For seven years, he had been imprisoned in a series of failures which had ended in retreat or defeat. 'I seemed to get my foot on the lowest rung of a ladder that led up and out of all this and my one desire was not to slip back.'[23]

During the fall and spring of 1927–8, he doggedly continued, teaching by day and taking courses at night. Sometimes he was too exhausted even to go to Dilworth's Thursday evenings. However, in mid-January he was again writing verses for Dilworth and the group. 'Read them my stuff on Fratrium the painter and a bad jingle on Sheila's hair.'[24] Sheila was Sheila Gillespie, a student he was tutoring; he had begun to think her quite attractive. Dilworth encouraged Daniells and offered to help him publish his verse with an Eastern firm.

In July 1928 Roy again returned to UBC summer school. Just before leaving Victoria on the morning ferry, he went to see Principal James Beatty at Sprott-Shaw Business School. He told Beatty that he would be unavailable to teach in the fall because he was entering UBC. Beatty's response was a revelation: '"Is there anything we could do to persuade you to stay?" He looked at me from behind his glasses ... a look that assured me in one moment that he understood me, Smith, Barnacle, the failure of Rocklands (it had gone under and its students had been transferred into the business college downtown), and the whole situation.' Roy replied politely that he could not continue, as much as he had liked the teaching. But he knew at once that this moment with Beatty was important. It told him that 'there are always people who are not in one's own field ... who have no contact with one on a religious basis, but who, nonetheless, *understand*.'[25]

During the 1928 summer session at UBC, Roy took second- and third-year history, medieval and Canadian, and French. In mid-July he applied to take honours English in the fall and was delighted when Dr Sedgewick agreed. 'Thank the Lord for that.' Roy spent the first three weeks of September preparing to return to UBC. Just before he left Victoria, he went to see Dilworth and had tea and 'a long talk,' presumably advice about UBC.

⎯⎯►◦◄⎯⎯

On 26 September, Daniells travelled to Vancouver, settled in his boarding house, and tried to find information about his courses at UBC. He was amazed to discover that there were at least 1,500 students on the campus. He saw Professors Sedgewick, Wood, MacDonald, Larsen, and Sage (of history) regarding his courses: history, English novel, a reading course in Elizabethan poetry with Larsen, Chaucer, Anglo-Saxon, and fourth-year French. Two days later, he was hard at work on a seminar essay on 'Poetic Truth' for Larsen's class.[26]

On 1 October he began to study Chaucer with Sedgewick; this was another milestone in his life: 'He taught Chaucer as nobody in UBC before or after could. He lived each part.'[27] A rather short, even diminutive man, Sedgewick made up for his lack of presence with an exaggerated personal style. Like his own professor, Kittredge, he was a consummate actor: he declaimed the part of each of Chaucer's pilgrims in a magnificent, resonant voice. Daniells admired Sedgewick from a distance. During his time as a student, and indeed for many years after, he did not penetrate beyond the public persona because Sedgewick 'was in every sense of the word, *worldly*, and I had been brought up to see the whole world differently, in a religious context.'[28]

Larsen presented no such barriers to Daniells' sensibility. He had come to Canada from Norway with his parents in 1890 and grown up in New Westminster, B.C. He was a graduate of the University of Toronto, graduating with a rare first-class honours in English language and literature, and was then a Rhodes scholar at Oxford. Roy admired his integrity and his character. His lightest word of praise or criticism carried the force of a pronouncement. 'His friendship was felt to be of inestimable worth. He taught Elizabethan poetry as though the texts were sacred.'[29] Shortly after the fall term started, Roy showed him some of his verses; Larsen responded with a little chapbook of poetry published in 1922 by the UBC people.[30]

Even at this early stage, Roy knew that Sedgewick and Larsen were the luminaries in the department and that between these two and the other three professors – Wood, MacDonald, and Walker – there was a clear drop in elevation. Moreover, the two worked together in harmony and did not appear competitive. In fact, they functioned in different spheres. Sedgewick took care of public affairs. He was the showman within and without the department. He pulled ties, rapped knuckles, and threw nickels and dimes at students who offered the right answers. In the larger Vancouver community, Sedgewick knew it was his role to spread the Arnoldian message of the 'sweetness and light' of the humanities. He lectured on Hardy and Shakespeare, gave innumerable talks, and, when radio broadcasts became popular in the forties, B.C. residents received their literature from Sedgewick. He was a capable scholar: his Alexander Lectures, 'Of Irony: Especially in Drama,' given at the University of Toronto in 1934, were highly regarded, and his publications on Chaucer were influential. But his chosen role, appropriate in boom-town Vancouver of 1924–48, was as teacher.

Daniells responded to both Larsen and Sedgewick. Larsen, remarkable for 'his learning, his love of literature, his modesty, and his kindness,'[31] introduced him to Elizabethan poetry and T.S. Eliot; Larsen also lent him a book on T.E. Hulme, which led Daniells to his first published article. Because of his Oxford connections, Larsen was in touch with contemporary books and scholarship, and in the late twenties was telling his students about T.S. Eliot and T.E. Hulme; later, in the thirties, he was directing them to I.A. Richards' *Practical Criticism* (1929) and the new theories of F.R. Leavis.[32]

Although Larsen guided Roy intellectually, it was Sedgewick's recommendations that launched his academic career. And it was Sedgewick's picture which he clipped from a Vancouver newspaper and kept in the cover of his diary for over a decade while he moved across the country from Vancouver to Toronto to Winnipeg and back to Vancouver again. Why? Roy wrote, 'I don't know why. It reassured me. It also terrified me. It was – like life itself – between a threat and a promise.'[33] This suggests that the young man carried with him an icon of the professor and head he was to become – recognizing instinctively, perhaps, both his future life and his anxiety about the kind of power Sedgewick represented.

When Roy Daniells arrived at UBC, the content of literature classes was imported. He later recalled that students were immersed in English seventeenth-century devotional poetry that quite another age and civilization had produced. 'Poetry written in Canada was indeed being encouraged, notably in the Letters Club, a charming and long lived group that published its own little magazine and encouraged its members to read their work ... But there was as yet no tradition of western Canadian poetry. Birney was in the future.'[34] In fact, Earle Birney, who was also Sedgewick's student, was an instructor on the campus during the summer of 1928 and later claimed to have marked some of Roy's student papers, one of which was written in verse.

Roy did well at UBC. In his first exam in third-year history in the fall of 1928, he received 98 per cent, the highest mark in the class, and an A+ for his English essay for Larsen.[35] Earlier that fall, he had been very pleased to learn he had been elected to the Letters Club, presided over by Larsen, and added characteristically, 'May I do God's will.'[36] In October he attended the first meeting. As formal dress was required, he bought a stiff collar, white shirt, and studs, proper evening dress to attend a second meeting at the home of another professor, Frederic Wood, where the group heard a new play by Eugene O'Neill.[37] The young man seems to have spent most of his first fall term either in classes or in the library. He wrote the last of his Christmas exams, Chaucer, on 20 December and took the night ferry back to Victoria for Christmas, sleeping on a row of chairs.

In January 1929 he returned to UBC and discovered he had done exceptionally well in his exams. During this term, he consulted Larsen on an honours thesis topic and was advised to work on the Elizabethan lyric.[38] He also made new friends through the Letters Club: fellow students Eugene Cassidy and Carol Coates (whom Cassidy was courting), both the children of missionaries. At the end of the term, Daniells was elected president of the Letters Club, and Carol was elected secretary.[39]

When the university term was over, Roy returned to Victoria for the summer, where he again taught at Sprott-Shaw. He cast an eye at several Victoria girls, notably Sheila Gillespie and Marjorie Rigler, but Sheila went to China on a mission, and Marjorie was unencouraging. He continued his spartan life, attending Oak Bay Hall regularly in Victoria, just as he had Mount Pleasant Hall in Vancouver the previous school year.

During 1929–30 he registered for courses in Tudor, Renaissance, and eighteenth-century literature, linguistics, English history, and the honours essay.[40] In his first honours class with Sedgewick, the professor 'after an hour's talk on matters Elizabethan ... gave an exam on summer reading (not done by me). I knew nothing about it. Prefaced an impudent ballad to my paper.'[41] Sedgewick did not hold his lack of preparation against him – at least not immediately. Roy had been shrewd enough to tell Sedgewick of his academic hopes for a graduate degree.

During this, his last year at UBC, there was a great expansion in Roy's life. When preparing to return to UBC for the 1929 fall term, he had completely updated his wardrobe and recorded this fact in celebratory capitals: first he bought an 'OVERCOAT' and a 'HAT'; a few days later, he bought 'FLANNEL SHIRT, TWO WHITE SHIRTS, TWO PAIRS WHITE SOCKS, ONE PAIR GREY SOCKS at Wilsons and WHITE RUNNING SHOES at Norman Maynard's this week.' To this he shortly added 'GREY FLANNEL TROUSERS.'[42] Daniells, who had made do with very little in the way of wearing apparel, had suddenly become very 'worldly,' and was concerned about his appearance.

He was now part of a series of groups, both in the Varsity Christian Fellowship and in the Letters Club. He astonished several of his professors by writing an exam in the metre of the Tudor lyric, and later the eighteenth-century couplet. They attributed this remarkable capacity to produce verse at will as spontaneous creation; very likely, however, they were roughed out earlier, and memorized by the Pelman system. During 1929–30 he was invited to a few dinners at Sedgewick's house with several other students. Sedgewick, like Dilworth, was a bachelor who lived with his mother, an imposing presence dressed in black, rather like Whistler's mother. Sedgewick liked to shock the more impressionable undergraduates by chasing her around the dinner table with a broom, pretending to hit her while she uttered blood-curdling cries. Such horseplay probably lightened Daniells' academic life – he studied continually and worked in the library for five hours on Monday nights – but he remained outside Sedgewick's 'inner circle.'[43]

However, his friendship with Eugene Cassidy blossomed. Eugene visited Victoria to spend three days with the Daniellses between Christmas and New Year's. More significantly, Roy began to see much of Carol Coates – in the Letters Club they often worked together – and she was in several of his classes. 'Seeing Carol home' becomes the most regular phrase in his fall 1929 and spring 1930 diaries. Carol was petite and dark-haired with a wide smile, and had a great interest in Japanese culture. When Roy met her, she was reading Arthur Waley and Amy

Lowell, poets whose work drew upon Chinese and Japanese sources. But Roy, Eugene, and Carol, as he versified, all considered themselves good friends:

We three in the gods are so riotous
They'll send up an usher to quiet us,
And put us in the clink
For a fortnight I think
On bread and on water to diet us.[44]

Privately, however, he was beginning to fall in love with Carol.

They had mutual interests and began to write verses to one another. They read plays together, had tea at the 'caf,' and he visited her at her home. Everything was going well until just after Valentine's Day: 'Took Carol home. Stayed at her house till late ... Had long confab. She loves me. But she will marry Eugene on May 23rd at 7 A.M. I greatly doubt if she would ever possibly have married me whatever the circumstances. God forgive me!'[45]

It is a peculiar diary entry. Daniells was confused – why, if Carol loved him, was she going to marry Eugene? More importantly, how was he going to deal with his emotions, which none of his Plymouth Brethren 'pashes' had ever evoked? Carol was flirtatious, yet she may have meant ideal, platonic love. They had studied Dante together, and their later letters are addressed 'Dear Beatrice' and 'Dear Dante.' But the platonic ideal was cold comfort. Although he adjusted to the idea that Carol would marry Eugene, Roy continued to adore her. He also continued his friendship with Eugene.

Over the Christmas holidays, he had acquired the poems of Wordsworth and Shelley and become interested in the contemporary romantic Humbert Wolfe, on whom he wrote a paper for Larsen. Dilworth lent him Wolfe's new book, Satire, to help him. He maintained his good grades, continued to write verse, and at the final meeting of the Letters Club was happy to receive the prize for originality: Sir James Frazer's The Golden Bough.[46]

On 30 April he wrote his exam on Shakespeare and the Renaissance period. When he got to the examination room, he was shocked when Dr Sedgewick dictated two questions for his exam, neither of which touched on the period of study. It looks as if Sedgewick was paying him back for his lack of preparation in the fall and, by the by, testing his mettle. Roy, in response, gave all he had. He took a seminar room and wrote from

10:45 in the morning until late in the evening. He got home around 11:30 and kept on writing until the small hours.[47] He must have done well because two days later Sedgewick suggested that he go to Seattle to see Dr Griffith, chair of the English Department at the University of Washington, regarding a position. Daniells did so, and he found Dr Griffith 'kindly.'

As might be expected, Daniells graduated with first-class honours. But he did not attend the formal dinner for graduates at the Hotel Vancouver, nor did he go to the chancellor's reception. He had a certain puritanical aversion to such festivities. His friends had also done well. Eugene obtained first-class honours, Carol a first-class pass, and Harry Hickman the Governor General's Medal. But after the graduation ceremonies on 8 May – processions, speeches, degrees conferred, and tea – Roy, Eugene, and Carol dined in the Hotel Vancouver's Oval Room, meeting with other acquaintances. Daniells had had his first taste of academic ceremony and discovered that he liked it: 'Whole affair new and very interesting to me.'[48]

A week later, he visited Sedgewick at his home, where Sedgewick gave him a whisky and water, and suggested that Toronto, Berkeley, and Seattle were the most desirable of the fellowships he had applied for. He also said that the UBC English Department would back Daniells whenever necessary. But if all fellowships failed, he should take a year at an American university, financing it himself, rather than take education at UBC. For several days, Roy lived in anxiety until Sedgewick phoned to say he had been granted an M.A. fellowship from Toronto. Roy was 'Very thankful for this.'[49] For the first time there is no reference to God in his habitual litany of thanks.

After graduation, Carol and Eugene married and prepared for a move to Japan, where Carol's parents lived. She planned to travel ahead, and her ship stopped at Victoria en route on 17 June. Carol had lunch with the Daniells family, and Constance Daniells took a great fancy to her because of her 'Englishness.' In the afternoon, after Carol sailed on the *Hikawa Maru* for Japan, Roy recognized that her arrival and departure had upset him badly: 'I get carried away by my emotions too easily I am afraid.'[50]

In fact, this first abortive 'crush' was to strongly affect his future relations with the opposite sex. Although Roy was very shy with young women, he appears to have genuinely loved Carol, and his mother liked her. Had she been free, he might well have married her. But circumstances had placed him as the third party in a romantic triangle.

Because of his friendship with Eugene, he was obliged to accommodate himself to this role, an accommodation which did not bode well for future courtships.

Shortly after Carol's departure, he returned a copy of Eliot's *The Waste Land* to the library and, perhaps in honour of Carol, got out a translation of *Divine Comedy*. He was coaching a Victoria girl called Hope Leeming, who taught at Oak Bay High School. Early in July, he took Hope out for lunch, and they talked about spiritual matters: 'She is in a bad way. Believes in no "world to come." I am considerably distressed.'[51] Again, as in past years, he became preoccupied with thoughts of the Second Coming as August drew near. On 2 July he wrote another long letter to W.E. Vine in England asking about his fears of being 'abandoned by Christ at the rapture'; he also asked again about the connection between the Feast of Trumpets and the Coming of the Lord. By the end of August, Roy was feeling miserable and depressed. But friendship helped. He and Max walked to Telegraph Bay, where they talked and enjoyed the last of their summer: 'Lay on the sand. Sun's rays slant now and the end of the summer is plainly here.'[52]

Daniells had come a long distance in the six years since his return to Victoria. Despite religious fears, he had slowly climbed the academic ladder to find that he, like Edmond Dantès, might escape from prison into a new world of freedom – the study of literature. For this rescue, he credited Divine Providence, then Maynard, Dilworth, Larsen, and Sedgewick. Nowhere does he acknowledge the intelligence, determination, and hard work of one J. Roy Daniells.

PART TWO

University of Toronto: 1930–1937

Chapter Four

A New World

The decade inaugurated by the crash of 1929 was to be dominated by the Depression, the Spanish Civil War, and the emergence of Adolf Hitler. But when Daniells began his long journey in September 1930, he was conscious only of the first: he desperately needed to save money. He boarded the CPR – travelling by coach – for Toronto. For several days and nights, he sat in his seat as he watched first the Fraser Valley roll by, then the Rocky Mountains, then the Prairies. After two longish stopovers at Calgary and Winnipeg (and five days of travelling in the same set of clothes), he arrived in Toronto.

His destination was Hart House, a gathering place for male students on the University of Toronto campus. There he showered, inquired about lodgings, and met another graduate student, Trygve Alstad, with whom he agreed to share a room on Willcocks Street. The next day, a Sunday, Daniells arranged to attend the Plymouth Brethren Central Gospel Hall. On Monday he set out to explore the campus.

The U of T, with its constituent University College, had been established as a single coherent entity covering the academic spectrum. When the church-related colleges were affiliated, six subjects were designated as 'college subjects'; the remainder, plus the professional faculties, were 'University subjects.' Victoria College was the United Church college, Trinity the Anglican, and St Michael's the Roman Catholic. Yet, by the turn of the century, all the colleges had become more secular; and, as A.B. McKillop has noted, the study of English in both Canada and England was becoming increasingly significant as the repository of cultural and moral values, a channel for developing and forming culture.[1] Daniells soon recognized that the Toronto colleges (not to become universities until later in the century), unlike the newly established UBC, were settled institutions, drawing students from a wide variety of professional families throughout Canada.

On Tuesday he went to University College, where he called on Dr Malcolm Wallace, the principal, who received him cordially. Wallace, a tall, white-haired man in his fifties, was Scottish and soft-spoken, a gentleman of the old school. Wallace was then teaching a course on the Romantics, but his tasks as principal included administering the six constituent departments of the college, managing the budget, and keeping the peace in a department of strong personalities.

The full professors in English at University College were Wallace and R.S. Knox; and the associate professors, Herbert Davis, W.H. Clawson, and J.F. MacDonald. A.S.P. Woodhouse was an assistant professor, as were two women, Miss Gladys Wookey and Mrs Hilda Kirkwood (later of Trinity). Both N.J. Endicott and E.K. Brown were lecturers. Many faculty had religious ties: Wallace and Endicott, for example, were sons of missionaries, and Davis had studied for Anglican orders. Similarly, at Victoria College, several professors, including E.J. Pratt, had been ordained as Methodist clergymen. However, religion was giving way to morality and culture through the study of literature. Matthew Arnold had been a major figure of study at the college for over thirty years, and by the mid-twenties his ethical idealism had been reinforced by Irving Babbitt's New Humanism, which also emphasized morality, but now buttressed by classical literature.

As the thirties moved into the forties, Woodhouse became the political power in the department. He was a graduate of Toronto who had studied under the university's first professor of English, W.J. Alexander, and then at Harvard, with Kittredge and Babbitt. Woodhouse was large, broad-faced, and fairly tall, with an imposing presence. His subject was Milton, and he respected the moral and classical emphasis of Babbitt's New Humanism, which he liked to call 'the higher Babbittry,'[2] punning both on 'the Higher Criticism' and Sinclair Lewis's *Babbitt*.

If Woodhouse's humanist, anti-romantic, history-of-ideas approach to literature represented one pole of English at University College, the other pole, 'the Dionysian, spiritual, aesthetic tendency,'[3] was embodied in Herbert Davis, an Englishman whose passions were Blake, Swift, and Lawrence. In later years, Daniells fondly recalled Davis looking like some 'visual ideal' of an Anglican bishop: he was tweedy, 'symmetrically built, without eccentricity of any kind, pink and white complexioned, a domed forehead with thinning hair, sharp features without acerbity, an air of gentleness without any loss of force.'[4] As a young man, Davis was so passionate an advocate for D.H. Lawrence, then the symbol of rebellion against English society, that his friends called him, not by his own names (Herbert John), but 'David' after Lawrence. Woodhouse had his academic disciples, but Davis, who inspired love and emulation, had his 'groupies.'[5]

The rising star in University College was E.K. Brown, in his midtwenties. A student at University College and a Roman Catholic, he had acquired his enthusiasm for a Canadian literature from Pelham Edgar, the principal of the United Church College, Victoria. He was also a great admirer of Babbitt.[6] Brown had recently returned from the Sorbonne, where he was preparing for his doctorate. He was an amiable man, of medium height, dark-haired, with a pleasant, assured manner and a clipped way of speaking both French and English. He appeared to get along with everybody, especially Woodhouse. In 1931 Woodhouse and Brown had helped G.S. Brett, head of the Department of Philosophy, found the *University of Toronto Quarterly* in an effort to raise critical standards. In 1933, when Brett became dean of the School of Graduate Studies, Woodhouse took over the editorship determined to make it 'a first class critical journal' which included articles and book reviews. In 1936 'Letters in Canada' was developed: 'an account of the work done in Canada in a given year ... writing, creative and critical.'[7]

Publication was becoming increasingly more important for professors, although the U of T, like British universities of this period, did not consider a Ph.D. essential: a good M.A., good teaching, and the possibility of a substantial book were sufficient for ensuring a long-term position – the equivalent of today's tenure appointment. Davis and Knox, for example, did not have Ph.D.'s, although Wallace did, and Endicott and Brown were acquiring theirs. Endicott, however, like Woodhouse, eventually ceased to pursue his Ph.D. studies.

Daniells was still an academic innocent. He did not see that the University College English Department was a Byzantine court with a nominal pope in Wallace, two rising cardinals in Davis and Woodhouse, and a number of factional bishops. But he did know that the graduate program in English that he was entering had a fine reputation. A study of the humanities in North America conducted in the early thirties rated the U of T with Harvard and well above Yale and Columbia.[8] The graduate program had high standards. As an M.A. student in his first year, Daniells was required to take three substantive survey courses and an additional course in bibliography; Ph.D. students were required to have Anglo-Saxon, Middle English, two modern languages, and two classical languages as well as full coverage in the area chosen for the dissertation.

His lack of knowledge of university politics was greatly to Daniells' advantage because he reached out on all sides. At first, he was taken up by Principal Wallace, who regularly invited him to tea and dinner. At Wallace's home, he met University College faculty and their wives in a social atmosphere where his intelligence, his puckish wit, and vulnerability recommended him. People wanted to help him. His initial social awkwardness, lack of money, and diffidence were all apparent. But he had a fine mind, probing and subtle; he could be quite humorous, and he was diligent. His professors soon acknowledged that this tall, craggy, older student from British Columbia was the best graduate student in his year.

In 1930–1 Daniells was thin to the point of emaciation, and neatly but modestly dressed. He had a narrow, bony face, and his hair tended to fall over his forehead. His personality belied a somewhat dour appearance. He had a nimble mind, and his face would light up when he began to talk. And he was mischievous: he enjoyed telling jokes.[9] Whatever his inner grief, he found other people infinitely interesting and he showed it. As one of his classmates recalled, 'the minute he spoke to you he made you feel as though he was terribly interested in you.' Once engaged in a conversation, he had a pleasant smile with a twinkle, a warm, recognizably south-of-England voice, and a sardonic wit.[10]

Yet during the first two months at Toronto, Daniells struggled to keep his emotional balance. He was lonely, frequently ill, and had very little money. He later told one of his own students, 'with a kind of wry but triumphant amusement, that he managed to get through that winter without an overcoat, by calculating to a T how far he could dash on the campus from one building entrance to the next without actually freezing to death.'[11] To assuage his loneliness, he began to write long chatty letters to 'Dear Parentums' at least twice a week, sometimes three times, and always on a Sunday. Some of these letters were signed 'Little Ethelbert,' echoing the name of the first Christian king of the Anglo-Saxons, who had been instrumental in the conversion of his countrymen. The allusion may have been a childhood family joke – Ethelbert had lived in Kent, the district from which the Daniellses had come – reflecting his parents' ideas about his future life. Even his nickname could be seen to place a certain pressure on him; he was now expected to minister to the heathen at Toronto, so to speak.

His letters, especially those to his mother, who became his chief confidante, tell of the people he met, what he did, the state of his studies, and his health. During 1930 and 1931, Daniells had trouble with his stomach, teeth, and tonsils. He had sore throats, frequent neuralgia, biliousness, and 'nerves.' There were a series of colds, an inflamed appendix, and painful kidneys. His teeth were filled, his migraines diagnosed, and eventually his tonsils removed, but there was little that could be done to help a continually upset stomach. As home remedies, he tried castor oil, a fruit diet, raw eggs, and enemas, as well as hydrogen peroxide for the sore throat.

None of these addressed the root problem of his distress – his depression. This Daniells attributed to his religious beliefs and to his concerns about his studies. When working on an essay on Arnold and 'Sweetness and Light' for his nineteenth-century group, for example, he felt 'horribly depressed about religious matters. I seem to slip and slip. Miserable. But I hope in God.'[12] These feelings of deep depression were accompanied by acute physical unease, nausea, and headaches, which made it impossible for him to eat properly. This, in turn, led to further stomach upsets and a further loss of weight.

All of these symptoms were now recurring: it was the autumn, always a bad time for him, and he was away from home. He also had a new reason to feel distressed – his parents were displeased with him. His father objected strongly to Daniells' correspondence with Carol Coates Cassidy. Letters were arriving in Victoria from Japan, at the rate of three a week. What did Roy think he was doing? He responded to his father by assembling a collage of quotations from their joint letters to him, to show they were not 'intriguing.' And he protested to his mother regarding a lack of faith: 'What worries me worst is the feeling that you and Pa regard me as a criminal of some sort. Even if you think I am being "entangled" or something I would like to ask what earthly purpose, other than a very pure and natural friendship, would induce a newly-married girl to write to a single man, who was 8000 miles away, – devoid of money, – of rigid morals – and of an entirely different religious conviction? Especially if she didn't expect to see him for five or ten years ...'[13] His parents, meantime, sent their son the sort of reading matter they approved of – a Bible.

He felt miserable. His two best friends were in Japan, his parents were disappointed in him, and he had a nagging suspicion that he was in the wrong. What was worse, his own unfulfilled sexuality was flaring up in what he called 'Eros.' He had been attempting to sublimate sexuality in religion and a long-distance courtly love; not surprisingly, it was not working. Now, when he received yet another letter from Carol, he felt 'rather rotten, downcast and miserable. Worried about Father & Mother, – their view of Carol. Also Eros now extremely bad.'[14] Two weeks later he still felt badly about Carol, but graduate school was making so many demands on his time and energy – a report on Cardinal Newman in his second week, an essay on Herbert and Crashaw a few days later – that he had no time to worry about himself. During his first year, Daniells took a special course from Brown in sixteenth- and seventeenth-century literature that emphasized the English humanists and Petrarchian and neo-Platonic ideas. He also took 'English Thought, 1640–1740,' which was taught by Endicott in the first term, and Davis in the second term, reading Milton, Herbert, Crashaw, and Donne. There was a nineteenth-century course taught by John F. MacDonald on figures like Mill and Bentham, and a bibliography course.

Early in the term, he recognized that he must 'get down to work.' He was reading late every night: *The Arcadia, Rosalynde, The Shepherd's Calendar, Lyrics 1557–1900, Cross Currents of the Seventeenth Century,* Louis Cazamian's *A History of English Literature* (1927), Babbitt's *Rousseau and Romanticism,* and the *Hogarth Essays.* He carried on a dialogue with his diary, telling himself to 'read less and think more,' but by mid-October he was doubtful whether he had made much progress despite long hours.[15]

A month later, he summed up his impressions of the U of T. Academic work was now more difficult: 'At UBC it was largely a matter of memory; here one has to have critical ability.' It was not easy to answer his parents' questions about whether he was happier in his work: 'Superficially yes. Fundamentally no.' The problem was that literary criticism as taught at the U of T extended into philosophy and aesthetics. He knew very little about either, and felt that he did not think easily or clearly. Furthermore, what he knew about religion could not be easily assimilated with what he was expected to know about literature: 'A synthesis between the moral and religious views I hold and the aesthetic & philosophic realms of thought [of the university] does not present itself.'[16] It was a shrewd analysis. It was not until later in his program, when his moral and religious understanding of Milton began to fuse with the aesthetic concept of the Baroque, that he was able to bring the two opposites together.

By late November he had successfully jumped a number of hurdles, and Brown had accepted his outline for his M.A. thesis. Consequently he felt more hopeful. But, continually pursued by the spectre of earlier failures, he continued to spur himself to work harder.[17] While in Victoria, he had thought that an M.A. was wonderful, but in Toronto he recognized that a man without European training or American experience seemed behind the times. His greatest problem was his age: 'at twenty-eight a now-or-never feeling seizes you. Seeing I have come so far in the last five years (even with three at Sprott-Shaw) I am extremely anxious not to make a false step now.'[18]

⎯⎯⎯➤◉◄⎯⎯⎯

As soon as Daniells' thesis topic had been accepted, he began the task of securing an adequate critical background for the lyric by studying the Christian humanists and the courtly love tradition. In addition, he began to read Babbitt's *Rousseau and Romanticism* chapter by chapter in tandem with the poetry of Babbitt's student T.S. Eliot, whom he saw as a contemporary humanist. The new ideas raised in Brown's lectures on the English humanists (and Brown's frequent references to Babbitt) caused Daniells to rethink some of his ideas on religion. Consequently it was with great interest that he went to hear Babbitt when he was invited to give the annual Alexander Lectures at U of T in November 1930.

Babbitt spoke on Wordsworth. His lectures were a *cause célèbre*. Many Torontonians – the *Canadian Forum* reported two thousand people – went to hear him. His message was blunt. He did not care for Wordsworth or for most Romantic poets. For a quarter of a century, he had opposed Romanticism, especially Jean-Jacques Rousseau, and advocated a return to the classics and a new humanism. Babbitt emphasized that man was not wholly good, as the romantics had claimed, but that his character contained a large admixture of evil. Thus, strenuous spiritual discipline was essential if man was to grow ethically.

Reaction to Babbitt's talk was mixed. E.J. Pratt wrote a poem called 'From Stone to Steel,' suggesting that man's evolutionary progress was, echoing Babbitt's terms, 'between the temple and the cave.' Barker Fairley, a professor of German at University College, wrote an 'Open Letter to Professor Irving Babbitt' in the *Canadian Forum*, complaining that 'you are a moralist and an historian of morals, using poetry and such-like for your own ends.'[19] Nonetheless, Babbitt had many supporters at Toronto, including J.S. Will, who responded indignantly; two years later, probably at Woodhouse's instigation, Paul Elmer More, a Harvard professor, wrote an article for the *University of Toronto Quarterly* explaining Babbitt's thought.[20]

Daniells was not impressed by Babbitt as a speaker; like Pratt, however, he responded positively to Babbitt's morality. He continued to read *Rousseau and Romanticism* with a view to applying it to his thesis. In Babbitt's view, man's dualism was the struggle between the egoism of 'natural man' and the moral sense (or conscience) of a civilized, ethical, humanistic man. Arguing that Romanticism and Freudian psychology are alike in that they excuse man of conscious purpose and so deprive him of his humanity, Babbitt contended that 'man becomes human in so far as he exercises moral choice.'[21] Daniells began to recognize some similarities between Babbitt's moral dogmatism and that of the Brethren. But although Babbitt believed in original sin, Daniells thought that morality might be achieved by 'classic discipline' rather than by the miraculous salvation of the Brethren. For the next few years, Daniells linked Babbitt's ethical dogmatism and Eliot's 'dogmatic ideas' when expounding his own religious beliefs.

Babbitt was an important bridge for Daniells between religion and literature. He absorbed Babbitt first-hand through his own reading and second-hand through Brown, whose career, especially his studies in France, illustrated the New Humanism's enthusiasm for French culture and the prevailing interest in Greek and Christian ideals, an interest manifested in Brown's Humanism course. The New Humanism, as understood in the thirties, joined literature with the graphic arts and music. It called for decorum and opposed the prevailing naturalism in letters. New Humanism did not quite succeed in reducing the judgment of art to a moral basis but – and this was the important point for Daniells – it introduced a reassuringly moral component.[22] He now considered himself a humanist.

In another respect, Babbitt was a very important figure in the reformation of North American education through an early book, *Literature and the American College* (1908), which had shifted the American university curriculum from an emphasis on Germanic language studies to a more humanistic, classically oriented curriculum. The 'Great Books of Western Civilization' courses that later emerged at Harvard, Columbia, and Chicago took their inspiration from the humanists' call for values and a return to the classics. Babbitt's humanistic combination of literature and morals had considerable impact, not only at the U of T, but throughout Canada, where at least five early and dominant heads of departments had passed through the Harvard English Department.

Brown, as Leon Edel reported, was carrying a copy of Babbitt's *The New Laokoon* (1910) when he first met him in Paris in the late twenties.[23] Now, near the end of the first term at Toronto in 1930, Daniells recorded that Brown's 'lecture on Humanists turned largely into discussion on the possibility of seeing other points of view if one holds dogmatic views. I holding the affirmative and E.K. the neg.'[24] The argument is a curious reversal of position because each man seems to be supporting the opposite of his own experience. To this point, Daniells had great difficulty in shifting his dogmatic beliefs even slightly, whereas Brown, as his biographer records, had changed his views from staunch Catholicism to a new 'religion of art' by way of the Sorbonne and Walter Pater.[25] Brown may have taken up an adversarial position in order to encourage his student to articulate his beliefs. In any event, this discussion marked a turning point in their relationship. Shortly after, on the last day of the first term, Daniells had a talk – first with Endicott, and then with Brown. He told both professors about the 'fixed dogmatic ethics' of his Plymouth Brethren beliefs.[26]

In the 1931 spring term, Brown and Daniells became friends. It was an intellectual friendship that began in late January when Daniells heard Brown's lecture on Matthew Arnold's French reputation.[27] Daniells asked Brown for a copy of his paper so that he could read it more carefully. The two young men – Brown was twenty-five and Daniells four years older – were interested in some of the same aesthetic and religious problems. They began to attend artistic and faculty events together – Brown invited Daniells to a lecture on Mazo de la Roche and then to a dinner for the American poet H.D. (Hilda Doolittle). In a college of older, settled professors, they were bachelors and free to come and go as they chose. They would often go to a literary event and then walk and talk into the early morning – 1:30 or 2:00 A.M. – discussing current topics.

Though also influenced by the New Critics, Brown retained the more eclectic approach of Matthew Arnold or Sainte-Beuve, which combined close reading of a text with biography and the history of ideas. A joint product of University College (plus Pelham Edgar's emphasis at Victoria on Canadian literature) and the Sorbonne, where Hippolyte Taine's emphasis on *race, époque,* and *milieu* combined with Louis Cazamian's encyclopedic approach to literary history, he was hospitable to the idea of a Canadian literature at a time when many scholars were not. Like Taine and Cazamian, Brown recognized and emphasized the interplay between culture and literature. A charismatic teacher, he set up an evening Canadian literature club, which Daniells attended, to discuss Canadian writers.[28] In his personal life and as a literary critic, Brown undertook the Arnoldian-humanist function of educating his readers. As a fellow student at the Maison Canadienne in 1929, he had influenced Leon Edel.[29] Now at the U of T in 1930, he turned to students like Daniells and the poet and historian Alfred Bailey. Bailey recalled that the Canadian literature group included the poet Dorothy Livesay and the social activist Stanley Ryerson. Bailey believed that 'people who were members of this group knew more about literature than any comparable group in Canada ... Each took a turn about each week in reading a paper. This was not a poetry club ... It was a club of literary critics.'[30]

In appearance, Brown was 'dapper': he was broad-shouldered, cleanshaven, and always dressed conventionally in suit, waistcoat, and tie, with his dark hair brushed back in T.S. Eliot fashion. By the 1930s, he wore wire-rim glasses, but earlier, as Edel recalls, his glasses were an accessory to his conversation: 'He wore pince-nez at that time, and used to take them off, pause, blink his eyes, and build up mystery when he had a story to tell. "Do you know ...?" And "What do you think happened ...?" And so on until he would come out with what he had to tell which was always some subtlety of observation. And he would chuckle very heartily.'[31] It is an attractive portrait. Brown enjoyed the art of conversation, and his talk was both subtle and humorous. He took pleasure in the role of professor and mentor, and Daniells was a willing student. What Daniells and Brown shared was a delight in the give and take of good conversation.

As they walked and talked, Brown told Daniells of his plans for advancement: 'E.K.B. said he was getting a book ready on Stoicism, Platonism, & c. in the 16th Century. Also he was expecting to offer ... a thesis on Mrs. Wharton & another bit of work on Matthew Arnold's prose works.' This information was punctuated by Daniells' regret that Brown was not 'a Xtian.' Brown, a Catholic, was not 'born again' and thus in Daniells' lights not bound for heaven. Brown, a careful observer and a shrewd judge of character, may well have seen – and discounted – these 'dogmatics,' for he continued to be kind. And Daniells continued to thank God rather than man. 'Saw E.K.B. in Hart House. He said he had spoken to Dr Wallace about the tutorial fellowship for next year & that there was apparently no obstacle to my getting it. So I praise God again for His very great kindness to me in spite of my perpetual sins & failures.'[32]

Brown was a good friend and an admirable thesis supervisor. He led Daniells to broaden the field of his thesis, pointed out deficiencies in his scholarship, and emphasized the importance of travel to Europe, especially France, if one were to become a cultivated scholar. He also advised him to apply for the University of Toronto Tutorial Fellowship. Daniells duly consulted Principal Wallace, who suggested he ask for renewal of the fellowship for the coming year.

In fact, both Brown and Wallace did their best for Daniells. On Christmas Day 1930, he was invited for dinner at the Wallaces. Daniells was quite impressed by the large Wallace home. As the family had been missionaries, it was furnished with Chinese chests and artifacts, which included two large vermilion dragons. There was pleasant company and a bountiful Christmas dinner, with paper hats and carols, followed by moving pictures taken in South America. Daniells arrived home at midnight after having a wonderful time: 'The generosity of the Wallaces makes me *gasp*.'[33] On Boxing Day, he was invited to dinner by a graduate student, Jimmie Knights. There he met Robert Finch, a young instructor of French at University College, who was to become a close friend. On Twelfth Night, Principal Wallace held another party for a few members of the UC faculty and several graduate students, including Daniells. It was an amusing evening with a good dinner, music, and charades, in which Daniells took the part of the serpent in Eden. It was here that he met Professor Herbert Davis, who would have a profound influence on his life.

In the spring, Davis became Daniells' instructor in the seventeenth-century course. His teaching, emphasizing God's 'divine Mercies and marvellous Judgements,' was far different from Brethren doctrine.[34] The old flaming portrait of hell was now subject to revision. The chief attraction to Milton's poetry, which was to become Daniells' main academic interest, was that, as it was taught by Davis, it bridged the old theology of the Plymouth Brethren and the world of humane studies. The familiar beliefs were now clothed in poetry and given rich classical and historical reference. 'I was now listening, not to the ministering

Brethren but to magnificent archangels, Raphael and Michael, who expound everything to Adam and Eve.'[35] Instead of thundering preachers like McClure threatening hellfire, Milton's whole structure, as interpreted by Davis, emphasized God's providence.

⟞⟝⟞⟝

He was now beginning to write his M.A. thesis. When Daniells arrived in Toronto in September, he had not finished his UBC graduating essay, 'A Century of Lyrics,' dealing with Renaissance lyrics. While completing it, he showed it to Brown, who told him his essay was 'full of material, but somewhat pointless.' He agreed, but he worked hard to complete it. It was not until late December that he finished and sent the essay to Dr Sedgwick. This essay was to lay important groundwork for his thesis, 'A Century and a Half of English Lyricism,' which Brown had agreed to supervise.

After Christmas he worked consistently on his thesis, which dealt with the period from 1550 to 1700. It discussed the lyric in terms of its paradoxes, its relationship to the English temper, and its genesis in religious thought, noting that it was not possible to understand the early Renaissance lyric without approaching it from the medieval period.[36] The literary structure which Daniells established draws on the Old Testament view of sinful man as taught by the Brethren, but is now filtered through Babbitt's *Rousseau and Romanticism* to indicate the transition from Christianity to the Christian humanists. In addition, he drew upon Oswald Spengler's *Decline of the West* (1926) for his exposition of the idea of cycles in human history. Daniells also discussed the expression of Puritan ideals in lyrics and the courtly love tradition.

He worked steadily throughout the spring term, combining his formal work with attending the Canadian Literature Club, the Graduate English Club, and the Inter-Collegiate Christian Union (ICCU), and playing badminton and squash. He appeared to have gained momentum because in late March he was sorting notes for chapter 3, but by the start of April he had nearly finished the chapter. Finally on 22 April 1931 he wrote in his diary: 'Finished ch. 4 & Conclusion of Thesis in a hurry & handed in to E.K.B.'[37]

At UBC there was great pleasure at the news of his speedy progress. Tuli Larsen, who had started him on the lyric, was especially pleased. 'It makes an enormous difference when one already has a background.

Moreover the subject looks to me to be the one that you can carry on for the Ph.D.' He added, perceptively, 'You now have your foot firmly on the ladder and in a few years I expect you will be ahead of us all.'[38] By mid-May Daniells had an oral examination with Davis, MacDonald, and Brown, which went very well. He achieved 85 per cent for nineteenth-century thought, and 85 per cent on his reading course with E.K. Brown on the humanists. Several months later, in Victoria, he received his M.A. certificate from Toronto in the mail.[39]

It had been a long, exhausting, and stimulating year. On 16 April he wrote in his diary that he was feeling 'pretty nervy and strung up.' He suddenly thought of going home to Victoria for the summer. His parents encouraged him, as his mother was very anxious that he rest and shore up 'some reserve nervous energy for next year ... You had these urges in Vancouver to work overhard, but dear boy where did it land you? Your summer last year was one of working on overwrought nerves.'[40] On 27 May he took the train for Vancouver and the ferry to Victoria, where he arrived on 1 June.

On his first day back home, he went to Sprott-Shaw to arrange some coaching work; he then visited old friends like Max Maynard, Dilworth, and Larsen, who were in Victoria marking papers. Daniells' days now assumed a routine; he taught himself German and coached a variety of students, primarily in English, but also in Latin. Over the summer, he cast a glance at an occasional girl but to no avail. His study was punctuated with diary entries noting friends seen, swims taken, and brief descriptions suggesting his pleasure at being home: 'Walked to Loon Bay for a dip. Countryside gorgeous; flowers and grasses beautiful.'

He went regularly to the public library, read plays and novels in preparation for fall teaching at the U of T, and slipped back into the routine of attending Plymouth Brethren meetings, often several times a week. In late June, he went with his father for a Bible reading 'on "Sin & Its Consequences." Spoke a little myself on pre-Adamic death.' His diary records his attendance at meetings at the Oak Bay Gospel Hall, and his regular stints of preaching are frequently accompanied by expressions of depression: 'Oak [Hall] Morn. Max [Maynard] to lunch & for walk. Oak eve. For walk afterwards. Feeling very depressed.' Nevertheless, he continued to attend meetings, and to preach. One Sunday he spoke on 'Habakkuk,' and a month later on 'standing fast and pressing on.' Early in the summer, Daniells and John McDonald walked to Mount Tolmie and afterward met up with Max. On the way home, Max had been 'outspoken on uselessness of our Xtianity. Very discouraging.'[41] Max was turning away from the Brethren, and it disturbed Roy.

By 1931 Max had taken an apartment above his brother's retail store in downtown Victoria, overlooking the harbour, and Daniells frequently came to talk or to look at Max's paintings: Max was now even more keen on paintings of stumps.[42] It is Max's apartment-cum-studio and his comments on the Plymouth Brethren that are reproduced in a semi-autobiographical sketch written by Daniells in the early forties. Max appears as Tarby, suggesting both 'tar' and J.N. Darby, a Plymouth Brethren founder, for by the early thirties Max had a reputation as a black sheep in the Plymouth Brethren community. Darby is a significant figure in Daniells' emotional pantheon because it was he who first conceived the idea of the Plymouth Brethren 'secret rapture.'

In Daniells' sketch, Tarby functions as a mentor who rejects Plymouth Brethren insularity:

> *'If you really want to know,' said Tarby, 'come up and I'll tell you ... Tarby kicked together a decayed fire ... He produced whisky from a locker ...*
>
> *'Nobody,' said Tarby, 'understands the Brethren unless he's been one of them. I doubt if even the most primitive Methodist or Baptist can quite grasp the inner world they have created. I know of nothing like it. Don't confuse it with mysticism, or the sacredotal authority or with the inner light ... Above all the Brethren are insular; they are founded on rock ... The rock, they say, is the Word ... It is at least the word, in the sense of the Bible. They have always the abyss, the fire in reserve'[43]*

Analysing, judging, dismissing, Tarby is in the process of rejecting Plymouth Brethren doctrine and practices, the latter rejection emphasized by his whisky-drinking. For the Daniells of 1931, Max was going entirely too far. Nonetheless, the rigidity of the Brethren point of view also bothered him. In mid-July at the Oak Bay Hall, several members had spoken out against a passion play to be staged that week. 'I arose & pointed out that we need not condemn the whole manifestation, medieval & modern, *en bloc*. Some thought I should not have done so ...'[44]

The biggest event in the Daniells household that summer was the sale in mid-August of the Cook Street house, and plans for the construction of a new home to be built by James Daniells on Cochrane Street. Daniells was a considerate son, and it was clearly a source of joy and comfort to his parents to have him around. But for him the experience was mixed. He, too, took comfort from his family, but the constant religious atmosphere caused inner turmoil. He did not return to Victoria for the summer holidays for almost five years.

By the end of August, he was planning his return to Toronto. A classmate recommended his landlady, Miss Jean Grant. She offered him, as a Christian young man, a room in her boarding house at a reduced rate. It was an irresistible offer – morality plus economy. He accepted promptly. And good friend that he was to Max, before leaving Victoria, Daniells loaned him seventy-five dollars.[45]

On 18 September 1931 Daniells boarded the train for Toronto, stopping in both Regina and Winnipeg to visit friends. He arrived in Toronto on the morning of Sunday, 27 September, and again went to Hart House for a shower and then to the Church of St George the Martyr. Only after this activity did he head for Miss Grant's and secured his room. She proved to be a solicitous, indeed over-solicitous, landlady.

He took on another heavy workload during the fall. Without a grant, he had to find money to help support himself. The teaching fellowship at University College secured by E.K. Brown helped: Daniells was given a freshman English pass course, and he taught four Shakespeare plays, modern novels by Bennett, Butler, Conrad, and Hardy, and modern plays by Galsworthy, Masefield, Shaw, and Synge. He also began teaching an extension course in composition and essay writing, and accepted a relief teaching position four times a week at Upper Canada College, where he may have taught the English novel to Robertson Davies. On top of all this, he began working two nights a week at the library.

His main activities, however, were associated with Ph.D. course work. He took a class on 'The Lyric' with Davis, 'Ancient Philosophy' with Brett of the Philosophy Department, and 'Wordsworth' with Wallace. He continued to attend Brown's Canadian literature group. Not surprisingly, his health suffered and his mother became worried, urging him to refuse more work: 'Dearest boy: We think and think of you and pray you will not overdo it.'[46]

This term Daniells was not so impressed by Davis's teaching,[47] largely because Davis was having difficulty discussing the lyric in literary and musical terms. Daniells was now elected president of the Graduate English Club and became increasingly busy when it sponsored a lunch for the Canadian literary figure J. Murray Gibbon, with a group that included Finch, Knox, Davis, and a student, Helen Kemp (who later married Northrop Frye). 'Gibbon spoke at (44 Hoskin St.); gramophone & lantern; pretty poor in some ways. I did not know what to say in reply at end.'[48]

Three weeks later, on 27 January 1932, Daniells himself gave a talk on T.S. Eliot and T.E. Hulme to the Graduate English Club, which turned out to be a 'smashing success.' Writing to his mother, he reported that nearly thirty faculty and students attended:

> The paper went off well; the discussion afterwards was extremely good; a number of people complimented little me; and Davis said the next day they would publish it (suitably cut down to 5000 words) in the University Quarterly. So I am immensely bucked: (a) it means $50 from the Quarterly if published. (b) the big guns got really interested and discussed it with vigour, meaning it was an *academic* success. (c) it was an attempt, in part, to present certain Christian beliefs in a new dress and make academic people listen: I have wanted to do this for a good many years & I take this small success as a Divine token of approval, – as a missionary rejoices over his first convert.[49]

The last comment may have been intended to please his parents. Little Ethelbert, or 'little me,' as he sometimes signed his letters, was carrying out his missionary work. His article had made a significant impression on the major professors at the U of T in respective colleges and departments – Wallace, Edgar, Davis, and Brown in English, and Professor Will from the French Department. What Daniells had done was to show how some of Eliot's ideas, especially his rejection of Romanticism in favour of a new Classicism, derived from the thought of Hulme.

After his talk on Eliot, Daniells went to Davis's flat more often than before to discuss Eliot, Lawrence, and other contemporary writers. The Davises enjoyed entertaining and had a pleasant flat dominated by a large piano, chintz upholstered furniture, and a number of paintings. It was a social centre for Toronto musicians and artists, for patrons of the arts like Douglas Duncan, and for bright young members of faculty like Finch and Wilson Knight. Knight, who was British, taught at Trinity College and was specializing in Shakespearean literature and myth criticism; he had already published *The Wheel of Fire* (1930). Davis, also English, had 'thrown in his lot' with Canada and was particularly interested in Canadian culture. He had several Group of Seven paintings, including one of Fred Varley's heads of a girl. Through Davis, Daniells began to sense the existence of a larger cultural world where art and literature and music were more important than theology.

Davis was an exceptionally pleasant companion. At first glance, he might be mistaken for a typical quiet Englishman. He was of average height and balding, but his amiable face was dominated by piercing and attentive blue eyes that suggested intelligence and sharpness. 'He was a kindly man, but if you made statements that were off the track, he would bring you up so that you would get a sense of erring, or of not being firmly based in your facts.'[50] A man of enthusiasms, he was constantly making invitations: '"Oh come and see ..." It might be a rose in the garden, it might be a picture that he'd acquired, it might be a song that he'd just found. But the enthusiasm was overpowering and you were just caught up in it too.'[51] Davis was a rarity, an enthusiast and an intellectual who held a genuine concern for his fellow man. He was also quite complex and private. An older Daniells recalled that 'he never revealed his inmost thoughts, not at least to me. I am not sure how he viewed me, – as a friend, a lonely student, someone who he had also found in his path to whom he could be kind.'[52]

Over the winter, Daniells and Davis played squash regularly and frequently went for tea or lunch afterward. They also swam, a habit Daniells continued for the rest of his life. In the spring of 1931, just before he returned to Victoria, Davis took him to a sumptuous lunch at Simpson's. 'We had tripe, very nicely cooked, in a magnificent dining room which I had never seen before, – glass dome, elaborate chandeliers, orchestra, etc. etc. & prices very reasonable. The more I see of Davis the more I like him. His manners are as near social perfection as you could very well ask for.'[53] At a dinner in mid-May, Davis and Daniells were joined by Barker Fairley, and the three men had a good discussion on Eliot. While visiting Davis, Daniells learned that neither he nor Brown had received the Royal Society fellowships for which they had applied to study abroad. Davis was unflappable. Daniells had been planning to go to England for the summer, and Davis counselled him not to change his plans. Daniells promptly arranged for study in England.

He had determined to write his Ph.D. thesis as an extension of his work on the English lyric. In fact, while studying the courtly love tradition, he was himself practising a kind of courtly love in his relations with young women. Carol had been his *'princesse lointaine,'* the 'Beatrice' to his 'Dante.' But he was now thirty and had never had a serious girlfriend. He had vague dreams of a special woman, even vaguer ideas of a wife, but no idea of how to conduct a courtship. When he wanted to initiate a friendship, he reverted to the Daniellses' family habits of giving chocolates and flowers and stockings. In keeping with his growing affluence as he gained scholarship support, he tended to go overboard – sending too many expensive gifts to young women who barely knew him and felt uncomfortable about his possible intentions.

In his choice of young women to court, as in everything else, his criteria were religious. The three young women who figured most in the early thirties were respectively very religious, not sufficiently religious, and atheist. The first, Muriel David, was a young American whom he had met at the Inter-Collegiate Christian Union. Daniells, initially attracted to her because of her religious beliefs, later found her too dogmatic. Muriel 'was always trying to uplift one. And was terrifically evangelistic. Well, there are limits to what one can stand.' The second, Elizabeth Lang, was a pleasant young woman from a good family. But 'Betty' was not religious enough. What she led him to recognize was 'the fearful difficulty that must confront people who have unsaved families.'[54] Daniells discouraged any deeper relationship with Betty: 'I feel totally unequal to the whole business of a home and children ... the thought that any child of mine might be damned freezes the marrow of me.'[55]

Then, too, Betty did not attract him as did her close friend Eugenia Watts, better known as 'Jim.' The daughter of a wealthy family, Jim was intelligent, vigorous, and impetuous. She had attended private school in Toronto with the poet Dorothy Livesay, and in the early thirties she was part of a group of young people at U of T attracted to the communism of Otto Van der Sprenkel, a Dutch professor of economics. This group, which included Stanley Ryerson, later a leader of the Communist Party in Canada, tended to meet at Charlotte's Coffee Shop, run by Jim's friend Ann Farwell. Jim was a complex young woman, sexually experimental and quick to initiate relationships.[56] In 1931, the summer before she met Daniells, Jim had travelled to Paris with Van der Sprenkel, where he had left her.[57]

Daniells knew little or nothing of Jim's past. He met her in February 1932 when Betty took him to Jim's apartment to have coffee. Tall and slim, she appeared to him as 'a beautiful creature [with] a mop of very blonde hair.' She had 'the face of a child with the most perfect complexion you ever saw – looks about sixteen and is twenty-three.' At Jim's apartment, Daniells found a group of U of T students, all concerned about the Depression, who frequently dropped in for lunch or dinner; a few years later, this group, now professing Marxism, rallied to the Loyalists in the Spanish Civil War.[58]

Jim's apartment was primarily a place to see Betty and the group. However, one evening he and Jim found themselves alone. Roy began to talk about religious subjects, and their discussion left them both intrigued. Subsequently, he took Jim to the Toronto zoo, one of his favourite places. Full of exuberant high spirits, she rolled down a hill. The next time they met, Jim 'told me what she felt about me.' Presumably Jim said she was attracted to him because he later recorded that Jim 'broke much more ice than I.' His diary entries for the next two days reiterate 'spent much of day with "Jim."' Jim's affections may have been transitory, but they were well worth having. An affectionate and warm-hearted woman, she saw through the facade of his literary posturings. Her letters asked the essential questions: Was he eating well? Was he sleeping? Was he wasting his time worrying about religion? It was time to have some fun! Three days later, when Daniells left by the midnight train to catch the boat to England for study at the British Museum, Jim phoned long distance to wish him 'bon voyage.' Perhaps they would meet on the Continent?[59]

Chapter Five

Following the Path

While crossing from Canada to England on the *Alaunia*, Daniells had met up with a classmate, Archie Hare, and notified his parents that he would 'push on' to Paris with Hare. There he expected to contact Jim through his U of T friends 'Dee' (Dorothy) Livesay and Stanley Ryerson. Jim had encouraged him in late May by writing: 'I am rather troubled with excessive thinking of you,' but then dashed his spirits by adding that she wanted to discuss Marx and Spengler.[1] He had arrived in Paris on 5 June and settled into the Hotel Lutèce on Rue Berthollet.

Daniells had been in Paris for nearly two weeks, long enough to see the sights, to discover Jim's absence, and to become desperately homesick. It was then that he undertook some serious mental stocktaking and wrote his parents from the Cimetière du Père-Lachaise, rejecting Plymouth Brethren doctrine: 'The whole urge that kept me going from 1924 till last year seems to have spent itself and I long for a rest, or oblivion, or death or something.' Although he had started research for his Ph.D., he feared he could not complete the work because of persistent ailments and 'nerves.' Indeed, he was convinced he was headed for a breakdown. But he promised his parents in a long letter to do what he could until his return to Toronto on 1 October. '*For the time being* I can see a straight road ahead and I shall not change my plans of seven years' standing rashly.'[2]

In this despair, his only comfort were the poems of T.S. Eliot. He copied out a few verses from 'Ash-Wednesday' for his parents, warning them that it was 'difficult stuff':

Because I know that time is always time
And place is always and only place

And what is actual is actual only for one time
And only for one place
I rejoice that things are as they are and
I renounce the blessèd face
And renounce the voice
Because I cannot hope to turn again.
Consequently I rejoice, having to construct something
Upon which to rejoice

And pray to God to have mercy upon us
And pray that I may forget
These matters that with myself I too much discuss
Too much explain ...

The final stanza is poignantly applicable to his own condition. The persona of Eliot's poem cries to God for help: 'Teach us to sit still / Even among these rocks, / Our peace in His will.'[3]

Daniells needed these words of comfort because he was in an emotional limbo. He had settled into 'Room 34 (up 83 stairs)'in the Hotel Lutèce, waiting anxiously for almost two weeks before he received a 'pneumatique' from Livesay, whom he described as 'a Canadian girl who writes poetry and has quite a reputation.'[4] Livesay and Ryerson expected that Jim and her friend, Ann Farwell, would arrive in Paris on 18 June. Livesay, who writes of Jim as Gina (short for Eugenia) does not mention this incident in her brief account of this period in *Journey with My Selves*. She refers to Ryerson as 'Tony,' who reads Marx and Engels and applies their theories to the capitalist system.[5]

While waiting for Jim, Daniells began a rigorous program of sightseeing, recorded in a diary-cum-letter sent to his parents. In effect, he took his parents sightseeing with him and gave them strict instructions to keep the letters for his future use. He found the wonderfully green countryside between Le Havre and Paris like a picture book, but the Seine was a disappointment: 'To us who have run beside the Thompson & Fraser it looks like a ditch for size.'[6] France's landscape did not compare with Canada, but Parisians were the last word in chic. He was self-conscious about his appearance, recognizably English with his grey flannel 'bags,' old brown camel hair overcoat, and muffler. He had also grown a sandy coloured moustache. And his French was atrocious: 'When I enquire, "Pardon, Monsieur, où est la rue St. Michel?" I find out, but there is a look of surprise in Monsieur's eyes.'

He was following the well-worn path of the student in Paris, seeing the sights, looking at classical art. At Notre Dame Cathedral he was so moved by a figure of Christ in a quiet corner of the cathedral that he lit a candle, although he knew that in the eyes of his parents this action was akin to popery. In the next few days, he went to the Bibliothèque Nationale, the Pantheon, and the Louvre. What he liked most were the early religious paintings by Giotto, Cimabue, Fra Angelico, and Ghirlandaio, most of whom were familiar from reproductions in *The Children's Encyclopaedia*. As he became more and more excited, his handwriting became crabbed and blackened the pages of his letters – the art of Europe was the aesthetic peak of his experience. He walked on the Champs Élysées, saw the Place de l'Étoile (Place Charles de Gaulle) and the Arc de Triomphe. Along the Bois de Boulogne there were birds singing, blossoms lying underfoot, and lovers on the benches – all of which accentuated his own sense of being alone.

He made a point of telling his parents that he had gone to the Folies-Bergères, perhaps goading them a little. On another occasion, when he was walking in Paris, the French Revolution came alive: 'I realized the full meaning of the cry, "À la lanterne!" during the Revolution. For the lamp post on some little alleys are just the right size & shape (right angle near top) to hang a man on expeditiously.' He also felt compelled to explain his trip to Paris. 'I hope you will see that, for my type of work, this kind of intensive sightseeing is really necessary. And I am economizing to the point of irreproachability.'[7]

He was counting his pennies. He had to because he had not yet received the next instalment of his fellowship. And there were other issues simmering. Despite the *gloire* that was Paris and his high hopes for Jim's arrival, she had still not turned up. He did not feel well, and there were no regular, comforting letters from home – his sudden change of plan meant it was almost a month before he heard from his family. All the old religious terrors were coming to the surface, accentuated by the religious art he had been seeing – crucifixions, tortures, and hellfire – and by his sense of disorientation. The day after writing home, 16 June, he had a 'neuralgia attack' – always the prelude to a period of depression. All these issues climaxed on the 18th – the day when Jim was supposed to arrive, but did not – at the Cimetière du Père-Lachaise.

A few days later, he was contacted by Ryerson, and they jointly discovered that Jim and Ann would be arriving on 22 June. Daniells met the train and was immediately caught up in a whirlwind tour of

Paris that banished his depression. Jim's obvious pleasure at being back in Paris was infectious. They walked to the notable landmarks: the Seine, Notre Dame, through the Tuileries to the Arc de Triomphe. She and Daniells 'sallied' out and sat in approved style on the 'trottoir' of one of the cafés, sipping coffee and talking. Daniells thought that the three Canadians were very conspicuous: he was clearly a foreigner, while Ann kept her coat collar turned up and looked like a man, and Jim was very pink and fair in her tweeds and woollies. 'As a trio we knock the eye out of the populace.'[8]

On Wednesday they went to Notre Dame Cathedral, and on Thursday to the Palace of Versailles. The girls allowed him to pay for the major expenses in public but then promptly repaid their share, which he found decent if humiliating. Jim knew exactly where to go to dine. She steered him through the menus, and his digestive system picked up: 'It is fitting, somehow, to end two weeks of serious observations & guide book with this tiny burst of pure pleasure.' He was finally having fun in Paris. On their last day, he and Jim went to Sèvres and St Cloud: they had ices while looking around at what he felt to be 'the most fascinating French people ... and everything so civilized, intelligent and ordered.'[9] Back in Paris, they rushed through dinner and hurriedly took a taxi to the St Lazare Station, from which Daniells was to depart for England.

These three days in Paris had been an oasis in a desiccated emotional life. Almost a decade later, he tried to recapture the enchantment in an unpublished sketch:

> *She lighted on the platform and he ran to meet her, scarcely noticing Ann. Too shy to kiss her, he took both hands and looked into the small resolute laughing face ... Then they all three went out and had dinner ... 'Look,' she said, 'the fountains are playing.' 'It is for you,' he said, 'they know you are here.'*

As he later recalled, '*they were in Paris, they were together, they were very happy.*' No doubt it was glamour, nonsense, and the moon. No doubt it was misconception, self-deceit, and illusion. '*But how sweet and intoxicating! And with what power to stir the roots of desire after beauty and order and freedom, in after years.*' Most importantly, as Daniells' fiction tells us, the overwhelming burden that he carried was lifted: '*It seemed as though an immense and stifling weight were about to be lifted from his heart and chest and lungs; as though someone had cut the cords of his burden and were on the point of taking it off his back.*'[10] Almost – but not quite.

Warm and outgoing, Jim was an ideal companion in many ways. She wrote him cheery notes, 'Hello darling how are you – do you still want to marry me? You should first have a counsel with Ann on all my bad points.' She urged him to do things, read things, see things that this ordinarily circumspect young man would have avoided. And she had a literary side. She wrote from Ireland saying how delighted she was to find copies of T.S. Eliot's poems in Galway. She had read 'Prufrock' while on a beach eating butterscotch – a little dig, perhaps, because Daniells, so emotionally timid, had many of Prufrock's qualities.[11]

He had begun to think that Jim would make a fine wife. His reasoning, developed after he reached England, was that his first girl had been too religious, his second not religious enough, but Jim was just right. As an atheist and a communist, she had escaped Plymouth Brethren theology and might be persuaded to live a scholarly life without children (the voice of the old Oregon grandmother, with her fears for 'the children,' still rang in his ears). He described this ideal situation to his parents. If they got married, she could go on with her work in psychology and education:

> Now, here is a girl whom I get on with perfectly, who is very taken with me, who ... would probably be willing not to have children and who is intellectually very good ...
>
> She inherits (I hate *mentioning* this) $10,000 next year and more later, and has a good deal of sense ... She knows my financial position and said simply she would pool incomes, as plenty of other people do.

They would live in a small flat, go to Europe every summer, work very hard, 'waste neither a cent nor a minute, and be extremely happy. I have never approached any arrangement which seemed so perfectly possible and devoid of all the common woes.'

As far as the 'too-little' religion was concerned, he had considered this also. He assured his parents that he didn't think that his religious life would suffer any more than that of Moses when he married Zipporah. But just in case Mrs Daniells had lingering doubts about an atheist as a daughter-in-law, he would 'pray very hard for Jim.' He couldn't bear to think of 'her very beautiful face and her whole very fine and delicate physique writhing about in hell for ever.' By marrying Jim, he would be increasing her chances for salvation. Even should the marriage fail, it would be perfectly all right. 'I should leave her (for she will have a big fortune) ... and go to some difficult and very dangerous missionary area like Mongolia where I could probably do something useful for the Kingdom.'[12] Daniells squared romance, theology, and economics. It all made perfect sense.

The problem was that it was all nonsense. What Jim represented was not so much a potential wife as a glimpse of another world – a little pleasure, a little warmth, and a spit in the eye at Plymouth Brethren teaching. His rebellion was starting with a vengeance. He and Jim were an ill-assorted pair, and both had serious doubts about the relationship: at first she, then he. They did not go to Germany after all, and in the following two months his meetings with Jim in London were hurried and unsatisfactory. But at the end of the summer when Jim said, as inevitably she must, that their interests were quite different, his subsequent feelings of loss and abandonment precipitated his most decisive emotional crisis.

⇒●⇐

They first parted in Paris on 25 June. Daniells took the overnight train to England (by way of Dieppe and Newhaven) and arrived at Victoria Station. He registered as a boarder at Westgate House and obtained permission to read in the British Museum. He visited Piccadilly Circus, the Houses of Parliament, Trafalgar Square, and the House of Commons. But his impressions of England were exactly the opposite of those of France. London was a great disappointment, dark and depressing and dirty: 'They are putting up these huge barbaric buildings ... which imperialistic civilizations always put up as they pass into the final stage.'

On the following day, a Sunday, he attended an Anglican service and then walked from Chelsea to Sydenham – the family's old neighbourhood. When passing the Crystal Palace Road, he suddenly saw a sign for 'Venner Road,' and walked down to their old home. 'Beg to report same greatly shrunken in size; our huge garden very small; high palings at back of lane now quite low; towering willows over rockery (leaf enclosed) very medium.'[13] He continued on to the Plymouth Brethren Hall on Mayow Road. There he found a number of people who knew his parents and made him feel welcome. The preacher was good and one of his parents' old friends, a Mr Kennedy, walked him back to the bus stop and provided him with bus fare – he had spent all of his money.

The next day his side hurt from the continuous walking, and the Plymouth Brethren service had set up unpleasant reverberations. Just hearing the word 'hell' upset him no end. This, he reminded his parents, was a simple psychopathic fact. What worried him most was that all the freedom, stimulus, and joy of his past few years had come from doing things which the Plymouth Brethren would call wicked or unprofitable. As an intellectual, he needed ideas, books, pictures, and discussion far more than food or clothing, but the Brethren were anti-intellectual and despised art. This dilemma put him in great straits: 'And Christ, whose name is Wisdom, help me.'[14] His solution was almost as bad as his problem, for it is at this point that he proposed to marry Jim, live happily, and have no children.

His continuing reflections on England suggests that he had absorbed some of Jim's Marxism: 'I am more than ever glad that we got out of England. London is not a healthy place: the lower class look terrible. You can see the marks of the Industrial Revolution everywhere on faces and bodies ... I shall always call myself a Canadian here and say I am from B.C.'[15]

On 28 June, Jim cabled from France that she and Ann were planning to join a walking party in Ireland and would stop off in London for two days. From the moment of their arrival, his meals became 'very amusing': the trio sought out German and French restaurants. There was another whirlwind tour: to Kensington Gardens, Hyde Park, St James's Park, the Houses of Parliament, Madame Tussaud's, and the zoo. The following day, they took a long bus trip to Kew Gardens. 'We felt pretty foreign. Goodness knows what I am by national characteristic,– I don't feel Canadian but I am certainly not English.'[16]

The girls left at 8:45 P.M. from Euston Station for Holyhead and Dublin. From that point onward, he became increasingly lugubrious and by early July was depressed. He censored his letters to his parents because they were so gloomy. Nothing out of the ordinary had occurred, only his usual melancholy, combined with anxiety about finishing his required tasks: 'I am rather swamped with thoughts of poverty, health, thesis, loneliness, etc. combined with the usual inability to manage practical affairs, dread of meeting strangers, and the sort of nervous disintegration that has been my peculiar curse ever since I can remember.'[17] Clearly he missed Jim, and he had no external routine to keep him busy. Furthermore, he had money problems – his grant had not arrived.

He had begun work at the British Museum, and the many spectacles of post-war poverty found in the street were distressing, especially an old woman with a basket of lavender, who asked him very pathetically to buy. He gave her all of his coppers, concluding that his generation lived in a damnably bad world. He was young, with ready money, supportive parents, and friends. 'And yet I feel the burden of my own life almost insupportable. What must it be, then, for these poor wretches?' Shortly after, to divert himself, he attended a service at St Paul's Cathedral. He greatly admired John Donne, the seventeenth-century Dean of St Paul's, and recalled that all through his poems and sermons, 'you feel a powerful and penetrating mind and the striving of heart after God.' Unfortunately, the service included a reading in which the Lord cast out dumb spirits: 'all things are possible to him that believeth.' This reference to belief – and probably his old fears that he could not believe – brought on a bad case of nerves. He was forced to flee and seek out a toilet.[18]

Unable to control his nerves, he could not concentrate at the British Museum. And to make matters worse, he was still sending letters into the void. There were no letters from his parents as yet and, although he saw a number of people in London, none was a friend. Miserably conscious that he lacked scholarly method, he could not get his research under way at the British Museum. After a night of a severe bilious attack and neuralgia, he recognized that his nerves were completely shattered: '... the slightest contact with people simply takes it out of me. And I get so depressed over my general ineptitude and lack of grip that I could call on the pavement to swallow me.'[19]

There was one ray of hope. Davis, now in Ireland, had sent a note asking him to inspect a house in Hertfordshire that Daniells might share with them. 'We shall be (1) our 3 selves (2) yourself (3) my aunt and maid (4) certain guests – one at a time.' He asked Daniells to see if there would be room, outlined his plans for the next few weeks, and added that they hoped to arrive by 16 July: 'So we can look after you from that date.'[20] Daniells promptly went to see the cottage and reported that it was located at a little settlement called Heronsgate, a few miles outside the town of Rickmansworth. The cottage had a large and beautiful garden and there were fields beyond. Daniells now began to look forward to the summer: 'Perhaps Davis will straighten out some of my scholastic tangles. I think in so confused a manner, it seems, even apart from intrusions of disturbing ideas. And a thesis is no small job.'[21]

He had arranged to meet Davis at Euston Station but went to the wrong train and they failed to connect. He lectured himself severely: 'I seem to have no sense of managing anything: life is a succession of blunders.' But when he came back to his lodgings that night, he found to his great delight that Davis had arrived. 'We had a long confab till the man in the next room asked for quiet.'[22] Davis took rooms overnight, was in 'great form,' and the next morning insisted that the two go shopping to fit out Daniells, still very much a provincial, with a new suit of clothes.

The move to Heronsgate took place the following Saturday. The house was charming, and there was a pleasant walk towards a neighbouring village, Chorley Wood. There were Gladys and Herbert Davis, his aunt and her maid, and Daniells. They were expecting Robert Lightfoot, a clerical friend of Davis. Daniells promptly took possession of the study, got down to work, and was delighted with his good fortune. 'Why the Davises asked me is not altogether clear, but they are kindness itself and the chance is a godsend ... Furthermore the stimulus of being with people on the English staff ... is not to be despised. It bucks one up to do more work.'[23] Davis was working on his edition of Swift's *The Drapier's Letters*, soon tagged 'The Diaper Letters' because the baby, Elizabeth Ann, was always at hand.

Daniells had not been able to find a branch of the Plymouth Brethren nearby, but in any case he did not want to find them. He thought that if Christians wished, they could save souls from hell by not having any children. As he was earnestly penning this information to his parents in Victoria, Davis entered the study bringing a letter from them. His father must have made some reference to his 'un-Christian' friends because Daniells immediately responded by saying, in effect, that he would rather be in hell with Davis and 'Doc' Wallace than be in heaven with the Plymouth Brethren preachers Lefevre and Mundy – 'for would not Christ and the Father at once move down to Hell and make it Heaven ...?'[24]

Daniells found the Davises' household infinitely interesting. He got along well with Davis's wife, the former University College assistant professor Gladys Wookey, and he enjoyed talking with Lightfoot, an older don who was preparing to give the celebrated Bampton Lectures in two years' time at Oxford. Daniells, who spent the better part of one Sunday looking up references to damnation in St Mark's Gospel, appreciated Lightfoot's biblical knowledge. He hoped to obtain from him further information on the Church of England doctrine of the soul. He also felt thoroughly at home at Heronsgate, and made himself useful cutting the grass, rolling the tennis court, and trapping wasps. He was obliging when he had to work in the garden or when his quarters were shifted from the upper bedroom to the garage as visitors such as Davis's old friends Lightfoot, Barker Fairley, or Chloe Volumay arrived. The group soon settled into a familiar routine with Davis and Daniells taking the train up to London to work in the British Museum or the Victoria and Albert Library.

On the train, he began to learn more about Davis, who had planned to enter the Anglican ministry but had become 'disturbed while at college and took refuge ... in believing for himself and leaving the world completely alone.' However, he returned to the world, joined up as a 'Tommy,' and fought in the First World War, where 'a chap ... introduced him to modern literature.' He was part of the British army of liberation in Germany, where he had met his first wife, Gertrud Lucas, the daughter of 'a good type of German of the political kind.'[25] In effect, Davis had passed through the same religious torment, the same conversion-narrative that Daniells had experienced, but he had found new meaning in life from his encounter with modern literature and a new vocation as a professor of English.

The more Daniells saw of Davis the more he liked him, but he was utterly mystified as to why Davis was so kind to him. 'Davis ... is one of the most delightful people to live with I have ever come across. Few people, in fact no one, has been so kind to me with so little reason ... Davis seems to give you everything and take nothing. Even allowing for my well-known temporary enthusiasms, he is a pretty Good Thing.' Much later in his life, when Daniells was in his seventies and Davis had died, he still found it a mystery. Yet Davis had told him, but so obliquely that the younger man had not caught the message. As he had said, his first wife, Gertrud, had been a beautiful and cultured woman who had been lost at sea. One of Robert Finch's most intense memories was a recollection of Gertrud, who suffered from tuberculosis of the spine, lying on a chaise longue reading aloud in a melodious voice from Goethe's *Iphigenia in Tauris*. It had forever changed the way in which he heard German. In 1929 when Davis and Gertrud were on their way to the Continent, after a period of intense depression about her illness, she had disappeared from the ship in mid-ocean. Davis's colleagues at the U of T were convinced that Gertrud, believing that Davis should have children and knowing that she could not recover, had taken her own life.[26] Davis knew only too well where severe depression led, and Daniells, so emotionally transparent, was severely depressed.

Davis saw that he could help Daniells, and he did so by taking him into his home and expanding his cultural horizons. He introduced Daniells to a number of English scholars, several knowledgeable about the Baroque, and he talked with Daniells about current literature, especially Eliot, on whom Daniells was then writing. The Davises regularly attended music recitals, the theatre, and films. Davis also introduced him to painting, especially watercolours, which he thoroughly enjoyed: 'I must say it rests the mind, – unlike writing. You sing as you paint; as you write you clutch your hair & bite your tongue.' He also took Daniells to a select gramophone shop in London, E.M.G. Hand-Made Gramophones Ltd, where Davis purchased some music and a huge papier-maché trumpet for his phonograph. Daniells was to maintain a standing order for classical music with this store for several decades. Davis also encouraged Daniells to travel: he found time to visit relatives, went to Bedford to see the Bunyan Museum, and to the National Portrait Gallery to see old friends from *The Children's Encyclopaedia*, such as Samuel Smiles, Faraday, Wordsworth, Hardy and Nell Gwynne, Marvell, Sidney, and Walton.[27]

The security of Heronsgate – the Davis family life, the pleasure of playing with the infant, Elizabeth Ann – helped him to get work done. Very slowly he gathered notes for his dissertation. And he and Davis continued to take long pleasant walks after supper, chatting about literary and religious matters. 'The weather is Hot. I am on the lawn with a chair & a card table & no collar. Last night it was so hot Davis & I went out toward midnight & walked along a field of grain being harvested. I climbed a haystack & walked along the ridge, & we leaned on a stile discussing the text of the N.T., etc., etc. It was rather good.'[28]

It was one thing to discuss the text of the New Testament, another to face his religious problems directly. A letter written to his parents documents these evasions. His reported that his research was going well and he had found several books on the Baroque. He and Davis had enjoyed a lunch in London. Daniells also reported a bilious attack. He said that he had felt ill coming home from the library, and had thrown up in the fields. But he rubbed on some Sloan's linament, felt better, and thought that his health would improve if he had his back teeth out.[29]

He was still attributing his physical illness to physical causes, not recognizing that it had a connection with his mental distress. During the lunch with Davis, they had a serious discussion about religion: 'he certainly does not believe as we do: he would apply exactly the same criticism to Isaiah as he would to Wordsworth. We should say he cannot be a Xtian. It is very puzzling. I am more & more suspicious that we are off the track somewhere.'[30] It was a day after this lunch discussion about religion that Daniells became so ill that he threw up.

Just two weeks earlier, on 25 July, Jim and Ann had returned from Ireland, and Daniells had had to face the inevitable. There was no hope of marrying. 'Jim is a communist and I am a Xtian and it seems impossible to bridge the gap. So nothing is likely to come of it, as I should have known from the first.' He also saw he was on the verge of a nervous breakdown, and his 'wild idea' about marrying Jim was simply 'a desire to escape' madness and the Brethren. Jim may have told him about her affair with Otto Van der Sprenkel because he explained to his parents that marriage to Jim was not possible because 'the communists ... seem to reject Christ, religion, and a good deal of what we should call morals.' A subsequent letter from Jim, then in Toronto, was frank: 'I just heard that Mrs Wallace had told Mrs Ryerson about my affair with Otto, and wondered why I wasn't kicked out if it were so widely known. I tell you this as everything else, so that you know what you're doing. All my love, my dear.'[31] Jim was honest, affectionate, and lovely – but she was a free spirit. This was not morality as he understood it.

Giving up Jim meant the loss of a bulwark against depression, which Daniells still characterized as madness. 'The fact remains that I did practically go mad once and am always hovering on the edge of mental disaster now ... Every winter I am fairly well, owing to lots of work. Every summer, the pressure of work being over and the weather hot I nearly fly off the handle and ever since Butcher gave me Baker's theory of the time of the Second Coming I have had a perfect hell of a time ... about the end of September.' As August wore on, Daniells' old problems with instability and the Feast of Trumpets intensified. On the same day Daniells wrote to his parents saying that it was impossible to bridge the gap with Jim, he spoke openly to Davis of his religious problems. A few days later, on 3 August, he had had a long talk with Lightfoot. Lightfoot emphasized Christ's redemption and addressed his fears about the damnation of children, pointing out that Christ in the New Testament says of the little children, 'Suffer them to come unto me.' When writing to his parents later in the month, Daniells described Lightfoot as a profound student of the New Testament and quoted the Lord's action with the children. Speaking of his own fears, he commented: 'Bunyan has nothing to compare in his *Grace Abounding*.'[32]

On 11 September, S.H. Hooke came to Heronsgate. Daniells recorded this information in his diary with an exclamation mark. Hooke, formerly of Emmanuel at Victoria College, U of T, was now a professor of Old Testament studies at the University of London. Northrop Frye recalled Sam Hooke as a man of bewildering ability: 'the very symbol of the radical theologian ... [who had] a bad-boy record at Victoria but became a world-famous scholar afterwards ... He was confident he could teach almost any subject you'd like to name – religion, anthropology, philosophy ... and he was a Plymouth Brother. And apparently busy revolting against that until he left Victoria.'[33] Daniells' exclamation mark probably registered his excitement at meeting Hooke and talking about the Brethren. For, on 30 September, he saw Hooke again at a lunch. 'Discussed religious matters. Feast of Trumpets.'[34] Hooke no doubt assured him that millenarianism was nonsense and that biblical references to the Feast of Trumpets should not be interpreted to mean the world would instantly end. He may have advised Daniells to leave the Brethren. Had he not done so himself?

The support that Daniells found in Lightfoot and Hooke – who covered between them the Old and the New Testament – is reflected in a later letter to his parents: 'I can still remember walking along Oxford Street in the sun, by Bumpus's book store, and feeling that if Lightfoot was right then I could breathe and digest things. It was not a case of "drifting into the world" but of being led out of Egypt, set free from McClure, Bar, Sutherland ... I don't mean to say that I am happy all the time now, but I do feel as though the chains had fallen off and the great iron gate had opened.'[35] The metaphors he uses, 'chains' and 'iron gate,' are those used by Bunyan when he explains how the Christian feels when the shackles of sin fall away.

In the early forties, Daniells wrote up his experiences with Hooke and Lightfoot as a fictional draft:

He walked along Oxford Street toward Bumpus' bookshop. Traffic filled the street from curb to curb ... All this while his mind was of its own accord turning over the problem that Lightfoot had put in the single injunction, 'Leave a door open.' But how could he leave a door open to the entrance of deadly error? The arch of truth was so constructed that every stone was a keystone and the removal of one would bring the whole thing crashing about his head. Yet Lightfoot had left a door open and was still a believer, one could not imagine then, if the Lord came ... Lightfoot could be left behind. It could not be. Hooke, too, had opened a door, more than one and had flung them wide. Yet one look [at] Hooke's great calm face assured you that he was not among the reprobates. Could he venture to open a door himself ... Suppose he should unlock a small wicket-gate ...[36]

Daniells gives a striking image of Lightfoot as a religious scholar and an academic, bending over a desk overflowing with books, attempting to determine the precise intention of the Holy Spirit. Lightfoot's suggestion that Daniells 'leave a door open' evokes perhaps to the hope proclaimed by Christ in Revelation (3:20). Could he, Daniells, open a door himself? The imagery of the 'wicket-gate' in Daniells's story is from *The Pilgrim's Progress* – he had visited the Bunyan Museum just a few weeks before his meeting with Hooke.

Although there was a great deal of internal change, he was still seeking physical causes for his problems. In early September, he visited a family connection, Dr Will Taylor, who gave him a physical examination, recommended reading glasses, and told him that his chronic appendicitis appeared to be causing indigestion. As his ticket to work at the British Museum had now expired, he continued to work at Heronsgate until everyone left in mid-September. It was tough slogging. However, there were spots of pleasure. He and Gladys Davis were working together 'famously': they collated the editions of Swift's *The Drapier's Letters* for Davis's book on Swift, which was due at the press. And the baby, Elizabeth Ann, was always a happy diversion. 'It is a great privilege in this household to converse with the Infant.'[37]

Daniells boarded the *Alaunia* for the return voyage to Canada on 1 October 1932. What had he accomplished? From his perspective, his primary accomplishment was the escape from religious dogma. A month later, reflecting on the past summer, he warned his parents: 'If a man has just escaped being swept into an abyss by an avalanche and gets on a path cut in the cliff surely his best move is to follow the path as far as he can see it.'[38] For Daniells, following the path meant abandoning the Brethren and theology in favour of Davis and the study of literature. With Davis's help, he had learned how to undertake research at the British Museum, he had completed an article on T.S. Eliot for publication, and his literary and aesthetic sensibility had dramatically widened. He was finding his way as a doctoral candidate in the discipline of English.

Daniells arrived back in Toronto on 10 October 1932, and again settled as a boarder at 125 Cumberland Street with Miss Grant. His fellow lodgers included an Englishman named Basil Ponsonby and a Swiss, Claude de Mestral. He continued to attend literary groups such as the

Graduate English Club and the English Association, and 'Doc' Wallace, head of University College, promised to do everything he could for him for the coming year. He saw much of the Davises, also returned from their summer research, while plays, movies, concerts, teas, and dinners marked his social life. On 16 November he and Robert Finch saw a production of *Romeo and Juliet* in which Wilson Knight, the British Shakespeare critic, now teaching at Trinity College, 'played Romeo with a high serious intensity that was somewhat wearing on the nerves.'[39]

Because 'Doc' Wallace had secured an open fellowship for him, Daniells did not have to lecture, but to make a little extra money he taught an extension course on Tuesday evenings and worked in the library Wednesday and Thursday nights. Besides a seventeenth-century literature course with Woodhouse and Anglo-Saxon with Professor Robins, he worked on Italian and German language requirements. During the fall of 1932, he reread Vaughan, Herbert, Crashaw, Traherne, and Donne, the primary English religious lyricists, and discovered the attractions of the moderate Anglican *via media*.[40]

At the same time, he rejected religious fundamentalism. Although he had been 'upset and torn to pieces inside' during his summer in England, the experience 'ha[d] resulted in a certain liberation and great relief, – for a time at least.' He had now definitely left the Brethren, and the relief was considerable. 'I feel as though the burden had rolled away. I wish I had had the courage to break away from the iron ring of dogma long ago. But I stayed till it was pretty well a choice between parting from them or sliding toward the abyss of a mental collapse.'[41]

James Daniells was very upset that his son had become a 'Prodigal.' He urged Daniells to attend Plymouth Brethren meetings on Sunday. Daniells would have none of it: 'I do not intend to risk another fall into religious dementia by associating with assemblies where hell and the nearness of an apocalyptic end to the age are continually mentioned or implied.' He had cut his connections with the Brethren. He knew how close he had come to the paralysis of 1919. 'I was pretty desperate this summer. If my fears had been realized I might now be in Victoria, unable to work, living on you, and repeating the miseries of D'Arcy ... Why should I return to people who will *immediately* rivet it about my neck?'

Daniells saw the religious dilemma in personal terms. He had just taken 'the most important step in the last fifteen years or more.'[42] But he was also undergoing the modernist revolution, shared by many of his colleagues at the U of T, in which religion was becoming increasingly secularized. For those who thought deeply, it was not possible to reconcile the bloodshed of the First World War with faith in a God of goodness and love. Daniells, who had responded to the war as an apocalypse and broken down under the strain, was now reading the starkly realistic poetry of Wilfred Owen. For modernists who had lost their faith, literature increasingly offered a medium for exploring such issues. Indeed, Eliot's breakdown, reflected in *The Waste Land* (1922), was first read as expressing the disillusionment of the post-war European sensibility.

Similarly, there were a number of faculty at the U of T whose religious beliefs had been assimilated into literature, and who also admired Eliot. E.J. Pratt had worked through his religious fears in poetry, and E.K. Brown subsumed his Catholicism into aestheticism and the New Humanism. Davis, in his professional life, turned to the literature of protest, especially the iconoclasts Blake, Swift, and Lawrence (all of whom shared a strong vein of Christianity), and in his private life he personified Christian charity by interesting himself in a number of academic waifs and strays, Daniells and Frye among them.

Woodhouse was a somewhat different case. Daniells considered him a Christian whose faith was historical and whose daily life was sustained by a Christian doctrine. His first book, *Puritanism and Liberty* (1938), a compilation of speeches from the Puritan Interregnum, demonstrated that for him liberty meant 'a freedom from the letter of the law and a liberation of intellect and spirit.' When Woodhouse taught Milton, however, what he taught was the theology of *Paradise Lost* – and with this in mind, Daniells jokingly likened him to a professorial shepherd driving his flock of students into the barn of Milton's doctrine and firmly bolting the door behind them. The security of Woodhouse's 'barn' attracted Daniells. He later remarked that Woodhouse's teaching of English, particularly Milton, became a reference and a reassurance to numbers of undergraduates – and he implicitly included himself in this group. From Woodhouse he learned the important lesson 'that intellectual labor is valuable in its own right and can absorb our personal idiosyncrasies and vicissitudes.'[43]

On 15 October, Daniells had his first lecture from Woodhouse. It was a Saturday and Woodhouse afterwards invited Daniells to come home with him to 24 Heathdale Road to have lunch with him and his mother. Woodhouse smoked continually while talking, gesturing, lighting a new cigarette from the stub of the old one. He had now been on the staff at University College for three years; before that, he had taught at the University of Manitoba. Woodhouse, as Daniells promptly reported to his parents, 'looks promising. He had me for lunch yesterday and I stayed on to dinner. We were talking more or less steadily from 11:30 AM to 8:00 PM.'[44] It is unusual for a professor to invite a student from a first class to lunch, and even more unusual for such a professor and student to sustain a conversation for seven and a half hours. However, Daniells was then a mature student of thirty, and Woodhouse was just thirty-seven. Obviously they had much in common and got along extremely well.

The two men talked first about his proposed thesis. Then they appeared to move to wider topics, probably Miltonic. As Daniells later recalled, 'Woodhouse believed in the historical criticism, in ascertaining the exact intention of an author when, in a particular time, place, state of mind, and context of circumstances he put pen to paper. He believed that truth can, by dispassionate and assiduous search, be found and, when found, can and must be communicated.' The beauty of Woodhouse's approach to literature was its absolute consistency. The weakness of this approach, perhaps not so obvious to Daniells at this time, was 'an unwillingness to note that, from another point of view or set of criteria, a different pattern might appear.'[45]

Woodhouse's class lectures stressed 'reason,' an emphasis on liberty and free will, and through his description of the Puritans of the seventeenth century, Daniells began to acquire a context for the creed of the Plymouth Brethren: 'It emphasizes ... the privileges of the Saints, and it looks forward to the millennium (which always seems to be just around the corner) when the Saints shall inherit the earth, and rule it with, or on behalf of, Christ.' This helped him to place his fears of the Day of Judgment into wider perspective. Any discussion of Milton and Puritanism would soon move to the subject of Milton's God, a matter of vital interest to Daniells. And Woodhouse would have found in this young provincial a mind with a knowledge of the Bible equal to, or greater than, his own. In later years, the two men sometimes communicated simply by exchanging little slips of paper alluding to biblical passages, the significance of which each could instantly decode.[46]

That year Daniells also met regularly with Alfred Bailey and Robert Finch to practise writing poetry. To Bailey he imparted his enthusiasm for T.S. Eliot and *The Waste Land*. Bailey recalls: 'One evening Roy Daniells called on me and my fiancée at her place and said, "Listen to this." And he read to us "The Hollow Men," "Prufrock," "The Waste

Land.'" Listening to *The Waste Land* gave Bailey the greatest excitement he had ever experienced from a work of literature. 'One can only think that the old symbols and intonations and meanings ... had become completely dead, that a great spiritual void had been created by a sense of the bankruptcy of nineteenth-century beliefs and standards ... Eliot supplied the catharsis. He, we thought, had pronounced an epitaph on the past.' Daniells also passed on his enthusiasm for Eliot to his English classes. The manager of a local bookstore reported that the lectures of this young instructor were causing a run on books by Eliot.[47]

He also explored the newer critical theories regarding the seventeenth century. Davis had brought to his attention a comment by Alexander Pope on the 'Baroque' quality of Milton's prose, and Daniells felt sufficiently intrigued to begin an essay on the Baroque for Davis. Intending to complete his course work in the spring, he began to cast around either for a job in September or for a scholarship that would allow him to do his research and writing in England. Again he applied to the Royal Society. On 28 January 1933 he wrote to L.J. Burpee, the secretary, summarizing his career to date, citing his work on the Elizabethan lyric, and noting that he was attempting to apply the theories of Babbitt, Hulme, and Spengler to Renaissance poetry. He proposed to do research at the University of London and the British and South Kensington Museums, arguing that he would be able to achieve results there that would be impossible to achieve in Canada. For safety's sake, he also applied to Mount Royal College in Calgary[48] and looked hopefully towards his professors.

Woodhouse directed much of his creative energy towards his students. For those he considered promising, like Daniells, he made great efforts. In early February, after a class lecture, Woodhouse asked Daniells what he was planning to do for the coming year. He first suggested some library work at University College, and then said, as Daniells reported to his parents, that 'if it came to the worst he would go to the President (Dr. Cody) whose personal friend he is and ask if there were not any way in which this outstanding graduate student engaged in research (this is me) could be kept from starving. Which I thought very decent.'[49] This personal interest was very much a part of English studies at the U of T during this period. Finch recalls that professors kept themselves informed about their students' economic circumstances as well as their grades. And a good student was known throughout the colleges.

On 5 February, Daniells learned that Woodhouse was not alone in thinking highly of his work. He was invited to a birthday dinner for E.J. (Ned) Pratt of Victoria College, a 'stag' where ten men gathered, including Wallace, Davis, Brown, and J.R. (Jim) MacGillivray, a specialist in the poetry of Wordsworth and Keats from the English Department at University College. Pratt's stags invariably meant good food, good drinks, and good talk. Shortly after Daniells arrived, Pratt took him aside to disclose 'a grand proposal' to get the young man a new position to be shared between Victoria College and University College. In effect, Daniells was being recruited to the priesthood of academe. Considering the matter late that night, he enumerated the problems. He was not a graduate of Victoria, there were other people in the running, and University College had no funds. 'But Pratt was most enthusiastic, had spoken to the Principal (a man I don't know, named Brown) and to Wallace and arranged a lunch for the four of us next Wednesday ... If I get taken on in the teeth of the depression it will be a miracle if ever there was one.'[50]

In mid-February, Walter Brown, principal of Victoria College, wrote asking for further information and referees. Daniells replied outlining his career at Rocklands Academy, UBC, and the U of T. A few days later, Brown invited him to lunch at Victoria's Burwash Hall to 'talk a little more about the plans for next year.' Following this lunch and a meeting with Pelham Edgar, Daniells wrote his parents explaining: 'It has been pretty nerve wracking. All my friends have risen to the occasion nobly: I wired Sedgewick and Beatty for recommends and got others from Tuli, Dilworth, Davis and Woodhouse.'[51] In the meantime, Principal Wallace of University College told Daniells that if there were any chance of putting in a junior member at his college, he would have done so to prevent Daniells from going to Victoria College.

Daniells kept hoping that the Royal Society Fellowship would come through. In April he was excited by a telephone call from Pelham Edgar: '... so I put on me little blue serge suit and trimmed me moustache and scrubbed me nails and toddled down to see His Literary Highness. And he led me to believe that I shall very probably get the Royal Society Fellowship. I hope he is right.' Before Daniells left his office, Edgar 'wished a bunch of essays on me for correction (presumably without pay) but *if* his committee awards me fifteen hundred dollars and he helps to get me a position in Victoria next year I forgive him that of course.'[52]

This April, his birth month, was going very well. Earlier in the month, he had seen Woodhouse working away on the *University of*

Toronto Quarterly, and he knew that it would appear fairly soon. Then, on 19 April, 'at last,' his article on Eliot appeared, demonstrating the connections between Eliot's poetry and T.E. Hulme's *Speculations.* Daniells argued that the poems of Eliot, which begin with the despairing 'Prufrock,' move through the aridity of *The Waste Land* to the hope of *Ash-Wednesday.* He thought that Eliot rejected progress, reaffirmed original sin, and advocated a return to religious dogma. Furthermore, Eliot's criticism showed the value of clear intelligence, detachment, and the ability to deal with literary problems.

Daniells was particularly interested that Eliot defined poetry as 'a superior amusement.' Poetry is not a criticism of life or morals, or an equivalent of religion, but has its own function, which is emotional rather than intellectual. He thought that Eliot had performed a great service by not asking more of poetry than it could give, by paradoxically separating it from transcendental truth, yet placing it in relationship to this truth. In proof of this thesis, Daniells cited several passages from *Ash-Wednesday* (1930), including the following lines:

> Distraction, music of the flute, stops and steps of the mind over the
>   third stair,
> Fading, fading; strength beyond hope and despair
> Climbing the [third] stair.
>
> Lord, I am not worthy
> Lord, I am not worthy
>   but speak the word only.

The concluding stanza demonstrates Eliot's desire for spiritual union with God. But Daniells did not describe it this way; rather, he used Hulme's terminology to suggest that Eliot's work presented the '"infinite straight line perpendicular to the plane."'[53]

The essay had just been published when he received a note from Douglas Bush, a U of T graduate teaching at the University of Minnesota, later the distinguished Harvard professor, asking for a reprint. A month later he received a similar request from S.I. Hayakawa, a graduated of McGill teaching at the University of Wisconsin, later president of San Francisco State.[54] This article was a substantial achievement for a graduate student; Daniells had published on the major modernist poet of his day in a manner that had attracted positive critical attention.

Edgar proved as good as his word. On 1 May 1933 he phoned Daniells to tell him he had been awarded the Royal Society Fellowship, providing living expenses for a year in England. Moreover, Daniells would be invited to teach in the U of T summer school along with full-time faculty members Endicott and MacGillivray. This job meant extra funds for his year abroad, but also extra work. Consequently, he postponed until the fall the Anglo-Saxon exam that he had been supposed to write in May.

However, he was now utterly spent. His diary entries record that he was 'feeble,' 'unwell,' 'rotten,' and suffering from neuralgia. The doctor advised that he have his tonsils removed. Near the end of May, Daniells was admitted to Toronto General Hospital and all his friends rallied round. After three days, he was released, staying with the Davises to recuperate. He then proposed to move into lodgings with a new friend, Earle Birney.

Chapter Six

Love and Politics

Who is Silvia? What is she,
That all our swains commend her?

William Shakespeare, *Two Gentlemen of Verona*

During the fall of 1932, the Depression had been a continual topic of discussion. Jobs were scarce and the future uncertain. In December, Daniells wrote his parents saying that politicians were 'defending an impossible system and that fact is bound to emerge sooner or later. I wish [J.S.] Woodsworth every success. If he doesn't succeed we shall probably get trouble on the Prairies and in the mining towns and such places.'[1] In the meantime, he was thankful not to be in the bread line. A year later, he concluded there was bound to be a revolution; the unemployed would not be forever patient.

Just after Daniells' return to Toronto from England, he had bumped into Earle Birney, a fellow graduate of UBC, and the two began to ice skate and play badminton together. Their friendship was competitive from the start: after one badminton game, Daniells recorded beating Birney 'after a grand struggle.' They began to see each other socially, Daniells' friendship with Jim Watts, a known Marxist, easing the way. Their political positions were the opposites of radical and conservative, but the problems raised by the Depression obscured such distinctions. Birney was a Communist, while Daniells, although distressed by prevailing social conditions, flirted with Marxism only to the extent that it was embodied in Jim. But he went regularly to Charlotte's Cafe, where the Marxists gathered, and might be, as Birney joked, 'a fellow traveller.' Consequently, he was viewed by Birney, then part of a Trotskyist cell at the U of T, as a good catch for the party. By the spring of 1933, he and Daniells were sufficiently good friends for Daniells to ask Birney to drive him out to the country to see Jim, then recovering from appendicitis.[2]

During the fall and spring terms, Daniells had attempted to avoid Jim, though their paths often crossed. But he kept aloof and Jim, hurt and angry, sent him a note: 'what a swell, mad time we had in Paris and in London ... My dear, *why* can't we still be friends ... wasn't I awfully *good* for you last spring, when you used to come around and we ate strawberries and went for walks. I made you young, you know and you *should* be young!' The PS to her note reveals that she understood his psychology perfectly well: 'I've just remembered the history of all your previous loves, and so of course know that you've simply passed over me, as you did them, in your transition. In that case, forget this and don't write.'[3]

Jim saw the pattern but not the cause. Some years later, when attempting to understand the 'why' of his behaviour, Daniells attributed his psychological reserve and sexual timidity to the Brethren, who 'had made sex something distant and forbidden, in my earlier years. Between 16 and 23 I had been, frankly, ill, and not only ill but isolated, changing jobs and locations, deprived of social life, *dogged by failure of all sorts.* Now, in Toronto, I met charming girls and they seemed like angels and about as approachable.' But he did not dance and had no interest in music or film or sports. 'My contact with the angelic girl[s] took the form of inviting them to lunch or writing verses for them.'[4] Daniells still associated sexuality with Adam's fall and thought that courtship consisted of writing love poetry. In fact, he had drifted into the pattern of the Renaissance courtly lover, which was to admire the Lady from a distance, write verse, and bestow presents. This was the literary *amour courtois* tradition displayed in the love lyrics that he had read for three years while preparing his graduating essay and his M.A. thesis. In these lyrics the Daphnes, Chloes, and Silvias were pursued by ardent lovers who never attained their desires; should the Lady prove cool or distant, as so often she did, the Lover himself assumed an air of disdain.

Unfortunately, literature had not been counterbalanced by life. Jim had reawakened his dormant emotional life, and for a few months in 1932, he had imagined himself in love. But the Jim who figured in his letters home was a kind of platonic ideal. Reality, with a flesh and blood 'Sylvia,' did not come crashing in until the spring and summer of 1933.

By then Daniells and Birney were close friends. They were physically very much alike – both were tall and lanky. Daniells described Birney as 'a long lean creature with reddish hair and a very good, tough intelligence.' And both had come from working-class families; Daniells' father was a house builder, and Birney's father a house painter. Each was an only son with a strong link to a dominant mother. Both had worked as labourers. Then there was the British Columbia connection and memories of happy days at UBC – both were protégés of Sedgewick. However, Birney had been forced to withdraw from his Ph.D. program at Berkeley and there had been problems associated with his teaching at the University of Utah. Daniells, by contrast, as Birney said, was clearly the 'golden boy' of the graduate program at the U of T.[5]

In the spring of 1933, however, their similarities were greater than their differences, especially as both were finding the academic program rough sledding. Then, too, both were writing the occasional poem. Their friendship was solidified by Birney when he brought his girl, Sylvia Johnstone, to have coffee with Daniells. Birney, as he later admitted, intended to teach Daniells a lesson: 'When I first met Sylvia I was almost impatient that she meet you – selfish desire to show off my brilliant friends to her, to show her off to you, plus scientific impulse to educate you into what seemed to me higher standards of feminine companionship.'[6]

His first evening with Birney and Johnstone was very stimulating for Daniells. The three had a long argument over communism. 'We had a long and very interesting discussion in which I opposed the theory of my pet philosopher Spengler to her overwhelming Marxism ... From meeting such people ... one gets an idea of the immense drive and force which the communistic ideal of a classless society can become (and has become in Russia). The fantastic misrepresentation to which it has been subjected by our Canadian papers is pathetic.' Birney also introduced Daniells to Maurice Spector, the only Canadian who had been on the executive committee of the Communist International.[7]

In May 1933 Daniells went to look at a shack in a Rosedale ravine in Toronto, a ramshackle building just behind the Group of Seven studio. He was beginning to feel restless under the omniscient, maternal eye of his landlady, Miss Grant. Wanting to establish his own digs, he invited Birney to share the shack with him as of 1 June. He was attracted to the shack by the privacy and the ambiance: '... the walls (of beaver board) are largely decorated with "frescoes" by various artists, some of which are Pukka works of art and quite a comfort to live with.'[8] The building, which had been used as a studio, was falling apart, but Daniells and Birney undertook repairs and jointly furnished a room. Daniells moved into the shack with his bed, some new china, and a long black table – later to figure in the title of one of Birney's novels.

Birney, who planned to leave on 16 June for Vancouver for the summer to establish a Trotskyist group, continued to have trouble with his eyesight, a problem that had developed from paint fumes when he had done a stint of house painting. As he was required to finish his doctoral thesis before leaving Toronto, Daniells helped him by reading aloud material and helping to type his thesis. The two young men then began an endless social round, entertaining friends and faculty. In early June, they invited the Davises, the Creightons, the Cassidys, Maurice Spector, and the Johnstones over for the evening; differing opinions were such that the night 'resolved itself into a tremendous debate on politics and social reconstruction.'[9] Daniells had earlier reported to his parents that Birney was becoming 'more Communistic every day'[10] and that he was smitten by Sylvia, a vivacious young woman from a Trotskyist family:

> At the moment we are all at the long table, Birney on his thesis, Sylvia on German ... and I writing this. It has been very gay and I shall miss them like anything when they are gone for good ... Earle's sympathies, as a Communist, are all away from the upper and middle classes and toward the factory workers, the unemployed and, in general, those whose shoulders bear the real burdens.[11]

In mid-July he wrote to his parents telling them not to worry about him keeping late hours, explaining that it was as much Sylvia as Anglo-Saxon as she had a few days to spare between her exams and leaving for Vancouver to meet Birney. Daniells included with his letter a few photos provided by Birney. 'Earle sends the enclosed photos. That of him is just as he left to drive to the coast. Those of the Shack are not bad, though you must remember that the *inside* is really very comfortable and nice. Earle has, rather neatly, quoted part of a poem by Eliot of which I am very fond, on the back. Its original subject is a beautiful *'Figlia Che Piange'* (maiden who weeps) and the twist to me is rather amusing. Can you read it?'[12]

The poem, spoken by a Prufrock-like observer, describes a young woman standing and weeping as a young man leaves:

So I would have had him leave,
So I would have had her stand and grieve,

...

She turned away, but with the autumn weather
Compelled my imagination many days,
Many days and many hours:
Her hair over her arms and her arms full of flowers.[13]

Eliot's scene is the familiar love triangle. That Birney should send a picture of himself leaving Toronto (with Sylvia tearfully waving and Daniells looking on) with a quotation from this poem on the back of one of the photographs suggests an arbitrary assigning of roles. He, Birney, is the departing young man, Sylvia the weeping beauty, and Daniells the disturbed (and impotent) observer. Not so subtly, Birney had flung down the gauntlet.

If Birney threw down the gauntlet, Daniells most certainly picked it up. The 'far-famed Sylvia' was a very attractive young woman: slim, fair-haired, always in motion, she had a heart-shaped face, a charming manner, and an infectious enthusiasm for life. Birney left for Vancouver by car on Friday, 16 June 1933, with Sylvia's brother, Ken Johnstone, intending to infiltrate Communist groups in Vancouver with Trotsky's ideas. The day after Birney left, Daniells wrote in his diary 'my head full of Sylvia.' The next day, he had 'a long confab' with Sylvia at her home; the day after, 'I kissed her.' In fact, Birney was still in transit to Vancouver when Daniells wrote him saying that he wanted to know what attitude Birney wanted him to take to Sylvia. But he didn't want to pry, and 'any discussion which treated me as a factor capable of seriously affecting your status and happiness seemed rather impertinent. This in spite of a number of remarks you made which I could never pin down as jest or earnest.'[14]

Birney had clearly been chaffing Daniells about Sylvia, and Daniells has assumed the role of good friend and harmless duffer. Nonetheless, his last remark about 'jest or earnest' suggests that Birney may have implied that Daniells – try as he might – did not have a chance with Sylvia. He had brought Sylvia to Daniells to show her off, no doubt anticipating that Daniells would also fall in love with Sylvia – *his* Sylvia.[15] Birney might then have the pleasure of comforting his love-struck friend while possessing the object of his affections.

What he did not consider was that Sylvia might also be attracted to

Daniells, the ineffectual 'Puck' or 'Pyk-Puk-Keewis,' as he was termed, a variation on the handsome son of Storm Fool in Longfellow's 'Hiawatha.' Daniells had written a poem on Hiawatha, which he read to Sylvia in her parents' sunroom. To his surprise (as he recorded in his diary), she reached up and kissed him on the cheek; this was the spark that ignited the flame. At the start of *l'affaire Sylvia*, all Daniells wanted was permission to become an attendant courtier, just as he had with Carol Coates and Eugene Cassidy. 'I made a straight request for the sort of relation I have with Carol, telling her I have refused to be considered as one of the suitors, that I hoped she would marry you, &c. &c.'[16]

This is very convoluted and probably false. Daniells had fallen for Sylvia, but he thought there was no hope. So he wrote both to tell Birney and to ask for permission to pay court to Sylvia. Unfortunately, he was incapable of maintaining an appropriate distance when it appeared that the Lady might respond. And Birney did not receive the warning letter; it arrived at the UBC English Department, where Garnett Sedgewick picked it up, brought it home, and did not pass it on to him for several weeks.

In the meantime, Daniells received a letter from Birney which did not say, 'Keep Off,' but even joked a little. He had spotted 'the superlatively casual remark that you "hope to see a fair amount of Sylvia between the seventh and the time she leaves." Hah! as Maurice [Spector] would say. Hah!' Birney knew the danger but since he was confident, he contented himself with advice. Daniells already knew twice as many people in Toronto as he, Birney, ever would, and he was already 'a mysterious Don Juan of the campus' – Daniells had a reputation for dating his female students. More importantly, he had access into the whole revolutionary movement in Toronto. 'Don't hang back from real life by convincing yourself it will harm you ... you're still clinging, unconsciously or not, to the notion that Marxism must be a religion.'

Above all, Daniells should undertake a proper regime of intellectual study. 'Real communism is ... a damned difficult study and a very careful application of that study to the world of human beings and human things.' Birney recommended Marx, Engels, Lenin, and Trotsky. 'Start now ... You'll find the intellectual labour of apprehending and absorbing them so compelling that your heart and kidneys and glands will be quite forgotten ... All right, keed, the dread voice is past.'[17] That Birney could joke suggested that relations were fine and that Daniells could continue as he had in the past. Or so he told himself.

He paid even more assiduous court to Sylvia. Four days later, on

19 June, Daniells' diary records that after he had done some Anglo-Saxon, Sylvia had come for tea in the shack and 'I kissed her.' The next day, she came down to the shack, very late, for dinner; 'Sylvia delightful beyond words.' With no oven and only one saucepan, he effected a culinary triumph of ox-tail soup, salad, lobster, cake, biscuits, and ice cream. Five days later, he read her his verses. On 2 July, he was disturbed to find Sylvia 'withdrawing into an extreme Platonic Position.' However, matters improved on 13 July, when she came for dinner, was very affectionate, and 'said she could wish to marry Earle and me together. Evidently very fond of me and dreading our separation somewhat.'[18] Sometime during this period, he seems to have attempted, and failed, to approach Sylvia sexually.[19]

On 14 July, Sylvia took the train to Vancouver, seen off by Daniells and her parents. His vivid sketch of Sylvia, boarding the train with her return ticket between her teeth, waving goodbye, is recorded in Elspeth Cameron's biography of Earle Birney.[20] With Sylvia gone, Daniells became very lonely. He began a long series of letters, urging her to write every day and enclosing stamps. But there was no letter. Near the end of July, he received a long chatty epistle. Sylvia had been sightseeing at Stanley Park and the Capilano Suspension Bridge. She had had tea with 'Doc Sedgewick,' who called her an 'Impudent Young Hussy.' She asked Daniells if he had been reading any communist literature: and had he had Jim Watts out to tea, yet?[21] The last question was an unkind dig.

Despite his disappointment at this letter, he composed a continuing saga to Hiawatha (Birney) and Minnehaha (Sylvia), which he transcribed on birchbark and sent to Vancouver. He then learned from her mother that Birney had wanted Sylvia to come to Vancouver so that they could be married. In mid-August, he wrote seriously:

Think, Minnehaha, you are very young; the world's your oyster ... To love intensely is to live but to get married at nineteen is – well, it's easy to pull the trigger with your very charming and kissable forefinger and then say, when the ambulance comes, that you didn't know it was loaded. If you were twenty-five I should be writing in altogether another strain. This dear Lady, is that rare and despised fruit of friendship which is called Good Advice ...

This was the admirable side of his affection. The next day, he continued as a love-sick swain. 'Sweetness and Light, am I boring you to death with all my stupid chatter ...?'

> Do you mind if I write to you nearly *every* day? It relieves the tension of
> just thinking about you ... Sylvia in the Shack, Sylvia in the sun-room,
> Sylvia in the kitchen, Sylvia on Bloor Street, Sylvia on Yonge Street ...
> Sylvia expounding Marx to me ... Sylvia in a thousand metamorphoses ...[22]

Sylvia has become Arnold's 'sweetness and light' and merged with the
'Silvia' of Shakespeare's song: 'Who is Silvia? What is she, / That all our
swains commend her?'

Daniells was confusing literature with life. Birney, meantime, became
convinced that his best friend was stealing his girlfriend and referred to
Daniells as Diomedes, thus casting himself as Chaucer's Troilus and
Sylvia as the faithless Criseyde.[23] Sedgewick had finally delivered
Daniells' first letter asking for instructions as to how he should behave
with Sylvia. Birney replied with stiff honesty that if Daniells continued
to see Sylvia, he would fall in love with her: Daniells might even believe
that he was a Marxist and convince Sylvia temporarily. Birney thought
that Daniells deceived himself, that he tended 'to idealize others who,
often much less capable than yourself, have assumed an imposing
front. You look for absolutes in people, often, rather than motives.'

Sylvia, Birney concluded, would be a danger to Daniells' intellectual
ideals, and stand in the way of his understanding of the Revolution.
What he really needed was sex: 'You need sexual release; physical
stifling is no doubt one cause of your nervous trouble ... I think you
ought deliberately to see a good number of women; single, unattached,
if possible ... You have years of normal contacts with the other sex to
catch up on yet.' Adding that 'we're very much alike here,' Birney
hoped that Daniells would realize that he was trying his best to help,
even while he was playing the part of the jealous lover: 'There's work to
be done – and that work isn't the *Beowulf* or wood-carving. It's the
reorganization of man's life – it's already begun, in Russia, in our
generation. It's coming here. Get into it.' His last words were 'Write me
and don't be angry.'[24]

Daniells was shaken but not deterred. He and Sylvia continued to
write each other. In early August, she and Birney composed a joint
letter, addressed to Daniells as Puck, saying she had met a number of
faculty members in the UBC English Department and listing the titles
of their most popular Trotskyist pamphlets. Sylvia, however, added a
plaintive and private PS. She and Birney had just quarrelled over a
stupid matter:

Oh well, what's to do about it – we don't fight often tho'. My mother writes and tells me how lovely you are [and] when I think of your calm serenity I heave a slight sigh – that's not exactly the state of affairs here. Both Earle and Mrs. Birney direct my time ... sometimes I ache for home ... it's just a case of different climes different customs ... We're always tearing round like mad here and everything is punctual you know how blighting to my soul that would be ...

She had just received his last letter and considered him 'a peach to bother so about me. I know you must be very busy yourself. Thanks for the stamps as a matter of fact I'm flat broke & they looked very welcome, do you mind if I use some on Mother's letters too?'[25] Sylvia's language flows in limpid artlessness. She may consider herself a revolutionary, but she is basically a gentle girl, inexperienced in the ways of the world, homesick, and kept on a short leash by the overwhelming Birney clan of mother and son.

Birney became annoyed when Sylvia received three letters from Daniells – one edged in black. It gave Sylvia, his mother, and him a fright. He thought it a piece of 'damnfoolery': 'Why don't you love the girl honestly and be honest with me too?' On the other hand, he did not want to lose a friend simply because he and Sylvia had decided to marry: 'there is no reason why we should not continue being the closest friends, the more so as you yourself seem to be swinging into at least a fellow-traveller's position ... I *do* feel, whatever you may say, that you are finely endowed intellectually and that you can do really important work for communism.'[26]

Daniells recognized that Birney considered his behaviour dishonest. Meantime, Sylvia wrote him in mid-September saying she intended to marry Birney. This was a final blow. He wrote a congratulatory note to the couple, and then left for research in Europe after sending a hasty note to Birney, asking for his assurance that whatever he might think of his 'shilly-shally in general *you do definitely stop short of calling me a crook and a liar?*' Birney responded promptly: 'You're an old billie-goat. You *know* I didn't mean any such thing. And you know I'm as tactful as a Nebraskan Rotarian in a French village.'[27]

What Daniells did not know was that Sylvia had already married Birney in haste, and that the couple had decided to keep the marriage secret. Incensed at Daniells' obtuseness, Sylvia wrote a long angry letter, forwarded to him in Europe, in which hurt pride and affection mingle. 'I feel only indignant at your bourgeois attitude of private *property* – *you* are the only human being ... who suggests that I will ever be barred in! ... do *you* consider you know what *I* feel? better than I do myself I suppose?'

The real reason for her anger comes in the next few lines, which are scribbled over and crossed out. She had tried to write to him on several occasions, but her pen halted and stumbled. His last letter was 'like a dribble of cold water – which chills & suppresses. You see you really committed yourself to no one course.'[28] There were two possible courses available; one was for him to reach out to her, and the other was to leave her alone. She felt that he should have decided one way or the other before writing her. What Sylvia sensed, but did not fully articulate, was that Daniells had misled her by professing affection he was unwilling to act on.

There is truth in Sylvia's assessment. Daniells was transposing from literature to life far too easily. In fact, at this point in his career, he could only cope with safe relationships and keep sufficient distance to avoid the danger of commitment. But Sylvia's letter and Birney's response gave him considerable distress. His next letter to his mother acknowledges that life had suddenly turned grey:

> [L]ife seems so terribly hard ... But when you think it over isn't life awfully sad for almost every body? ... And now the religious trouble has passed away I still feel I want to leave all my wretched books and my friends, whom I never *quite* make contact with, and the girls I fall in love with unsuccessfully about every three months, and come home and straighten it all out. But we shouldn't be able to.[29]

At Christmas, Daniells sent a card to Utah addressed to Mr and Mrs Birney, a salutation that would have been painful for Birney because the couple were not living together. Indeed, on Christmas Day, Sylvia wrote Daniells to tell him that she and Birney were not planning to marry after all. She did not, however, tell him the whole story.

They had indeed been married in September but, as Birney's biographer reports, under bizarre circumstances. Birney had proposed that Sylvia drive with him by car to Utah, where he was teaching for the coming year; from there she could catch a train to Toronto. But on the journey, as Sylvia reported much later to Birney's second wife, Esther, he became worried about an American regulation against transporting minors over the Canadian-American border. Sylvia, a minor, was distressed when Birney told her that if authorities at the University of Utah discovered this, he might lose his job. He also argued, as she later explained to her husband, David Easton, that if he were married, it would help him retain his position.[30]

Sylvia didn't want him to lose his job, but, on the other hand, she was not ready to get married. She made an agreement with him that if the marriage licence bureau was open when they got to Salt Lake City, she would marry him and then go back to her mother as planned. The bureau was open, Birney got the licence, and the bride cried through the wedding ceremony. Sylvia then caught the train to Toronto. But as Birney did not think to give her any money and as she had only ten cents in her purse, she 'starved' for the two days it took to get home.[31]

Birney wrote, he phoned, and he wired, but Sylvia would not come back. Her mother would not let her. Perhaps Mrs Johnstone saw through Birney's arguments. Throughout the trip from British Columbia to Utah, sitting grimly in the back seat of the car with purse, hat, coat, and gloves had been Mrs Birney – at Sylvia's instigation.[32] Birney could not have been charged with transporting a minor when such an obvious chaperone was present. The intriguing question is why did Birney marry Sylvia? Marriage without consummation was the opposite of his later practice. Perhaps he genuinely wanted to share his life with Sylvia, and his mother approved. Both then put pressure on a reluctant Sylvia, correctly expecting that her good nature would catapult her into marriage. But the stratagem was successful only temporarily as Sylvia obtained a legal annulment on the grounds that the marriage had not been consummated.[33]

However, at some time during those last unhappy days in Utah, Sylvia forever cast a shadow on the friendship between Birney and Daniells by confessing to Birney that she preferred Daniells to him.[34] Birney had warned Daniells during that long Vancouver summer, 'If you were to capture Sylvia, I should never forgive you, however much Sylvia shared in the capture,' and although his rational side may have wanted to retain Daniells' friendship, hurt pride, anger, and envy were eventually to militate against it.[35] It is strange how random and seemingly unrelated events can decisively shape lives; Birney's struggle with Daniells over Sylvia was to condition Daniells' future academic career – and to some extent Birney's – in a way which neither could foresee: what began as male bonding within the academy was to resurface as professional rivalry.

It is clear from the start that the relationship between the two young men, especially as expressed in Birney's letters, was just as important, if not more so, than their relationship to Sylvia. The language of both academics (Daniells saw her as 'Silvia,' and Birney implied she was a 'Criseyde') suggests that each saw the young woman within the framework of his particular academic specialty: by implication, theirs was a literary affection. Moreover, despite this first *contretemps* between them, Birney in September 1933 maintained his friendship with Daniells, replying warmly to Daniells' expressions of regret, while in November he told Ken Johnstone that his ardour for Sylvia had cooled.[36] For the next two decades, the two men saw a fair amount of each other, but curiously neither appears to have seen very much of Sylvia. The following year, she contracted tuberculosis and spent some time in a sanitarium before returning to University of Toronto. Subsequently, Sylvia married David Easton, later a professor at UCLA, and enjoyed a happy family and professional life.

But how are we to interpret the situation between Daniells and Birney? Birney's biographer, Cameron, sees the relationship between the two men as part of 'a classic love triangle,' and suggests that this time 'Birney had no intention of being cheated of his girl, as he had been cheated of Barbara Barrett by Hank Gartshore' at Berkeley.[37] This is an endorsement of Birney's later claim that once again, as formerly at Berkeley, his best friend had stolen his girl. However, given that Birney had already experienced this problem in the past, why did he recreate it by setting up a second triangle with Daniells? Possibly because his *amour propre* required restaging the situation, but with a less aggressive rival, thus ensuring a successful outcome. And why did Daniells, who had behaved with an excess of gallantry with Eugene Cassidy and Carol Coates, suddenly feel impelled to fight for Sylvia Johnstone? Possibly because Birney's chaffing, and especially the quote from Eliot's poem, struck Daniells where he was most vulnerable – with the suggestion of impotence – thus pressuring him into action.

What Birney seems to have intended was to consolidate his bond with Daniells, a friend and possible future colleague. A critical study from the 1980s, Eve Kosofsky Sedgewick's *Between Men: English Literature and Male Homosocial Desire*, suggests that a major factor in establishing such erotic triangles is the desire to forge social bonds and demonstrate social power between two men. Thus, in introducing Daniells to Sylvia, Birney was both offering friendship and indicating his superiority (by possessing the superior kind of girl he thought Daniells should be seeking). But Birney not only wanted to 'show off'

Sylvia, he also wanted to encourage Daniells to join the Toronto Trotskyist circle by way of Sylvia.

Birney's letters suggest that he wanted to intensify a fraternal and political bond with Daniells. But when the danger of an attraction between Sylvia and Daniells arose, Birney repudiated this position. He concluded that should Daniells fall in love with Sylvia, he would become 'the reddist of radicals – for a couple of months. Then there'd be an annihilating reaction. Now I hope with all my heart that you will become an active Marxian. But I know you'll never be that if you enter through the backdoor of emotionalism.'[38] Therefore, Birney urged his friend to seek out other women.

The impetus, then, appears to be academic power politics with incipient rivalry a close second. As Sedgewick also points out, there is a 'calculus of power that [is] structured by the relation of rivalry between the two active members of an erotic triangle.' The woman in question often has less value in herself than as currency between the two men, for 'the bond that links the two rivals is as intense and potent as the bond that links either of the rivals to the beloved.' What is more, such bonds of 'rivalry' and 'love,' although differently experienced, are equally powerful and can be equivalent.[39] This is very raw, very strongly experienced emotion. In later years, when Daniells once again did not respond positively to Birney's overtures of friendship and requests for special consideration, Birney retained a large stratum of negative emotion which, in turn, led to serious division within the UBC English Department. In this game of love and politics, the idealistic and charming Sylvia finally becomes a signifier for power relations in the academy.

Chapter Seven

Europe

With a Royal Society fellowship to support him and access to England and the Continent assured, Daniells' primary concern for the next year and a half was to write the dissertation required for his degree: 'An Inquiry into Some Formal Problems in English Non-dramatic Literature of the Seventeenth Century.' He wanted to discuss seventeenth-century poetry in terms of the Baroque, a new way of looking at the formal aspects of literature and culture. Unlike Woodhouse, who would have been content with a history of ideas approach, Daniells was gravitating towards Davis and Brown, who emphasized formal analysis, a close reading of the text, and a consideration of the other arts. His own developing interest in the Baroque subsumed the history of ideas, New Criticism, and comparative art criticism, and drew upon H. Wölfflin's pioneering studies of the Baroque.

The concept was new in English literary criticism, but recent European criticism had revealed some parallels between the English lyric poets and the Continental Baroque: a similarity between George Herbert and the early Jesuits, for example, or between Richard Crashaw and the Catholic Baroque. Daniells wanted to extend these arguments to prove that many seventeenth-century poets, and for that matter the period itself, could best be described in terms of the Baroque. This was a highly ambitious project. The new concept was still in the process of definition, the area to be covered was vast, and, most importantly, the term involved several of the arts – architecture, sculpture, painting, and music – as well as poetry, the ostensible subject of his dissertation.

Daniells knew that the term 'Baroque' in the English nineteenth century had been synonymous with 'absurd' or 'frantic.' But in 1916 the German critic Fritz Strich had designated a body of German verse as the *Barocklyrik* and attempted to show that this verse was characterized by tension and by strained conceits which were in themselves 'Baroque.' Since then, Italian critics had developed the concept, particularly Mario Praz, who had discussed Donne and Crashaw in his study of mannerism in England, *Secentismo e marinismo in Inghilterra* (1925), and also Benedetto Croce in *Storia della età barocca in Italia* in 1929. In North America the Princeton professor Morris Croll had written an influential essay, 'The Baroque Style in Prose,' published in *Studies in English Philology* in 1929.

To work on this topic, Daniells had to learn sufficient German to consult primary sources and obscure critical publications, and he had to see examples of Baroque art and architecture on the Continent so that he could consider the possible parallels with English poetry during the same period. This was a daunting task. He began by stopping off, en route to Europe, on 30 August 1933, at Saranac Lake, New York, to visit Professor Croll. Croll, just retired from teaching at Princeton, was taking a rest cure at Saranac. Daniells found him 'a very likeable old boy' who gave him some 'good tips,' apparently suggestions about ways to approach the subject.[1] Daniells then travelled up to Montreal and sailed for Europe two days later on 1 September on the *Aurania*.

By 11 September he was in Paris. He spent several days there, attempting to construct a bibliography on the Baroque and seeking out relevant art. On 14 September he travelled to Bonn by way of Belgium. He stayed the first night with Davis's first wife's parents, 'Frau Geheimrat Lucas, whose husband was a Landrat, a very big pot in the German system of government.' The next day, Daniells moved to a Frau Reinecke's on Joachimstrasse and began to work hard on his German. On 9 October he travelled to Horn, where he stayed with a Fraulein Herrmanns, a 'voluble old dear, tremendously Protestant and rooted in the land.' She dictated German hymns to Daniells, but as he did not know many of the words, he relied on phonetic transcription: 'When I come to translate some of it won't make sense. But it's all good practice.'[2] He borrowed a bicycle and rode around the towns outside Bonn through the wine-growing districts.

He sought out books on the Baroque. He also tried to understand Nazism and bought a book on Hitler entitled *Von Sieben Mann zum Volk* (From seven followers to the whole people). At first he was captivated by Nazi youth's energy: 'It's like being in a dream or a picture book here. The air was thick with bells ringing and flags – the National flag of red, white, and black and the Nazi flag with the swastika on it – because the new council or Steirrat meets in Berlin for the first time today. Even the Churches flew these flags.'³

Nazi propaganda was attractive but transparent, and after two weeks he had tired of the endless bombardment of politics: 'I was never so sick of politics in my life. I am back to the ideology of the good old individualist and if the Fascists or the Bolsheviks wish to shoot me they may go ahead.' He disliked the idea of the collective state, but recognized that Germany was attempting to pull itself up by its boot straps. When in Bonn, Daniells was not blind to the menace the Nazis represented, and he saw that 'a war might start ... You never saw anything like the fervor there is here. And they have absolutely smashed the Socialists and Communists to pieces. Nor are the Jews enjoying life.'⁴

A month later, attempting to convey a sense of his time in Germany to friends in Canada, Daniells remarked that his five weeks in the Rhineland had been amazing: his initial feelings of hostility had changed to admiration. He explained that he had lived with three different families, been exposed to varying political creeds, and concluded that it was the nation that the Reich was determined to revive and strengthen, the result being 'a necessary, if unpleasant, period of intensified nationalism all round.'⁵ What this really meant Daniells did not attempt to confront; in several letters, he confesses frankly that he was relieved that he was an academic rather than an actively political person.

Daniells' attitude was not unusual in 1933. He saw a Germany that had been broken by the First World War and reparation payments, a country where a totalitarian regime had emerged to pull the country together. He recognized that Hitler was a despot, but like many travellers seeking German culture, did not fully understand the campaign against the Jews until *Kristallnacht* in November 1938. Nonetheless, his admiration for what he saw as the constructive aspects of Italian and German fascism at this period would have been repugnant to Birney, to whose letters he replied while still in Germany. Birney seems to have gossiped about this at the U of T because some months later Daniells received a letter from a mutual friend there inquiring whether he had become a 'convinced fascist.'⁶

On 21 October, Daniells travelled to Bruges and Ostend, arriving in London on 23 October. While sightseeing in Belgium, he had an unpleasant experience: 'Unfortunately I chanced to ascend the belfry with an Italian lawyer of homosexual tendencies. My first – and very slight – experience with these people. But it confirmed what I should have expected to feel: pity for the person and horror of the thing.' Daniells, raised on the biblical view of Sodom and Gomorrah, had kept himself surprisingly insulated regarding all forms of sexuality or 'carnal intercourse' as the Brethren would term it; a few years earlier, Max Maynard had written him to speculate that Sedgewick was a homosexual; Daniells did not appear to know this.[7]

When he arrived in London on 24 October 1933, he took a 'rotten room' at the Channel Island House, off Russell Square, but promptly made arrangements to live with his cousins, Mal and Mabel Stevens in Catford, a distant suburb of London. He travelled almost daily on the train to work in the British Museum. During his first week in London, he contacted H.V. Routh of King's College, London, who had agreed to act as his advisor, and got another temporary 'ticket' for research in the British Museum. Near the end of October, he took an essay on the medieval poets to Routh, and on 8 November he formally enrolled at King's College.

He reported to Davis that he frequented 'the B.M. with religious regularity and am actually getting definite slabs of work done.' His work consisted of a cycle of preparing papers and going to see Routh. 'But one naturally cannot push round the place and talk to people as in BC or Toronto. The insulation they carry is so effective that Routh had never heard of Sam Hooke, though they are in the same college.'[8] In addition to research, he was also trying to finish his Anglo-Saxon course by completing an essay on *Beowulf*, which took most of November. Then, in late November, he applied himself to his dissertation, working out some ideas in a brief paper, which Routh approved.

Daniells was, nevertheless, dissatisfied with his work and concerned about his future as an academic. Uppermost in his mind were fears about whether he would be appointed to Victoria College for the coming year. He wrote to Edgar and Pratt (telling the latter of the German beers and brandies he had drunk), asking both for help, saying he had asked Principal Brown about a position for next fall: 'I am willing to take *anything* they like to offer ... But I must leave it to you, if he shuts down on me for financial reasons, to let him know very definitely that I will jump at anything whatever that will keep me off the street.' Daniells knew that Pratt had gone out of his way to help him and reiterated how grateful he felt: 'I assure you they are not "benefits forgot."'[9]

The Christmas holidays found him suffering with a severe cold. On the 23rd and 24th he stayed in bed most of the day. As his cousins and the children had left Catford to spend Christmas with relatives, he spent Christmas Day alone with the housekeeper. Despite a bad attack of neuralgia, he listened to the King's Christmas message on the radio. The following day, Boxing Day, was a pleasant surprise. He was invited by a Toronto friend, the Englishman Basil Ponsonby, to the home of his uncle, Lord Noel Buxton, and the company fried sausages and buns at an open fire. Among the other guests were Basil's employer, the Bishop of Gibraltar, and Charles Buxton, well known for his humanitarian work. The next day, Daniells received the letter from Sylvia Johnstone, written on Christmas Day, telling him that she and Earle Birney 'are only on a friendship basis now.'[10]

It was good news, but Daniells was in no condition to act upon it. 'Silvia' had disappeared into the Baroque complexities of the seventeenth-century lyric. Throughout January, he was plagued by ill health, overwhelmed by the task of writing the dissertation, and on tenterhooks about the Toronto job. He attributed his ill health to depression about religious matters and urged his mother to get a copy of William James's *Varieties of Religious Experience*, saying: 'People talk about Bunyan. His experience was a joke compared with mine.' He continued his work at the British Museum and took out innumerable books which he read without understanding: 'I must have been born to lie under a palm tree on a warm beach and count the coconuts on my fingers.'[11] The last humorous twist was meant to divert his mother, but in fact he was beginning to wonder whether scholarship was really his métier.

What was worse, his migraines and stomach upsets continued. He sought out a London doctor but considered him of no use because the physician could not find anything physically wrong, but suggested that he go to a psychiatrist: there was 'probably a sort of permanent kink in my mind due to religious fear and sex-repression. He may be right – probably is – but it's of no immediate use to know it.' A year earlier, when hoping to hear from Victoria College, he had reflected sadly, 'Hope deferred maketh the heart sick.' This was now quite literally true. But he did not have the energy to deal with the psychological implications of his ill health. For the moment there were only two issues he could entertain: the first was a job; the second was the dissertation. Finally, on 31 January, he could stand the suspense no longer and cabled Davis for news. Davis, as always, came through, responding with the news that Principal Walter Brown and Edgar had definitely recommended him for a post at Victoria College.[12]

———➤◦◄———

He turned back to the dissertation with new heart. Davis had been keeping a close eye on Daniells' progress – or lack of it. In response to Davis's Christmas letter, Daniells failed to mention that he had been alone on Christmas Day, but emphasized a happy Christmas with the Ponsonbys. He also set out a table of contents for the dissertation, which included nine points, covering all possible aspects of the Baroque. Davis replied promptly: 'damn your long-breathed efforts.' He thought a perfectly adequate dissertation could be written without all this material. Davis advised the younger man to approach writing the thesis as though he were finishing a job: 'You can do work as solid in one year as three. It's only a matter (difficult enough) of deciding *which part to finish first*. Never mind about your completed baroque cathedral. All we want – all a PhD is worth – is a single doorway, solid and beautiful and promising.'[13]

This was excellent advice. Davis was a fine senior supervisor, promptly reading what Daniells produced and devising a work plan for his student: 'a few separate articles and after that – a year or so after the PhD is done – out comes a real book!' He also understood that all work and no play makes Jack a dull boy, and he urged Daniells to get outdoors and enjoy the English spring. When he returned, his spirits refreshed, the dissertation would not be so difficult to complete. A month later, Davis addressed Daniells' worries: 'I don't think you need to be anxious, as Pelham [Edgar] is clearly so keen to get you appointed as soon as possible. Therefore *get the thing done and keep it within bounds*.'[14]

Daniells tried. Nonetheless, the dissertation went 'incredibly slowly. I seem to be always tired. Heaven knows why I can't accomplish a little more.'[15] He warmed to his English supervisor, Routh, whom he found pleasant and helpful. Routh, unlike Brown and Davis, was quite excited about the idea of applying Oswald Spengler's cycles to his dissertation. Then, to his horror, in the spring of 1934 Daniells read the advertisements for a new book on the Baroque, *Die Geistesgeschichtlichen Grundlagen des Englischen Literaturbarocks*, by a German, Paul Meissner.

As it was to include English poetry, it 'scooped' the subject of his dissertation.

Early in March, he drafted a careful letter to Routh, saying that he would take the book seriously into account. It was a brave letter, designed for damage control. He also wrote to Davis. Davis was appalled, but for entirely different reasons. He said he had no confidence in Routh if he recommended Spengler. 'Read the Occult and talk about the 4th and 6th round (Lawren Harris last night) or go back to the Plymouth Brethren but for heaven's sake *no Marx and no Spengler*. I mean is there nobody has any interest in anything but "thought" ... This period's philosophy is the devil – will Spengler help you to understand John Donne?' There is no indication as to how Daniells replied. But the introductory sections of his completed dissertation make it very clear that his primary emphasis is poetry, and his real concern is to develop a definition of the Baroque that adequately reflects English conditions and English poetry. Spengler appears very briefly.[16]

Daniells now looked for examples of Baroque art. 'Last Friday I hunted up the statue of John Donne in St. Paul's. It is very old, almost the only thing saved from the Great Fire which destroyed Old St. Paul's. It represents Donne in a shroud, rising out of a burial urn.' He went to Cambridge for two days to copy an article by Mukarovsky at King's College Library, after which he returned to his routine of working in the British Museum and meeting with Routh. Barker Fairley, formerly of Toronto, who had just been appointed head of the German Department at Manchester University, used his contacts to put Daniells in touch with Mario Praz, and another professor, O.H. Edwards. In late February, he went to see Praz whom he found 'an excellent chap & full of good critical ideas.' His response to Edwards was similar: 'Awfully nice chap and very keen. Promises to be most useful: knows Meissner.' He now began to try to 'get a nominal 10 pages per day done.'[17] Daniells was finally into the swing of academic research.

He fitted in some social life around the fringes of his dissertation. First, there was his involvement in the family life of his cousins, with whom he played draughts and attended movies. Then there was music and theatre in London. He saw his first opera, Gounod's *Faust*, and began attending the Sadler's Wells opera, over the spring seeing *Cavalleria Rusticana*, *I Pagliacci*, *Carmen*, and *The Barber of Seville*. He heard Stravinsky at Queen's Hall. He also kept up his interest in T.S. Eliot. Early in February, he went to St Martin-in-the-Fields to hear Eliot read 'Gerontion,' 'What the Thunder Said,' 'Song for Simeon,' and 'Ash

Wednesday,' and a week later purchased Eliot's *The Use of Poetry and the Use of Criticism*.[18] However, a social life without a special girl to share it with seemed rather flat. He wrote to his U of T friend Ruel Lochore, a New Zealander, admitting frankly: 'I perish emotionally for lack of feminine sympathy ... I have no reference, as you know, to carnal intercourse ... What is your prescription, my dear fellow puritan?'[19]

On 1 March he went to Oxford for a week of research work and sociability. Another friend from Toronto, Gerald Riddell, was finishing his Ph.D. at Oxford. He also met several other Canadians, including James Gibson from British Columbia and Geoffrey Andrew from Toronto. Daniells spent some time looking up texts in the Bodleian and then enjoyed Oxford life. He also heard Robert Lightfoot give a Bampton Lecture on the Gospel of Mark. Later in the week, they had lunch together and 'discussed old troubles.' He also went to a meeting at Rhodes House, where he heard a discussion on CCF policies, noting that David Lewis, Riddell, E.B. Jolliffe, and (later Sir) Stafford Cripps had participated.

Daniells had arranged to visit Barker Fairley after his week at Oxford. On 9 March he travelled to Birmingham and thence to Buxton, where Fairley, his wife, Margaret, and their three children were living. Fairley had begun to paint and showed Daniells 'good and numerous water colors of his own and some oils. We discussed a scheme of his to contrast Wdswth. & Goethe (recollection of nature confused with fresh observation vs. consistent immediacy).' Several days later Fairley and Daniells went to Manchester, where he visited the Rylands Library to look at manuscripts and the Whitworth Galleries to see watercolours.

En route back to London, he visited relatives at Beeston and went to Nottingham, where he saw 'some good pictures: a Vandyke of Sir William Killigrew, some Lelys (e.g. Nell Gwynne), and a very Baroque picture of the Magdalene (skull, fair hair, cross, shoulder bare) by Trevisani.' He also visited relatives at Olney, Rugby, and made a pilgrimage of sorts to Long Buckby, Davis's family home, where he visited with Davis's aunt, Miss Bosworth. Daniells had hoped that Davis would be coming to England over the summer, but it now appeared that this would not be possible. As he wrote his parents, 'Davis is almost certainly *not* coming to Europe this year: the inevitable result of having a baby. It's a fatal sequence. You start with a wife. The wife has to have a baby. The baby has to have a garden. The garden needs a house in it. The house swallows all your money and you can't go to Europe any more. And so it goes on.'[20]

Nonetheless, Davis had given him his marching orders: 'Don't go making yourself too comfortable in the old B.M. ... if you get a nice sunny morning ... go off to the West Country for a few days, Dartmoor, or the Quantocks or the Cornish Coast – and just take a raincoat and a small knapsack and a stout pair of boots. You may never have the chance of another Spring in England – so don't miss it altogether.' He had joked, 'If you don't do something like this, I'll tell Pratt you will really be much too learned for Vic.'[21]

In mid-April, Daniells took his advice. He and Jerry Riddell set aside a week for a bicycle trip up the west coast of Ireland. They cycled from Cork to Killarney to Limerick, then north and west to Galway, Roundstone, and Maam Cross, and back east through Ballinasloe and Athlone to Dublin. 'The country is enchanting: low, wet meadows, high bare rocks, rushing waters everywhere, primroses in hedges, hollys, laurels, ivy, and the intense and surprising greens.' The two men put in long days, biking in mixed weather and on some difficult roads; they made from fifty-six to ninety miles a day. And they enjoyed themselves. 'Bad road and grand wild country ... Glorious time.' They arrived in Dublin on 20 April and took a train to Dalkey, where they stayed with a hospitable couple, Captain and Mrs D.M. Frazer. On his return to Canada, Daniells sent them reproductions of the Group of Seven, including Varley's *Stormy Weather near Georgian Bay*.[22]

This bicycle trip with Jerry became inextricably mixed with his feelings about the Plymouth Brethren because, just a week before they left for Ireland, there had been a long tirade from his father about the Brethren. Daniells later wrote a short story describing his discussion with Jerry:

> *'You've had a bad time with your religious upbringing, Dick, but I wouldn't brood over it if I were you. Look to the future.'*
>
> ...
>
> *'But it's a terribly hard job ... Besides they did me in very thoroughly; I'm having to rebuild my nervous system piece by piece.'*
>
> *'Well, never say die. You've got your life before you. There's plenty of time for changes. And you have friends.'*
>
> ...
>
> *'Damn them!' (he cried suddenly). 'May they burn in hell! May they writhe in the flames they condemned others to!'*
>
> ...
>
> *Jerry went to the window. 'Look,' he said, pushing the casements out wide. The moon stood, pale silver over the midnight blue of Connemara hills.*[23]

Daniells had let it slip in a letter to his friend Frank Hamilton in Victoria that he had left the Brethren, and Frank had told others. They, in turn, castigated his parents for the backsliding ways of their son. When Daniells remonstrated with Hamilton for breaking his confidence, Hamilton retorted that if Daniells believed that he was right, then he should not mind telling the Brethren: '... your new position is pure Modernism, as I see it, and it simply will not stand the test of Scripture ... I know the problem of heathen, eternal punishment, etc. is very terrible, and apparently inexplicable, but I feel that we must leave that with God.'[24]

Daniells was then plunged into an acrimonious correspondence with his father in which he attempted to show, by many references to the Bible, that what the Brethren taught was contrary to his father's belief. He pleaded: 'Now what I want is *that* YOU *and I stand together* AGAINST THE BRETHREN *in this matter.*' In the ensuing debate, he drew upon much of his new university knowledge (on the fallacies of historical judgment) and advanced logical syllogisms. His father, predictably, was not convinced. In mid-May, Daniells tried a new tactic: he sent a letter with a little drawing. It sketched 'R.D.' singing on a mountain, heaven above him, a smiling sun beaming rays towards him, birds in the air – all contrasted with three figures huddled in a 'P.B. cave' deep in the mountain.[25]

A few days later, Daniells wrote again, surprised that his parents had not commented about the Victoria job: 'The really bright spot is the job for next year. That is a great relief. I am rather amazed that you make no comment upon it, since about it revolve the matters of financial life and death.'[26] At the end of February, he had received a formal offer from Principal Walter Brown of an instructorship at $1,200 per year; the appointment would involve work as a reader of papers, that is, as a marker, and some lecturing. This offer was very low, even by Depression standards.

But Wallace and Davis cannily raised the ante by securing a competing offer for Daniells from Bishop's College. Daniells described the whole strategy to his parents with great satisfaction:

Davis writes to say that I have had the chance of a job at Lennoxville, Quebec (no particulars) of $1800 plus board and lodging. Mark the wisdom and faithfulness of my backers in Toronto (Davis & Doctor Wallace): they approach Principal Brown, of Victoria, & extract from him the fact that his own offer to me is a perfectly genuine one; then they sensibly decide that I would prefer a meagre stipend in Toronto to a good one in

Lennoxville; they thus make the right decision and at the same time strengthen the hand which I play with Victoria. God bless 'em![27]

Meanwhile, Birney wrote saying he was coming to East London College to work with Ifor Evans, and asking for help to secure accommodations. He added sarcastically: 'You will no doubt see my beloved wife if you return to Toronto ... perhaps your big moment is still ahead.'[28] Birney was clearly angry about Sylvia (she had now annulled their marriage), but Daniells does not appear to have responded.

The summer passed quickly with steady writing and a crisis or two on the home front. He had managed to get his upset stomach under control, and he was beginning to think that he might get the thesis roughed out by September. In May he sent chapter headings to Routh, and, as Woodhouse was now also working in the British Museum, Daniells consulted with him regularly. They began to have the occasional lunch together to discuss the dissertation.

In July, Davis came to England after all, and Daniells had an opportunity to accompany him to Oxford to do some research and visiting: 'It is a grand opportunity. Davis is about the best friend I have ... Lightfoot, too, is a thoroughly good person, and I am looking forward to the stay with great anticipation.'[29] During this trip, Daniells stayed at New College, travelling to Woodstock, near Oxford, to see Blenheim Palace, a vast mansion belonging to the Dukes of Marlborough, which he considered the best example of the Baroque in England. Davis read the work that Daniells had completed and, with reservations, agreed with his thesis. A few days later, Woodhouse also read the completed sections; he approved of the thesis in general, but he was uneasy about the treatment of Milton, which he considered weak, possibly because Daniells' Baroque approach was so different from his own emphasis on the history of ideas.

In late August, the old religious issues with his father again flared up over the question of how he was spending his Sundays. Daniells became quite angry as he attempted to reason with his father, asking him to make an effort to understand the problem. He pointed out that after several years of seeking Christ passionately and eagerly, when he finally came to the conclusion that the doctrines he had been taught were 'in part false, and when I definitely said, No ... then some degree of peace and light began to break on me ... No amount of argument can convince me that I haven't come out of prison into freedom. It's an undeniable experience of the mind and heart ...' Despite his father,

Daniells concluded that he '*must* go in the path I am going: there is no other way under heaven by which I can be saved.'[30]

On 13 September, Daniells returned to the British Museum, where he finished his work and met the Canadian scholar Douglas Bush, now teaching in the United States, who had earlier requested a copy of his Eliot essay. Bush was soon to initiate a distinguished career with the publication of *The Renaissance and English Humanism* (1939). The following day, he sailed on the *Berengaria* with plans to stop off in New York to see the city's museums and art galleries. Daniells had survived his first year as an independent researcher. He was returning to Toronto with a growing conviction that he might be, after all, cut out to be a scholar.

Chapter Eight

A Narrow Circle

In the fall of 1934 Daniells began his new position as an instructor at Victoria College. He taught second-year and fourth-year honours classes, the latter an early combined American and Canadian course. In addition, he taught two hours a week in classes in which J.D. Robins and Pelham Edgar were the principal lecturers. Early in November he gave what he thought was a poor lecture on Holmes and Lowell, promising himself, 'Must do better in future.' His class was difficult, 'most unenthusiastic,' and American literature was not his subject.[1] However, matters improved considerably in the second term, when he taught Canadian poetry. He enjoyed his contacts with students and faculty, but thought that Principal Brown, Edgar, and Pratt ran a looser ship at Victoria than did Principal Wallace, Davis, and Woodhouse at University College.

After a year in the college, Daniells recognized that 'one is inevitably driven in on a very narrow circle for actual companionship even in a place like this. Jerry, Carson and Frye in this college; Davis, Finch and possibly Endicott in University College: and that about makes up the list. Fortunately it's a very choice list if a short one. It would be hard to find six more satisfactory men for one's intimates.'[2] Life at the University of Toronto was indeed 'a very narrow circle' – or concentric circles – radiating around the university, the *Canadian Forum*, the Davises, and the Pratts. Many of his friends became prominent in the development of Canadian life and culture: Riddell became assistant to Lester B. Pearson in External Affairs and permanent representative for Canada to the United Nations; Frye became the most distinguished Canadian literary critic of the twentieth century; Birney became one of Canada's major poets; Finch, a professor of French, became a Governor-General's Award–winning poet and a distinguished musician and painter.

The cultural matrix that formed this group is very revealing. Benedict Anderson has pointed out the close connections between the waning of monarchy and religious belief and the emergence of new nationalisms that are given impetus by print culture and by the sense of 'imagined communities.'[3] In Canada, in the thirties, the older religious idealism had funnelled not only into Arnoldian idealism (in which the teaching of English was seen as the repository of cultural values) but also into Christian socialism and a new, post-war Canadian nationalism that carried with it the desire for a Canadian art, politics, and literature. All of these ideas were expressed to the nation through the *Canadian Forum*.

But a Canadian was still a British subject. And even though some U of T faculty, like Davis, Fairley, and Daniells, had been born in England, all were now committed to Canada. For Daniells, Canada had come to mean a combination of history, geography, and personal contacts. His sense of the country, deeply felt, was above all geographic: the freedom of land and sea he experienced in Victoria, the unending flatness of the prairie, and the landscapes of Ontario and northern Quebec now reflected in the art of the Group of Seven.

By 1934, this image of Canada had been fleshed out by a greater knowledge of individual provinces and by a clearer sense of what was meant by 'things Canadian.' In this evolution, the *Canadian Forum* and those connected with it – particularly Davis and Pratt – were significant factors; so, too, was the Canadian poetry to which Daniells was introduced by E.K. Brown. Also important were his personal discoveries, his recognition when in England that he was a Canadian and not, as he had once supposed, an Englishman. Another moment of insight came 'when at some party in Malcolm Wallace's house, [I became aware] that Canada possessed highly intelligent, active and significant citizens whose compass needle did *not* point straight to London.'[4]

In his new position as an instructor at Victoria (and don in residence), he continued to see his old friends at University College – Davis, Brown, Finch, Woodhouse, Endicott, Fairley, and Wallace. Victoria friends included Edgar, Pratt, Principal Walter Brown, Riddell, now in essence the dean of men in residence, Bert Carson, a fellow don and budding lawyer, and Northrop Frye, a graduate student in theology, who became the equivalent of Daniells' teaching assistant in English the following year. Riddell, a historian, was a man of action; Frye had a 'pure ... intelligence'; and Finch was a 'pure aesthete.' With Riddell he had fun, with Frye he talked about literature, and with Finch he wrote poetry. Despite shyness and an intense reserve, Daniells appealed to widely different persons: 'He had that wonderful way of revealing himself to people when he was attracted to them.' As such he was a foil, drawing people out creatively without ever seeming to pry.[5]

During his first few days back in Toronto, he got in touch with the Davises, who continued 'absolutely fool-proof and unfailing as friends ...'[6] Daniells was helping Davis with a new edition of *Representative Poetry*, a text used by U of T undergraduates. He saw a production of Shakespeare's *Henry VIII* in which Finch played a small part, and he reported that Brown was back in town. But the friend he saw most was Riddell. At Victoria their friendship was now institutionalized, for Daniells reported to Riddell on matters pertaining to the residence. As Riddell joked, the authorities at Victoria 'having secured brilliance, wit and erudition for their staff by appointing you, must needs add balance, stability, sanity by appointing me.'[7] It was a happy arrangement. Riddell's quarters were nearby on Charles Street, so that Daniells could nip out of Burwash Hall and be at Riddell's front door in less than two minutes. Roars of laughter would then erupt from behind Riddell's closed study door. Both were obliged to be serious in their professional lives at Vic, but when they got together they let off steam.

As a United Church college well known for its theological school, Emmanuel, Victoria had a reputation for sanctimoniousness – no drinking, no smoking, no cards, and no violations of the Sabbath. The Old Testament theologian S.H. Hooke, Frye recalled, was rumoured to have lost his faculty position at Emmanuel for coming in to work on a Sunday morning. The students, as Daniells soon noted, 'are all docile and decent, so far. Vic. is noted for that quality in its student body which has a large element of missionary and other church sentiment behind it.'[8] *Acta Victoriana*, the college publication, featured biographies of eminent Methodists and the poems of Canadian poets such as Charles G.D. Roberts and E.J. Pratt. In the early thirties, when Frye became an editor, these biographies disappeared in favour of articles on contemporary political figures like Gandhi and J.S. Woodsworth, and modernist writers like Virginia Woolf and T.S. Eliot. However, *Acta's* perennial 'ragging' student humour with obvious targets – in this case, Frye's courtship of a fellow undergraduate, Helen Kemp – remained:

Frye: 'So you asked Helen to marry you.'
Romanes: 'Yes, but I didn't have any luck.'
Frye: 'Why didn't you tell her about your rich uncle?'
Romanes: 'I did. She's my aunt now.'[9]

The principal of Victoria College, Walter Brown, was a short, round man with a ruddy complexion; he was gentle, kind, and helpful, but 'no sharp scholar.'[10] Pelham Edgar, head of English and son of Sir James David Edgar, Speaker in the House of Commons from 1896 to 1899, was sometimes a figure of fun. His admiration for the British nobility (manifested by repeated allusions to his friendship with the Duke of Dufferin and Ava)[11] coexisted with a passionate belief in a Canadian poetry and the institutions required to support it. More than any other person, Edgar had supported the cause of a Canadian poetry, and Daniells reported several lunches at which Edgar gave 'wearisome accounts' of the new Canadian Bookman's Association, founded to 'boost' a Canadian literature.[12]

Edgar's enthusiasms were trying, but his campaigns for Canadian poetry were triumphant. Although Pratt was a theological student, Edgar recognized his poetic gifts and appointed him to Victoria's English Department in 1919. There, from a position of relative security, Pratt waged guerrilla warfare against Methodist piety in verse like *The Witches' Brew* (1925), which Lorne Pierce (another of Edgar's students and, as editor of Ryerson Press, the primary, church-supported publisher of Canadian poetry) did not dare publish. When teaching summer school at Columbia in 1929, Edgar had declaimed verses from the Confederation poets so persuasively that Carl F. Klinck, later to edit the *Literary History of Canada* (1964, 1976), wrote his thesis on the group.[13] Edgar had also taught E.K. Brown, later to write *On Canadian Poetry* (1943). Brown was responsible for several recruits, including Daniells, who, in turn, taught Desmond Pacey, later to publish *Ten Canadian Poets* (1958). In 1930 Edgar befriended Frye, who initially considered Canadian literature 'decadent and commonplace' and primarily for women.[14] But Frye liked 'Ned' Pratt and his poetry, he chummed with Daniells, who was teaching Canadian poetry, and admired the landscapes of the Group of Seven; by 1943, when reviewing A.J.M. Smith's *The Book of Canadian Poetry*, he had changed his mind about the merits of a Canadian poetry.

Appointed by Edgar to Victoria College, Daniells found himself in the middle of this nationalist ferment. He and Riddell, their academic horizons stretched by study in England, viewed Victoria College with amusement. They were soon composing a Gilbert and Sullivan epic that lampooned the U of T faculty, especially the Methodist worthies: 'the president of the music club here having offered to put it to music (*if* good enough) with a view to having the club perform it next year.' Daniells spent some happy evenings 'writing a chorus for a group of Indians, another for a band of Voyageurs, and a song (in Scotch) for the Hudson's Bay cook.' As both men were chafing against institutionalized piety, and had targeted prickly individuals, their opera, 'The Orkney Lad,' might have landed them in hot water. Fortunately, it never appeared. It was vetoed by a faculty member, J.D. Robins, who claimed 'the songs won't sing and the dialogue isn't funny enough.'[15]

The positive side of Methodist piety was Methodist social concern as translated into the social gospel and social action. Earlier, in 1919, an undergraduate Victoria College magazine, *The Rebel*, had been transformed by Barker Fairley and S.H. Hooke into the most influential Canadian journal of the twenties and thirties, the *Canadian Forum*, which sought 'to trace and value those developments of art and literature which are distinctively Canadian.'[16] Throughout the twenties and early thirties, the *Forum* had raised questions about a Canadian identity, a Canadian art and literature, and a new socialism suitable for Canadian conditions. In mid-February 1935, links between the *Forum*, the CCF and Victoria College were close. After speaking to a few graduates 'very sensibly and humanly,' J.S. Woodsworth, leader of the CCF, came for coffee with Riddell and Daniells in the former's rooms.[17]

Daniells recognized that the impulse that motivated Riddell, whose father was principal of United College in Winnipeg, and his future wife Kay Dobson, daughter of a missionary, was a transposition of Christian ethics to social service: 'My two friends ... had converted all that idealism and sense of conscience and responsibility into social and political channels ... Their generation exhibited this ability to seek the kingdom of God in the ordinary necessary professional labour that Canada needed.'[18] What Daniells did not see was that he and Frye, as well as their predecessors, Pratt and Davis, exemplified the same conversion: they had transferred religious idealism to the professing of English.

At Victoria in 1934 Daniells' new responsibilities as a don in residence carried certain obligations, such as socializing with students, enforcing curfews, chaperoning dances, and establishing regulations for visits by women. Daniells enjoyed repartee with individual students, but was uncomfortable at undergraduate dances and fêtes. Nothing in his Plymouth Brethren background had prepared him for them. When first-year students staged a dance at Burwash Hall in the fall, he reflected ruefully: 'In the presence of all this *jeunesse dorée* having a gay time I feel about a thousand years old and like the inhabitant of another planet. So, I suppose, they go on, year after year passing into, through and out of the College while the staff petrifies slowly in its own especial cell.'

In the midst of these ruminations, the door of Victoria College opened, 'Ned' Pratt came out, and Daniells enthused: 'He is really one of the nicest people. Has been exceedingly kind to me and was largely instrumental in getting me on here in the first place ... On the whole I get on very well with the staff here. But it's queer how each individual lives his own life behind his own mask, and what strange things there are behind when you manage to lift it a little. And the same with students: each a complete little world in himself. It's either a very splendid or a very terrible thing. Probably both.'[19]

One of the graduate students with whom Daniells' own reticence dissipated was Northrop Frye, who also lived in residence. One February weekend, the two men walked down the Rosedale ravine to the zoo and then had tea on the way back. Daniells described this new friend to his parents: 'Frye is about the best example of pure unadulterated intelligence I have ever met (small, thin, bent, spectacled, with no physique to mention, but with a brain like a glass cutter). It's good to have him round the place. Though I admit one couldn't live in a society composed of nothing else but Fryes.'[20]

Frye, in turn, liked Daniells more and more. He wrote his fiancée, Helen Kemp, then studying at the Courtauld Institute of Art in London, that 'a friend ... has moved into the inner circle, my colleague Roy Daniells ... a damned good head, doing a PhD thesis on Baroque ... He likes me, and I certainly like him – we have somewhat similar types of mind, and somehow the ten years between us don't seem to matter so much, unless someone else is around.' By 'somewhat similar minds,' he may have meant Daniells' proclivity for talking about religion, his enthusiasm for Spengler (one of Frye's passions), and his developing interest in myth – Daniells had been reading Frazer's *The Golden Bough* since 1930.

Three weeks after Daniells arrived at Victoria, Frye discovered that he was 'brought up among the Plymouth Brethren, and bears the scars of some terrific religious experiences.' Frye would have been sensitive to this because it corresponded to elements in his own background. His own mother was quite religious; as a child, he had experienced nightmares after seeing an image of Faithful being burned at the stake in *The Pilgrim's Progress*; and a sister had been active in the Holiness Movement, which led into Pentecostalism.[21] Daniells was also quick to take Frye's measure, having, as Frye told Helen, 'an embarrassingly high estimate of my ability.'[22]

The two walked together, visited friends, yarned 'endlessly,' and spent free time on the weekends together. They attended films and plays, including *The Barretts of Wimpole Street*, a film based on Tolstoy's *Resurrection*, *The Lives of a Bengal Lancer*, a Chaplin film, *The Count of Monte C(h)risto*, and Walt Disney's *Goddess of Spring*, a treatment of the Persephone story.[23] Daniells' way of spelling Cristo reveals his mythic bent; it was the archetype of Christ in *The Count of Monte Cristo* and the question of rescue or deliverance that fascinated him, in a tale that he reread regularly for over forty years.

What Daniells and Frye provided for each other at Victoria was intellectual companionship. Frye felt he knew Blake 'as no man has ever known him,' but he was 'damnably lonesome, intellectually ... And besides, there are only two people in Toronto who have the remotest idea what I'm talking about, Roy Daniells and Wilson Knight; and Knight won't read Spengler, Roy won't read Shakespeare, and neither one will read Blake.' To be sure, Frye was studying theology, not English, but Pratt had switched his field twenty years earlier. And a new possibility was opening up because of the death of a Victoria College professor, C.E. Auger. In early December, Frye had written to Kemp: 'I may have to swing over and devote my whole time to English. Roy Daniells, naturally enough, wants me to, and Edgar wants me to.'[24]

Each week was crammed with activities. Daniells and Frye's circle also included Mary Winspear and Margaret Roseborough, graduate students living in an apartment on Huron Street. On Monday nights, the whole group studied German together for their comprehensive exams. As well, Daniells and Frye tended to visit many of the same people, such as the Davises and Pratts, singly or together. On Remembrance Day 1934, Daniells noted that Riddell and his girl were 'due at any moment' and that they were all going to the Davises for tea. On another occasion, 'Jerry, Frye and I went up to Davis' place to hear some Bach records (harpsichord variations) and had the usual comforting ... time ... one always has with the Davises.'[25]

Daniells enjoyed the music, the art, and the conversation at Davis's house. But most of all, he appreciated the opportunity to talk. In early March, Davis's wife, Gladys, who was expecting another baby, was resting, and so the two men trekked out into the snow. 'Davis and I had a good long walk out in the country and then dinner together and a tremendous yarn which was quite like old times and very enjoyable.' Davis was Daniells' supervisor, friend, and confidant. When plans began at University College to also offer Daniells a position, it was through Davis that the news first, and unofficially, reached him. 'Saw Davis, who spoke of EK's going to Manitoba and [me] possibly being offered a job in U.C., at the bottom.' When a formal offer came from Principal Wallace, Daniells agonized over the question for some time, consulting with Pratt and with Edgar. In fact, Edgar had given Daniells good advice a year earlier when he was first considering a position at Victoria: 'You will be ... in an important Department and you shall go far when resignation or death has gathered in the grey heads.'[26]

After much thought, Daniells refused Principal Wallace and University College. But he felt badly. Principal Wallace had been good to him for many years. Yet, after consultations all round, he decided to stay at Victoria, where he thought the surroundings more congenial and the opportunities greater. It was an important decision; as Daniells recognized, 'I may have decided, in effect, where I am to spend the rest of my life.'[27] This new job offer was a confirmation of Daniells' high status in both colleges – his was one of the rare appointments in English during the Depression – but by turning down Wallace and University College, he may have dampened his prospects for a future offer.

―――❧―――

But although Daniells' academic future seemed assured, his personal life was unsettled. In late November he took stock of the academic life:

> In many respects this is a peculiar life. To sleep in a residence with a definite, if small responsibility for twenty or thirty men; to have meals at high table, in semi-public as it were; to have all your activities part of the college work & play is, I suppose, rather narrowing. But it has its compensations and suits me very well indeed. One large question is whether or

not to marry; and, if to anyone, to whom. I certainly don't want children if I can avoid them. But to live always alone is not too pleasant ... I haven't seen the face yet that I could guarantee I would want to see for forty consecutive years ... I think the older you get the less real enthusiasm you feel for marriage. But also, the less enthusiasm you feel for the single life. It's bad either way.

Near the end of the spring term, he was visited by a former student who assessed his situation quite astutely: 'Wedded as you are to your books, your work, and your comfortable quarters, a fair lady would need to be what Alfred's [Tennyson's] father designated as a "No 1" girl, gifted with brains, beauty, and wealth, to lure you into the bonds of holy wedlock.'[28]

In fact, Daniells had come across several 'No 1' girls. He was attracted to a young woman called Leith Ferguson, a student in his 1-D English class whom he nicknamed 'Valerie' (because she took the part of a woman called 'Valerie' in a play called *The Crime at Blossoms*).[29] She recalls that Daniells, revolting against the Plymouth Brethren, was passionately fond of theatre. 'Valerie' took part in a Hart House production of John Steinbeck's *East of Eden*, and looked especially lovely 'in a green dress looking like leaves with a red flower in her hair.'[30] Another young woman, Doris Traill, wrote chatty, informative letters when he was out of the country. But Daniells, in response, withdrew. He pronounced himself doubtful about marriage; it meant settling down with one person and bringing children into the world, thus condemning them to damnation.[31] Finally, there was a young Finnish art student-instructor at Victoria, Eva-Lis Wuorio, later a member of the *Maclean's* editorial board, who led him a merry dance. Daniells showered her with presents of money, stockings, even a pair of shoes until she finally wrote a formal note reminding him that only flowers, books, and candy were appropriate.[32] But throughout all of these 'pashes,' his long friendship with Evelyn Stewart, a classically beautiful student, remained constant. Evelyn was engaged to another student, Ted Avison, who broke their engagement just before the two were to leave for Europe. Daniells then gallantly offered to marry her, much to the amusement of their friends.[33]

He was now established in a secure teaching position, but the Depression was taking a heavy toll on his friends: Frye could not get funding to study in England during the summer; Winspear lost a good job as headmistress of a girls' school in Montreal; Roseborough and

John Creighton failed to get Royal Society fellowships.[34] Ever since the previous fall when he had exchanged his return trip tickets so as to be able to accommodate Davis's schedule, Daniells had planned to return to England and the Continent in the summer of 1935 to work on his thesis. Because Frye had not obtained a scholarship and had no funds to support himself, when Daniells was ready to leave for England in April, he offered Frye his room in East House for the summer.

⊫•◦•⊨

Daniells then took passage for England on 18 April. On arrival, his first stop was Oxford, where he worked briefly at the Bodleian and then went to stay again with his relatives at Catford. From there he commuted regularly to London to the British Museum to work on his dissertation.

He had a secondary project to try to publish a manuscript which he had found while working on his dissertation, one written by Thomas Traherne, the seventeenth-century mystical poet. He contacted T.S. Eliot at the publishing firm of Faber & Faber. A year earlier in 1934, as a result of hearing Eliot read his poetry, Daniells had sent him a copy of his essay on Eliot and Hulme.[35] Eliot had replied courteously saying that he thought there was very little to amend and that he had enjoyed reading the essay very much. At that time he had suggested that Daniells might be interested in his recently published pamphlet *After Strange Gods*. Thus encouraged, Daniells made an appointment to see Eliot about republishing Traherne's 'Centuries of Meditations.' Fundamentally, it was a document of religious mysticism and possibly of interest to Eliot personally, but not likely to be a saleable book for Faber & Faber. This Eliot had recognized, replying that he did not think that the press was the right one to publish Traherne.[36] However, it is worth speculating whether Daniells' inquiry spurred John Hayward, with whom Eliot shared a flat, to reprint Bertram Dobell's edition of 1908 in 1950 with a brief introduction.[37]

Daniells spent much of his summer at the British Museum, plugging away at books and manuscripts, occasionally aware that he lacked 'method.' He was aware that he accomplished relatively little. Many years later, he reflected: 'It's clear, reading between the lines of the diary, that, although I'm in London to work on a thesis and going up to the British Museum Reading Room and so forth, I haven't the foggiest notion of what I'm doing, what methods to pursue, how to use other people's work, how to organize my own presentation, how, in short, to act like a professional academic, which is what I'm hoping to be.'[38] At the museum, he again met a number of fellow Canadians, including Douglas Bush, Alfred and Jean Bailey, William Robbins, Birney, and Helen Kemp.

With Robbins he organized a bicycle tour around Devonshire and Wales. They took the train to Exeter, then biked across Dartmoor in the wind. The next day, they went to Plymouth and Lostwithiel and stayed overnight in a pub. The following day, they cycled to Tintagel and Bideford. 'Thence to Ilfracombe, next morning, which is most disappointing being a regular resort full of things which please tourists. A boat to Cardiff, where we spent the night in a dreadful boarding house ... Left Brecon about eleven in pouring rain, but with a fine wind behind us ...' They finished their tour at Crewe. During the trip, Robbins excitedly drew Daniells' attention to several old mailboxes that had the initials of Victoria Regina as well as George Rex. 'That's nothing,' quipped Daniells, 'I saw William the Conqueror down there.'[39]

Frye wanted his fiancée, Helen Kemp, then in England, to meet Daniells, and wrote her saying: 'I very much want you two to meet, as it will close up a gap in the circle.' They arranged to meet outside the British Museum and went for tea: 'We talked about an awful lot of things ... about living on two planes of existence, one being unhappy and lonely and the other of quite simultaneous enjoyment of life about one ... He does admire you a good deal, and he seems to be very diffident himself.'[40]

It was one of those long, wet English summers when the rain fell for twenty-one days and then, suddenly, the sun came out. Kemp celebrated by again inviting Daniells for tea. She liked him and told Frye: 'I was looking for someone to walk or cycle or get to Vienna with – I want to see the Brueghels there. And his face lit up and he said: "Why I'm looking for someone to cycle to Vienna with! Let's go together!" I pondered a moment and said I'd go, and was full of plans in an instant. But he said no, it just wouldn't do, not for a member of the Victoria College staff.' Kemp was disappointed, but Frye understood at once. 'Roy has had a good many years of grubbing around without a job in considerable poverty and more anxiety, running up debts and not seeing anything ahead of it. Now he's landed his job, he still feels insecure and frightened, and works himself up into hysterical nervous fears about the prudery of the powers that run Vic ... Too bad, but he'll recover eventually.'[41]

When Daniells returned from his bicycle trip with Robbins, he found a letter from Riddell, whose father was looking for a new man for the English Department at United College in Winnipeg. Daniells wired back, recommending Robbins. But he was worried about the latest issue of *Acta Victoriana*, which seemed to implicate him. Apparently it was a student 'rag' about tea at an instructor's – clearly Daniells – and a young lady who never refused a dare. Daniells was worried about the reaction at Victoria: there *were* students in his room, but they were there in quantity 'and the girl Coleman left *with the rest* ...'[42] Riddell's reply was reassuring, reminding him that lecturers are always fit game for ragging.

Daniells continued to fret, and Riddell, in his next letter, told him not to be so worried about the Victoria authorities: 'Norrie tells me that you turned down a cycling tour to Vienna with Helen Kemp because of your Victorian responsibilities – if that was your only & genuine reason, you ought to be kicked, & I invite you to present each buttock in rotation for kicking on your return.' But, of course, Daniells may now have been wary of seeing too much of young women engaged to his friends. Riddell also passed on the latest news on Pratt and Frye: 'Pratt also is working – poor old Ned – imagine being reduced to marking Mature papers when one has achieved his status – apparently as a plain common or garden variety of worker, too ... Norrie works away like a busy little termagant (no, I mean "termite") and thinks he is sitting firmly on the neck of one Blake rubbing his nose and his ink pot.'[43] Robbins, in the meantime, had turned up at Toronto and appeared to be a satisfactory candidate for Winnipeg. He sent Daniells a grateful note: 'deepest thanks for what you've done. If I land the job, I won't let you down.'[44]

Just before he left England for Germany, Daniells received a letter from Frye that included a very personal, stock-taking sonnet written on the latter's twenty-third birthday, 14 July. In it Frye explores the Miltonic question of vocation and spiritual 'gifts':

Milton considered his declining spring
And realized the possibility
That while he mused on Horton scenery
Genius might join his youth in taking wing;
Yet thought this not too serious a thing
Because of God's well-known propensity
To take and re-absorb inscrutably
The lives of men, whatever gifts they bring.

> Of course I have a different heritage
> I have worked hard not to be young at all,
> With fair results; at least my blood is cooled,
> And I am safe in saying, at Milton's age,
> That if Time pays me an informal call
> And tries to steal my youth, Time will get fooled.[45]

This sonnet is a play on Milton's famous 'Sonnet VII' ('How soon hath Time, the subtle thief of youth, / Stol'n on his wing my three and twentieth year'), but Frye's questioning seems genuine. His youth is passing, but he has spent all his life attempting to achieve. There is a ring of truth as well as self-parody in the statement 'I have worked hard not to be young at all, / With fair results.' The young Frye was a product of the Maritimes, where education as a preacher or teacher was often the only way out of poverty. This is the point at which the lives of Frye, Daniells, and Pratt intersect – for Pratt had followed the same arduous path from Newfoundland and theological studies some twenty-odd years earlier to become a professor of English.

Frye's escape from the problem ('Time will get fooled') – and from the sonnet – is also revealing. For Milton, it was still possible to have faith in God's plan for man, however inscrutable; for the modern Frye, resolution is achieved through irony. That Frye sent such a self-revealing verse to Daniells indicated that he considered him a friend who would understand. Daniells did understand. He, too, felt that his life was slipping away and that he had not yet established himself. But the differences between the two men are also shown in this sonnet. Frye's picture of himself is more wryly comic than deeply sad; he sees himself as one who was never young as opposed to Daniells' darker sense of a blighted youth. Unlike Frye, Daniells still found religious questions far too serious to be dispatched with irony.

In late August, after receiving yet another letter from his father about his backsliding ways, he was goaded into an impassioned response: 'My dear Mother':

> It's about time that *mon père* looked at the situation from a common sense point of view. I followed his teaching and nearly went mad twice ... Try for goodness sake to convince him that I'm not a reprobate or a rake but only a poor tormented soul once sunk in the depths of despair and now only too glad to have come to the surface & be in the sun and air.[46]

In the last week of July, Daniells crossed the Channel to Antwerp to continue his language studies. He cycled from Antwerp to Aachen to Bonn, where he bought a number of books on the Baroque and contacted Davis's former in-laws, the Lucases: 'Evidently they feel the political tension.' He then travelled to Horn via Brühl and Cologne. There he met a Quaker, Karl Koch, whom he had earlier befriended, but for most of the time he cycled alone, finally reaching Frankfurt, where he recorded in his diary: 'Am enjoying trip very much. [Idea: a novel on Canada as a refuge for English culture when Eng. goes under.]'[47]

Throughout his trip, he visited churches, cultural sites such as Goethe's house, and Baroque landmarks such as Nördlingen and Neuburg. Finally he reached Vienna and went to the Barock Museum (which was disappointing) as well as a number of landmarks, including the Schönbrunn, which he thought compared favourably with Baroque Versailles. He pushed on to Stuttgart, where he spent the night. In Molenkur he was delighted by the scenery: a 'rising slope, with its cultivated patches vanishing into woods; flags at top of hill; the Schloss, a red stone ruin; downstream, red roofs & trees & green & brown fields melting away into far-off mistiness.'[48]

He was now on his return journey by way of Heidelberg, Mannheim, and Bonn. While in Germany, Daniells had some marks wired into the country but failed to declare them, possibly because he meant to give them to Germans who had befriended him. However, he left sooner than expected and still had 400 more marks than he would have been able to explain at the border. So he left 200 marks with a journalist, Dünnwald, in Bonn and put the other 200 inside his bicycle tires.[49] But after he had biked from Aachen to Brussels in the pouring rain, he discovered to his dismay that his paper money had disintegrated. He continued on to Ostend and crossed back to Dover and England, finally leaving for Canada on 15 September on the *Berengaria*. He now had sufficient experience of Baroque architecture to complete his Ph.D. dissertation.

Chapter Nine

Professing English

By late September 1935 Daniells was again teaching at Victoria College, now assisted by Northrop Frye. In the next few years, he was to discover the real nature of university teaching: its joys, its tensions, and the problems that a cloistered life presented to a person like himself. Several of his contemporaries were creative poets, artists, and critics as well as professors of English, closely connected with the new Canadian literature and criticism. He was soon to follow their example.

He also carried on the mentoring tradition that had assisted him. Many U of T faculty attempted to meet the financial as well as intellectual needs of their better graduate students. Daniells wrote a letter to Pelham Edgar, his head, outlining a fourth-year English drama course – including *Everyman*, *King Lear*, and *The Duchess of Malfi* – in which Frye was to assist him. He then asked a favour. As the preceding year's first-year honours course had not done very well in their examinations, he proposed that Frye be paid to give an extra hour of instruction. Daniells was attempting to find additional work for Frye, who needed the money.[1] Edgar agreed.

His own teaching was now going more successfully, despite his riding a Baroque hobby horse. At the end of the first term, he reported ruefully that he had gone to see A.S.P. Woodhouse, as his students wanted 'more on Milton's thought and are tired of fiddling about with form.'[2] As a modernist, Daniells knew that the 'form' could not be separated from the meaning, or thought, of Milton's poetry. But, like many a new instructor, Daniells offered far too much (and too woolly) an analysis of form to a class that would have been happier with Woodhouse's potted notes on Milton's religious and political thought.

Daniells regularly visited with Frye, Woodhouse, and Pratt. He had always made the parallel between Woodhouse and Dr Johnson. A few years earlier, he had observed that 'Woodhouse is puffing away at editing the *Quarterly*, like a second Dr. Johnson.'[3] Some time towards the end of this period, when repainting and rearrangement of offices was taking place, Daniells removed a reproduction of a portrait of Dr Johnson by Joshua Reynolds from an office and placed it above Woodhouse's desk. For successive generations of U of T students, Woodhouse became associated with this portrait of Dr Johnson. For Daniells, the analogy was clear. To him the Reynolds portrait revealed 'the same evidences of inner struggle resolved by force of will and dedication to a task; the same robustness of intellect with a use of common sense and downright reason; the same kindness half hidden by a formal manner of speech; the same indefatigableness in intellectual pursuits and capacity for mental exertions.'[4]

Although Daniells' circle included both Woodhouse and Frye, Woodhouse excluded Frye from his own group of intimates. In September 1937, a young graduate student from Manitoba, George Ford, attended the Graduate Club to hear Frye, just back from Oxford, give a talk on Chaucer. There was a good crowd and Ford thought that Frye, with his floating hair, looked very much like some pictures of Tchaikovsky. Frye began his talk by saying, 'No one has understood the writings of Geoffrey Chaucer as well as William Blake.' It was an audacious assertion because, although Chaucer was acknowledged as the father of English literature, Blake was still viewed by some scholars as something of a madman. There was a hushed silence; some of the faculty and graduates were embarrassed. Woodhouse was indignant. He looked around, catching the eyes of several faculty as if to say, 'This young fellow with his Oxford notions.' He later said to Ford, '"Well what do you think of these new people? You know, in our kind of scholarship, you go along like this," and I can still see him and his hand, just above the ground, "but you stay close to the ground. But young men like this, they go up in the air, and they stay up there."'[5] It was an encounter that explains much of Woodhouse's early reservations about the kind of scholarship that Davis's students, Frye and Daniells, practised. Frye's scholarship, especially his later criticism, was 'up there,' far from the ground of historical criticism. And indeed this is how he was later seen by the artist Martin Douglas, who painted a portrait of Frye, sitting on the clouds, his legs dangling, his fair hair haloed: the portrait now in the Pratt Library at Victoria University at the U of T.

Pratt, however, got on with both Frye and Woodhouse. Indeed, for Daniells, Pratt's personality always bridged the great divide between the teacher and the taught. 'No more "Professoring" of me, if you please.'[6] And he practised the art that he taught. Already an established poet, Pratt was now in his prime, his mid-fifties. His appearance was striking: 'a dome-like head, partly bald; an active and animated frame that gave the impression of continuous movement; great intensity of utterance, even if it were only a friendly word in passing.' Many years later, Daniells recalled Pratt responding to an inquiry about his daughter, Claire, who suffered from polio and required repeated operations which left her permanently lamed. 'As he answered, his face was suffused with such agony that one could never forget it. He felt everything with great intensity.'[7]

Pratt was exceptionally kind to students and younger faculty. A Newfoundlander, he brought to Toronto his native habit of celebrating happy occasions, and inventing them when they did not exist. He was also something of a socialist. In December 1934 he gave a dinner that included Daniells, the Wallaces, and Hugh Eayrs, president of Macmillan Publishing. In such circles, the discussion ranged from the immortality of the soul, to Marx's doctrines, to the miserable wages paid by large department stores: 'tremendous concern over the unemployed and the capitalistic system, and indignation over the disparity between the vast sums raked off by men like Flavelle & the wages they pay clerks in Simpsons and the Bank of Commerce.'[8] Many U of T faculty of the period, including Frank Underhill, were prominent socialists.

Daniells also recorded a New Year's stag dinner at Pratt's attended by six men: 'Wilson Knight, the Shakespearean critic, was there – a very clever, sensitive and likeable man; also Frye; Ned himself, the epitome of kind-heartedness; two lads who recently graduated in English; and meself. Ned had a grand dinner, based on a "Muscovy duck," and embroidered with sherry and blackberry brandy. We had a very pleasant time, and a tremendous discussion of Shakespeare.'[9] Knight, usually reticent, appears to have participated fully in this conversation. If *Wheel of Fire* is any indication, his comments could have run to a discussion of religious ritual, myth, and archetypal pattern in Shakespeare – matters of interest to Pratt, Daniells, and Frye – and later undoubtedly influencing Daniells' and Frye's mythic conceptions of literary form.

Several U of T faculty, including Pratt and Robert Finch, published poetry in the *Canadian Forum*. In 1934 they, together with A.M. Klein,

Leo Kennedy, F.R. Scott, and A.J.M. Smith from the Montreal Group, got together to produce the first modernist anthology of Canadian poetry, *New Provinces* (1936), at their own expense. Now, in the fall of 1935, Pratt had finished a new long poem called *The Titanic*. Daniells later recalled the 'plain heroic magnitude of mind' with which Pratt approached the struggle of writing the poem: 'when he would expound his intention, when floor-boards became deck-planks under one's feet as the long narrow office shuddered under the impact of ice and slowly sank, leaving one struggling – with Ned's problems, his efforts to shape the narrative, to find diction, to achieve catharsis. (I doubt if he really got help from anyone).'[10]

Daniells heard Pratt read *The Titanic* on 13 November. His large Toronto audience was enthusiastic about the poem, but Daniells was less so. The narrative bore no resemblance to the elliptic and allusive manner of Eliot, which, for Daniells, defined modernism. Daniells, who considered it 'a middling poem,' did not perceive that the iceberg section of the poem (drawn from Pratt's Newfoundland experience and A.Y. Jackson's painting *Iceberg, Near Godhaven*) provided the shock of recognition for an audience newly sensitive to the Canadian North as a symbol of Canadian nationality. Nor did he see that the poem was structured by myth and archetype in a way that Wilson Knight would have approved. Daniells knew that he had had a blind spot in relation to Pratt's poetry; nonetheless, he retained an affection for the man: 'What I learned from him is that one must accord as full a response as one possibly can to goodness and to excellence, even though it is not in one's own small groove of experience or within one's limited imaginative grasp. His memory is very dear.'[11]

The mid-thirties were the height of Pratt's party-giving days, clubby Chestertonian 'stag nights,' where the writing of verse, especially parodied sonnets, was part of the evening's entertainment. Paradoxically, Pratt's own poetry, although rarely solemn, was deeply serious, often preoccupied with religious issues. Daniells shared many of these concerns, which suggests a reason for their friendship. This new generation – Daniells and Frye, and Birney after 1936 – may well have reminded Pratt of his own early days in Toronto as a poverty-stricken student. Consequently he befriended them all.

Simply coming to 'Ned's' for dinner, with good food, lots to drink, and jolly company, encouraged the writing of verse. Daniells attended another such 'stag' in the fall of 1936, one at which John Creighton was 'half seas over' and Daniells was expected to contribute the limericks.

He did:

> There once was a promising writer
> Who all night, with a bishop, got tighter
> Till, precisely at 4:00,
> They were found on the floor
> Playing craps with two bones in a mitre.[12]

Shortly after hearing Pratt read, Daniells felt encouraged to submit a verse on astrology to *Acta Victoriana*.

By the spring of 1936, Daniells was trying desperately to finish his dissertation. He occasionally visited with two of his students who later distinguished themselves as poets – Margaret Avison, who, he reported, was 'filled with life and fanciful imagination,' and George Johnston.[13] Daniells had become a faculty advisor to the Dramatic Society and was also helpful to a small group who were attempting to transform *Acta Victoriana* into a more intellectually ambitious paper. There were objections to this, but Johnston recalled 'Roy was strongly on our side.' Johnston had published a poem called 'Annabelle' in *Acta*, to which fellow student Desmond Pacey had objected. 'Daniells said stoutly, "As for Annabelle ... I love her very dearly."'[14]

Margaret Avison remembers Daniells' introduction to Old English, Spenser, Milton, and Donne in the Victoria College survey course of 1936. The classes were held in what is now the Birge Carnegie Library, and the ground-floor casement window opened directly to the lawn. The class was intrigued by this young man who swept into the class, gown fluttering, lectured brilliantly, and then left by way of the casement window. Because some students were not in his seminars, a few of the men contrived a prank to get his attention.

The lecturer usually spoke from behind a massive oak table on a raised dais, but Daniells often stood to the side and leaned on the desk as he lectured. Two of the men moved the heavy desk so that it stood just on the edge of the dais. Daniells arrived, leaned on the table, and – predictably – it began to fall. With one hand he reached out, grasped the desk, and righted it; with the other, he caught his flying papers. The class, astonished, made no effort to help. He again lectured, his face a deep crimson, and again left by way of the casement. As Avison reminisced: 'We learned two things about him. He was strong, and he blushed.' During this academic year, Avison drafted a verse about Daniells called 'Gregory':

Gregory was handsome in a tweed sort of way
His accent was Oxford; and his moustache, his moustache,
You don't see a moustache like that every day.

He liked the theatre and tea at 4 o'clock,
He liked to lean his head back, and listen to Bach;
He liked Victor Hugo, and rain in the night:
And all of his handkerchiefs were scrupulously white.

Nothing ever happened; this isn't a story
In stories things happen; in real life never ...[15]

'Handsome' and 'clever,' Gregory is an aesthete patterned on the British model, a young man who retained his privacy.

Once when Johnston was visiting in Daniells' office at the Victoria College Library, Birney came through the open window. Despite Sylvia, the two men saw quite a lot of each other that spring. Daniells had been very helpful to Birney in the preceding two years and had responded to Birney's plea for advice about study in England. At that time Birney, on a Royal Society fellowship, had described himself as 'an anchorite, remote upon a gorsy hill, pecking ... out Chaucer,'[16] which was not quite accurate because Birney had met Esther Bull Heiger, an attractive young Trotskyist, who was typing his dissertation upon that same gorsy hill. As Esther wanted to leave England and the Party had recommended that the two comrades join forces, they set themselves up as a couple and left for Canada together.[17] In 1935, when Daniells had returned to Toronto and Birney was still in England without a job, Daniells advised him that the medievalist W.H. Clawson might be resigning from University College. Birney sent back a grateful letter: 'I wish you would continue to spy out the land ... But I don't want to look like a lean young buzzard swooping before the old carrion has dropped.'[18] Daniells was supportive of his friends, and he appears to have spoken to Principal Wallace for Birney.

In the spring of 1936, he and Birney struggled to get through their Ph.D. oral examinations, especially Anglo-Saxon, which they studied together: 'Birney and I having a stiff time.'[19] At one point, Daniells was ready to give up, but he took the first *viva* in Anglo-Saxon and, to his surprise, 'got through pleasantly, d.g.'[20] This final period of examination was extremely stressful, and at one point he fainted in the washroom. However, he finished his dissertation and turned it in.

On 27 May he took his final Ph.D. *viva* in the morning and rejoiced in a celebratory lunch with Frye and Kemp. They were probably as relieved as he was to have him finished.

His dissertation, 'An Inquiry into Some Formal Problems in English Non-dramatic Literature of the Seventeenth Century,' begins with the assertion that it will define the Baroque style and show the way in which the poetic mind works in a Baroque milieu. In practice, this meant that Daniells discusses the major metaphysical poets, Donne, Crashaw, Herbert, and Traherne, and Milton's epics, especially *Paradise Lost*. He maintains that the seventeenth century is characterized by two primary strands of thought: one transcendental and the other rational. Consequently, the keynote of the period is complexity with persistent 'conflict, tension, an unstable combination of opposing principles.'

For Daniells, the Baroque sensibility in lyric sermon and prose pamphlet is 'tormented, introspective and ratiocinative, oppressed and afflicted, yet struggling to liberate itself, to see, to grasp, to realize, and, above all, to unify its experience' – which is not too far from a description of Daniells himself. A primary example of the Baroque sensibility is John Donne, whose intelligence shapes the form of his expression. Daniells discusses one of Donne's sermons, which is a meditation on the biblical text 'Thy Kingdom Come':

> From a contemplation of two kinds of death – natural and spiritual – he rises ... to the apprehension of a third and mystical death, that of S. Teresa, in which the soul finds the presence of God. And the period ends in a fine, flagrant, Baroque image out of the red wounds of Christ, as out of red paradisal earth of Adam's making, his soul shall burst forth into fresh blade and flower of the resurrection.[21]

This section of the thesis, with its exegesis of a biblical text, would not be out of place in James Daniells' notes for Sunday morning Assembly in the Plymouth Brethren Hall; what is different is the exuberant poetic language. Throughout the dissertation, a number of pressing points of doctrine are raised and discussed: for example, Daniells pauses to discuss the torments engendered by an overly fervent Evangelical Protestantism; he also wonders, a question which recurs, whether we can accept Milton's self-justifying God?

When Daniells and Birney completed their examinations, they headed off together to British Columbia by train. This was the first summer that Daniells had been home since 1931. He got in touch with Max Maynard,

John McDonald, and several other old friends, and spent a great deal of time walking and enjoying the countryside near Victoria. He also spent a day in Vancouver, staying with Birney and Esther. Birney had still not found a job by the end of the summer but at the last moment, on 6 September, Principal Wallace offered him the lectureship at University College which Daniells had first suggested. Birney accepted with pleasure.[22]

On his return to Toronto in the fall of 1936, Daniells continued to see much of the *Canadian Forum* group. After he met Fairley at the Davises in Heronsgate in 1932, he learned of Fairley's and Davis's close connection with the magazine. Fairley always considered himself the bridge between artists and the *Forum*.[23] Pratt, who was a friend of Fred Varley and influenced by the Group of Seven, also published early poetry, including 'The Ice-Floes,' in the *Forum*. All these individuals strongly supported the idea of a Canadian nationality symbolized by the Group. The art of the Group, Pratt's poems, and a retrospective analysis of Canadian poetry was later to lead Frye, who began to write for the *Forum* in the late thirties, to argue in his review of A.J.M. Smith's *The Book of Canadian Poetry* (1943) that 'a tone of deep terror' was characteristic of Canadian poetry.[24]

Daniells had acquired a taste for the art of the Group of Seven in 1933 when he had rented the 'shack' where the walls had been painted by Tom Thomson. In November 1934 he discussed ideas expressed in F.B. Housser's book on the Group with Maynard.[25] In 1936 he saw a 'Superb exhibit of Group of Seven' in the Art Gallery of Toronto, and in March 1937 he saw the Tom Thomson show at Mellors.[26] Sometime during this period, Daniells became friends with Lawren Harris, probably through Davis and Fairley. In the mid-thirties, Daniells sent some replicas of Group paintings to the Frazers, his hosts in Ireland, who responded: 'What a lovely surprise today when your Canadian pictures walked in! They are extraordinarily attractive, and have an air of youth & energy and freshness that becomes a new country.'[27]

It was this strongly pictorial sense of Canada, held by his friends and advocated by the *Forum*, that Daniells shared. But, by the mid-thirties, socialism was an equally strong component of the *Forum* agenda for Canadians, and it became overt in articles and verse depicting social dislocation. Pratt contributed 'A Prayer-Medley'; A.M. Klein, 'Barricade Smith: His Speeches'; and Norman Bethune, 'Red Moon.' With his thesis now completed and more free time, Daniells also turned to poetry. He had earlier published a conventional verse, 'Emelye,' in August 1932 under his own name, but he now wrote several politicized and subversive poems which he submitted to the *Forum* under the pseudonym 'Aquarius,' possibly because he may have felt that his own position as an instructor at Victoria was too tenuous for such frankness.

'A Modern Marvell' was a contemporary version of Andrew Marvell's poem 'To His Coy Mistress.' The poem depicts a Depression world followed by the Spanish Civil War and Baldwin's appeasement. 'Had we but hope enough and Spring / to propagate were then the thing ...'

> But at my back I hear the cough
> of old Sir Basil Zaharoff
> and yonder all before us show
> Oswald, Adolf, Benito.

What lay ahead was inevitable war with Germany: 'Then all my love's outrageous flood / shall fall in wastes of German mud.'[28] A few months later, in October, he published another political verse, 'To a Generation Unemployed,' parodying A.E. Housman:

> Many a lad like you and me
> To save the Empire crossed the sea
> And fought for right and swallowed lies
> In Flanders fields and there he lies ...[29]

Again he signed his poem 'Aquarius.' The *nom de guerre* is not surprising, as he suggests that both the Prussian and the Canadian soldier are equally unemployed and only 'Big Business' will profit from war. The tenor of this poem suggests various entries in his diary which express his reactions to conversations at Pratt's stags.

In the same month, *Saturday Night* published his 'Look Homeward, Angel,' a sonnet alluding to the Spanish Civil War: 'Where men die grim and hope dies yet more hard.'[30] It is clear why Daniells submitted this poem anonymously – this was just before F.H. Underhill got into hot water at the U of T for his views on war. In the next year, Daniells published a number of poems and articles in the *Forum*, invariably signing the articles but usually publishing the poems, all satires, with a pseudonym.[31] Letters of congratulation arrived from Maynard, Robbins, and Riddell, as well as, one suspects, friendly words from his U of T circle. By October 1936 Daniells verse was sufficiently well known for him to be invited by Eric Havelock, a member of the *Forum* editorial board, to become its literary editor. Daniells refused. The next spring, in April 1937, Birney received the same invitation and accepted.

━━━➤◦◄━━━

Daniells could now publish everything he wrote. But he had served a long apprenticeship with Alfred Bailey and Robert Finch. He had first met Finch, a faculty member at University College, at a dinner party in 1931, and was astonished by his abilities: 'most extraordinary chap, a pure aesthete. About thirty, has spent some three years in Paris, plays beautifully, writes poetry ... and is a sort of authority on Elizabethan music.'[32] Finch was a talented artist and pianist: closely in touch with Continental art and music, he had some knowledge of Baroque art and literature.

Finch saw Daniells primarily as a poet, and it was as fellow poets that they met weekly with Bailey. Bailey recalls that it was Daniells who first introduced him to *The Waste Land* and that he felt 'transfigured by this experience.' The whole group recognized that a great spiritual void had been opened by the failure of nineteenth-century standards and beliefs and that 'the economic system under which we lived was in a state of disintegration.' What Eliot offered was a catharsis – a way of dealing with chaos in poetry. In their regular poetry sessions, the group would select a topic or a verse form and each would write a poem. Bailey recalls: 'These meetings, exercises and criticisms, were among the most valuable that I ever took part in as far as developing my own writing of verse was concerned. We were following Eliot's dictum, favouring constant practice, so that our technique would be ready.'[33] This Toronto poetry group, and the later example of Montreal's *Preview* (1942), led Bailey to start a similar group in Fredericton that founded *The Fiddlehead* (1945), one of the outlets for Canadian poets from the mid-1940s to the 1980s.

As Finch later wrote, his friendship with Daniells grew, 'talking of why and how a poem grows.'[34] But they had friends and other interests in common, as well. When Finch was acting in *L'Habit Vert* in 1932 and needed a quiet retreat, he exchanged lodgings with Daniells on Cumberland Street. When Daniells went to Paris to see Baroque art,

Finch gave him advice for a bibliography and directed him to examples of Baroque architecture. When Daniells returned to Toronto in 1932, distressed about Jim Watts, Finch walked him about town, attempting to cheer him up. They went to plays and concerts together and were guests at the homes of mutual friends like the Davises and the Wallaces.

Finch, slightly above average height with classic features, saw Daniells as large, tall, bluff, in 'rugged good health.' What he remembered was his 'nimble mind,' and the way his face would light up when he began to talk about a subject. Finch's sense was that he would open a door, and Daniells would suddenly be there, full of mischievousness. He found characteristic Daniells' habit of beginning to talk about quite a serious subject and then deftly turning it into a humorous quip.[35] Compared to Finch, Daniells felt himself a blunderer, a Caliban to Finch's Ariel. Years later, Daniells found a scrap of paper in his diaries containing a number of comments from Finch on his social behaviour, such as: 'I put bald leading questions to people; I tend to regard people as specimens, not as companions in distress; I ask people for their schemes and theories and fail therefore to get the best out of them; I should try to entertain rather than dissect my companions.'[36]

Aside from their shared aesthetic, their friendship was a classic case of opposites attracting: Daniells was a willing student of Finch's culture; Finch liked to be helpful to Daniells. Near Christmas of 1935, Finch suggested that Daniells travel with him to Mexico. He would pay most of the expenses, and Mexico would provide Daniells with an opportunity to see further examples of Baroque architecture. Daniells explored the idea for a while and mentioned it to one of his friends, Muriel David, who replied firmly, 'You wouldn't like Mexico & Mexico wouldn't like you.'[37] Her reasons were simply that his queasy stomach would not take to Mexican food and that the Mexican, bastardized version of Baroque would not be helpful for his thesis. Daniells declined, citing the pressures of time and work to be done at Victoria College.

But there was perhaps another, more important, reason expressed in this poem that Finch later wrote about Daniells:

> Well I remember how you came one night,
> My attic study was a cube of light
> Deluged with books, there was a sofa there,
> A waste-basket, a table and a chair
> Where I sat writing on this same occasion

When you appeared (by now a rare invasion),
You looked worn-out and I did no inviting
But pointing to the sofa went on writing.
You lay there quietly and at length you slept

...

While on my sheet of paper grew a maze
Of verse that wrote itself in words so clear

...

The window shuddered like a guillotine
And fell. Your eyelids opened and your eyes
Met mine with no expression of surprise,
Showed you were rested, asked if you might share
What I had written, but the page was bare.[38]

These lines, written one evening when Daniells dropped in to see Finch at Middle House, reveal an unexpected depth of feeling on Finch's part, but apparently unexpressed except in these lines. Given Daniells' Plymouth Brethren background, he would have found it difficult to acknowledge Finch's affection, much less respond. Finch understood this. He recalled that he did not show this poem to Daniells, nor did he attempt to publish it.[39] Daniells appreciated Finch as a friend, as 'a palm in the desert,' and their friendship, although it lasted until Daniells' death, remained nurturing but not intimate.

Throughout the thirties, they continued to write poetry together and to advise each other. When 'A Modern Marvell' appeared, Finch wrote commenting that 'form, content, and style in the poem by Aquarius are unified, and the *genre* may well prove to be the one best suited you.'[40] Max Maynard was equally complimentary. 'Your "Modern Marvell" that came out in the Aug. *Forum* I liked extremely. But why the pseudonym? ... Do you ever think of getting some of your best poetry together for a small volume?'[41]

Daniells did not have sufficient poetry to publish a book, but he was writing plays and had been contemplating a novel since the early thirties. He wrote a one-act play, a take-off on civic politics, produced by George Johnston, now a fourth-year student, through the Victoria College Dramatic Society at Hart House.[42] Daniells also wondered if perhaps his own tumultuous childhood could be expressed as a novel. Edmund Gosse's *Father and Son* had arisen from the anxieties of a child surrounded by Plymouth Brethren dogma, and he admired the treatment of religion in Somerset Maugham's *Of Human Bondage*. A year

later, in March 1937, after reading George Moore's *The Brook Kerith*, a
fictionalized account of the biblical Joseph of Arimathea who provided
a tomb for Jesus, Daniells told his father that he wanted to write. He
recognized that it meant years of labour, 'about as painful as having a
child and much longer in the process. But, then, a book – a good one –
lives longer than a child so perhaps it's worth it.'[43] Not surprisingly, it
was a book with a biblical theme that crystallized his desire to write
fiction.

Daniells returned from his 1936 summer holiday in Victoria in poor
health. He travelled by train, stopping in Winnipeg to see E.K. Brown,
who had recently wed a vivacious young Minneapolis society woman,
Margaret Deaver. Back in Toronto, he had a series of 'violent' bilious
attacks, once or twice accompanied by fainting. In mid-July he had an
attack at the Davises. Davis solicitously looked after him, got him tea
afterwards, 'and was charm itself.'[44] That summer he saw a fair amount
of Pratt and Endicott and kept a close eye on the international situation
in Spain. He was still unlucky in his girlfriends. Evelyn Stewart refused
him, and Eva-Lis Wuorio alternated between lukewarm and cold. But
Stewart was now in crisis with her fiancé and Daniells appears to have
been helpful. She wrote in October to say, 'The one bright spot in the
hellishness of the last six weeks has been your friendship.'[45]

⎯⎯➤◆◄⎯⎯

Daniells felt ill all that fall of 1936; in fact, he was working up to a crisis.
There was a great deal of confusion at the start of the term; he was still
camping in Riddell's old rooms in the midst of kettles, ink pots, tennis
racquets, and clothing. He expected that matters would be sorted out
shortly when both men moved into new quarters. But physical confusion appeared to accentuate his nausea. One day in mid-September, he
felt so miserable that he could not get up. Davis came, dug him out of
bed, and took him to lunch. He may have advised Daniells that it was
time to see a doctor because the following day Daniells went to see a Dr
Amsden. 'He spoke of religion, calcium, metabolism, and etc. etc. Good
man I think.'[46] Throughout 1936 he saw this doctor once a week for a
variety of treatments and nostrums. Also, in mid-September, Daniells
went with Davis and Fairley (now back at Toronto) to see a ruined stone
farmhouse near Inglewood. They had evolved a scheme to buy a place
in the country shared by all three, but the farmer refused to sell.[47]

By the fall of 1936, Helen Kemp had returned to Toronto, and Frye had gone to Oxford on a Royal Society scholarship. She duly reported to Oxford that R.K. Arnold, a professor of German at Victoria College, had told her that 'Roy had an incurable habit of falling for some girl, distrusting his own powers, and proposing on the spot before someone else ran off with her.' This distressed Helen, who thought she ought to 'try and marry Roy off to somebody.'[48] Frye rallied to his friend's defence, but he cautioned Helen: '... don't try to marry Roy to anybody. He's a man to be discouraged from marriage.'[49] Daniells had reached similar conclusions a year earlier: 'I can't afford to marry for some time and, in any case, I don't know that anyone so chronically depressed as I ought to get married. It's a great problem.'[50]

Helen continued to keep Frye up to date on Daniells' amours. He had been smitten by Leith Ferguson when she was a 'freshette' (the usual term for a first-year woman student). Now, in 1936, Helen watched him attempting to make a date, keeping up 'a certain adolescent vivacity whenever she was anywhere near. I recognized the symptoms for I've done it myself lots of times.' Evelyn Stewart's room-mate also reported that after Daniells left their flat, a Finnish girl (undoubtedly Eva-Lis Wuorio) phoned and asked crossly for Daniells' phone number: '... so you can see that poor old Roy is being fairly hounded to death at this rate. The Finnish girl is in charge of the art group and is very attractive. There's really nothing like a fascinating foreign accent, especially in a foreign girl.'[51]

Every now and then, Daniells consulted with Woodhouse, no longer his advisor but a colleague and friend. He reported to his parents that he had had a 'pow-wow' with Woodhouse, 'who is, as usual, furiously busy and has two or three books under way. He is most refreshing to speak to. Has a bedroom-study on the top of his boarding house (he and his mother got back from England too late to get good rooms) where he sits surrounded by books and papers, devouring the time with his labours.'[52] It was an attractive picture that he painted for his parents. Given that Daniells had now reached his mid-thirties and was still having difficulty finding a suitable girl (although his father had waited until late in life to marry), his mother may have begun to think that Daniells might also in his later life reside comfortably with his mother, as did Dilworth, Sedgewick, and Woodhouse. The difference was that it was socially convenient for all three to have their mothers as their housekeepers, but Daniells, although deeply and emotionally tied to his mother, nonetheless saw himself with a wife of his own. Because of this, he continued to court a number of young women, hoping to find the right one – one who could inspire him to leave his first family circle.

In December 1936 Daniells was delighted to get a wire from James H. Hanford, the Milton scholar at Western Reserve University in Cleveland, asking him to teach a summer session from 20 June to 29 July for the princely sum of $540. He accepted with alacrity. He was happy to have the experience of teaching a summer session at an American university, where he could meet new people and see the American system. As there would now be a little extra money coming in, he decided to go home for a vacation before summer school.

By February, however, he had clearly fallen into another cycle of depression. To be sure, the dissertation was finally done, and he had a faculty position. But now there was the inevitable let-down after the struggle. He did not feel settled in Toronto. And he had finally been rejected by Eva-Lis Wuorio, although many of his male friends and acquaintances were going 'the way of all flesh.'[53] First Birney, then Riddell, then Frye, even Pelham Edgar! Recently widowed after many years of marriage, Edgar confounded his colleagues by retiring, remarrying, and producing an infant with impressive speed. Daniells, who visited Edgar in early spring 1937, must have been conscious of the ironic contrast between Edgar and himself. He would be thirty-five on 6 April 1937 and still did not have even a steady girlfriend.

His unhappiness over Eva-Lis is expressed in a sad letter to his mother. He was so depressed that he had cancelled his class for the morning, something he rarely did. 'Wish I were there with you and the trees & the sea & the growing things and away from all this high pressure and heartbreak.'[54] His mother responded by sending a large bouquet of flowers: iris, fern, carnation, daffodils, and tulips. The flowers brought back memories of how much enjoyment there was in gardening and spring bulbs, even in the bad old days at Cook Street:

It's curious that, looking back on this last June, it seems I had innumerable things to say to you which never got said ... Chiefly, I suppose, that I love you very much, so much that I don't dare think of it. On a different and deeper plane, somehow, than anything that I experience here and now. We always got on so well. I can remember so many things. And so far back. Us walking about the island on D'Arcy together when things were at their worst, for instance. You were always so good & patient. And the Brethren had done for us, really, so completely and for so long. Life was intolerable then, but real. It's more tolerable now, but less real. This Toronto is a smoke, signifying nothing.

Why I can't say what I want I don't know. I don't know *what it is*. Only that I've loved you inexpressibly much and I hate growing up and having to live a separate life.

Daniells realized that he was caught in a double bind: it was not just his fixation with Plymouth Brethren doctrine but also his overly strong connections with his mother. At this point, he saw that the idea of marriage was 'a problem. There are no end of attractive girls here, one way and another, but my technique is bad, as witness the affairs with the Wuorio and the Harvey girl, to mention the two latest only.' Caught up in memories of the past, he found it impossible to make new connections: 'I keep thinking of the past, of our whole life among trees at Cook Street. And how much the rain & snow, the seasons coming & going, &, above all, the flowers, meant to us. And these you now send bring it all back.'[55]

Like D.H. Lawrence's Paul Morel in *Sons and Lovers*, he now perceived the bond with the mother and determined to write of his early life, possibly to understand it. He wrote his father, '*I think I have matured my experience to the point where it may profitably be set down*' (his italics).[56] However, it is doubtful whether Daniells had matured his experience to the point where it could be written about: the real trauma of his mother and the 'rapture' was now far from the surface of his consciousness, and he tended to fix upon hectoring Plymouth brothers as the origin of his distress.

He continued to see Helen Kemp, who acted as hostess for the teas which, as a don at Burwash Hall, Daniells was obliged to give for the male residents. She found Daniells quite irritating at times: '... the only time he asks me to do anything with him is when he has to have a gorgon attend his teas.' But, she told Frye, 'when I feel the need of masculine company I 'phone him up and feel very fond of him. I suppose it is his courageous bachelor whistling in the dark that annoys me – he keeps on telling me how wonderful it is to live in Burwash as he does, blissfully without care – and then he tells me how wonderful Evelyn [Stewart] is, and then Dorothy [Drever] tells me how devoted he is and Roy [Kemp, Helen's brother] tells me how the men have diagnosed Daniells as needing a woman badly and how they speculate about his feminine friends.'[57] Frye was reassuring: 'Roy isn't insulting you, sweetheart. He's being scrupulously honourable about you, and he doesn't do it well, that's all.'[58] Frye had asked Daniells to 'look after' Helen when he first went to England, and Daniells appears to have been doing just that. After the Birney-Sylvia imbroglio, he probably felt that he could not be too careful.

However, there was truth in Kemp's observation that Daniells was both too fussy and too absorbed in himself.[59] In fact, Daniells was going through one of the most difficult periods in his life. Because of his solitary twenties, in his mid-thirties he was undergoing the emotional *sturm und drang* usually associated with much younger men. He was also curiously immature in social relationships. He recognized that he adored his friends, had an uncritical loyalty to the institutions he worked for, but had no real depth of self-knowledge: 'If I hurt people's feelings, as I did by sudden shifts of interest and attention, it was out of the purest inadvertence. I had no aim except to succeed in what I was immediately doing – some simple job involving the handling of words – that is, I had a burning intention to avoid failure ... But it is odd now to realize what was hidden from me then, that at 35 I was a very immature, well meaning but blundering fellow.'[60]

Nonetheless, he was canny in terms of institutional politics. Loyalty to his friends led Daniells to caution Frye when in England to be sure to keep in touch with Edgar and Principal Brown. Frye, immersed in Blake, failed to do so, and his scholarship was not renewed. Kemp suggested that Frye borrow some money from Daniells, and he, once again, obliged. Meantime, Daniells urged Frye's case through Edgar, Pratt, and Brown, attempting to secure a position for Frye at Victoria. A position seemed likely, but it became definite only when it appeared that he himself might leave Victoria. As Kemp told Frye: 'There is just a chance of a very interesting shift here ... E.K. Brown is coming to Toronto and Roy Daniells may go to take his place.'[61]

⟫•◦•⟪

In that miserable spring of 1937 the Spanish Civil War raged, and Daniells recognized that 'things look worse than ever in Europe ... probability of a war. If there is one, what will Canada do?'[62] Just as he was feeling most bereft, Davis told him that he was planning to accept an offer from Cornell. It must have been a devastating blow; on two earlier occasions, Daniells had recorded how badly he felt about the possibility of Davis taking a position in Australia. He had hardly digested this news when he received 'exciting news' from Brown regarding a possible move for himself. It was not quite a surprise; Davis a year earlier had made an 'astonishing remark ... with regard to E.K.B. – myself – & Winnipeg.'[63] Brown, now head of English at Manitoba, had been invited back to University College, probably at Woodhouse's instigation. Daniells, although he had just finished his Ph.D., was Brown's choice to fill his position as head. It was an exceptionally flattering offer.

Because of his depression, because he had had an earlier intimation of the offer, and because Davis himself was leaving Toronto, Daniells was more receptive than he might otherwise have been. Brown came to Toronto to explain the situation in full on his way to the annual meeting of the Learned Societies at Queen's University. He said that Sidney Smith, president at Manitoba, would be contacting Daniells for an interview.

Daniells informed Edgar of the pending offer. Explaining the possibilities of a job at Manitoba to his parents, he said that he was highly attracted because there would be a chance to do 'a real job of organization.'[64] And his two mentors, Brown and Davis, wanted him to take it. As he said, 'I have been in Toronto or looked upon it as a place to return since the autumn of 1930 ... Davis in whose judgement I have great confidence writes ... "a real chance of breaking loose – away from Vic and a college residence, and to a real job on your own."'[65]

He had expected to hear about the University of Manitoba job prior to leaving to teach summer school in Cleveland. However, as no word came, on 14 June he left for Cleveland, travelling by way of St Catharines, stopping to visit the parents of his latest flame, Grete Estrup. On 17 June he arrived in Cleveland where his contact was G.C. Robinson. He described Robinson as grey-haired and 'rather subdued, I thought at first,'[66] but the two men appear to have quickly developed an easy rapport. His lectures began on 23 June to an 'attentive, if not very advanced class.'[67] In fact, he was teaching two graduate classes, one in sixteenth-century and the other in seventeenth-century.

At last, on 26 June, a letter came from President Smith at Manitoba asking him to come to Winnipeg for an interview. As soon as his Friday classes were over, he boarded a train on 2 July and travelled to Winnipeg, by way of Chicago and Minneapolis. There he spent most of Sunday and was interviewed by Smith and J.W. Dafoe, the chancellor, whom Daniells described as 'the editor of the *Winnipeg Free Press* and a grand old boy, about seventy.' He had met Dafoe earlier in Toronto at a farewell tea for Davis and had apparently made a good impression. He reported to his parents that 'they both seemed favourable to the appointment and my name comes up before the board this week, I hope, but you never can tell till you get a *fait accompli*. However, it looks extremely promising. Now, of course, I begin to wonder whether it wouldn't be better to stay in Toronto and wait for slower-but-sure promotion.'[68]

He had discovered, much to his surprise, how highly he was regarded at Victoria College. He had received an urgent letter from Frye: 'Hope you will quash all hideous rumours about your leaving Toronto.'[69] And both Principal Brown and the chancellor had contacted him regarding staying on at Victoria. 'I was agreeably surprised to find how solidly I seem to be entrenched here and how anxious the Principal is to retain my services. Incidentally, and distinct from this altogether, they have put my salary up a double amount this year; – $300 (less 5%) instead of $150. It is very gratifying.'[70] Pelham Edgar told him bluntly that he had written to President Smith at Manitoba telling him 'you were so good that we did not want to lose you, and that you had an assured future in this place ... you will be foolish to accept. Toronto is a far better place than Winnipeg, and a much better jumping off place ... You fit in here ... It is a proud thing to be in the offer market, but you need not accept the offer.'[71] This was sober fact and it caused him to give further thought to his precipitous decision. Daniells was flattered by the offer, had not been sure that he would be hired, and was carried along by the flutter of trying. When on 9 July he received a telegram from Smith offering him the job, he wired his acceptance but recorded his reservations in his diary: 'Hope it's the best thing.'[72]

That same night, he wrote his parents to explain both the advantages of the position and his obvious uncertainty: 'It's a toss up whether in the very long run the job beats my present one, but I think I've done the right thing in accepting it, and certainly the *immediate* rise in salary is a point. Instead of 2400 less 5% this next year, I am to get 4500 less of 20% (i.e. 3600).' There would be no don's allowance in terms of free meals and accommodation, but he would be considerably closer to his family: 'by two nights and a day in the train, to be exact. I am also, from July 1st, a professor (!) and head of an English Department (!!) – a small one, but mine own, so to say.'[73]

Daniells knew that the Department of English at the University of Manitoba was not Victoria College, U of T. Edgar was quite right. When the greybeards fell by the way, Daniells could have become the senior professor, going on, as his successor Frye later did, to be principal of Victoria College. In the interim, he could have developed his scholarly rather than administrative skills. But Daniells may have countered these arguments with the thought that Woodhouse and Brown had been called back to Toronto, so why not he as well? By mid-July, he was psychologically persuaded that he should go. 'Want to start a new life in Winnipeg & constantly think of it.'[74] Davis's reasons for encouraging Daniells to make the move might have been more complicated. Davis himself had stayed at University College for thirteen years before accepting the offer from Cornell. But he had seen during the past year that Daniells was in a rut: he needed to leave his cloistered Toronto life, and take on the rough and tumble of running a department in Winnipeg. In the process, he would be forced to strike out and make a new life for himself.

The decision to accept the University of Manitoba offer plunged Daniells into furious activity. He was full of plans, packing, getting himself and his belongings to Winnipeg, trying to determine whether to buy a car, whether to take Davis's gramophone (a gift) with him, whether to spend August in Toronto, where there was a good library, or to go down to Massachusetts and use the Harvard library.

What he regretted most about leaving Toronto was parting from the Davises. When he had first gone with Davis and Brown in late May to arrange for the American immigration papers, Daniells had 'a fearful bilious attack' followed the next day by 'another frightful bilious attack' – so bad, in fact, that Joe Fisher, later a faculty member at Victoria and UBC, stayed with him overnight.[75] In June, Daniells gave an impromptu speech at the farewell dinner given for Davis by the university. Now, at the end of August, just before leaving for Winnipeg, he had his last lunch at the Davises' household with Fairley. As always, there was good conversation and he had a wonderful time. 'Shall not forget the atmosphere of that house, ever. Feeling pretty depressed.'[76]

He would miss Davis, who had been 'good to me and good for me.'[77] The clearest acknowledgment of his feelings about Davis are found in the dedication to his doctoral dissertation, which is simply: 'To David (2 Sam. 9:13).' We expect some reference to the friendship of David and Jonathan, but Daniells is citing the passage which says, 'So Mephibosheth dwelt in Jerusalem: for he did eat continually at the king's table and was lame on both his feet.' At one level, the citation is a humorous admission that Daniells, who could be depended upon to turn up at dinner time at 'David's,' was a lame duck of sorts. It also suggests their relative positions. The biblical King David, having vanquished his enemy King Saul, wanted to be kind to his grandson, Mephibosheth, Jonathan's son. King David promises him: 'I will show thee kindness for Jonathan thy father's sake ... and thou shall eat bread at my table continually.'

That Daniells, who knew the Bible so well, should choose this passage indicates that it expressed his own position. Davis was kind to him. Why? Possibly because of his Christian charity, possibly because of the loss of his first wife, Gertrud. The quotation also illustrates Daniells' own sense of their unequal relations. Davis was indeed kind; however, their relationship was not quite as lopsided as the younger man imagined. Daniells was always an amusing companion, a colleague of sorts, and a man Friday to the Davises: he fixed toasters, rolled lawns, looked after the baby, checked items in the British Museum, and read proofs of *The Drapier's Letters*. On at least two occasions, he did Davis the great favour of changing his sailings without demur – in one case, from one year to the next – to accommodate the latter's bookings so that both could travel together as he had requested. It must have been a horror for Davis to travel to and from England on boats so like the one from which Gertrud had disappeared. But Daniells did not recognize all that. Nor did he see that in accepting the position of head of English at Manitoba he had taken the most decisive step in his career as an up-and-coming professor of English. He still thought himself a handicapped beginner – the object of David's kindness.

PART THREE

University of Manitoba: 1937–1946

Chapter Ten

'This Winnipeg!'

With very mixed feelings, on 9 September 1937, Daniells took the train from Toronto to Winnipeg. Toronto had been good to him, and he recognized that uprooting connections which began in 1930 would be more painful than he had anticipated. E.K. Brown, outgoing head at the U of M, was helpful to his successor with advice and advance information, but it had become clear to Daniells that conditions at Winnipeg would be very different. He was also a little worried about his academic future – had he made the right choice in leaving an established position at Victoria College? As Pelham Edgar had pointedly remarked, 'After all it isn't Harvard calling.'[1] On the last night on the train, he was sick, probably anxious about his arrival the next morning. As he stepped off the train on 12 September into the bustling railway station, he stepped into a fixed slot in the cultural elite of an important mercantile centre in Canada. He was to have two free years to reorganize the English Department before the Second World War started.

Winnipeg had had its genesis as the Red River Colony. In succession, the city became headquarters of the Hudson's Bay Company, hub of the new continental railroad, and a centre for immigration. Since to the north of the city was wilderness and to the south the United States, people and goods had to pass through Winnipeg to reach the far west. As early as 1900, the city had become a distribution centre and large resource base for grain, fur, textiles, and cheap immigrant labour, and by 1914 it became a labour movement centre for J.S. Woodsworth's downtown mission and for socialist thought. By 1937, when Daniells arrived, there was support not only for the traditional Liberal and Conservative parties, but also the new Co-operative Commonwealth Federation (CCF) and, on the more radical fringe, the Communist party.

The city had a vibrant cultural life, reflecting the interests of Scots, English, Germans, Ukrainians, Jews, and Icelanders, as well as the large French-speaking community in St Boniface. Besides a number of active theatre groups, there was a celebrated young men's choir at All Saints Anglican Church; and, a year after Daniells' arrival, in 1938, Gweneth Lloyd and Betty Farrally started the forerunner of the Royal Winnipeg Ballet. Daniells took dancing lessons from a 'Miss Lloyd.' Winnipeg also had the liberal *Free Press*, considered by many the best newspaper in the country, edited by John Wesley Dafoe, also considered by many the best editor in Canada. As well, there was the conservative *Winnipeg Tribune*, a daily Yiddish paper, and two Anglo-Jewish weeklies.

Winnipeg society was strongly divided by class. The English and mercantile Scots were still at the top of the heap, especially those who had made their money through land speculation at the turn of the century: they attended the Anglican and Presbyterian churches, belonged to the Winnipeg Winter Club, and intermarried. This hierarchy was challenged in the thirties as Jewish immigrants from Russia and Poland moved from small farms to small shops to manufacturing plants; their children began to attend the U of M, but subject in medicine to a Jewish quota.

The U of M included the university proper and the affiliated colleges of St Paul's (Catholic), St John's (Anglican), and Wesley (United Church), as well as Brandon College. Each college could teach what it liked, but it presented students for the U of M's examinations. A.R.M. Lower, who joined Wesley College in the late twenties, recorded that this situation 'was to make Winnipeg just about the most unpleasant academic centre in the country. The various colleges and the university behaved towards each other like competing business firms. Jealousy was everywhere ... They suspected each other's probity.'[2] As head of English at Manitoba, the most prestigious institution, Daniells felt some responsibility for holding the affiliated colleges together and could influence standards for the group as a whole.

Much of this he had been told by E.K. Brown. He had also heard from Herbert Davis (who had now left for Cornell) that Brown had said Daniells had won his position against several rivals: 'you should plan to give them five years or so of your best, and then see what you feel like.'[3] From Northrop Frye came a long, chatty letter, which said that Daniells' departure left large gaps in the first-, second-, and third-year honours program at Victoria. As Daniells' replacement, Frye wanted advice, and he reported that he had prepared stencilled handouts for the students: 'I shall spoon feed these children till they retch.'[4] From A.S.P. Woodhouse came the magisterial observation: 'EK has shown his usual wisdom, in selecting his successor.'[5] From the undergraduate Leith Ferguson came a lament that Daniells was 'skipping out westward': 'What's the dramatic society going to do? What's the *Acta* going to do?'[6]

There were warm congratulations from all of his friends in British Columbia, especially Garnett Sedgewick, head of English at UBC. Sedgewick's letter had copious biblical allusions. Now that the younger man had joined the 'dishonourable company of Heads,' he would find that the position brought with it all the 'boils,' 'whelks,' and 'bubuckles' that had plagued Job. His situation at Manitoba 'must indeed be perennially delicate. It will require the unremitting exercise of nice feelings, fine shades – nicer & finer than ever [George] Meredith imagined.'[7] Sedgewick was alluding to the complicated structure of power at the university. But there were further financial complications. In 1932 chancellor and treasurer of the U of M, John A. Machray, was discovered to have embezzled university funds. Threatened with bankruptcy in 1934, the board of governors had hired President Sidney Smith to clean up the mess.[8] He, in turn, hoping to raise academic standards, had hired the most promising young scholar in English in Canada – E.K. Brown. As Brown's successor, Daniells was inheriting a financially troubled position, a weak department, an unequal student body, and a president whose expectations were exceptionally high.

To be sure, there were compensations, not all financial. As Sedgewick pointed out, Daniells would find departmental friends, notably William Robbins and Lloyd Wheeler, both from BC. He also said Arthur Phelps at Wesley United would be 'a very fair and generous man.' Sedgewick advised Daniells against forming a 'BC clique' and gave him some good advice: 'First, lie low for a while till you have seen everything for yourself. Second, in Manitoba, of all places, a "Head" must endeavor to wear a cheerful & unperturbed front. He is expected to be something of a social figure ... If he feels the need of being abstracted & solitary, he had better obey scripture and shut himself up in his own closet for a while ... he must learn to affect a measure of joy in suffering fools – even when he feels like Jeremiah within. Here endeth the Lesson.'[9]

Sedgewick had read the situation astutely. Daniells was uncomfortable with the superficial socializing that made up much of the public role of head of English in a city like Winnipeg in the thirties and forties. When he was depressed, he showed it; and he was partial to his friends, a dangerous quality for a head. Above all, he had little sympathy for fools, or for those who did not keep up with their academic work. On the positive side, he was intelligent, exceptionally hard-working, and an inspired speaker. He had a strong sense of duty, which, coupled with his seven years at University of Toronto, enabled him to judge how the department *should* be run. Finally, he was in the prime of life – thirty-five – capable of taking on large administrative responsibilities.

On his first day in Winnipeg, Daniells booked into the St Charles Hotel. He had tea that afternoon with his old friend William Robbins, followed by dinner the next day with Robbins and his new wife, Margaret. The next day, he met Doris Saunders, an eighteenth-century specialist and the only woman in the department, and Arthur Phelps, head of English at United College. Phelps, a small, dark, balding man, had done graduate work at Toronto and was a close friend of E.J. Pratt; he was also a Sunday poet and a popular but somewhat eccentric lecturer. He tended to galvanize a class's attention by such histrionics as springing nimbly onto desks and chairs.[10] Even his good friend Lower recalled that 'his lecture notes were mostly jottings on the backs of envelopes.'[11] Phelps was astute and could be formidable when crossed.

On 14 September, Daniells met for the first time with six departmental colleagues.[12] The two senior professors were William Talbot Allison, a graduate of Yale and a Shakespeare specialist, and Aaron Jenkins Perry, who held an M.A. from Yale in Anglo-Saxon. Lloyd Wheeler, Sedgewick's former student, was 'gaunt, lean, medium height, stooped and very earnest, and totally devoted to Shakespeare.'[13] Wheeler was an encouraging teacher. He socialized with students in a theatre group, and each spring took four or five upper-level students to his summer cottage: there they worked on his road by day and talked about literary topics at night. As he was not a publishing scholar, he was bypassed for promotion, but Wheeler did not appear to harbour grudges. He was friendly to Daniells and promptly invited him to lunch. Other English faculty members were Robert Fletcher Argue, an assistant professor in English and education, Clark Hopper, an assistant professor who was later dean of men, and Saunders, whom he had already met.

The student population for arts and science at Manitoba in the fall of 1937 was 1,411. There is no information regarding the number of English students other than a registrar's list for 1937–8 with the notation that forty-two students were writing specialist exams. However, because the English Department was a service department, providing training in English for all the other faculties, English would have been one of the largest university departments.

The first shock at Winnipeg was the layout of the university. There were two campuses, widely separated, and faculty haphazardly taught at both. U of M's downtown campus was housed in a large school-like structure across Broadway from the provincial legislature. One brick building was connected to several ramshackle wooden ones, left over from the First World War, all of which stank of chemicals from science classes. The Fort Garry campus, consisting of the Administration, Agriculture, Arts, Commerce, Engineering, and Science Buildings, was a long distance from downtown and took three-quarters of an hour in a jolting streetcar. Daniells complained: 'I never had anything to do with so queerly organized a University before; we are bound by the most bizarre regulations and having to operate on two sites six miles apart makes everything just six times as fantastic as it would be otherwise.'[14]

Then there were problems with the faculty, which consisted of 'Perry and Allison (both due to retire soon), Argue and Hopper (both badly trained), Wheeler (a B.C. man and very good) and Miss Saunders (... willing and energetic).'[15] The English curriculum, which Brown had started to reorganize, needed complete revision. Standards for entering students were particularly low. What was worse, a tradition of misrule existed at the U of M. Daniells got his first taste of the 'Wild West' when entering students, as was their custom, attempted to make a 'goat' of their instructor. Woodhouse, recalling his own experience with U of M classes, had earlier told Brown that 'broad shoulders' would be far more helpful to him at Winnipeg than a D.Litt. from the Sorbonne. Brown, faced with students who would not subside for a mere professor, stood in front of his classes waiting and smiling for long periods.[16] Allison, a former head, white haired, slight shouldered, expounding *Antony and Cleopatra* and challenged to define 'harlot' by a bullying first-year student, stood before the class, embarrassed but unable to secure order;[17] Daniells, faced with similar provocations, was initially polite but then lost his temper: he picked up a chair and threw it across the room.[18] Order prevailed in his classrooms.

Students in English, many first-generation Canadians, worked very hard. But such students had problems with spoken English and composition. Daniells met a class briefly to get a sense of the student body, but it was not until 20 September that he gave his 'first real class in this Broadway building – an introduction to [Sir Thomas] Browne to a ɪɪ year class.'[19] He was also responsible for the senior honours course, English ɪV, but because of the press of other business, did not meet them until 25 September, inspiring a stiff reproof from President Smith. Despite being head, Daniells was accountable for every small action. In this, as in many other matters, U of M was quite different from U of T.

He had been very busy since his arrival. Besides attempting to get classes under way, he had been looking, unsuccessfully, for a place to live. In mid-September, he settled into his office, which overlooked the Parliament Buildings, 'about the nicest looking building there is in Winnipeg.'[20] His office effects had arrived, and he 'unpacked books, to my great relief for I feel queer without them, and got carpet down, which also helps.'[21] That day he also signed a lease for a flat which he saw advertised. But it was not until 1 October that he moved into a suite at 121 Carlton Street, owned by a Jewish family named Wolinsky; they kindly helped him settle in, and he subsequently reported that 'my opinion of Jews has acquired a reservation.'[22] His attitude points to a casual acceptance of Jewish and other cultural stereotypes.

Daniells brought from Toronto most of the essentials for his apartment, including chairs, carpet, and bedding. Wheeler helped him move his 450 books and assisted in setting up Davis's gramophone with the huge papier mâché horn.[23] He had also brought some fine Japanese artifacts and photographs that Eugene Cassidy had sent to Toronto. But he had not yet acquired curtains, kettle, or bookshelves. Everything took a great deal of effort, and he was uncomfortable with these rapid changes in his routine, so different from the prescribed and orderly pattern of Toronto.

Nonetheless, he enjoyed many aspects of his new life: 'I am busy as a gopher, with innumerable things to find out and arrange.' He did not know how long he would stay in Winnipeg, or whether he really wanted to remain an academic. But, taking Sedgewick's injunctions to heart, he cultivated a 'social front,' making calls to persons like J.W. Dafoe and George Ferguson of the *Winnipeg Free Press*. He communicated regularly with President Smith, writing informative memos on the departmental activities. He saw various heads of English at the affiliated colleges and attempted to make friends. He also made a point of getting to know his colleagues in other departments. That he rapidly became respected at the university is indicated by his prompt election to the Faculty Council, the governing board of the faculty.

He also bridged the gap between gown and town by giving countless lectures on poetry and novels to library groups, poetry groups, high school teachers, university clubs, and business associations. The president, keeping tabs on his progress, told him that his first public talk to the Poetry Society was a great success: 'I have heard great praise ... The cordial and unsolicited commendation came to me from laymen and academic colleagues.'[24] Daniells also, after a year at Manitoba, began a series of radio programs that brought literature to the general public. As Brown had been somewhat reserved in his public persona, Daniells was seen as a great improvement. Again President Smith expressed his approval.

By October the weather had become cool, with a hint of winter. Daniells found himself on a treadmill, attempting to combine administration, teaching, and socializing. 'The routine of the Department is to a great extent still unfamiliar to me, and I dislike routine of this sort and am not good at it.'[25] Nonetheless, he found the actual teaching encouraging: the upper-level students were quite intelligent, and the staff was welcoming. He was now established in Winnipeg. He found the landscape severe, the weather trying, the town nearly as provincial as he had expected. But there were compensations. He appreciated the wide skies and austerely beautiful prairies, and he learned to live with the weather, acquiring a huge fur coat and hat. And he joined the Winnipeg Winter Club. There he could swim, exercise, dine, and meet other young single professionals.

Meeting with his counterparts, the heads of English at the affiliated colleges, Daniells began to survey the program at the U of M and plan course work and examinations. He soon discovered that Manitoba, unlike Toronto, was basically a frontier institution in which the president and board of governors often represented the views of big business, and university faculties were expected to comply. The fiscal problems of the university, complicated by the Depression, made matters worse because there were no funds to hire good faculty. Moreover, the English Department was expected to impart rudimentary English to nursing and agriculture students, and to support other professional faculties in training students for careers. This emphasis was not wildly amiss for burgeoning Winnipeg with its large immigrant population. However, it meant that the English curriculum was basic, that it had not been substantially upgraded for some time, and there was less interest in graduate work than in the university as a whole.

Daniells wanted to restructure the English program, and for this he needed the cooperation of the heads of the affiliated colleges. Initially he found Phelps, head of English at United College, relatively congenial and Father Gerald Lahey, head of English at St Paul's College, welcoming. Lahey, a sandy-haired man with a fine sense of humour, was a Jesuit trained at Oxford who had written *Gerard Manley Hopkins* (1930), one of the first critical studies of the poet. A sophisticate, he found Winnipeg something of a backwater and dryly explained to colleagues that in order to communicate with his students he had been reading the funny papers.[26] His wit, interest in poetry, and possibly his exotic Catholicism appealed to Daniells. Lahey became one of his first real friends. After he joined the department in 1941, Max Patrick, also an Oxford man, sometimes joined the two for lunch on a Friday at the Hudson's Bay Company restaurant: 'Smiling coyly Father Lahey would tell us that as a Jesuit he had the right to dispense with the R.C. rules about fasting ... Much encouraged by Roy, Father Lahey would order a copious meal – and enjoy it very enthusiastically,' while Catholic patrons of the restaurant 'used to gaze, somewhat constrained, on the Father's breaking the dietary rules of eating with such gusto – and so much! Roy delighted in this.'[27]

Although making friends at Manitoba, Daniells remained uncertain about his future and considered posts in the United States, at Toronto, and at UBC. As he recognized from the onset, 'I don't know how I shall like Winnipeg. It will be a halting place only, I hope.'[28] Meantime, his old colleagues at Toronto, like J.D. Robins at Victoria, kept in touch. 'O Willie, we have missed you! Not only have we missed you, but so have the students, greatly ... I think we have no one left with your gift for exciting the creative impulse in the youthful into activity. It is a pity, for the deficiency in that quality is a deficiency in the very heart of university work. Frye may develop in that way, and I hope he will.'[29]

His Toronto colleagues and students, several doing postgraduate studies in England, continued to write. And Jerry Riddell wrote to give him all the latest news. Birney was publishing one of Daniells' scurrilous poems in the *Forum;* Margaret Avison, his former student, was doing very well; the post-Oxford Frye was a vast improvement: 'his competence is more impressive than ever, and he himself mellower and no longer devastating.'[30] Desmond Pacey appealed for help in applying for a Rhodes scholarship; when it fell through, he asked for a recommendation for a Massey scholarship, which he received for study in England.[31] When Pacey did well at Cambridge, Daniells helped him to secure a position at Brandon College, affiliated with U of M. Henry

Noyes, later a distinguished American professor, wrote from the University of London in November to tell Daniells about F.R. Leavis's criticism and to thank him 'for the good advice you gave me about coming over here and getting this research work cleared out the way of a career.'[32] A Romantic specialist, Noyes was one of the first younger faculty members that Daniells hired at Manitoba.

<hr />

Daniells was aware of the new directions in English criticism. A few years earlier, he and Larsen had discussed I.A. Richards's techniques, and he was now developing a seminar in practical criticism with a third-year honours group. Ernest Sirluck, one of his students during these first years, recalls that his critical views reflected 'Eliot, Richards, Empson, and Leavis,' and that 'he gave us a sensitive and exciting introduction to Donne and the Metaphysicals,' but that he was somewhat ambivalent about Milton, whom he contrasted with the Metaphysicals. As a personality, Daniells appeared to his students as elegant in manner and appearance, but 'thirty-five, unmarried, whimsically moustachioed ... harried and on the verge of despair, hurrying along at a kind of restrained lope.' As a lecturer, however, Daniells was captivating. Sirluck considered his lectures 'studied performances' that won immediate approval from his students – 'superficially self-deprecating, humorously humble, irreverent about monuments or institutions, but absolutely serious about poetry and criticism.'[33]

Daniells' teaching methods with his honours students were based on those of Herbert Davis. As he later remarked: 'My friend, Professor Davis, pursued this method of throwing his house open to groups of students and it was remarkably successful.'[34] Among the first honours group were Alan Adamson, Margaret Ann Bjornson, better known as 'Baby,' Ogden or 'Oggie' Turner, and Sirluck. As the Fort Garry campus was so inconvenient, the group frequently met during 1939–40 at Daniells' flat, now at 577 Stradbrook Avenue. The group was extraordinarily talented, but diverse. Adamson was tall and witty; his fiancée, Bjornson, was a striking blonde with a theatrical presence; Sirluck was charismatic and intellectually confident; Turner, a former country schoolteacher, was a tall, ungainly man, exceptionally courteous.

As Adamson recalled, 'a typical meeting would begin with Roy circulating a poem, with author, date, and anything else that might identify it omitted. We were asked to decide who had written it, and when, justifying our conclusions by reference to the poem's technical, verbal/syntactic and thematic features. A group of us – Bjornson, Sirluck, Turner and myself,' as Adamson recalls, 'picked up the discipline ... and began to play it as an ultra-mural game.' In addition to practical criticism, there was always music. Daniells still used Davis's machine, which was an old RCA Victor hand-wound victrola, its wooden needles needing to be carefully sharpened after each side was played. He liked Elizabethan madrigals and Purcell, with the Alfred Deller singers and consort performing on ancient instruments. Adamson remembered the robust counter-tenors: 'To thee, to thee and to a maid / Who kindly will upon her back be laid.' And:

> I kissed her once, I kissed her twice
>   I gave her sack and sherry
> I kissed her once, I kissed her twice
>   And we were wondrous merry.

Adamson, who still considered himself 'an uncombed prairie dog,' found Daniells' precocity intimidating. 'Maybe we got too much of Herbert and not enough of Milton and the early Donne. But you have to remember the time and the place. Eliot's influence as a canoniser was immense, Auden, Spender, C. Day Lewis were devoured even in Fort Garry and we grasped desperately at anything that would lift us out of the middle-brow, middle class, middle west, Middletown that Winnipeg symbolized.'[35]

It was precisely because Daniells lifted a whole generation of bright students out of the Winnipeg 'Middletown' that they found his teaching so exciting. He stimulated their literary interests, helped them start their careers, and directed them to graduate study and work in Toronto, Ottawa, and Montreal. He also brought new life to English studies at the University of Manitoba. Bjornson, later Lady Elton, recalled, 'The advent of Roy marked the end of the Palgrave's *Golden Treasury* era in the English Dept. Before he married, he had us to his flat, and rapidly became a friend as well as a tutor.'[36] Sirluck, in his autobiography, *First Generation*, remarks that 'Daniells formed closer relationships with students than was usual, and I benefited greatly from his friendship; in and out of the classroom he helped me widen my horizons, sharpen my perceptions, and above all discipline and modulate my responses.'[37]

However, it was Turner, who taught English at St John's-Ravenscourt School and at U of M, who became one of Daniells' closest student friends, largely because he was the first student representative for the *Manitoba Arts Review*.

The support which Daniells gave to this student-generated review represented one of his initial attempts to bring a larger cultural life to the university. Turner, associate editor for 1938–9 (fall and spring), appears to have done most of the editorial work during this first year.[38] Daniells was listed as advisory literary editor in the first issue, and subsequently as faculty advisor. He served as a sounding board for student submissions and helped secure articles from established scholars and critics. During its first two years, the *MAR* carried an article by R.O. MacFarlane, 'What is a Canadian?'; an essay by Brown on Robinson Jeffers; and an amusing essay on academic individualism by Daniells featuring a bull named Ferdinand – modelled on a popular illustrated book of the period, *Ferdinand the Bull*.[39]

The students Daniells saw most of during his first three years at Manitoba were those associated with the honours course, the *Manitoba Arts Review*, and the 'Morons,' an undergraduate club of bright sparks meant as an alternative to the official English Club. It had been founded just before Daniells arrived by Stanley Jackson, later of the National Film Board, Frank Pickersgill, a Canadian who would be killed by the Gestapo while working for British security, George Ford, later an English professor, and Bjornson, later a film-maker. It was controlled by the undergraduate members, and membership was by invitation only. The group met once a month: 'the undergraduate members would read papers to one another, after which a long and often violent discussion would take place, often ending close to dawn.'[40] As the club was student-generated, faculty came only by invitation. Wheeler was a regular, and Daniells was soon invited.

During the first two years, 'Baby' Bjornson, who was engaged to Adamson, became a friend and confidante. In 1940–1 Adamson and Bjornson married and left for Ottawa to join the National Film Board under John Grierson, where Adamson became Grierson's personal assistant and Bjornson a film-maker – producing, among other films, *Iceland on the Prairies*. After her divorce from Adamson, she married British film-maker Arthur (later Lord) Elton. Adamson, briefly a socialist, later became professor of history at Concordia. Sirluck, recommended to Woodhouse by Brown and Daniells, received an award of free tuition and $500 to begin graduate study at the University of Toronto, beginning a distinguished academic career as a Miltonist.

When Daniells first came to Winnipeg, the young women he met were either university students, such as Cynthia Roblin and Jean Landreth, or young Winnipeg society women. Once he was having dinner with a young woman when 'she came out with a burst of material ambition & must marry a rich man – which really startled me. This Winnipeg!'[41] Certain aspects of Winnipeg society, particularly an emphasis on material possessions, bothered Daniells. He was uncomfortable in the presence of wealth; it went against the grain of his Puritan background, and he was miserably aware that he, like Eliot's Prufrock, did not fit in with society, much less did he 'dare to eat a peach.' Nonetheless, he was smitten by a young woman from a wealthy family, Frances Aikens, better known as 'Dime.'

Dime was part of the student group who travelled to the Fort Garry campus for a night class during 1938–9. Often when Daniells was standing at the bus stop, she would zip by in her roadster and pick up whoever was standing there. Frances was pleasant, courteous, and quite unlike the type of person he disapproved of. She fully appreciated his kindness, interest in art, and sensitivity. Daniells showered her with flowers, art books, and recordings, but she was in love with someone else. He continued to be enamoured, sending her roses for her graduation and roses and lilies-of-the-valley when she took a trip to Europe.[42]

Daniells recognized that he was infatuated and that he and Aikens lived in quite different worlds. Perhaps to clarify matters, he explored his own feelings in an impressionistic essay, which was part diary in that it recorded actual events, and part fiction in that he sees himself through the literary persona of a Prufrock. He called it 'Impressions of Riley Tea-party' (Dec. 1938):

> ... I smile and bungle 'May I pay my respects to your tea-party,' ... I pass on through a dimly glowing room where dancing is in progress, with a drop of my heart within [dancing: Burwash-Wymilwood-Valerie-Cynthia-lessons-clumsiness-hands with swollen veins – nerves tense, eyes staring, smile fixed] – then to a room where cups & flowers & silver are to be seen on a long table – Jack Coyne near the door... finally I go on to get some tea... I see Frances, in

blue ... I feel I should step forward & speak to her but am afraid & do nothing
... back to cloakroom & glance in mirror, hoping I looked all right – rubbers,
scarf, hat, coat, gloves, & so homeward.[43]

Frances married Conrad Riley, and both joined up for the duration of the war. Jack Coyne later became an Ottawa lawyer; his brother, Jim, a governor of the Bank of Canada.

Daniells had now started writing seriously. During the summer of 1939, he had returned to Victoria to rest and work on his novel after a difficult winter of administration. He was happy to be at home on Cochrane Street with his parents and old friends. When not working, Daniells visited Max Maynard, Jack Shadbolt, John Mcdonald, and another member of this group, Gwladys Downes, a young Victoria teacher with reddish hair and a quick intelligence, later a poet and a university professor of French. She had first met Daniells in 1930 when she was in high school and he spoke to her class. Now they met as part of the group of friends who frequently picnicked, took walks, met to discuss ideas, and travelled up island for outings. Their friendship developed quickly into a deeper relationship.

Downes recalls that 'in the summer of 1939, we met in Victoria at the home of friends and found ourselves with so much in common that we started to see each other daily. Within three weeks I had agreed to marry him. It was quite conventional in some respects. He took me to meet his parents, we discussed plans for European travel the next year, budgets, the role of faculty wives who must be prepared to entertain students but never interfere ... in faculty and Departmental affairs.' However, as she soon recognized, Daniells came with resident demons: 'He was frank about his troubles as well as previous emotional attachments. It was clear that he was living on a knife-edge of nervous tension ... and the more one moved into a labyrinth of psychic strains – fear, guilt, and memories of collapse, the more one realized what a terrible legacy the Plymouth Brethren had left an unusually intelligent and sensitive child with a temperament closer to Baudelaire's than to Milton's.' She saw Daniells as a classically divided personality. One side of the man was pessimistic, caught up with philosophical and spiritual questions, and with a sense of himself as doomed to suffer. The other side of the man was warm and outgoing, the 'inspired teacher' and friend. In essence, she felt that Daniells had been crippled by temperament and circumstance.[44] By spring 1940, it was apparent to both that marriage was impossible.

But the summer of 1939 had been an idyllic time for the couple. Daniells was relaxed and Downes recalls 'real joy, much fun with friends, shows, swimming ... [as] Roy spread the most charming aspects of his intense nature before me.' Until he returned to Winnipeg, she recalls, 'we were both on the surface acting as though marriage would take place after the winter term, i.e., May-June 1940.' Downes spent the winter writing a French M.A. thesis. But Daniells, back in Winnipeg, began to doubt the wisdom of marriage. He wrote her attempting to pull back.

When Downes next saw Daniells in the summer of 1940, he was 'completely shattered and in a state of nervous misery.'[45] Contemplations of suicide and a debilitating sense of his own unworthiness haunted him. Stress, combined with memories of past unhappy courtships, and the advice of Maynard the previous summer – Maynard did not think that the two were suited – contributed to his depression.[46] On his part, Daniells felt the relationship 'such a strain that it feels as if my reason would give way.'[47] For the first time, he recognized his psychosomatic symptoms for what they were: 'Was to have gone over to Gwladys's for tea but woke with really dreadful bilious attack; frightful headache, inability to talk properly, gasping, and weeping. The origin, the chief one at any rate, I think is in Gwladys's desire to bring our relation at once into marriage.'[48]

Downes had made some decisions about her future career based on their understanding at the end of the summer of 1939; understandably, she was now trying to face her own disappointment as well as make Daniells realize the repercussions of his actions. However, it is apparent that he was incapable of marriage at this time. He could not make room for a wife in his emotional life when his parents, his unresolved psychological problems, and the English Department at Manitoba occupied such a large part of it.

When Daniells returned to Winnipeg in September 1939, he began to pull the department together and to develop new courses for entering freshmen. One of the English honours students recalled that he was an excellent administrator: 'This was either a transformation or a coming of age, or both. Very professional. Otherwise he would have found provincial Winnipeg rather tiresome, but he detected where the promise was, and built on it, perhaps even enjoying it. Yet he was as pains-taking with the lesser talents (such as I was) as with the brightest.'[49] However, his personal life remained unsettled: he continued to be very troubled about Downes, and shortly after fell in love with another of his students, Ruth Schlass, who was editor of the *Manitoba Arts Review*.

Although Daniells enjoyed teaching the brighter students, they were only a small section of the student population. He was soon aware that the whole English program desperately needed modernizing. Both the faculty and the curriculum were too old. Brown had changed the fourth-year honours program to emphasize the nineteenth century and his own interests. Daniells now revamped the third-year program towards the seventeenth century and established additional courses in composi-tion for entering students whose English was inadequate for university work. He also began to ease out faculty as they reached retiring age, especially those whom he considered ineffective. He was a good ad-ministrator because he continually evaluated both faculty and curricu-lum. He also recognized that the Manitoba English Department could not improve without properly trained scholars and began to seek them out, relying heavily in his first years on the advice of Brown, Davis, Woodhouse, and Wallace.

His first appointments were Henry Noyes, who replaced Allison, and George Ford, who replaced Perry. Ford had been a student of Brown's in 1935 at Winnipeg and again in 1937 at Toronto. He did an M.A. at University College and then began his Ph.D. at Yale. While working on his dissertation, he applied to the U of M for a teaching position. The year after, 1940–1, when Noyes went to Missouri and Hopper had taken leave in order to command the U of M Military Training Unit, Daniells hired George Brodersen, an Oxford B.A. who lectured in English at one of the affiliated colleges, Ford, and Max Patrick, a U of T graduate with an Oxford B.Litt.[50] These three young men completely changed the tenor of the English program at Manitoba: Brodersen augmented Wheeler's interest in drama; Ford brought needed expertise in the nineteenth century; and Patrick, later the founding editor of the *Seventeenth-Century Newsletter*, was already a published scholar.

Brown, a shrewd judge of character, had earlier warned Daniells that both Patrick and Brodersen might well cause him difficulty, possibly because both were flamboyant in manner. When Ford and Patrick were assigned to teach English to the traditionally staid home economics students, Patrick became annoyed at one talkative girl and allegedly shouted, 'Hey you, you with the big breasts.' The girl complained, the head of home economics went to the president, and the president called in Daniells. Patrick then smoothly claimed that he had said: 'Hey you, you with the red dress.'[51]

Despite some rough edges, Patrick was a fine seventeenth-century scholar and an effective teacher. Daniells liked him. Patrick soon cast a shrewd eye on Daniells' chairing of department meetings. 'He would introduce matters for discussion and then run the discussions like a Quaker meeting ... [he] would keep discussion going, avoiding bringing matters to a vote. Eventually, after prolonged delays, he would say that the consensus of the meeting appeared to be – and then encouraged more discussion on that. Eventually I recognized that in practice discussion had to continue until he declared what the consensus was, i.e., What he wanted! This was a quiet way of domineering though it seemed democratic.' Patrick was also aware of Daniells' health problems and felt sufficiently free with him to speculate on their causes. 'Roy suffered from occasional severe migraine attacks – rather frequent ones and certainly hard on him and the rest of us. He got quite disturbed when one day I pointed out that they occurred at times of strain or crisis – to the extent that I could prophesy when they'd come.' At the time, Daniells strongly resisted facing this truth, and as time went on his attacks became less frequent.[52]

Once Daniells got good men into his department, he tried to keep them, but the U of M was exceptionally low-paying, and the earlier financial crisis and the new treasurer, Crawford, who severely controlled expenditures, made it difficult for Daniells to retain good, younger scholars. He was continually sending pleading letters. Even as late as February 1942, he was writing to Smith urgently requesting him to recognize that the English Department was costing the university $164 per annum less than it had at the height of the Depression and pointing out that if Smith did not authorize some small salary increments, the department would lose good younger faculty.[53]

Daniells had 'fought a good fight' for two years – struggled with large numbers of students, inadequate faculty, and back-breaking teaching.[54] He had initiated curriculum reforms, attempted to bring together a coherent program in English throughout the affiliated colleges, and endured the lack of intellectual peers. By 1939 he hoped to leave Winnipeg and return to Toronto. Brown, who was considering leaving Toronto for an associate professorship at Chicago, wrote Daniells in April 1938 regarding a vacancy in the University College department. But Davis, in the meantime, cautioned Daniells. He would be no better off than when he left the U of T. It was unlikely that Principal Wallace would appoint him above Knox and Woodhouse, who were both senior to Daniells in experience, but below him in rank as associate professors. Meanwhile, Brown decided against Chicago, and University College simultaneously raised both Brown and Woodhouse to full professor.

Since his return from Manitoba in 1937, Brown had been working closely with Woodhouse to reform the curriculum at Toronto and fend off attacks on the *University of Toronto Quarterly*, so that their friendship was a close one. Daniells, on the other hand, was known to be strongly affiliated with the Davis camp and to enjoy support from Principal Wallace, Woodhouse's superior. Wallace had long expressed the wish that Daniells return to Toronto. At Christmas 1938, Daniells bussed to Toronto to spend Christmas Day with the Wallaces before going on to the MLA in New York.

Daniells very probably expected to return to University College eventually, as had Woodhouse and Brown. The problem, perhaps, from Woodhouse's point of view, was that Daniells might have proven a rival and, as a full professor, might have contested Woodhouse's historical and textual approach with his own alternative Baroque views of the seventeenth century. Like Davis, Daniells took a broader approach to literature, emphasizing cross-currents between art, literature, and music. Again like Davis, he made friends of his brighter graduate students, a familiarity Woodhouse strongly disapproved of in theory.

Significantly it was during 1937–8, when Davis had left and Brown was talking about moving elsewhere, that Woodhouse, who lacked a Ph.D., took time off to consolidate his academic position by going to the British Museum to complete his first book on the seventeenth-century Puritan pamphlets. It was at this point that he wrote a familiar verse to 'Dear Daniells':

The Bursar, Dean and Registrar,
I hear their voices from afar,
And, thank my stars, am not right under
The seat of Presidential thunder,
But feed my sheep a good way off,

A humble Asso-cí-ate Prof. –
Yet sometimes stand in urgent need
Of moly or more potent weed ...

A.S.P.W[oodhouse][55]

The verse is pleasantly chaffing, but the rhythm of line six in stanza two underscores a more serious message when the reader is required to halt on 'Asso-ci-ate Prof.' Woodhouse in February 1938 was just that. Daniells, by moving to Manitoba, had become a not-so-humble full professor, which may have raised some professional animosities as well as whimsical satire in his former mentor. Since those 'gone good days, Baroque and all,' Daniells had finished his work, obtained his Ph.D., and moved into administrative spheres, whereas Woodhouse had not. By doing so, Daniells may have fallen into the great divide that separated Woodhouse and Davis.

Later, in 1941, Brown did receive an offer to go to Cornell. He wrote to Daniells giving him information on the faculty in University College in case he wished to apply. But Brown was now less encouraging. As he said, 'it is strongly felt (and I can't help agreeing) that the 18C is a staring gap ... For the 18C there is only Woodhouse, and he wants to leave the field.'[56] Woodhouse may have made a pre-emptive strike. By arguing that he, who had formerly taught both the seventeenth and eighteenth centuries, now wished to devote all his energies to one area – the seventeenth century – he forced the department to shift the new senior appointment to the eighteenth century only. Certainly Daniells could not have been easily accommodated into the program of seventeenth-century textual studies at University College as Woodhouse hoped to develop it. Two weeks later, a senior eighteenth-century scholar declined their offer, and University College made two appointments at the junior level: Claude Bissell and Douglas LePan. With Davis and Brown leaving University College for greener pastures and Principal Wallace's retirement imminent, Woodhouse was then the pre-eminent candidate for head of English at University College, which he became in 1944.

Relations between Woodhouse and Daniells, however, were again amiable as there was no longer any possibility that Daniells might be parachuted into University College. When Woodhouse was appointed head, Daniells' letter of congratulation must have suggested some Miltonic *double entendre*, for Woodhouse replied: 'I am delighted that you approve of what the powers design – it is not yet done, but I suppose will be. I will not speak of my hesitation, but only of my final ground of acceptance: that I see much that needs to be done for English.'[57] He and Daniells were to continue to work together congenially and profitably for the next two decades.

———

In November 1938 at a dinner at the Wheelers, Daniells met a young professor from the U of M Mathematics Department, Carson Mark, and his wife, Kay. 'Car,' as he was known by his friends, was very like Daniells: almost six feet tall, with bright blue eyes, and a good sense of fun. During the summer vacations in the late thirties, he and Kay had canoed on the Severn River and befriended David Milne, the artist. Several of his sketches hung on their walls. Carson had a strong aesthetic sense, was a good pianist, and was keenly interested in literature. The Marks became his intimate friends, and they considered Daniells a bridge to the outside world. He went regularly to their home on Ainslie Street for dinners, and their evenings were filled with good talk, games such as charades, and parties with other faculty members. Apparently Daniells disliked passing the landlady's part of the house – he considered her too nosy – and always climbed the outside fire escape and entered through the living-room window. These high jinks were characteristic. He and Carson also liked to set bonfires on the frozen river.[58]

In 1940 Daniells proposed that he and the Marks share a house together. Thus, in the spring of 1941, they rented 578 Stradbrook, where the Marks took the ground floor and Daniells most of the top floor. On one occasion, a census taker came and Daniells noted 'a shock to *hear* Car say he is 27 and Kay 29, and to hear myself confess to 39.'[59] But the age difference did not seem to matter. The Marks enjoyed Daniells, and he, once again, discovered the pleasures of living in a family. With both Car and Kay, he could speak freely about the university, literature, and his personal life.

During the summer of 1941, Carson Mark was at Brown University to 'help the war effort.' Although he could not know it at the time, he had taken a step which was to lead him to become director of the theoretical group for the development of the hydrogen bomb at Los Alamos. The two men corresponded regularly and discussed, among other subjects, Kafka, about whom Daniells was writing an article, and Eliot's allusions to the Upanishads in *The Waste Land*. But one of Daniells' letters, which made reference to days which 'did not come up to expectations' alerted Mark to the fact that something was amiss. He was sorry that there was nothing that he could do to help for he admired and respected Daniells. Moreover, Mark suggested, Daniells had 'been granted the keys to his own happiness; and it remains only to find the door.'

Mark's use of Bunyan's images of the 'key' and the 'door' suggests that these are topics that he and Daniells had discussed, and that the latter had explained his deep unhappiness. This was a period when Daniells quite literally felt himself in sackcloth and ashes, with no hope of finding a wife whom he could love, and who would love him. His future, single and unhappy, stretched ahead of him. His explanation for his failure to connect with the young women whom he was dating was that his 'technique' was inadequate. Carson Mark had a wider perspective:

> You sometimes fear that happiness cannot come for you; but this, I am confident, need not be true. And yet the spirit dwelling beyond the door which will open to you will probably not reveal itself fully, at once; but only gradually ... In the case of women in particular, should the door be through her, the body is the threshold of the spirit, and is one means of approach to it ... If I were to offer 'criticism' of your 'technique' it would be this: that I wonder if you are not ... setting a course by the map rather than moving through the stream itself? ...
>
> My dear Roy, could you by any means take up work again at the novel? You say there is no one to do it for. Do it for itself, for yourself. Do it for your friends' sake, who would be so pleased with it not for its wit, its value, its excellence, its success, only – although they would delight in those – but because it would be yours.[60]

Shortly after receiving this letter from Mark, Daniells began again on the manuscript of his novel. Now entitled 'Oh Canada,' it was the story of a young man who had been killed during the Second World War leaving behind a trunk of papers from which the narrator, an archivist of sorts, attempts to determine a personality, a cause, and a nation. It prefigures Timothy Findley's The Wars.

Chapter Eleven

'The End of an Era'

Dear Roy,

I've been trying to imagine where you are at this particular moment – 12.25 hours June 5 in this Year of No Grace 1941 ...

Most of all I get a sinking feeling in my tummy when I see again the lights of the 'Empress of Britain,' God rest her soul, fading into the night with you on board, and me on the Cherbourg tender with the C.P.R. agent. That was the end of an era. After that the pressure and the pace became almost too much for sanity.

Evelyn[1]

It was the end of an era. Not just the end of the troubled peace of the thirties, but the end of a whole way of life: the nostalgia that Evelyn Smith (née Stewart) felt was for the Toronto world of the thirties and Europe just before the debacle in 1939. In Winnipeg the newspapers had ceased to rail against A.R.M. Lower, who insisted that Canadians should have a choice regarding their participation in war, and were instead reporting the bombing of Britain, the fall of Belgium and France, and the deaths of young Manitobans in Hong Kong.

Throughout the late thirties, the probability of war loomed, especially after the invasion of Ethiopia and the Spanish Civil War. But for some the war had already begun. In 1938, when Daniells had gone to England after Cleveland summer school to research Traherne's poetry, he was conscious of war preparations. There, in London in late August, Daniells had had lunch with Evelyn Stewart, who was worried because her new fiancé, Arnold Smith, was overdue from Spain. Similarly United College's Meredith Thompson, working in England the following summer, reported: 'Atmosphere very tense. Everyone *expects* war. Cheer or

Hiss Chamberlain in a News Reel. We had a "black-out" the other night while planes "attacked."'[2]

After 1 September 1939, the war in Europe impinged on life in Canada. Up to this point, Daniells had been preparing for the press Traherne's *A Serious and Pathetical Contemplation of the Mercies of God, in Several Most Devout and Sublime Thanksgivings for the Same*, which had appeared anonymously twenty-five years after Traherne's death in 1674, but which had been long out of print. In his brief introduction, Daniells suggested that Traherne's readings in hermetic philosophy made possible his joy in religion and his freedom from a sense of sin.[3] His attraction to Traherne's poetry is explicit in his 1936 Ph.D. dissertation, in which he remarks upon the happy astonishment of Traherne, who counts up God's blessings like a child counting his Christmas presents. Traherne's paean of thanks includes all the visible and invisible world:

> Light and Darkness,   Night and Day,
>   The Seasons of the Year.
> Springs, Rivers, Fountains, Oceans,
>   Gold, Silver, and precious Stones.
>   Corn, Wine, and Oyl,
>   The Sun, Moon, and Stars,
>   Cities, Nations, Kingdoms.
> And the Bodies of Men, the greatest Treasures of all,
>   For each other.
> What then, O Lord, hast thou intended for our
> Souls, who givest to our Bodies such glorious things![4]

Malcolm Wallace, who delivered the manuscript for Daniells to the University of Toronto Press, expected that war activities would impede printing. However, he found 'Burns [the editor] evidently quite willing to consider it.'[5] The reprint appeared in 1941 with very little editing.

Davis wrote at Christmas that year to say that various friends had attempted to keep him in England the previous summer. However, he did not see much point in taking his wife and two daughters into what he thought would soon be 'a war game.' Davis knew what it would mean to stay in North America: 'It won't be pleasant to stay here in plenty while they starve and bleed one another over there. But God knows how anybody can stop it now. And yet the mess ultimately will be worse if one side gets knocked out.'[6]

Daniells was worried about this. Earlier, in May 1940, he wrote terse notes in his diary on the fighting in Europe: 'War news dreadful. Belgians have folded up'; and 'War news still most alarming.'[7] A month later, he began to read Tolstoy's *War and Peace*. He felt he ought to 'join up' and wrote to Davis saying this. In February 1940, Davis replied whimsically, 'I propose that you get married in term time, and do some writing in the vac. and let the war get on without you. Do you happen to know that in England the academic profession as a whole and the literary profession too is a reserved occupation for all who are over the age of twenty-five?' Davis thought that Daniells might as well accept the same ruling for Canada.[8] Later in the war, Margaret Bjornson, now Adamson, wrote from the National Film Board with news of England: 'I forgot to tell you this, which comes via Elizabeth Smart via George Barker from some English poet [probably W.H. Auden] in New York. T.S. Eliot is now a fireman in London running around with sacks and buckets. Reported to have told aforementioned poet that he has never been happier that he is obeying the orders of somebody like Lil's husband and feels he has an important, significant, social function to perform. "Out of the fire Lord, thou pluckest me burning burning."'[9]

In the early 1940s, intellectuals across Canada were particularly worried about the war. F.R. Scott, formerly a pacifist, abruptly changed his mind when it appeared that England might fall. Northrop Frye was also greatly worried. The decline of the West, envisioned by Spengler, was becoming all too literal. France had fallen and he feared for England. What he had earlier termed the undergraduate's excuse, 'war jitters,' was interfering with his work, to the extent that he was reading Wilkie Collins for diversion instead of Montaigne. His emotions splash across the page in a letter to Daniells:

> England can't lose. England can't lose. England can't lose. Smug, rich, moral, perfidious Albion has played Moby Dick to a long string of exasperated continental Ahabs, and what's Hitler got that Philip II or Louis XIV and Napoleon and the Kaiser didn't have? England can't lose ...
>
> ...
>
> I suppose this war will end with the total destruction of Germany. The feeling that that may be only one of a long series of similar annihilations is what gives one futurist nightmares. I wish Spengler had gone in for collecting butterflies.[10]

Frye did not find equilibrium until mid-August during a stag at Birney's, where Pratt read a new poem, 'The Truant,' in which an ordinary – but courageous – man defies a Grand Panjandrum, the embodiment of totalitarian force. Frye later confessed that the poem had given him heart: 'I heard Ned read "The Truant," and felt ... that the voice of humanity had spoken once more, with the kind of authority it reserves for such moments as the bombing of London, when the powers of darkness test the soul and find once more that "The stuff is not amenable to fire."'[11]

For Daniells, who was a decade older than Frye, but two decades younger than Pratt, the anxieties generated by the war took other forms. It accentuated his desire to 'do something' for Canada. At first he threw all his energies into building up the Manitoba English Department, and then he turned back to writing his novel, 'Oh Canada,' an attempt to give meaning to the Canadian war experience. In addition, throughout the war years he sent aid to Britain in the form of food, money, books, and letters to POW's and the Stevens family.

One recipient was George Kane, a young British Columbian taking graduate studies in England, who enlisted in the British army. He was taken prisoner at Dunkirk and spent the duration of the war in a camp in Germany. When the war was over, Daniells attempted unsuccessfully to hire Kane, 'an absolutely first-class man,' who later became the eminent *Piers Plowman* scholar.[12] A second charity was E.M.G. Hand-Made Gramophones Ltd. This was the firm to which Davis had taken him early in the thirties to buy a gramophone and from which he still ordered classical recordings. His first food parcel was received by the workers at this London firm with delight and incredulity. Eventually a warm correspondence developed. He knew what was most required – the secretary at EMG prepared a list: 'lard, suet, *dried* fruit, (preferably apricots as they contain iron and do not weigh much), fruit or tomato juice. And chocolate, of course, or sultanas, currants, and raisins.'[13] All of these items were either rationed or unobtainable.

Daniells was eventually called up in January 1943. He talked with President Smith about the ramifications of leaving his post and believed that notice was imminent for military service. But Smith told him they would 'go to the board about it.'[14] When his notice was returned in early March, he found he was classified 'E' and rejected for army service because of his poor health and migraine headaches. He was much relieved: 'His Britannic Majesty will probably dispense with my services as trailing a pike or carrying a musket, at least for the present. I am not sorry; for one thing I *can* do something for Canada here, there are opportunities and responsibilities of no mean order.'[15]

For Daniells, as for all university administrators, two of the more serious problems created by the war were the difficulties in getting teaching staff and the declining enrolment of male students. By 1942 the war had made itself felt in all aspects of university life. As war dragged on, the universities developed policies with the Canadian government about their role and the role of students in the war effort. The 1942–3 president's report stated the policy clearly: 'The Canadian Government and the Canadian universities do not intend that university students should be put in a privileged class.'[16] During the war period there were conditions attached to entering university: male and female students were expected to take advantage of special training and, upon completion of a program or degree, offer their services to the war effort.

As tenured faculty, graduate, and undergraduate students signed up to go to war, universities scrambled to find staff and students. Making the best of the situation, Daniells hired T.A.W. (Chester) Duncan and Max Maynard, 'whose teaching of English promises to add a salutary broadening of interest into related fields of music and fine art.'[17] Duncan replaced Ford. He was a music teacher rather than an English specialist, but he had a talent for reading and understanding poetry.[18] The same might also be said of Maynard. In late summer 1942, Max Patrick had wired him to say he was accepting a job at the University of Buffalo if he (Daniells) did not prevent him. Hiring a replacement so near to the beginning of a new term placed Daniells in a quandary, and in late August he consulted President Smith and subsequently offered Maynard a job.[19] Maynard wasted no time in settling into lectures on art as well as English, and in February 1943 Daniells reflected: 'He is a good fellow and I like him as much as ever, in spite of his shortcomings. A series of lectures on art which he gives at the Fort Garry site are going very well: he gets fifty or sixty people in every Tuesday afternoon.'[20]

By 1943–4 there was a shift in tone in the president's report. The end of the war was in sight. Smith recognized that there would have to be a greatly expanded program if the university was to serve adequately the men and women who would return to it under the Post-Discharge Re-Establishment Order, which provided liberal grants to ex-service personnel for university training.[21] Staff, equipment, and accommodation would all need to be augmented and upgraded. For ten years after the war, Canadian universities would struggle to fulfil this commitment.

As the war intensified, the pronounced shift in university demographics meant that the majority of students were female. This situation allowed a number of intelligent young women to obtain recognition, free from the competition of their male counterparts. The dominance of women during the war years is reflected in their participation in all aspects of campus life, such as in the *Manitoba Arts Review*. Until 1940 the editors had all been male, although a number of women, including Frances Aikens and Margaret Bjornson, were on the editorial staff. In 1941 the editor was Ruth Schlass, who produced the winter 1941 and spring 1942 issues. Another student, Patricia Murray, who later married George Ford, was the assistant editor for the spring edition.

These issues of the *Manitoba Arts Review* were among the best published during the forties. They contain a short story by Sinclair Ross, articles by Birney on Chaucer and Daniells on Kafka, and Frye's 'On Anatomy.' Daniells recollected that Northrop Frye had given a student paper on the 'Anatomy' to the Graduate Club at the U of T, and, because Frye had recently told him that he needed to get into print, Daniells urged him to submit it as an article to *MAR*, thus encouraging him to develop a topic that led to the most important book of criticism written by a Canadian, *Anatomy of Criticism: Four Essays* (1957). Mildred Shanas, a fellow student, contributed an article on Tolstoy and Dostoyevsky. Schlass, Shanas, and Fredelle Bruser were highly gifted Jewish Canadians, children of immigrants. Schlass believed that the issues were so impressive because Daniells solicited articles, but, like Murray, she had a fine literary sensibility.[22]

Daniells was enamoured of Schlass, but he recognized the ability of all three young women. Fredelle Bruser and Mildred Shanas also took English honours, and in June 1941 he noted that Bruser had been for tea, probably to discuss her academic work. Shanas first met Daniells in her second-year classes and remembers the excitement of learning to *read* poetry for the first time. He would arrive at the honours class, where students were sitting around a seminar table, and hand out carbons of unidentified scraps of poetry. He would ask: 'Who wrote that?'

> From our first blank bewilderment we gradually came to focus on all the internal details of content and language that bespoke the scrap's period and sensibility, and later, on the subtleties of imagery and structure, so that literature opened up like a flower. And then prose, and – clever us – we had the fun of working out a writer from the inside, by being assigned to write something ourselves 'in the style of ...'

That this focus on the autonomy of the composition itself was a New Critical method Shanas discovered much later, but an initial close reading of the literary text remained fundamental to all of her future work as a professor of English. She also noticed that Daniells' teaching had another quality, the mark of a truly gifted teacher, 'the almost indefinable capacity to make me arrive at a complex point a moment before he articulated it.' Shanas also recalls his sly pleasure in pointing out to a class of women the joke in John Donne's poem 'Love's Alchemy': 'Hope not for mind in women; at their best / Sweetness and wit, they are but mummy possessed.'[23]

Fredelle Bruser was recalled by George Ford, then teaching at Manitoba but later head of English at the University of Rochester, as 'the most brilliant student I ever had in my life.'[24] In Bruser's memoirs, *Raisins and Almonds* (1964), she writes of first hearing about Eliot's *The Waste Land* as taught by the new English professor, a seventeenth-century specialist, recognizably Daniells. It was the first poetry that ever moved her deeply:

It was Spender's 'I think continually of those who were truly great, / Who, from the womb, remembered the soul's history / Through corridors of light where the hours are suns, / Endless and singing ...' I'm not sure, now, that I understood what the lines were about. Only I had the impression of dazzlement. Words rang like coins in a fountain of bright water, light streamed about me in a chime of colors.[25]

When Maynard came to teach in the English Department, Daniells assigned Bruser to be his 'reader' or marker. Her explanation was that Daniells, knowing something of Maynard's history with women, 'took pains to provide, as assistant essay-reader, a student surely impervious to seduction.' To no avail. Maynard was an artist with a Byronic melancholy, which contributed to his sexual attractiveness, and his voice was mesmeric, hypnotic.[26] He had now separated from his wife, and Bruser found him irresistible.

Daniells recommended both Bruser and Shanas for graduate study at Toronto, where both came face to face with Woodhouse. Woodhouse's attitude towards women students who were not obviously 'bluestockings,' that is, not clearly designated for the single academic life, often led to a reluctance to supervise their work. Bruser undoubtedly possessed extraordinary intelligence and the additional advantage of a photographic memory, which she described as a 'freak ability to visualize pages.'[27] She brought this capacity – and a determination to succeed – to Toronto.

Such a formidable talent was highly disconcerting. Ford, who had enlisted in 1941 and dropped in to see Woodhouse while in Toronto, found him in a snit about Bruser. '"Oh," he said, "I hate the word, I hate the word, but she's a genius."'[28] Patrick, now at Buffalo, but still paying his respects to Woodhouse at Toronto between semesters, gleaned further information. He wrote Daniells: 'In deep, deep, deep confidence I shall share with you what the Toronto Department wishes her not to know: she got the highest mark they ever gave on the preliminary comprehensive exam.' Bruser was beginning her dissertation on seventeenth-century chastity, but Patrick was doubtful about this: 'Woodhouse, by virtue of his nature, habits and *Comus* article has left the subject a rather unsatisfactory one in some respects. I think that you were wrong not to push Bruser for Chicago.'[29]

Woodhouse wrote to Daniells that 'Miss Bruser is very good indeed' and foresaw 'years of a really distinguished career.' But not at Toronto. 'I wish we could keep her here, for the doctorate (and I think she wants to stay) – that is, I wish we could keep her with a clear conscience. But the openings for women in Canada are so few and so uncertain that I have felt obliged to advise her to go on to the States for her doctorate. What, in general terms, do you think of her prospects in the Canadian West? ... Would her race be a serious impediment? I warned Sirluck about this; but he courageously determined to go on with us. But added to the limited openings for a woman, is not the difficulty almost insuperable – or is it? What do you think? I would bend every effort to get her fellowship renewed or increased here.'[30] Two months later, he reported that 'Miss Bruser has a number of attractive offers. I have advised her to take Radcliffe (= Harvard) as the place most likely to open the American field to her and offset the double disability (academically speaking) of sex and race.'[31]

Fredelle Bruser enrolled at Radcliffe, where she did well. However, in her first year abroad, she succumbed to Maynard's urgent pleas to marry him. She then became a mother and a part-time academic: despite her record, she appears to have received no job offers from either Toronto or Manitoba. She later wrote two books of memoirs: the first, an idyllic portrayal of an immigrant daughter who did well; the second, a bitterly honest story of a failed marriage and a blighted career. Mildred Shanas, after completing her M.A., returned to U of M to teach part-time. She married happily, had a family, and later became a professor of seventeenth-century literature and assistant head in the English Department. Ernest Sirluck did extraordinarily well at Toronto. A fine student, he became a distinguished Milton textual scholar and ultimately was appointed president of the U of M. Woodhouse, who had supervised his graduate work, offered him a position teaching at Toronto, and recommended him to Manitoba, Queen's, Cornell, and Chicago. Woodhouse subsequently wrote to Daniells: 'If you have produced any more Sirlucks or Brusers, let me know in good time and I will get them either fellowships or teaching fellowships.'[32]

E.K. Brown, now a settled family man, continued to be concerned about Daniells' single state. Writing to his former student Ford, he remarked that Daniells was 'born to be married.'[33] In early November 1941, Brown wrote Daniells directly: 'May I make a personal remark? I think you can not be far from 40. Have you made up your mind whether or not you will marry? The more I see, the more I think that it is unwise to marry before one is really under way, but also unwise not to marry before 40 if one is to marry at all.' He understood that it was difficult to make a final decision about this, and he hoped that Daniells would not consider that he was prying: '... on the other hand I can see a very happy life for the bachelor-scholar. The news that in some fashion you are sharing the house of the Marks made me think that perhaps you were now deciding against marriage and (wisely in that event) shaping a home for yourself.'[34]

It took Daniells two months to reply. He had decided to ask Brown frankly for advice. He explained that he was sharing a house with the Marks because for the moment it suited both parties. 'But marriage would be infinitely better than this. The reason I haven't married long ago is that I haven't found the girl ... You remember the girl Watts, in Toronto, now Mrs. Lawson? The bar there was her convinced Communism. It was an excessively painful matter. Since then, three, but the results always the same. Just now, indeed for the past year, it has been one of my own students ... delightful, but, alas! Jewish by family connexion and with a father who would rather see her dead than joined with a Gentile ... What to do? What? If the alternative is a rational marriage with some "suitable" person, I will stay in purgatory, indeed, go to hell, first. The heart has its own dictates, which, too, are reasonable .'[35]

Daniells was explaining to Brown about Ruth Schlass. Predictably, he was infatuated with Schlass, whom he saw, in literary terms, as 'the schloss,' or castle. He was reading Kafka's *The Castle* in the summer of 1941 and sensed that there were aspects of Ruth's character that he could not approach. Tall, slim, and dark, she was a flamboyant beauty, but rather sensitive and even shy. Her classmates recognized in her quiet brooding manner the *femme fatale*. That Daniells saw her in aesthetic terms is apparent in an early October 1941 comment when she came for tea: 'Ruth here ... and had a long talk about life and personality, in which Car[son Mark] joined. R. looked superb sitting on green settee under lamp, in camel hair coat, very red and white, massive and individual. I love her, if anything, more than ever.'[36]

Despite her youth, Ruth Schlass saw Daniells' character clearly. She was fond of him – her letters were lively, often containing little jokes – but she kept her distance, recognizing the divisions created by religion, Winnipeg society, and the difference in their ages. During the late summer of 1941, when he was still in Victoria, she wrote telling him about the wedding of Alan Adamson and Margaret (Baby) Bjornson, which, in some ways, had been a conventional society wedding – Adamson's father was a member of the board of governors at Manitoba, and Bjornson's father was a prosperous Winnipegger. Schlass said she had 'bounced down [the aisle] in a highly-flowered yellow dress and felt about as at home as a tiger-lily in a morning-glory bed.' About to leave the wedding early, she had an exchange with Lloyd Wheeler. She had told Wheeler, 'I feel like a Philistine here.' He countered, 'Just try to feel like a Gentile.' She finished her letter to Daniells: 'But I couldn't, so I left.'[37]

Predictably, in 1942, again when Daniells was in Victoria for the summer, she wrote to say that she planned to marry a young Jewish doctor. Heartbroken, he wanted to know why: 'I can't bear to lose you ... You've always been so verbally reserved and unwilling to give yourself away. Won't you for *once* write me a page as though you loved me or had at one time loved me, or at least recognized how much I loved you?'[38] Ruth was sympathetic but understood the differences between them: '... whereas I would just want to forget, you must pursue everything to its conclusion – even though you may think it will be bitter for you.'[39]

Daniells also poured out his unhappiness to his friend Carson Mark. 'Why these particular eyes and lips and hands and breasts should seem to me the centre of the universe God only knows.' He felt that 'the silliest things she said were oracles to me ... And when she did, on rare occasions open up, and the last occasion was just as I left Winnipeg, there was nothing like it. And all the time one could feel an immense reserve of something in her quite untapped.'[40]

Mark rebuked him, 'You say there never was any real chance for you. That I do not believe. For, for a while at least, she did love you, as you, possibly, may wish you could forget.' He diagnosed the differences between them as those of race and religion: 'You are English: for a time you were primarily a Plymouth Brother, and again, a Humanist with a sense of Tragedy(!), and possibly yet to be what? A good Jew is always a Jew.'[41]

This observation has the ring of truth. Winnipeg society was strongly divided between Jew and Gentile, and Ruth's parents did not want her to marry outside the Jewish culture. Then, too, the courtship had started when each was recovering from an unhappy romance. Finally, Daniells was overly insistent but perhaps not emotionally present. Ruth's explanation was simply that he had misconstrued her feelings. 'I think this phenomenon was due often to the feeling of the teacher-student relationship which sub-consciously was always with me. I could not, somehow, assert my innermost thoughts because of it. And after all Roy – I was only eighteen years old.'[42] Although Ruth was willing to be a 'good friend,' he wrote a painfully honest letter saying that he cared for her too much to continue a friendship.

Finally, there was undoubtedly a third party in their relationship, his mother, still in Victoria. A decade earlier she had written: 'There is a Rachel some-where waiting & will be willing to "Go with this man" when the proper time comes & doubtless she will be 'very fair to look upon" possibly feeding sheep now or in other words – teaching.'[43] But Mrs Daniells could not have adjusted to a real Rachel – a Ruth Schlass who taught first-year engineers – any more than Ruth's parents could have adjusted to a Plymouth Brethren fundamentalism that condemned the Jews for crucifying Christ.

Brown, who had married a vivacious and outspoken society woman, sympathized with Daniells' predicament by return letter. He, too, disagreed with prudent marriages. Nonetheless, he recognized that Jim Watts would have been an unsuitable wife for Daniells, and that 'marriage with a Jewish person is the very devil in our society! Even strangely liberal people have their wrong reactions to this, and one would suffer terribly in the end.'[44]

Brown was all too familiar with the societal prohibitions. As a Roman

Catholic academic in Canada, he was fortunate when University College offered him a position. As the former head of English at Manitoba, he knew the additional great divide that separated Jew from Gentile. He was soon to make the further unpleasant discovery that Catholics would not be considered as candidates for the post of university president at the U of M. It was indeed the end of an era, but the old prohibitions against women, Catholics, and Jews fell very slowly.

The early 1940s were also the end of an era with reference to the rigidly hierarchical relationship between faculty and university administration. Daniells, a spokesman for U of M faculty, eventually found an unexpected ally in President Sidney Smith. In the long run, their aims were not dissimilar – each wanted a better university.

In his first two years, Daniells completely remodelled the lower- and upper-level literature program. Individual courses were replaced with a single course in poetry, which treated authors chronologically and allowed for study of periods and literary movements. He had countered a 'low standard of writing,' particularly in first and second years, with 'special instruction ... given to those most obviously deficient.' This was a great success. Daniells decided that thereafter, all incoming freshmen were to be tested at the beginning of term and special classes established for those requiring them. This move raised the standard of composition for all years. Above all, Daniells aimed to reconcile the disparate elements of the study of English at Manitoba: 'provision of five years of work in Arts, collaboration with four Arts colleges, the duplication of courses on two sites, the growing enrolment and demands of the Faculty of Agriculture and Home Economics, and the teaching of composition.'[45] Despite limitations in staff, a lack of reading materials, and the ambitious nature of the project, he was quite successful.

Revision continued. In 1939–40 the second-year prose course was changed 'so as to present three separate *genres*: satire, the essay, the short story.' In 1940–1 a new course, English 21, was created for commerce students which dealt exclusively with the mechanics of composition. Daniells implemented practical, common-sense solutions to refining the English curriculum and responding to students' problems.

He also took a leadership role in a university-wide committee whose recommendations for the arts curriculum had wider philosophical implications. This committee, made up of Daniells, H.N. Fieldhouse, C.M.

Jones, and W.J. Waines, was established to investigate the belief that the arts course had no practical application and was not intellectually stimulating. The group met between 1941 and 1943 and produced a report that recognized there was a decline in the liberal arts because course offerings 'had ceased to furnish a synthesis, or at least a general pattern of knowledge ... a *speculum mentis* for the educated man.' They recommended the addition of a Western civilization course to the already standard four courses in first and second year in order to provide 'a survey of the historical, aesthetic and scientific development of the western world,' and so give students an opportunity to bring their various studies into mutual relationship.[46]

President Smith devoted a large portion of his 1943 report to the committee's recommendations, especially the recommendation that a more interdisciplinary and liberal approach be adopted. All students in general arts would be required to take 'Western Civilization' courses to fill gaps in 'aesthetics ... various forms of order and beauty developed by musicians, painters, sculptors and architects.' [47] By the third-year level, stress would be placed on an examination of a small number of great works exemplifying the principal literary genres: 'Emphasis will be placed on the creative role of the artist and on the power which literature possesses to illuminate its own cultural background and to explore and solve the problems of human life.' The fourth year, the realm of 'fine arts,' was intended to instil an appreciation for culture and to quicken creative impulses.[48]

The emphasis on the artist, the integration of English with wider subjects in the arts, the desire to teach students to perceive beauty – all these aspects of the Western Civilization Program reflect Daniells' concerns and his New Humanism as derived from Irving Babbitt. This important program, as W.L. Morton identified it, a 'brave and well-considered attempt to deal with an urgent problem,' indicates that Daniells was not only attempting to incorporate current views in English to rehabilitate the prestige of the liberal arts program, but he was also encouraging artistic expression in University of Manitoba students.'[49] In this aim, he was to be exceptionally successful.

———————

In mid-April 1943, Smith wrote a hasty note to Daniells to wonder 'about research and creative writing by members of the various departments. Could you let me have a list of papers written in your department in the last four years?'[50] Daniells, profoundly shocked by the request because it revealed how little Smith understood the problems facing English departments in Canada – and especially English at Manitoba – temporized, saying that the department would hold a meeting about the issue as soon as exams were over.

His report reveals six years of frustration. He stated that although he had worked very hard to make the English Department more effective, he was willing to resign without resentment if the board of governors was unsatisfied. He then provided the department's publishing record for the past four years: Brodersen, Maynard, and Wheeler had each published an article, Patrick two articles, and Daniells himself one article and an edition of Traherne's *Contemplations*. The department had discussed the issue and although there was a strong desire to publish more if conditions would permit, there was an unwillingness to be apologetic.

Of the eight most active department members, Patrick, who had left the department, was potentially a publishing scholar, but was kept from publication by an excessive workload. Ford was publishing his thesis, which had won first prize for his year at Yale. Brodersen had no articles planned. The war had stalled Duncan, who had a book of songs at Oxford University Press awaiting publication. Doris Saunders' good research on Samuel Johnson and Maynard's M.A. thesis were also delayed. Summer was the only time professors could do research, and Wheeler, for financial reasons, had taught summer school for a number of years.

Daniells then discussed his own lack of publication, explaining that by the end of each teaching year he was completely exhausted. It was not just the difficulties of coping with frequent staff changes, but the fact that he had to carry over half the teaching load of the three senior years. In Toronto he was understood to be a seventeenth-century specialist and passable elsewhere: '... here I must be prepared to teach some *forty* major authors, besides minors, and not taking into account the Junior Division or the Third Year Honours. Until I know a great deal more about those forty men and their works, their times, their significance, their inter-relations, their whole spiritual background (and they range from Chaucer to T.S. Eliot) there is no sense in my spending time in writing specialized articles.'[51] He saw no relief for this situation in sight.

He also referred to Desmond Pacey at Brandon College, praising Pacey's training and efforts to both carry his heavy teaching load and publish. But the result of this exceptional load had been Pacey's break-down halfway through the term. Daniells again asked: 'Why have I not, as head of the Department, done more to promote research and publication?' And his answer was:

> Four men, all excellent scholars and potential writers, have left us ... The winter is too severe, the community too inimical, the registrar and the comptroller too insistent, the colleges too numerous, the need for constant elementary instruction too crying, the numbers of students too great, for any state of mind to develop which would make for a fruitful school of English studies. We are missionaries – and missionaries are seldom theologians.

Daniells, whenever profoundly moved, expressed himself in biblical language: indeed, for him to profess English was akin to professing religion.

And he was a master of academic polemic. As he argued, the chief responsibility of any professor of English in Canada was to teach, but in Manitoba the peculiarly Canadian conditions were such that for 'chief' it was necessary to substitute 'only.' Other departments might teach and maintain a good publishing record, but the English Department was unable to do so under current conditions. Had Daniells remained at Victoria College, he would have developed his work on the Baroque and become a publishing scholar. However, he had chosen to go west and develop his own department – to become an academic missionary of sorts. He was now being forced to justify this decision – and so he did. He invited comparison in performance between his department and other Canadian universities, which worked under conditions much better than Manitoba's. Despite this, 'Professor Sedgewick, perhaps the best head of an English Department anywhere in Canada, has the most meagre list of publications at an age approaching sixty. Even the justly celebrated English staff of University College publish very little, as the yearly reviews of the *University of Toronto Quarterly* will show.'

Daniells proposed several solutions, none of which he believed feasible. The first was to hire a man with a 'flair for research' to reduce his load, isolate him from the running of the department, and let him publish. The second would be to divert everyone's energies away from 'the always overwhelming task of the teaching.' He cited Patrick's teaching load: '85 First Year students, 62 Second Year, 51 Third Year, 101 Agriculture and Home Economics, 42 School of Agriculture ...' To undertake any research at all, Patrick had to work long periods at night and on Sundays; understandably, he had accepted a vastly better offer from the University of Buffalo. A third solution might be for faculty to publish ephemeral articles, but this went against the grain. Lastly, he proposed that the university could establish 'a series of University studies in the humanities and elevate the *Arts Review* into a University Quarterly, so that graduate students doing research, as well as members of the staff, might have a ready vehicle for publication. This has been done in Toronto with fair success.' In conclusion, he affirmed that the Department of English had no apologies to make. As long as the 'present situation persists, with its exhausting demands upon our slender resources, our list of publications will remain a small one.'[52]

Smith read Daniells' letter with deep interest. Perhaps feeling a little chastised but unable to admit it, he remarked, 'I have no apologies to make about raising the question. I feel sure that the discussion will promote the best interests of the Department.' He agreed that no administrator could requisition creativity and closed warmly: 'In all sincerity I assert that I am proud of the advances that have been made by the Department of English which was, to say the least, not one of the strongest when I joined the University in 1934.'[53]

The issues raised by Smith's letter were significant ones. It was the question of the amount of academic publishing possible for university professors in Canada given the extraordinarily heavy teaching load carried throughout the forties and into the fifties. The issue of academic publishing was to become paramount in the next decade, the fifties, and the arguments which are raised in Daniells' letter – large enrolments in English, huge classes, inadequate faculty, long teaching and marking hours, no time for research – give us some idea of the practical problems faced by professors and administrators who were increasingly expected to be good scholars as well as good teachers.

Daniells had pulled the English Department together, and both persuaded and refuted Smith. In January 1944, he took a further, precipitous step by writing a letter to Smith stating that Manitoba university faculty were unsatisfied with the direction taken by the board of governors. For over six years, Daniells and other department heads had chafed under the limited vision of F.W. Crawford, the comptroller, who had refused essential expenditures, especially salaries. Smith was at first indignant, then responsive: 'Terrific time with Sidney Smith at his home, in late evening. He had never received such a letter of mine (it stated we had no confidence in the board) in fourteen years ...'[54] Daniells then wrote Brown. Brown's response was revealing: 'I meant to refer to your interesting account of Smith's surprise at hearing the staff don't trust the governors. I think this shows his surprise at criticism of Crawford was genuine. I always thought it "tactical." What a dream world!'[55] When, in the summer of 1944, Smith left Manitoba to become president of the University of Toronto, he wrote an affectionate note to Daniells: 'I have enjoyed and benefited from working with you ... you have helped me in seeing more clearly the highest ideals of Universities. I pray that you will never lose that spirit so sensitive to the best. I am proud of your appointment.'[56]

Daniells as well as Brown lived in a 'dream world.' When Smith resigned, Daniells put forward Brown's name to the board of governors as a possible candidate for president. Brown might have made a good president: he had been trained at Toronto and the Sorbonne, was highly regarded as a faculty member at Toronto, understood conditions at Winnipeg, and had been sought out as a faculty member by prestigious American institutions such as Cornell (where he was chair) and Chicago. However, negotiations lapsed unaccountably, and Brown was not contacted. He was not surprised, telling Daniells he had not supposed it would work out.[57] Later, Daniells received a letter from Saunders in his department, who had been told by Crawford, also a member of the presidential search committee, that the committee had reduced the number of candidates for president from fourteen to a convenient four by a criteria of: '(1) No Catholics, (2) No clergymen (3) None over 50, (4) No Medical men!'[58] The end of an era was at hand. But not quite gone.

Chapter Twelve

'O Canada'

My eyes were formed [in a small Prairie town] ... Towns like ours, set in a sea of land, have been described thousands of times as dull, bleak, flat, uninteresting ... All I can say is – well, you really have to live there to know that country ...

In winter ... the sky would be black but not dark, for you could see a cold glitter of stars from one side of the earth's rim to the other. And then the sometime astonishment when you saw the Northern Lights flaring across the sky, like the scrawled signature of God ...

Margaret Laurence, *Heart of a Stranger*, 238

For Canadians, the 1940s brought a shift in political allegiance from England to Canada, making possible a shift in artistic allegiance. For the first time, Canadian novelists, although still drawing on European forms, could fully claim their own landscape and construct their own myths. In this new wave of literary nationalism, the Second World War was a catalyst. When Daniells had first arrived in Winnipeg, he had found himself among a group of Canadian nationalists, such as J.W. Dafoe, who regularly wrote editorials for the *Winnipeg Free Press* about Canada as 'a North American nation' that should determine its own destiny rather than blindly follow Britain into war. With the outbreak of war in 1939, the newspaper carried articles by the U of M historian W.L. Morton and the United College historian A.R.M. Lower urging greater independence in Canadian affairs. Lower, a member of the Canadian Institute for International Affairs, was also part of a Winnipeg group that included Dafoe and Robert (Pete) McQueen, head of the Economics Department at Manitoba, which set out what they thought ought to be Canada's international position. Daniells met with a similar CIIA group, which considered the wartime curtailment of freedom of speech. He had close connections with both Dafoe, the university chancellor, whom he considered 'a great man,' and McQueen, and visited frequently at both men's houses. Dafoe was tall and heavyset, with a shock of white hair, commanding in manner. Winnipeggers liked to boast that 'when Dafoe spoke, Mackenzie King trembled.'[1] There was a certain amount of truth in this jest, which alluded partly to the power of the *Winnipeg Free Press* as a national paper. Daniells now found himself at the centre of the West's views on business and foreign policy. He did not always like what he heard. There was, he believed 'a subtle but deep antagonism between the responsible financial and business element in the community and the cultural interests of the University ... I doubt if there exists anywhere in the country a more ruthless set of *entrepreneurs* than in this city ... To fashion the elements of a Canadian culture here is truly to make bricks without straw.'[2]

Middle- and upper-class Winnipeg was strongly mercantilist, conservative, and anglophile. It was not until 1941 that correspondents like 'Mother of Six' finally stopped writing letters to the editor of the *Tribune*, the Conservative and British-oriented paper, attacking 'wicked nationalists' like Lower.[3] The high degree of pro-British sentiment is understandable, given that Britain was fully engaged in fighting against the threat of Germany and its allies. But national issues were becoming increasingly important, especially Canada's need to assert itself as an independent nation rather than a colony of Britain. It was to prove beyond doubt that Canada had become a nation that Lower began his important historical study *Colony to Nation* (1946).

There was also an equally strong desire to establish a Canadian literature, which would demonstrate literary independence from Britain. In the early forties, Ralph Gustafson put together an anthology of Canadian poetry for the Canadian forces at the front, and two years later A.J.M Smith compiled an anthology for use in universities and colleges. This literary nationalism of the forties paralleled that of the twenties, when the primary question had been: Can there be a Canadian literature? By the mid-forties, this question was no longer asked. Pratt was widely acclaimed as Canada's major poet for *Brébeuf and His Brethren* (1940), and Frederick Philip Grove had emerged as the major Prairie novelist because of novels such as *Fruits of the Earth* (1933). Both received their first honorary degrees for literature in the mid-forties at U of M at Daniells' instigation.

But nationalist aspirations still focused on poetry. The desire for a

Canadian poetry (proving beyond doubt the existence of a Canadian culture) was so strong in the decades between the wars that Paul Hiebert, a professor of chemistry at U of M, invented a poet, Sarah Binks, who embodied the weakest aspects of the nationalist movement. Daniells was delighted in late March 1939, when Hiebert introduced Sarah to the Morons.[4] His eventual satire, featuring 'the sweet song-stress of Saskatchewan,' incorporated Sarah's life, letters, and a critical biography. Sarah was the heroine of a parodic romance, and her verse reflected the wide, flat reaches of the Canadian prairies: 'I heard your dear voice calling / To the piglets and their mother ... "Hi, Sooky, ho, Sooky, / Come and get your swill!"'[5] In 1947, when *Sarah Binks* was published, Hiebert supplied an appropriately parodic preface: 'From Shakespeare's "England's my England," to a Saskatchewan wheat farm may seem a far cry. But that same patriotism, that same confidence, and joy in his native land which is a heritage of all poets, is also Sarah's.'[6]

Canadians in 1940 were willing to spoof the idea of a 'Canadian' literature; yet a new literature was definitely coming into being – especially in Montreal, Toronto, and Winnipeg. Daniells had close connections with many of the writers and critics of the period, including Birney, Frye, Hiebert, Desmond Pacey, Sinclair Ross, E.K. Brown, and A.J.M. Smith. Moreover, he was training in his English department a number of young writers and critics – Fredelle Bruser, A.C. Hamilton, Jack Ludwig, Adele Wiseman, and Jean Margaret Wemyss (better known as Margaret Laurence), whose careers would show that Winnipeg, after all, could produce a literary culture. The importance of the Western Civilization Program and honours English in developing highly literate writers cannot be over-emphasized.

———————

One of the first Prairie writers Daniells befriended was Sinclair Ross, whose short stories were appearing in *Queen's Quarterly*. Max Patrick, who had met Ross at the Young Men's Musical Association choir, had organized an evening reading for him.[7] Shortly afterward, on 23 October 1940, Daniells invited Ross for dinner. Two years after Hiebert had introduced Sarah's verse, some of the same faculty members who had howled with laughter over Hiebert's parody – the very idea of trying to capture the essence of the prairie in verse! – sat and listened gravely to Ross's prose:

It's an immense night out there, wheeling and windy. The lights on the street and in the house are helpless against the black wetness, little unilluminating glints that might be painted on it. The town seems huddled together, cowering on a high, tiny perch, afraid to move lest it topple into the wind. Close to the parsonage is the church, black even against the darkness ...[8]

When *As for Me and My House* was published in 1941, Daniells read it at one sitting, telling Ross: 'It's fine, it's really excellent ... you should be able to produce that phenomenon we've been waiting for since Confederation *the great* Canadian novel. *As for Me* is very close to it.'[9] He also wrote an appreciative review.

Ross was overjoyed. 'There's no use pretending that a word of praise isn't sweet. I find my appetite for it enormous.'[10] In mid-May, Daniells proposed to make the book a first-year English text at U of M and affiliated colleges, including United. But he ran into trouble, as he explained to Ross: 'Phelps, Lahey, and other members of the English Committee have given the matter careful consideration and we feel that *as a teaching instrument* for students just out of High School it is better to have a text in which the traditional approach to character, plot, setting, theme, characterization, etc., are more easily made.' However, it was decided to use *As for Me and My House* in upper-level courses, where Margaret Laurence first read it.[11]

Daniells was one of the chief boosters of the novel. In the fall of 1941, he introduced Ross's fiction to a national audience on the CBC. The first broadcast described *As for Me and My House* to Canadians as a story that concerns 'a minister and his wife, who live in a small prairie town fitly called Horizon.' Ross, Daniells pointed out, was 'eminently faithful to the actuality of life as he sees it on the prairies.'[12] In his second broadcast, Daniells showed why the novel was so important. Ross's Prairie characters are 'combatants in the midst of a war, and since this war is against the inclemency of heaven and earth, the forces of nature, we feel the dignity of their struggle, even when most hopeless.'[13]

Later Daniells visited the novelist at his home in Winnipeg. Although he had come to see 'Jimmy,' Ross's mother talked throughout the visit, overriding her son,[14] like the fictional Mrs Bentley. Ross also recalled meeting Daniells in the forties. He had liked him, felt his kindness, but recognized a great social chasm. Daniells had to 'unbend': he, Ross, was a bank clerk with a grade eleven education, whereas Daniells was a university professor. Ross remembered that Daniells had 'spoken of his

concerns about religion as if [Ross] would understand.' However, as a
Unitarian, Ross did not know what the Plymouth Brethren believed. He
also considered Daniells a little 'naïve' because he had told him he was
agitated by the frequency and strength of his sexual feelings.[15] Daniells
was confiding in Ross, a younger, unmarried man, on the assumption
that he shared his puritanical hang-ups about sex before marriage,
unaware, though Patrick and George Ford knew, that Ross was homosexual.[16]

As for Me and My House is now considered by many critics the first
major English-Canadian novel. For Daniells the novel may have had
personal significance as well. Major elements in it corresponded to
similar elements in his own life – the emphasis on a confining religion,
the overwhelming mother-wife figure, the problem of the artist who
attempts to find a vocation and establish a satisfactory sexual relation.
He later wrote an influential introduction to the first New Canadian
Library edition of the novel, which describes the internal action of the
novel as the struggles of 'the Puritan soul' to find a way. Later critics
objected to his reading of the character of Mrs Bentley as 'pure gold,'[17]
but Daniells – perhaps reflecting on his mother's role in his own life –
acknowledges the virtues of the strong, nurturing mother figure against
whom the artist must eventually rebel.

Through his support of writers like Hiebert and Ross, and his role as
advisor to the *Manitoba Arts Review*, where he published Northrop Frye,
Daniells attempted to raise literary standards at Manitoba. He now had
a national reputation as a critic of Canadian literature on the CBC. He
spoke favourably in 1942 on Birney's first book of poetry, *David and
Other Poems*, noting that 'David' reflects the Alberta landscape and
questions of survival, and that the shorter poems display the new war
sensibility. A.J.M. Smith, largely on Daniells' advice, included 'David'
in *The Book of Canadian Poetry* (1943). Daniells played a major part in
developing this book, the most important modernist anthology of Canadian poetry, because he and Pratt were the Canadian 'readers,' or
assessors, of the manuscript for University of Chicago Press. W.H.
Auden was the American reader. Pratt advised Smith to include more
popular poets like Wilson MacDonald, and he warned him about the
Canadian Mrs Grundy's likely reaction to erotic verse: 'Before you
decide on anything, get Daniells' reaction.'[18]

Daniells, like Auden, questioned Smith's division of modern Canadian poets into 'Native' and 'Cosmopolitan' streams, a division which
was to cause much negative critical comment in later years. He was also

concerned about the structure of the book, which he thought included too many selections from bad, early poets and insufficient representation from good, younger poets like Birney, Robert Finch, Floris McLaren, A.M. Klein, and Ralph Gustafson. He also appears to have implied there was too much Pratt. Smith thanked him for his 'painstaking and helpful criticism ... As you mentioned, there is some inequality of attention. In the cases of Finch and Birney this will be remedied.'[19]

In a second letter, a month later, Smith was more frank: 'I am much more conscious of my debt to you ... I have tried to carry out almost all of your suggestions.' He had streamlined Pratt, cut out 'big hunks' from the early material, and added 'David' and 'Anglo-Saxon Street,' as well as new poems by Floris McLaren, James Wreford, A.M. Klein, and Ralph Gustafson. Smith incorporated Daniells' idea of different poets being 'stages on a road' into a division of the book entitled 'Varieties of Romantic Sensibility.' In line with Daniells' remark that he had overpraised some poems, 'I cut out most of the emotive adjectives and made a number of specific revaluations – all in the direction of honesty.' Daniells had criticized Smith's remarks on Finch and Birney, and as a result Smith had added commentary about them. 'On the whole, you see I have reason to be deeply grateful to you.' Smith also argued with Daniells, who had withdrawn permission for publication of two of his own poems. 'I must ask you to let me insist on keeping your two poems. They are good, and should be in.'[20] Daniells, however, continued to refuse. He did not think his poems sufficiently polished.

He also had other reservations because he planned to use Smith's anthology at the U of M. If one of Smith's selections was 'To Sir O ... D ...,' a poem on the fascist Sir Oswald Mosley, published in the *Canadian Forum* in 1937, this is likely. Parodying Wordsworth's sonnet on John Milton, Daniells wrote: 'England has need of Oswald now! / End not with ill directed blow / This darling child of Fascismo':

He'll bring contempt upon his cause
Without your breaking England's laws.
Give, give him time enough and scope
And ample length of hempen rope,
He'll hang himself.
                So if the fit
Comes on again, to make a hit,
Shun stones and shy a lump of dirt.[21]

The last word was originally 'shit,' thus rhyming with 'fit' and 'hit.' But this was a little strong, even for the *Canadian Forum*. Birney, then literary editor, wrote Daniells asking if he might follow Skeat's edition of Chaucer and substitute 'dirt'?[22] Astute readers of the *Forum* promptly spotted the substitution and wrote Daniells congratulating him on his fine satiric poem. Such verse passed muster for magazine publication, but Daniells may have thought it unwise to publish in an anthology intended for university use, especially in conservative Winnipeg.

Smith's anthology was a landmark. For the first time, Canadians recognized that there existed a reputable body of national poetry. Frye, who reviewed the book in the *Forum*, declared that Canadian poetry was characterized by a fear of nature, a hypothesis that dominated Canadian literary criticism for the next forty years.[23] Daniells often discussed Canadian writing with Desmond Pacey, who was teaching at Brandon, and now received a proposal from him: 'Suppose this new Smith anthology is as good as it should be, couldn't we put it on say First Year instead of that nauseating *Golden Book*?'[24] As Palgrave's *Golden Treasury* was still the recognized collection of English poetry, substituting Smith's book, as was done, was a distinct challenge to all who taught 'English' literature.

Daniells also introduced E.K. Brown's critical study *On Canadian Poetry* (1943) to a national audience on the CBC. In it Brown explained why it had been difficult for a Canadian writing to come into being: a country bordering the United States, always subject to competition from its writers; its English-French political and linguistic division; a Puritanism that prevented writers from speaking honestly; and a 'frontier mentality' that devalued literature. Daniells spoke favourably of the book and wrote a further generous review. In fact, ever since the late thirties Daniells had 'boosted' Canadian writing on national radio. In November 1942, speaking about 'The Future of Canadian Writing,' Daniells reminded his listeners that Canadian writing 'must depend on our discovering an idiom, an outlook, an approach independent of English or American models.' He praised Earle Birney for the ability to 'write as a Canadian with the most intense consciousness and poetic realization of particular British Columbian landscape.'[25]

———◆———

Daniells' students in honours English at the U of M were responding to the Canadian nationalist impulse which his public broadcasts and university lectures stressed. In 1944 the *Literary Supplement* of the student paper *The Manitoban* published an 'Editorial' strongly supportive of a Canadian literature, and suggestive of Daniells' recent broadcast on Brown:

> We in Canada suffer from what our psychologists term 'an inferiority complex' ... When John Smith, Canadian, publishes a poem, novel or short story, the reviews tell us that his work is like that of some English writer or some American artist. No one has ever said that it was typically Canadian.

The young editor, Jack Ludwig, later to become a novelist and academic, concluded that there was no reason why Canadians should not be able to turn out first-class poetry and prose.[26] This editorial would have been seen by Margaret Laurence, at that time a close reader of *The Manitoban*.

The same issue of the *Supplement* published a verse called 'Atrocities,' which took off from a newspaper report in which Prime Minister Mackenzie King had condemned Japanese atrocities against Canadian prisoners of war. The anonymous student poet wrote: 'The fault of war / Is that it kills the wrong people. If only the tortures inflicted upon these men / Were inflicted upon these on the home front / It would all be a matter / Of rejoicing.' Politicians and home-front patriots, the young poet argued, proclaim their willingness to die for democracy, knowing they will never have to. Today such verse might raise an eyebrow, but in the intense war climate of 1944 such sentiments were 'treasonous.' The verse, the journal, the English Department, and the university became a *cause célèbre*. The RCMP were brought in to investigate. At first it was thought that the verse had been written by Ludwig, but A.C. Hamilton, a fifth-year honours student and president of the Students' Union, came forward as author.

While an uproar about 'traitorous malingerers' went on in Winnipeg daily newspapers, the *Canadian Forum* contacted Daniells with a question regarding infractions of the student's freedom of speech, a difficult question to answer in terms of peace-time definitions because war changes the meaning and use of speech. Daniells, who refused to identify the author, declared that the poem was 'well over the border between what can be said in war time and what cannot.'[27] Hamilton felt that Daniells had not supported him – not an unreasonable assumption considering that during a class lecture Daniells reportedly pointed to a tree outside the classroom window and said that whoever had published the poem deserved to be hanged.[28] However, the head had been placed in an awkward situation: as a university administrator, he had a responsibility to the department and members of the community who had been angered by the writer; yet, as a teacher and writer, he had a responsibility to support the use of free speech.

President Smith judged the incident severely. Ludwig and Hamilton were allowed to finish their year and write their final exams, but their degrees were to be withheld until they had proven themselves worthy. Hamilton served in the armed forces until honourably discharged, and Ludwig (who had a health problem) until he had done a year's special service.[29] Both men finished their degrees to become professors of English and later acknowledged a debt to Daniells.[30] Ludwig, who taught at State University of New York at Stony Brook, published a number of novels, including *Confusions* (1967). Hamilton, who taught at Queen's University, became a distinguished scholar of Renaissance literature and of Frye's criticism. First introduced to Frye in the *Manitoba Arts Review* in 1942, Hamilton was later advised by Daniells to look up Frye when he went to graduate school at the U of T. In his preface to *Northrop Frye: Anatomy of His Criticism* (1990), Hamilton remarks that he had come late to literature, but that when attending lectures by Daniells at the U of M, 'it struck me that there must be something in a subject that could involve so passionately such an intelligent and sensitive person.'[31]

In a far more provocative way, four young women writers were to emerge from Daniells' revised English program at the U of M to become major figures in the Canadian literary community. While most of the male students responded intellectually, developing ideas and criticism, a number of young women, notably Adele Wiseman, Patricia Blondal, Fredelle Bruser Maynard, and Margaret Laurence, turned to narrative, to fictions which explored some of their professor's ideas and which, in certain cases, narrowed down to a psychological study of Daniells himself. Three of these narratives bring in considerations of the professor and the university context, and all bear witness to the writer's training in English at the University of Manitoba.

In Fredelle Bruser Maynard's fictionalized memoir, *Raisins and Almonds* (1964), written from the perspective of a Winnipeg university student, Daniells is portrayed as a charismatic professor of seventeenth-century literature, nicknamed 'Ogden Agonistes,' who first introduced the narrator to poetry. (Daniells, who taught Milton's *Samson Agonistes*, had once referred to himself during a bout of melancholia as 'Daniells Agonistes' and the term stuck.) In Bruser's narrative, the young woman student is highly attracted to Agonistes and his teaching; nonetheless, she marries another English professor, recognizably Max Maynard.[32]

Adele Wiseman's first novel, *The Sacrifice* (1956), set in Winnipeg, draws upon the Jewish tradition as well as Daniells' classroom emphasis on myth and biblical archetype. Wiseman's focus is upon the religiously determined personality of the main character, Abraham, and the novel builds up to a ritual murder presented as an Old Testament sacrifice.[33] Several years later, another U of M student, Patricia Blondal, wrote two novels which were published posthumously. In her first manuscript, *From Heaven with a Shout* (published as a second book in 1962), she presents two brothers, twins, 'The Doctor' and 'The Professor,' whose rapport suggests a single personality. When Gwladys Downes, Daniells' former fiancée, read the novel, she recognized the brothers as expressing the two sides of Daniells' personality.[34] The links with Daniells' life story are further underlined by a framing journey from England to Victoria, the Vancouver Island locale of the story; by the novel's title and epigraph, with its Plymouth Brethren millenarian text ('For the Lord himself shall descend from heaven with a shout . . . with the trump of God'); and by a reference to a clergyman named Oldham, who bears the same name as the Plymouth Brother who waved goodbye to the Daniells family when they emigrated to Canada.[35] In Blondal's novel, the inevitable conclusion is the death of one twin, the dark side of the personality, and the marriage of the other, the outgoing professor side. Specific allusions suggest that Blondal had access to Daniells' life story. This fact would be apparent to Margaret Laurence when she read this book and its Winnipeg-based successor, *A Candle to Light the Sun* (1960), in manuscript for McClelland and Stewart. Laurence, who had known Blondal at Manitoba, envied her skill in capturing Winnipeg life, and was spurred to emulate her; indeed, this was part of the impetus which led Laurence to write her first Canadian novel, *The Stone Angel* (1964).[36]

Margaret Laurence's connections with Daniells began in the forties but extended to the seventies. During 1944–5, while Ludwig and Hamilton were under censure for their verse, Laurence was an interested bystander who frequented the Broadway office of *The Manitoban*. She began as one of Arthur Phelps's literary protégés at United College, more of a poet than the novelist she would become,[37] but in 1945–6, when Daniells was still head of English at Manitoba, she took an Honours course in his department, English III, a survey of English from the Renaissance up taught by Malcolm Ross, and came to know in person a man already known as a public figure.

His was a familiar voice, speaking on literature, on the national CBC and on the Winnipeg station CKY-CKX. In 1942, Laurence's and Wiseman's freshman year, Daniells gave a talk on man's search for self, emphasizing the mythic quality of ordinary human life. Speaking of Prospero and Caliban in Shakespeare's *The Tempest*, he commented, 'Each of us is Caliban, and if we do not recognize ourselves, it is only because we do not know ourselves very well.'[38] In a another broadcast, on T.S. Eliot and *The Waste Land*, he emphasized Eliot's use of archetypal myth – the story of an aged king ruling over an infertile land – and its link with literary pattern. Daniells spoke about Eliot's method of 'free association of ideas, emotions, and images so that things which seem to have no *logical* connection are found together and make a whole.'[39] This was a new and exciting exposition of what became known as myth criticism. Two years later, in October 1944, Daniells gave a CBC broadcast with Phelps, speaking on the importance of including Canadian landscape in the new Canadian writing, a talk which elicited letters of praise from Northrop Frye and Marshall McLuhan – and was likely heard by Laurence.[40]

Between 1941 and 1945, Daniells taught many English classes consisting largely of young women. With so many of the male students at the front, these young women had more opportunity to speak out, to interact, and to develop their literary abilities for, in addition to literary criticism, Daniells regularly assigned topics for their own creative writing of poems and prose. Inevitably, there was some personal interest in their professor. Daniells was 'a catch,' once described in the *Winnipeg Free Press* as 'the year's most eligible bachelor.' A member of this class, Nathan Divinsky, recalls that in 1946 there was much student gossip about Daniells, his courtship of a former student, and his sudden move to Vancouver to accept a faculty position at UBC.[41] By the spring of 1947, when Laurence won the graduating prize for poetry awarded to honours students at Manitoba, Daniells had become a subject of considerable interest. He had published several verses in the *Manitoba Arts Review*, including a whimsical sonnet in which he took on the persona of Prospero: 'I never met Miranda ... I'm going berry-picking with Caliban.' Upper-level students wondered if Daniells was Prospero, who was Caliban? And why had he not found a Miranda? Daniells' friend Ogden Turner, then teaching in the English Department at Manitoba, wrote Daniells to say that honours students – who included Laurence and Wiseman – were reading his sonnets and 'professing to identify two characters!'[42]

An attractive, unmarried head of an English department, even a former head, had little personal privacy. A year later, in May 1948, students had some new gossip, namely that Daniells had married a young woman, a Winnipegger, whose Scots family had links with the Métis and Louis Riel. Four months later, he published a book of poetry, *Deeper into the Forest*, which contained 'Farewell to Winnipeg.' It was one of the first assertions that the Riel story was 'a tale of wrong':

> The fiery face of Riel turning again,
> Reining his horse a moment, into the rain
> Galloping ...
> ...
> He set his foot down on the surveyor's chain
> Challenging empire, challenging law, in vain.[43]

It was over a decade later, at UBC in 1957, when Laurence was writing short stories and novels, that she next encountered Daniells. He had now become head of the English Department and hired her husband, Jack Laurence, to teach English and later hired her to mark essays. It was likely during this year that Laurence registered the striking physical resemblance between her husband and Daniells: both were English professors, both were tall and slim, both had a sandy-coloured moustache and a British accent.

Later, in June 1967, after Laurence had published *The Stone Angel* and *A Jest of God*, Daniells had the pleasure of presenting her at the Governor General's literary awards in Ottawa. Laurence had returned to Canada from England, and, before and after the awards ceremony, she stayed with Wiseman, a close friend. It is likely (as Bruser's *Raisins and Almonds* had appeared three years earlier) that the two writers would have discussed their old connections with honours English and 'Daniells Agonistes' because it was during this period that Laurence told Alice Munro that Daniells had played a very important role at the U of M.[44] Two years later, in 1969, Laurence, Wiseman, and Daniells appeared together in a special issue of the U of M journal *Mosaic*, which reprinted that section of Daniells' poem 'Farewell to Winnipeg' which dealt with Riel, perhaps reminding Laurence of the biographical connections between Daniells' story and Riel.

These connections reappear centrally in her last novel, *The Diviners* (1974), a self-reflexive and autobiographical study, where much of the foregoing material, augmented by other sources, became grist for Laurence's fictional mill. Morag Gunn of *The Diviners* is a young woman of Scots ancestry who studies honours English at a college in the city, clearly Winnipeg. There she publishes a poem in a student literary magazine which brings her to the attention of Dr Brooke Skelton. Skelton 'teaches the Seventeenth-Century Poetry course and the Milton course. He is English (from England, that is) ... He is, of course, swooned over by various bird-brained females in the class.'[45] Daniells, English born, regularly taught the seventeenth-century and Milton courses. He was tall, charismatic, and had a well-deserved reputation as a ladies' man.[46]

James King, Laurence's biographer, points out that Brooke Skelton's 'condescending attitude' is meant to reflect Jack Laurence.[47] However, I would argue that this fictional professor of English combines aspects of Roy Daniells as well as Jack Laurence. This combination is first signalled by his name, which is an amalgam of two poets: John Skelton and Rupert Brooke. However, 'Brooke' is a name given to an imperialist Englishman in Laurence's early African fiction, husband to a young woman much like herself, whereas 'Skelton' may be associated with Daniells, who gave a special, advertised lecture on the English poet, John Skelton, in the fall of 1945, to the Manitoba Poetry Club, when Laurence, then a poet, was taking an English course which included Skelton.[48]

Like Daniells – and, for that matter, like Jack Laurence – the fictional Skelton is attracted to a student who publishes in the campus literary journal. Both Daniells (when he came to Winnipeg) and Skelton are in their mid-thirties, each has had a disturbing childhood, each marries a student, and each then moves to a university in a big city to become at first a professor, and then head of an English department. Laurence's Skelton, also like Daniells, suffers from depression and nightmares. Morag recognizes 'his terrible need for someone who could bring him light, lightness, release, relief. How could you fight that? How could you withdraw from the terrors of the cave in which he lived almost always alone?'[49] The most telling detail of Laurence's portrait of Brooke Skelton, however, is his fear of having *any* child, a fear that characterized the Daniells of this period, whereas Jack Laurence simply did not wish to have *another* child. Laurence uses Brooke's fear of children as a basis for the eventual failure of the relationship between Morag and her husband.

When Morag leaves her husband to become a writer, she travels to England, where she is hired by J. Sampson, proprietor of the Agonistes Bookshop.[50] Here Laurence incorporates a little joke – Bruser's reference to Daniells' nickname, 'Agonistes,' from *Raisins and Almonds*. Laurence also offers the reader a clue to her technique as a novelist when she gives Daniells' first initial (he was then professionally known as J. Roy Daniells) to Sampson and develops the passage to emphasize myth and archetype – the parallels between Mr Sampson, the bookseller, and Samson, his mythic prototype. In his honours courses and in his radio broadcasts, Daniells emphasized myth and archetype. Indeed, it was during Laurence's first year at United College that Daniells had remarked, 'Each of us is Caliban' – and she, too, had learned by the sixties to recognize in her own writing the connections between myth, archetype, and universal human psychology. One of her characters, Stacey, from *The Fire Dwellers*, says, while watching her two sons fight: 'Cain and his brother began that way.'[51]

One section of *The Diviners*, describing Winnipeg student life in the mid-forties may also be read to give us a sense of how Laurence as student may have felt in relation to Daniells, the English professor. Her fictional character, Morag, becomes indignant when Dr Skelton teaches John Donne's poem 'The Canonization,' with its admonition: 'For God's sake hold your tongue, and let me love.' (I well remember this passage from classes in seventeenth-century poetry with Daniells in 1963 – his resonant south-of-England voice, the waves of shocked delight from the class.) But in this class in the forties, the student Morag misunderstands Donne's syntax. She thinks the poet has told the woman to keep quiet. She says, 'Supposing the lady had been able to write poetry – I mean, you wonder what she might have said of *him*.' Morag's argument is that it is possible to accept 'He for God only; she for God in him' from John Milton, but that '"you wouldn't have expected it of Donne, so much."' The class erupts in laughter, and Dr Skelton is amused. He suggests that she is a student who wants to go back into the past 'to discuss the matter' with the poet. 'That's right,' Morag says.[52]

I suspect that Laurence is going back into her own academic past to discuss the matter with the poet and the professor who were combined in one figure. Specifically, she addresses what Daniells, as head of English at Manitoba, represents in view of her position as student of

English, would-be writer, and a woman in a gender-biased academy. In *The Diviners*, Morag marries Skelton, partly to get closer to the world of literature, which he represents. But when she realizes he intends to keep her in a child-like state, she begins a novel, 'Prospero's Child,' in which the young woman writer must break with her English husband-professor – and the dominance of English literature that he represents – in order to assert herself as a woman and a Canadian writer.[53] Here Laurence interrogates the figure of Skelton/Daniells as representative professor and characterizes the study and canon of English literature as male, English, and dominated by religion.

It is clear that *The Diviners* is intended to make a political statement on the literary colonization of Canada. While at UBC in the early sixties, Laurence had read O. Mannoni's *Prospero and Caliban: A Study of the Psychology of Colonization*, which argues that the typical colonial was 'compelled to live out Prospero's drama.'[54] Thus her personal associations with Daniells, Prospero, and English literature were now overlaid with Mannoni's concept of colonization and the repressive political context which she later assigns in *The Diviners* to Dr Skelton as Prospero and to English literature. To become a Canadian writer, Morag (and by inference Laurence) must reject the symbol of British imperialism to create a Canadian literature.

But why did Laurence present as a British imperialist a man who was one of the best-known Canadianists of the forties, fifties, and sixties? Perhaps simply because *he was there* – embedded in her Winnipeg memories and inextricably associated with her negative memories of her divorced husband, Jack, whom she left because he had disparaged her first Canadian novel, *The Stone Angel*.[55] Brooke Skelton symbolizes the type of 'English professor' whom Laurence wanted to portray, one sufficiently monumental to fully justify the rigours of her own continuing struggle to find a Canadian voice in fiction. In the early 1970s, when she completed *The Diviners*, Daniells was such a figure. Elected president of the Royal Society in 1970–1, he was recognized as one of the most distinguished English professors in the country.

Undoubtedly, Daniells was one of the strongest advocates of a Canadian literature during Laurence's university days. And, as the architect of the honours program at the U of M and affiliated colleges, he brought to honours students like Bruser, Laurence, Ludwig, and Wiseman a broad understanding of the English literary past as well as the archetypal myths and techniques of contemporary writing. Yet it is not surprising that Laurence darkened her fictional portrait.[56] As Morag,

Young Roy with his parents, Constance and James Daniells, Victoria, B.C., ca. 1914

Jack Shadbolt, John McDonald, Roy Daniells, and Max Maynard at the Daniells
home in Victoria, ca. 1926–7

Roy Daniells, graduation photo, University of British Columbia, 1930

Northrop Frye, graduation photo, University of Toronto, 1933

Roy Daniells, Winnipeg, Manitoba, 1937

Laurenda Francis, Winnipeg, 1948

Garnett Sedgewick and his mother, Bessie, with Laurenda and Roy Daniells, Vancouver, B.C., 1948

Roy Daniells, J.B. Priestley, Earle Birney, University of British Columbia, 1956

Laurenda and Roy Daniells with their children, Sara and Susan, on the ship
Homeric, 1960

Roy Daniells and Desmond Pacey in Fredericton, N.B., 1961

the writer-narrator of *The Diviners*, remarks of her own calling as novelist: 'A daft profession. Wordsmith. Liar, more likely. Weaving fabrications. Yet, with typical ambiguity, convinced that fiction was more true than fact. Or that fact was in fact fiction.'[57] In this case, Laurence's art – and her sense of where she stood in relation to her past, the academy, and her former husband – required a larger metafictional statement. This was despite the fact, as she told Al Purdy, that the truth about the relation between *The Diviners* and the 'so-called-reality' of living individuals was far more complex.[58]

——————

Ironically, during this period in which Laurence later depicted Daniells as the typical 'English' professor, he saw himself as a Canadian attempting to write 'The Great Canadian novel.'[59] In the early thirties, while still a graduate student at the U of T, Daniells wrote to his mother urging her to save his early diaries because some day he might need them for a novel.[60] In 1937, then teaching at Victoria College, Toronto, he remembered 'the thing I really have to do in this world is to *write*.'[61] In 1939, when head of English at Manitoba but back in Victoria for the summer holidays, he 'began last night on the actual text of *The Island*, which I hope will prove a really good novel.'[62] The material was clearly autobiographical, describing Daniells' early childhood in England and the family's emigration to Canada. He saw his book in terms of geography: 'The Island, the Lakes, the Plains.'[63] Each unit of geography was a metaphor. The island, for example, encompassed England, Vancouver Island, the English in Victoria, the Plymouth Brethren, and the young Daniells himself – a sensitive child isolated both from the Brethren and his classmates.

The middle-aged Daniells wrote introspectively: he needed to understand the child he had been in order to understand the man he had become. He also wrote symbolically, using myths and metaphors as keys to understanding. In 1939 and 1940, he described the small boy and his religious terrors. In 1940, back in Winnipeg, he read out the first completed pages to Carson and Kay Mark; again, during the summer of 1942, he reported 'working on novel and on verses.'[64] In June 1943 he sketched the whole scheme of the novel to a sympathetic E.K. Brown. By 1944 he had evolved a framing structure for his story. In this version, called 'Oh Canada,' the boy's story is incorporated within the story of

John Davidson and a larger Canadian epic. In this new version, through the name of his protagonist, Daniells may be seen as changing his psychological relationship with his mentor, Herbert Davis, commonly known as David. The Daniells persona is no longer 'Mephibosheth,' the lamed object of Davis's charity, as he identified himself in his thesis dedication to Davis, but rather Davidson or David's 'son.'

'Autobiographical Fragments – Fictionalized' appears to be part of a first sequence begun in 1939 and written over the next two years.[65] There are references to the boy's early life, a story regarding C.H. Mackintosh's book on biblical exegesis, a train journey, a Plymouth Brethren picnic, and a Joycean stream-of-consciousness passage which revealed the experimental writer. The picnic story depicts Mrs Butcher, who had befriended Daniells on Vancouver Island. She is a slight, frail woman with sloping shoulders and skin the colour of Sunlight soap for whom speech was *'a simple function like breathing, the beating of the heart or the digestion of food.'*

In another drafted section, free association, puns, and an almost total lack of punctuation allow the narrator to effectively contrast the life in the 'cave' of primitive days – the struggle for survival and the making of sacrifice – with man's present situation: *'Come let us even where the cave yawns deepest penetrate even in roaring torrent cleft in the cliff wild in the wilderness O roof swallow built O fire of sticks.'* This monologue is interrupted at several points. The narrator reflects that life in the cave is no longer possible 'as for me belonging to Canadian scene orientation more difficult.' He was glad to leave England and return to his own country, but now: *'what to do.'* He thinks of *'symbols signs human soul long conscious of itself and struggling to express results of insight . . . and myth symbol ritual story tale parable ...'*[66] As Daniells later participated in Birney's creative-writing group in Vancouver, a group also attended by Laurence, she may have heard him read this excerpt with its allusion to the lonely 'cave.'

The papers called 'Autobiographical Fictionized Fragments' appear to have been written in 1941. This group contains thirties material, including the story of Jim Watts in Paris and of S.H. Hooke and Bumpus's bookstore in London. There are several stories about the boy, one describing his experience with poetry and another in which he makes a friend at school, but is rejected when he has a breakdown. One of the most powerful sections provides a reason for the adolescent breakdown, showing a boy of ten in the 'torture chamber' of the Plymouth Brethren Hall. Brightly lit walls and a narrow corridor lead to a preacher, who becomes a black portal through which the boy passes into a small chamber where gratings made visible the red and gold of a fiery furnace. There he was arrested by a dark robed figure with a kindly face. As the boy attempts to escape, this figures warns him: *'This land is for you ... Infinite is the mercy which bestows it upon you. You have but to take possession ... "The fire is ready," said a voice from beyond the grating.'*[67] This passage powerfully conveys the confusingly paradoxical nature of his childhood experience: a God figure who professes mercy but inflicts cruelty. It also suggests Kafka, whom Daniells was reading early in the forties.

The manuscript 'Oh Canada' is dated 1 June 1944 and is written on several exam booklets. It is addressed to Carson Mark because, as Daniells explains, *'I need a listener and you have been so good a one in the past; because you are Canadian and this is about Canada; because you are a mathematician, a solver of problems.'* The story begins with an anecdote from Marco Polo, who had come across a city where the inhabitants laid up great heaps of clay to weather so that their children and grandchildren might later use it to manufacture porcelain. *'This,'* Daniells says, *'is exactly what I want to do in telling the story of John Davidson ... Our Canadian territory has not yet yielded much in the way of china clay and still less of precious metals ... This heap is for the future.'*

Davidson, who has been killed during the Second World War, has left with the narrator a small suitcase containing three cardboard boxes filled with cards and some exercise and loose-leaf books. Consequently, the story is told by the older narrator, working from Davidson's papers, and the emphasis is both nationalist and spiritual. Canada itself is presented as a puzzle with the properties of a geographically shapeless torso: *'cut off at the waist from the economic belly of the continent, its head lost somewhere in the dreaming Arctic, its right arm, flung up toward Russia, amputated, and pressing about the heart, the ice of James Bay and rocks of the Canadian Shield.'*

This proposed novel is also a form of Daniells' autobiography. While the narrator states that his role is *'to lay up in as clearly and orderly a fashion as I can, the heap,'* he also urges any Canadian writer who might read it to consider whether parts of it could be turned into a novel, or play. It is an odd sensation for a biographer, even in these days of self-reflexive prose, to have one's subject address one directly – a voice from the past speaking to the present.

Davidson's life parallels his creator's in parents, school, books read, and the journey from England to Vancouver Island. Clearly, Daniells intended to insert here the earlier material written regarding the child in Victoria. But Davidson differs from Daniells in that he goes to war: *'wanting nothing, asking nothing ... a steady flame of joyous action.'* Why? The narrator tells us that psychologists might say that Davidson is now thirty-nine (Daniells' age when he started this revision of the novel) and thus had reached a degree of maturity. The narrator, however, prefers to make an additional connection with the maturing of Canada:

> *Perhaps, too, this country of ours, butchered, buggered, and bewildered by politicians, whirled on the economic wheel, battered by the elements, cursed with two incompatible cultures, its navigating instruments perpetually deranged by the proximity of powerfully charged poles of Great Britain and the United States – may at last waken out of the nightmare ... to realize its own deep dream of patient calm, steady endurance, the clean coolness of a northern morning, the intuitive stirrings of its own awakening life.*[68]

The next version of Daniells' novel, entitled 'The Island: A Study in Insularity,' can be dated post-June 1944. The story of a sensitive child is now punctuated by a number of prologues, interludes, and epilogues interspersed between successive chapters, which allowed for a more objective and ironic perspective. The prologue, for example, included 'the Island, the City, and the Child,' and he now planned to insert some passages written earlier describing Vancouver Island and to incorporate the whole under 'Oh Canada.'

There are some fine landscape passages on the geography of Vancouver Island, which the traveller first sees as low cliffs and forested hills, a sober tapestry of repeated colour, and descriptions of early traffic on the roads. Above all, Daniells stresses the insularity, the separation of island from mainland, the boy from both the Brethren and his school chums. The boy is now called Philip (suggestive of Philip Bentley of Ross's *As for Me and My House*). There is an allusion to the boy as 'P.Q.,' and a later manuscript spells out the full name as Philip Quest – indicating that this is to be a symbolic treatment of Philip's quest.

By bringing in a narrator through whom his subject is viewed, Daniells also adopts a structural device from Ross's novel. In effect, he viewed his own past through a fictional narrator in much the same way as Ross views himself through descriptions of the artist Philip in the diaries of Mrs Bentley. However, Daniells' narrator is ironic and dismissive: *'I myself knew Philip at this time: his views and solutions not necessarily complete or correct.'* His stage directions to himself as author included the comment that he wished to *'manage the [narrator's] contempt'* so that the reader resents it.[69] In effect, Daniells as author attempted to mitigate some of the problems of himself as subject. By setting up an antagonism to the narrator's comments, he brings the reader alongside, sharing his concern for the boy. This is an ingenious solution to the problem of maintaining sympathy for a boy whose sufferings are repetitive.

Despite several attempts over a decade, Daniells never finished the novel. It did not get any further than a number of stories regarding the boy, the adolescent, and the man, and a few dozen pages of jottings and notes. Other than for the summer holidays in Victoria, continually interrupted by Winnipeg crises, he had no time for writing. More importantly, his greatest emotional energy was centred in the boy. The novel is quite literally, as Daniells once explained to his father, his 'child.' It floundered because he could not detach himself from it.

Nonetheless, he kept trying to tell his story. Because it was easier to snatch a few moments here and there for verse, Daniells developed a series of autobiographical sonnets. At the same time, he regrouped some of the childhood material, omitting some darker passages. The hero's name continued to be Philip Quest. A section from this revised version of the novel entitled 'Overture' was published in 1949 in the little magazine *Here and Now* .

It begins with the boy at a Sunday morning service: *'"Lit-tle chil-dren, lit-tle chil-dren, who love their Re-dee-mer." There was no part of him not covered by this flood of singing, heavy as gold honey in a bowl.'*[70] The story delicately details the rest of this day and the next through Philip's eyes: Sunday school, school, his parents, prayer, the beach. He and his parents have recently arrived from England, and his musings reveal his confusion over the changes. In Canada everything is different. Freedom for the boy is found at the beach, where he delights in the ocean and hillside. The next day, he returns to the beach with his cousins, Tom and Molly, and at low tide finds kelp, *'the long thin wet rope of it wound round and round the waist and over the shoulder ...'* Together the children make a raft from beach logs.

That evening the family is visited by an old friend of his father's, Mr McCaul, a humourless, harsh, deeply religious man whose prayers before and after tea were lengthy. On departing, he asks Philip if he is saved, and the child panics: *'He must tell a lie and say Yes, he was ... It was a lie because how could anyone except people like Mr. McCaul ever be sure.'* In bed that night as he drifts into sleep, he sees himself *'on a headland jutting into the sea.'* He and his cousin Molly are building a raft with proper tools. '*The sea reached its arms up the rounded slope of the rock, eager to receive his raft. He would have a mast and sail; he would sail beyond the rocks and the tangle of the kelp beds, right out into the main ocean.*'

Had he sufficient leisure and motivation to develop his fictional drafts, Daniells might have become a fine novelist: the same qualities of observation, deep feeling, and fluency in language that he brought to the teaching of literature could also have been brought to its creation. But unlike Earle Birney, who combined teaching with the writing of poetry, or Northrop Frye, who combined teaching with the writing of criticism (except for a period of administration in the fifties), Daniells' entire academic life consisted of teaching and time-consuming administration. This decision was precipitated by his acceptance of the appointment at Winnipeg and his late start in the profession: as he later remarked in September 1947, 'when I first came to Winnipeg I lost my chance to be a productive scholar and became a pusher & puller of things; having got used to pushing & pulling I itch to continue.'[71]

Chapter Thirteen

Casting Anchor

During his nine years in Winnipeg, Daniells came to know himself a little better. It was partly that he was attempting to write fiction; seeing objectified on paper the boy he had been helped him to understand the man he had become. As well, he had begun in 1941 to read Franz Kafka's novels, which gave him unexpected insight into his own personality. Kafka's allegories he recognized as 'the quest of an individual for salvation,' a modern version of Bunyan's *The Pilgrim's Progress*. But whereas Christian's path was prepared by divine help, Kafka's protagonists were 'cruelly' alone, and found themselves faced with a supreme power that had elements of both good and evil.[1]

In an essay published in the *Manitoba Arts Review*, Daniells relates the individual's unhappy relation with himself, his world, and his God to Kafka's unhappy relation with his father, 'a forcible and domineering character ... a being incomprehensible and awful on one hand, yet necessary and desirable, on the other.' He also saw that it was Kafka's failure to achieve independence from his family that conditioned the way in which his anti-heroes developed. Moreover, in Kafka's diaries he found constant 'the desire to achieve through woman, a rapprochement with the highest authorities (i.e. with God).' Searching for a definitive image for Kafka's relation with women, Daniells found it in one of his diaries where the novelist describes a girl, who is the object of his attention, surrounded by a ring of spearmen facing outwards. Kafka explains: 'I too was surrounded by armed men, whose spears were turned inwards, that is towards me. If I tried to reach the girl I was caught first on the spears of my own spearmen ... Perhaps I never reached the girl's spearmen, or if I did, I was bloody and fainting with the wounds of my own spears.'[2]

This is a revealing psychological study of a person with whom Daniells clearly identifies. By linking Kafka's allegories with Bunyan's allegories, he connects his own world with Kafka's. And his remarks that Kafka's novels are concerned with a quest for salvation by 'an individual with an over-active conscience' and the process of 'ratiocination' apply equally to Daniells. He, too, possessed a troubled Puritan conscience, idealized women and was sexually timid. But, as Kafka remarked, such manifestations, or beliefs, 'represent the attempts of a human being in distress to cast his anchor in some mother-soil.'[3] This can also apply to Daniells, and evokes a dream which he had had in the mid-thirties: 'Dream of descent through fertile brown earth into Chartres-like glass & stone ribs, that I had some time ago in Canada, a return-to-mother [earth?] motif?'[4]

At that time and later, Daniells began to write prose in a Joycean stream-of-consciousness manner with free association. In one piece of fiction, the narrator effectively contrasts the life of primitive days with man as hunter – 'Now will climb ladder of fortune to the hills high crest with pelt of wolf slung over shoulder, weapon on thigh flint and steel at waist' – with his present, more passive, situation. And, like Joyce's Molly Bloom anticipating the arrival of her husband in bed, the narrator dreams of orgasm. He thinks 'bed most welcome spot and without woman unhappily legs spreading in response touch firm belly and good breasts kisses unending and release of permanent power release but not enough.' In this section there is also a reference to the 'depth of cathedral under blue windows of Chartres and myth symbol ritual story tale parable ...'[5] Daniells' older, fundamentalist Christian beliefs, which prohibited sexual sin, are breaking down to the point where sexuality can be accommodated in a framework that contains both religion (Chartres) and modernist references to myth and symbol, possibly by way of Frazer's The Golden Bough, which he had been rereading.

Above all, Daniells was ready to cast his anchor, to settle down. To be sure, he had friends, close friends, but up to the mid-forties he despaired of finding the right woman to marry. He now recognized that his successive love interests, like Kafka's, had been blocked by his own internal resistances and his failure to achieve independence from his family. In the thirties, he had recognized the need to escape from the prison of religious dogma, the kind of escape that he associated with The Pilgrim's Progress and The Count of Monte Cristo. In Bunyan, he found an image for his situation when Christian turns the key in the lock in Castle Despair. In the early forties, when rereading Eliot's The

Waste Land, he saw this image extended to imply escape from the prison of self – as suggested in Eliot's line *'Le Prince d'Aquitaine à la tour abolie.'*[6] Now, in the mid-forties, he recognized that such escape involved freeing his natural sexual impulses. He was to learn that he must loosen the apron strings that bound him to his mother and change his relation with his father (and his father's cruel God). He was finally able to break down these religious and parental rigidities – his internalized spearmen – by reaching out to a young woman and committing himself emotionally. Between 1944 and 1948, he found the courage to 'cast his anchor' and take a wife.

He had been reading a number of books on psychology and religion. Some were the standards of the period, notably two psychological textbooks: *The Varieties of Temperament: A Psychology of Constitutional Differences* (1944) by W.H. Sheldon and S.S. Stevens; and *Common Neuroses of Children and Adults* (1937), by Oliver English and Gerald H. Pearson. As well, he read more general biological studies, such as G.P. Wells's *The Science of Life* (1934) and Julian Huxley's *Essays of a Biologist* (1923). His reading also included Karen Horney, a Freudian, who had published three books during this period, including *The Neurotic Personality of Our Time* (1937). In the chapter 'Sexuality in the Neurotic Need for Affection,' Horney speculates that in some cases the Oedipus complex 'is brought about by the child clinging to one parent for the sake of reassurance.'[7]

These more general studies led him to see the world in a scientific, rather than a religious, frame of reference. He found helpful an early article by Julian Huxley, 'Why I Am a Scientific Humanist?' which, building on Daniells' earlier interest in New Humanism, suggests that man is central to the world and that the idea of God is man-made.[8] Huxley suggested downplaying the idea of God and concentrating instead on finding purpose in the world: thus sin can be interpreted in the light of modern psychology. Daniells was attracted to Huxley's suggestion that man can ally himself with psychological forces such as righteousness, truth, and love with the aim of building a better human society. After reading Huxley, he reminded himself in March 1946 that he must 'cut with the past' – the fearful child in the Cook Street garden – and 'teach the mind new tricks.' These new paths of thought included the recognition that he was an agnostic, that God was not personal but in the universe, and that he no longer needed to fear the sin of blasphemy. The important thing was 'personal integrity and wholeheartedness.'[9]

This new sense of himself and his world affected his view of the young women he continued to court. During the mid-forties, he took out Virginia Cameron, Mary Elizabeth Bayer (to whom he was briefly engaged), and Phyllis Abbott, Kay Mark's younger sister. None of these relationships finally worked out – largely because Daniells was now in his early forties, while many of these young women were in their early twenties. The end of each new romance left him feeling increasingly bewildered and unhappy. His good friend Carson Mark understood: 'A young person, just free of the period of formal preparation looks *forward* to romance, homes, etc. in the *future*.' Such a person is willing to marry as an embarkation on the sea of adventure. But Daniells, as Mark reminded him, had already experienced these things and was 'anxious for a home, a lover, anxious to come back from the sea ... Realization of this must surely terrify people of that age in a much more fundamental sense than any mere statement of difference in age.'

Mark continued to explain: 'You insist that in seeking a mate you cannot direct or school your choice. This must be left to fancy, to the irrational motive.' He knew that Daniells had a horror of an arranged date, yet there was no doubt that his needs were appreciable to others. Mark's advice was succinct. It was time that Daniells adjusted his ideas of the feminine to 'actively seek the best part of what we include under the word "home": an intimate, personal haven; a place in which your own private acts can assume significance; to be held dear ... Your prerequisite of exercising an absolutely untrammeled fancy is, I should say, rather a luxury.'[10] Daniells appears to have taken this good advice to heart; a year later, he acted upon it.

In May 1944, Daniells was working late one evening in his office at the downtown campus on Broadway. When he got home, he jotted in his diary: 'Laurenda Francis (in slacks) dropped in during evening; I walked home with her (pushing her bicycle) & had coffee. She is very simple & charming.'[11] The following evening, and the evening after, the same notation occurred. Laurenda's recollection is somewhat different. She had been rehearsing for a play, and as she passed Daniells' office, he suddenly popped out like a jack-in-the-box. The following evening, he did so again, but as he had pushed her bicycle and walked her home, she invited him in to have coffee and to meet the family.

Laurenda's father, Charles Ross Francis, was an intelligent man with literary interests; Daniells liked him at once. Her mother, Mary Rhodes Francis, was astute and dignified. There were two boisterous younger brothers, Donald and Ross, and a dog, Carli – all contributed to the sense of family that he missed. Daniells felt welcomed. The family had an open-door policy with frequent visitors, and during the next month he contrived to arrive at their home in time for teas and dinners.

He discovered that her family was firmly rooted in Canadian history. On the Francis side was her great-great-grandfather, Alexander Ross, who had written *The Red River Settlement*, detailing the settlement's 'rise, progress and present state with some account of the native races and general history.'[12] His wife, Sally Ross, was the daughter of an Okanagan Indian chief whom he met when working in the Columbia area as a clerk with the Pacific Fur Company. One of their children, James, became a lawyer; later, he was a close associate of Louis Riel. Laurenda's mother and her family were from Lancashire, but when the woollen industry collapsed in 1912, her family emigrated to Calgary. One of the chief attractions for Daniells, besides Laurenda herself, was her family and their history. As she recalled, 'at that point Roy was really looking to be a Canadian rather than an Englishman.'[13]

Daniells received a rude shock on 28 June, Laurenda's twenty-first birthday, when he came to visit and found that she had received a ring from a soldier at the front. A few days later, when he and Laurenda took a walk on the railroad tracks, he exuberantly gathered her up in his arms and twirled her in a circle. Utterly astonished, she landed on her feet, but the normally sure-footed Daniells fell on the tracks, and skinned parts of his face.[14] On 7 July he left Winnipeg to spend the summer in Victoria, and did not see Laurenda again until the fall term. Then, at registration, she was the first person he saw. By Thanksgiving, he was again walking her home, and staying for tea or dinner with the family. During the next two months there are many diary references regarding shows, theatres, and museums, followed by the comments 'very nice,' 'very enjoyable,' 'very charming.' He was thoroughly enjoying himself. Laurenda was dark-haired, petite, and vivacious, a good companion with a highly developed sense of humour, sharp but not malicious. At first he was attracted to her personality and her conversation, then her sound values and perspicacity. After a month, he was aware of a familiar, overpowering emotion: 'Have fallen in love with Laurenda.'[15]

A week later, he decided to tell her. He had had lunch with her at the Bay's dining room, and they had walked back to his office, where 'she sat in the green chair with the white rattan frame and I told her I loved her and said I knew she would feel inclined to end things there. She looked at me and said something, I forget what, perhaps, "O dear!" ...'

> She said, Has anyone ever told you about me? And I said, No. She said she eloped [with Angus] ... when she was 19 ... Has hoped, she confessed, that he would fall in love with someone else.[16]

Daniells' diary entry elides some details, which testifies to his shock when Laurenda told him about Angus. To her parents' displeasure, Laurenda had begun dating Angus when she was still in high school. Subsequently, he asked for her parents' permission to marry Laurenda before he went overseas with his unit. They refused. But Angus found an Anglican minister to marry them the day before he left for boot camp. Their respective families were distressed, and, at her mother's insistence, Laurenda agreed to stay at home as if she were a single woman. Daniells was initially a father figure to Laurenda, 'a great relief after having my guard up for two years,' but Angus had been writing home telling Laurenda he had been seeing other women in England.[17] This upset her badly, and their correspondence had begun to cool.

Daniells asked her if she had thought of getting a divorce, but she did not think that would be right. He soon discovered that this astonishing young woman had great reserves of feeling balanced by common sense. She told Daniells that she had been worried about seeing him as he might take her further from reality: 'She had not made a friend for a long time, she said. I spoke long and seriously & I hope, decently. She agreed to go on as we are going.'[18] What this meant was that Daniells continued to call on the family. On Christmas Day he went to 'Laurenda's to take her some records (Bach & Hungarian Rhapsody). She in a white housecoat with pajamas and stockings slipping about her heels but amazingly feminine and altogether charming. I got my desired kiss; she offered it.'[19]

He had Christmas dinner with the Wheelers but saw a great deal of Laurenda until the New Year. Then he had another glimpse of Laurenda's capacity for genuine feeling: 'She spoke deeply and intimately of herself and the expression on her face changed at one point to simple human grief and uncertainty that seemed to reveal the depth within.'[20] Laurenda had begun to care for him and was honest in expressing both this affection and her sense of responsibility to her first love: 'In the kitchen, kisses of the most passionate attachment and the statement that whichever way she chooses she will cause unhappiness & be made unhappy.'[21] Several letters had arrived from her soldier stating his intention to set up a home with her on his next leave: she 'was reading these as I left & came out with me & walked a few score yards. The car came & I left her wide & grey eyed on the corner. Things like these it is that bind me to her so hopelessly.'[22]

For the first time in Daniells' emotional life, liking, respect, and deep emotion fused with passion: 'Wish we could sleep together now, but must wait.'[23] Both recognized that things were going too fast. Laurenda was about to write her graduate exams in social work; he was desperately overworked with setting and marking spring examinations. A series of steamy leave-takings was followed by an abrupt halt. 'L and I have decided passionate good-nights are too hard on the nerves at this time of year.'[24] Nonetheless, he had no doubts about her commitment.

In July 1945 Laurenda graduated, and the following week he joined her and her family at a holiday cottage. On their return, she became a social worker with the Children's Aid Society of Winnipeg, and he went back to the English Department. But the question of her youthful marriage had not yet been settled. As he told his parents, 'Laurenda's friend ... has not yet come back and I have no idea when he will, except that it will probably be before Christmas. So the matter will be decided one way or another fairly soon.'[25] When, in late November, a wire came saying that Angus was on his way home from war, 'L wept in the kitchen, after Mr. & Mrs. were in bed, was clearly much disturbed.'[26] Laurenda was conscious that she was violating all the social mores of the period, especially given the stigma against divorce. The whole situation was further complicated by the rectitude of the Francis family and the fact that, as 'a returned man,' Angus deserved more from the society he had fought to protect.[27]

The soldier finally did arrive at Sprague Street. In tragicomic fashion, Daniells arrived for dinner to find that Laurenda had taken to her bed and the young man was sitting beside her in a chair. Mrs Francis would not ask him for dinner, but Mr Francis brought him something to eat. Daniells, meanwhile, marked papers in Laurenda's room, while Ross, the younger brother, studied there. It was all very crowded, all very tense, and all very trying. After the young man left, Laurenda 'spoke sorrowfully ... and her tears rolled out.'[28] In the next few weeks, she grieved deeply, became exhausted, and lost weight.

But she soon took hold of the situation. As she explained (and he recorded), she and her young man might have made a go of it if things had been tackled differently. But she was willing to wait a while and see it through, rather than break off immediately and perhaps regret that she had been hasty. 'She said she thought things would come out all right for everybody.' She considered a divorce difficult, but thought their situation would level out by January and he 'had best not worry.' Daniells had discovered her remarkable strength of character. 'I may be mistaken, but it does look as if she intends to break off with Angus in the New Year. I am amazed at her kindness, her competence, her coolness.'[29]

Christmas Day was again spent at the Francises' home: 'Christmas Day. To L's and had some breakfast there. Great store of presents. I gave Mr. F. a leather cigarette case, Ross a flashlight, Mrs. F. a jug and some sachets, L a pin from Birks, Donnie a tie.' He also gave Laurenda, privately, 'four "Saxon" knives and four soup spoons' – they were beginning to collect silverware for their future. All this was followed by Christmas dinner at the Wheelers and an immediate departure with George Ford from English and Harry Steinhauer from the German Department for the MLA in Chicago.[30] There, following a paper by René Wellek, he presented a well-received paper on the Baroque, later published in the *University of Toronto Quarterly*.[31]

On 1 January 1946, Daniells declared his intentions: 'I asked if she would marry me, when all this present stress is over. She nodded she would.'[32] She was as open in her affection as the later Valentine's card she gave him: 'The story of my heart since I met you – Going, Going, Gone!' But she also intended to establish herself as a social worker, and put off their marriage for two years.

It was impossible to keep their courtship private, and as Laurenda attempted to keep their relation – and Winnipeg reactions – in balance, Daniells' feelings went up and down like a see-saw. Most of the time he recognized that they could have a happy life together; occasionally, he had second thoughts: 'Trying, painfully but not unsuccessfully, to disengage my mind from L and get ready to stand on my own feet when we break it up, – if we break it up ... Feeling pretty wretched.'[33]

That he was consciously attempting to record his symptoms and change his reactions both then and in the preceding year is apparent from a passage recorded in a special diary:

– Effort to stop tumult in brain: imaginary axes splitting head from all directions; flames from level of eyes upwards consuming the brain; oneself as very small indeed, an infinitesimal seed, too minute to suffer, to feel pressure of millstones upon one.

– Good effect of reading, during June 1945, *The Varieties of Temperament* by Sheldon and Stevens, especially their discussion of the cerebrotonic type.[34]

The cerebrotonic personality was characterized by internal tension, mental intensity, and the substitution of thought for direct action. Such a person is overly responsive psychologically, subject to fatigue, is secretive, and dislikes large social gatherings.[35] This is pre-eminently the sensitive scholar or artist. Because Daniells felt that he fitted this classification, he recognized a need to change his behaviour. After first reading Sheldon and Stevens, and again a year later in June 1946, Daniells renewed his earlier affirmation to 'sit among the dandelions, and let go,' to cease worrying for a year, and to try to be happy: 'to give Laurenda joy.'[36]

Making both himself and Laurenda happy meant establishing a new life together, away from Winnipeg. By the spring of 1946, Daniells had started negotiating with UBC president Norman MacKenzie for a position in the English Department. He had tried for a position there before, in 1940, when his old mentor and friend Ira Dilworth had left the department.[37] There was no position then available, but in early March 1946, the new UBC president, MacKenzie, had approached Daniells in Winnipeg to ask his advice on hiring for the English Department. In response, Daniells recommended Desmond Pacey and Earle Birney, describing both as 'temperamentally a bit difficult but they have unusual energy and intellectual vigour.' He asked if he might also be considered for a position, as the ultimate shape of the English Department interested him. He thought that 'extraordinary results can be achieved by quite ordinary means and within the limits of ordinary budgets.'[38] Daniells was obviously closely in touch with Birney, who wrote thanking him for suggesting his name to MacKenzie, and adding, 'I hope very much that he gives you an offer. It would be grand for U.B.C.'[39]

Daniells also wrote to Sedgewick. It was a difficult letter, and he admitted destroying his first four attempts. In the end, he wrote a brief note providing the names of possible references and saying: '... if there is a chance of my returning to U.B.C., on any reasonable terms, I should be very grateful. Father is now very old and unwell. It will not be long before I must provide a home for my mother which is very difficult in this lethal climate.'[40]

Both MacKenzie and Sedgewick replied the same day, Sedgewick writing twice. In his first letter, he quipped: 'If I had any good teeth left (which I haven't), I would gladly give them up in order to have you at U.B.C. (I *might* even lay my Dentures – Geez! – on the altar).' He told Daniells the university would need junior instructors for the 'locust swarms' of returning war veterans. The university was pressed for money, but Sedgewick promised to put forward Daniells' case. He closed by saying that he did not need references: 'Good wine needs no bush, as you may have heard.'[41]

While Sedgewick was writing this letter, MacKenzie was dictating one of his own. He told Daniells that he already had him in mind for the department at UBC, but that he had postponed discussion until the retirement of the senior members of staff (clearly Sedgewick) took place.[42] However, after MacKenzie and Sedgewick conferred later that day, Sedgewick wrote a second letter: 'Put bluntly & unofficially, & strictly Sedgewickedly ... how little will you come for?' He and the president realized that Daniells could not take anything less than a full professorship: '*How* Full do *you* think the Professorship should be? *Our* Minimum Fullness is Four Thousand Bucks *per annum*.' If President MacKenzie could meet Daniells' terms, he would offer him a position. What exactly did Daniells expect?

As far as Sedgewick himself was concerned, he wanted Daniells: 'the holy saints & angels know how much I should admire to have you as support for me in my brief span remaining of academic life. As usual, you see, I keep Number One close in view: in fact I huggle him to my bosom.' The workload, he said, would be heavy: four hours a week of first-year English; three hours a week for about ten weeks of second-year English, which had an enrolment of over one thousand; and three hours a week of an upper-division class. Sedgewick closed: 'Of course you had better remember Dante's inscription over the Infernal Gate. Ah well, I am *not yet* Abandoning Hope, tho' inside the gate.'[43]

On 20 March, Daniells received another letter from Birney, who had a firm offer from UBC: 'I am in your debt for giving MacKenzie my name; it is the only rank, and almost the only University, I was interested in. The CBC is trying hard to keep me ... but I know that an academic job is the only one that will give me the spare summer-time for writing.'[44] This fact may have prompted Daniells to telephone Sedgewick, who told him 'he had me in mind to succeed him, & would ask MacKenzie for $4400 for me this coming year. President MacKenzie then wrote to say that the board of governors had approved a permanent appointment for him.[45]

Daniells immediately contacted Albert Trueman, the newly appointed president at Manitoba, and asked Laurenda Francis for her opinion: 'As I see it, the offer from UBC merits very careful consideration, especially if I do not wish to stay in Winnipeg all my life and *do* wish to stay in Canada.' Nonetheless, he gave her freedom to decide upon their joint future: '... everything depends on what *you* want ...' He anticipated that if he went to UBC for 1946–7, they could join up again in the summer. 'If, however, Sweetheart, you have any doubt as to whether you can stand periods of separation, I shall stay here.'[46]

In fact, Laurenda was in complete agreement with his plan to move to British Columbia; she knew she would miss her family, but, like Daniells, her 'sea of adventure' was behind – she intended to divorce Angus, and she was willing to settle down wherever Daniells' work required. On 1 April he telegraphed President MacKenzie saying that he would be happy to accept his offer if it was a safe assumption that the UBC board would in due course approve Sedgewick's recommendation for Daniells as his successor.

Daniells' reply alarmed MacKenzie. He replied that the board could not state that an individual would be made head of a department at some future date.[47] Sedgewick was also troubled by the telegram, and explained that the headship would be vacant in the next year or two, and that Daniells would be his choice as successor, but he could not guarantee it.[48] Daniells, in turn, was rattled; he was leaving a secure position as head of English at Manitoba for a mere professorship at UBC with no assurance of a future headship. However, after a long telephone conversation with Sedgewick, he accepted the position.

E.K. Brown sent Daniells his warm congratulations. Daniells was returning to B.C., where, in a very short time, he would lead 'the best undergraduate department in the country on its record, and with the chance to do what you think wise to make it a good graduate department too.' He reminded Daniells that between the two of them they had 'pulled the Manitoba department right out of its slump, and the lion was you and not me, for you had the more difficult part of the job by far.'[49] Birney also sent congratulations: 'I am more pleased than I can say that you, too, are coming to Acadia [university residence] this fall.'[50]

Daniells now began to look for a replacement for himself at the U of

M. His old friend William Robbins was a possibility, as was a new senior faculty member, John Watkins, who had described Daniells' departure as a '*disaster*.' Meanwhile, several members of the faculty wrote a letter to President Trueman pointing out that Daniells had consistently stood for the highest values of scholarship, tact, and kindness and had built up a high sense of loyalty in the English Department. His loss would be felt deeply. As his possible successor, they put forward Dr Wheeler, the senior member of the department.[51]

Daniells then wrote to President Trueman supporting Wheeler, not as a candidate for the headship, but for full professorship on the grounds of a long record of faithful service to the university. Wheeler (also recognizing that his promotion could not be justified on academic grounds) wrote Daniells that his comments to the president had been 'generous and dexterous. It reminded me of your nimble footedness over "rocks and stones and trees" at Sooke and the Lake ... Whatever happens I will try to make the prophecy come true.'[52] In the end, however, none of Daniells' preferred candidates came to Manitoba. Robbins, who had moved to UBC, had been offered a raise in salary and decided to stay there.[53] And Northrop Frye, a second candidate, described a similar process. His head at Victoria College went to the board of regents: 'They raised me to Associate Professor and jumped my salary to the point it normally would have been at in about three years ... So your kind intentions regarding me met with complete fulfillment, and I have a great deal to thank you for in consequence.'[54]

In June, with the president's encouragement, Daniells had telegraphed A.J.M. Smith to inquire whether he was interested in the headship.[55] Daniells knew that although Smith had been teaching at Michigan State for some time (where he was comfortably established with a salary of $4,500, congenial colleagues, and upper-level courses), his academic interests were Canadian.[56] 'I am keen on having you come here [to Manitoba] ... if you are to continue as an interpreter of Canadian culture, you should live for a time in this region and preferably in this city ... unless you do acquire some first hand knowledge of the best that is thought and known between the Rockies and the Canadian Shield, your critical approaches to Canadian letters will be forever somewhat mutilated and incomplete.'[57] This was a fair judgment; Smith's later work suffered from his distance from Canada. Nonetheless, by mid-August, Smith had determined to stay on at Michigan.[58] For a temporary replacement, Daniells then spoke to Wheeler, who, as he wrote to

President Trueman, was 'willing to step in for the session 1946–47 and will undoubtedly, as always, put his best into the job.'[59]

For the first time, the hitherto most important people in Daniells' life, his parents, learned of his new appointment at UBC, not through him, but through a friend. He apologized, but excused himself on the grounds that he did not feel he should speak about it because there might be misunderstandings at both Manitoba and Vancouver. He said he was 'going to U.B.C. at less money than I should be getting here – six hundred dollars to be exact. But that is only a fraction of the total pattern. Over a period of years I expect to make as much at U.B.C. as here and the initial loss is not so important. There are other factors: locale, type of work, board of governors in each place, climate, etc. etc.'[60] The fact was that he had determined that he must leave Winnipeg. He had reached a point in his emotional and professional life where he knew he had to make a clean start. Yet because he was consciously breaking ties, he no longer wrote to his family so openly as he had in the past. His deepest confidences had been shared with Carson and Kay Mark until they left for Los Alamos in 1945, and then after 1946 with Laurenda Francis.

PART FOUR

University of British Columbia: 1946–1960

Chapter Fourteen

Anatomy of a Department

Daniells arrived in Vancouver in early August 1946. The UBC department he was joining was, in effect, a teaching department, characterized as such by Birney a year later when he attempted to persuade a friend to apply: 'You would find some likeable people in the dept. and the general age level agreeably below fifty ... I think you would like an atmosphere where nobody expects you to grind out books so long as you seem to be a competent teacher. You would probably have about 8 hours a week with quite a lot of essays to mark.' At this point, Birney thought that Sedgewick and Daniells were alike in that neither was too puritanical in H.L. Mencken's nay-saying sense: '... we haven't had much trouble with Puritans in these parts so far, and Sedgewick himself is a liberal soul, as well as a brilliant teacher. His likely successor is similar, and a good friend of mine.'[1]

Reflecting its origins as a service department, the UBC English Department was staffed by many former high school and college teachers. Full professors included Sedgewick, W.L. MacDonald, Frederic Wood, Thorleif Larsen, Dorothy Mawdsley (also dean of women), Birney, and Daniells. The acknowledged scholars were Sedgewick and Larsen, both members of the Royal Society of Canada.[2] Only Sedgewick, Birney, Daniells, MacDonald, and Mawdsley had Ph.D.'s. In his quiet way, Larsen had remained the most significant scholarly force in the department, guiding younger individuals in their work: learned and patient, he loved literature and believed that poetry could liberate the mind.[3]

In the associate professor rank, Dorothy Blakey-Smith, Edmund Morrison, William Robbins, and R.E. Watters had, or were acquiring, a Ph.D. Of the assistant professors, G.P.V. Akrigg and M.W. Steinberg had Ph.D.'s, and John Grant and R.C. Cragg would obtain theirs by 1950.

There were also a number of lecturers, most with B.A.'s or M.A.'s, including Edna Baxter, also a former schoolteacher. In all there were twenty-two full-time faculty and forty-three persons in the English Department to meet the challenge of teaching huge classes of returning veterans.

Very little had changed in the department curriculum since Daniells had been a student in the late 1920s. The department offered first-year students two hours in English 100, a general course in literary genres, and two hours in English 101, a course in composition. Second-year students took English 200, a survey course, from the beginning to the Romantics. Third- and fourth-year students were offered a choice of courses ranging from Shakespeare to 'English Literature of the American Continent,' which included some Canadian writing. But the offerings were ad hoc, and the whole curriculum badly needed restructuring.

Moreover, the faculty possessed widely divergent qualifications, and the department was top-heavy with 'political' appointments. In 1947–8, just before his retirement, Sedgewick promoted Robbins and Morrison to full professor, while President MacKenzie, who had appointed an old friend Stanley Read to the English Department, also parachuted into the department his personal assistant, Geoffrey Andrew. By 1954 Andrew, who had earned a B.A. in history, was a dean while still functioning as a full professor in English.[4]

The two newcomers to this group were Daniells and Birney. Birney, briefly an assistant professor at Toronto, had now been raised two steps to full professor. His promotion was not for academic reasons but based on the fact that he had enlisted, and war regulations specified that a man ought not to fall behind in his field because of war service. President MacKenzie also liked having a popular poet in the department, and *David and Other Poems* (1940) had secured Birney a national reputation. Daniells, in contrast, had been a full professor and head of a department for almost a decade .

Daniells was also to inherit a department and a university which, by today's standards, had a 'chilly climate' for women, a climate which undoubtedly shaped some of his own actions. The old seminary model of the professor as priest with a young male scholar as his acolyte had persisted into the late forties and fifties. Daniells had been the grateful recipient of the kindness of Malcolm Wallace, E.K. Brown, and Herbert Davis, but there were few or no corresponding mentors for women. The rhetoric of the day still referred to the university as 'a man's university,' and in the English Department, as in no other UBC department, introductory classes were segregated by gender until 1941.[5] Blakey-Smith, like Mawdsley, had been hired to teach the all-female sections of the introductory courses. This division was different from usual practice and reflected Sedgewick's desire to teach only bright young men.[6] A forties woman graduate later said that once a woman had proven herself, Sedgewick treated her as a person.[7] However, this sexist hurdle did mean that the woman student or professor in English at UBC operated under a systemic handicap.

When Daniells arrived at Garnett Sedgewick's 'court' in 1946, the head was an absolute monarch with a half-dozen dukes or full professors. Sedgewick had an affable, joking manner with his faculty. A short man who always wore a bow tie, he tended to be puckish in manner and speech and was still best known for his Shakespeare classes. Sedgewick, like Kittredge, still declaimed the great Shakespearean dramas, striding the podium of the lecture hall, his gown flying, becoming in turn an Othello, an Iago, an Ophelia.

During this period, the personality of the head determined the nature of the department, and Daniells now saw Sedgewick much more clearly than when he was a student. He was 'a small man with a large head, not deformed, but oddly shaped. He hailed from the Maritimes. He was a homosexual and like many bachelors with that tendency (overt or covert) he had a mother who lived to be about a hundred. He entertained us and made us his friends.'[8] Even when Sedgewick was autocratic, his students and faculty accepted his judgments without a murmur, partly because many recognized good will under his strictures, partly because he had taught or hired all of his colleagues, and partly because the thirties and forties were difficult times for professors of English. UBC had nearly shut down during the Depression, and there were stringent financial restrictions as a result of the war years. Faculty members had good reason to fear for their jobs. Thus no English Department member would contradict Sedgewick.

Daniells and Robbins fared no better. In the summer of 1947, Daniells had been asked to set the summer supplemental exams for students who had failed their course. After doing so, he left for Victoria to spend some time with his family. On 8 September he received an urgent letter from Robbins describing a 'typical bit of Sedgewickery': 'He just blew up in a taxi with all the second year supps for you to mark, and was amazed that you weren't here, what with the Registrar's office howling for the marks.' As Robbins explained, he had told Sedgewick that Daniells was in Victoria, and that someone else could mark the exams. Sedgewick had tried to recruit Robbins, but he was busy with other marking. Robbins continued: '... the upshot is that you are to mark them, with what help you can get.'

Robbins was also annoyed that Sedgewick had considered the exam too difficult for the students: 'He marked one himself, giving 75/150 to (he says) a paper deserving only 40/150. Does that mean people writing supps are all mercy cases? That we failed too many in the Spring? That a "hard" paper means automatically doubled grades? I give up.'[9] What was most aggravating to the two men was the combination of Sedgewick's absolute power with his disregard for the wishes of other members of faculty.

Daniells soon discovered (and this was not unusual during this period), that Sedgewick considered English a personal fiefdom, instructing Walter Gage, of the registrar's office, to scan the list of incoming students and 'cream off' the brightest young men for his own classes. F.W. Watt, then a freshman, recalls Sedgewick, entering the class, peering over the top of his spectacles and pronouncing: 'This may be the cream of the cream ... but it looks pretty sour to me.' Sedgewick announced the course requirements, the reading list, and the expectations for the final exam. Then he said: '"I'm not doing any of *that*. That's *your* responsibility. *This* is the book I want you to buy (an anthology of his choice). This is the book we're going to be using." And he was true to his word. He totally ignored the curriculum.' Watt, who later became a professor and an administrator, reflected on how far this behaviour was 'from the sense of responsibility of a Head like Woodhouse, who spent hours and years of his life building and fortifying the formal academic structures of English studies ... clearly thought out and hammered into permanent forms that nobody, least of all the Head, could decline to follow without awareness of sin or heresy, subversion or anarchy.'[10]

In his classes on Chaucer and Shakespeare, again like Kittredge, Sedgewick shut the classroom door at 9:30 sharp. A student, late for class, once opened the back door and was tip-toeing towards an empty seat when Sedgewick boomed, 'Enter the Bastard,' the stage directions from the Shakespearean play they were reading.[11] It was common for students to refer to English 409 as 'the course in Sedgewick' rather than Shakespeare because of the personal element in the lectures. Daniells recalled that Sedgewick would talk about himself, about his mother and how badly she treated him, and about centres of learning he had known at Harvard, Berkeley, and Chicago: '... this discourse he would vary by long sessions of bullying some innocent football-player, some chosen victim who would be verbally pilloried for his shortcomings (real or imagined) whose deficiencies were slowly canvassed with sadistic joy.'[12]

Some students, however, enjoyed Sedgewick's antics. Watt recalls that those sitting in the front row were frequently 'taken aback by his habit of seizing you by the ears and bumping his huge forehead against yours – he was so short that standing he met the sitter's face at the right level – while he intoned ... on the subject of your bottomless ignorance and intellectual laziness ... But I have to say that in my class everyone seemed to enjoy these bizarre moments, even the unfortunate center of attention, usually some big, red-faced, gangling young man with a sheepish grin from ear to ear after release, rather proud of his supporting actor's turn.'[13]

Bullying students, especially athletes, is reminiscent of the athlete/aesthete conflicts at Oxford University. But for some, such as the returning veterans, these antics were not so amusing.[14] Sedgewick himself, on the eve of a term in 1948, recognized this. He would be facing classes of forty to fifty of the 'awe-struck multitude for the 31st time.' Although he was unhappy about the class sizes, and although he sensed that the old methods no longer worked, 'I just can't & won't try to, change my old methods: I'm too old to learn new tricks.'[15]

For Daniells, department meetings were another potential source of conflict. At Manitoba they had become exchanges of opinion directed towards academic policy, although Daniells reserved the right to make final decisions. At UBC, however, Sedgewick decided such issues and informed the department. Most of the department 'knew enough about his methods to realize that he had sought many opinions before reaching his own ... the tension centred on his relationship with the Senior Committee, who ... chafed at being ignored in meetings.'[16] The UBC structure nominally recognized that senior professors in all departments should contribute to policy decisions. But Sedgewick, a founding professor, ignored this. For him, department meetings were for the purposes of grade reports and the rubber stamping of texts for the coming session. Morrison, an established member of the department in 1946, recalls 'it was a fine department':

We used to have meetings, and Sedgewick [would] bustle in late and flutter around, and would say, 'Well, we've got to choose a Freshman book, a book for the Freshman.' Well, we'd either choose it then or we'd defer the choice. And then we would say, 'Well, what will we do in the course, the Freshman course, what will we do?' And someone would say, 'Well, we'll do what we did last year.' 'Fine. We'll do that.' End of the meeting.[17]

Daniells was appalled. As he explained to Pacey, after his nine years at Manitoba the situation at UBC astounded him: 'No committee meeting in the Department beyond the most mechanical & perfunctory gatherings to distribute papers & such. Courses regarded as private preserves so that no one in the Department knows or need care what anyone else teaches.'[18] As an experienced head, he understood how relations between the head and the faculty should be conducted. But as a new member of the department and Sedgewick's successor, he had to bite his tongue, teach his huge classes, and mark endless papers until two and three in the morning.

When he started in 1946, Daniells was assigned a large section of English 100, consisting mainly of veterans, given a share in the lectures for the survey course, English 200, and also a third-year seventeenth-century course. In addition to this full load, he was assigned the Romantics. He soon gained a reputation as a fine teacher. One of the freshmen recalls Daniells as an 'interactive teacher': '... in the slowest and shyest of classes he would eventually find at least one student who could produce and volunteer at least one word to begin to describe some literary reality he was talking about. That one word, however frail, he would pounce on as a choice specimen and proudly write down in bold letters on the board. Fifteen minutes later the huge blank board would be full of words, and the classroom humming with raised hands and words called out for Daniells to cram into corners, and extend into further and further comments, and amplifications and refinements. Those were classes alive in the work and loving it and caught up in the process of learning.'[19]

One of the student veterans in the 200-odd second-year English survey class, Jan de Bruyn, later a professor at UBC, remembers that the course was taught by a group of professors who moved from class to class teaching a section of literary history. On the day Daniells was to take over, the room was overrun with students from his former class: '... they were everywhere – on the stairs, on the floor between the podium, on the podium itself, draped over radiators, standing in every available space and not a seat was empty.'[20] An evicted student still remembers Daniells' response: 'I'm sorry, this is just impossible. I shall come back in twenty minutes and I want to see nobody in this classroom who is standing, or sitting on the steps ... a lot of you will have to leave.'[21] Two weeks into the teaching term, Daniells discovered that the syllabus for English 200 was 'too heavy to cover.'[22] The curriculum, the procedures, the administration all cried out for change, but he had no power to effect it. As a result, his diary is peppered with exclamations of dismay and anger: 'Feeling very much wrought up over Garnett's autocratic methods.'[23]

At the turn of the year, he reported to Laurenda Francis that he was attempting to 'steer between an oily subservience to Sedgewick and a brusque & critical independence. Luckily I like him immensely & I *think* he likes me so things even out. But next week I am to present a report calling for the revision of II year English (15 years overdue), & I look forward with mingled feelings.'[24] However, Sedgewick blandly ignored the report. The following term, at the start of 1947, Daniells again consulted Sedgewick about his report. Still no response: 'Depressing interview with G.G.S. who will keep to the status quo in English #200.'[25] Then, arbitrarily, Sedgewick changed his mind and announced the changes. Throughout all of these ups and downs Laurenda commiserated: 'I am glad to hear that Mr. Sedgewick came round to your reforms. His method of expressing a lack of interest in change and then suddenly embodying a good many of them sounds rather frustrating. However I guess he is probably feeling rather insecure and feels he must assert his authority.'[26]

Sedgewick knew that reform was necessary, but reform implied there was something wrong with his procedures. Thus he see-sawed back and forth between acceptance and rejection, taking pleasure in tripping up his would-be successor. In early November 1947, Sedgewick wrote to his friends and former students Bob and Ruth apRoberts: 'The week has passed without much excitement of unusual sorts. There promised to be a bit of flurry about the English 2 exam, Roy Daniells having a bee in his bonnet, but the bee flew off or stopped buzzing under the Head's soothing (but firm) hand. *Après moi, le déluge?* I feel as egoistic as Louis xv, looking forward to my retirement next May.'[27] Sedgewick liked manipulating Daniells. There was a degree of malice as well as mischief in his character, and he was aware that the department, long checked, might well rebel after his retirement.

Daniells understood much of this, but could not detach himself emotionally, be pragmatic, and leave the department behind at the end of the day. Nor could he fight back directly. As a result, his first year at UBC was difficult. Birney, an astute judge of character, later pinpointed his character precisely when he commented in relation to another matter that 'aggressive malice is not in [Daniells'] nature ... he has a great capacity for innocence'[28] While Daniells expected to be appointed head of the department, he knew it depended on Sedgewick's fluctuating approval, the dean's recommendation, the president's concurrence, and ratification by the board of governors. Consequently, he could urge change, but he could not afford to rock the boat.

As he went about his teaching, he continued to assess the department. In May 1947, rereading his seventeenth-century course outline, he told Laurenda it was 'really an impassioned defence of my way of teaching the century as against the poor way we have to teach it here.'[29] They had been apart for over a year by December 1947, and the combination of missing her and continuous marking and stress had taken its toll: 'Papers, papers, papers ... Everyone's pretty nervous and on edge with the strain of marking for 8000 people. Our system in English of asking innumerable small points, marked separately, is not only bad pedagogically but hard on the marker.'[30] He continued to be angry at Sedgewick: 'I am sorry to be so tired and dull. All today I've been filled with a sense of annoyance and grief over Sedgewick's inexcusable egotism and dictatorial mismanagement of things. But that will end, too.'[31]

Daniells also saw that the big problem for English departments across Canada in the post-war period would be financial. Birney, for example, who was living with his wife, Esther, and new son, Bill, in army housing at Acadia Camp, was having trouble living on his salary. Daniells saw no relief in sight. As he told Laurenda in 1946, 'it means – à propos of running English Departments – that whereas a few years ago you could get a person like Chester [Duncan] for 1500 or 1800 and hold out the hope of say 3000 as a prize if he was a good fellow and got on with his graduate work, now you can't hold out any prizes ... And how to induce the younger ones to do anything if you haven't any inducements of a financial nature I don't quite see.'

In late 1947 Daniells took stock, recognizing that being head of the English Department at UBC would be full of contradictions for him: 'a financial gain, but how much I am not sure; a gain in capacity to get reforms made and new ideas tried out; a loss in that it would absorb a great deal of my time & energy (I can't do the grand seigneur as G.G.S. does); & so on & so on.'[32] He understood that by accepting a position as head at Manitoba, he had lost his chance to become a productive scholar and became instead an administrator. But chance, favour, and his own ability had slotted him into the role of head. And he had acquired a facility for administration as well as a taste for power and prestige. Daniells fulfilled the expectations for department head very well. He understood what an English curriculum ought to be; he had the academic contacts to build up a strong department; and he had the wit and social polish to carry off the public role of a head with distinction. What he lacked, as Sedgewick had earlier noted, was the ability to suffer fools. Instead of allowing his difficult colleagues a long rope, Daniells tended to pull them up short and bluntly disagree with them. This became a problem because he was inheriting a department that was already chafing at the bit for more autonomy.

Nonetheless, the intelligence, wit, and urbanity which made Daniells a fine English professor also made him a welcome guest at dinners and parties. The university world extended into the city's cultural and business circles, and he soon met prominent Vancouverites: H.R. MacMillan, the lumber baron, Dal Grauer, later chairman of B.C. Electric, and a host of other notables, including several judges and a 'Mr. Corning' of Alaska White Pine.[33] This was Walter Koerner, the noted philanthropist, who became a friend. He had an immediate entrée into art circles because of his earlier friendships with Jack Shadbolt and Lawren Harris. He was especially pleased to be invited to Harris's home with its elegant appointments: 'e.g. large fragile-looking white tulips in a room predominantly cream, buff & gold.'[34] He and Shadbolt frequently visited Mabel Mackenzie, an old friend from Victoria who was close to Max Maynard. On one of these visits, all three made papier mâché models of their heads: the effect, rather like death masks, was eerie.

In 1947 Harris, Shadbolt, and Daniells gave a series of lectures at the Vancouver Art Gallery in which Daniells spoke on 'The Gothic, the Baroque, and the Metaphysicals.' In the next few years, he gave innumerable talks on radio and in person on poetry, education, and art, introducing himself to Vancouver audiences. Most of his friends, however, were at the university. Aside from Walter Gage (an old friend from Victoria), who often dropped by for a chat, and members of the department such as the Birneys, the Robbinses, and the Reads, he regularly visited the Volkoffs. George Volkoff was a brilliant young physicist who later became dean of science. He and his wife, Olga, have warm memories of Daniells sitting down on the floor and playing with their two-year-old daughter, Elizabeth.[35] After Daniells' marriage, the Volkoffs became part of a close-knit group of friends who included the Skerls and the Mackedies, all families living in the campus neighbourhood.

Daniells was now well situated at a university concerned with social and cultural issues. He was soon invited to join the advisory board of the Civil Liberties Association, of which Sedgewick was honorary chairman and Duncan Macnair, Dorothy Livesay's husband, executive secretary. One of the group's first acts was to support repeal of the Chinese Immigration Act, passed in 1923, which discriminated against Vancouver's Chinese.[36] Then, in 1947, President MacKenzie was appointed to the Massey Commission, the Royal Commission on National Development in the Arts, Letters and Sciences. There, under the rubric of encouraging Canadian culture, MacKenzie helped direct government funding towards Canadian universities. The larger recommendations of this commission were to make possible many of the academic projects with which Daniells was to be associated in the next two decades.

From the summer of 1946 to the spring of 1948, while Daniells continued to size up the UBC English Department, he was also attempting to assess what he saw as his own 'neuroses.' He had become aware of the close connections between creativity and neurosis; in 1946 he sent Laurenda one of Dostoyevsky's novels with an introduction by Thomas Mann stressing this connection. Ironically, the sensitivity and introspection that complicated his personal and academic life were also the qualities that made him an inspiring teacher and generated his poetry and prose. In these qualities, Daniells had affiliations with the archetypal poet of the period – the suffering narrator of Rilke's *Duino Elegies* and Eliot's 'Prufrock.'

As Daniells recognized, the cause of his extreme sensitivity was religious trauma. At the end of his first session at UBC in June 1947, he attempted to record his most immediate worry, the old deep-seated fear that he considered the source of his neurosis:

Manifestation: fear of committing the unpardonable sin by saying that Jesus had a demon. This is so powerful that it still stops my breath, paralyzes me with fear, inhibits action, induces the drug of dreamings. Cause: probably deep down and far back perhaps a hatred of Father, his power and authority as husband of Mother and as my parent; perhaps a hatred of Jehovah, felt as a tyrannical god who would not save me or give me peace.[37]

But the struggles that had made life so bitter in the past, the fight to make a living, the search for sexual tenderness and response, were no longer so pressing. The job at UBC and Laurenda's promise to marry him had taken the edge off these fears. He decided that when familiar fears arose, he would relax and 'trust God that it is all right for me to go on with what I am doing, knowing that all this is a neurosis out of my control, and that God can take care of it all.'[38] He considered psychoanalysis, but ultimately decided against it in favour of reading psychological literature and talking with friends.

That the agent of these doubts and fears had been his father was a fact that surfaced in mid-January 1948: 'I dreamed recently that I was with Father & went up to him in a very straight line and said that we always disagreed when we were together for a few minutes. This brings out my very deep-seated fear & dislike of parental authority and teaching.'[39] He had been working up to this discovery for over a year. Early in 1947 he had visited Robbins, an agnostic, and discussed his 'religious terrors' with him. To Laurenda he wrote: 'That night I thought over all he had said and determined to free my mind as much as I could from all inhibition and especially from the fears and restrictions of my Plymouth Brethren–dominated childhood. I succeeded all too well in releasing my subconscious mind into innocent unrestraint. In the morning, to my *horror*, I had wet the bed, like a very innocent child indeed! I told Birney, who was much amused. He thinks I shall wake up some morning in the bureau drawer, a step *farther* back'[40] – presumably as an infant. Robbins and Birney were pragmatists and unsympathetic to such issues.

The following month, he chanced upon an article discussing some letters of John Ruskin and his marriage to Effie Gray, who left him for the painter Millais because Ruskin had not consummated their marriage. Later, when Ruskin fell in love with another young woman, her family contacted the former Mrs Ruskin. Her explanation of the breakdown in their marriage revealed to Daniells, as he told Laurenda, the essence of Ruskin's abnormality: 'his excessive and too long continued devotion to his parents and (I suspect) to religious and moral concepts which they had implanted in him as a child. As one L.F. often says, "Very interesting."'[41]

Laurenda Francis, who had not seen the article, shrewdly followed his argument to conclusion. As Daniells' interpretation of Ruskin's breakdown was influenced, in part, by his identification with him, she wondered whether his own behaviour was motivated by his relationship with his parents. She put the issue tactfully, as a question: the fact that Ruskin found it impossible to reject his parents' principles proved 'that their neurotic hold over him must have been tremendous ...?' But, if Ruskin 'rejected the religion & morals of his father, he is rejecting his father, a thing he is afraid to do, because his father in teaching him fear of God and of breaking moral codes has managed to teach him fear of the world & he has only his father to protect him.'[42] Laurenda recognized that in Daniells' belief structure his father had coalesced with the cruel Jehovah. She asked: 'I often wonder how much of your feelings against religion is really that, and how much it is a feeling ... against the person you associate with the religion that you hate.'[43]

Daniells conceded: 'Your remark about my resentment against such forms of religion being only a form of a family resentment is an intriguing one.'[44] Ultimately, however, he saw that his love for her had overcome the psychological fears that had blocked his earlier relationships. 'Sweetheart, I don't know *how much* I love you because I've never got to the bottom of it. But a great deal: so much – and you will understand what this means – that I who have transferred the original terror of religion to so much else in life, *am not in the least afraid of getting married.* I can't pay you any higher tribute nor say in any clearer way how much I love you.'[45]

There was other good news. In March 1948 he wrote her to say that he was nearly finished a manuscript of poems, which included a reference to their life together: 'Escape into our refuge of green hope, / The forest wild, the fortress heart of life.' He added, 'The "our" is yours and mine. The wedding occupies some two lines, being buried in the welter of public affairs as all weddings of thinking people are bound to be now.'[46]

Earlier, in 1947, the couple were making plans for her to move to Vancouver, where they would finally be able to marry and set up their own home. Laurenda Francis's divorce had been finalized on 11 January 1947. The Winnipeg papers printed divorce news and people were talking, but she hoped to maintain their privacy: 'I have led all my friends to believe that things are pretty well all off between us. Of course, the family can hardly be led to believe that we are separated forever, in view of the fact that I get mail practically every day from you.'[47]

In January 1947 Daniells wrote to say that he had had an important dream about their lives together:

> We were in a canoe. I was paddling ... We were moving so as to be in line with one boat in which were Ogden and (possibly) Birney ... I brought the canoe round so as to be at the head of one of the long open lanes ... An outstretched oar from a boat almost caught me across the neck, but I avoided it ... You called out to warn me of breakers or rocks ... Now, as we ran into these breakers or rocks I said twice, 'I can't see a thing.' I was, it became clear, quite blind though not painfully or distressingly so. We tumbled on a shore. My sight was suddenly and completely restored. We were out of the canoe, dripping wet, climbing obliquely a grassy hill.[48]

It is a complex dream, full of Freudian symbolism, but the import is clear. Ogden and Birney had already embarked on the 'sea' of matrimony, and Daniells, although blind in his dream, trusted Laurenda's direction and no longer feared sexual love.

Nonetheless, in the spring of 1947 a wedding date had not been fixed. At this point Laurenda's father providentially suggested a camping trip to British Columbia. The Francis family arrived in Vancouver on 9 August 1947, and the two lovers found a little time to make plans. On 14 August, Daniells took the Francises to Vancouver Island to meet his family in Victoria. There Mrs Daniells provided tea in the garden and the visit went well. That night Daniells told his mother 'about L & our plans for next year.'[49]

When the party returned to Vancouver, Daniells formally told Mr Francis that the couple expected to be married the next summer. After courting so many young women and backing off, Daniells was finally ready to marry. Laurenda Francis was an exceptional woman. It was not just that she was attractive with an uproarious sense of humour, it was also her fortitude and her sense of family, combined with a generous understanding of his nature.

His parents were overjoyed with the news. When he was considering buying a house in Vancouver, his father told him, 'I think I'll pack up my tools & come over and build you a house.' It was not a realistic offer since his father was now old and frail, but after so many years of difficulties between them over the Plymouth Brethren, the gesture meant a great deal. As he told Laurenda, 'I could have burst into tears, I don't know why.'[50]

⎯⎯➤•◀⎯⎯

January 1948 brought to Daniells 'one of the strangest few weeks in my life. Four things (*not* in order of importance) that I have wanted very badly and for a *very* long time are becoming almost daily more concrete and definite, and *simultaneously* so.' Laurenda Francis was coming to Vancouver as his wife; the headship of the department had been settled; it seemed that he might be able to buy a house (it did not work out); and he was about to have a book of poetry published. But of these, only Laurenda really mattered: 'I suppose a year from today the book will be forgotten ... and the headship will turn out to be a headache ... [but] I have no fear of your losing your sweetness of disposition.'[51]

They had decided to marry on 29 May 1948. The wedding was to be announced just a day or so ahead, and the ceremony kept mostly to the Francis family. In March, Daniells bought Laurenda a fine sapphire, and a month later she bought 'a dress to be married in ... plain and very nice sort of a blue.' Her mother, she wrote Daniells, was 'having the time of her life planning all the details. A kitchen to be painted, a room to be decorated. A *cake* (I never thought of it) to be made ... I am overwhelmed with all this. As far as I am concerned it could be tomorrow and I would be ready and willing to go ahead.'[52]

Daniells was also dealing with practical arrangements. In early May he wrote to say: 'I've got plane reservations for the 29th at 5:30. "Name," said he over the phone. "Daniells," I said. "Mr. and Mrs. Daniells?" he said. "Yes" I said.' After so many years of waiting for this moment, he could not believe it was happening. 'That we are actually going to be married is, of course, a myth. A very beautiful one, but a myth nevertheless. I can't bring myself to believe that we are actually going to be living together ... It's too good to be true.'[53]

On 23 May, Daniells arrived in Winnipeg and spent the next few days visiting with old friends and the Francis family. At four in the afternoon on the 29th, he and Laurenda were married at her parents' home. Only the family, the Turners, and another friend, Joyce Irvine, were present. By six-thirty they were on the plane for Vancouver. Because of a delay in their flight out of Calgary, they did not arrive until five in the morning, but as they crossed the mountains they could see 'the most majestic landscape below us as the light of dawn broke. The Fraser, flooded disastrously, was also clearly visible.'

As the Birneys planned to be away, the new couple stayed at their home in Acadia Camp, where Earle and Esther had made thoughtful preparations. The house was beautifully clean and well ordered, with an open book of poetry – Fitzgerald's translation of Omar Khayam: 'A Book of Verses underneath the bough / A Jug of Wine, a Loaf of Bread – and Thou.' They spent the first weeks of June walking around the campus and going to teas and dinners. A month later, Daniells took his 'brand New Wife' to meet Sedgewick, who liked Laurenda and pronounced in capitals, 'She is very quiet but she seems pleasant and competent – if not a Woman of the World.'[54] On 1 July, Daniells noted: 'Today I officially succeed G.G.S. as head of the English Department.'[55]

On 15 September they moved into Mabel Mackenzie's house at 1832 Allison Road, while she began the Ph.D. program at the University of Toronto. In addition to his duties as head, Daniells taught classes, wrote citations for Ira Dilworth and Kaye Lamb, who received honorary degrees at the fall convocation, and prepared for a CBC broadcast on Emily Carr's prose. Laurenda's first official act as wife to the head of the English Department was to cook a Thanksgiving turkey for E.M.W. Tillyard, then well known for his work on Shakespeare's history plays. Tillyard gave two lectures at UBC, the Daniellses being his hosts.

This was the first large public event where Daniells and Sedgewick appeared together as head and ex-head. The new man, Daniells, presented the legendary Sedgewick to the audience a little awkwardly, as if by inadvertence seeming to direct his predecessor a little, but really just trying to honour him: '"And Professor Sedgewick will now introduce our distinguished visitor." Then Sedgewick, at the lectern, after one of his trademark long pauses, peering over his glasses, grinned, growling: "Around here – for those of you who know me – I do pretty much ... WHATEVER I DAMN WELL PLEASE."'[56]

While he and Laurenda were still separated, Daniells had completed a book of poems, *Deeper into the Forest*. He had begun to write many of the poems during the fall and spring of 1947 as 'a relief from the tensions of marking papers.' He felt that he was advancing technically; the writing was freer, and he was using more modern images. He told

Laurenda self-deprecatingly: 'A few people who care about the technique of verse will write to me. Two students will want to borrow the library copy. And several of the vaguer faculty wives will get you confused with Mrs. Birney.'[57] In May 1948 he worked on an introduction that ultimately, in emulation of T.S. Eliot, became concluding 'Notes.' Daniells dedicated the book to Herbert Davis, but his title, *Deeper into the Forest*, is a phrase is from a Jacob Grimm tale.

The first sequence, 'Anthony,' is a long semi-autobiographical poem composed of fourteen sonnets. The issues raised suggest that Daniells was attempting to gain insight into his own psychology through writing poetry as well as through reading psychological textbooks. To do this, he split himself into two parts: the 'I'/eye of the passive observing poet is fixed upon Anthony, a rebellious alter ego figure. For Anthony, Daniells drew on aspects of the character of Max Maynard – perhaps because Max had represented the unexpressed side of his own character when they were young. It is probable that when Patricia Blondal and Margaret Laurence later came to construct characters based on Daniells, they remembered this dualism from his poem.

Anthony, complete with 'the fivefold sign the tiger made,' could have stepped from Eliot's pages. He is the *enfant terrible de nos jours*, a thirties Childe Harold of sorts, who reflects Freud, Jung, and Frazer. Like Daniells at St Paul's in London in the thirties (or, for that matter, like Maynard at the Anglican cathedral in Winnipeg in the forties), his response to church and doctrine is to be 'most confounded sick' and throw up.[58] Anthony becomes the spokesman for the disillusioned moderns spanning the Spanish Civil War and the Second World War. Although he goes to Spain, he feels great guilt because he did not die with his comrades – an indirect comment, perhaps, on Daniells' own feelings on not enlisting. Religion offers Anthony no comfort, social life no diversions, the New Year no hope. Instead, like a soldier on leave, he goes on a 'bat,' getting thoroughly drunk:

New Year's is over: Anthony has pulled through
But it was bad while it lasted. He came in
Crying, 'God is a concept!' and 'Original sin!'
Then he threw his head back with, 'Cock-a-doodle-do!'
My Aunt came down and Uncle he came too
To see what happened and calm the bloody din.[59]

Uncle and Aunt (transparent substitutes for Daniells' father and mother) are distressed at this mockery of theology.

Anthony, a poet whose life is presented as a quest which is shared by the narrator figure, has some affinities with the ascetic Saint Anthony as well as the narrator of *The Pilgrim's Progress*: sonnet 12 offers 'A straight road right to the Celestial City,' and sonnet 13, 'Look, the Bough of Gold!' By combining references to *The Pilgrim's Progress* and Frazer's *Golden Bough* in the conclusion of the sequence, Daniells presents the modern road to salvation. And since Anthony finds the golden bough, presumably he (and Daniells) is now equipped to navigate the underworld of the psyche.

We can associate Anthony with Max Maynard because both were Plymouth Brethren (thus one of the 'Saints') and also because sonnet 8 unmasks a Maynard-like aesthete delivering art criticism. Anthony also resembles Maynard in his repudiation of theology, in his Pan-like qualities (his attraction to women, his excessive drinking), and in his name. Fredelle Bruser, when she first met Maynard, was irresistibly attracted by his resonant voice, which she called an 'Antony' voice, after Shakespeare's *Antony and Cleopatra*.[60] The most important link with Maynard, however, was his drawing of two Pan-like figures ('Modern Enigma') which Daniells published in the *Manitoba Arts Review* in 1945. Maynard explained that the larger of the two figures 'was the Everyman of this Wasteland world' and that the smaller figure was his alter ego. The sketch is accompanied with a few lines from Eliot: 'What are the roots that clutch, what branches grow / Out of this stony rubbish? ...'[61] It is this visual structure – transformed into poetry – that Daniells' sonnet sequence offers. For above all, 'Anthony' evokes the personal tumult and aridity – the Waste Land world – that Daniells experienced in the forties before he met Laurenda Francis.

The second section of *Deeper into the Forest* is a series of sonnets on various occasions. One, sonnet 5, alludes directly to a divided consciousness – 'Double I am and daily conflict rends me' – and the delicate language of sonnet 9 evokes the mythic unicorn, that fabulous beast that can only be caught in the lap of a chaste maiden:

See the white stillness of the unicorn
Remotely moving through the purpled wood.
Light lift the fetlocks, freckled with bright blood
Of wretched jewellers, pierced, trampled, torn,
Who coveted the slim and spiralled horn.
See now, he turns to where the maid's quiet mood
Waits, and in that chaste lap the head o'erbowed
With crested magic on the forehead borne,

Under cool hands caressing rests.
　　　　　　　But hark!
The loud note sounds. The hunter gallops nigh
With furious baying of the hound led on
Hateful and deadly – till the kindly dark
Draws down. And now toward an evening sky
He veers, a pale star gleaming, and is gone. (35)

The book also includes a long poem, 'Farewell to Winnipeg,' and 'Epithalamion in Time of Peace,' a wedding song for their marriage.

One of the first reviews was on the CBC by Sedgewick, who regularly reviewed on the program 'Mainly about Books.' This 26 January 1949 broadcast was also his last, and he spoke of Daniells' book and Robert Finch's, *The Strength of the Hills* together, noting both were fine collections of poetry, rich, and 'not obtrusively larded with allusion.' Sedgewick read 'Anthony' as a description of a guilt-ridden man searching for a golden bough that will give him safe conduct through a dark world, and he admired the 'delicate and elusive power of the second sequence, "Deeper into the Forest."'[62]

Hugo McPherson recognized that the forest was a 'Grimm-Eliotian tangle' where the quest was an attempt to penetrate the tangle of contemporary experience, and W.G. Stobie remarked on the power of Daniells' images, a characteristic 'not unique amongst Canadian writers, but no other possesses it in so marked a degree.'[63] James Reaney, who reviewed the book for the *Toronto Telegram*, found that by 'going deeper into ourselves we find the greater reality.' He thought that the 'Anthony' sequence had the effect of a 'compressed novel, unfortunately no Canadian novel that one can think of' – a suggestive remark given that his own later books of poetry were narratives.[64]

Herbert Davis thought it something of a miracle that Daniells was able to teach and write about literature 'without destroying the love of making it.'[65] Mabel Mackenzie, who knew Max Maynard very well, said: 'It is almost impossible to avoid fitting real people to the incidents in your poems ... Can I say I feel as if I know something of what you felt. Not the last part ... but the first part, "Ant[h]ony" and how he felt.'[66] Desmond Pacey concluded that Daniells' 'special gift ... shines brightest in the poems about the ostrich & the unicorn: the subtle evocation of peace-in-terror, of the green shade in the sun-dried desert, of the vague menace without and the momentary, insecure but splendid calm within.' He considered the book 'the freshest, purest, most intense little book of poems we've had in years – perhaps ever.'[67]

Dorothy Livesay liked the book, as did novelist Ethel Wilson and poet James Wreford Watson. Indeed his poems spoke to many of the younger writers of the forties and early fifties in a persuasive combination of myth, wit, and erudition. Reaney was later to acknowledge the importance of *Deeper into the Forest* to his own poetry, and, a decade later, Eli Mandel wrote to Daniells to say that Anthony was one of his earliest heroes and suggested that he began to write mythic poetry because of Daniells' influence.[68] In 1956 Phyllis Webb published a book of poetry, *Even Your Right Eye*, in the same Indian File series as Daniells' book. She inscribed a copy of her book: 'To Roy Daniells a great teacher from Phyllis Webb student.'[69] Daniells, as an early mythological poet, has had a larger influence on modern Canadian poetry than has been recognized. Furthermore, the mythic and allusive structure of his long poem 'Anthony' would have been of interest to Margaret Laurence, a poet at its time of publication.

The book came out in the fall of 1948, and one December evening he and Laurenda took a copy of *Deeper into the Forest* to a faculty friend, Stanley Read. The couple were now settling into UBC life. The following year, they built a modern new home at 1741 Allison Road, and moved in in August. On that first Christmas on Allison Road there was 'a perfect Christmas card scene here: quite deep snow, packed and piled everywhere, crisp underfoot.'[70]

On 17 December 1949 their first child, Susan Catherine Mary, was born, and Daniells found Laurenda 'very composed, & brave & beautiful.' The baby was born at seven in the evening: 'I found L still somewhat under influence of ether, but rational, very calm & happy, full of love for the child & for me. I was sick briefly, but all right at once.'[71] As usual, Daniells' queasy stomach gave way under stress – even joyful stress. Two years later, their second child, Sara Elizabeth Ann, was born on 27 November. For the next decade, most of Laurenda's time was occupied with raising the children, making a home for her family, and acting as official hostess for the English Department. But although the couple saw many of the English faculty socially, Daniells kept his home and office lives relatively separate.

Chapter Fifteen

The New Head

When Daniells had been formally confirmed as head of English at UBC, Sedgewick had introduced him at a department meeting with the comment: 'This is your new head. You will find him very different from me.' William Robbins, who had arrived three years earlier than Daniells, interpreted this to mean that Sedgewick was saying that Daniells would run a tight ship. He also wondered if Sedgewick's interest in Chaucer and Shakespeare would give way to Daniells' in Milton and the Metaphysicals.[1] Edward Morrison, appointed six years earlier, also listened carefully. He knew that Sedgewick, who had a tendency to speak bluntly, could also be cautious. Was he warning the department against Daniells?[2] There is no record of what Earle Birney thought, but his subsequent actions suggest he was unhappy with the succession: it indicated that Sedgewick had favoured Daniells over him.

Aside from these normal expressions of faculty self-interest, Daniells faced a turbulent decade. UBC had grown little in the thirties and early forties, but enrolment had suddenly ballooned because of returning veterans. To meet this challenge, a number of minimally qualified instructors were added to the English faculty. After the mid-fifties, when newly trained Ph.D.'s were hired, there was an inevitable clash between the two groups because of changing requirements for the profession. Added to these problems were the increasing expectations by women faculty for equality and the conflicting views of departmental governance held by Canadian, American, and British faculty. For the next two decades in universities throughout North America, the struggle was both for faculty independence – which led in the sixties to the change from department 'heads' to department 'chairs' – and for greater autonomy of departments within the university.

Daniells encountered many of these problems earlier and in a more acute form than elsewhere in Canada. Not only was the UBC English Department a microcosm of other departments, but the necessity for change was intensified by tensions in the university and the department, many entrenched when Daniells arrived. These tensions resulted, in part, from President MacKenzie's 'personal' style of administration, very different from Sidney Smith's at Manitoba: one department member whose research involved James I, said that his knowledge of MacKenzie gave him a 'thorough-going understanding of Scottish cronyism.'[3] Given that Daniells and Birney both joined the department in 1946, a dust-up between the young Turks and the old gang might have been expected, but that did not happen.

In fact, Sedgewick had approved of the new head. As he had explained to the apRoberts: 'It is Roy Daniells. I am glad of the appointment – which, indeed, I warmly recommended. He will do very differently from G.G. – in some few ways not so well, in others better. The Dept. is not likely to be so free and easy but it will be better organized & made to experiment with new ideas. R.D. is puritanically conscientious: that is a virtue surviving from the Plymouth Brethren ... He will be *good*.'[4] However, some members of the department had sensed the underlying ambiguity in Sedgewick's introduction – on second thought, and after some experience with Daniells' proposed reforms, Sedgewick was not entirely sure he wanted the department to be different.

When, in January 1948, Daniells' succession to the headship was indicated, he was puzzled by Sedgewick's reaction: 'The way is being opened for changes in the calendar ... Sedgewick is really very amusing: he did not say he was glad to have me succeed or shake hands or anything.'[5] Daniells did not know how to read Sedgewick. Robbins later speculated that the two men were simply not compatible: 'Sedgewick was no Puritan and Daniells had been brought up as one in Victoria.' Moreover, 'at one point, this was just between Roy and me ... he thought Sedgewick was evil. A fellow brought up in a Victorian family of a certain kind used that word deliberately ...'[6] It was not just Sedgewick's hedonism versus Daniells' puritanism, it seems, but more specifically Sedgewick's homosexuality. On occasion, Sedgewick could be sexually aggressive; several veterans and one young UBC instructor in the 1946–7 group reported uncomfortable attempts to repulse him.[7] Birney knew about this behaviour; he told his wife, Esther, of being propositioned by Sedgewick.[8]

For many students, however, the homosexual element in Sedgewick's address to them was less conscious and less threatening. In late 1947 early 1948, F.W. Watt went to Sedgewick's office to ask if he might be admitted to honours English: 'Yes, he did glare gleefully over his spectacles, and savoured my discomfort ... Yes, he joked a little about having seen me the other afternoon from his car in my "little shorts" running after the football on the green grass of the Thunderbird English rugby team practice grounds ... Yes, ... he bumped his forehead against mine for an interminable period. But "aggressive"? Not an apt phrase for that encounter. I left in a sweat of astonishment, amusement and social embarrassment, not thinking about sexuality at all clearly but aware that it was there in the background somewhere. Also feeling that this improbable little volcano, if it ever had done much erupting, was now extinct, although still strange, awesome and scenic.'9

Daniells appears to have become concerned about Sedgewick's antics after he returned to Vancouver, and he wrote to his old mentors, Ira Dilworth and E.K. Brown, apparently asking for information; he was aware of potential problems because there had been a threat of legal action at Manitoba against a professor at one of the affiliated colleges.10 But Dilworth refused to gossip. He said he hesitated to reply for a month because of Daniells' 'suggestion that I speculate about your "chief." Good Heavens ... If I ever pluck the heart out of the Sedgewick mystery I should feel myself ready to tackle many of the baffling problems that surround me with a great deal more courage & assurance than I have passion. I know how you have suffered under him ... And I have had some experience in that connection myself.'11 Brown replied more promptly but equally discreetly: 'From time to time I hear disturbing stories about currents of feeling in your Dep't. To which I always reply that I know nothing about these things, but hope the succession goes to you.'12

When, in February 1948, Daniells received a letter from President MacKenzie asking him to form a committee to steer the English Department over the transition period for the next few months,'13 English Department dynamics changed immediately, with a fine set of comic scenes over the headship: 'Sedgewick ever so reluctant, underneath the disclaiming words, to relinquish power. Larsen, dear good honest fellow, not wanting to succeed himself at all ... yet shyly wanting the President and me to realize that he has a sort of prior claim and *is* withdrawing, not just being neglected.' The situation, as Daniells recognized, was 'funny as hell' and highly predictable: 'It has really been quite relaxing to whisk round the old familiar whirlpool round and round the old familiar vacant vortex of the headship of an English Department.' He foresaw the next step. 'Everyone in the department will suddenly discover that he should be giving a seminar in his own favourite course and please will I arrange it.'[14]

Sedgewick had taught at UBC since 1918 and his classes were still crowded, but when he retired in 1948 he was in failing health. The next spring his kidneys failed and he was hospitalized. Daniells had a last chance to repair his friendship with Sedgewick when, just before the latter's death, he gave a CBC broadcast, 'Garnett Gladwin Sedgewick,' which Sedgewick heard and liked. Birney had suggested that several faculty members go down to see him in the hospital, and Daniells recalled: 'We went down together. He seemed lively and cheerful. I told him we had his classes under control and that he could resume just as soon as he was well enough and wanted to. "That's as may be!" he cried, hopping back into bed. He was gone with[in] a day or so.'[15]

In his broadcast, Daniells had described Sedgewick's great impact on students.[16] He had brought Chaucer and Shakespeare, the prototypes of English culture, to generations of British Columbians: 'He took us into Chaucer's multifarious mediaeval world and, without saying so, made us see that it was the world of Canada, our own world ... That human nature is eternally enduring, though changing in its idiom and vocabulary. Beyond this, he made literature seem incredibly important.'[17] Why, Daniells asked in his CBC broadcast, did more than two hundred people, including the honours students, sit through his lectures with rapt attention? 'Because between the personalities and the horseplay, scenes of Shakespeare were read and interpreted with unmatched clarity and precision. Because the whole warmth and tragic value of the Elizabethan drama would suddenly seem to flower:

We are such stuff
As dreams are made on and our little life
Is rounded with a sleep ...'[18]

It was clear to the younger members of the department that Daniells intended to develop the curriculum, improve teaching, hire better-trained faculty, and introduce a degree of participatory democracy. In

Manitoba he had developed a system of one man, one vote. In practice this meant that he encouraged department discussion and called for a vote, but he made the final decision. This was considerably better than Sedgewick's ultimatums – but probably not sufficient for a faculty kept from power over so many years. Daniells also wanted to establish standardized marking by having essays marked by an instructor other than the one who assigned them. Finally, he wanted to reorganize the curriculum, which had changed very little since the twenties.

The danger for a head who takes his role as a new broom too seriously is that he, too, may be swept out of office. Daniells' first serious dust-up came in the spring of 1948, shortly before he took over officially as head. Birney had been talking to an honours graduate, Hilda Thomas, who proposed to write a book of lyrics for an M.A. in creative writing. Birney thought this a fine idea and nipped in to the next-door office to clear it with Daniells. After ten minutes, the voices in the adjoining office became louder and louder until finally Thomas heard a roar from Birney: 'What the hell do you think I've been doing in my creative-writing class all this time if you can't evaluate creative writing?' But Daniells was adamant. He did not think that the UBC English Department should give an M.A. for a group of lyrics; he had gone a long way by agreeing to an M.A. in creative writing in prose.

In retrospect, Thomas thought that Birney had sprung the question on Daniells too quickly and that their opposing positions had hardened. The issue of credit for creative writing, however, was larger than the persons concerned. Many faculty members did not think it could be taught; others objected to hiring whom they saw as unqualified people to teach senior students. The American poet Karl Shapiro once joked that American heads of English departments considered creative writing a Trojan horse: they tried to keep it out because once inside the gates, a door opened up, and hordes of barbarians overran the department.[19] Creative writing was still quite rare in the United States, with only two existing programs, one at Iowa and the other at Stanford.

As a new department head, Daniells was concerned about maintaining academic standards. Birney, however, thought of UBC as a department where writers from across the country could come to take degrees in creative writing. As Thomas recalled, 'he would have seen Daniells as stuffy, intractable, and leading the department down a quite narrow academic path that was squelching the possibilities for innovation.'[20] Birney put up a spirited argument about the decision, writing the first of a long series of letters to Daniells regarding 'my disagreement with a decision of yours.' As he acknowledged, 'it is a department chairman's right to make a decision and my duty to see it is carried out; but it is also my professional right and perhaps even duty to say if I don't agree, and why.'[21]

This would be reasonable were it not for Birney's claim that Daniells was to become 'chairman' of English. In fact, Daniells was to become head of English. A chair consults with his colleagues before making decisions; a head may well consult, but has the power to disregard advice and make his own decisions. The English Department at the University of California at Berkeley, which both Birney and Morrison had attended in 1929, had already moved to a system of rotating chairs, but no Canadian department had done so, and the tradition of the head was firmly entrenched at UBC. Yet, in some corner of Birney's mind, he had transposed categories: Sedgewick had been a head, but Daniells would be a chair.

Birney's descriptions of Daniells as a 'chairman' characterize his subsequent letters of complaint. It was a wilful misperception that may have existed for reasons that even Birney was not clear about. As a young instructor and would-be poet at the UBC summer school in the late twenties, Birney had marked Daniells' exam paper, written in polished verse.[22] For a poet who struggled with continuous revision, it must have been devastating to come across good verse by an undergraduate, apparently dashed off at will. Then, too, Birney and Daniells had been aggressive rivals in their games of badminton and tennis in the early thirties, and Daniells then – as now – did not intend to be beaten.[23] Finally there was Birney's dare, the snippet from T.S. Eliot's poem, on the back of the photographs of the Shack, referring to himself, Daniells, and Sylvia Johnstone, now seemingly forgotten. What Birney remembered, as he complained bitterly to Gwladys Downes in the late 1940s, was that Daniells had stolen his Sylvia.[24] Now he had lost the headship to Daniells. The stage was set for strife.

Sedgewick – 'the man of all men who has stood nearest in the role of father to me' – had been extraordinarily important to Birney.[25] In later years, Birney claimed Sedgewick had intended him to be head, but that seems unlikely given his radical Trotskyism, his failures at Berkeley and Utah, and the fact that Woodhouse had reservations about having him back at University College after the war.[26] Also, Sedgewick's letters indicate that Daniells was his candidate for head. Creative writing provided Birney with his first and continuing reason to object to Daniells, but had it not existed he might well have found another. Now that their friendship had been ruptured, his long-repressed rivalry found a focus in the cause of creative writing.

English professors are generally highly articulate. Language is their stock in trade, and they can wield it as a rapier. It was Daniells' misfortune to have in his department a man who was becoming the best-known poet in the country, and who now nursed a grudge against him. When verbal aggression is combined, as it was in Birney's case, with a respected position, a cause, and a militant personality, it can rupture a department, especially if the head is not equally bellicose.

Birney's first loyalty was not the English Department but his poetry, and the only subject he was happy to teach was creative writing. He was continually frustrated as Old English, Chaucer, and departmental responsibilities got in the way of his poetry. Unwilling to take responsibility for his own situation, Birney began to disagree with Daniells soon after it was announced he would succeed Sedgewick. These disagreements were about course work that took time from Birney's writing, about departmental reorganization that also took time from Birney's writing, and about who should be hired to teach creative writing. Major flare-ups occurred in 1954, 1957, 1959, and 1963. Birney was to claim that a condition of his appointment at UBC was that he would be allowed to teach creative writing regularly, but his letters requesting this privilege suggest this was not the case.

Daniells, when he had initially considered coming to UBC in the mid-forties, had believed that he would be able to work amiably with Birney, Morrison, and Robbins. But Robbins and Morrison, who had come earlier to UBC, had stronger connections to the older professors. Moreover, they considered themselves Daniells' peers. Although Robbins owed much to Daniells, who had helped him in the early thirties and found him his first academic job, he had become closer to Birney at the U of T in the late thirties: his affiliations were now with the older professors, especially Sedgewick. Actions taken by Daniells to reform the department were seen by Birney, Morrison, and Robbins as disrespectful to his seniors.[27]

Birney also enjoyed close connections with Geoffrey Andrew, President MacKenzie's personal assistant. Andrew, when literary editor of the *Canadian Forum*, had published Birney's 'David.' And, as an ex-army man, Major Birney had affiliations with Major Read and the UBC military hierarchy. Dean Sperrin Chant was ex-army, and President MacKenzie, a First World War veteran, was proud of his service as civilian head of a government board in Ottawa during the Second

World War. This was a fraternity from which Daniells was excluded. More importantly, Daniells' plans for limited departmental democracy were a decade too early: both Andrew and Read disapproved of his notions about one man, one vote.[28] Thus Birney was in an ideal situation to mobilize discontent. He did so, as his biographer remarks, by the classic technique of establishing a small committee, an oligarchy, to change the direction of the larger group, a Trotskyist process later described in his novel *Down the Long Table* (1955).[29]

In practice the Trotskyists were dedicated, hard-working leftists who, when working with other organizations, tended to meet in caucus separately in order to establish the direction in which they wanted the organization to move. This tactic sometimes conflicted with the aims of the larger group, and they were occasionally expelled from organizations on the grounds that they were manipulating the group. Birney, espousing democracy, was actually a Trotskyist in his English Department activities, although he does not appear to have recognized this. Near the end of the fifties, he summarized his view of the decade to an economist friend:

> I don't know if I ever told you about the sonofabitch we have for an English Dept. 'Head.' For five years he ran the dept. both incompetently and bureaucratically, making confidants of the handsomer young instructors and freezing out the senior men from any share in the deptl administration. Then we had a revolt of the full professors (all 9 of us, united by desperation) which I led. We had the full support of the Dean of Arts, and the tacit support of MacKenzie, with the result that we got Daniells' powers reduced to that of chairman.[30]

In this memo, Birney implies that Daniells, like Sedgewick, was attracted to the younger male instructors. Daniells was handsome and witty, attracting both male and female friends, but other than the normative male bonding of the period; there is no evidence of homosexuality in Daniells' papers, or from interviews with colleagues and close friends. However, Birney himself acknowledges that he went through a bisexual period; his biographer reports an affair in the thirties with a male American professor in the UBC English Department, and his wife, Esther, believes that Birney had an affair with Sedgewick.[31] It is therefore probable that aside from all of the other differences between the two men – and Birney's public profession as a Don Juan – there was an element of sexual rivalry in Birney's animus.

Daniells' version of what happened in the English Department would be quite different from Birney's. Very probably, he would not have recognized himself in Birney's portrait. Moreover, he would very likely stress the problems involved in rebuilding an English department when the senior members of the department saw no reason for reform.

⟩•◦•⟨

From 1948 to 1951 Daniells carried out an energetic program of curriculum revision. For the first-year English textbook, *A Century of Short Stories* (1935), edited by department members Larsen and MacDonald, he substituted two textbooks, *Masters of the Modern Short Story* (1955), edited by Walter Havighurst, and *A Little Treasury of Modern Poetry* (1950), edited by Oscar Williams, which were more up to date. Havighurst begins where Larsen and MacDonald end. Williams' emphasis was on modern twentieth-century writing, and his anthology included two poems by Margaret Avison. By introducing these new texts, Daniells improved English 100 but annoyed two senior faculty members who received royalties from the sale of the text.

By 1950–1 he had instituted prerequisites for the study of English; no student who had failed English 100 or 101 could take further courses, and English 200 was a prerequisite to English courses above 400. The second-year course of study now ran from Chaucer to the Victorians, and a new course, English 205, 'English Composition and Literature,' was designed for the non-specialist student. Students could choose a variety of courses for their third and fourth year, ranging from a creative-writing course, a European classics course, period courses from Chaucer to contemporary literature, and North American literature. There were also theatre courses, literature and language, bibliography, theory, and 'aesthetics.' In addition, honours students continued to write a 'graduating essay.'

Daniells had systematized the curriculum, plugged the more obvious holes, made American literature a separate field of study, and provided instruction for specialists as well as for those who simply wanted to acquire functional English. In effect, he brought the curriculum up to date. His proposals were not radical but constructive, and he did try to listen to faculty suggestions and to incorporate them into policy.[32] But departmental democracy, new at UBC, was time-consuming, and this extra work came on top of the grind generated by the veterans. By introducing more advanced texts, by insisting that new areas of the discipline be covered, and by instituting departmental committees, Daniells increased the faculty workload. Birney soon complained to Lister Sinclair, the playwright, that much of his time was spent preparing new lectures and attending committees, 'since we haven't re-organized in a way that satisfied any of us yet':

We are suffering the benefits of Democracy after 25 years of Benevolent Patriarchy. Under Sedgewick, dept. meetings occurred rarely and suddenly; we gathered and were told as little as possible about what to do, and no argument. Under Daniells, the lowest teaching-fellow has a voice 'as cleere, and eek as loude' as the Chairman's – in fact louder and clearer, since Roy insists on being a non-voting observer in any committee involving a course he doesn't personally teach. It's wonderful, we love him, the stables are being scoured down to the white of the beams, aged professors work off twenty-year suppressions – but it takes one hell of a time, and actually forces us to think.[33]

Daniells also took steps to raise the level of teaching in the department. As one 1947 student recalled, some of the senior professors were 'pontificating bores: they were dull, dull, dull.'[34] In 1948 he concluded that MacDonald's teaching was not up to par and refused to allow him to continue to teach beyond retirement; in 1950 he had a talk with Ruth Humphrey, an intelligent woman who tended to be forthright and outspoken in class, and was alienating the veterans with sarcasm.[35] They, too, complained to the head. And then there were complaints about another professor being absent from class, or, worse, that he was present but intoxicated.[36]

The problems associated with Birney were perennial. At first Daniells worried about his attentions to young women students. To be sure, Daniells had courted students in the preceding decade, but he had been single, whereas Birney had married in 1940. As Daniells had earlier marvelled to Laurenda Francis, Birney and his wife believed 'that married people should be quite free to come and go in their relations with others':

Birney, when in England, and in the army, had an affair with an English girl who writes poetry. Not only so but he is thinking of publishing a series of sonnets which he wrote at that time and which are most palpable and obvious references to his physical relations with the girl ... Furthermore, he propositioned a local gal recently, and suggested she might like to come round and see him and sleep with him. All this with a kind of childlike innocence which is queer in a person of his maturity. He is, as you know, a most honest and scrupulous fellow and delicate in his relationships, which makes it all the stranger. It all strikes me as amusing and a little pathetic.[37]

After Daniells' marriage, Birney's rivalry took a sexual tone. In 1948 he gave some film to another faculty member, Stanley Read, a photography enthusiast, to develop. In the resulting photographs, Birney was shown naked, 'all ... erect,'[38] on Bowen Island with a girlfriend. He apparently made some wisecrack about Daniells, drawing invidious comparisons; Daniells replied to the effect that *his wife* was not complaining.[39] This sexual rivalry accelerated in a manner unknown to Daniells when Birney told some of the senior professors and a student in creative writing that Daniells was a homosexual, producing as evidence the fact that he had waited so long to marry and that Sedgewick had favoured him as his successor.[40] Sedgewick's long tenure and personal prestige had protected him against the public at large; indeed, most of the university community kept very quiet about his personal preferences. But times were changing and Daniells was another matter. Members of the department, like Morrison and his wife, Mary, and students like Phyllis Webb had no reason to disbelieve Birney. And, as Birney recognized in another context, Daniells with his 'great capacity for innocence and not-knowing-what-has-happened,' seemed to have had no idea that such stories were circulating.[41]

Until 1953 these issues had not become public. Birney and Daniells would disagree and shout at each other, but then they would accompany one another to university functions with their wives. The beginning of a more serious difference came in 1952 when Birney asked Daniells to give him a reduced teaching load to accommodate his writing. *David*, which had won a Governor General's Award, had been rapidly followed by two more poetry books and a novel: *Now Is Time* (1945), *Strait of Anian* (1948), and *Turvey* (1949). Now, Birney was working on the radio drama *Trial of a City* (1952) and wanted more time for a novel that later became *Down the Long Table*. He urged Daniells to approach the dean and president supporting a sharply reduced teaching load.

Daniells refused. Enrolment in English had continued to soar, the department was overworked, and he had given Birney a teaching reduction the year before when he had asked for a series of favours which would 'reduce my lecture load to six hours, retain Med. Lit. every year, retain creative writing every other year, and fill in three other hours on the alternate years either with sophomore or freshman work.'[42] As Daniells explained, Birney's timetable already showed only a nominal six and a half hours per week of classroom instruction for the current session: 'The truth is that I am at the end of my resources and cannot, in any fairness to students, to the rest of the Department or to myself, promise you anything more than a very sympathetic consideration ... it may well be that in any given year, next year for all I can tell, you will have to assume a fuller load.'[43] Birney's first special request had been to teach creative writing every other year; now he wanted to teach it *every year*, a difficult request when the department was so understaffed. Moreover, his teaching schedule was far better than the nine to twelve hours taught by other members of the faculty.

At this point, Birney began a series of supplicating letters to President MacKenzie. Since his arrival in 1946, he had cultivated MacKenzie, asking for his advice, offering to attend educational conferences in Europe, and interesting himself in the war memorial volume, which was MacKenzie's pet project. Now he asked for, and received, special raises.[44] In 1955 Daniells was jolted to discover that he had received a raise of $100 in contrast to Birney's $800.[45]

Daniells also antagonized Robbins and Morrison. They had proposed to develop a new textbook for English 100 and invited him to join them as a third editor. If he had no time to edit because of the pressure of department work, they would enlist R.E. Watters and give Daniells full credit. It was a seductive offer. Daniells would have received financial benefit and would have been credited with editing a textbook. Why did he decide against it? Perhaps because he had already replaced the Larsen and MacDonald 100 textbook with two texts that he considered superior. As head he did not want to take an advantage he had already denied to two other faculty. Had he been a more 'political' man, he might have avoided trouble by agreeing to share in the anthology and by passing along Birney's request to the dean with sufficient department statistics to ensure it would be rejected. Instead Daniells frankly told his faculty where he stood: 'Wrote Bill declining to interest myself in the anthologies proposed by him and Ted. Wrote Earle declining to get involved in promises of a permanently reduced programme for him. Feel better now these are dispatched.'[46]

Sedgewick might have gone along with both proposals in the interests of departmental peace. If he had been forced to say 'No,' he would have been more likely to go to the persons concerned and give them his reasons, face to face, and argue them down when they objected. But Daniells disliked personal confrontations; he preferred communication by letter. He also played his cards closer to his chest assuming, erroneously, that his faculty would understand. A year later he further antagonized Morrison, a charming and witty man in person, but uninspiring in English 300 for engineers, where he regularly began lectures with a list of the students' most egregious errors. Many engineers hated English, and they too complained.[47]

Ensuring that instruction is given to the best of each professor's ability is the normal task of a department head. But Larsen, MacDonald, Morrison, and Robbins were all senior professors, Daniells' peers in rank. They saw the end of Sedgewick's regime as the beginning of their freedom. They had expected Daniells (who, after all, had been taught by two of their number) to be their spokesperson rather than their head. The differences between Daniells and the majority of the senior professors related to the way an English department should be run. It was epitomized by the difference between the old concept of head and the new concept of chair. Consequently, Daniells was, as Birney cheerfully told me in 1975, 'aggravating everybody.'[48]

Including his dean. In January 1954 Daniells wrote to Dean Chant asking for additional support for teaching faculty. The appeal was based on a comparison of conditions in 1947–8 during the peak of veteran enrolment and conditions in 1954. Although enrolment in first- and second-year English was down by approximately 16 per cent, the teaching staff had been reduced by 30 per cent. When compared to other departments, English, Department faculty were carrying a ratio of two and a half times as many students. Furthermore, because of curriculum changes designed to teach students to write, there were now eight assignments in introductory English and the hours of instruction had been doubled in English 250. Even to maintain 'the very bad conditions' which prevailed in 1947, the department needed additional instructors.

Daniells had been elected by the faculty to the UBC Senate, the administrative body that considers such academic issues, and in the next meeting he complained. In response, he received a stiff note from the dean, who was 'a little perturbed by your statement in Senate regarding the load that is carried by the staff in English.'[49] Chant appended a list showing that the class workload in terms of hours taught for departments like classics, French, economics, and math was like that in English. However, the marking load for essays in English is usually far greater than that of other disciplines, the department had instituted additional requirements for first-year composition, and none of this work was reflected in scheduled class hours. Nonetheless, by protesting that English was treated unfairly, Daniells had gone to Senate over the head of Dean Chant, his superior. This was not politically wise because a head is fundamentally middle management: he can function with the goodwill of either department or dean – but not without both. Trouble was in the offing.

Chapter Sixteen

'The Revolt of the Dukes'

By simultaneously antagonizing his department and his dean, Daniells placed himself between a rock and a hard place. The dynamics of academic departments are such that if the senior members of a department are not governed, or represented, by their head to their satisfaction, they may object to his procedures and go over him to the dean and president and attempt to unseat him. Daniells' diary records the process, and Birney's letters reveal the impetus. One young professor, observing the clash, found a convenient tag from English history, describing it as 'the revolt of the dukes.'[1] At Runnymede in 1215 the power of King John, who had incurred the hostility of his powerful dukes and barons, was curbed when they forced him to enter into a new agreement, *Magna Carta*. This was a reactionary document intended to ensure that the king would not encroach on baronial privilege; ironically, it was later interpreted to guarantee the rights of individual citizens. At UBC in 1954, Daniells was placed in the situation of King John, with the senior professors cast as dukes and barons.

Birney, by his own admission, was the instigator. In 1953 he had been in France on a Canadian Government Overseas Fellowship, but when he returned to UBC in January 1954, he was angry about his teaching schedule, unhappy with new departmental committees, and annoyed about new appointments, not just faculty appointments but also about the appointment of R.G. Baker, better known as Ron, an RAF veteran, former student, and now a lecturer in the department, who was acting as Daniells' secretary. Birney and some other senior professors did not like to see a junior faculty member in a position where he might exert undue influence.

Birney, forgetting that he had asked to teach creative writing every other year as a special favour, told his friend Herman Singer, 'I found, on returning, that my Creative Writing course had been taken away from me ... In replacement, I was given so much frosh and soph work that I had to mark, without reader assistance, 300,000 essay-words since Jan. 15.'[2] He had had a year off, a privilege no one else had enjoyed, and he had been warned that he would have to take a larger load when he returned. But he still resented the time that teaching and department business took away from his creative work. He also recognized that democratization of the department would threaten the power of the senior professors. Earlier he had been critical of Daniells for introducing time-wasting democratic procedures, but now, as his biographer remarks, he took the opposite argument: 'Our dept head has, over the years, been quietly eliminating whatever democracy was inherent in our departmental set-up. I returned from a year's leave to find all the senior men cleverly isolated, power shared with a crop of new faces, kids with a couple of years' experience, imported by the Head to be henchmen of the New Order.'[3]

Birney is specifically objecting to Daniells' policy of one man, one vote, but his language is thirties Trotskyist rhetoric. He soon found common cause with a number of senior professors on the grounds that Daniells was eliminating democracy in the department. Indeed, as Birney told me in a taped interview in 1977, there were eleven full professors and 'each of us separately apparently had our quarrels with Daniells and on not being consulted for decisions.' In notes which he archived relating to this incident, Birney listed a number of issues: no consultation for the freshmen and sophomore exam; the department was overworked, underpaid, and forced to work in four locations; there was insufficient emphasis on research and graduate work.[4] However, consultation for lower-level exams was not part of the department climate, and a department chair in a service department has little control over many of the other issues. Nonetheless, the senior professors met and sent a delegation to the dean of arts and science, Sperrin Chant. What they wanted, Birney recalled, was 'to appoint Daniells as chairman. He [the dean] reluctantly agreed.'[5]

Daniells' diary confirms this sequence because on 1 March 1954 he was 'perturbed about complaints to the Dean.' A week later there is a 'stinking letter from Bill [Robbins] re Dept.' On 23 March the whole department was invited to the president's house in the evening: 'A strange and confusing discussion.' Apparently President MacKenzie spoke to faculty members individually on this occasion. On 14 April,

Daniells began the first of three unpleasant meetings with the senior professors, in which Geoffrey Andrew, MacKenzie's assistant, made a parallel between Daniells' administration of the UBC English Department and the unsatisfactory British Columbia Liberal-Conservative coalition, which had been defeated at the polls in 1952. What was needed, Andrew opined, was a strong Senior Committee at the helm.[6]

Birney had been back in Canada for less than four months when he wrote to Herman Singer taking full responsibility for a coup. As his biographer remarks, Birney gathered the senior professors 'into something remarkably like a Trotskyist cell, and, in his own words, they "had to organize a *coup d'état* and take dictatorial powers from the ... Chairman."'[7] By Easter, Daniells was told by Dean Chant that he must 'consult' with the senior professors before taking major administrative action. As Birney told Singer, the administration had been sympathetic to his claim that he was overworked: 'but since the Head was their man we had to plot cleverly to save faces all around. This has taken up what spare time we had between essay-marking. Happily, we've been successful. Power has passed to a Committee of Senior Professors, the Head reduced to a nominal Chairman.'[8]

It is difficult to determine the degree to which there was a valid academic cause for the coup. Certainly, Sedgewick would not have consulted on such decisions, and his faculty would have accepted his authority. A more probable reason was that the senior professors had become restive under Daniells' administration. There were philosophic as well as political reasons for this. Most of this group, former pupils of Sedgewick, were strong Arnoldians: they defined literature as the best that had been thought and felt and expressed – thus it should be the staple of the department's teaching. However, this definition meant English literature up to the end of the nineteenth century and a history-of-ideas approach, neither of which satisfied Daniells. He had begun as an Arnoldian, but he was now broader in his views of department curricula, largely because his experience as a student of Sedgewick and A.S.P. Woodhouse had been leavened by the teachings of Herbert Davis and E.K. Brown. He wanted to include new literatures in the curriculum, especially Canadian, and he placed importance on modern literature. He also encouraged myth criticism, cross-cultural approaches to literature, and, later in the decade, Freudian and Jungian readings of texts. Another of his later innovations was a new third-year course, 'Approaches to Poetry,' basically a course in New Criticism, and he encouraged faculty to maintain ongoing academic research to the best of their ability. As head of English, he had made these preferences evident by the mid-fifties.

This new emphasis was galling to a number of senior professors who, up to the mid-sixties, emphasized the classic English authors, disparaged Canadian literature (Birney excepted), and considered mythic and psychological criticism inadequate as scholarship. Birney and this group nonetheless made common cause because these objections were accompanied by practical considerations: the senior professors wanted a greater share in the governing of the department, which necessitated lessening the decision-making powers of the head.

In the past, the head had been supported by a junior faculty member, who acted as 'right-hand man' and occasional secretary. The senior professors now wanted to employ a paid, full-time, non-faculty secretary (who could work for all members of the department), to modernize the English office and to centralize department business, as instructors were housed in at least four different locations. Previously, the Faculty of Arts office had taken telephone calls and carried on the general business of the English Department, while the head relied on this junior member of faculty and a part-time secretary/stenographer. Daniells had agreed to this general office reorganization, but as it was already end of term, he kept on Jan de Bruyn, an instructor with a young family, earlier approached regarding a part-time secretarial position over the summer. His mistake was that he did not formally notify the committee that he had done this.

Daniells then made the cardinal error of following through on an invitation to give the de Carle lectures in New Zealand during the summer. It was a great honour, but it meant that he would be away at a time when faculty were restive. He was hardly on the plane winging his way across the Pacific when Birney and members of the Senior Committee discovered that Daniells had asked de Bruyn to be secretary. There was an immediate uproar on the grounds that Daniells had acted undemocratically. This was not a large issue, but wielded skilfully it became the justification for broadening the Senior Committee's powers.

There were meetings at faculty homes; Birney and Andrew again went to the dean; the president was consulted. De Bruyn was released from his duties but reimbursed. Daniells' half-time secretary, Mrs Toynbee, was fired; a new telephone was installed in his office (Daniells was known not to want the distraction of a telephone when working in his office); a new Gestetner was purchased, the general office painted, and a new secretary, Mrs Cromie, 'a honey,' according to Birney, hired. As Birney later recalled, he had been appointed acting head when Robbins went on summer holidays. 'I had fun exercising power, fired the deptl sec ... hired an American poet, Melvin La Follette, who appears in the last Chi[cago] *Poetry*' and 'generally played hare-and-hounds in the general faculty paperchase.'[9]

Daniells, in New Zealand, knew nothing of all this. He was out of the country because of the de Carle lectures, which brought a guest from another Commonwealth country to New Zealand every four years. He had been invited to lecture on Milton's *Samson Agonistes* and Canadian literature for about six weeks at the University of Otago, located in Dunedin, a small and picturesque mountain town. He was then scheduled to lecture at several other universities. On 4 August he flew back to Vancouver.

The first issue facing Daniells was the Senior Committee. He knew what to expect. Before his departure from New Zealand, he had received a distressed letter from his secretary, Mrs Toynbee, saying that her job was in jeopardy. He promptly cabled Dean Chant asking for an explanation. Chant did not reply, but forwarded the cable to Birney and the Senior Committee. Daniells then received a letter from Baker detailing the immediate crisis. Apparently it had all begun at a social evening at Morrisons, where de Bruyn had innocently remarked to some senior members of the department that he could not rent his house for the full summer session because he was taking over the departmental secretarial job.

A few days later, Daniells received a measured letter from Robbins, who outlined the actions of the Senior Committee. They had elected Birney as interim head, made new appointments for the fall, replaced his secretary, and approached the administration for funding. Robbins said that he had given the grounds of Daniells' policy as faithfully as he could, but the Senior Committee had concluded that a gain in centralization and efficiency was an end that Daniells himself (they hoped) would desire; moreover, there were assurances from the dean regarding finances: 'I hope you will be content with this change, and even see advantage in it; I *earnestly* hope that the whole committee will evolve harmoniously and cheer my distant struggle with the sources of sweetness and light.'[10] Robbins is putting the matter reasonably, in the best Arnoldian language possible, but the Senior Committee had supplanted the head.

When Daniells returned on 6 August and found the office repainted and new equipment installed, he jotted in his diary: 'Evidently Geoff [Andrew] and [Dean] Chant felt nothing was too good for the senior committee.'[11] Although he could not get additional funding for teaching, there was now a large budget for decoration, office equipment, and a full-time secretary. Daniells, somewhat shortsightedly, thought that departmental work could just as well have continued to be done in the dean's office, as it had been until the late forties. But enormous postwar enrolments had made it essential that departments function independently, a fact that probably underlay Dean Chant's assent to modernization.

What rankled, justifiably, was that the dean had given credence to Birney and Andrew but not to the head. But Andrew was now also a dean as well as a member of the English Department. Because he, as assistant to the president, held a position on the senior executive of the English Department – whereas the normal lines of communication are from head to dean to president – Daniells was placed in a situation where several department members, notably Andrew, Read, and Birney, could short-circuit his communication with dean and president.

In essence, the issue of hiring a half-time secretary had been a rallying cry to consolidate additional powers in an elitist Senior Committee. Daniells had arranged, before he left, that the Committee include assistant and associate professors. But on his return he discovered there was no representation from the junior group. Assistant professors would therefore not have any input on important departmental matters. Daniells' diary entry of 18 August records his distress: 'Have been much obsessed lately by failure of senior committee to include asst. profs. as agreed, & by failure of Chant & Andrew to give me any backing.'[12]

Birney now attempted to exclude even associate professors. G.P.V. Akrigg, at that time an associate professor, recalled Birney saying to him that the Senior Committee was much too large with the associate professors and they should resign.[13] Campaigning in the name of democracy, Birney actually wanted a small oligarchy to govern the department. This Daniells had immediately recognized: 'Much worried about grab of power by Senior Committee.'[14]

Birney had been placed in charge of a subcommittee of the Senior Committee to suggest reorganization of departmental procedures. In September his proposals for reorganization were brought to the whole department. They were rejected. In mid- and late October there were further departmental meetings, giving Daniells hope that the exclusive power of the Senior Committee would be broken. However, on 29 October a general meeting of the department disappointed Daniells: 'not enough of the juniors spoke & not persuasively enough, either.'[15] Finally, in mid-November there was a meeting of tenured members of the department. To Daniells' astonishment, the junior members of the department gave away their vote: 'Meeting of full, asso & asst profs at which, amazingly, the solution of an executive of full profs only was agreed on.'[16]

Tempers had flared at the earlier English Department meetings, and the tension surrounding the Senior Committee had become so extreme that it alienated the associate and assistant professors. Junior members especially felt threatened and fearful for their jobs. Unwilling to take part in what they considered 'a mess,' they had voted to leave the administration of the department to the full professors alone.[17] This reactionary step was exceedingly disheartening to Daniells. Not only had his own power been curbed, but the department as a whole, below the rank of full professor, had no part in departmental governance.

There were now two centres of power in the department: the powers associated with the head, who controlled the purse strings and was officially entrusted with responsibility for the department; and the powers associated with the full professors who constituted the Senior Committee. This committee, nominally chaired by the head, now determined who should be hired, who should be promoted, and what policies the department should follow, although these tasks were formally defined as the head's job. This bifurcation of authority was not instituted in any other department at UBC.

Daniells briefly considered resignation. 'Saw President and the possibility of an out for me emerged. I can, it seems, drop the headship and keep on at the same or an increased salary!'[18] However, after nearly two decades of administration, he had fallen behind in his field as a scholar. Moreover, he was now fifty-two years of age, he had two children under five, and he worried about jeopardizing the additional salary that came with the position of head. Resignations were then very rare; and there was some danger about retaining a position in a department from which one had resigned as head. To some degree, he was trapped.

Yet he knew that he had been a good academic head. He may have believed that the department troubles would have resolved themselves were it not for Birney's rivalry and Andrew's connections with the dean and president. Certainly, he was convinced that he had been treated unfairly. His earlier reaction to bullying by the Plymouth Brethren began to surface again as he decided 'not to let the bastards get him.'[19] Daniells, when convinced of the justice of a cause, was intractable. He determined to soldier on. Not surprisingly, the following year he developed a severe stomach ulcer.

With crisis Daniells' susceptibility to depression came to the fore. He still suffered periods of deep and recurrent depression about which most of the department knew nothing, but which disturbed his days and nights. He again suffered fearsome migraines. Daniells was a highly responsible person, probably overly sympathetic to the underdog because of his own experience. For him the continued battles with Birney were especially wearing because of the depression from which he could never entirely escape. He was not a bipolar affective depressive, but he did have periods when he was animated, excited, and could work prodigiously and at length. During these periods of sustained wit and animation, he was an engaging person to talk to and be with.

But his lows were very low. He lost all energy, was physically sick when he attempted to eat, and lost all pleasure in day-to-day life. Thoughts of his own unworthiness, of sin and death, predominated. Curiously, the migraines, which rendered him incapable of action, did not come during the attacks of stress or depression, but occurred when the stress was lifted. One morning in the late fifties, he dictated a letter to his secretary; when she came back in the afternoon, she stood by his desk for a few minutes, checking the letter. Suddenly she heard a small, other-worldly voice that came from nowhere: 'Could you please pull the door behind you as you go out?' It was Daniells, wearing an eye-shade and huddled under the desk to get away from the light because it made his migraines worse.[20]

Daniells was (even under the desk), as Robbins later reminisced, 'head and shoulders over us all.'[21] Because he felt he had been treated unfairly, because the majority of department members were now deprived of a vote, he worked to subvert the Senior Committee, making decisions on his own whenever he could, redefining issues broadly so that they would have to be brought to the full department for consideration. Like King John in response to the barons, he cultivated junior professors like de Bruyn, Craig Miller, A.E. Sawyer, and M.W. Steinberg, informing them of new initiatives, attempting to determine how they felt, acquiring the information he needed to push his academic directives successfully through the department executive.

The juniors responded favourably because, as Steinberg remarked, 'I trusted Daniells' vision for the department.' Moreover, 'that [was] his way of doing things anyway. He made up his mind on the basis of his judgment, his principles ... I think that provoked a fair amount of resentment, and that built up over the years.'[22] Some members of the Senior Committee, recognizing his 'Proteus-like ability' to slip out of nets, redoubled their efforts to contain him.[23] And so the process continued. The repercussions of this division of authority in the English Department plagued the institution for over twenty-five years. Significantly, the year after the coup, in 1955, when Dean Chant established a committee of heads in the Faculty of Arts, they promptly elected Daniells as *their* chair. The lesson of what had happened in the English Department had not been lost on other heads, who promptly drafted a document establishing what ought to be the proper relation between head, dean and president.[24]

Birney carried on the battle by caricaturing Daniells in *Down the Long Table*, a tale about Trotskyist politics and the Depression. E.J. Pratt recognized 'a gorgeous bit of autobiographical analysis,' and, as Birney later admitted, Daniells is caricatured as Sather.[25] Drawing on his unhappy courtship of Sylvia Johnstone, Birney casts the trio in the characters of Sather, Gordon, and Thelma. Sather (who also reflects aspects of the Communist Maurice Spector) steals the girlfriend of the young Trotskyist hero, Gordon:

> Gordon turned to Sather and caught again something (was it only the hawklike poise of his face?) something cunning, ruthless, inimical, which, despite all his reason, he could have sworn was directed against himself. And it was a little odd, surely, that Sather ... seemed deliberately to be avoiding any reference to his engagement, or to Thelma at all.[26]

The chapter in question is about stealing a girlfriend, but the novel as a whole is about the fraternal relationship between men, with strong homosocial overtones. Moreover, the name of Sather, as Birney knew from his year of graduate study at Berkeley, was associated with lectures on classical antiquity and Greek humanism given annually at that institution; as such, it was a neat tag for Daniells, who advocated both Hulme's classicism and Babbitt's humanism.[27] The name also implicitly suggests a psychological carry-over from Birney's earlier unhappy engagement at Berkeley in the late twenties, where his best friend did indeed woo and win Birney's fiancée. It is the psychological truth of his relationship to Daniells that Birney expresses in his portrait of Sather. In one sense, the enmity is beyond reason – there was no sound academic cause for the fifties flare-up between the two men. This was a product of Birney's situation as a writer, aggravated by his resentment over his loss of Sylvia. As Birney soon explained to President MacKenzie on 18 March 1955, he was both a writer and a professor, and his duties and responsibilities as a professor had brought him to the point where 'I must either cease writing, or cease teaching.' But in another sense, Birney's anger is entirely understandable; he felt betrayed by a close friend from whom he had expected academic favours, and he was unable to get beyond that feeling, especially when it seemed that Daniells continued to block his path.

Chapter Seventeen

Developing English

During the fifties at UBC, Daniells aimed to transform what was, in effect, a strong undergraduate teaching department into a teaching and publishing department with an effective graduate program. To this point, the professor of English, almost invariably male, took undergraduate training in Canada and did graduate work in England or in the United States despite Toronto's Ph.D. program. But conceptions of the profession were rapidly changing. There were growing expectations that students should be able to take graduate study in Canada, that professors of English should be scholars as well as teachers, and that faculty could be female as well as male. In English studies, criticism was supplanting textual work, and the new, close reading of texts was becoming increasingly important, often augmented by Freud, Fraser, or Jung. Several of these issues, including the training of faculty, the developing of graduate programs, and the new importance of criticism were raised at the first meeting of Canadian professors of English convened by Daniells in the late fifties.

The strongest support for a well-qualified faculty and increased graduate education came from the Humanities Research Council and A.S.P. Woodhouse. When Daniells first became head in 1948, he received a letter from Woodhouse indicating that he expected that 'the hearty cooperation of the two Departments will continue and increase to (I hope) their mutual benefit.' Woodhouse, who had sent the names of several Toronto graduates for consideration as UBC faculty, continued: 'If you want more (or different) names, let me know. We have others of this kind, and some with more training, but at a rather higher price.'[1] Woodhouse had set up dossiers for each graduating student because there was no appointment office associated with Toronto's School of Graduate Studies and he wanted to fill Canadian needs before these students were attracted to the United States. 'My idea is that this University (and as time goes on any other Canadian University that feels itself able to undertake the task) should do everything in its power to furnish graduate instruction to such able Canadian students as wish to come to it, and should help them to pay their way through, and to get some necessary teaching experience, by means of teaching fellowships.'[2]

This was the beginning of almost two decades of a close, reciprocal relationship between Daniells and Woodhouse, not only in graduate education but also in the development of the humanities in Canada. As Malcolm Ross has remarked, 'I *do* believe that next to Woodhouse Daniells was the main architect both of the Humanities Association and ACUTE. Humane studies in Canada had in Daniells the most eloquent and witty of advocates. He should and must be remembered above everything else for his unique and compelling contribution to the intellectual life of this country.'[3]

At UBC, Daniells had initially followed the educational pattern that had produced him. He had been passed from a feeder college, to a provincial university, to the established centre for graduate studies at the University of Toronto. That is, he had been passed from Dilworth to Sedgewick to Woodhouse – all of whom had trained at Harvard and absorbed Kittredge's 'personal' style of teaching. They shared close professional and personal ties. M.W. Steinberg, a student of Woodhouse, recalls a meeting in 1946 between 'the two greats in Canada' – Sedgewick, small and pixieish, taking umbrage with something said by the big and hefty Woodhouse: 'He poked him in the stomach – "Oh Arthur," he said, "go to Hell."'[4] Now, in 1949, Daniells was taking up Sedgewick's position in relation to Woodhouse, but their connection was not so free and easy. Daniells had been Woodhouse's former student and had been, at one point, a possible rival. Nonetheless, they were to sustain a close but formal bond based on their shared love of Milton, their common desire to develop research and graduate education in Canada, and the fact that both were seasoned academics, able to work fruitfully together through the old Humanities Council, which set the direction for scholarship in Canada.

Throughout Daniells' first decade at UBC, he continued to send students to the University of Toronto for graduate work. His revisions to the UBC English curriculum and his changes to the honours program produced strong graduates in English. Although he accepted forty to forty-five students for upper-levels courses, he worked hard to secure small classes of twenty-five to thirty students for first-year courses, understanding that for many students English 100 would be their only encounter with the civilizing humanities. Also, if students were discouraged in their first-year English courses, the department would not get good honours students. Consequently, he always made sure that the honours section of the department was given sufficient resources to flourish. Honours students took a comprehensive program of study, were responsible for independent reading, and wrote special examinations and a graduating essay. The difference between the UBC honours program and that at U of T, was that UBC students took additional courses rather than an additional year. This program was the backbone of UBC English, producing graduates with a firm grasp of the whole sweep of English literature and the capacity to do independent research.

Woodhouse was generous with his praise, saying that his best graduate students came from Daniells and UBC.[5] He could afford to be generous, for he tended to view outlying universities as feeder schools for graduate study at Toronto. Toronto had by far the largest and most prestigious graduate department: from 1920 to 1962 only three Canadian universities had given Ph.D.'s in English: Toronto (82), Ottawa (22), and Montréal (24).[6] But as both Ottawa and Montréal were French-speaking institutions which graduated a large number of teaching nuns with Ph.D.'s, Toronto was the primary research institution. Since academic standards and the attrition rate were high at Toronto, there were few Canadian graduates during the fifties. Furthermore, an increasing number of Canadian students gravitated to the United States to undertake graduate work and then remained to teach. Thus there was only a small pool of Canadian graduate Ph.D.'s in English available for teaching. But for those who successfully completed their U of T exams, Woodhouse found starting positions in universities across the country. Consequently, his remark in the late fifties to a woman who wanted to undertake the Ph.D. in English at Toronto, 'I can't prevent you from taking the degree, but don't expect *me* to find you a position,' carried a threat.[7] Because he had the last word on both training and placing, he effectively controlled the Canadian professoriate.

Birney grumbled justifiably that Woodhouse had a 'stranglehold' on Canadian higher education because he was the head of the largest graduate school in English in the country and, as a founding member of the Humanities Research Council of Canada, the individual who set the standards for the discipline. When Woodhouse came across an exceptionally good student like William Blissett, W.J. Keith, Allan Pritchard, or F.W. Watt, he tended to replicate his own experience at Manitoba. Usually, although he sometimes hired directly, he sent the young graduate elsewhere for some experience (three of the above were graduates of UBC, Pritchard returned briefly to UBC). Then, a few years later, the now-experienced professor was invited back to teach at University College with contracts no other institutions could match: little first-year teaching, marking assistance when papers exceeded a set number, a good pension plan, generous leave for research, a superior salary, and, of course, the prestige of teaching at the University of Toronto, the largest university in the country. For the head of even the second-best English Department in the country, it was inevitably a no-win situation.[8]

In the early fifties, like most English departments in the country, UBC had too many students, too few faculty, and too little classroom space. Because of administrative delays in approving budgets (which were keyed to the UBC fall student enrolment), Daniells often did not know if he could hire a faculty member until early October. Then, if Woodhouse could not supply a candidate, his solution was to look south, to the Universities of Washington, Oregon, and California. Daniells enjoyed good relations with Robert Heilman, the Shakespeare specialist who was head of English at Washington, and he frequently hired Washington graduates. He attempted to recruit British graduates to UBC by asking R.G. Baker, undertaking graduate work in England between 1954 and 1955, to contact the British Council and advertise for British faculty. He also relied on individuals like Herbert Davis, who first from Smith College, and then from Oxford, directed scholars to UBC, including Ian Ross, a young Scot who became one of Daniells' successors as head of English at UBC.

Daniells encouraged his own promising graduates to take further study at Toronto. Over the next decade, he sent, among others, George Baldwin, Michael Booth, Fred Flahiff, Jean Mallinson, Allan Pritchard, Sheila Watson, and F.W. Watt. Some returned to UBC to teach, but Daniells could rarely keep them. It was partly UBC's teaching conditions, especially the large burden of freshman teaching carried by every faculty member, and partly the fact that by the mid-fifties the UBC English Department had become so contentious. That UBC was a service department also seriously affected Daniells' attempts to keep young

faculty who wanted to become serious scholars. Other English departments in Canada, notably Toronto's, were more successful in persuad-
ing their administrations that they should concentrate on upper-level
English studies.

The combination of overwhelming teaching loads, new vexations
about promotions, and the jockeying for power between Daniells as
head and Birney and the Senior Committee placed considerable pressure on junior members. Jack Robson, later the distinguished John
Stuart Mill scholar, who taught at UBC during the fifties, was heard to
remark that he was leaving UBC because he found the atmosphere
uncongenial, but Robson apparently also objected to Daniells' promotion procedures, considered the pay scale unfair, and disliked the large
burden of freshman marking.[9]

Daniells himself continued to carry a large number of honours students and to creatively influence their future careers. Flahiff, later a
professor at St Michael's College, recalls a discussion with Daniells just
after an honours English seminar in 1957. Apparently they were chatting when Daniells flipped a nickel (then the cost of a phone call)
towards him: 'If you ever figure out what happens at the end of *Wuthering
Heights*,' Daniells said, 'give me a call. Anytime.' Brontë was a highly
significant figure to Daniells – he was particularly moved by the way in
which her landscapes are informed by spiritual forces. And he knew
Flahiff to be interested in theological issues. Several years later, then at
Toronto and struggling with a massive body of information on Tobias
Smollett for his Ph.D. thesis, Flahiff remembered this comment. He put
Smollett aside, read the Brontës for the rest of the summer, wrote his
dissertation on Charlotte Brontë's poetry, and then edited *Wuthering
Heights*. Flahiff recognized the power of Daniells' pedagogical device–
the throwing out of a question – and its importance on his own research
and teaching career.[10] Similarly, Daniells' thirties student Desmond
Pacey once told me that he began a study of Ethel Wilson in an attempt
to answer Daniells' question: 'Why did she call her novel *Swamp Angel*?' I began my own academic career in the mid-sixties with another of
Daniells' questions: 'What really happened in Canadian poetry in the
1920s?'

———————◆———————

By the mid-fifties, the number of British Columbia students wanting to
attend university was growing by leaps and bounds, the University of

Toronto was turning out very few Ph.D.'s, and Daniells could not find sufficient Canadian faculty to staff his department. Because he was frequently forced to turn to American universities at the last moment, the demographics of the department shifted as a number of young Americans, just out of graduate school, were hired as lecturers. Daniells had an unofficial formula for an ideal English Department of one-third Canadian, one-third British, and one-third American. But these proportions never applied in practice. In the mid-fifties, the faculty was almost entirely Canadian with an occasional British or American scholar. But by 1962–3, 50 per cent of the assistant professor group were Americans, with the other 50 per cent divided between Canadians and British immigrants. Thus there were sufficient new American appointees to change the character and direction of the department. These faculty demographics illustrate the nature of the change taking place in a number of other Canadian universities.

The pivotal year was 1956.[11] The department hired four Americans as instructors: E.B. Gose, W.E. Fredeman, Warren Tallman, and J. Zilber; three Canadians, G.V. Hopwood, Jack Robson, and George Woodcock; and an Englishman, John Hulcoop. The new appointments brought new stresses and strains because the inevitable struggle between the young Turks and the old gang, which might have been expected to occur at the start of the fifties, had simply been delayed to the late fifties. It was no longer simply a struggle between newer concepts of the discipline of English – a more comprehensive curriculum, the Ph.D. as a requirement for teaching, greater emphasis on publishing as opposed to the traditional emphasis on good teaching – but a struggle between differing Canadian and American conceptions of the discipline and the nature of graduate and undergraduate education. However, not all faculty tended to think, or to vote, along national lines, and the struggle was further complicated by the fact that the department was now governed by an oligarchy. Daniells could not unilaterally make the changes some of the younger faculty wanted.

Further serious frictions developed regarding the administration of the department. With the expansion of the department there was suddenly a large proportion of the faculty who had little sense of the traditional teaching of English at UBC, or elsewhere in Canada. American professors were accustomed to a broader curriculum and more freedom in developing their courses than Canadian professors were; they did not expect to be told what texts to purchase, or what authors to discuss. Some resented the group meetings which Daniells organized to establish parity in marking standards. Weren't they trusted?[12] Moreover, they held, on the whole, different attitudes to departmental governance. It is only a slight exaggeration to say that many Canadian professors who had come through the U of T graduate program tended not to speak at the rank of assistant professor, to ask questions at the rank of associate professor, and to engage seriously as an equal member of a department at the rank of full professor. Young American lecturers, and for that matter British lecturers, felt free to speak up in department meetings in tones that offended some of the more reserved Canadian faculty.

While Daniells and the Canadian faculty emphasized the honours program, the new American faculty were unfamiliar with a system that emphasized comprehensive coverage at the undergraduate level. They wanted more graduate courses addressing specific areas because they were accustomed to systematic requirements leading to the Ph.D. This group, although as yet inexperienced as teachers, also tended to be more professionally oriented. They knew they had to finish their Ph.D.'s. As some incumbent UBC English associate professors in the late fifties did not have degrees higher than the M.A., the newcomers disparaged their 'lack of professionalism.'[13] However, many of this group of associate professors had been UBC students, had taught for over a decade, and thought the newcomers put too much stress on the Ph.D. and publishing, and not enough emphasis on good teaching. Most lecturers now had M.A.'s; instructors tended to have Ph.D.'s and, after 1956, could expect promotion within a few years.[14]

It was a difficult transitional decade. At the start of the fifties, finances were strained, and President MacKenzie, who favoured firing weaker members of faculty, had sent a memo in 1954 suggesting this. But Daniells would have had to dismiss faculty hired by Sedgewick who had given excellent service during the earlier, arduous years. A second possibility was to support the faculty he had and encourage them to continue with their degrees while augmenting his staff with bright new graduates. Not surprisingly he chose this second route, which left him open to charges from the conservative right that he was fostering weak faculty. George Woodcock, who had no university degree, was hired at this period, but with the agreement of senior members of the department.

Daniells was also thought to 'play favourites' by supporting the promotion of weaker faculty when he thought the person's circumstances and contributions to the department required it.[15] To some extent this was a justified criticism. However, the current UBC system also evidenced a high degree of cronyism, and it is probable that Daniells wanted to acknowledge his supporters, as well as those who had given good teaching service. Finally, the department coup seems to have been a watershed. After this, a disillusioned Daniells recognized that if he were to remain as head, he would have to maintain tighter political control. But he was now limited in his power to shape the department because hiring and promotion were determined by the Senior Committee. And even when this committee agreed about faculty to be recommended, these recommendations were frequently rejected by the dean or by the ultimate authority, the university-wide Tenure Committee.

English department candidates for promotion did not always understand this, nor were they privy to the way in which power was actually distributed. They believed that the head, as in Sedgewick's day, was all-powerful. Consequently, candidates who were not successful in achieving promotion tended to think that if the head had supported their candidacy, they would have been successful. But the head of UBC English was now a virtual chair whose powers were restricted to persuasion, indirection, and the purse strings. Academically, Daniells was very persuasive. He advised new faculty such as D.G. Stephens and John Hulcoop to finish their Ph.D.'s; he encouraged M.W. Steinberg and Elliott Gose to publish; he invited Warren Tallman, a new American appointee, to help him teach a new course, 'Approaches to Poetry'; and he asked William E. Fredeman, another young American who advocated graduate courses, to gather information for a Ph.D. program.

One effect of an increasing emphasis on professionalism in the department was to put pressure on senior professors to publish and on all faculty members to complete their Ph.D.'s. Robbins, Akrigg, and Birney all took time off to do scholarly research, the first two producing books and the latter a series of scholarly articles. Robbins, who went to the British Museum in 1955 to work on *The Ethical Idealism of Matthew Arnold* (1959), wrote to Daniells to say that it was not just inertia that kept him from getting on with his book for the last decade:

A man can only do this kind of thing by having a year off. I worked steadily for 3 months at the B.M. reading and note-taking, from mid-Sept. to mid-Dec. And I mean *work*, 8–10 hours there and at home till my eyes bugged out. Then 2 more of the same, Jan and Feb. Then steady writing at home for March and May, with J[une] and J[uly] still to come and lots to do ...[16]

Robbins was putting into context the problems experienced by all Canadian scholars at this point. It was impossible to carry the heavy teaching and marking loads most UBC English professors carried – sometimes ten to twelve hours teaching at least three courses per week, with as many as 50 to 150 students in one undergraduate introductory course, each of whom produced at least two long essays and two exams per year – and still have energy left to undertake original research. If scholars were also to become researchers, if promotion was to depend on publishing, time and support to undertake research had to be built into the academic system. This reasoning, inherent in the report of the Massey Commission, led the newly founded Canada Council to support academic research.

Another effect of the new professionalism was the development of Ph.D. programs across the country. At UBC, Birney and R.G. Watters had been among the strongest advocates of the Ph.D. Birney had long resented sending UBC graduates to Toronto and saw no reason why the department could not develop its own doctoral program. Yet, when a department does not have enough faculty to cope with undergraduate teaching, as UBC did not, it is unwise to embark on an ambitious graduate program. Moreover, there was also some feeling in the department that the Ph.D., like academic professionalism, represented Americanization of the Canadian university. Nonetheless, by 1956–7, practical considerations were intervening. In that year, UBC needed six Ph.D.'s in the Mathematics Department, but Canada had produced only one.[17] There was suddenly recognition among university faculty and administrators across the country that Ph.D. programs must be supported. That UBC and the University of New Brunswick began such programs in 1957 was a direct response to such concerns and to the newly founded Association of Canadian University Teachers of English.

Daniells had been a catalyst in the formation of this association. For some years, teachers of English in Canada had wanted to develop a specialized association and had twice, unsuccessfully, attempted to organize. In 1950 at the International Conference of University Professors of English at Oxford, Woodhouse, F.M. Salter from Alberta, and H.J. Alexander from Queen's tried again. The founding group was joined by Daniells from UBC and Claude Bissell from the U of T. At a 1952 meeting, Daniells was appointed chairman, William Robbins secretary, and H.J. Alexander a member at large.[18] Over five years, Daniells applied to the Rockefeller and Carnegie foundations for support for this project, since, at this time, the main source of funding for humanities projects in Canada came from such American philanthropic foundations.

Daniells was a highly effective fund-raiser and in 1956 persuaded the Rockefeller Foundation to support a meeting to establish an association of Canadian professors. In November 1956, he wrote to heads of English in Canada suggesting that 'the next move should be the formation of an Association of University Teachers of English in Canada.'[19] In June 1957 eighty-two teachers of English met with the Learned Societies at the University of Ottawa and voted to continue to meet on an annual basis as a nationwide professional organization. The founding members included, among others, Baker, Birney, Bissell, William Blissett, H.G. Files, Joyce Hemlow, Carl F. Klinck, Henry Kreisel, Jay Macpherson, Desmond Pacey, F.E.L. Priestley, A.M. Ross, J.M. Stedmond, G.M. Story, Clarence Tracy, and Woodhouse.

Daniells asked Frye to speak on criticism at the opening session. Frye's talk stressed the importance of a professional organization at a time 'when literary criticism was beginning to be recognized as a field of study in its own right, and when creative writers too were tending to reflect in their work a sense of the underlying structures of literature.'[20] This founding address underlined the importance of literary criticism and mythic structure – as opposed to textual studies, or history of ideas – thus formally setting out new directions for research in English.

In the afternoon, Murdo MacKinnon, then of the University of Western Ontario, spoke on the practical problems of a university department of English, 'how curricula should be set up, how faculty should be deployed, how an individual could devote adequate attention to his own scholarship in the face of all the claims that are made on his time.' Discussion centred on Woodhouse's emphasis, already known to most universities, on 'the need for expanding graduate education in English in Canada.'

Lastly the group discussed the formation of a permanent association and in a unanimous vote formed the Association of Canadian University Teachers of English, the name altered at the last moment from CAUTE or CUTE to form the more appropriate acronym ACUTE. The history of ACUTE (or ACCUTE as it is now known) attributes the acronym to Frye, but Hugo McPherson explains that it was coined by Daniells. When 'a distinguished scholar quipped that an organization of Canadian University Teachers of English might be properly abbreviated to CUTE, Roy Daniells' rejoinder was that such a distinguished group, united in an "Association" must surely be recognized as ACUTE.'[21] His own diary record of the occasion is brief, making little claim for his efforts: 'Meetings of English teachers in Universities. We got an association formed.'[22]

ACUTE brought together members on an annual basis. For the first time, members of English departments from across the country could share their research, meet younger scholars, and hire faculty in a congenial atmosphere. It became, as Jean-Charles Falardeau, the Quebec sociologist, once remarked of the Learned Societies, a 'spring-time strawberry festival' because it brought the year's work in scholarship to an end-of-term relaxation.[23] Everybody attended; everybody caught up with events of the previous year. A junior professor, such as myself, attending ACUTE in the late sixties could meet Daniells, Frye, Klinck, Pacey, Ross, Milton Wilson, and other major figures.

The inaugural meeting of ACUTE stimulated academic criticism and graduate programs. In May 1957 at UBC the English Senior Committee had appointed Birney as chairman of a subcommittee on graduate studies to consider a Ph.D. in English. But he resigned in October, saying he did not have time and that a Ph.D. program did not have the wholehearted support of the department.[24] Despite his eventual unwillingness to support the program, Birney in early 1957 had written to Dean Chant to complain that Daniells 'resisted the development of graduate work and continues, privately, to do so.'[25]

In fact, Daniells favoured a Ph.D. program. The department had hired new faculty, the administration now appeared willing to support graduate work, and his own planning for the ACUTE program had emphasized the importance of graduate work. As it appeared that none of the senior professors was willing to develop a graduate program at UBC (Watters was finishing a book and slated for leave in Australia in

1958), Daniells turned to the newly hired Fredeman, who recalled him saying: 'If you want a Ph.D. program, draw one up and submit it to me and I will submit it to the department.'

Fredeman, an instructor, sent out requests for information to thirty American universities asking about their Ph.D. programs. 'I got their programs and then I picked what I thought were the best requirements based on my own graduate experience.' He drafted a proposal, which went to the full department for discussion and revision. The program eventually offered a stiff Ph.D., very like the existing program at Toronto, requiring examination in eight of twelve areas: English Language, Old English, Middle English, the Renaissance, Seventeenth Century to 1660, Restoration and Eighteenth Century, Romantic, Victorian and Early Modern, Twentieth Century, American Literature to 1900, American Literature – Twentieth Century, and Canadian Literature. When the candidate had submitted an acceptable thesis, he or she then sat a final oral examination on the thesis and its field. Because of the extensive areas to be covered, the UBC degree, like the Toronto degree, produced well-trained scholars.

In an attempt to get the Ph.D. under way, Daniells wrote to Frederick Soward, dean of the Faculty of Graduate Studies, arguing that the English Department had sufficient faculty for graduate work – fifteen to twenty people with advanced research degrees, of whom half a dozen had done advanced graduate work. Moreover, there was sufficient library support for graduate work in English. The UBC library holdings were excellent in the Canadian field and good in nineteenth- and twentieth-century American. The Milton collection was fairly good, and nineteenth-century prose and poetry, as well as contemporary literature, were well represented. Daniells considered the library adequate in Middle and Old English, but weak in aesthetics, drama, and the Renaissance.

Up to this point, UBC offered a solid training in honours followed by either graduate study at Toronto, in which case the student left the system, or a UBC M.A. followed by a Ph.D. elsewhere. For the M.A., a student took undergraduate courses, studied independently, and wrote a thesis, which, as a new faculty member noted, sometimes matched a Ph.D. in length.[26] The student did not take graduate courses because there were none, or very few. The first graduate seminar was given by G.P.V. Akrigg in Tudor literature and consisted of poetic drama – the plays of Shakespeare and the Elizabethans, augmented by other figures.[27]

Among the new proposals for a Ph.D. program were a series of rotating graduate seminars in various areas, which were promptly implemented. The UBC Ph.D., like that of Toronto, maintained high standards; consequently, although many students enrolled, there was a high failure rate. The first Ph.D. was awarded in 1962 to Beryl Rowland, who had written her thesis on Chaucer and later became a faculty member at York University. In 1968, a decade after the program had been initiated, three students had graduated. In that year, Anthony Bellette, later a professor of English in New Zealand, and I were the fourth and fifth graduates.

While Canadian and American faculty members debated the issue of professionalization, women faculty members objected to their unequal status. Women in the fifties regularly began at a lower salary than men, and they were especially affected by a correspondingly slow rate of promotion. The first two women hired in English at UBC, recognizably 'bluestockings,' were Dorothy Blakey (later Blakey-Smith) and Dorothy Mawdsley, both single women. Marion Smith, divorced and supporting a family, was hired in 1948–9 to teach Shakespeare. The qualifications of many women members of the UBC faculty were equal to, if not better than, those of their male peers. Blakey-Smith, who left in 1951, had two M.A.'s (UBC and Toronto) and a Ph.D. from London. Daniells considered her the best scholar in the department and later attempted, unsuccessfully, to persuade her to return to the department after she married a Victoria resident.[28] Mawdsley had a McGill B.A., a UBC M.A., and a Chicago Ph.D. Dorothy Somerset had an M.A. from Radcliffe, and Marion Smith a Ph.D. from Pennsylvania. Ruth Humphrey, who had been head of English at Victoria College, had an M.A., as did Edna Baxter, who was working for her Ph.D. in Old English. Mabel Mackenzie, a former UBC student, was now teaching at UBC as an instructor but completing a thesis for her Toronto Ph.D.

Women faculty members were convinced that they did not get the courses, salaries, and respect that they deserved – although some male faculty protested that they did not either. There was a lingering misogyny in the department (which Mawdsley claimed was Sedgewick's legacy),[29] but a more important reason was the overly conservative stereotype of women held in that period. Steinberg, a supportive faculty member who had undertaken a study of the 'woman question' in literature, recalls the gap between theory and practice when discussing the issue of women in the department with Daniells: 'We didn't question their intelligence [but] ... we felt, they're going to get married or leave, going to have families.' Both wanted to establish a solid English Department at UBC, which required long-term scholarly commitment. There was a perception that women faculty couldn't 'cope with a crisis, they were flying off the handle ... Now that could be modified maybe – in the light of the experience we had actually with women like Marion [Smith] and Ruth Humphrey.' They, as Steinberg reminisced, were 'strong-minded women,' as intelligent or more so than most in the department, as devoted to teaching and scholarship.[30] In time, their presence helped ameliorate the prejudice against women faculty.

Daniells' teaching was not gender-directed, but, as his discussion with Steinberg indicates, he shared the prevailing view that since men were supporting families, they should be given first consideration. In the late forties, Daniells sent to the University of Toronto George Baldwin, later chair of English at Alberta, and Jean Mallinson, later to become a college instructor. Mallinson's comparison of Daniells and Woodhouse as professors is illuminating. She found Daniells an intellectually challenging professor, spoke of the excitement generated in his honours courses ('he was a passionate lecturer on the Baroque'), and was stimulated to undertake graduate work in English at the University of Toronto.[31] However, her experience in Woodhouse's graduate program led her to write 'Paradise Lost,' an autobiographical fiction based on her perception that at Toronto her sex barred her from the paradise of literature.

Woodhouse appears as 'Professor Woodholme,' the head of the Graduate Committee, who quotes from Book IV of Milton's *Paradise Lost*: 'He for God only, She for God in him.' This irritates the young woman; but it is one thing to question Milton's poetry, and another to question the conventions of scholarly life. In the following excerpt, 'Emily' has been summoned to the office of the head of the Graduate Committee:

'Now, Mrs,' he hesitated, as if unable to recall her name, she filled in 'Anderson,' and he went on, 'Yes, Mrs. Anderson, of course, that's it. You know, it took us weeks to locate you on our student list after the fall term started, we had you down as "Miss Johnson." Wasn't it rather peculiar of you to go off and get married without informing the University?'

'I'm sorry sir, I thought it was a private matter, just personal. It didn't occur to me that the University would be interested.'

'Personal' – he mused over the word – 'I dare say it might have seemed personal to you at the time. But I must tell you, Mrs. Anderson'– having found her name, he kept repeating it, as if to remind her of her married state – 'that it makes a good deal of difference to your academic career here and elsewhere. There is no future for married women at Canadian universities, marriage, as you no doubt know, tends to have certain consequences' – he paused, as if to let the direness of these consequences sink in. '"Hostages to fortune," as Francis Bacon called them, eh Mrs. Anderson?'

He paused again, pleased with his literary allusion. The delicate matter of sex hovered between them. Emily hoped he would let it drop. He went on, 'Had you remained single, Mrs. Anderson, we could have placed you in the Ph.D. Programme at Smith College, a prestigious women's college in America, where the head of the English Department is – or was – Canadian [Herbert Davis]. But here, I must tell you, we'll see you through the MA Program, having admitted you – albeit under another name – and then we can do nothing for you, though of course we cannot prevent you from enrolling in the Ph.D. Programme.'

He beamed at his magnanimity, paused, lit another cigarette and blew smoke in her direction.

As Emily leaves the office, a male student enters, and she hears, as she walks down the corridor, bursts of shared laughter from behind the door.[32] Mallinson's fiction reaffirms numerous reports that graduate study at Toronto during the forties and fifties was unwelcoming to female students.

This notion Woodhouse would not have understood. 'Literature was essentially ideas to him, not WORDS ON THE PAGE or a haunting in your ears.' A deeply conservative man, he had his own kind of passion. 'He was far more concerned with preserving the traditional good things about his world, the rigorous early twentieth-century world of the Oxford or Harvard scholar, than trying to eradicate or ameliorate conditions that later generations saw as unfair conditions for women scholars in the 1940s and '50s.' The wisdom of his generation was that most women students married and thus disappeared from the profession. 'Was he anti-Semitic? Racist? Anti-woman?' From his perspective (as seen by his associate head, F.W. Watt), the answer would be 'No.' From years of living in the corridors of power, he was simply being realistic.

'There were very few Jews, women, or people of colour in the profession in Canadian universities. They had to face prejudice. If they were tough enough and brilliant enough to survive, then he would help them. Otherwise, they would be better off trying something else – and he had no compunction about saying so.'[33]

Daniells' position was further along the road to equality. He did not, like Woodhouse, discriminate against the female student, although Hilda Thomas, later to join the UBC English Department, reports that she experienced the 'I-cannot-prevent-you' formula when she suggested graduate work to Daniells in the early sixties, possibly because she had not been a good student in his 1940s seventeenth-century course. However, she felt that he did support those women whom he considered serious about their work.[34] Daniells clearly admired Blakey-Smith, thought Baxter and Helen Sonthoff committed teachers, and encouraged Sheila Watson, a sessional lecturer at UBC during 1948–50, to undertake her Ph.D. When Watson learned of the fiasco involving Daniells and the Senior Committee, she wrote him from Paris: 'I saw a suit of armor which belonged to Francis the first – the headpiece was the head of a lion – the colour a magnificent bronze. I thought: If only Roy had that to slip into.'[35]

Daniells also had a high regard for Dorothy Somerset, who joined the English faculty at UBC as assistant professor in July 1947. She later also taught French and drama. He supported her requests to put on public performances of plays at the end of the third-year English drama courses. In 1956, when drama was becoming so popular with students that it was expanding into esoteric courses like 'stage management,' which had little relation to the normal English curriculum, Daniells helped Somerset orchestrate a campaign to establish a separate Drama Department. He was also sympathetic to the problems that such women faced when dealing with their male peers. After her presentation to the English Department Senior Committee concerning the proposed Drama Department, Daniells reported cheerfully: 'D. Somerset brilliantly defended herself against the boys.'[36] Later, the Frederic Wood and Dorothy Somerset Theatres at UBC were the legacy of third-year English Department drama courses.

The angriest reports regarding the status of women in the English Department at UBC came from working wives like Smith and Mackenzie, who needed an adequate salary and resented the double standard. This also applied to some faculty members' wives with Ph.D.'s who were teaching in the department, including Kay Stockholder, but her case extends beyond Daniells' tenure. It is evident that Smith was treated unfairly. In the 1980s, when universities attempted to equalize the salaries of male and female faculty, committees of redress were directed to look at the rank at appointment and the speed of promotion of a female faculty member contrasted to a male cohort. When this standard is applied to Smith and a male colleague, Steinberg, for example, it is apparent that although both possessed the same qualifications, the Ph.D., the former was initially hired as a lecturer in 1948–9 whereas the latter was hired at two steps higher as an assistant professor in 1946–7. Moreover, during the four years when Smith was a lecturer, all the other lecturers listed in the calendar had possessed only an M.A. Smith was promoted to an instructor for one year, 1953–4, and then became an assistant professor for three years. In 1956–7 Steinberg became an associate professor, and the following year, 1958–9, Smith was given an equivalent rank. However, Smith had been deprived of an assistant professor's salary for five years. It is also apparent that she had to fight for promotion. This is very demoralizing. When she complained to President MacKenzie (described by Birney as a 'male chauvinist') that her salary was below the norm, he allegedly responded that she did not need salary increments as badly as male faculty – her widowed father would leave his house to her.[37] This response is markedly different from MacKenzie's response to Birney's requests for additional salary for family needs.

Nonetheless, Smith blamed Daniells for her slow rate of promotion and satirized him bitterly in a sonnet which portrays him as a Puritan, a scholar who favours male academics above female academics:

Secure, elect, in youth I bore His Light
And sowed His Truth in every rocky field
...

My casuistry
Impresses learned doctors, and a host
Of young disciples, all delightful chaps,
Extol the Father of Lies made Man in Me,
And blind John Milton as Our Holy Ghost.[38]

Here, as in Margaret Laurence's novel and Mallinson's short story, Milton becomes a signifier for the oppression of women, perhaps because Milton formed so large a part of the English canon in Canada.

Smith's comment that Daniells impresses the 'young disciples' of the English Department also raises the important issue of male bonding. Women joining English departments in the fifties and sixties were almost always excluded from male socializing, a significant exclusion because department business is often conducted through one-to-one mentoring and social contact.

The case of Mabel Mackenzie illuminates the personal element in the old-boy network in Canadian graduate education, which could sometimes work to the advantage – as well as the disadvantage – of the woman faculty member. A woman with broad social interests, Mackenzie had begun her formal university training in her forties to supplement her husband's pension. When she graduated with a first-class degree from UBC, did well on her M.A., and applied to take a Ph.D. at the graduate school at Toronto, Woodhouse was initially nervous about accepting her, as he told Daniells: 'Your assurance that Mrs. Mackenzie can return to you removes my one misgiving. I did not know, or at least had not grasped this, when I said that I was frightened of having her on our hands.'[39]

Mackenzie then left Vancouver for Toronto, renting her house to the newly married Roy and Laurenda Daniells while she was away. She kept both informed of her progress, saying that she liked Professor Woodhouse: 'I like his somewhat pompous urbanity, and I thoroughly enjoy his polite manner to students. I have to run like a hare to get to his lectures from a class I teach, so he said "Please Mrs. Mackenzie feel free to come in at any time. Even if you are late I shall be glad to see you."'[40] There is chivalry in Woodhouse's response to Mackenzie, then an older woman student. She told Daniells that her thesis subject was to be '"The literary influence of the Scottish Ballad in the 18th Century, with special reference to Burns"' and added, 'Don't be appalled. I had to do literary history. Philosophical abstraction was too much for me, as was literary criticism.'[41]

The Ph.D. candidate took required courses and then sat a preliminary oral exam to demonstrate mastery of the subject before starting on the dissertation. Mackenzie thought she had done badly on her comprehensive orals, and later described them to a fellow instructor at UBC:

She said ... she went in and they started asking her all sorts of things that were on the list. And she was flubbing every one of these. And finally she said, 'At home I just knew things like that, now I don't understand!' And she said she finally got up, picked up everything, and walked out. And I said, 'Mabel, where'd you go?' and she said 'Go, go? I went to the wash-room, I was sick!'

It turned out that Mackenzie had been supplied with a different copy of the requirements for the exam than the one which the examiners had.[42] Nonetheless, when the results were announced, she discovered she had done exceptionally well and provided Birney with a full report: 'The exam – it was most gratifying. 26 took it, 8 failed completely, 8 failed to get the over 70% mark required for acceptance. And I, through what luck I cannot imagine, came third.'[43]

The problem was that Mackenzie's initial sense of her Ph.D. oral appears to have been correct. What she did not know was that the examining committee had judged that she had not done well but acknowledged extenuating circumstances. Woodhouse had telephoned long distance to Daniells, and they had discussed what ought to be done. Finally, Woodhouse struck a bargain with Daniells. If Daniells would guarantee Mackenzie a position at UBC and not give her senior courses to teach, Woodhouse would permit her to continue the Ph.D. program. Daniells accepted these restrictions.[44] Mackenzie, it appears, was then passed at a distinguished level, possibly to ensure that she retained a position at the University of British Columbia.

For Daniells was not the sole arbiter of Mackenzie's fate. Even as he assured Woodhouse that she would have a faculty position, two members of the Senior Committee saw Dean Chant in relation to the fall roster. When the subject of renewing or replacing Mackenzie came up, Morrison recalled that Chant had offered to let her go. But Morrison and Robbins refused because, as Morrison said, 'we were, both of us, cream puffs. We took a heaven-sent academic opportunity and said, "Well, Sperrin [Chant], she's just having her orals at Toronto this week, let's see what happens." We had no reason to think she would get it.'[45]

The situation was complicated by the fact that senior faculty may have simply judged Mackenzie by the familiar yardstick of whether or not she appeared to be a scholar – that is, a 'bluestocking,' which she was not. Moreover, Daniells could never explain the situation to Mackenzie; not only did he regard her as a friend, but he also was bound by professional confidence. Meantime, influential Senior Committee members held the view that she was not a strong scholar and should not be rewarded. In the spring of 1954, Daniells noted in his diary that this committee had been 'discussing Mabel Mackenzie with distressing chilliness.'[46] Mackenzie, however, once she had completed her degree and proved herself a stimulating classroom teacher, felt that Daniells, in his capacity as head of the department, stood between her and senior courses. She appealed to Birney, who in 1956–7 mounted a mini-campaign to the dean accusing Daniells of ill-treating women faculty. It was probably in the wake of this campaign that Marion Smith achieved her deserved promotion. Mackenzie, in the meantime, continued to teach with distinction and, along with Ruth McConnell, an education professor who taught English courses, including 'The History and Structure of the English Language,' became a role model for young women students in the early sixties.

Throughout the fifties, Daniells had been an active member of the Humanities Research Council. Indeed many of the academic directives taken during this decade, including ACUTE, had been formulated and financed through this organization. He had been elected to the council in 1949, and for the next fifteen years he and Woodhouse were central to the organization, with Daniells serving as president in 1951 and again in 1953. He also proved to be a successful fund-raiser.

The council had begun in 1943, largely because the Depression and the Second World War had had a devastating effect on financing to universities, especially the humanities. At the founding meeting in December 1943, Watson Kirkconnell summarized the 'perilous' state of the humanities, which were neglected by federal and provincial governments as well as the general public. The organization established a membership of sixteen scholars actively involved in research, elected for limited terms, and representative of a wide range of disciplines. At the first plenary meeting in Montreal in May 1944, they adopted aims: 'to analyze problems facing humanistic research in Canada; to aid research through direct funding; to lobby government agencies and universities; to organize direct and indirect contacts among universities and learned societies; and to assist scholarly publication.'[47]

The new organization began by surveying the humanities in Canada with an $8,000 grant from the Rockefeller Foundation. The resulting report, entitled *The Humanities in Canada* (1947), was written by Watson Kirkconnell and Woodhouse, and analysed organizational needs and scholarly standards. For this report, Woodhouse polled professors of English with the question: 'What aim do you set yourself in the honours course in your subject?' Daniells' course was in Milton, and his response to this inquiry was: 'My original answer to this question, *The glory of God*, is still the only one. In the same way that the Christian in a world inimical to his profession must keep his eye on an invisible goal ... so we set up standards of scholarship and objectives in terms of the knowledge that are realized by rather less than two students per annum, on the average.'[48]

Daniells is writing only slightly tongue-in-cheek. As he was to write in a later study of Milton, the object of Milton's scheme of education was to lead the student to know God. Should we wonder how literature and history lead us to God, Milton's answer is simply: '"Our understanding cannot in this body found itself but on sensible things, nor arrive so clearly to the knowledge of God and things invisible as by orderly conning over the visible and inferior creature [i.e., creation]."' Indeed, Daniells argues that for Milton education is closely associated with God and with nationalism: 'a reform of education "for want whereof this nation perishes," is, quite seriously, "an opportunity to try what God hath determined."'[49]

Funding remained an outstanding problem for the Humanities Research Council, and prior to the founding of the Canada Council, the HRC was forced to apply to the Rockefeller Foundation and Carnegie Corporation for funds to administer its programs. In 1953 Daniells had been highly successful in raising $68,000 for the association, which was used for the purpose of furthering scholarship.[50] One of the HRC's primary concerns was the establishment of a national funding council for the arts, humanities, and social sciences; consequently, HRC representatives had appeared three times before the Massey Commission in 1948–9. Pressure was exerted on the federal government to create a funding council, and at the national conference 'Humanities and Government' in 1954, Prime Minister Louis St Laurent announced his government's intention to create a funding body. In 1957, when the Canada Council was formed, it assumed complete financial responsibility for the funding and expansion of the existing aid-to-research and aid-to-publication programs of HRC.

The HRC acted as a clearing house, encouraging and funding scholarship. Through this body in the mid-fifties, R.E. Watters was commissioned and funded to begin work on a massive checklist to determine holdings in Canadian literature in Canadian libraries – by synecdoche, English-Canadian literature. This work was to lay the groundwork for the later *Literary History of Canada* (1964), also supported by the HRC. By 1960 the HRC determined there was need for a new national survey of the humanities in Canada, and a number of scholars, including Daniells, were asked to visit their respective regions in order to 'consult the greatest possible number of university presidents, rectors, deans and professors and prepare reports on the problems facing research.'[51] As one of the primary originators of academic policy in the HRC, Daniells was thus actively engaged in shaping the discipline of English in Canada.

In 1957 Woodhouse had invited Daniells to vary his usual summer vacation by coming to the University of Toronto to teach summer courses on Milton and Canadian literature. This was a welcome invitation. Daniells enjoyed lecturing, and visited many old friends, such as Northrop Frye, and former students, such as F.W. Watt. He also met a pleasant younger couple, Roland McMaster and his wife, who shepherded the family around Toronto.

Daniells usually escaped from the pressures of the UBC English Department by spending his summers in Victoria, primarily to be near his family. Although his father had died in 1951, his mother was delighted to see her grandchildren, and he enjoyed teaching at Victoria College, B.C. There he had no institutional responsibilities, and his good friend, Roger Bishop, was head of English. Roger and Ailsa Bishop joined the couples' list of close friends. The Bishops lived on the waterfront in Victoria, and the Daniells family often found accommodation nearby. After the day's teaching was over, there was always time for swimming in the ocean, socializing with mutual friends, and visiting his mother.

Daniells' ties with his mother were strong until her death, and these yearly vacations provided opportunity for long visits. Daniells also wrote or telephoned several times each week. But in the mid-fifties her health worsened, and in April 1957 she was hospitalized, suffering from dizzy spells. She appeared to rally and returned home, but in October she fell and suffered a fatal heart attack, dying shortly after. The last gathering of the old Plymouth Brethren friends from Daniells' childhood took place at her funeral. Sid Burdge, the farmer for whom he had worked in Alberta, said the last prayer at the graveside. Daniells was comforted by this outpouring of love and affection, but he grieved about not being with his mother at her death.

Laurenda Daniells' father had died a year earlier, at the beginning of October. Because plans had been already made, in November 1957 she and the children went to stay with her mother. With everyone gone, Daniells felt especially bereft. He wrote to Susan and Sally (the family's pet name for Sara) saying, 'I miss you ever so much. The garden looks very quiet and nobody plays there. And the toys in your room are waiting and waiting.' The girls, now seven and eight, loved the stories that their father told them, and he ended his letter with the promise of another tale about

> Lady Greensleeves
> and a big pink rose
> and Big Black Bear
> and a little gold pin
> and Wee Willie Winkie
>
> ...
>
> So give a big kiss to Grandma and a big kiss to Mummy,
> and
>   come
>   home
>   soon![52]

Throughout the fifties, his family had remained a source of love and comfort. And as the children grew, his own horizons widened. To his daughters, Daniells was an indulgent father and, above all, a wonderful storyteller. Like his own Grandfather Stevens, he continued the family tradition of the oral story, made up as he went along. On their family trips, his accounts of 'When I Was a Little Red Headed Girl' – so bad, and a feminist to boot – a favourite of his red-headed daughters, were augmented with stories about 'Lady Greensleeves,' who was beautiful and kind like Laurenda:

> She lived in a forest outside Chartres where, if you walk deep into the forest, the path is covered with little black feathers. But when you get to her house, if you know where to look, there is a little piece of holly. You fit the holly in the keyhole and you hear 'snick' the sound of the key turning the bolt.[53]

Chapter Eighteen

A Canadian Literature

In the mid-fifties Daniells could look back on almost a quarter century of highly successful activity in developing a Canadian literature. In the early thirties, he had taught one of the first combined American and Canadian literature courses to English honours students at Victoria College, Toronto. In the forties at Manitoba, he had encouraged Sinclair Ross, Adele Wiseman, and Margaret Laurence, institutionalized the *Manitoba Arts Review*, and regularly spoke on the CBC on Canadian topics. In fact, one of his 1944 broadcasts about the importance of landscape in Canadian writing was so stimulating that both Northrop Frye and Marshall McLuhan promptly sent letters of appreciation. McLuhan wrote: 'Your remarks about Canadian literature are still caressing my grateful ears ... as for Canadian scenery, its effect is either to paralyse or to muscle-bind, and it will continue to act that way until there are 80 million people here to reduce this horrendous stuff to human terms.'[1]

In 1954, in response to Daniells' growing reputation, he had been invited to New Zealand to speak about Canadian writing. He set out the primary figures, defined what each had accomplished, and deftly summarized the difficulties of establishing a Canadian literature. He was particularly interested in the larger geographical features that had conditioned the history of the country – especially the experience of entering the country through the St Lawrence (a concept later developed metaphorically by Frye in his Conclusion to the *Literary History of Canada*) – and the importance of landscape on all forms of new writing.[2] Daniells also recognized the importance of religious themes in the new novel, especially in Hugh MacLennan's *The Precipice* (1948), Morley Callaghan's *The Loved and the Lost* (1951), and A.M. Klein's *The Second*

Scroll (1951). After his return to Canada, he continued to keep New Zealand audiences informed of developments in Canadian writing by writing an annual 'Letter from Canada' for *Landfall*, the New Zealand literary magazine edited by the poet Charles Brasch. This was the first time Canadian literary events had been reported abroad annually.

Now, in the mid- to late fifties, he was a catalyst in the institutionalizing of Canadian literature. A major figure in the Kingston Conference (1955), he was a central member of the editorial committee that began to meet in 1956–7 to initiate the *Literary History of Canada* (1965) and the prime mover for the journal *Canadian Literature*. Daniells genuinely wanted a Canadian writing to come into being, and as a dominant member of the Humanities Research Council of Canada, he was ideally placed to bring these projects to fruition.

In July 1955 Daniells agreed to help the poet and legal scholar F.R. Scott organize and chair a conference at Kingston, 'The Writer, His Media and the Public,' funded by the Rockefeller Foundation. From the media came Ralph Allen, Kildare Dobbs, Jack McClelland, and Robert Weaver; critics and prose writers included Morley Callaghan, Henry Kreisel, John Marlyn, Joyce Marshall, Hugo McPherson, Desmond Pacey, Malcolm Ross, John Sutherland, and Adele Wiseman. Among the poets were Birney, Elizabeth Brewster, Leonard Cohen, Irving Layton, Dorothy Livesay, Jay Macpherson, Eli Mandel, A.J. M. Smith, and Phyllis Webb. One of the unexpected results of this conference was the establishing of an infrastructure for the development of Canadian literature as a scholarly discipline.

Smith introduced the conference with a talk, 'The Poet,' which began by quoting Daniells, who had said (drawing on his own experience) that the excellence of Canadian poetry existed because of the 'vision' and the 'self-taught craftsmanship' of a handful of individuals, despite 'immense public indifference, deadly though unspoken.' Such indifference existed not, Smith thought, because poetry is obscure, but because the poet is too critical, 'the teller of unpleasant truths, the secret conscience of society, the revealer of unconscious guilt.'[3] Witty but combative, Smith argued that poets wrote for other poets. Irving Layton, equally pugnacious, took the opposite tack, saying that the poet wrote for the public.

Those who agreed with Smith were forced to defend their positions, while those who did not, notably Layton's followers, carried the battle to the barricades. Macpherson later wrote to Scott: 'I found myself again and again crammed into a corner with Reaney & Mandel and bitterly defending myth against everything else possible.'[4] The central split of the conference as far as the poets were concerned was the debate between Smith and Layton. As Eli Mandel recalled, at this point a shift in sensibility in Canadian poetry began to manifest itself: 'to move from whatever the modern period means – Smith, Scott, Klein, Pratt, Finch and Kennedy – to Layton, Dudek, Souster on one hand, and Reaney, Mandel, Macpherson ... on the other.'[5] As both Reaney and Mandel acknowledged their indebtedness to Daniells' *Deeper into the Forest*, there is a sense in which he, as well as Frye, was a progenitor of the new myth poetry.

The closing session was chaired by Daniells and Scott, who attempted to pull together the opposing factions, and to bring forward resolutions to support Canadian writing. The first three resolutions urged all provinces to give a more prominent place to Canadian literature in school curricula, textbooks, colleges, and universities and to support Canadian libraries. After 1956, a number of Canadian universities, notably UBC, included Canadian literature as a separate course, not part of 'North American' literature. The fourth resolution stated that in order 'to establish a continuing literary tradition in Canada significant works by Canadians must be kept in print and if necessary republished in inexpensive editions for use both by students and by general readers.' McClelland and Stewart's New Canadian Library series – the reprinting of classic texts in Canadian literature – was encouraged by discussions between Malcolm Ross and Jack McClelland at Kingston, and linked to this resolution.[6] The resolutions further suggested that the Canada Council, then being formed, should subsidize Canadian books and help Canadian writers through the provision of literary fellowships and scholarships. The importance of the Kingston Conference in giving direction to the Canada Council cannot be overestimated. It quite literally laid the foundations for the future academic study of English and Canadian literature.

After the Kingston Conference, Scott, with several others, gave a radio broadcast on the CBC's 'Fighting Words' describing the resolutions of the final session. He augmented this with an article published in October 1955, pointing out that 'there does not exist in Canada a literary magazine of the type of *Partisan Review, Hudson Review* or the

Sewanee Review, where a coterie of writers and critics maintain a constant watch for new talent ... Indeed ... criticism of Canadian literature scarcely exists at all.'[7] Daniells was already attempting to remedy this situation. Returning from Kingston to B.C. by way of Toronto, he sat with the poet Dorothy Livesay and the Vancouver lawyer and short story writer W.C. McConnell on the plane. Jointly they evolved a plan for a conference on B.C. writing modelled after the Kingston Conference.

Over the next six months, Daniells held a number of meetings at his home with a small committee. The Conference on B.C. Writing was held from 27 to 29 January 1956. Fifty-five delegates attended. Discussion was stimulating and centred on such topics as the situation of the Canadian writer, the difficulty of obtaining Canadian books, and a request that the CBC increase its coverage of Canadian writing. Alan Crawley, editor of the important British Columbia poetry magazine *Contemporary Verse,* and George Woodcock, formerly associated with a number of British little magazines, presented papers on 'The Critic's View.' At the closing session, a number of committees were established, including a continuing executive with Birney (who wanted a creative writing magazine, later to become *Prism* [1959–]) as chair, and a periodical committee consisting of R.E. Watters, Woodcock, Robert Patchell, and Inglis Bell. In the autumn following the Kingston Conference, Woodcock had written an article for the *Dalhousie Review* alluding to the 'Fighting Words' broadcast and also suggesting 'a Canadian Journal devoted specifically to the critical consideration of native and world literature' – although Woodcock's own interests inclined to the cosmopolitan.[8] The subcommittees established at the conference were given the responsibility of calling a second meeting the following year. When it was all over – an outstanding success – Daniells held a celebratory lunch with Birney and Woodcock. However, the project then lapsed as Birney took a year off and Woodcock went to France.

Also in the mid-fifties, Daniells was approached by the American sociologist Julian Park, who had earlier published a study of French culture, regarding a volume on the culture of Canada. That the 'Canadian' context of writing was considered questionable at this time is pointed up by Park's introductory remarks that one or two individuals had declined to contribute to his volume on the grounds that Canada was culturally immature. Daniells strongly disagreed. His own chapter is a spirited assertion of the existence of a Canadian literary tradition. In his chapter, 'Literature: Poetry and the Novel,' which introduces the book, he brought his earlier de Carle lectures up to date by surveying the Canadian field to this point. Daniells' concern is to distinguish the Canadian experience from the American, and to isolate the essentials of Canadian life. He begins gracefully by remarking that 'the people of the United States are North Americans whose national identity begins with a revolution and who settled their greatest internal problem by a decisive civil war between the states. The people of Canada are North Americans who have avoided both these solutions.' The large facts of Canadian life are 'first the land itself, the great terrain, and second the juxtapositions of race, nationality, and creed within the country and upon the continent.'

Within this structure, Daniells writes skilfully and sensitively of the novels and journals that deal with national issues (Hugh MacLennan's *Two Solitudes*, Susanna Moodie's *Roughing It in the Bush*), sketches the major texts in poetry and prose, and points to what he sees as the emergence of a Jewish tradition in Canada. He also attempts to place Canadian literature by quoting MacLennan, who had once told Daniells that the nationalism of his early novels represented an attempt to communicate with Canadians: 'Fiction in Canada is at the stage of fiction in the States a century ago ... Hawthorne particularly felt the problem we feel – the need of creating a perspective into which an American fiction could fit.'[9]

Daniells felt a similar need to create perspective. When reviewing the work of poets and novelists, he alluded to the general perception that Canada had produced no major literary figure, a De Maupassant, 'someone capable of producing a large number of stories which are united by a sensibility, a style, a locale, and a selection of material,' and suggested Morley Callaghan as a possibility.[10] It is a pleasant irony that two women, a former Manitoba student Margaret Laurence, and Alice Munro, Carl F. Klinck's former student at Western, were to become the chief contenders for this distinction in the early seventies. Furthermore, Kevin Brooks, arguing on the basis of this essay in the Park volume, and Daniells' work in founding the Association of Canadian University Teachers of English, suggests that Daniells' literary criticism 'promote[d] the idea of a national identity in scholarship.'[11]

———◆◆———

Between 1956 and 1964 Daniells was working on the most ambitious project yet undertaken to promote a Canadian literature. He had been meeting with a small group of individuals, several of whom were members of the HRC, to develop a literary history of Canada. The idea of a history had first been raised by R.E. Watters, in correspondence with Carl Klinck regarding their joint textbook, *Canadian Anthology*, but it was Klinck who carried the idea forward.[12] In September 1956 Klinck had attended meetings of the English Institute at Columbia University, where he had been greatly impressed by a paper given by Northrop Frye. He asked Frye 'whether he could reconcile his *high* criticism with respect for Canadian literary works.' Frye assured Klinck that he could. Indeed he was preparing a paper on this topic called 'Preface to an Uncollected Anthology.'[13]

After consultation with Frye, and assured of support from the HRC, Klinck invited Daniells, Frye, and Alfred Bailey to form an advisory board to produce a literary history that 'interprets Canadians in terms of the literary vision of those who have written here ... It could be solidly based on a substantial body of Canadian writing, much of which would thus receive its first critical examination.'[14] Desmond Pacey and Claude Bissell soon joined the project, and all five became editors, with Klinck as general editor. Klinck's model was Spiller, Thorpe, and Canby's *Literary History of the United States* (1946, 1953), which had an implicitly nationalist agenda. Daniells was the primary fund-raiser for the endeavour, contributed four chapters, and, throughout the project, engaged in a dialogue with Klinck to establish critical parameters.

Initially, when planning for the *Literary History* began, the greatest problem faced by the editors was the small pool of contributors to choose from (as opposed to the sixty or more contributors for the American history), fewer still of whom were specialists in Canadian literature or cultural history. Consequently, completed chapters varied dramatically both in style and critical approach. Early in the project, Watters had been irritated because he thought that the 'Daniells-Frye-Pacey' group had been assigned responsibility for too much of the text.[15] Then, as successive parts of the book took shape, Daniells became concerned: 'Where is our boundary, the boundary between Canadian literature and Canadian writing? I don't think much of the production of our social scientists qualifies as literature.'[16]

When the drafted chapters were submitted to the advisory board for commentary, Daniells was alarmed. 'I doubt if it is going to be possible substantially to harmonize styles (and approaches).'[17] He told Klinck he saw 'two problems, quite separable, one of sentence-by-sentence felicity or correctness, the other of scale, density, method of approach.' As Daniells acknowledged, little could be done about the second problem. Once the editors had decided 'to let contributors go their own way within a simple limit of number of words,' they had also decided 'to run the risk of incompatible and incongruous contributions.'[18] The most important question about the nature of the projected book was the question of literary value. As Daniells bluntly asked Klinck, 'is the book to be a *literary* history or a literary *history*?'[19] It was in this aspect of the undertaking that Frye provided critical support for Klinck by carving out in his article, 'Preface to an Uncollected Anthology,' a special place for the critic of Canadian literature 'somewhere between' the descriptive function of the social sciences and the ordinary standards of literary judgment. Klinck knew that certain examples of Canadian writing were not up to snuff. But he pinned his hopes on future revised editions of the *Literary History*, where succeeding scholars could undertake evaluation in depth.[20] In the meantime, he hoped to make the volume as definitive as possible. Daniells was more pragmatic: 'I doubt whether L.H.C. can be in any sense definitive. It will provoke discussion, reply, emulation and criticism: this is perhaps its main function, in the present dearth of real critical interest in Canada's literature outside the universities.'[21]

As a Milton scholar, Daniells tended towards a 'greats' theory of literature which distinguished between major and minor figures. 'What I am afraid of is that a reader in England might have difficulty in knowing who our major authors are and what they may be supposed to have accomplished.'[22] As a compromise, Daniells suggested that Klinck should set out his principles in a preface, while Frye should write a summarizing conclusion. Meantime, Daniells as contributor (as opposed to editor) went his own merry way, ignoring Klinck's editorial directives and writing his chapters on poets of the Confederation precisely the way he thought they should be written: with appreciation and judicious selection from the text, and under the categories of major and minor poets. The predictable result, as Klinck later ruefully admitted, was that Daniells' chapters and Frye's conclusion were considered by critics to be the best pieces in the volume.[23] The process of developing the individual chapters and the structure for the *Literary History of Canada* was to engage all of the contributors from 1956 to 1964.

In the meantime, in 1958, the proposed new UBC journal for the study of Canadian literature had been temporarily derailed. The editorial committee of Birney, Watters, and Woodcock had dispersed, and, with no action in sight, Daniells attacked the problem from a new direction. He spoke to his colleague Stanley Read, who was a good friend of President MacKenzie. While the two men were playing golf, Read extracted from MacKenzie a promise of initial support for a periodical on Canadian literature. An office and a salary for hiring an editor were agreed upon.[24] With MacKenzie's support assured, Daniells knew that the next step in founding a journal was to establish continuing financial support. Daniells wrote to the Koerner Foundation committee setting out the academic guidelines for a new journal on Canadian literature, the tasks of an editor, his proposed salary, and an overall budget. Basically, Daniells wanted to continue the aims now set out by the editors of the *Literary History* in charting the history of writing in Canada and reassessing literary works and periods. To everyone's astonishment, his application was successful, possibly because of his friendship with Walter Koerner. With this financial backing, it was possible to establish *Canadian Literature*.[25]

As this was to be an in-house journal, the committee's first choice for editor was Watters, then a full professor who had recently published *Canadian Anthology* (1965), co-edited with Klinck. Watters was the Canadian literature specialist at UBC and was then preparing the most extensive list of Canadian library holdings in the subject, *A Checklist of Canadian Literature and Background Materials, 1628–1950* (1959; 2nd ed., 1973). However, Watters had just accepted an invitation to visit Australia and would be away for a year. The committee's second choice was Woodcock, and Daniells personally invited him to take on the job of editor. In *Beyond the Blue Mountains: An Autobiography*, Woodcock recalls that in February 1956 Daniells invited him to tea with Earle Birney: 'we discussed my joining the Department of English. While wandering around Roy's winter garden, the suggestion was made that someday soon U.B.C. might decide to compete with Queen's and Toronto by publishing its own quarterly and that I might be the person to give it a special editorial tone.' The rest of the story is best told by Woodcock, writing in the *British Columbia Library Quarterly* in 1959. He states that in 1958 the idea of publishing a review of Canadian studies had been circulating at UBC when

a group including Roy Daniells and Stanley Read of the English Department and Neal Harlow and Inglis Bell of the University Library narrowed down this rather general idea to the specific proposal of a journal for the criticism and reviewing of the literature of Canada, a journal which would fulfill more or less the same function as *Canadian Art* for the visual arts. I was a late comer to the proposal; I had been studying in France during the

year of 1957/58 and did not return until August, 1958, when I was approached with the suggestion that I might become the editor of such a magazine.
I accepted ...[26]

In later years, Woodcock was mistakenly credited with the conception and founding of *Canadian Literature*[27] – indeed, he sometimes claimed this himself. However, it was very much Daniells' project and supported by the English Department. Department members such as Read, Tallman, and Hugo McPherson wrote articles for early issues, and literary figures like A.J.M. Smith and Ethel Wilson, with whom Daniells had close connections, also contributed. Daniells also acted as a behind-the-scenes literary advisor to Woodcock up to the seventies, performing the same function that he had earlier done for the *Manitoba Arts Review*.[28] The new journal, which provided a focus for the emerging Canadian literature, immediately became essential reading for all scholars in the field. Younger poets (such as Margaret Atwood) as well as university teachers and students eagerly read each issue. This journal had a major function in consolidating the growth of Canadian literature as a discipline.

PART FIVE

University of British Columbia: 1960–1970

Chapter Nineteen

The Lions' Den

In March 1959, Daniells received a great surprise when he opened a letter from Albert Trueman, now head of the just founded Canada Council, which stated that he had been awarded a special $8,000 Canada Council Fellowship with research travel expenses. Daniells had not applied for this grant, and only three were awarded across Canada. He decided to take his first sabbatical in twenty-eight years of teaching English and to use the grant to research his long-projected book on the Baroque. His doctoral thesis had been augmented by several papers in the forties and fifties, but what he needed now was leisure to reconsider the Baroque in the light of recent criticism and to undertake field work in Italy. He also wanted to work in a library with adequate resources on Milton for his project; this meant the British Museum.

Such sabbaticals, usually a year's research leave free from teaching but supported with some salary, are commonplace today, but in 1959 they were rare. Moreover, his thesis about the Baroque was a large critical assertion, as yet not satisfactorily proven. In the introduction to his eventual book, Daniells felt obliged to argue that 'the arts of a given period form a total pattern, the same impulses expressing themselves in a variety of forms.'[1]

On 22 August the whole family sailed from New York for England, and, after some sightseeing in Scotland, they boarded a ferry for Calais a month later. They drove to Rouen, continued on to Chartres, and then on 27 September the Daniellses arrived in Menton on the Côte d'Azur. They decided to rent a flat, enrol the children in the local school, and stay for at least three months. Menton was ideally situated: Rome, where Daniells would be doing much of his research, could be reached overnight by train.

Their days assumed a leisurely routine: the girls went to school; Daniells worked on his book; he and Laurenda took walks and visited museums; and in the evenings they all went to the beach. In early October, Daniells began working steadily on his book, examining connections between Milton's poetry and the Baroque style, and concepts of unity, power, and will. The work was not without frustrations. As often happens in such large projects, especially one which broke new ground in relating literature to the other arts, his progress was discouragingly slow. As he admitted to Desmond Pacey, 'in a fumbling, creaking, repetitive manner it is possible to think and I chop off daily a fragment from the lump of research to which I've been committed for so long and with so little result.'[2]

In early December, he went to Rome, walking to St Peter's on his first day: 'got my first sight first of the dome & then of the whole piazza & facade ... could not go much further toward the cathedral than Bernini's columns over the papal altar ... very impressive nevertheless & my belief that the whole is a monument to papal power very much strengthened.' The following day, he went to see the Spanish Steps and attempted, unsuccessfully, to get into St Peter's. On his last day, he made arrangements to use the British Council library and went to the Colosseum, where he was overawed by its massive, brutal stonework. He then returned 'to good old Menton, so small and quiet and French with the curve of green lights on the bay and glad to be home.'[3]

Christmas was spent in Menton, complete with an English plum pudding, a chicken, and champagne. It was a bright sunny day, one of his happiest Christmases ever: 'so many old fears and obsessions being stilled, & so much of the happiness implicit but not realized in my childhood being now realized.'[4] In the New Year there were a number of research trips to Pisa, Florence, Siena, and Milan. March and April were spent chiefly in Rome, where he gained a better sense of the sculptors Bernini, Borromini, and Cortona. It had become apparent to Daniells that there was a movement in Milton's poetry from struggle to a regaining of balance, which, in his earlier poems, could be seen as style changes associated with Mannerism, the form between Renaissance and Baroque.[5] To see Mannerism in greater detail, he travelled with the family to Florence, to the palace at Caserta, and to the Church of Santa Maria della Salute in Venice.

In March the family drove to Pisa, and on to Florence. There Daniells went to the Laurentian Library and the Medici Chapel, where he had the great joy, after years of interest in the subject, of seeing Michelangelo's rendering of the Medici tombs with their statues. Michelangelo's works fascinated Daniells: he felt that a creative spirit of great power was 'telling us something about death ... there is paradoxical reversal and denial in this chapel.'[6] He went several times to the Uffizi Gallery, where he became 'saturated with masterpieces,' and to St Mark's Monastery, where he saw 'the Fra Angelicos & the cells, particularly Savonarola's own, with two pictures of his execution.'[7]

The Baroque appealed to Daniells because it seemed to suggest 'causal sequences [and] connecting threads' which allowed him to make sense of a whole historical period; thus the culmination of each historical period is seen as worthwhile in itself, not simply the dead past.[8] Furthermore, as his daughter Sara later recalled, although he rejected the Puritanism of the Reformation, he felt that Mannerist and Baroque art and architecture embodied 'the spirit, the essence of it all, the higher thing that he was always trying to find.' She recalls once standing with him in front of Michelangelo's *Moses*, where Daniells was so overwhelmed with emotion that he burst into tears. The whole architecture of Rome itself seemed to be designed to express the power of God, especially St Peter's, where the embracing columns seemed to bring the worshipper closer to the spirit. 'That's why he was always so charmed by Rome and so overwhelmed by Rome at the same time.'[9]

The family later took sightseeing trips to Athens, where they visited the Parthenon, the theatre of Dionysus, and the Roman agora. In Corinth, Daniells was struck by an old marketplace 'facing an extremely ancient, small well preserved temple on a small hill, which Paul must have seen as he argued with the Corinthians.' From there they continued to Argos and Epidaurus. As they continued north, he enjoyed the 'carpets of flowers among the rocks & fragments of old structures,– poppies, daisies ... a fine herb-like smell in the air ... At Mycenae we stood in the ruts of Agamemnon's chariot, saw the ruins of the palace & the fresh-looking cement of the floor, admired the views up into the hills or down the valley to the sea.'[10]

Letters had been arriving regularly from Vancouver. In the fall, Woodcock had written to say that he was 'pleased with the initial success of C[anadian] L[iterature],'[11] and at the start of 1960 R.G. Baker wrote saying that Meredith Thompson, a newly appointed senior professor, together with William Robbins, were attempting to set the clock back with relation to the powers of the Senior Committee.[12] This news reawakened his miserable anxieties of 1954. For nearly a week, Daniells 'couldn't stop thinking about UBC' and found himself 'still in great turmoil about the department.'[13]

The worry gradually receded but was replaced by self-reproach: 'I am rather sad about not getting more done & determined to pull up my socks.'[14] On 2 March 1960 he noted, 'At about 8 am today half of my formal year of leave was up. My only resolution, as I review it and look forward, is to commit myself instant by instant wholly into the hands of God.'[15] In fact, he was using his time fully. Not only was he researching his study of the Baroque, he was also working on his chapters for the *Literary History of Canada* and trying to write a few poems every week.

On their last day in Rome, 8 April, Daniells went on a final tour of Baroque churches. The following day, the family left Rome for Naples, Pompeii, Assisi, and Ravenna. During the next few weeks, the family drove through the Austrian Tyrol to Switzerland and from there to Germany, Holland, and France. They lingered a little in Paris but left the Continent in early May for England, stopping at Canterbury to see the cathedral, and continuing on to London. There Daniells received by mail 'the news of Tuli Larsen's death, who I suppose inspired more affection than any other person in the Department.'[16] Another chapter of his life had ended. Larsen, more than Sedgewick, had inspired Daniells with a genuine love of literature.

In London, Daniells went to the British Museum each day to read Milton criticism, and the family continued to take day trips. He and Laurenda celebrated their twelfth wedding anniversary – 'much happiness to recall during all that time.'[17] There were various visitors from home, mostly colleagues in English, and the family visited one of his Manitoba students, Margaret, the former 'Baby' Bjornson from Winnipeg, now Lady Elton and keeper of the Elton papers, in Kensington.

In Oxford, Daniells saw Herbert Davis and the new Bodleian Library. The family attended the wedding of the Davis's daughter Jane, where Daniells met, to his great surprise, old friends like Donald Creighton and S.H. Hooke in the gardens of Worcester College. One of his last pilgrimages was with his cousin 'Mal' to see their old houses at Sydenham and Catford, including his old home at 188 Venner Road: 'the place appeared very run down indeed and narrow[er] (about 18 or 19 feet) than I would have believed.'[18] It was to be his last visit to his birthplace.

The family sailed for Canada on 23 August, disembarking at Montreal on 30 August. Laurenda Daniells and the girls left for Winnipeg by the 'Canadian,' and he took another train to Kingston to work on his chapters for the *Literary History* in the Rogers Library in the Lorne Pierce collection of Canadiana. He found H.P. (Pete) Gundy, the librarian, very helpful, and also saw George Whalley and Malcolm Ross. He spent several days looking at the Isabella Valancy Crawford files and 'could have wept at the evidence of that poor girl's struggle. She seems to be our Brontë, Keats and Chatterton, all in one.' Later, when writing on the Confederation group, Daniells gave Carl Klinck his impressions of Crawford: 'How likeable, how loveable, she is compared with those two dummies, Roberts & Scott.'[19] Before Daniells left, Ross presented him with a paperback copy of *Canadian Poets of the Confederation*, which he had edited, one of the first texts for university use produced as a result of the Kingston Conference.

In Toronto, Daniells discussed publication of his manuscript with University of Toronto Press and had a visit with 'Norrie' and Helen Frye, probably about the *Literary History*. Then he took the train to Winnipeg, where he met the family, and they continued on to Vancouver, arriving 7 September. In retrospect, it had been a stimulating and enjoyable year. Although he did not realize it, Daniells now had the basis for a book, and the time he had spent with his family had been important – he constantly noted in his diary his delight in activities with his wife and daughters. After this year of freedom, getting back into administrative harness was to prove a great strain.

When Daniells returned to UBC in September 1960, the old problems of departmental administration – fractious personalities, inadequate funding, lack of support at the administrative university level – began again, but now complicated by new problems associated with promotion and tenure. The effect of these severe pressures on a sensitive and creative individual can be crushing. Visitors to his office in the early sixties, in order to reach Daniells, had to navigate a virtual barricade of bookcases. Although his public image was that of the polished and urbane professor, the man beneath the facade (or behind the barricade) sometimes appeared to have been as vulnerable as the small creature, the mole, of one of his early sonnets who, when threatened by dogs, 'squeaked and thrust and thrust his head in anguish / Telling his pain and grief in a mole's language / And tried a refuge in the earth to tear':

For that's the best-laid scheme of moles and men,
To get down under in the healing gloom,
Calm in the dark and soundless in the ground.[20]

Daniells also seems to have sought 'healing gloom,' but the temper of the hippie sixties and the requirements of his office as head of English precluded this.

Earlier, in the fifties, hiring and tenure were less controversial. Individuals who had continued their teaching and academic work at a reasonable level were eventually granted an appointment 'without term.' But department members were now increasingly vocal about appointments because the choice of candidates hired affected the nature of the department. Moreover, new UBC tenure requirements, established in the late fifties, were far more stringent: the contracts of faculty who did not complete their Ph.D.'s or publish sufficiently within five years of their initial appointment were not renewed. Because of these regulations, and because the department had split into a self-styled 'left' which put more emphasis on teaching and a 'right' which put more emphasis on publication, it was now necessary to get 65 per cent of the vote of tenured professors in the department to give a young professor a permanent appointment. Thus it was far easier for the right to get 35 per cent of the vote and deny tenure than it was for the left to get 65 per cent and grant a permanent appointment. The undeclared middle of the department was always vulnerable to the argument that better scholars could be found.[21]

Even when the department members and the tenure committee could agree, the English Department's recommendations were frequently rejected by the University Tenure Committee. Anxiety was high. When popular young instructors were not given permanent positions, students, other faculty, and sometimes the public at large protested that they had been unjustly treated. Students then organized petitions and rallies; the student newspaper, *The Ubyssey*, came out in favour of the instructor; and the department divided on the merits of specific cases. Throughout all this turmoil, the head was obliged to keep the department together, placate both sides, and find adequate funding and new faculty to staff overflowing classes. Daniells' diary of December 1961 repeatedly records his concern about appointments and about other curriculum issues: 'Departmental meeting; protests from [Charles] Mitchell & [Fred] Stockholder.'[22]

Stockholder, then considered one of the younger radicals, recalls that he and his group regarded Daniells as a 'machiavellian saint, which meant that he was witty, amiable, generous, as well as a devious authoritarian playing groups and individuals against each other. I know that he found jobs for at least three people who had to leave because they could not get tenure at UBC ... I also know that he gave money to faculty who needed [it], and glasses of sherry when it helped. I think he also regularly reached beyond his personal prejudices to befriend people who were very different from himself (myself among them). He was a rare thing, a colleague who acted affectionately with nearly all of us.' Stockholder also believed that the biggest conflicts in the department were generational rather than ideological.[23]

The department had divided: on one side were the senior professors, largely Canadian, with a relatively fixed view of the discipline; on the other side were the American younger professors with a high degree of professionalism and a more diverse sense of what ought to be taught. These were the difficult years of the Vietnam War, with American Ph.D.'s coming to Canada angry about their country. Daniells, who rarely shared his private feelings with his faculty, appeared to be remote from such issues. To some of the younger professors, his gentlemanly concerns about good teaching and about 'equity' throughout the department may have seemed passé, although they would have shared his belief in the importance of research.

To make matters worse, the sixties had brought social unrest and the questioning of established values. It was not simply a matter of student unrest and American activists like Jerry Rubin occupying the UBC Faculty Club with a pig, but rather a new, sixties sense of faculty rights and freedoms – all of which overflowed in departmental meetings. This was offensive to Daniells, who expected decorum in department meetings. He didn't like being challenged, but the challenging of authority was what the sixties was all about. And when aggravated, he had a hot temper and could fly into a passion of righteous indignation. In one department meeting, Philip Pinkus, a young professor who tagged Daniells as anti-Semitic, accused him of running department meetings like a Nuremberg rally. 'Put that down in the minutes!' shouted Daniells.[24]

Undoubtedly, he could be autocratic when conducting department meetings – he was 'Old School' in his sense of the relation between a head and faculty members – and he shared some of the unthinking, middle-class anti-Semitism of an earlier period.[25] Pinkus considered him anti-Jewish because Eli Mandel had once told Pinkus that A.S.P. Woodhouse had reported that Daniells had refused to hire Mandel on the grounds that he already had a Jewish person, M.W. Steinberg, on the staff. Yet Steinberg was one of Daniells' few confidants at UBC. On another occasion, after a trying department meeting, someone sent

Daniells a few lines from Milton's *Paradise Lost*, rearranged as a found poem:

ROY
With head uplift above
   the departmental wave
And eyes that sparkling
   blazed.[26]

Of course, it is Milton's Satan, defiant even in defeat, who raises his head above the wave.

Daniells was appalled at himself when he lost his temper. Early in 1961 he copied a series of prayers, recording on 1 January, 'Help me O God, even today at this hour when I must begin my work, to take the first steps on the way and to enter into the blessed life. Control my thoughts, full of sorrow and anger and rage.'[27] His turmoil was generated by English Department problems – especially Birney – partly by a troubling world situation, and partly by his own genetic predisposition to depression: 'Help me, O God to preserve a mind at peace with Thee and with itself in the midst of these troubles in Laos ...'[28] In the spring of 1962 he went to see Dean Chant 're grief over promotion list and also re Birney, who is raging over the failure of his attempt to get Layton appointed here.'[29]

The early sixties brought to a head the long simmering disagreements between Birney and Daniells. As time went on, each became more set in his ways. Hilda Thomas, then an English Department lecturer, recalled: 'I think they became more and more separate in the paths they pursued because of their different temperaments. Everything in Daniells that said upright, respectable, disciplined, morally correct was reinforced as time went on until that became his métier if you like, and everything in Birney that said romantic, free, untrammelled, explorative, wide-ranging, developed until they completely diverged.'[30] The divide was growing too great to be bridged.

As a child, Daniells knew well the Old Testament story about his namesake, the prophet Daniel, who was thrown into a lions' den (Daniel 6:22). This story must have seemed particularly appropriate to Daniells in April and May 1962, with Birney cast as his persecutor. Providentially, he was to escape from this predicament when his relationship with Birney changed. Until 1963 Birney had made his own agenda prevail within the department and the university, but after 1965 and the publications of *Milton, Mannerism and Baroque* and the *Literary History of Canada*, Daniells rose in academic prestige. Conversely, although Birney continued to be respected throughout Canada as a poet, he lost stature as a professor at UBC. The change in their relative positions again pivoted on creative writing and questions of hiring.

It is curious that the two men differed so profoundly, because their interests were so similar. The creative – or creating – aspect of English had always been a strong part of the English Department at UBC under Daniells' leadership. In the fifties, he had encouraged the Poetry Centre talks, organized by Steinberg, through which poets like Dylan Thomas, W.H. Auden, Stephen Spender, and Theodore Roethke had read at UBC. In the late fifties and early sixties, Helen Sonthoff, an instructor in the English Department, became secretary for the Poetry Centre, and she and the novelist Jane Rule assisted Steinberg in bringing in visiting poets. This group, acting on advice from both Warren Tallman and Birney, invited several poets from San Francisco, including Robert Duncan, Lawrence Ferlinghetti, Michael McClure, and Jack Spicer. In 1961, when organizing the year's roster of poetry readings, Sonthoff invited Daniells to read some of his new poems.

On 20 October 1961, Daniells read several poems later to be published in *The Chequered Shade* (1963), including 'Menton 1,' 'Re-Creation Grounds,' and 'With Children in the Protestant Cemetery' (at one point, when Daniells had become gravely ill in Italy, he and Laurenda had briefly talked about the possibility that he might be buried there):

Kneel in the grass with them. And when you say,
'He was a poet, you will love him, he died young,'
...
Go on, go on, to tell what day by day
Through years nor Keats nor Shelley could prolong
You've learned, that bitterness and grief and wrong
Time hurls upon us, friendship lifts away.

The large Buchanan lecture hall was crowded, and he was wretchedly ill with a cold; nonetheless, the reading went well. After his reading, he received several notes of appreciation, including one from Birney: 'Your range in and control of the sonnet would be hard to equal among living English writers. I felt I was listening to a distillation of a technique that could only have been achieved by a long loyalty to the craft, and a love of the essence.'[31] It was a kind message, all the more remarkable because Birney and Daniells were not getting on. This hiatus in their thirty years of on-again, off-again disagreement is all the more significant because 'With Children in the Protestant Cemetery' was written with Birney in mind, and recalled their youthful friendship.[32]

These poems were published in his second book of poetry, *The Chequered Shade*, largely a collection of sonnets. Daniells' emotional range is large: from the urbane and lovely 'Dear to God and Famous to All Ages,' in which the speaker refutes Milton to affirm that only personal love matters, through the slightly comic 'Psalm 23,' where a good landlord and a good roast beef stand in for the parable of the Good Samaritan, to the bitterly honest 'Psalm 37':

> Fret not thyself because of evil-doers.
> Good advice but very hard to take.
> Too many bastards always on the make ...

To be sure, God has promised retribution: 'But in the meantime how to go about / Containing myself. For that there is no provision. / Anger and hope deferred eat out my bones.'[33] These sonnets reveal a passionate sensibility held in check by conventional form. Louis Dudek, reviewing *The Chequered Shade*, finds that Daniells' irony puts him in the company of modernists like Edwin Muir and John Crowe Ransom.[34]

Although Daniells preferred to write the old-fashioned sonnet, possibly because the sonnet provided formal control over experience, the UBC English Department was well staffed with faculty who advocated free-flowing modern poetry. Several American assistant professors had close connections with the earlier bohemian, and later hippie, movements at Berkeley. Department members such as Warren Tallman and his wife, Ellen, provided a meeting ground for Black Mountain poets like Allen Ginsberg, Robert Creeley, Robert Duncan, Jack Spicer, and Gary Snyder. In the early sixties, Tallman invited Duncan to visit UBC; the excitement generated by his visit led Frank Davey, George Bowering, and Lionel Kearns to start *TISH* in 1961, a poetry little mag intended to shock – the name is an anagram.

Tallman was not originally a poetry enthusiast. When he had first come to UBC in 1956, his specialty was Henry James and he taught the fiction of Hardy, Lawrence, and Conrad. However, Daniells invited him to help teach a new third-year course, an introduction to poetry, which he was developing.[35] His wife, Ellen Tallman, recalls that with his erudition, wit, and classroom manner, 'Roy charmed [Warren], utterly charmed him ... it was a kind of literary seduction and he loved it.' Tallman felt singled out by Daniells at that point; 'he [Tallman] was clearly captivated with the mind, the vision, the poetry ... he'd never really met anyone quite like that, or at least anyone who'd paid attention to him.' Tallman's academic interests suddenly changed: 'it was his doing the poetry with Daniells ... that made him realize that that was the way he was really interested. And from then on he really was in poetry.'[36] Daniells also gave Tallman a copy of Sinclair Ross's novel *As for Me and My House*, to which he had just written an introduction. From then on, Tallman began to read Canadian as well as American writing, building on his understanding that both were New World literatures.

Daniells and Tallman got along very well – for Tallman, although a maverick, was not political. 'I think that Roy had a great tolerance with a maverick, as long as it wasn't a hostile maverick.'[37] Tallman was now a mentor to a group of active young poets who congregated at his home – the *TISH* poets – and he wanted to widen their experience by bringing some of the chief figures of the new Black Mountain poetics to Vancouver. This group was particularly interested in a poetry that approximated natural speech and was written in lines set out by oral rhythms. When Tallman proposed the idea of a poetry summer school, Daniells was supportive.

Tallman began planning in the spring of 1962, although the summer school was not held until a year later. As Birney recalled, 'the idea was to have [Charles] Olson and Ginsberg and Duncan and they [Tallman, Zilber, and the creative-writing group] asked for my advice and how to raise money. I told them I had planned for a trip to Central America – had applied for a grant ... They tried to find a replacement and started with Irving [Layton].'[38] Birney, who had been appointed by Daniells to chair the department's creative-writing offerings, had some autonomy in seeking out sessional appointments for such courses. He wrote to Layton asking him if he would be interested in coming for the summer session. To his surprise, Layton was interested in a permanent position: 'to help make Vancouver the centre of good writing in this country.'

Birney was delighted with the possibility of having a poet of Layton's stature at UBC. But a permanent appointment could only be made through the English Department. Accordingly, Birney approached Daniells, who, he reported, 'clapped [his] hand to [his] head and said, "Not Layton!"'[39] Undoubtedly Daniells feared that Layton would be a difficult colleague, multiplying by two the difficulties with Birney. Nonetheless, on Birney's insistence, he agreed that Layton could submit an application. This procedure was putting the cart before the horse because usually a department determines whether it needs a faculty member in a specific area, gets a funding commitment from the dean and/or president, and then advertises. None of that had been done.

Layton applied to Daniells on 7 May 1962, explaining that he had a B.Sc. from Macdonald College and an M.A. from McGill. He had taught part-time at McGill and at Sir George Williams. 'If I may slip into an unhabitual bit of immodesty, I can add that my courses have always been well attended and that I am regarded as one of the more popular lecturers at the University.'[40] He mentioned his last book, *The Swinging Flesh* (1961), just reviewed by Daniells.

Layton's application was not a strong one, for although his poetry compensated for a lack of graduate study in English, the question to be asked by any administrator is why Layton, who had received his undergraduate degree in 1939 and an M.A. in 1946, had not obtained a permanent position in the intervening twenty-odd years. Was it a question of academic competence? Or was it his reputation as a difficult colleague? Layton was known to have carried on a number of literary feuds throughout the fifties, attacking colleagues such as Northrop Frye, A.J.M. Smith, and F.R. Scott, sometimes in vituperative verse.

Daniells wrote to Desmond Pacey, then vice-president at the University of New Brunswick, acknowledging these concerns and asking Pacey, whom he knew to be Layton's friend, for his advice. He also contacted Frye, then principal of Victoria College. As the former editor of 'Poetry: Letters in Canada' for the *University of Toronto Quarterly*, Frye was well qualified to assess his poetry. Finally, he wrote Harold Files, head of English at McGill, Layton's old professor. Layton had secured references from the head of English at Sir George Williams, Wynne Francis, a friend and professor, and from Pacey, his closest academic friend.

Meantime, Daniells called together the English Department tenure committee, which consisted of himself, John Creighton, and Meredith Thompson, to consider Layton's file. It was now an English Department appointments committee, rather than the Senior Committee, that considered Layton's application because of a new tenure document developed at UBC in the late fifties which restored to Daniells some of the powers earlier held by the Senior Committee. The committee met on 8 May with the creative-writing committee, which consisted of Birney, J. Zilber, and A.M. Friedson. During this meeting, Daniells mentioned that he had no funds allocated for a permanent position for Layton. Birney's response was that Daniells 'must request money from the dean.'[41]

At this point, Birney became alarmed. He was already chafing about the delay in reaching a decision. He was scheduled to leave for Mexico in early June and wanted the matter settled before he left. On 14 May, a week after the date on Layton's application, Birney wrote directly to President MacKenzie submitting his own dossier. This consisted of a covering letter together with a number of supporting letters from students taking creative-writing courses, notably Bowering, Davey, and Kearns, and instructors such as Zilber, Friedson, Tallman, and Phyllis Webb. He did not inform Daniells that he was doing this, again bypassing both the department and the head.

Daniells appears to have still been considering the matter. Between 14 and 17 May, the appointments committee had met and recommended against offering an appointment to Layton. Nonetheless, Daniells wanted to talk over the matter with Dean Chant before making his own recommendation. On his arrival in the dean's office of 17 May, Chant told him that Birney had written directly to the president. By now Daniells had endured these tactics from Birney for fourteen years. He would have no more. He went back to his office, bundled up all the material relating to Layton's application, dictated a covering letter, and sent it all to Dean Chant. The decision was now removed from the department level to the dean's level.

Daniells' letter acknowledged that at face value Layton was a good appointment for a Western university with a program of creative-writing. However, other considerations applied. The principal objection was that the department was well staffed by faculty who could teach the program. There were then only fifty-odd students in the creative-writing courses, who could be taught by faculty including Birney, Zilber, Friedson, and Robert Creeley (the American poet, due to start work on 1 July). Other members of the English Department such as John Hulcoop, Tallman, and the novelist Jane Rule could teach in the program. Daniells was also worried about Layton as a colleague. Would he want to attack – or to take over – *Prism* or *Canadian Literature*, both of which needed nurturing? Above all, he was concerned about Layton as an academic. As he pointed out, Layton's own referees had said that 'Mr. Layton's teaching is not scholarly, and that even in the field of Canadian literature his prejudices are such as to produce distorted views.' Finally, 'in spite of reports that he attracts students – which is undoubtedly true – he has not obtained in Montreal any sort of settled teaching post. Sir George Williams employs him on an hourly basis.'[42] It was all very damning, and true. Even Pacey, who got on well with Layton, had no illusions that he would fit into his own English department at UNB.

Birney, impatient, phoned Daniells at home on 18 May. Daniells told him that Layton's application was now with Dean Chant and hung up. In the following weeks, Birney attempted to corner Daniells in corridors, in front of his office, in the coffee room in front of colleagues. Daniells evaded him, refusing to discuss the matter. Birney quite literally wanted Daniells to stand up and fight. What Daniells wanted was for Birney to go away – far away – so that he could get on with English Department business. But he had no intention of being boxed into a corner. One day, suffering from a severe migraine (probably the after-effect of the decision), he bundled up in scarf and overcoat and wore dark glasses to the office to protect his eyes from the strong light. Birney later wrote a scathing letter claiming that Daniells was attempting to disguise himself.[43]

Dean Chant considered the references and the student and faculty letters of support, and he read Layton's *The Swinging Flesh*. All Layton's letters of reference were mixed, praising his strengths as a poet but acknowledging unprofessional behaviour. One of the most astute assessments was made by his old professor, Harold Files, who thought Layton an *enfant terrible*, a kind of Jekyll and Hyde: a man so insistent upon his own genius that it had crowded out collegiality, good sense, and any conception of humour.[44] Dean Chant, after reading this material, recommended against the appointment. This information was communicated to both Birney and Layton by the end of the month, but the reasons for the decision were not released.

By 14 June, Layton had received Birney's account of the hiring process. He then wrote to Daniells objecting to a world where 'a neurotic bug like yourself can be the head of an English Department with the power to all but decide whether someone like myself should be kept

from doing what he likes best, namely, teaching.'[45] He ended his letter
with a flourish, an 'Epigram for Daniells':

Just men for stys think him fit
And thinking on it, do spit;
And colleagues tamed though they be
Find none so gelded as he:
A professorial ox

...

I, for now and for all times
Toss this Daniells to the lines.

This verse was published in *TISH* 13 (September 1962), where Davey
took up the cudgels for Daniells, saying there was no cause for condem-
nation. If the poem was generated by disappointment over an academic
position, then it 'makes quite accurate any appraisal Daniells may have
made of Layton at the time of his consideration.'[46]

Pacey, good friend to both Daniells and Layton, was upset. He believed that Daniells had acted responsibly. Pacey wrote Layton pointing out there was no established vacancy in the English Department,
his proposed appointment had been Birney's idea, and Layton should
apologize: 'You've got yourself caught in a Birney-Daniells feud that
has its roots in the fact that Birney wanted the headship Roy got.'[47] To
Layton's credit, he wrote Daniells a letter of apology for his 'intemper-
ate letter': 'the whole business proves to me once again, and this time
conclusively, that I'm not cut out for the academic life.'[48]

Birney, now in Mexico, let off steam with a long indignant letter
written to Daniells, Chant, MacKenzie, and the chair of the creative-
writing committee, Zilber. It was basically an angry chronology that
presented Daniells as a dishonest administrator, and the 'intolerant and
sectarian Puritan' he had known thirty years earlier. The Layton affair
had crystallized all Birney's unhappiness at UBC in relation to Daniells:

Ten years ago every one of the nine full professors in your department
rebelled against your incompetency and undemocratic ways and jointly
created an Executive Committee which you were forced to accept, at the
Dean's insistence, or be removed from the headship. Ever since, you have
plotted and manoeuvred and played shameful favouritism among the
innocent new members of staff ... You have succeeded so well that once
more the Executive Committee is reduced to a cipher ...[49]

In a subsequent letter, Birney threatened that if the dean and president did not give him a creative-writing department of his own by 31 January 1963, he would leave UBC.

The letter to Daniells had become an impassioned justification of Birney's position, a kind of last-ditch struggle. There was merit in Birney's position; indeed, Layton could have been a major figure in a revitalized creative-writing program, but only assuming that he and Birney got along. Birney also failed to see that bullying tactics were unacceptable. Moreover, there was the opinion of the creative-writing students to consider. Although several had written in favour of Layton, they privately considered his poetry too rhetorical as they were more interested in oral rhythms. While the Layton case was generating fuss and debate, Daniells hired Louis Dudek to teach summer school in 1962. The young writers found Dudek, who was interested in direct speech, useful for their poetry, and the result of his visit to UBC was that he produced a Vancouver issue of his Montreal little magazine, *Delta*. This helped the Vancouver poets with their careers because they became known across Canada. Davey, therefore, saw Daniells as 'benign, removing roadblocks.'[50]

Birney, however, saw the failure to hire Layton as a symbolic defeat. He extracted revenge in a verse entitled 'Testimony of a Canadian Educational Leader,' a bleak account of the intertwined careers of the two men first published in *Near False Creek Mouth* (1964). The first two stanzas introduce a puritan and imply a Plymouth Brethren background. 'Sixty years it took to make me. / Church taught me first: all men are sinners, / and Women Eves ...' There are references to Daniells' early fears and his breakdowns in stanza two – 'I'd been saved for lone damnation' – and an allusion to his study of Milton: 'religion / and literature, I twigged, were synonyms.' Stanza three introduces sexual timidity and raises implications of homosexuality: 'Was I too timid? Or was it youthful Adam / that I craved?' This stanza alludes directly to the summer of 1933 and to Sylvia Johnstone (although, in fact, Johnstone and Birney were not then married): 'I tried, and failed, to bed / my best friend's wife ...'[51]

Stanza four introduces the Second World War and Birney's resentment that while he joined up, Daniells remained as head of English at Manitoba: 'Some rivals lost their lives, and all lost time. / I was the humanism they were fighting for, / rose to be Head, ate better and wrote sonnets.' The last stanza deals with UBC in the early sixties when President MacKenzie ('the Prexy') retired in 1963 and the new president, John Barfoot Macdonald, thought highly of Daniells:

> Then just as my Satanic colleagues had it fixed
> with the Admin. to cast me out from here –
> my God is good! – the Prexy's plane went down,
> and I was quickest to the New Man's ear.

In January 1964 Daniells was asked by President Macdonald to give his opinion on the separation of creative writing from the Department of English. As he saw it, the primary purpose of the academic study of literature was to provide the student with historical and textual knowledge together with critical appreciation. However, the primary function of creative writing was to liberate individual experience. 'It follows that academic people with reason resent the granting of formal English credits for poems and stories that seem emitted rather than composed, while creative writers find academic restrictions intolerable.' He therefore recommended 'the separation of the creative-writing operation into a department of its own.'[52] He later suggested the novelist Robert Harlow for the post of head of creative writing.

When President MacKenzie retired and his replacement, John Barfoot Macdonald, a former dentist, was announced in 1961, Birney sent him a letter of regret with a joke, which nonetheless expressed genuine feeling: 'The cavity left when Larry went / Was one no dentist could cement.'[53] In 1963, with MacKenzie and Chant gone, and with Tallman's new prominence in creative writing, Birney's influence had been curtailed. Perhaps because of this, and because matters were not going well in his personal life, he decided to leave Vancouver for a year to take a writer-in-residence position at the University of Toronto. He did not return. His biographer speculates that 'Birney had been looking around for someone to replace him as head of the creative writing program, which – now that he had freed it from Daniells' English Department – no longer challenged him.'[54]

Although this is possible, it is more probable that Birney acted on his earlier ultimatum and left UBC because Harlow had been named head of the new department for which Birney had fought so long. Birney did not tell his colleagues this; he said that administration bored him, but it is clear that he left UBC in a great huff, removing his papers from the UBC library's Special Collections, just before his departure, with the explanation that he needed to tidy them up. In 1966 he sold them to the University of Toronto for the equivalent of a year's salary.[55]

Midway through this process, Daniells encountered F.W. Watt, a former student but now associate head of English at University College, who explained that he had been asked to evaluate Birney's papers for the U of T librarian. Watt recalls, 'Roy stopped me to look me in the eye and struggled to express something he had to say about Birney ... [his] face becoming flustered and agitated while his grin showed that he realized how outrageous it would seem to me if he spoke his mind. It was along the lines of, "I have to tell you something about that man ... what he really is ... Earle Birney is a BASTARD, he is EVIL."'[56]

Harlow, the new director of UBC's Creative Writing Department, in response to a new criticism of the program by Birney in 1970, wryly summarized that the Creative Writing Department as then constituted 'would be a hell for [Birney] to work in. It does have to reflect competence and at least the structure of an academic department to remain viable inside the university ... Earle's revolutionary stance was before its time – a revolt for his own ends and comforts and not in aid of any particular cause, as are so many of the young's revolutions now ... All of which doesn't diminish my respect for his good work and his good works. I could only wish that he had better information about the baby he bore.'[57]

Once at the U of T, Birney explained to a number of Eastern academics that Daniells had been a despotic head at UBC, and that he had been obliged to leave in protest. In the early seventies, he told this to Frank Davey, who was writing a book of criticism on his poetry, and to me when I interviewed him on E.J. Pratt.[58] However, by the late seventies Birney had mellowed considerably. He then said, separately to Allan Pritchard and to me, that he regretted the estrangement between himself and Daniells.[59] Ironically, Daniells had experienced the same change of heart, but neither man felt free to approach the other.[60]

⊷⊶

The UBC Summer Poetry Conference, supported by Daniells, was held between 24 July and 16 August 1963. It proved to be one of the most important literary events held in Canada in the early sixties and resulted in the consolidation of a specifically West Coast school of poetry. By now Tallman was the most charismatic advocate of the new American poetry on the campus. Predictably, a split along national lines had developed between Tallman and Birney. The large crowds generated by the American poets were a threat to Birney and the creative-writing program as he had conceived it. Jane Rule recalls: 'I can remember Ferlinghetti being here, and the old gym filled to the rafters ... Warren was interested in the American crew – found them much more interesting than the Canadian poets, and wanted his young poets to be exposed to better writing.'[61]

Poets (including Margaret Avison) and their audiences congregated on the lawns and under the trees between the UBC library and the arts building, a colourful collection of people in shirts and sandals – rather shocking for the conservative suit-and-tie campus. Two years after the poetry conference, Phyllis Webb published *Naked Poems* (1965) in a new spare idiom, a complete departure from the long lines of *The Sea Is Also a Garden* (1962). Even Dorothy Livesay, a thirties poet a little to the side of the new movement, responded to it, and to the oral rhythms which she had absorbed in Zambia, with *The Unquiet Bed* (1967). The fact that Birney and his poetry had also strongly influenced some of the younger poets associated with *TISH*, especially George Bowering, was now obscured by the unfortunate separation between *TISH* (which was seen as representative of American poetry) and other schools of Canadian poetry.

Daniells did not make these distinctions. He offered practical help to younger writers and critics, and made sure that Bowering and Davey, studying at UBC, received opportunities to teach. Davey recalls Daniells as a large but isolated figure: 'very big, broad-shouldered, a bit like a buffalo, hunched over, very private.' Davey would receive little notes from Daniells asking if he would like to teach courses, such as the summer linguistics course in 1962. But he was never put in a position where he needed to feel grateful. Davey felt that Daniells was self-sufficient and 'did not require being buttressed by our generation' – which suggests that Daniells was continuing in Pratt's tradition.

Most importantly, Daniells supported *TISH*. He did not say anything directly to the group, but *TISH* members were informed by the English Department secretary that the head had said that he considered it an appropriate extracurricular activity. This meant that secretaries sometimes ran off early copies of the magazine and *TISH* members could occasionally filch an odd box of paper for the magazine while everybody would look the other way. The group saw themselves as rebelling against authority, but Davey, himself later chair of English at York, recognized that 'we were encouraged in being rebellious'– by Daniells.[62]

He also helped a number of young writers and critics financially. One secretary, whenever funds arrived anonymously in the head's mail, knew them to be repayment on what she called 'the Daniells bursaries.' However, many of Daniells' gifts were anonymous. One of Daniells' colleagues disapproved of what he saw as Daniells' habit of furtive giving to charities like Tibetan relief, but for Daniells who had been raised with a belief in the 'widow's mite,' any other form of giving would have seemed ostentatious.

In the early sixties, Daniells had supported hiring Robert Creeley, one of the most lyrical Black Mountain poets, in the hope that he would provide new energy to the UBC creative-writing program. He also offered Margaret Atwood a sessional appointment at UBC in 1965–6, and asked Helen Sonthoff and Jane Rule to help her get settled. Rule recalls Atwood as very hard-working and conscientious about her teaching.[63] While in Vancouver, Atwood wrote *Surfacing* on UBC exam booklets, and a book of poems later published as *The Circle Game* (1966). Daniells also made a point of supporting writers by buying their books, some of which he distributed to graduate students. One morning in 1966, I found outside my carrell door in the UBC library a copy of *The Circle Game*, put there by Daniells, and shortly after a copy of *Hundreds and Thousands: The Journals of Emily Carr* (1966), which I lent in the mid-seventies to the SFU historian Douglas Cole for his wife, Maria Tippett, who had sat in on our joint classes on Emily Carr. She later published *Emily Carr: A Biography* (1979).

Chapter Twenty

Academic Publishing

In the fall of 1963, Daniells had been totally dispirited. His department was fractious; he felt he had not received adequate support from the dean and president; he had a wife and family to support; and in four years, he would be sixty-five. But he could not get any clear statement from the UBC administration about whether he could continue to teach beyond retirement age. He decided to apply to Simon Fraser University, then in the process of construction.

In November he met with Patrick McTaggart-Cowan, the designated president of SFU, and formally applied for a position to Gordon Shrum, chair of B.C. Hydro and chancellor of SFU, saying that SFU offered a fresh opportunity to build up an English Department. Two months later, discussing the matter with Kaspar Naegle, who succeeded Chant as dean of arts in January 1964, Daniells was more frank. His motives for applying to SFU were both positive and negative. On the positive side, he had worked well with R.G. Baker in the past, now the academic planner for Simon Fraser, and foresaw good possibilities for the future. On the negative side, he was depressed by the commitment of President Macdonald at UBC to a concept of research modelled on science. He was worried that a new dean of arts might follow the same path, and that English would be again relegated to a service department.[1]

But events took a sudden turn for the better near the end of 1963 and positively turned around by 1965. It was partly his increasing reputation as a teacher and leader in the discipline, and partly that Daniells' scholarly work was finally being acknowledged at UBC. Academic publishing helped: his new book, *Milton, Mannerism, and Baroque* (1963), came out to good reviews; then, two years later, after the publication of the *Literary History of Canada* (1965), Daniells stature in both seventeenth-century studies and Canadian literature was recognized.

The immediate result of his new book on Milton and the Baroque was an invitation to leave UBC. Daniells, who was invited to lecture on Milton at the University of Western Ontario in early December 1963, discovered on his arrival that Carl Klinck and Murdo MacKinnon, then head of English, proposed that he come to Western as one of the new 'senior professors' subsidized by the government of Ontario, or as head of one of the departments. With this unexpected offer in hand, Daniells approached his UBC dean and president asking for a definite statement regarding his situation.

Macdonald assured Daniells he could take a year of research leave in 1965–6, and reduce his load. More importantly, he could anticipate a year-by-year reappointment at the full professor level without administrative responsibilities, between sixty-five and seventy, if he maintained a high level of teaching and research. To this commitment from Macdonald was added the appointment of Naegle as dean of arts, a humanist who respected Daniells' views on the development of the English Department. Suddenly the whole administrative horizon at UBC had improved dramatically. Daniells promptly withdrew from consideration at SFU and Western. As he whimsically explained to MacKinnon at Western: '... having put my hand to this little plough I had better go on to the end of the furrow.'[2]

The publication of *Milton, Mannerism and Baroque* had changed his academic status because it was a pioneering study, one of the first to investigate the relationship between Milton's poetry and the art and architecture of the seventeenth century, and beautifully illustrated with photographs of the Italian Baroque. The concept of interdisciplinary work was just beginning: Wylie Sypher in his *Four Stages of Renaissance Style* (1955) and *Rococo to Cubism in Art and Literature* (1960) had done similar cross-disciplinary work, although not so specifically with relation to Milton.

Daniells' study, a synthesis of his many years of teaching and research, and informed by his own religious belief, was more personal in nature. He continues to argue that the seventeenth century was a continuation, as well as a dislocation, of the classical Renaissance, but he now acknowledges new critical divisions in the period and maintains that early poems of Milton, such as 'Comus' and 'Lycidas,' are Mannerist (1520–1600), whereas later works, Milton's *Paradise Lost* and Bunyan's *The Pilgrim's Progress*, are best approached as Baroque (1630–80).

Baroque, as a description of a period and a mode of composition, carries all of the qualities of 'complexity,' 'conflict,' 'tension,' and 'the unstable combination of opposing principles' that he had identified in his Ph.D. dissertation; however, his earlier, brief references to the architectural qualities of specific poems are now fleshed out.[3] For example, Daniells allows that there are few examples of Baroque architecture in England. Nonetheless, he conjectures that English Puritanism in its movement towards power, unity, and will shares many of the qualities of the Catholic Counter-Reformation, which produced Baroque architecture. Furthermore, he points out that poetry can call up in the imagination the effects of architectural splendour. Thus, the structure of *Paradise Lost* can be compared with the architecture of a High Baroque church:

> The universe of *Paradise Lost*, if we are willing to look at it with a fresh eye, reveals a complex plan. It is axial in that heaven and hell are antipodal and no other polarity can compete with the dominance of this one. It is also cruciform, in a psychological rather than planimetric fashion. When we are in heaven all is drawn up to God and there is little if any tendency to think laterally ... Similarly hell draws all in it down so that lateral space outside its walls scarcely enters as a possibility.[4]

In the Acknowledgements to the book, Daniells remarks that his debts to his former professor A.S.P. Woodhouse are 'so many and of such long standing they can neither be itemized nor summed up.' And indeed, in Daniells' initial treatment of Milton's poetry, he explicates Woodhouse's concept of Christian Liberty. Nonetheless, his own emphasis is placed elsewhere, upon a redefined description of the relation of the individual soul to God – the straight axis from man to God which characterizes his understanding of Puritan (e.g., Plymouth Brethren) theology – and, in addition, upon the Baroque elements of 'naturalism, allegory, grandiose dignity, severe tensions, Counter-Reformation doctrine, and courtly life.'[5]

Specifically, in his discussion of Milton's 'Comus,' Daniells invokes Woodhouse's important essay on the order of Nature and the order of Grace as it relates to the doctrine of Chastity in 'Comus' – only to show that his former professor's history of ideas approach is inadequate as a way of explaining doctrinal and aesthetic discrepancies in the poem.[6] Daniells identifies Mannerism with 'a simultaneous eagerness to employ traditional [Renaissance] forms and determination to rupture their prescribed rules' – particularly as it relates to the handling of figures in space.[7] Thus, the reliance on Renaissance forms together with numerous aesthetic and doctrinal discrepancies in 'Comus' are best characterized as Manneristic. He further shows that each character in this poem inhabits his own space, and that these spaces are never brought into a common perspective, as required by Woodhouse's interpretation.

Daniells reasons that although there is nothing in 'Comus' for which traditional Renaissance sources cannot be cited (and so readers tend to see the poem as an expression of Christian humanism), nonetheless, odd 'lapses and dislocations are such as to evoke an aesthetic response of a new and intensely gratifying kind.'[8] Implicit in this argument is the idea that the distortions of Mannerist art reveal deeper psychological and aesthetic truths. Frequently, the reader is directed to analogies with Italian Mannerist art and architecture, some carefully and convincingly presented.

The interpretive and exegetical practices of the Plymouth Brethren, as well as Daniells' own literary sensibility, shaped *Milton, Mannerism and Baroque*. In particular, his treatment of the great Puritans – Spenser, Bunyan, Milton, and Defoe – reflects his understanding of the priesthood of all believers, the rejection of authority, and the recourse to one's own inner illumination in relation to God or to the text, be it sacred or secular. Throughout this book, he is often fascinated by the aesthetic expression of Christian doctrine in the structure of *Paradise Lost*. For example, Adam tells Eve of 'the Power that made us' who requires simple obedience, 'Among so many signs of power and rule / Conferr'd upon us, and Dominion giv'n / Over all other Creatures.'[9] But at the same time – and this is yet another manifestation of his religious heritage – Daniells rejects unleavened dogma. Thus he points out complexities, stressing what he saw as Milton's presentation of 'counter-will' as shown in Satan's misdirected struggle and humanity's assertion of individual will.[10] He finds the 'will to power' everywhere present in *Paradise Lost* – Satan, Eve, and Adam all disobey God, and without convincing reasons. This argument may be read to suggest that Daniells is reading his own spiritual struggle into the text – a justification of his own counter-will in response to the commandment that man obey God and receive grace. Indeed, we may suspect that he revels in concepts like Mannerism and Baroque because they are not Puritan (that is, not Plymouth Brethren), and thus not overly simplified.

His approach forced the reader, as Sid Warhaft (a student of both Daniells and Woodhouse) remarked in *Queen's Quarterly*, to 'see Milton ...

as a thoroughly seventeenth-century artist dynamically at home in the cultural life of his day.' Warhaft did wonder 'whether *precise* parallels between architecture and literature can properly be made to touch this side of infinity ... The fact is that all too often we are required to make a Kierkegaardian leap of faith, to jump trustingly from architecture to literature, from form to content ... from orthodoxy to Milton's beliefs.'[11] For Marshall McLuhan, however, it was precisely Daniells' ability to 'unify disparate facets and experiences by directing attention to the moment of change' in the art of the Baroque that he found most impressive; McLuhan quotes from the book approvingly when making comments on visual perspective in *Through the Vanishing Point: Space in Poetry and Painting.*[12]

Most reviews of *Milton, Mannerism and Baroque* were favourable; the book was well received and promptly went into a second printing. It was an original study and moving in a direction in which other scholars have followed. Paul Stanwood, Daniells' younger colleague in seventeenth-century studies at UBC, suggests that Daniells' 'influence may be felt, if not explicitly acknowledged, in John Dixon Hunt, *Encounters: Essays on Literature and the Visual Arts* (1971); Joseph A. Wittreich, *Angel of Apocalypse: Blake's Idea of Milton* (1975); Murray Roston, *Milton and the Baroque* (1980); and in Roland Mushat Frye, *Milton's Imagery and the Visual Arts*, and in recent books by James Grantham Turner (on landscapes), Marcia Poynton, and Estella Shoenburg.' Although contemporary critics may not necessarily reach the same conclusions as he did, 'one must grant that [he] was innovative; he also wrote in a style that is elegant and immensely civilized.'[13]

Daniells published a number of articles on seventeenth-century literature during this period, including 'The Mannerist Element in English Literature' (1966) and 'Milton and Renaissance Art' (1973).[14] That younger scholars found Daniells' work on Milton fruitful is indicated by a letter from Richard Levin, then a graduate student at Stanford, and later to write *Love and Society in Shakespearean Comedy* (1985). He wrote: 'Your pages on Milton's humour opened for me an entirely new appreciation of the work. Your comments on Adam in Book x and the material that follows (epic enfolds and assuages the imperfectly healed wounds of tragic conflict) seem to me superb.' Levin was travelling to the Continent, and Daniells provided him with an itinerary so that he, too, could read seventeenth-century poetry while viewing Mannerist and Baroque architecture. He later recalled: 'I was tremendously impressed by *Milton, Mannerism and Baroque*: it [was] distinctive and bold; it got away from the prim and proper Renaissance of Tillyard's *Elizabethan World Picture* and made Milton and the period far more interesting.'[15]

⟶►●◄⟵

In 1965 the landmark first edition of the *Literary History of Canada* finally appeared. Developing the *Literary History* had taken seven years and the work of thirty-five contributors. Reaction to the book was prompt and generally positive. The immediate perception was that Klinck and his editors had demonstrated that Canada possessed a literary history and, thus, a literature. There was special praise for Frye's conclusion and for Daniells' chapters on the Confederation poets.

The critical principles guiding the contributors were later identified in a brief talk given by Carl Klinck to graduate students at Leeds in 1965 as those cited in Northrop Frye's essay 'Preface to an Uncollected Anthology,' which makes the point that 'the cultivated Canadian has the same kind of interest in Canadian poetry that he has in Canadian history or politics. Whatever its merits, it is the poetry of his own country, and it gives him an understanding of that country which nothing else can give him.'[16] Drawing on comments in the *Literary History* text made by both Daniells and Frye, Klinck's summary emphasizes the importance of the Canadian landscape on literature and culture and quotes further from Frye's 'Preface to an Uncollected Anthology.' Canada, divided by two languages and great stretches of wilderness and prairies, a country that has developed a nation out of stops on a railroad line: 'this is the environment that Canadian poets have to grapple with, and many of the imaginative problems it presents have no counterpart in the United States, or anywhere else.'[17]

Daniells' own contributions included an overview of the Confederation period. Although he found no simple correspondence between the political and the literary, nonetheless, in the literary journals of the period, he found the desire 'to preserve, justify, and substantiate national unity.'[18] He emerges as an incisive historian of Confederation writing, who shows how the major poets differed from their English predecessors. As an immigrant, he was sensitive to the efforts of nineteenth-century critics to establish a Canadian context, and he saw the period stretching from Confederation to the First World War as one in which literature creates a world: '... its centre in the Canadian home, its middle distance the loved landscape of Canada, its protecting wall the circle of British institutions, associations, and loyalties.' He also asks several important questions: 'Why did the fact of Confederation prove so powerful (though brief), a stimulus to Canada's literary culture? Why does the land, in the sense of terrain, play so dominant a role in Canadian experience?'[19]

In his discussion of individual poets, Daniells realigned traditional views of the canon by placing Lampman before Roberts and by dealing with what is distinctive – as opposed to derivative – in this group. His chief interest is how the Confederation poets transmuted the Canadian landscape, and his commentary on Lampman emphasizes poetic process – 'at the centre of his [Lampman's] being there burned a small clear flame.' The metaphor is Walter Pater's, but Daniells' analysis is astute: Lampman's major poems show that he has a personal 'sensation in the face of nature which, without alienating him from his surroundings, lifts him into another sphere.' Elsewhere, Daniells quotes a concluding line from one of Lampman's best-known poems illustrating this 'pleasure secret and austere.'[20] His chapters firmly anchor the Confederation poets in a continuum of nineteenth-century transcendentalism, and correctly identify the source of their poetic impulse in the Canadian landscape.

In Frye's conclusion to the *Literary History*, Daniells' arguments regarding the lack of a major figure in the Canadian tradition are introduced, but neatly reworked; 'Canada has produced no author who is a classic in the sense of possessing a vision greater in kind than that of his best readers.' Frye deals extensively with 'the imminence of the natural world,' that feature of Canadian poetry that Daniells had distinguished as 'an absorption in landscape.'[21] He attributes to this landscape the impetus for what he considers a characteristic note of 'terror' in Canadian nature poetry. And, like the avowedly nationalist critics of the 1880s and 1920s, Frye asserts the continuity of a Canadian tradition: 'I keep coming back to the feeling that there does seem to be such a thing as an imaginative continuum, and that writers are conditioned in their attitudes by their predecessors, or by the cultural climate of their predecessors, whether there is conscious influence or not.'[22]

Frye's conclusion, Klinck stated, was 'exactly what was needed to capture the spirit of the book ... written in Norrie's inimitable style.' However, in a letter to Daniells in the early seventies, Klinck was less circumspect, remarking that Frye's conclusion had not emphasized (as he and Daniells had expected) 'a factual-critical record, but more particularly ... a factual-descriptive record of what there is in English Canadian literature.'[23] In the late seventies, he was more frank about the conclusion, commenting to me that 'integration is something I think is necessary and we left that to Norrie [Frye] ... But mind you, it doesn't do justice to the material ... it's beautiful ... because ... of the insights from his point of view but it's far from being a literary history.'[24]

Daniells maintained that Frye's chapter, although a splendid conclusion, evaded the whole question of what Canadian literature was all about and expressed the hope that a new literary history would spotlight the best that Canadian literature had to offer in a summary chapter quite different from Frye's:

> To present a record of the good, bad and indifferent in an undifferentiated continuum does, I think, drag down the whole operation ... I mention this, not with any thought of diverting the main-stream of opinion in the committee and without disrespect to those, like my dear friend Desmond [Pacey], who hold to the historico-informative concept. But I do think that problems remain and that some effort should be made to spotlight the best we can offer to the world, perhaps in an penultimate brief summing-up of a character and intent different from Norrie's.[25]

In fact, Frye was to write a second conclusion, but again generalizing about the nature of the Canadian contribution to literary history.

The most incisive review of the first edition of the *Literary History* was by A.J.M. Smith, who praised the volume for 'catholicity, variety, and fullness' but, like Daniells, expressed his concern that reviewers had not been adequately critical: 'I have always believed that evaluation *is* the end, purpose, and *raison d'être* of criticism.'[26] Lionel Stevenson, a Canadian, now a professor in the United States, also made a telling point when he remarked that contributors to the *Literary History* were 'haunted by the spectre of provincialism.' The poets of the Confederation were accused of being influenced by their contemporaries, 'whereas it is all to the credit of poets of the present era that to quite as great an extent they are the disciples of Donne, or Eliot, or Wallace Stevens.'[27]

The general response to the *Literary History of Canada* was that it generated new and informed criticism of the national literature. Now that the historical periods had been delineated and the major writers identified, more intensive study was possible. A sidelight of establishing the Canadian historical canon may have been the fact that in 1965 the University of Toronto English departments at last offered an undergraduate course in Canadian literature alone; a half dozen other universities, including UBC, had been offering such a course for some years.

In the early sixties, Daniells had given a heartfelt address on Emily Carr at Carleton University, later published in *Our Living Tradition* (1962). As one who had also been a child in Victoria, a full generation later, he admits to feeling quite intimately 'Emily Carr's predicament, which was, by the recoil of her strong will and the intensity of her effort, a main source of her unique artistic achievement.' There was little in the history of the West Coast for the mind of a child to fasten on, but abundant natural beauty was at her door, especially the wildness of Beacon Hill Park. Daniells also offers a shrewd psychological analysis: he acknowledges that Carr's relations with her family were ambivalent and that her adult life was filled with annoyances, frustrations, and 'rage.' Candidly, he counts himself among the Philistines who had not bought her work in the early forties. What he finds to be the persuasive note in all of her work is 'an extreme sensitiveness to direct impressions ... there was a great reciprocal flow of power between her soul and the spirit of the woods which makes of her later paintings and sketches a series of statements in which the objective and subjective elements are perfectly and permanently fused.' Her art was a continued autobiography which recorded 'the life force which beat with equal pulse in her and in the green current of the foliage.' Carr, he argues, 'was not primarily interpreting Canada to the world. She was interpreting herself to herself by the symbols which the forest provided.'[28] Similar observations, particularly on Carr's 'rage' and her identity with nature, were to be made in subsequent biographies of Emily Carr.[29]

In 1964, after E.J. Pratt's death in April, both Daniells and Frye wrote spontaneous appreciations of Pratt's role as a mentor at Victoria College for the journal *Canadian Literature*. Daniells emphasized his hospitality, his kindness, and the enormous difficulty under which Pratt, the poet, had struggled to bring poems such as *The Titanic* into being. He acknowledged that Pratt was somehow 'larger' than any of the other figures which he had encountered as a young student and professor in the thirties, but besides this psychic dimension Pratt 'possessed the complementary virtue of being responsive to people, of being intuitive, spontaneous, *uncalculating*. No one of his innumerable beneficiaries ever felt he had to do something in return.'[30]

A few years prior to the publication of the *Literary History*, Daniells had written an article entitled 'The Long-Enduring Spring' for *Canadian Literature*, in which he speculated on some of the causes for the slow development of a national literature, but argued that a blossoming was at hand.[31] One of the harvest years was certainly 1965 because of the *Literary History* and Margaret Laurence's *The Stone Angel*, published simultaneously in London, New York, and Toronto during that year. Daniells, a member of the jury, voted in favour of this book for the Governor General's Award for fiction. Laurence did not get the prize, although her book can now be seen as the point at which the Canadian novel came of age. However, two years later, Daniells had the triple pleasure of officially presenting Laurence to the governor general for *A Jest of God*, Atwood for *The Circle Game*, and Woodcock for *The Crystal Spirit*.[32] The new Canadian literature had indeed blossomed. And he had some personal influence on all three writers: on Laurence's literary sensibility and education at the U of M; by hiring Atwood as an instructor; and by appointing Woodcock to the editorship of *Canadian Literature*, a salaried position which allowed him leisure to write biography.

Two years later, in an address on 'Literary Studies in Canada' for a symposium held by the Royal Society, Daniells observed that 'literary critics in the native tradition consciously or unconsciously do their work within the framework of this concept.' However, he acknowledged that the Canadian Arnoldian historical and ethical perspectives which in the past had brought forth important work from scholars such as A.S.P. Woodhouse were changing into concepts not yet articulated. 'Should we not, then, cheerfully abandon all thought of [Canadian] scholarship and think rather of scholarship in Canada?' He recognized that Canadian literature as a subject of critical inquiry was now guaranteed by a stream of reprints through the New Canadian Library and the Carleton Library, by a permanent place for papers on Canadian literature in the annual program of ACUTE, and by the success of the quarterly *Canadian Literature*. In the course of this talk, Daniells raised some larger questions:

> What do we hope from literary studies? An addition to Canada's gross national scholarly product? A contribution to the common market of humane studies in the western world? An increase of knowledge? An accession of wisdom? An attainment of insight? A means of protest? A sense of glory? Could it be that we shall return to the old belief that the

humanities have the power to make the student of them humane? And beyond all this, is there something unpredictable and incalculable, that self-justifying search for beauty and order which inspires not infrequently a passionate commitment beyond discussion or argument?[33]

In 'High Colonialism in Canada,' published in *Canadian Literature* in 1969, Daniells refers to W.D. Lighthall, the nineteenth-century editor of a popular anthology, *Songs of the Great Dominion* (1889), to praise a vision of Canada which was intimately tied to Britain, and which looks forward to political independence but not instantly. The organic unity of this ideology is 'the power of imagination to project a vision of Canada having its own logic and consistency.'[34] His aim is to acknowledge the importance and the usefulness of this vision in this period, an acknowledgment also made by Carl Berger in *The Sense of Power: Studies in the Causes of Canadian Imperialism 1867–1914* (1970).

In the late sixties, Daniells had also prepared a report on 'English-Canadian Writing' for a conference on Commonwealth literature, later published in *National Identity* (1968), edited in Australia by K.L. Goodwin. There he again surveyed Canadian writing from the nineteenth century to the present, commenting that 'the true alpha and omega of Canadian national consciousness is, of course, in the last analysis, the land.'[35] Nonetheless, Daniells advanced a relatively sophisticated argument, quoting Marshall McLuhan and Northrop Frye, to the effect that Canada was moving '"towards a post-national world ... What is important about the last century, in this country, is not that we have been a nation for a hundred years, but that we have had a hundred years in which to make the transition from a pre-national to a post-national consciousness."'[36]

Daniells headed the Canadian contingent of scholars at Brisbane, and this section of his paper anticipates a direction to be taken by a number of younger Australian scholars attending the conference, including Helen and Christopher Tiffin. Helen Tiffin came to Canada shortly after to study Commonwealth literature at Queen's University. It was at this point, as W.H. New remarks, that 'younger scholars began to recognize, both at the Brisbane Conference and at the next, more polarized Australian/Canadian Conference of the Commonwealth Association that there was a different way of looking at literature. It was no longer so much the influence of English works on Canadian or Australian works but rather literature as seen from a Canadian or Australian point of view.'[37] Daniells' nomenclature at Brisbane was 'post-national' (and, in another article 'High Colonialism'), but as Helen Tiffin and her co-editors later defined the contemporary situation, it became 'post-colonial' in *The Empire Writes Back: Theory and Practice in Post-Colonial Literature* (1987).

In his Brisbane paper, Daniells had also briefly referred to Alexander Mackenzie, the eighteenth-century Scottish fur trader whose biography he had contracted to write. In the next two years, Daniells followed the trail of Mackenzie, who from Montreal and the St Lawrence 'moved into the land of the Great Northern Lakes and from there, in 1789, he first penetrated to the Arctic, then, by another voyage, four years later, pierced the Rocky Mountains to reach Bella Coola on the Pacific Coast.' In order to tell Mackenzie's story, Daniells began in Scotland, then picked up Mackenzie's trail back in B.C., and followed it to Bella Coola and Great Slave Lake.

In the summer of 1967, he and Laurenda undertook the British Columbia leg of Mackenzie's journey, starting from Vancouver by car on 9 August with the intention of reaching Great Slave Lake. They travelled by way of Lac La Hache, Williams Lake, and the Chilcotin down to the Bella Coola River valley, back to Williams Lake, Barkerville, Hay River, and finally Great Slave Lake, where Daniells had a swim before starting their return journey on 18 August.

In 1968 *Alexander Mackenzie and the North West*, was published. There, partly from his own experience, Daniells gives the reader a sense of the geography that Mackenzie had to traverse and the Indian world of which he had to become a part, emphasizing the 'particularly Canadian' aspects of Mackenzie's voyages:

> He never fired on an Indian; he never lied or deceived; he never lost a man of his party; yet he was constantly in danger and amid hardships; his material resources were very slender; he was operating from a base thousands of miles distant from the settled parts of Canada. Watching him on one of his carefully timed journeys, filled with hair's breadth chances and studded with menacing obstacles, is to become convinced that imagination, courage and power of will can be effective in the affairs of men, and that decisive turning points in the history of a country are often reached without excitement or fanfare.[38]

The Mackenzie biography was his most successful book from a sales point of view. It also had a strong influence on the architect John Woodward, who later went on to spearhead the effort to create the now great Alexander Mackenzie Heritage Trail, dedicated in 1987.

Chapter Twenty-One

University Professor

Daniells' research was long delayed by administration, and the book that was to be his *magnum opus* was not published until late in his academic life. Many of the friends and colleagues of his youth were now dying. In April 1964, E.J. Pratt had died. Later that spring, after receiving an honorary LCD degree from Queen's University and while attending a meeting of the Royal Society in Montreal, Daniells was asked an odd question by A.S.P. Woodhouse, a question he did not fully understand until later in the summer. Then, after Daniells had been formally told that the University of Toronto also proposed to offer him an honorary degree at the spring 1965 convocation, Woodhouse wrote to explain: 'I ... send you my warmest felicitations. This was the subject of my cryptic (because cautious) questions in Montreal, whether you had lately heard from Toronto. You had not at that time and I beat a hasty retreat, preferring an impression of idiocy to indiscretion.' This was the last, typically careful, missive that Daniells received from Woodhouse.[1]

On 1 November, Daniells learned Woodhouse had died: 'Died of a heart-attack Ted Morrison surmises. Found dead in his house. A great blow. Such a good, good man.' Primarily, Daniells thought of Woodhouse as a Christian academic.[2] His tribute to Woodhouse had been expressed in an article written in 1961 for the U of T *Varsity Graduate*, where he remarked that in Woodhouse's teaching of English, particularly Milton, the student recognized 'that ideas are imperishable and belong to the eternal world of Plato and the Gospels; that to grasp the ideas of great minds and perceive that they form coherent frames of reference is among the highest activities of man.'[3]

Daniells appreciated Woodhouse in a way that my generation, the sixties' generation, could not. He understood, in the words of Woodhouse's younger colleague F.W. Watt, that Woodhouse 'was wedded to his discipline, the needs of which he put above his own vanities, and I'm sure he believed that any deviousness or administrative manipulations or downright skullduggery he might have to sully his hands with were for a higher cause. In particular, he was wedded to the Honour Course.' To appreciate this edifice, the structure on which everything else in English literary studies, including graduate work and scholarships depended, it is necessary to pursue the old University of Toronto calendars from the fifties and Woodhouse's massive detailed notes, which he circulated, for his honours Spenser, Milton, and nineteenth-century-thought courses. Woodhouse spent the last years of his life 'planning how he would conserve and bolster the Honour Course long after he was gone by leaving the bulk of his estate to the funding of English Language and Literature scholarships. I'm not sure he ever faced the reality that the great system which he had done so much to create and order was actually about to be transformed out of any existence he would recognize.'[4] In fact, the study of English, as both Woodhouse and Daniells had understood it, was about to radically change under the influence of the new European criticism .

At the end of December 1964, Daniells learned that he, too, was not immune to the ravages of age. His doctor had found a 'heart murmur likely due to cusps on a valve which do not function impeccably & permit some turbulence. But ... he [Dr. Rennie] does not think it will develop into anything worse ...'[5] However, 1965 began very badly. Daniells was unwell, and there were still more problems in the department about appointments, promotions, and inadequate funding for teaching.

Throughout January and February 1965, he was 'greatly troubled' about departmental appointments, largely because the 'English budget [was] short of what it should be by extrapolation from last year, – by over $10,000.'[6] There were now nearly a hundred teaching faculty in the department, constant battles regarding procedures, and hordes of students seeking entrance to English courses. Daniells now had a fine scholarly department, possibly one of the largest academic departments of any discipline in the country.[7] But a UBC head, unlike his counterpart, the business CEO, had little power to restrict admittance, fire incompetents, or refuse services when funding was inadequate. By 1965 Daniells was 'more than a little depressed and disturbed by inability to do a good day's work, general mental confusion, ... and continuous anxiety about the administration of the Department. How I am to accomplish what must be done in the next few months I do not know. I pray to God & struggle to organize myself but remain terrifyingly inefficient.'[8]

The pressures of university life sometimes became more than individuals can bear. Two persons whom Daniells knew and respected at UBC – a dean of arts and a member of the English department – took their own lives during this period. Only too aware of the pressures to which each had been subjected, Daniells responded deeply to both deaths. At a memorial service in 1967 for the faculty member – an older woman suffering from a terminal illness and a former member of the Plymouth Brethren – Daniells broke down and wept. Some faculty who knew nothing of his religious history (for he kept this information private) believed that he wept because he felt guilt for the woman's suicide.[9] However, we may suspect that Daniells, like Milton grieving for himself in *Lycidas*, also wept for the direction in which his own life might have gone had he been unable to escape the Brethren.

During the spring of 1965, *Discipline and Discovery*, a report initiated by Dean Naegle on undergraduate education in the arts, was released. Committee members included Naegle, Steinberg, Margaret Prang of the History Department, C.W.J. Elliot of Classics, and Lionel Tiger of Anthropology. It proposed that education for undergraduates be integrated under the general theme of man in relation to specific disciplines rather than through the usual disciplinary structure. Both Daniells, as head of English, and Malcolm MacGregor, head of Classics, strongly opposed the four-year program. After years of insisting upon graduated levels of study in their core subjects, each was unwilling to give this up for what might prove to be a diluted thematic study. Nonetheless, Daniells supported the highly successful interdisciplinary program, Arts I, which emerged from this report.

———————

Daniells had always been known as one of UBC's best teachers; now he was acknowledged as one of UBC's distinguished scholars. On 11 May he reported that he was called in by the president, 'who proposed to recommend me for a special chair & gave me the choice of retaining or dropping the headship of the English Department. All very exciting!'[10] President Macdonald proposed to establish a special University Professorship, and whether he retired as head or stayed on did not matter. Daniells would be the first to be honoured.

Daniells was certainly qualified for the chair; the question is whether it was implemented in order to make changes in the department. Undoubtedly any individual who has been in a department for almost twenty years has run out of steam. But Macdonald's offer was not couched in this manner. He had specified that Daniells could stay on as head of English if he wished. Consequently, if this was a motive behind the offer, it was presented in a manner that both acknowledged Daniells' stature and allowed him some freedom to negotiate. Daniells accepted happily and immediately.

His last day as department head was 30 June 1965: 'O joy, O rapture!'[11] Coincidentally, his old friend Max Maynard visited that evening and shared the family celebration. As Daniells had earlier negotiated a year's research leave for 1965–6, to be spent largely in Rome under a Canada Council Leave Fellowship, he and Laurenda began to make plans for their trip abroad. Just before the family left on 4 August there was an English Department lunch arranged by Stanley Read, William Robbins, John Creighton, M.W. Steinberg, and Edmund Morrison, at which the group presented Daniells with an Inuit carving. Read, always warm and gracious, had composed a special poem for the occasion, acknowledging Daniells' own facility with occasional verse.

On 11 August, Roy and Laurenda Daniells travelled by rail to Montreal, embarking on the *Ryndam* with an elegant send-off, a bottle of champagne provided by good friends, the Steinbergs. They arrived at Rotterdam on 3 September and drove immediately to Rome.

Daniells found it difficult to settle. He seems to have been a little homesick and was seriously ill with flu. It is also possible that his heart condition was beginning to affect his health, as he was disoriented and depressed. After a day at home spent in bed, he roused himself one evening with the thought 'that, God willing, we shall all be home again in a few months time, that my book on Mannerism is a feasible project regardless of present confusions, and that I come of a family that never lacked courage but stood firm and worked hard and put their faith in God.'[12]

To search out Mannerist art and architecture, he took a number of side trips by rail to Copenhagen and to Basel, and numerous trips with the family to Florence, Venice, Vienna, Innsbruck, and Paris. On the second trip to Basel, travelling by himself, Daniells was overcome by feelings of 'horror & confusion of the mind.' He had slept before dinner and 'woke up into spell of extreme lowness & a feeling of horror that upset me quite badly. Contemplating skipping Parma & going straight home to Rome tomorrow, but shall probably stick to original plan.' Puritan that he was, he soldiered on. The following day, in Parma, checking some Mannerist art, he was again conscious of 'some horror & confusion of the mind.'[13]

Back in Rome, he found abundant mail from Canadian students and faculty, including a generous letter from an old friend, Walter Koerner of UBC's board of governors, taking 'particular delight in the fact that proper recognition has been given to you after so many years of dedicated service to our University. You have brought distinction, in spite of many difficulties, to our University and therefore you deserve a position of special standing in British Columbia.'[14]

In December, Laurenda's mother, Mrs Francis, came to visit, and the family travelled in southern France and Spain. On Christmas Day, Laurenda ingeniously contrived a Christmas tree out of a massive bureau with a mirror, and Daniells recorded in his diary: '... we had our usual fun and pleasure. A fine green leather box, an agate egg, a lovely tie, a beautiful small red leather box, slippers, razor blades, tea, &c fell to my share.'

By 14 January 1966, the Daniellses were back in Rome, and, shortly after, Laurenda set off on a two-month journey to Nairobi – she wanted to visit some national parks and do some bird watching. Daniells stayed at home with the children. Although he was busy, he missed her and his old anxieties surfaced: 'Today is the halfway mark between Aug 1st/65 and Sept 1/66; also the halfway mark of our tenancy of this flat, if all goes as planned. Deeply concerned about the amount I've accomplished and how much remains to be done.'[15] He wondered if he had been so far behind during his first trip to Menton, but on reflection realized that he had.

One morning in early March, Daniells awoke with a migraine and 'filled with thoughts of my dear Father.'[16] He had recently seen a reproduction of Christ as a carpenter that had reminded him of his father and his vocation. Daniells, who had been so angry with his father as a young man, was now, like his father, in his sixties; not surprisingly, he was changing his perceptions of him. Thoughts of his own mortality also may have been spurred by a letter from Canada from the novelist Ethel Wilson, telling of the death of her husband, Wallace. When Laurenda finally came back, he had a 'horrible cold & sad depression, keeping poor L awake & uncheerful. But feeling better this morning.'[17]

On 2 August, they left Europe for England and a whirlwind tour of London, where they met William Robbins of the UBC English Department, and Allan Pritchard, a former UBC student and instructor, now teaching at University College, U of T. A few days later, they drove to Oxford, where they met F.W. Watt, a former UBC graduate but now part of the administration of the English Department at University College, U of T. There was just time for a brief visit with Herbert and Gladys Davis. Davis made heroic efforts to link up with Daniells both in London and at Oxford, as he was leaving for Australia the next day. Sadly, this was to be their last visit, as Davis died on 29 March 1967. A decade later, Daniells recalled him with affection and gratitude: 'My friendship with Herbert Davis, the Swift scholar, was ... of incredibly more importance than the materials of my PhD thesis.' In these early days of failure, 'it was friends alone that shone in the general murkiness of things.'[18]

After seeing the Davises and taking a jaunt to Haworth, where Daniells made a pilgrimage to the Emily Brontë Museum, they left for Canada on 17 August on the *Empress of England*. The family disembarked at Montreal on 24 August and drove back to Vancouver by way of Winnipeg.

━━━━●◆●━━━━

Daniells was now officially leaving the Department of English at UBC after nearly two decades as head. He had put the curriculum on a solid academic footing, raised standards for teaching and research, consolidated a strong academic faculty, redeveloped the graduate program, and introduced the Ph.D. Through his department had passed some of the best scholars in Canada, and he, himself, was now recognized as one of the best teachers in the country.

However, he had not been able to reconcile the divisions between the old guard and the younger members of the English Department, a conflict that had its roots in personality differences as well as in different national cultures – all accentuated by the abyss of the sixties revolution. Ian Ross, head of English in the eighties, saw Daniells sympathetically as a man who understood that with the university expanding rapidly in the post-war years, it was important to have a large English department that could cope with a substantial experience in English literature, composition, and rhetoric:

I could see his sincerity in wanting this kind of department, but others were not accepting of this ... I felt he was trying to do his best as a decent human being in extremely difficult circumstances. Trying to be fair, trying to achieve equity in marking for the benefit of students, trying to make English a very good part of university education, and with so much against him – colleagues who didn't like him, and didn't understand him, and opposed him – just intractable problems.

Ross also remarked that if originally Daniells thought that his vocation would be preaching but that he ended up teaching, 'there's quite a balancing act to handle all of that. I myself thought he did remarkably well. He radiated, to some degree, a bit of good humour.'[19]

Outside the English Department, as UBC University Professor, Daniells taught English classes and was available for special lectures. In November 1966, he lectured on the architecture of *Paradise Lost* in the old Arts 100 classroom where, as he noted, 'GGS used to lecture.' Sedgewick's mantle as UBC's master teacher now rested on Daniells. Students flocked from all faculties to this lecture. Daniells was easy, scholarly, witty. He drew diagrams showing Milton's view of the proximity of Heaven, Earth, and Hell, sketched the ladder climbed by Satan as he left Hell to infiltrate Eden to tempt Adam and Eve, and brought his sense of the poignancy of the fall of man to the lecture hall. When he had finished, he asked for questions. Afterward, he waited by the lectern for the shy students, the ones who preferred to ask their questions privately, but when he left the room he was surrounded by a cheerful crowd.

Daniells had the essential qualities of an inspiring teacher: he was emotionally involved with his subject, loved to teach, and genuinely wanted to know what his students thought. He asked probing questions and entertained answers (even foolish ones) kindly. Students went away from his classes, not just informed, but impelled by the urge to discover more. He also understood the explosive power of real teaching. One of his sonnets, 'Three lecture hours per week' – the description of the time allotted to a typical class in the university calendar – alludes to knowledge as a genie, drowned under old drugs, and imprisoned in a bottle. Most lecturers water down knowledge: what they offer is a teaspoon of 'the thick dark liquor that might incite the soul,' diluted in warm water, three times a week. For such knowledge is dangerous, the speaker warns: 'Take care ... / You do not wake the genie ... He is a spirit ... Able to wither you with one slight breath.'

The paradox is that those teachers who dilute knowledge, who do not wake the genie, invariably 'go down into death.'[20]

In 1968 UBC established the Dorothy Somerset Theatre in honour of the former English professor. She wrote to Daniells, whom she particularly wanted to speak on the occasion of its opening, saying that she found it very difficult to associate herself, the 'Me,' with the formal Dorothy Somerset of UBC. Nonetheless, as she recalled: 'But D.S. and "me" are *one* when remembering all of the generous and active encouragement you gave to the development of theatre as a recognized and legitimate branch of the Humanities and the Arts at UBC. Bless you, dear Roy!'[21]

A few years later in 1973, he received a similar letter from an old student from the forties, Fredelle Bruser Maynard, mother of writers Rona and Jocelyn Maynard. She said that she had no idea, when she first entered the University of Manitoba, what 'literature was all about (or what I was all about). It was sitting in your classes that I first acquired a passion for language – and a standard of value.' Maynard comments, '... that viewed *sub specie aeternitatis*, what a great teacher does is ephemeral. But my God what reverberations it can have through, say, a half century':

> Certain poets, certain lines, live in my mind because of the way you read, the comments you made ...
>
> Thirty years after, I marvel at the wizardry of certain performances ... You came in one day, just before exams, when George Ford was out sick, and volunteered to talk about anything, anything in the entire course. Someone proposed Bacon's *Essays* and you began, 'A single essay is like a box of nails. Individual sentences are hard, sharp, uniformly cut. You can lift out any statement and hang things on it. Order is irrelevant ...' And then you proceed to throw off a dazzling series of comparisons illuminating half a dozen distinctive essay styles. Bacon and Lamb ... Bacon and Cowley, Bacon and Overbury, Bacon and Addison ... Pure joy.

She added, 'You will be amused to know I've had many letters – from all across Canada – correctly identifying Ogden Bartlett (though heaven knows he's the merest shadow of a portrait).' Bartlett was the portrait of Daniells in Bruser's autobiographical *Raisins and Almonds*.[22]

Peter Howarth, a B.C. actor and playwright, recalls Daniells' course on Milton and the seventeenth century, the course 'that had the greatest influence on me, and my life.' It was his ability to make the student engage with the subject that Howarth most admired:

I remember him coming on the last day when we were finishing *Paradise Lost*, and that was the only time he wore his gown. And he began to read the last lines of *Paradise Lost* and he broke down. This was when Adam and Eve were forced to leave the garden of paradise: 'They hand in hand with wand'ring steps and slow, / Through *Eden* took their solitary way.'

Daniells did not weep, but deep emotion showed as his voice broke. Howarth thought, 'If a man who's taught that course all those years is still so moved by this poetry, there's something there.' In retrospect, we can speculate that it was not only Milton's poetry but the whole trauma of the loss of Paradise that resonated in Daniells' voice.

Although his standards as a professor were high, his corrections to students' work were often kindly. On one essay on Thomas Traherne, a seventeenth-century cleric, he wrote to the student: 'Your handwriting is like the trail of a lame but amiable spider. Do you use underwater ink?'[23] His files overflow with letters from students – good, bad, and indifferent. Good students wrote asking for recommendations, and to acknowledge his influence on their lives. Failed students also wrote. One woman said: 'It is some years since I took English 425, but it may please you to know that although I did so badly that I was obliged to write a supp., I was left with a deep and abiding love for Milton's work and read him to this day, purely for pleasure. Indeed, I may truthfully say that no other course in any subject did as much for me, intellectually and spiritually, as did English 425.'[24]

A Manitoba high-school teacher, David Duerksen, wrote in the late seventies to say: 'It is now thirty years since our paths crossed briefly in English 425. But, as Goethe says: "Eternity lies in the moment" – that moment of meaning and truth which never fades. What these moments of inspiration have contributed to my life in terms of literary and pedagogical insights, I have mentioned in the past ...'[25] Nine years earlier, in another letter to Daniells, Duerksen had written: 'As a matter of fact, my receiving a Centennial Medal for service in my profession in 1967, may be to a large extent attributed to the seeds of appreciation for literature and thought sown in your class. It is amazing and staggering what a prolonged influence three lecture hours a week can have.' He concluded by saying:

Just in case the negative criticism such as found in Irving Layton's 'Epigram for Roy Daniells' (*Balls for a One Armed Juggler*) or Earle Birney's poem on an educational [leader in] *Near False Creek Mouth* may have discouraged you along the way, might I say that your influence on many of your former students and your reward for it, is more aptly described in Daniel 12:3a. 'And they that be wise, shall shine as the brightness of the firmament.'[26]

━━▶◄━━

In 1970 Daniells' established reputation as a Milton specialist and as a Canadianist was acknowledged by his election as president of the Royal Society of Canada. He was also awarded the Lorne Pierce Medal that year 'since he alone has made a significant contribution to the development of Canadian literature as poet, critic, literary historian, administrator, and, last but by no means least, inspired and inspiring teacher.'[27] In September 1970, the *UBC Report* named these honours and added his honorary degree from McMaster University.

At the same time, his career, and life, were winding down. Daniells began to feel the chill wind of mortality: at first, smaller physical ailments, a brush with cancer, the deaths of old and dear friends; finally, his own increasing illness and a sense that time was running out. In 1959 he had had his first intuition of 'a return to the ultimate,' but by the seventies, this recognition had become much more intense.[28] In August 1971 he records feeling 'oddly disoriented, during the past day or so, reminding me of my experience at Zurich. I've felt Pascal's terror, the blankness [of] religious doubt, a sense of an immediately impending unconsciousness, a sense of the shortness of life remaining, an extra-awareness of flowers, trees &c and of people I knew long ago. Very strange.'[29] Two months later, he felt a 'sense of anxiety and impending stroke or heart failure. Dr. ... came and checked me over, finding nothing wrong. Now gradually recovering but with odd differences of outlook: feel rather fragile in myself, more kindly, more perceptive of natural and human beauty, more concerned about people, especially family and friends. No apparent diminution of intellectual grasp ... But I feel a change of a sense of having, like Christian, come through the valley of the shadow of death.'[30]

What made him happiest during these last years was his love for his wife and daughters, and the affection of his many friends. He started the seventies as a fairly vigorous sixty-eight-year-old, carrying nearly a full teaching load. Although he was no longer formally responsible for the English Department, when consulted he advised both Geoffrey Durrant, the new head, and his successor, Robert Jordan. The department did not function any better after his retirement; indeed, factions worsened.

When Daniells was elected president of the Royal Society in 1970, he was apprehensive about its future. But he proved to be an energetic president – he encouraged local branches and a strong central committee, and set the organization on its feet for the next decade. The past president, Claude Dolman, had begun to reorganize the Society, and Daniells continued this work. A new and efficient secretary was hired, the office reorganized, the fees raised to support expenses, and, as he reported, the society did indeed 'measure up to our chief raison d'être, the provision of a common forum for humanists and scientists, for Franco- and Anglophones ... our symposia in 1970 and 1971 (Influence of Climate on Canadian Culture and Survival of the Essential Human Values) were broadly based and yet acute examinations of important issues.'[31] In 1972 Daniells spoke to the Royal Society, urging the creation of a Cultural History of Canada as a centennial project:

> I would argue that a cultural history of Canada should be as comprehensive in the range of its concerns as the great encyclopedias are; that a purpose should be established with care and its acknowledgement made a condition of all editorial appointments; that potential contributors be asked, not merely to do their scholarly best, but to transcend themselves and produce something hitherto unknown in this country.[32]

What Daniells had in mind was a study that dealt with the relations between French and English, with ethnic minorities, and with the development of newspapers in order to show the way in which the culture of Canada really works. This idea of a cultural history was a project dear to the hearts of Daniells, Pacey, and Klinck, but, unfortunately, it did not come into being.

As his term drew to a close, he was preparing the Alexander Lectures for presentation at U of T in the spring of 1972. He hoped to try out some of the ideas developed for his book on Mannerism, 'to establish a working definition of Mannerism (as I endeavoured to do for Baroque in the other book) and then to apply the concept to Donne, Bacon, Browne, Marvell, one or two plays of Shakespeare ... The attempt to cross over from Italy and the graphic arts to English poetry is, in itself, stimulating.'[33] To the managing editor U of T Press, Francess Halpenny, he suggested that the draft lectures could form the basis for a book. She agreed. Daniells was more frank with his old friend Pacey. 'I am to give the Alexander lectures in Toronto next month, and quake inwardly.'[34]

Because of his full teaching and administrative schedule, he had little time for extended research, yet he continued to work on his book. Family life and his beloved garden at 1741 Allison Road were completely satisfying. 'After a dismal winter, the pussy-willows and jasmine (or is it forsythia) are out and the bulbs poking up. Signs of hope!'[35] In the late sixties, as they had earlier agreed, Laurenda had continued her career by taking librarianship at UBC. She was now employed as the UBC archivist in Special Collections. Susan and Sara both attended UBC, Susan taking honours English and theatre, and Sara honours English and fine arts.

The family had acquired a dog, a beautiful black-masked blond Afghan hound they named Shalimar. The two – the tall, slightly stooped older professor and the tall dog with her thin, elegant face – became a familiar sight on the UBC campus. He was now more accessible at home, and his daughters' classmates dropped in 'by the dozens' – frequently ending up in the kitchen talking with Daniells and drinking tea. For the first time since 1949, the couple made changes to their home: 'We have spent a fortune enlarging the kitchen (to contain a breakfast room) and stretching the dining room. The girls' numerous friends were once toddlers who packed in easily; they are now young giants and goddesses with far-flung limbs.'[36]

In early 1972 Daniells opened the first World Shakespeare Congress at SFU with some witty doggerel which played on Shakespeare's name:

Take Holy Writ, by Shakespeare prized, –
The version King James authorized.
Then open it between your palms,
Turn over to the book of psalms,
Psalm forty-six, to be precise,
Then change the focus of your eyes
And count the words, with penciled ticks,
Until you've numbered forty-six.
That word is SHAKE: take note, my friend ...[37]

He received a standing ovation. The event, organized by Rudolph

Habenicht, editor of the *Shakespeare Bibliography* and a professor of English at SFU, was an outstanding success. Habenicht's letter of thanks reminded Daniells how he had helped him from the start: '... five years ago you may recall sitting in my car in a melancholy rain urging me to carry on regardless of timid, negative advice just given me; and of course you helped all of us at the Congress itself. I have therefore real and sincere thanks for all that you have done.'[38]

Daniells' Alexander Lectures on 7, 8, and 9 March 1972 were a personal triumph. Accompanied by slides, his topics were 'Mannerism in English Literature: Can It Be Defined?'; 'Mannerist Prose and the Strange Case of Francis Bacon'; and 'Mannerism in Drama and Poetry: Shakespeare, Donne, Marvell.' He commented in his notes for one lecture on 'Donne's affinity to a general movement in Europe, a rising wave of aspiration ... distressed, divided and driven back on itself; creating, in such moments of internal stress, permanent expressions of a strange and troubling sensibility.'[39] The lectures were a continuation of the explorations of Mannerism he had begun in Italy, and bridged English literary traditions and art and architectural traditions encountered in Italy. His lectures reapproached the devotional, metaphysical, and mystic in light of the period and its art.

Norman Endicott, his old friend and professor, had been asked to thank the speaker. As W.J. Keith recalled, he 'got up and said the conventional things, what a pleasure, etc., and two minutes into his talk he began to say that the speaker had said such-and-such on Mannerism, but what he might have said was ... For what seemed like ten minutes he went off on what the speaker might have said.' Later, just before the dinner in Daniells' honour, Keith approached Endicott and said, '"You certainly put Daniells in his place." Endicott appeared quite surprised and said, "Did I come across like that?"'[40] Daniells, however, was unperturbed; he knew Endicott's ways when tracing a line of thought.

Many old friends and former students were there: Northrop Frye, Robert Finch, Barker Fairley, Donald Creighton, Kay Riddell, and even a former girlfriend from Victoria College days, Leith Ferguson, now Mrs MacDonald. Hugh MacCallum and his family were kind hosts, and there was a splendid reception at Massey College by Robertson Davies, 'at whose right hand I sat.'[41] Daniells had several breakfasts with Finch; Frye gave him a special lunch at the York Club; and he caught up with friends such as Douglas LePan, Jay Macpherson, Douglas Lochhead, Tuzo Wilson, Ann Saddlemyer, Ken MacLean, and others. Daniells enjoyed his few days of glory, but he returned to B.C. aware that his decision in the 1930s to leave Toronto had been for the best in terms of his personal happiness.

He later received a letter from Finch, questioning a point made in his lectures: '... there is a division of opinion among scholars as to whether Marino belongs to the mannerist category or the baroque. My basic problem in this case is therefore: How will your book deal with such a division? ... how are you to "confirm" that Marino is not in one category but in another, when two sets of scholars have already "confirmed," the one set that he is in one category, the other set that he is in the other?'[42] It was a vitally important question implicit in Endicott's impromptu monologue, but Daniells was not willing to speculate further.

On 6 April he celebrated his seventieth birthday with the family and neighbours. On 12 April he was invested with the Order of Canada at Rideau Hall, an honour he attributed to Pacey: 'If, long ago, you had not – at a time when I was very distressed and confused – lifted up your voice to nominate me for various Royal Society offices and then as vice-president, I should never have come out of my shell on this Pacific beach.'[43] Laurenda attended the ceremony with him and shared his pleasure. More important to both was the UBC convocation on 24 May: 'Our dear old Susan went smiling across the platform with an honours BA in English, first-class. L & I most grateful.'[44]

In response to the Order of Canada, Finch sent Daniells a present which he had found in Ireland. As he explained, 'somehow it disappeared from sight but suddenly the unicorn has come out of hiding – so here it is.'[45] It was a graceful allusion to one of Daniells' finest sonnets on the unicorn in *Deeper into the Forest*. Finch's unicorn, originally a shoe scraper made of black iron, was later sculpted into Daniells' house next to the front door.

That July, Daniells had the first of a number of worrisome illnesses, a cancerous growth on his cheek. At the same time, Pacey informed him that he was undergoing a serious operation for cancer. However, Pacey was sufficiently recovered to join the *Literary History* group in November, which celebrated a 'Carolingian Festival' at the University of Western Ontario in honour of Carl Klinck. As Daniells deftly explained, 'the Carolingians were followers of Charlemagne, that is Carolus Magnus or Carl the Great.' Daniells composed one of his celebrated pieces of witty doggerel for this last meeting of the original *Literary History* editors:

Cheers for our Carl! for he's a hoarder
   Of Can Lit. in its fine disorder:
  From vivid tales that shock the censors
To gentle hymns, like Edmund Spenser's;

Tales that Sir Walter Scott's may rival
   Of hero's triumph all unaided,
  Or tales on Atwood's theme, Survival
With heroines who've barely made it ...[46]

The editors, meeting to discuss a revised edition of the *Literary History*, decided to bring in some younger scholars to contribute to the revision. Daniells had suggested as contributors two former UBC students, 'Sandra Djwa / Bill New,' on the grounds that both were rather like Klinck and Daniells,[47] and Frye was later to suggest one of his former students, Margaret Atwood. However, Klinck did not know me at the time, but he had met New when visiting Leeds to lecture on the *Literary History* in the mid-sixties. Moreover, both Daniells and Klinck were uncomfortable with the thesis of Atwood's *Survival*, then just published: as Klinck wrote Daniells, 'I will not stand for Atwood's impressionistic nonsense; with your help we shall maintain the *LHC* as it *substantially* has been – a bulwark against such drivel.'[48] Eventually, New was invited to join the group to write on prose fiction, and George Woodcock was invited to write on poetry.

With a new group of contributors to the *Literary History*, Daniells and Klinck still continued to debate the nature of the project, and to be active editors. In September 1972 Daniells had told Klinck, 'As you know, I am regretfully in complete disagreement with Norrie's view that the revised version should be primarily descriptive and only secondarily critical ... I am now quite fervently of the opinion that evaluation and criticism and incitement to clearer views on the part of the reader are the desiderata for this decade ...'[49] Two years later, both men were busy editing the submitted typescripts: they were candid with each other, but considerate with colleagues. On Malcolm Ross's drafted chapter on criticism, for example, Daniells told Klinck that he had placed pencilled marks in the margin, easily removed, in about sixty places: 'Nevertheless, I like Ross's chapter very much. It is alive and kicking, mewling, puking, soiling its diapers, crowing with excitement and wanting to be picked up.' This he contrasted to another drafted chapter which he considered 'a kind of still birth.' Daniells added a P.S. to this letter, saying that where his comments would hurt anyone's feelings, Klinck should cast them into the waste basket.[50]

Specifically, Daniells was most irked by the encyclopedic nature of drafted contributions to the *Literary History*; he thought that contributors would be better advised to follow the more urbane example of Baugh's *Literary History of England*: failing this, Klinck and Frye (then scheduled to write the conclusion) would have a difficult task. In fact, Frye was again to write the conclusion himself. 'Typically Northropian,' Daniells concluded. 'The reader feels thrust into a number of fresh and unresolved questions rather than getting a firm grip on the knot at the end of the rope.' During this period, as Klinck reflected, he relied heavily on Daniells as the 'conscience' of the revised *Literary History*.[51]

In 1973 Roy and Laurenda Daniells celebrated their twenty-fifth wedding anniversary with a special dinner at a seafood restaurant, with Susan and a good friend and neighbour, Doris Skerl. It was an introspective moment for Daniells: 'But for Laurenda, I should by [now] likely have gone insane or committed suicide. Her love & affection, her strength, wisdom, tact and common sense are beyond all praise.'[52] Their marriage had indeed been exceptionally happy; almost every anniversary is marked in his diary with a reference to his continued joy. Laurenda provided more than simply a happy home: her good sense, intelligence, and kindness nurtured a secure domestic setting that left him free rein in the areas where he worked best. Throughout the seventies, he fretted that she carried such a heavy load of family life, archival work, and university responsibilities, although she was always cheerful and never complained.

In May 1973 the Alumni Association gave a formal dinner at the Hotel Vancouver, at which Daniells was honoured: '[S.I.] Hayakawa spoke very effectively about Univ. problems. I was given a fine Indian mask, as a mark of recognition (which I hardly deserve, I think).'[53] The event was written up in the *Alumni Chronicle* and published with a photograph of Daniells. It brought a spate of letters from former students: one wrote that the article 'is tolerably well written but clearly fails to do anything like justice to the ... perpetually amazing depth and rigorous honesty of your thought ... We theologs worshipped you. Other professors had students, but you had disciples.'[54]

In 1974 Daniells, Marion Smith, now of the University of Guelph, and Henry Kreisel, vice-president of the University of Alberta, were asked to assess the English Department at Simon Fraser University. Like many new universities in the sixties, SFU had had a troubled history, and this was the first external review of the department. The committee visited SFU between 19 and 21 February, meeting faculty, students, and administrators. Morale in the department was low. The larger American contingent veered to the political left, and the more conservative Canadians were outnumbered in departmental voting. The committee's report finally acknowledged the large degree of mistrust in the department as well as the fact that a split seemed imminent. Daniells, who wrote the report, revealed his implicit assumptions regarding the role of the head of an English Department when he suggested that 'a chairman without moral authority, reduced to adjusting the routine mechanisms of a Department in the hope that it will somehow achieve greatness is an implausible figure.'[55]

In the same year, he spoke at a convocation at UNB at which Pacey had been made University Professor. Pacey had been a candidate for president of UNB, but his ill health had intervened. Two years earlier, when Pacey had been invited to apply for the post of president at the University of Victoria, Daniells had expressed to him his views on the role of the Canadian university president: 'It's clear that a president, from now on, can't act as a mother hen to whom all the chicks come peeping. He will be at the head of an armoured column defending its homeland ... To put it another way, a president, in the 70's and 80's of this century will be a public advocate and defender of the educational principle in our Canadian culture. A wonderful chance!'[56]

During the early seventies, Daniells caught up with a number of old friends from Victoria, Toronto, and Winnipeg. Fredelle Maynard wrote: 'Looking back, I see the university [of Manitoba] in 1938 as provincial, isolated, heterogeneous, in some ways comic ... and yet it was there, not at Toronto or Harvard, that I had my only great experiences in education. How lucky I was to encounter you at just the right moment!'[57] Daniells also wrote to Max Maynard, asking him if he understood why Birney had plagued him the way he had, and confessing that he had been unable to find intellectual peace. Maynard responded: 'Why, for heavens sake, should you be writing *me* about Birney? And what can I say to you, after all your reading, about finding "a stable point of rest"?'

> But first, Birney. Why did he plague you, as you say he did? From Mabel Mackenzie and Jack Shadbolt, I heard whispers about this. But nothing that made sense. Could it be that Earle resented your being head of the Dept. – your superior rank in relation to himself? And was he (a defected Marxist) perhaps a bit scornful of your Arnold-Babbitt-Woodhouse-Bush type of humanism? I don't know, but it seems to me that this was quite possible. Furthermore, both of you were poets (i.e. rivals) & had great reputations as classroom performers. One final observation: you have (had) a tendency to allow your exuberant wit to frolic unleashed. And at times it became not wholly (or innocently) playful. My reading of Earle is that he was a very sensitive & somewhat open man. You were quite capable of sallies that would hit vital nerves.[58]

Maynard's analysis was astute, particularly his suggestion that Birney was an exceptionally sensitive and easily wounded man. Daniells' wit could be cutting.

Daniells did not serve on the ACUTE executive after its initial forma- tion, but in 1976 was honoured at the annual banquet in Quebec City 'to recognize in a public and formal way your outstanding contribution to the work and concerns of our profession.'[59] Paul Fleck, president of ACUTE, R.G. Baker, then president of the UPEI, his UBC colleague Jan de Bruyn, and F.E.L. Priestley of U of T paid tributes. At the centre of all their tributes were the light poems and doggerel (their own and Daniells') for which he was celebrated. Fleck, who had been taught by Daniells as an undergraduate, and later as an M.A. student supervised by him, joked that Daniells 'has distinguished himself as a poet, scholar, teacher and humanist. He manages his eyebrows with elegance and finesse, and he is the best damn limerick-writer in Canada.'[60] Fleck was allud- ing to the fact that when amused, Daniells twitched his thick, bushy eyebrows, inviting the observer to share his sense of the absurdity of the human situation. The ACUTE banquet represented the tribute of his peers, both to the man and the academic. Daniells was now acknowl- edged as one of Canada's outstanding professors of English.

PART SIX

Vancouver: 1970–1979

Chapter Twenty-Two

The River of Time

Seven Scotsmen stood above (when I lay bounden
In dread of the channering worm and the coals of hell);
Two men from Ulster, three from the east of London
Stood on a platform the gospel for to tell.

They were cobblers, blacksmiths, bricklayers and a labourer,
They shouted and stamped and leaned and levered and swung,
They hammered with hard hands on the holy pages,
And cried in a high, round, loud, uprising tongue.

They are all gone now except old Andrew Smart,
They worship the Lamb in the mist of the golden street
In a world of light. And I sit lingering here,
For their awls have pierced, their pinchers have clenched my heart;
In my skull their forges roar, their sledges beat;
And the labyrinth walls they built ring round my fear.

Deeper into the Forest, p. 42

This poem, echoing Henry Vaughan's 'They are all gone into the world of light, / And I alone sit lingering here!,' expresses the predicament of both the young and the old Daniells.[1] Vaughan's poem is the quintessential statement in English poetry about the fear of the loss of salvation, the primary fear of Daniells' religious life. In his own poem, he explains that the bullying theology of the seven Scotsmen, the ministering Brethren, had cut off the young man, and now the adult, from Vaughan's eternity, 'the world of light,' and confined him to his own skull, where, through frightful migraines, the forges roared and the sledges hammered. In his last years, after 1970, the old man turned inward in an attempt to come to terms with his early religious teaching.

Attempting to clarify his thoughts, he corresponded with long-time friends, Northrop Frye, Desmond Pacey, and Robert Finch. Frye and Pacey had been ordained as United Church ministers, and Finch was a highly (though privately) religious man who chose not to publish his devotional poetry. Daniells also wrote to a number of theologians, including Wilfred Cantwell Smith, who wrote *Belief and History* (1966), and consulted a number of people at UBC, including William Taylor, principal of Union College of British Columbia. At UBC he had been attending the local University Hill United Church and reading a number of texts on the historical Christ, including *The Jesus of the Early Church* and *The Jesus of the Early Christians*.[2]

Although Daniells had worked his way through many religious fears, he had not quite come out on the other side. One evening at a dinner at our home in the early seventies, he told guests that he had just come back from a trip during which two of his fellow passengers on the train had been members of the Plymouth Brethren. One said, very soberly, 'Are you saved, Brother?' and Daniells recalled, 'I instantly slipped back into the groove.'[3] Intellectually he had rejected the Brethren in his thirties and forties, but emotionally he had not been able to resolve issues regarding sin, salvation, and the nature of God, and these recurred in his seventies. His childhood fixation that the Day of Judgment was imminent, and that his mother would be saved while he was left behind, now re-emerged in the fear that he might be saved while his family, his wife and daughters, might be left behind.

As a young man in the thirties, he had welcomed Milton's *Paradise Lost* as a paean of forgiveness. He believed that God had sent the angel Raphael to Adam so that man might be armoured against the serpent. Nonetheless, God gave man an opportunity to choose so that he was, in Milton's terms, 'sufficient to have stood, yet free to fall.'[4] A younger colleague recalls asking Daniells which scene he liked best in Milton: 'Roy said it was that wonderful scene in Book v where Raphael comes as God's emissary to meet with Adam. It is the first contact as it were between God and man, between heaven and earth. Roy liked it for its harmony and grace and balance.'[5] He found such qualities a welcome antidote to the stark black and white of Plymouth Brethren theology.

Although Milton was initially very liberating for Daniells, in time he began to question the nature of Milton's God, assigning essay topics on this subject to his classes. One such occasion was later recalled by a former student: 'Do you recall a paper Harold Giesbrecht wrote for you on the topic "Is Milton a Christian?"' Using fundamentalist definitions, Giesbrecht had argued a negative thesis statement, apparently to Daniells' satisfaction:

> You commented 'Do you really think Milton is in Hell?' We talked about the implications in a seminar, and your observation about the demarcation line between salvation and damnation being no wider than a hair-breadth from our vantage point, has frequently helped me to preserve my sanity as it has also helped to strengthen my faith in 'a divinity that shapes our ends.'[6]

The incident may have helped confirm the student's faith, but it also suggests that Daniells was open to the idea that Milton's God shared some of the attributes of the cruel Jehovah. It also implies that Daniells, like Woodhouse, sometimes viewed literature as a religious text in that it had a theological message to teach.

His old fears about an unforgiving God and human sin surfaced every now and then. For Daniells, the long decades of English Department difficulties were not just conflicts of opposing egos and agendas – which no individual could hope to resolve – but, rather, when he was depressed, a measure of his own failure. In response, he actively searched for theological answers to his concerns about the nature of God and the hereafter. He wrote to his old friend from Winnipeg days, Father Patrick Plunkett, who offered to remember him in his prayers. To Jim Manly, a former student and friend, who was a United Church minister, he asked: 'How can members of Churches which take the Bible literally rejoice at Christmas time?' His reasoning was that the newborn Christ of Christmas would, 'by inexorable sequence of events, become the judge at the last Judgment. ' For Daniells, the fear was that relatives and dear friends who did not accept orthodox Christianity 'will be consigned to endless torment.'[7] Manly preached a Christmas sermon in December 1974 responding to these questions. But Daniells' apprehensions persisted.

He wanted to understand the nature of the Christian God. Is he the forgiving Christ of the New Testament? The wrathful Jehovah of the Old Testament? Or worse, because one does not know what to expect, is he a combination of both? He wrote to Frye, asking him for his views. Frye responded that '"a" God is only a vague notion of Something

Upstairs. Christianity, which unites the conception of God to a specific man whose characteristics and attitudes are described, is more concrete than this.'[8]

Daniells then suggested that the two discuss religious questions by mail. In a subsequent letter, Frye jokingly responded to what he called (alluding to Martin Luther) the first five of Daniells' 'ninety-five theses.' In these letters, we find some of Frye's most explicit statements on his own religious beliefs. He said that for him there was a difference between scientific truth and imaginative vision, that 'the gospels present their story as a myth, an imaginative vision,' and that Blake says that '"God only acts and is, in existing beings or men."' He did not see a historical Jesus behind the New Testament because from the very first moment that we see him, 'Jesus is imprisoned within gospels, presented within a framework of assumptions derived from the early church.' But he agreed with Daniells that the historical tradition of Christianity has been 'overwhelmingly in favour of persecution.'[9]

While Daniells continued to worry these questions, he taught his classes, graduate and undergraduate, encouraging young scholars in both seventeenth-century literature and Canadian literature and, in the fall of 1974, slowly began to prepare for retirement. He moved his office, bringing home to Allison Road his scholarly books for sorting, many of which he donated to the UBC library. In early December 1974, he gave his final lecture in English 305, the last in some fifty years of teaching. Daniells found himself in 'a state of euphoria, now that I am free of so many burdens.'[10] On 11 December the department held a farewell lunch. Forty-five members of the English Department and the new UBC president, his old friend from Victoria days, Walter Gage, attended. Stanley Read, Gage, and Robbins made brief speeches, and Daniells was presented with a fine art book of Rubens reproductions.

Another burden lifted was his manuscript on Mannerism, which he had finally finished. The book had been completed under difficult circumstances: he had been unwell for the preceding two years, had had several small heart attacks, and suffered continuing back pain aggravated by a serious fall. But he determined to submit it to University of Toronto Press before starting out, in December, on a fellowship for further research on the same subject in Rome.

The trip did not begin well. Laurenda Daniells had barely arrived home from the hospital, where she had had a hysterectomy, when it was time to get on the plane. Their eldest daughter, Susan, who saw them off at the airport just before Christmas, wrote cheerfully: 'I hope you made it. It was unnerving watching Major Surgery in a wheelchair and I'll Never Travel Like This Again lose the boarding passes.'[11] However, the couple had a few days of rest over Christmas while visiting Laurenda's brother, Ross, now settled in England with the Canadian diplomatic corps. They reached Rome on 28 December.

As always, Daniells found it difficult to function in new surroundings, and his depression and disorientation were accentuated by the overwhelmingly pictorial religious art and sculpture of Italy. He may also have been conscious that this would be his last research trip. During their earlier visit, he had initially felt 'peculiarly unnerved, dispirited, and convinced of my inability to speak any language (even English), to read a map, tip a waiter, find an apartment, or ask for a hair cut.' He had written then to Pacey: 'I feel like Christian in Giant Despair's dungeon before he thought of the key in his bosom. I wish you were here to say like Faithful "Pluck it out, good brother!"'[12] Cut off from colleagues and students, Daniells was lonely and reached out through correspondence.

As he now told Pacey, 'the past month has been hectic in the extreme. Laurenda ... by sheer will power pulled herself together after the minimum period of recuperation, faced the Vancouver-London flight ... and even drove a new BMW from Munich to Rome. These women you and I were lucky enough to marry, Desmond, are they not wonderful beyond belief?' But now, as earlier, Daniells' religious concerns were paramount. He explained that he had organized his research 'so as to include a study of images of God in Italian paintings and concepts of God the Father in 17th Century (and some other) Eng. Lit. ... God is pictured as an old man, often remote, sometimes beneficent, occasionally wrathful. This suggests human qualities rather than eternal ones; it omits the penetrating, vivifying & fructifying elements of divine power.'[13]

Pacey saw that Daniells was still troubled about the question of the wrathful Jehovah, and joked a little: 'Naturally one sees God as the highest manifestation of one's own kind, so that in periods when the stern father was seen to be the human ideal, God would be picked as the stern father. I wonder how "hippies" see God? – I suppose as a long-haired, bead-bedecked, "stoned" old man!'[14]

Their correspondence languished in February and March, primarily because Pacey's cancer recurred. Unaware of this, Daniells in Rome continued his correspondence on religion with Frye, who reiterated that for him 'poetry and myth are interchangeable':

> Some clunkheads talk about trying to 'demythologize' the Gospels or the Bible, subtract everything that seems incredible and keep a historical residue. If you tried that with the Gospels, all you'd have would be something like 'Jesus wept.' Not until EVERY GODDAM SYLLABLE of the Bible has been translated into myth does it even pretend to make any sense. Historical meaning: the Jews and Romans crucified Christ. So what? Mythical meaning: you and I crucified Christ. That at least makes sense in its own terms, whether one accepts it as faith or not: the essential thing is to get rid of it as fact.

The 'clunkhead' to whom Frye referred was undoubtedly Rudolph Bultmann, whose ground-breaking essay 'New Testament and Mythology' begins with a discussion of demythologizing the New Testament; but he does not, as Frye suggests, propose to subtract the incredible and leave a historical residue. What Bultmann calls for is a reinterpretation of biblical myth, not its elimination: 'Whereas the older liberals used criticism to *eliminate* the mythology of the New Testatment, our task today is to use criticism to *interpret* it.' Bultmann, who states that 'the facts which historical criticism can verify cannot exhaust, indeed they cannot adequately indicate all that Jesus meant to me ...' holds a position close to that expressed by Daniells.[15]

In his next letter, Frye told Daniells very frankly that in early adolescence he had realized that 'the whole apparatus of afterlife in heaven and hell, unpardonable sins, and the like was a lot of junk.' There remained the influence of his mother and the fact that he had agreed to go to college as a church student. Nonetheless, he had decided, without quite realizing it at the time, that he would accept from religion only what made sense to him as a human being:

> I was not going to worship a god whose actions, judged by human standards, were contemptible. That was where Blake helped me so much: he taught me that the lugubrious old stinker in the sky that I had heard so much about existed all right, but that his name was Satan, that his function was to promote tyranny in society and repression in the mind.

Frye did not think he had learned anything from his professors at the University of Toronto: E.K. Brown he considered a Platonist, and the Emmanuel faculty 'dazed professionals.' As a student, he had concluded that the New Testament was full of pious frauds, and that the Gospels obliterated any historically accessible Jesus. In fact, he believed that the gospel writers had somehow turned 'something historical, assuming it was there, into myth.' At this point, Frye had realized that myth was the opposite of history, that it described what is expected to happen in the reader's mind while he reads:

> This is what Milton calls the Word of God in the heart and ultimately gives the highest authority to. So the whole drama of the human movement, which was also a divine movement, incarnating itself in the world and pulling the world up with it at the Resurrection seemed to me to make sense. In this process everything demonic gets left behind. Hell and torture and punishment and revenge and unpardonable sins all vanish into nothingness in that upward movement. So the Gospel writers weren't really liars, any more than poets are.[16]

Frye's responses suggest that he was now thinking out the structures that were shortly to appear in Book I of *The Great Code* (1981). In his Introduction, he remarked that this book 'expresses only my personal encounter with the Bible.'[17] The intriguing question is the degree to which some of these encounters were triggered or encouraged by his correspondence with Daniells.

Nonetheless, Frye's answers were totally unsatisfactory to Daniells. He still saw the Bible as the divinely inspired word of God. To say, as Frye did, that the Bible was all myth and poetry was not to address his question at all. Despite his considerable intellect, despite his training in literary symbolism, at a deep emotional level Daniells could not escape from the tyranny of literalism in relation to the Bible although he recognized that the gospel narratives were filled with contradiction and invention. Nor could he escape the Plymouth Brethren theological questions that it raised in his own life. A fragment of a letter suggests some of his problems:

> The concept of *myth* is a useful device for packaging ideas that have been powerfully operative in human history. It has its limits, however. A medical man, choosing between two opposing myths concerning the origins of

disease, should be able to sort the more nearly true one from the others. Otherwise, he kills the patient. If the resurrection is a myth, then what truth, if any, does reside in it? When we read that in Adam all died and, similarly, in Christ all are made alive, we take the first half of the statement as myth and as *misleading* myth. What, then, do we do about the second half? In a world of myths, some true, some half true, some dangerously false, who knows where to turn?

Daniells added that he still found Julian Huxley as useful as anyone he had read. 'His frank acceptance of religious experience as a guide to human experience ... and his sense of human experience as a retrospective, presently active and everlastingly hopeful guide to ultimate truths strikes me as admirable.'[18] These notes appear to be a response to some of the issues raised by Frye.

While still in Rome in March 1975, Daniells received a letter from University of Toronto Press rejecting his manuscript. It had been read by two readers, both of whom recognized that Daniells was remarkable in his capacity to discuss art, music, and literature. Reader A, apparently a literary critic, thought that dating Mannerism was 'a slippery business' and placing a period definitively nearly impossible. Reader B, apparently an art critic, completely disagreed with Daniells' definitions of Mannerism and could not recommend publication.[19] As a result, the Press recommended against publication. Daniells wrote Jean Jamieson, the humanities editor, and explained that, as he had written the manuscript under duress, he would make revisions.

He had been working on this book for at least a decade. To have it rejected at this stage in his life must have been a crushing disappointment. During the same period, however, two prominent members of the U of T English Department were also turned down by University of Toronto Press for publication.[20] Had Daniells been aware of this, the rejection might have proved less devastating. As it was, there was no one to whom he could turn to discuss the matter. Pacey was again ill, Frye was too successful, and Finch had already warned Daniells that the whole Mannerist area was a minefield as far as definition was concerned. Nonetheless, it was to Finch he eventually turned – but not immediately and not for discussion of his book, but rather for discussion of some of the religious issues that lay behind the iconography of the book.

The disappointment about his Mannerist book came on top of his religious fears and his worsening health. Indeed his poor health aggravated his religious worries. When he first arrived in Italy, he had felt disoriented: he was finally retired, but he did not like it – his students were the focus of his life. Seriously ill with the flu and despondent in Rome, he had been given a strong sedative, similar to Valium, at too high a dosage. At the same time, he was taking pills, recommended by a Vancouver doctor, to steady his heart. This combination of medications interfered with his normal functioning so severely that he tried to do without them. Several days later, on 3 May, he had a heart attack and was rushed to hospital.

Despite this serious setback, he decided to return to Vancouver in late May to receive an honorary degree at UBC's spring convocation. The degree, a final acknowledgment of his extraordinary contributions to teaching and scholarship, was proposed by President Walter Gage and the board of governors. Unfortunately, Laurenda Daniells missed the ceremony – 'All those honorary degrees ... six honorary degrees, and I never made it. There was always some ridiculous reason why I couldn't.'[21] Although it was too expensive for her to fly home, a student fare for Sara was possible, so that Daniells and his youngest daughter left together in mid-May for the trip back to Vancouver. On 29 May, Daniells gave the convocation address to the arts faculty and graduates at a ceremony where he and Carl Borden, a UBC anthropologist, were both honoured.[22]

His three weeks in Canada were spent with Susan, Sara, and the neighbours, and consulting various doctors. He went to a Dr Hamilton about his heart problem, to a Dr Sawchuk about his back problem, and to the cancer clinic for a check-up for a small growth which he had removed from his face. The results were generally favourable, and he returned to Rome via England on 16 June.

But he had hardly arrived in Rome when he received a telegram from Mary Pacey, telling of Desmond's death from cancer: 'A sad, sad loss.'[23] Daniells had known Pacey since the mid-thirties, first as an eager student, then as a trusted colleague, and then as one of his closest friends. When Pacey had suffered a nervous breakdown in the forties, Daniells had written him supportive letters, describing his own difficulties; when Daniells had troubles with Birney and Layton in the sixties, Pacey had done his best to mediate the situation. Daniells had introduced Pacey to the study of Canadian literature, and at the time of his death, Pacey was one of Canadian literature's most important critics. They had a strong friendship, proven by time and based on mutual respect. That Pacey, the younger man, should die before Daniells was a blow. Daniells expressed his grief in a personal memoir of Pacey for publication in *Canadian Literature*.[24]

Three days after he heard the bad news of Pacey's death, Daniells was feeling ill himself: 'I am far from well and considering a return to Canada, for a check up, poss. in August.'[25] A lasting effect of his earlier over-medication was that he now experienced some mental incoherence on his return to Europe. His response to this new problem, Pacey's death, and increasing troubles with his heart was a serious depression. It had been coming for some time.

Clearly the strain of scholarly work was now too high. During this summer in Rome, in August 1975, Laurenda Daniells persuaded him to set aside Mannerism for a while and to write instead about himself, family life in England, and immigration to Canada. She suggested that he write these reminiscences to their daughter Susan, now at home in Vancouver. Throughout their stay in Rome, Susan had kept them amused with a series of chatty, informative letters, some about the beloved family dog, Shalimar. Responding to Susan about his early life was also a literary activity, but with none of the pressures demanded by Mannerist theory.

In early September, the family took a trip to Switzerland to meet Laurenda Daniells' brother and his family. They travelled to Bellagio, Lugano, and Bologna and returned to Rome by 25 September. Daniells continued to sketch out his autobiographical letters for the next two months. On 2 December they started on their journey back to Vancouver with Laurenda remaining in England for a few weeks to visit with her brother and his family, and Daniells and Sara returning to Canada. He arrived in Vancouver on 5 December and recorded heartfelt thanks: 'I am so glad to be home & so thankful for having lasted the year.'[26]

The next day, he went to the doctor, who was reassuring, but in subsequent days he had several blackouts: 'Last night I seemed to have gone upstairs to where G'ma and Sue were playing scrabble and said something about not knowing where I was and going back to bed without remembering a thing ... Sue came and sat with me and talked to me helpfully and with great love and sweetness.'[27] Later, in January

1976, he had a more serious attack: 'Was taken to hosp. in ambulance, suffering from convulsion similar to that in Rome. What anxiety I do give my dear L.'[28]

His ill health, the failure of his Mannerist book, and the medication he was taking left him more open to anxiety about religious issues. He began a long and intense correspondence with Robert Finch, apparently initiating it with a comment about his own spiritual difficulties and a remark to the effect that Finch had found in the arts 'a kind of ultimate meaning and satisfaction.'[29] Finch responded indignantly, saying that they had not corresponded sufficiently for Daniells to know this. In a following letter, he remarked, 'What odd correspondents we are! – First, you introduce a major issue. Then I reply, then you thank me for my reply, but drop the issue. I am not solely referring to our recent exchanges, but to our exchanges over the years.'[30] Finch was right to take umbrage. Daniells wanted to talk about religion in the abstract, but did not want to bare his soul. But in the next twelve months, Finch's searching questions forced him to do so.

Their correspondence began in January 1976. Daniells was once again convinced of the cruelty of Jehovah, the fact that 'many are called but few are chosen,' and that most people were destined for hell. He saw the existence of at least three Christs in the Bible. The first was the Christ of the Plymouth Brethren, whose coming will restore the dead in Christ: '"Then we which are alive and remain shall be caught up together with them in clouds so shall we ever be with the Lord."'[31] The second Christ was the 'Person' presented in the New Testament. This Christ did not 'disown or repudiate the Law and the Jehovah who towers behind it.' In Daniells' view, this is the Jehovah who kills the firstborn of Egypt and, indeed, the whole population of earth, for trifling offences.[32] The third was the historical Christ, a figure difficult to find because the Gospels could not be verified.

Finch had no patience with this formulation. To him, such arguments were negative, coming entirely from the mind: '... in the case of your treatment of the third Christ, who, I presume, is the one you choose to accept. I should have expected a trace of feeling or warmth, instead of which I find no trace of a person at all. Could you say something positive about him? Or am I impertinent?'[33]

Daniells found this question difficult to answer. 'On the positive side, there does seem to be some evidence of a teacher, with a message of grace and truth, who was put to death.' He had recently discovered that comparisons of the Greek and Aramaic languages suggested that there were insertions in the Gospels by members of the early Church. This gave him enormous relief. Imagine, he said to Finch, that Frye and Daniells were to be burned at the stake because neither could take the Scriptures in the literal sense demanded by the Church, when suddenly it was discovered that this appalling picture had been created by the human imagination rather than by divine inspiration. 'That is my condition. I feel as though I had emerged from some frightful place of confinement, got through the gate, fallen on my face in the grass and was simply for the time being lying there. I am not being rhetorical. I am just, my dear Robert, being quite candid with you.'[34]

He had come to an overpowering emotional and intellectual block. Finch recognized this. Now retired and living at Massey College, Finch was a devout Christian who knew the Scriptures well. He did not allow Daniells to get away with what he considered misinterpretation of texts. The two men wrote regularly, on an average of three or four letters a month – sometimes several in one day – for almost a year. Their correspondence is curiously like those long pages of foolscap on which James, Daniells' father, recorded his observations regarding biblical passages for the Sunday morning Plymouth Brethren Assembly. Many letters are strictly exegeses of specific passages. Finch went over much of the old theological ground travelled by Daniells from 1914 to 1936, dealing with issues such as God's grace, unforgivable sin, the promise of redemption, and the nature of God. He assured Daniells that God would not reject anyone who truly repented.

Finch told him that it was impossible to have committed an 'unforgivable sin' if one has fears and worries about it. The whole point about a sin being unforgivable is that the individual himself had turned away from God's love. In response to Daniells' old problem that he had never had the sense of salvation, Finch reassured him that even if the person himself were not aware of it, God's love extended to him. When Daniells described the God of the Old Testament, Finch refused to accept Daniells' statement that '"it was God who arranged it so that Adam and Eve would be tempted"; etc.'

Throughout their long correspondence, Finch continued to put forward the God of the New Testament. He pointed out that God, who is

Love, created two human beings who had the power of choice. Moreover, he had been taught 'to look on Adam and Eve's interlocutor as an attractive person, the word "Serpent" being the part used for the whole, the charm of subtlety standing for all the other charms ... His utterances, though, fall apart when measured against the utterances of the One who is the Truth.'[35]

Finch's letters reveal a probing, incisive, but entirely orthodox intelligence. Eventually he demanded, 'How can I understand and appreciate your views when you have never stated them positively? I know that you are anti-Bible, anti-the Christ-of-the-Bible, and so on, but I have not the least idea of what your beliefs are, nor whence they are derived. Are they, for instance, your own, or from someone else, or do they belong to a sect, or group, or philosophy? Your statements, throughout your letters, are of a negative nature and whenever I asked you to be precise and positive you made no reply.'[36]

Daniells was now forced to speak of his own situation:

> I used to believe in the Bible; as a boy, I accepted Christ as my Saviour ... [but] I never experienced what the Plymouth Brethren used to call 'assurance' and I became increasing[ly] disquieted ... As you know, I broke down under the strain of it all ... Suffice it to say that I finally broke free, with the sensation our friend Dantès [of *The Count of Monte Cristo*] had when [he] shot up to the surface after his immersion.

But Daniells no longer thought that God had rejected him. He confided some new information to Finch: 'I have had two visions as decisive (for me) as anything Paul ever had; First a sudden sense of unity with my Mother, who died nearly twenty years ago ... coming as an assurance that *time and space are transcended by love.* I can't explain how. Second: that the Last Judgment is a kind of stage set which blows over and disappears when there sways over it the great wind that "bloweth where it listeth and (I) cannot tell whence it cometh or whither it goeth."'[37] For Daniells at this point, the sense of God as a merciful spirit seems to have overcome the cruel God of judgment.

Finch's response was that he had become convinced that to love God was simply to obey him, and this could be achieved by an act of will.[38] On the same day, near the end of this round of correspondence, Daniells wrote a verse suggesting that Finch rested on 'the Rock' of faith, whereas he was lost on an iceberg in a polar 'sea':

Robert, your feet are on the Rock
Behind, a continent stands high,
While I squat on an iceberg's block
With nothing round but wind and sky.[39]

In reply, Finch tackled him angrily. If Daniells was going to use the stereotype of the 'rock,' then he should think about the stereotype of the 'sea' – an allusion to Christ taming the waves.[40] Nonetheless, the process of writing to Finch about his deepest fears elicited from Daniells the admission that he had experienced a sense of God's grace which, in turn, had moderated his fears.

During his last four years, Daniells took inventory of his life, partly through autobiographical letters to Susan, partly by connecting with old friends. 'Of course,' as Laurenda Daniells recalled, 'he'd had several small heart attacks by then and we were aware of the fact that he was mortal.'[41] Earlier in the decade, he had written to Max Maynard to ask him how *he* had come to terms with his Plymouth Brethren legacy. His wife, Fredelle Maynard, found the question highly ironic. 'Truth is, he never made his peace with it, [n]or with his complicated family; he was wounded, perhaps mortally, very young.'[42] Maynard reiterated this himself in 1979: 'It was good to hear from you and to read your comment about the old days in Vict – how full of the future they were, though we didn't know it. But actually, both of us knew, I think, that the cloth was already woven and only the details had to be added.' Surprisingly, Maynard added that he had 'just received letters from Fred Brand and Jack Shadbolt telling me that I have been very important in their intellectual and spiritual development. Try not to flinch when I say that you were, I think, the most important influence in my whole life – apart from Fredelle. But it was you who introduced me to Fredelle.'[43]

The 'details' of life now preoccupied Daniells. He had begun the first letter of his autobiographical reminiscences, which he alphabetized, on 9 August 1975 and continued to write into 1976. The first, letter A, addressed to 'Dear Susan,' begins: 'One of your Mother's brilliant suggestions ... is that I should go over my recollection of England and of our coming to Canada.' He knew that his story was one of escape, but he believed that it was an escape from failure and life as an itinerant labourer: 'To achieve a B.C. degree with honours was like having got over a wall and into the open. To get to Toronto was like crossing to a new continent. To get even the poorest paid and lowliest academic job was like being crowned king of a small kingdom.'

From a distance of sixty years, he could now see himself from the outside; at the time, he could only experience life from the inside: 'That I was self-centered, self-protective, and self-concerned was, of course, a dreadful and continuing fact ... Luckily there was one compensating quality which I had in abundance. That was the capacity for admiration, gratitude, emulation and love.'[44] His life, he saw, had been governed by long-term friendships with Maynard, Robbins, Birney, Frye, Finch and others. Even when these friendships had been chequered, as with Birney, 'I retain the most definite emotional residuum. Birney has recently broken his hip and I am debating whether to write to him or not. Would he be gratified or offended? I can't guess.'[45] Concerned that he might be hurt by Birney's possible negative response, Laurenda Daniells persuaded him not to write.

Attempting to discover whether there was a pattern in his life other than the simple desire to escape manual labour, Daniells tried to formulate what Canada had meant to him. 'By CANADA is meant the combination in one image of geography, history, representative people (often friends), government, international relations, permanent problems, future possibilities, and uniqueness among nations. These combined into one vision, deeply charged with emotion.'[46] There is no doubt that the freedom that Victoria, the small town, offered to the boy, and the sense of a developing culture that Canada offered to the young adult, was extraordinarily important. Canada was the envelope surrounding his present and promising a future. Yet this does not explain what he was attempting to escape from.

When writing these letters to Susan, Daniells at first relied on his memory. Then he turned to old letters and diaries, where he was struck by 'the air of innocence that they radiate.' He was also baffled about how he was to deal with this material; he did not think that he had a 'story,' or that he was skilled in developing incident.[47] All he had were his memories of the people he encountered – Davis, Brown, Pratt, Riddell, Dilworth, Robbins, Pacey. He also wondered why his own plans, unlike those of Birney and Frye, lacked direction. Eventually, he concluded that the whole course of his life had been shaped by religious trauma:

> I had made so long and painful an effort (successful) to regain my mental balance, shake off the worst horrors of the Brethren, escape the manual labour and casual jobs, and get an education that I may have been exhausted by the effort.

This was true. The attempt to retain his mental balance had indeed affected his whole academic life. What he could not recognize was the enormous triumph that this struggle represented. Another large factor, also not mentioned, was his nearly thirty years as an administrator; these were troubled years, when to be head of the English departments at Manitoba and UBC was a stressful, full-time job. Then, unlike now, department administrators could not easily resign – heads either stayed in office or they rolled. Nonetheless, he believed there was more to his story than just the attempt to escape and if he had the courage to keep facing the past, the rest of the pattern might emerge.[48]

Up to this point, Daniells had been unable to deal with the Plymouth Brethren. He made several attempts to talk about his religious views, but each time he had to stop because the process of recall was too painful. Consequently, the most important aspect of his life story, his escape from Plymouth Brethren theology (really, his transmutation of some aspects of fundamentalism as a student and professor of English), had not been explained. In his last letter, 'X,' describing himself in the early twenties, he got as far as saying: 'I am clearly *learning to teach.* I am also clearly strait-jacketed by the Plymouth Brethren.' Both were important articulations. Daniells had profound influence as a teacher, far beyond that of the usual professor of English. And the fact that he recognized that he had been confined by a particular theology implicitly acknowledged the missing part of his story.

He identified the dominant motif of his life as escape and deliverance, and reminded Susan of the many times that she had seen him rereading Alexandre Dumas's *Count of Monte Cristo*, which deals with the long imprisonment and final deliverance of the unjustly accused Edmond Dantès. His own notes, written on the last pages of his copy of the book, go one step further in itemizing 'despair, deliverance, triumph, and vengeance.' (Curiously, Daniells does not deal with vengeance.) The story also resonated with other personal myths – Christian's escape from the tower of Giant Despair, and the Israelites' escape from bondage. In May of 1976, when confiding to Carl Klinck that he regretted that he could not do more for the *Literary History*, he added that 'Wait and hope' were the last words in *Monte Cristo*, and said that he took them, with the return of the swallows, as a good omen.[49]

For Daniells the escape from bondage was quite literally the escape from the Plymouth Brethren, personified by 'the seven Scotsmen' of his poem, who 'cried in a high, round, loud, uprising tongue' on the platform of the gospel hall. Behind the Scotsmen was the cruel Jehovah of his childhood, merged with his father and with God the Father. His final coming to terms with the theology which this represented was expressed in his correspondence with Frye, Finch, and others, the writing of 'Letters to Susan' during 1975–6, and the preparing of two CBC talks on his childhood. By 1977 he had been taken off the prescription for seizures, an action that restored his previous mental abilities. Having successfully completed letter X, he began to write a talk for the CBC on *The Children's Encyclopaedia*.

On 1 July 1977, while he was in the midst of this work, I had visited Daniells at home, to ask his advice about an application to the SSHRC for a project on English-Canadian poetry. To make sure that I recorded his comments, we left the tape recorder running. After we had tea in the garden, our talk drifted into his memories of his connections with professors and friends at Toronto in the thirties. He was still in the process of recovering the past:

R.D.: The people I was first impressed with were people like Malcolm Wallace, the Principal at University College ... in English and immensely kind. What his intellectual scope was I don't know, but he was doing all the right things – making it possible for people to develop ... Then there was Woodhouse with his Miltonic obsession so dominant that it was very much like hearing a strongly denominational preacher three times a week.
S.D.: What was his most strong obsession, do you think, about Milton? ...
R.D.: I think it was probably Milton's handling of the will ... And he was at the same moment immensely helpful because he was always there as a great centre of reference, and he would do things for students. Obviously, if he wrote a letter for anybody it would carry a lot of weight. When he came to finalize what he thought, it was a bit like an elephant trying to swim in the sea. There was so much of it and so much of him. And you remember that after he was gone, his friends scurried around and gathered up his papers, and made a book because it was Woodhouse in personality and in operation rather than anything else.

Let's put it another way. I think it would be easy, for an enemy of Woodhouse, to make him look very ridiculous. But as he was so useful and kind and good to most of us, none of us would ever wish to do so ... Now Brown, of course, was totally different, subtle and penetrating, but they were very good friends.

S.D.: Dapper and elegant, too.

R.D.: Yes, a bit reminiscent of T.S. Eliot, this control, penetration. What he would have become if he hadn't died, of course nobody would know ... One thing that happened after his death which always baffled me, of no importance, but as I remember we sent a Christmas card the year after he died to Peggy [Brown] because we always had done. And we got the most curious thank you note indicating that she was starting a new life somewhere else. A clear indication that she wasn't going to have any contact with us. I thought about that very often. Let's put it this way: the sort of man who would marry that sort of woman must have been very self-controlled, capable of holding everything in place, not being easily disturbed. His whole life must have been extremely orderly, I think.[50]

Daniells, although a little unfair to Margaret Brown, was remembering and clarifying the similarities and differences between Wallace, Woodhouse, Brown, and himself. His remarks on Woodhouse, acknowledging the doctrinal foundations of his teaching, also indicate that his sense of gratitude to Woodhouse as teacher and scholar erased the possibility of any negative judgment. His comments on Frye (who had not yet published *The Great Code*) suggest that Daniells could not then recognize, as Jan Gorak was later to argue in *The Making of the Modern Canon* (1991), that 'Frye sees literature grounded on universally appealing spiritual foundations': so that, in effect, both the world of English literature and of Frye's own criticism form 'a visionary canon.'[51] From this perspective, both Daniells and Frye may be seen as approaching literature through religion.

In 1977 Daniells was also writing to his old friend Carl Klinck. Klinck, in turn, was sending letters and essays, some on religious topics, to Daniells. Included in one of Daniells' letters was a reworking of Hardy's poem 'The Oxen,' with its poignant line 'hoping it might be so.' It is Hardy's hope that, as recalled in the old stories, the oxen did indeed kneel to Jesus on Christmas Eve. Daniells, in opposition, expresses the hope that animals can meet death quietly, without theology: 'not closed in Calvin's pen / Not closed in Luther's halter.'[52] These stanzas indicate how strongly the issue of predestination bothered him.

A year later, Daniells again wrote to Klinck about his fear of eternal punishment, contrasting his own views with those of their mutual friends:

As for our friends: our good friend Norrie sees most of the Bible as myth and for his own spiritual life (who can blame him?) dwells on, say, the Paradise of Dante and not the inferno. I am not critical of Norrie; I admire and cherish him. Robert Finch is a believer in the manner of George Herbert and that's that. Wilfred Smith believes that something can be rescued from the wreck of church doctrine ... And so it goes on.

For myself, my experience of the Bible and of the church, has, over so many decades, been so dreadful that I would like to escape, like the raven.[53]

What Daniells appreciated in Klinck was 'a friend who has the ability and the desire to discuss what used to be called "spiritual things."' He now recognized, he told Klinck, that there may not be a 'hereafter' in the old sense but nonetheless he now had a strong sense, of '*not losing*' his parents:

It could be put this way; having been, they *are*, and not merely in memory. You will recall that, at the close of *Wuthering Heights*, a small boy (an innocent) and some sheep (without theology) are on the road, and as they move onward they become aware of Catherine and Heathcliff just ahead of them. The narrator speaks of it as an illusion but neither Emily Brontë nor the reader takes it as such. It is a reality, having been, they are.

Again, Daniells' sense of the 'reality' of religious experience is akin to theologian Rudolph Bultmann's exposition of the reality of the person of Jesus: 'his person is just what the New Testament proclaims as the decisive event of redemption.'[54]

In the fall of 1978, Daniells became intrigued by a CBC radio program on religion entitled 'Celebration.' He wrote to the producer, John Reeves, offering to write a talk on his own experience with the Plymouth Brethren. Who were they? What did they believe? And how had the Brethren influenced his childhood? As he was now writing autobiography rather than academic criticism, this approach gave him a sense of release. In the spring of 1979, he began to articulate how his terrible fears as a child had begun and for the first time described the terror he felt when he believed that his mother had been taken away in the 'rapture.' But at this point, when he could have written his full story, he suffered a fatal heart attack.

His heart had been failing since the start of the seventies. In 1972, 1975, 1976, and again in 1978 there had been seizures. In the spring of 1979, he confided to his diary, 'Very tired; angina. I begin to think I must live one day at a time.' He had gone to see a heart specialist, Dr Kinahan, who diagnosed aortic stenosis and suggested open-heart surgery. Daniells was then hospitalized by his family doctor for an angiogram. But the results of the test made it clear that he would not be a good candidate for open-heart surgery. The arteries around the heart had deteriorated because of a series of small attacks, and they were no longer strong enough to support an operation. After a discussion with both husband and wife, the specialist decided against surgery. Daniells, who dreaded the operation because he feared he might again lose some mental competence, was delighted: 'Home – and oh! how good to be home!!!'[55]

Spring was just around the corner. For him, the sense of spring life and renewal was epitomized by his garden. He had always loved to putter, and to feed the birds, especially the swallows whose return every year made his heart 'leap with joy.' On this 9 April he again recorded their return: 'Not at all well. Swallows are back; I have put their house up this morning, in great haste, hoping to attract them.'[56] Two days later, on 11 April, his beloved dog, Shalimar, died. Daniells wrote the date in his diary, but for the first time in over sixty years there is no accompanying entry beside it.

Shalimar had been his companion for twelve years, but she, too, had been failing for the previous two years. When Laurenda Daniells had taken her to the vet that morning, she had had a convulsion and the vet said that it was cruel to allow the dog to continue living. Laurenda agreed, but with great reservation. She said, only half in jest, 'This will kill my husband.'[57] She then went home, told Daniells the bad news, and returned to the UBC archives.

While she was at work, a friend happened by and saw that Daniells looked flushed and miserable. He had gone into the garden to dig the compost, but digging into the hard earth had precipitated another small heart attack. When Laurenda got home for lunch, she found him lying on the sofa with a manuscript by his side. She told him she was going to call an ambulance. He grasped her strongly by the wrist and said, 'No, no ambulance.' She said, 'Well, I'll call a doctor.' And he replied, 'No ambulance, no doctor.' She replied, 'Roy, I won't call the hospital, but you must let me call a doctor.'

The doctor came at once and announced: 'We must get you to hospital.' Daniells replied, 'I won't go.' The decision rested with Laurenda, who considered her husband perfectly capable of determining what he wanted to do. It was agreed that he could stay at home in bed. There, he refused to obey doctor's orders and kept trying to get up. He had known for some time that he might die at any moment. Indeed he had written a brief farewell to his family over a year before, the manuscript found by his side, and he had worked on it earlier that spring, when it was decided that an operation was not feasible. But he had not expected the end to come so soon. He was looking forward to broadcasting his 'Plymouth Brother' talk later in the week on the CBC, and was very disappointed to be ill for a short time, as he now explained to the producer on the telephone.

Daniells died two days later on 13 April, Good Friday, a significant date given his religious sensibility. He had called to Laurenda, and she had gone to his bedside, where he spoke of their happiness and how fulfilled his life had been in the years after they met. He then said that he was getting very tired, and she should 'turn off the light.' As she stood up to do this, she saw he was having another seizure. She called to their daughters and to Dennis McCrea, Susan's friend. Dennis attempted to keep Daniells' heart going, and he was still breathing when the ambulance arrived.[58] But he had suffered a massive heart attack, and died before reaching the hospital.

So I saw in my dream that just as Christian came up to the Cross, his burden loosed from off his shoulders and fell from off his back, and began to tumble, and so continued to do, till it came to the mouth of the Sepulchre, where it fell in, and I saw it no more.

John Bunyan, *The Pilgrim's Progress*, p. 39

Daniells left behind a manuscript, 'Now I saw in my dream,' later published as a small pamphlet, *The Current of Time*. Earlier, in September 1976, he had told Finch that he had experienced a vision that convinced him that those who die are not finally separated from those whom they love. This experience seems to have led him to write a narrative which in May 1978 he sent to Finch, Frye and Klinck. It was 'a familiar allegory of a man named Thoughtful,' familiar because it was written in the style and sensibility of Bunyan's *The Pilgrim's Progress*. As Daniells' wife and their two daughters appear in this account, it suggests that he had reached some resolution in his spiritual life and wanted his family to know this. Characteristically this resolution took the form of a story with allegorical overtones and a character, Thoughtful, borrowed from Bunyan.

In this allegory, Daniells takes on the persona of a thoughtful pilgrim who tells his life story to a Mr Watchful: '*In truth*,' said Thoughtful,

> *my experience upon the road has not been as theirs [as Christian and Hopeful], for though I came in at the wicket gate and looked for straight and narrow paths to follow, yet was I in continual doubt as to the right way. In difficulties by day and in forebodings by night I have come hither through many combats and with few comforters. Yea, for long years I lay in prison.*

This is, as we know, the story of Daniells' own life. He is, in effect, like Bunyan in *Grace Abounding*, writing the conclusion to his own conversion-narrative. In this account, Thoughtful is comforted by Watchful, who explains that the great river called by some the river of death '*is perceived by those who have long regarded it as the river of change and of life, for it flows towards the sea whence life came when the spirit of God moved on the face of the waters.*' Thoughtful, amazed, says: '*What must I do to be saved?*' Like Bunyan's Christian at the end of his journey, he finds a friend who helps him to cross the river to reach the shining spirits:

> *Watchful, with much affection, saith to him, 'My brother, the time of my own departure is come. Let us enter the river together.' So the two of them stepped in and Watchful, leading Thoughtful into the deepest part of the current, swam with easy strokes downstream, supporting Thoughtful who rested one hand upon his shoulder. So I saw them no more.*

Daniells' narrator, who tells this story, awakes and finds that it was a dream and that it was his birthday (April 6), and that even as he woke, his good friends and members of his household greeted him with tokens of love: '*Then, looking with fresh vision upon them, I saw as it were the countenances of Thoughtful and of Watchful and in the faces of my wife and daughters the likenesses of angels.*' It was then that he recognizes that *'thus was all fulfilled and the promise of Watchful concerning the river already in adumbration, it being in truth the river of life's revival and of renewal without end.'*[59]

━━➤•○•◅━━

We may ask whether Daniells finally achieved the emotional peace that *The Current of Time* affirms. He lived a year or so after it had been written, and he was still attempting to work out his religious and intellectual life in essays like the projected broadcast 'Plymouth Brother.' His colleague, the late Craig Miller, in the forties one of the 'juniors' in the English Department and a long-time friend, remarked after reading a draft of this biography, that he saw more duality at the end of his life than I acknowledge. He was also critical of a biography that presented Daniells as a 'representative professor': Daniells, Miller insisted, was far more than this. 'He was a leading light. His life shows that he was a fighter beyond belief. There was nothing that defeated him in the end. He got everything he wanted. He outlasted all of his enemies. He was unique. He had special gifts.' Miller, himself a religious man, also spoke of Northrop Frye as 'one of the comforters that failed.'[60]

To be sure, it is 'Mr Watchful,' Daniells' literary creation, who provides final assurance, yet behind this symbolic figure stands Bunyan, Daniells' vision of his mother, and his correspondence with good friends, Frye and Finch. There is also the evidence of his last two, peaceful days when, surrounded by family, he had lost the fears of the young man in the Père-Lachaise cemetery and waited for death without any desire to prolong his life. Yet I suspect that Daniells might have agreed with Miller to some degree. This is because in his radio script 'Plymouth Brother,' Daniells tells us frankly, 'Let me admit that I have never completed my escape from [the Plymouth Brethren].' 'It was many years before I could leave the Brethren and even pull the door to behind me. Even then, I closed it slowly and quietly and waited for the latch to click. I am not sure that it ever did quite click.'[61]

In retrospect, we may ask why an intelligent person, a product of the modernist twenties, was preoccupied by fundamentalist teaching for so much of his life? In this secular age, the whole concept of religious belief is incomprehensible to many. Yet for Daniells, both his nurture by the Brethren and his nature, subject to depression, focused his imagination on apocalypse: no intellectual process could erase a structure of belief that was emotionally compelling because imprinted in child-hood. At the end of his life, he produced a striking metaphor for the malleable boy he had been: '... if you wind a wire round a piece of soft iron and pass a powerful electric current through it, you have a magnet that points north and south. The same thing happened to the mind of a young person wound round by the Brethren's doctrines and subjected to the current of their preaching. Heaven and hell were the only reali-ties ...'[62] His oldest friend, Max Maynard, used another simile: for Daniells and himself, the cloth of their lives had been woven in their Victoria childhood – all that remained was the laying out of the pattern.

Most admirable is the pattern that Daniells created from the 'soft iron' of his childhood. Despite constricted beginnings, he liberated himself through education. After his conversion experience in the Père-Lachaise Cemetery, he turned his life around to become one of the most distinguished professors of English in Canada, a man whose broad humanity extended to several generations of friends, colleagues, and university students. Ultimately, his life story can be seen as a triumph of the human spirit against heavy odds.

Explaining the evolution of his own faith in 1979, he said that through literature and through nature he had found the 'keys with which to open prison gates' and 'doors that swung open into direct sunlight.' Other people, he confessed, were often of little direct help because Canadians are often reluctant to talk about ultimate issues. However, in literature there was Emily Brontë's *Wuthering Heights*, which he ad-mired because 'she accepts wickedness, violence, and suffering as part of the human scene but a spirit of abundant and unquenchable life supervenes.' Similarly, Dylan Thomas in 'A Refusal to Mourn the Death by Fire of a Child in London' sees a 'dead child as clasped safely in the arms of her mother, the immemorial earth, while the ever-flowing stream of the Thames triumphantly assures the continuity of life.'

What was most important to Daniells at the end was nature itself – a fir tree and the swallows – in which he rejoices in some of the cadences of the King James Bible:

> Across the road from where I live is a magnificent fir tree whose branches are never still, for we live close to the sea and its varying winds. Do not be offended if I confess that this tree, which is older than I am and will outlive me, in its steady growth, endurance of all weathers and aspiration toward the light – this tree is more to me than the tree of Calvary, with its message that without shedding of blood there is no remission of sin.

And do not, furthermore, be offended if I say that the pair of swallows, violet-blue, who come and build in the nest I put up for them in April and feed their chirping young ones, fly swiftly out for food and swerve on sunlit wings – if I say that these give me more comfort and hope than any Biblical story of angels descending on Jacob's ladder.[63]

Notes

Primary Unpublished Sources

References to Daniells' unpublished papers are followed by the box and file numbers of the Roy Daniells Papers [RDP] at the University of British Columbia. A number of previously undated letters have been dated with reference to the context and to Daniells' daily journals; in these cases, the dates established are indicated in square brackets. Other abbreviations used in the notes are given below in square brackets. Full references to all published texts cited in the notes are provided in the Bibliography.

Archives Consulted

Earle Birney Papers. Thomas Fisher Rare Book Library, University of Toronto Library. [EBP]
Frank Davey Papers. Special Collections, Simon Fraser University. [FDP]
English Department Papers. Rare Book Room, University of Manitoba.
Northrop Frye Papers. E.J. Pratt Library, University of Toronto. [NFP]
Carl F. Klinck Papers. Special Collections, D.B. Weldon Library, University of Western Ontario. [CFKP]
Desmond Pacey Papers. National Archives of Canada. [DPP]
E.J. Pratt Papers. Victoria University Library, University of Toronto.
F.R. Scott Papers. National Archives of Canada. [FRSP]
Garnett Gladwin Sedgewick Papers. Special Collections, University of British Columbia. [GGSP]
A.J.M. Smith Papers. Trent University Rare Book Room. [AJMSP]

Selected Papers Consulted in Daniells Collection

'Autobiographical Fictionalized Fragments.' RDP 16-9.
'*The Children's Encyclopaedia*.' Typescript of broadcast, 17 July 1978. RDP 14-11.
'*The Children's Encyclopaedia*.' 1978–9. RDP 14-10.
'Classics of Tomorrow: *The Waste Land* by T.S. Eliot.' Typescript, 13 October 1944. RDP 14-6.
Constance and James Daniells Diaries. RDP 41 to 43.
The Current of Time. Privately printed, 1981.
Diaries and Sundry Notes, 1947, 1957, 1960. [Also contains entries dated 1946.] Property of Laurenda Daniells.
Draft of review of *The Heavenly Muse: A Preface to Milton*, by A.S.P. Woodhouse. Toronto: University of Toronto Press, 1972. RDP 16-32.
'The Future of Canadian Writing.' Transcript, 18 November 1942. RDP 14-5.
'The Island.' Autobiographical fragment. RDP 16-8.
'The Island: A Study in Insularity.' RDP 16-8
'Letters to Susan.' RDP 16-6. [LS]
'Milestones of Thought: Man Discovers Himself.' Transcript, 22 March 1942. RDP 14-6.
'Ms for Magnum Opus: Work in Progress' ['Oh Canada']. RDP 16-13.
'Overture.' Autobiographical fragment. RDP 16-36.
'Profile of Garnett Sedgewick.' Transcript, CBC broadcast, 26 January 1949. RDP 29-3.
Roy Daniells' Diaries. RDP 11-1 to 45.
'Sinclair Ross – Short Stories.' Transcript, CBC broadcast, Dec. 1941. RDP 14-5.
'Sundry Notes (for Novel).' RDP 11-45.
'Tribute to Garnett Sedgewick.' 29 August 1949 – first broadcast. RDP 14-6.
'Trip Diary.' RDP 11-35.
Untitled review of *As for Me and My House*. Transcript for CBC broadcast, 25 November 1941. RDP 14-5.

Prologue

1 Letter to parents, 18 June 1932, RDP 40-7.
2 Ibid.
3 Letter to parents, 14 August 1934, RDP 40-6.
4 CBC broadcast, 'Tribute to Garnett Sedgewick,' 29 August 1949, RDP 14-6.
5 Draft of review of A.S.P. Woodhouse's *The Heavenly Muse: A Preface to Milton*, RDP 16-32.
6 Rose Sheinin, 'The Changing Space for Women in Academe: The "Engender-ing" of Knowledge,' in *The Illusion of Inclusion*, 96–7.

7 Gerald Graff, *Professing Literature*, 23, 85.

8 Matthew Arnold, *Literature and Dogma*, xix.

9 A.B. McKillop, *Matters of Mind*, 204.

10 Patricia Jasen, 'Arnoldian Humanism, English Studies and the Canadian University,' 553.

11 Editorial, *Canadian Forum* 1, no. 1 (Oct. 1920): 3.

12 Margaret Bottrall, *Every Man a Phoenix*, 85–6.

13 Malcolm Ross, letter, 5 May 1995. Ross makes the point that Woodhouse and Daniells were the two most important figures in the Humanities Research Council during this period.

14 Irving Babbitt, *Literature and the American College: Essays in Defense of the Humanities*.

15 Introduction, *As for Me and My House*, by Sinclair Ross, v.

16 Graff, *Professing Literature*, 20.

17 Elspeth Cameron, *Earle Birney: A Life*, 107.

18 Heather Murray, *Working in English: History, Institution, Resources*, 195.

19 Chaviva M. Hosek, 'Women at Victoria,' in *From Cobourg to Toronto: Victoria University in Retrospect*, 58–9.

20 Viola Pratt translated articles and chapters of books dealing with the German Higher Criticism for her husband; Gladys Davis checked the proofs of her husband's first book on Swift and regularly undertook research tasks; Helen Frye introduced her husband to the principles of art criticism; Jeannie Smith helped prepare both texts and notes for Smith's anthology *The Book of Canadian Poetry* (1943).

21 Fredelle Bruser Maynard to R.D., letter, 20 January 1973, RDP 8-9.

22 Max Maynard to R.D., letter, 19 December 1936, RDP 2-12.

23 Margaret Avison, interview, 30 October 1998.

24 Earle Birney to Frank Davey, letter, 7 April 1966, FDP 3.1.2.2.

25 Frank Davey, discussion, 7 June 1999.

26 Jean Strouse, 'Semiprivate Lives,' in *Studies in Biography*, 114.

27 William Fredeman, interview, 18 December 1997. The vote of censure passed because members of ACUTE felt that the young man's flippancy compromised the newly founded association. (Walter Swayze, letter, 18 December 2000).

28 G.P.V. Akrigg, interview, 30 June 1992.

29 James Clifford, '"Hanging Up Looking Glasses at Odd Corners": Ethnobiographical Prospects,' in *Studies in Biography*, 50.

30 W.H. Sheldon and S.S. Stevens, *The Varieties of Temperament: A Psychology of Constitutional Differences*, 69–94. 'Cerebrotonic' in 'Diaries and Sundry Notes, 1947, 1957, 1960,' ca. 1946.

31 A.J.M. Smith, *The Classic Shade: Selected Poems*, 77.

32 'Human Values and the Evolution of Society,' in *Our Debt to the Future, Studia Varia* ser. no. 2, 117–19.
33 Kevin Brooks, 'Writing Instruction in Western Canadian Universities: A History of Nation-Building and Professionalism,' 172.

Chapter 1: Plymouth Brother

1 'Plymouth Brother,' *Canadian Literature*, no. 90 (Autumn 1981): 25.
2 Ibid.
3 Gwladys Downes, interview, 27 July 1997. During the early forties, Daniells had told Downes, then his fiancée, of his parents' courtship.
4 'Wanted!' Miscellaneous papers, RDP 4-6.
5 'Plymouth Brother,' 27.
6 LS, letter A.
7 'Sundry Notes (for Novel),' RDP 11-45.
8 LS, letter A.
9 'Sundry Notes (for Novel).'
10 James Stevens to R.D., letter, 12 May 1929, RDP 1-2.
11 LS, letter A.
12 James Daniells to R.D., letter, 3 July 1908, RDP 1-1
13 'Sundry Notes (for Novel).'
14 Ibid.
15 'The Children's Encyclopaedia,' typescript of broadcast, 17 July 1978, RDP 14-11.
16 Arthur Mee, ed., *The Children's Encyclopaedia*, 1027.
17 LS, letter J.
18 Ibid., letter A.
19 Ibid.
20 Ibid.
21 CBC broadcast, 'The Children's Encyclopaedia,' 1978–9, RDP 14-10.
22 'The Island,' autobiographical fragment, RDP 16-8.
23 'Sundry Notes (for Novel).'
24 Ibid.
25 'Overture,' RDP 16-36.
26 LS, letter B.
27 Ibid., letter F.
28 Sonnet 21, in *Deeper into the Forest*, 47.
29 'Autobiographical Fragment,' RDP 16-7.
30 'Plymouth Brother,' 28.
31 Letter to John Reeves, 10 November 1978, RDP 14-11.

32 John Bunyan, *The Pilgrim's Progress*, 146.

33 Ibid., 37.

34 'Plymouth Brother,' 28.

35 'Sundry Notes (for Novel).'

36 I am grateful to Mildred (Shanas) Gutkin of the University of Manitoba for pointing out this connection.

37 Letter to parents, [April 1933], RDP 40-5.

38 'Plymouth Brother,' 28.

39 Ibid.

40 William Styron, *Darkness Visible: A Memoir of Madness*, 79–80.

41 André Haynal, *Depression and Creativity*, xiii, xiv, 17.

42 'Autobiographical Fragment,' RDP 16-17.

43 Ibid.

44 'Plymouth Brother,' 29.

45 Ibid.

Chapter 2: Breakdown

1 'Sundry Notes (for Novel),' RDP 11-45.

2 Constance Daniells, diary, 21 August 1917, RDP 42-4.

3 James Stevens to R.D., letter, 20 September 1917, RDP 1-3.

4 Letter to parents, 14 August 1934, RDP 40-6.

5 Constance Daniells, diary, 7, 10, and 11 October 1917, RDP 40-6.

6 'Sundry Notes (for Novel).'

7 Constance Daniells, diary, 22 June 1919; 15 and 17 July 1919, RDP 41-2.

8 'Sundry Notes (for Novel).'

9 C.J.B., *'The Coming of the Lord Draweth Nigh': An Examination of the Scriptures on the Length of the 'Times of the Gentiles,'* 27, RDP 47-3.

10 Constance Daniells, diary, 17 July 1919, RDP 41-2.

11 LS, letter C.

12 Letter to parents, 14 November 1932, RDP 40-4.

13 LS, letter E.

14 Ibid., letter D.

15 Ibid.

16 Letter to parents, 14 November 1932, RDP 40-4.

17 Roger Bishop, interview, 9 January 1996.

18 Letter to mother, 8 May 1933, RDP 40-5.

19 LS, letter K-1.

20 Ibid., letter K-2.

21 Diary, 16 May 1921, RDP 11-1.

22 *Pelmanism: The First Principles of Pelmanism.*
23 'Plymouth Brother,' *Canadian Literature,* no. 90 (Autumn 1981): 30, 31.
24 Letter to mother, 16 April 1922; verse, 21 May 1922, RDP 40-1.
25 Letter to parents, 27 July 1932, RDP 40-4.
26 Ernest Sirluck, interview, 31 October 1992.
27 Conversation with the author [ca. July 1963].
28 'Autobiographical Fragment,' RDP 16-9.
29 Sidney Burdge to R.D., letter, 20 April 1923, RDP 1-2.
30 Notes for 'Plymouth Brother' article, RDP 14-11.
31 'Autobiographical Fragment.'
32 'Plymouth Brother,' 32.
33 Letter to father, n.d. [ca. Summer 1923], RDP 40-1.
34 W.E. Vine to R.D., letter, 4 September 1923, RDP 1-2.
35 Sidney Burdge to R.D., letter, 20 April 1923, RDP 1-2.
36 LS, letter J.

Chapter 3: Rescue

 1 Jack Shadbolt, interview, 8 September 1993.
 2 Diary, 27 November 1924, RDP 11-2.
 3 LS, letter L.
 4 Diary, 8 January 1927, RDP 11-5.
 5 Jack Shadbolt, interview.
 6 Max Maynard to R.D., letter, n.d. [ca. December 1979], RDP 8-21.
 7 Diary, 27 July 1924, RDP 11-2.
 8 Ibid., 29 December 1924, RDP 11-2.
 9 Ibid., 4 June 1928, RDP 11-6.
10 Maria Tippett, *Emily Carr: A Biography,* 196–7.
11 Jack Shadbolt to R.D., letter, 30 June 1979, RDP 8-20.
12 Diary, 22 January 1926, RDP 11-4.
13 Jack Parnell, interview, 20 July 1993.
14 John McDonald, conversation [ca. December 1990].
15 Diary, 8 March 1928, RDP 11-6.
16 William Robbins, interview, 11 June 1992.
17 Jack Shadbolt, interview.
18 John McDonald, conversation.
19 Jack Shadbolt to R.D., letter, 30 June 1979, RDP 8-20.
20 Jack Shadbolt, interview.
21 *Pelmanism: The First Principles of Pelmanism,* vi, 4.
22 G.P.V. Akrigg, 'Sedgewick: The Man and His Achievement,' 2.

23 LS, letter O.

24 Diary, 12 and 19 January 1928, RDP 11-6.

25 LS, letter L.

26 Diary, 27 and 29 September 1928, RDP 11-6.

27 LS, letter L.

28 Ibid.

29 LS, letter M.

30 Diary, 26 October 1928, RDP 11-6.

31 'Thorleif Larsen: 1887–1960,' *Transactions of the Royal Society of Canada,* ser. 3, 55 (1960–1): 127–8, RDP 29-1.

32 Jean Mallinson, interview, 22 June 1995.

33 'Profile of Garnett Sedgewick,' typescript, 1949, RDP 14-6.

34 LS, letter N.

35 Diary, 27 October and 2 November 1928, RDP 11-6.

36 Ibid., 17 October 1928, RDP 11-6.

37 Ibid., 13 November 1928, RDP 11-6.

38 Ibid., 20 March 1929, RDP 11-7.

39 Ibid., 19 March 1929.

40 Roy Daniells, UBC student transcript, 12 February 1930, RDP 10-3.

41 Diary, 27 September 1929, RDP 11-7.

42 Ibid., 9, 17, 21, 23 September 1929.

43 David Williams, a biographer and former B.C. judge, who attended UBC in the mid-forties, recalled that Sedgewick met with two groups of young men: the group that he was sexually interested in, and the group that he was not: generally known as his 'inner' and 'outer' circles respectively (David Williams, discussion with the author, 7 May 1994).

44 Diary, 20 January 1930, RDP 11-8.

45 Ibid., 17 February 1930.

46 Ibid., 22 March 1930.

47 Ibid., 30 April 1930.

48 Ibid., 8 May 1930.

49 Ibid., 14 and 21 May 1930.

50 Ibid., 17 June 1930.

51 Ibid., 5 July 1930.

52 Ibid., 29 August 1930.

Chapter 4: A New World

1 A.B. McKillop, *Matters of Mind,* 466.

2 Northrop Frye, interview, [ca. 1975].

3 Mary Winspear, interview, 8 January 1996.

4 LS, letter T.

5 Mary Winspear, interview.

6 Leon Edel, interview [ca. April 1974]. I am grateful to Edel, who provided access to his collection of Canadian materials and correspondence then held at his home in Hawaii.

7 R.D., 'A Quarter-Century of the Quarterly,' *University of Toronto Quarterly* 25 (1955): 4–5.

8 Mary Winspear, interview.

9 Robert Finch, interview, 9 October 1994.

10 Kay Riddell-Rouillard, interview, 11 October 1994.

11 Mildred (Shanas) Gutkin to the author, letter, 5 December 2000.

12 Diary, 18 March 1931, RDP 11-9.

13 Letter to mother, 21 October 1930, RDP 40-2.

14 Diary, 23 October 1930, RDP 11-8.

15 Ibid., 30 September and 11 October 1930.

16 Letter to mother, n.d. [ca. 25 November 1930], RDP 40-11.

17 Diary, 3 December 1930.

18 Letter to parents, n.d. [ca. 27 December 1930], RDP 40-2.

19 Barker Fairley, 'Open Letter to Professor Irving Babbitt,' *Canadian Forum* 11, no. 124 (Jan. 1931): 136.

20 J.S. Will, 'In Defence of Professor Babbitt,' *Canadian Forum* 11, no. 125 (Feb. 1931): 177–8.

21 Irving Babbitt, *Rousseau and Romanticism*, 262.

22 Robert E. Spiller et al., *Literary History of the United States*, 4th rev. ed., 1148.

23 Leon Edel, interview.

24 Diary, 15 December 1930.

25 Laura Smyth Groening, *E.K. Brown: A Study in Conflict*, 185.

26 Diary, 19 December 1930.

27 Ibid., 22 January 1931, RDP 11-9.

28 Ibid., 29 October 1931, RDP 11-9; 7 January 1932, RDP 11-10.

29 Leon Edel, interview [ca. 1981].

30 Alfred Bailey, interview, [March/April] 1974.

31 Leon Edel to Robert L. McDougall, letter, 27 July 1977.

32 Diary, 7 February 1931, RDP 11-9.

33 Letter to parents, 26 December 1930, RDP 40-2.

34 Herbert Davis, 'John Milton,' *Dalhousie Review* 8, no. 3 (Oct. 1928): 302.

35 'Plymouth Brother,' *Canadian Literature*, no. 90 (Autumn 1981): 33.

36 'A Century and a Half of English Lyricism,' 5, RDP 16-5.

37 Diary, 22 April 1931, RDP 11-9.

38 Thorlief Larsen to R.D., letter, 30 March 1931, RDP 1-5.

39 Diary, 10 August 1931.

40 Letter from parents, n.d. [ca. April 1931], RDP 1-4.

41 Diary, 10, 23, 28 June; 4 July; 9 August; 13 September, 1931, RDP 11-9.

42 Ibid., 9 July 1931.

43 'Autobiographical Fragment.'

44 Diary, 19 July 1931.

45 Jean Grant to R.D., letter, 28 August 1931; diary, 2 September 1931, RDP 1-6.

46 Constance Daniells to R.D., letter, n.d. [ca. September 1931], RDP 1-4.

47 Diary, 19 October 1931.

48 Ibid., 20 November 1931.

49 Letter to mother, 31 January 1932, RDP 1-8.

50 Ian Ross, interview, 10 February 2000.

51 Robert Finch, interview, 9 October 1994.

52 LS, letter T.

53 Letter to parents, 27 March 1932, RDP 40-3.

54 Ibid., 17 July 1932, RDP 40-4.

55 Ibid., n.d. [12 June 1932], RDP 40-4.

56 Dorothy Livesay, *Journey with My Selves: A Memoir 1909–1963*, 72. Livesay records a letter from Gina [Jim Watts] of February 1930 in which Gina said, 'I keep seeing people, *my* sort of people, suddenly, anywhere and wanting to talk to them and have an affair.'

57 Dorothy Livesay, *Right Hand Left Hand*, 31.

58 Letter to parents, 26 June 1932; 'Sunday' [12 June 1932], RDP 40-4. Others who frequently visited the apartment were Alfred Bailey, Henry Noyes, Jane Grey, Olga Vipond, Marjorie James, Harold King, Ross Parmenter, and Colin Jarvis.

59 Diary, 15, 22, 26 May 1932, RDP 11-10.

Chapter 5: Following the Path

1 Jim Watts to R.D., letter, n.d. [ca. May 1932], RDP 1-8.

2 Letter to parents, 'Saturday' [18 June 1932], RDP 40-7.

3 T.S. Eliot, 'Ash-Wednesday,' in *Collected Poems 1909–1962*, 95–6, 105. Quoted by R.D. in letter to parents, 'Saturday' [18 June 1932], RDP 40-7.

4 Letter to parents, 11 June 1932, RDP 40-4.

5 Dorothy Livesay, *Journey with My Selves: A Memoir 1909–1963*. Livesay's principle of selection in this autobiography is to tell the truth but, echoing Emily Dickinson, to 'tell it slant': she gives fictitious names to three lovers,

one called 'Tony,' recognizably Stanley Ryerson, who was part of Livesay's earlier left-wing circle at Toronto. Daniells' diary identifies Livesay's companion as Ryerson. Also, Leon Edel met Livesay and Ryerson together in Paris when he was studying at the Sorbonne (Leon Edel, interview, 1974).

6   Letter to parents, 5 June 1932.
7   Ibid., 7 June 1932; 15 June 1932.
8   Ibid., 22 June 1932, RDP 40-7.
9   Preceding quotations from letter to parents, 'Saturday' [18 June 1932]; 25 June 1932, RDP 40-7.
10 'Autobiographical Fragments,' RDP 16-9.
11 Jim Watts to R.D., letter, 16 July 1932, RDP 1-9.
12 Letter to parents, n.d. [12 June 1932]; 26 June 1932, RDP 40-4.
13 Ibid., 25 June 1932.
14 Ibid.
15 Ibid.
16 Ibid., 28 June 1932.
17 Ibid., 2 July 1932.
18 Ibid., 2, 3 July 1932; n.d. [July 1932], RDP 40-4.
19 Ibid., 11 July 1932, RDP 40-4.
20 Herbert Davis to R.D., partially dated letter, 1 July [1932], RDP 1-9.
21 Letter to parents, 3 July 1932, RDP 40-4.
22 Ibid., 11 July 1932.
23 Ibid., 17 July [1932], RDP 40-6.
24 Ibid.
25 Letter to parents, 21 July 1932; n.d. [ca. 5 August 1932], RDP 40-4.
26 Ibid., n.d. [ca. 5 August 1932], RDP 40-4; Robert Finch, interview.
27 Letter to parents, 18 July 1932, RDP 40-4; 25 August 1932.
28 Ibid., 19 August 1932.
29 Ibid., 10 August 1932.
30 Ibid. Daniells uses the example of Dean Wren, a seventeenth-century divine who said that the earth cannot move because the Scripture says that the sun moves and the earth is still. These arguments, he reminded his parents, were very similar to the those used by the Brethren. 'Here is a man, sincerely it seems denouncing those who said the earth moved & pointing to Scripture after Scripture to support his stand. If the method led *him* into simple stupid error what is to prevent its leading *us* there? I don't question the Bible. But I am distressed to see men following it literally ...'
31 Letter to parents, 27 July 1932, RDP 40-4; Jim Watts to R.D., letter, 29 August 1932, RDP 1-9.
32 Letter to parents, 27 July 1932, RDP 40-4; 27 August 1932.

33 Northrop Frye, interview, 23 August 1983.

34 Diary, 30 September 1932.

35 Letter to parents, 'Saturday' [25 February 1933], RDP 40-11.

36 'Autobiographical Fragments,' RDP 16-9.

37 Letter to parents, 6 September 1932, RDP 40-4.

38 Ibid., 2 November 1932.

39 Ibid.

40 Letter to parents, 'Monday' [21 November 1932], RDP 40-4.

41 Ibid., 'Friday night' [ca. 11 November 1932]; 24 October 1932, RDP 40-4.

42 Letter to father, n.d. [ca. 2 November 1932], RDP 40-4.

43 A.S.P. Woodhouse, ed., *Puritanism and Liberty: Being the Army Debates (1647–9) from the Clarke Manuscripts with Supplementary Documents*, 18; draft of review of Woodhouse's *The Heavenly Muse: A Preface to Milton*, RDP 16-32; R.D, interview, 13 July 1977; 'He burnished ideas till they shone like revealed truth ...,' *Varsity Graduate* (Spring 1961): 72.

44 Letter to parents, n.d. [ca. 15 October 1932], RDP 40-11.

45 Diary, 15 October 1932; draft of review of *The Heavenly Muse: A Preface to Milton*.

46 Notes for article on Woodhouse, *Varsity Graduate*; R.J. Baker, interview, 27 September 1994.

47 Alfred Bailey, interview, [ca. March-April 1974]; Mary Winspear, interview, 8 January 1996.

48 Diary, 10 January 1933, RDP 11-11; letter to L.J. Burpee, 28 January 1933; George Walters to R.D., letter, 9 February 1933, RDP 1-12.

49 Letter to parents, n.d. [ca. 5 February 1933], RDP 40-3.

50 Ibid.

51 Letter to Walter Brown, 13 February 1933; letter from Walter Brown, 14 February 1933, RDP 1-12; letter to parents, 'Saturday' [misfiled as 1930, ca. February 1933], RDP 40-2.

52 Letter to parents, n.d. [ca. April 1933], RDP 40-5.

53 'T.S. Eliot and His Relation to T.E. Hulme,' *University of Toronto Quarterly* 2 (1932–3): 391.

54 Douglas Bush to R.D., letter, 27 April 1933; S.I. Hayakawa to R.D., letter, 31 May 1933, RDP 1-12.

Chapter 6: Love and Politics

1 Letter to parents, 14 December 1932, RDP 40-4.

2 Diary, 31 October 1932, RDP 11-10; Earle Birney to R.D., letter, 28 August 1933, RDP 1-13; diary, 5 March 1933, RDP 11-11.

3 Jim Watts to R.D., letter, n.d. [ca. 1 March 1933], RDP 1-13.

4 LS, letter Q.

5 Letter to Beatrice Wallace, 21 June 1933, RDP 1-12; Earle Birney to R.D., letter, 10 July 1933, RDP 1-13.

6 Earle Birney to R.D., letter, 15 July [1933], RDP 1-13.

7 Letter to parents, n.d. [15 April 1933], RDP 40-5; Lita-Rose Betcherman, *The Little Band*, 18.

8 Diary, 1 May 1933; letter to Beatrice Wallace, 21 June 1933, RDP 1-12.

9 Diary, 10 June 1933, RDP 11-12; letter to Beatrice Wallace, 21 June 1933, RDP 1-12.

10 Letter to parents, n.d. [April 1933], RDP 40-5.

11 Ibid., 14 June 1933.

12 Ibid., n.d. [13 July 1933].

13 T.S. Eliot, 'La Figlia che Piange,' in *Collected Poems 1909–1962*, 26.

14 Diary, 16 June 1933, RDP 11-11; Esther Birney, interview, 16 August 1995; diary, 17–19 June 1933; letter to Earle Birney, headed 'Shack/Sunday night' [ca. 18 June 1933], RDP 1-13.

15 Earle Birney to R.D., letter, 15 July [1933], RDP 1-13.

16 Letter to Earle Birney, n.d. [ca. 18 June 1933], RDP 1-13.

17 Earle Birney to R.D., letter, 10 [July 1933], RDP 1-13.

18 Diary, 20 June 1933; 2 and 13 July 1933.

19 Alan Adamson, interview, 16 March 1997. Adamson's first wife was the former Margaret Ann Bjornson, in whom Daniells had confided in the early forties at U of M.

20 Elspeth Cameron, *Earle Birney: A Life*, 93.

21 Sylvia Johnstone to R.D., letter, 25 July 1933, RDP 40-5.

22 Letter to Sylvia Johnstone n.d., copy [17 August 1933]; [18 August 1933], RDP 1-13.

23 Earle Birney to R.D., letter, 10 [July 1933] RDP 1-13; Cameron, *Earle Birney*, 107.

24 Earle Birney to R.D., letter, 15 July [1933], RDP 1-13.

25 Sylvia Johnstone to R.D., letter, 6 August 1933.

26 Earle Birney to R.D., letter, 28 August 1933, RDP 1-13.

27 Letter to Earle Birney, copy, 20 September 1933; Earle Birney to R.D., letter, 9 October 1933, RDP 1-14.

28 Sylvia Johnstone to R.D., letter, n.d., [ca. October 1933], RDP 1-14.

29 Letter to parents, 18 September 1933, RDP 40-5.

30 Esther Birney, interview, 16 August 1995; David Easton, interview, 5 February 1997.

31 Esther Birney, interview. This account is confirmed by David Easton, Sylvia Johnstone's husband.

32 David Easton, interview, 5 February 1997.

33 David Easton to the author, letter, 31 August 1998.

34 Earle Birney repeated this remark to Gwladys Downes (Gwladys Downes, interview, 27 July 1997).

35 Earle Birney to R.D., letter, 15 July [1933], RDP 1-13.

36 Cameron, *Earle Birney*, 124.

37 Ibid., 107.

38 Earle Birney to R.D., letter, 15 July [1933], RDP 1-13.

39 Eve Kosofsky Sedgewick, *Between Men: English Literature and Male Homosocial Desire*, 21.

Chapter 7: Europe

1 Letter to parents, n.d. [1 September 1933], RDP 40-5.

2 Ibid., 14 September 1933; 9 October 1933.

3 Ibid., 15 September 1933.

4 Ibid., 2 October 1933; 7 October 1933.

5 Letter to J.D. Robins, 11 November 1933, RDP 1-14.

6 Claude de Mestral to R.D., letter, 11 June 1934, RDP 2-1.

7 Letter to Ruel Lochore, 24 October 1933, RDP 2-3; Max Maynard to R.D., letter, 28 October 1930, RDP 1-3.

8 Diary, 8 November 1933, RDP 11-11; letter to Pelham Edgar, 21 November 1933, RDP 1-14.

9 Letter to Pelham Edgar, 21 November 1933; letter to E.J. Pratt, partially dated, copy, December 1933, RDP 1-14.

10 Sylvia Johnstone to R.D., letter, 25 December 1933, RDP 1-14.

11 Letter to parents, 6 January 1934; letter to mother, 30 January 1934, RDP 40-6.

12 Letter to mother, 27 January 1934, RDP 40-6; letter to parents, [April 1933]; Herbert Davis to R.D., letter, 10 February 1934, RDP 1-17.

13 Herbert Davis to R.D., letter, 10 January 1934.

14 Ibid., 28 February 1934.

15 Letter to mother, n.d. [ca. 18 February 1934], RDP 40-6.

16 Herbert Davis to R.D., letter, 14 March 1934, RDP 1-17; 'An Inquiry into Some Formal Problems in English Non-dramatic Literature of the Seventeenth Century.'

17 Letter to parents, n.d. [18 February 1934], RDP 40-6; letter to father, 28 February 1934, RDP 40-6; diary, 1 and 11 April 1934, RDP 11-12.

18 Diary, 9 and 15 February 1934.

19 Letter to Ruel Lochore, 22 February 1934, RDP 2-3.

20 Diary, 19 and 20 March 1934; letter to parents, 18 February 1934, RDP 40-6.
21 Herbert Davis to R.D., partially dated letter, 10 January [1934], RDP 1-17.
22 Diary, 15–20 April 1934; L. Frazer to R.D., letter, 5 July 1934, RDP 2-2.
23 'Sundry Notes (for Novel),' RDP 11-45.
24 Frank Hamilton to R.D., letter, 23 February 1934, RDP 1-17.
25 Letter to parents, 8 April 1934; 12 May 1934, RDP 40-6.
26 Ibid., n.d. [16 May 1934].
27 Ibid., 26 March 1934.
28 Earle Birney to R.D., letter, 30 May 1934, RDP 2-1.
29 Letter to mother, 22 July 1934, RDP 40-6.
30 Letter to father, 14 August 1934, RDP 40-6.

Chapter 8: A Narrow Circle

1 Diary, 2 and 23 November 1934, RDP 11-12.
2 Letter to parents, 17 March 1935, RDP 40-7.
3 Benedict Anderson, *Imagined Communities: Reflections on the Origin and Spread of Nationalism*, rev. ed., 5–7.
4 LS, letter R.
5 Letter to parents, 23 February 1935, RDP 40-7; partially dated, December 1930, RDP 40-2; Kay Riddell-Rouillard, interview, 11 October 1994.
6 Letter to parents, n.d. [ca. October 1934], RDP 40-6.
7 Gerald Riddell to R.D., letter, n.d. [ca. May 1934], RDP 2-1.
8 Northrop Frye, interview, 23 August 1983; letter to mother, 7 October 1934, RDP 40-6.
9 'Acta Locals,' *Acta Victoriana* 55, no. 5 (Feb.–March 1931): 35.
10 Kay Riddell-Rouillard, interview.
11 Viola Pratt, interview, 19 January 1976.
12 Diary, 10 December 1935, RDP 11-13.
13 Carl F. Klinck, *Giving Canada a Literary History*, 11–12.
14 Northrop Frye, 'The Case against Examinations,' *Acta Victoriana* 56, no. 6 (April 1932): 29.
15 Letter to parents, 19 February 1935, RDP 40-7; 31 March 1935.
16 *Canadian Forum* 1, no. 1 (Oct. 1920): 3.
17 Letter to parents, 19 February 1935.
18 LS, letter S.
19 Letter to parents, n.d. [ca. October 1934], RDP 40-6.
20 Ibid., 23 February 1935, RDP 40-7.
21 John Ayre, interview, 11 November 1999. See also John Ayre, *Northrop Frye: A Biography*, 25.

22 Northrop Frye to Helen Kemp, letter 94, postmarked 19 October 1934, in
    The Correspondence of Northrop Frye and Helen Kemp, 1932–1939, ed. Robert
    D. Denham, 1:354.
23 Diary, 24 February 1934; 8 December 1934, RDP 11-12; 2 February 1935,
    RDP 11-13; 29 February 1936, RDP 11-14.
24 Northrop Frye to Helen Kemp, letter 114, postmarked 3 May 1935, in
    Denham, ed., *Correspondence*, 1:435; letter 99, postmarked 12 December
    1934, in ibid., 1:378.
25 Letter to parents, 19 February 1935, RDP 40-7.
26 Ibid., 17 March 1935; diary, 28 February 1935, RDP 11-13; Pelham Edgar to
    R.D., letter, 20 February 1934, RDP 1-17.
27 Letter to parents, 8 March 1935, RDP 40-7.
28 Ibid., 2 November 1935; T.J. Keenan to R.D., letter, 23 April 1935, RDP 2-5.
29 Leith Macdonald, interview, 21 October 1998.
30 Diary, 1 December 1935, RDP 11-13.
31 Ibid., 26 September 1935, RDP 11-13.
32 Ibid., 24 and 25 August 1936; 11 September 1936; 15 September 1936, RDP
    11-14.
33 Helen Kemp to Northrop Frye, letter 146, 21 September 1936, in Denham,
    ed., *Correspondence*, 2:563.
34 Letter to parents, 31 March 1935, RDP 40-7.
35 Diary, 9 February 1934, RDP 11-12.
36 T.S. Eliot to R.D., letter, 23 February 1934, RDP 1-17; diary, 11 May 1935,
    RDP 11-13; T.S. Eliot to R.D., letter, 29 May 1935, RDP 2-6.
37 I am indebted to Walter Swayze, formerly of the University of Calgary, for
    this information.
38 LS, letter W.
39 Letter to parents, 14 June 1935, RDP 40-7; William Robbins, interview,
    11 June 1992.
40 Northrop Frye to Helen Kemp, letter 112, postmarked 23 April 1935, in
    Denham, ed., *Correspondence*, 1:425; Helen Kemp to Northrop Frye, letter
    115, postmarked 13 May 1935, in ibid., 1:440–1.
41 Denham, ed., *Correspondence*, letter 118, 20 June 1935, 1:454; letter 123,
    postmarked 24 July 1935, 1:478.
42 Letter to Gerald Riddell, 6 June 1935, RDP 2-6.
43 Gerald Riddell to R.D., letter, 11 July 1935, RDP 2-7.
44 William Robbins to R.D., letter, 28 June 1935, RDP 2-6.
45 Northrop Frye to R.D., letter, n.d. [ca. 14 July 1935], RDP 2-5.
46 Letter to mother, n.d. [ca. 26 August 1935], RDP 40-7.
47 Diary, 23 and 30 July 1935, RDP 11-13.

48 Ibid., 23 August 1935.
49 George Johnston to the author, letter, 1 December 1996.

Chapter 9: Professing English

1 Letter to Pelham Edgar, 26 September 1935, RDP 2-8.
2 Diary, 12 December 1936, RDP 11-14.
3 Letter to parents, n.d. [April 1933], RDP 40-5.
4 'He burnished ideas till they shone like revealed truth ...,' *Variety Graduate* (Spring 1961): 69–74.
5 George Ford, interview, 21 October 1993.
6 E.J. Pratt to R.D., letter, 28 February 1934, RDP 1-17.
7 LS, letter S.
8 Letter to mother, 2 December 1934, RDP 40-6.
9 Letter to parents, 5 January 1936, RDP 40-8.
10 'The Special Quality,' in 'Ned Pratt: Two Recollections,' *Canadian Literature*, no. 21 (1964): 10–12.
11 LS, letter S.
12 Diary, 17 October 1936, RDP 11-14.
13 Ibid., 25 January 1937, RDP 11-15.
14 George Johnston to the author, letter, 1 December 1996.
15 Margaret Avison, interview, 30 October 1998.
16 Earle Birney to R.D., letter, 11 May 1935, RDP 2-6.
17 Esther Birney, discussion, 16 August 1995.
18 Earle Birney to R.D., letter, 31 October 1935, RDP 2-8.
19 Diary, 8 May 1936, RDP 11-14.
20 Ibid., 12 May 1936.
21 'An Inquiry into Some Formal Problems in English Non-dramatic Litera-ture of the Seventeenth Century,' 32, 201,184.
22 Earle Birney to R.D., letter, 6 August 1936, RDP 2-11.
23 Barker Fairley, interview, 3 February 1974.
24 Northrop Frye, 'Conclusion,' *Literary History of Canada*, ed. Carl Klinck, 830.
25 Max Maynard to R.D., letter, 22 October 1934, RDP 2-3.
26 Diary, 22 May 1936, RDP 11-14; 22 March 1937, RDP 11-15.
27 L. Frazer to R.D., letter, 5 July 1934, RDP 2-2.
28 'A Modern Marvell,' *Canadian Forum* 16, no. 187 (Aug. 1936): 18.
29 'To a Generation Unemployed,' *Canadian Forum* 17, no. 189 (16 Oct. 1936): 10.
30 'Look Homeward Angel,' *Saturday Night* 51, no. 48 (3 Oct. 1936): 1.
31 Articles and poems published in the *Canadian Forum* include an extended satiric verse on Gertrude Stein (Feb. 1937), a verse on a dollar bill, 'La

Dollabella' (April 1937), a review of a book on current educational practices, 'The Muse in Chains' (July 1937), a critical article on Eliot, 'The Christian Drama of T.S. Eliot' (Aug. 1937), and another satiric verse 'To Sir O... D...' (Dec. 1937).

32 Letter to parents, 26 December 1930, RDP 11-8.

33 A.G. Bailey, interview on the literary development of the University of New Brunswick, March/April 1974. Tape supplied by Bailey.

34 Robert Finch. 'I,' in 'A Letter: To Several Poets Addressed As One,' copy of unpublished typescript, in the possession of the author.

35 Robert Finch, interview, 10 October 1994.

36 LS, letter W.

37 Muriel David to R.D., letter, 23 November 1935, RDP 2-9.

38 Finch, 'VII,' in 'A Letter.'

39 Finch kindly provided copies of his poems, identifying those which referred to Daniells.

40 Robert Finch to R.D., letter, 25 August 1936, RDP 2-12.

41 Max Maynard to R.D., letter, 19 December 1936, RDP 2-12.

42 George Johnston to the author, letter, 1 December 1996.

43 Letter to father, 13 March 1937, RDP 40-9.

44 Diary, 19 July 1936, RDP 11-14.

45 Evelyn Stewart to R.D., letter, 5 October 1936, RDP 2-12.

46 Diary, 19 September 1936, RDP 11-14.

47 Letter to parents, n.d. [ca. 27 September 1935], RDP 11-14.

48 Helen Kemp to Northrop Frye, letter 146, 21 September 1936, in *The Correspondence of Northrop Frye and Helen Kemp, 1932–1939*, ed. Robert D. Denham, 2: 563–4.

49 Northrop Frye to Helen Kemp, letter 151, postmarked 1 October 1936, in ibid., 2:580.

50 Letter to parents, 6 June 1935, RDP 40-7.

51 Helen Kemp to Northrop Frye, letter 155, 30 September to 10 October 1936, in Denham, ed., *Correspondence*, 2:595.

52 Letter to parents, 12 December 1936, RDP 40-8.

53 Letter to mother, 22 March 1934, RDP 40-6.

54 Ibid., 20 February 1937, RDP 40-9.

55 Ibid., 4 March 1937.

56 Letter to father, 13 March 1937, RDP 40-9,

57 Helen Kemp to Northrop Frye, letter 175, postmarked 10 January 1937, in Denham, ed., *Correspondence*, 2:673.

58 Northrop Frye to Helen Kemp, letter 183, postmarked 9 February 1937, in ibid., 2:692.

59 Helen Kemp to Northrop Frye, letter 187, 8 March 1937, in ibid., 2:708.
60 LS, letter Q.
61 Helen Kemp to Northrop Frye, letter 207, 11 June 1937, in Denham, ed., *Correspondence*, 2:765.
62 Letter to parents, 28 March 1937, RDP 40-9.
63 Diary, 29 April 1936, RDP 11-14.
64 Letter to parents, n.d. [ca. May 1937], RDP 40-9.
65 Ibid., n.d. [ca. 14 July 1937], RDP 40-9.
66 Letter to mother, 19 June 1937, RDP 11-15.
67 Ibid., 23 June 1937.
68 Letter to mother, n.d. [ca. 7 July 1937], RDP 40-11.
69 Northrop Frye to R.D., partially dated letter, July 1937, RDP 3-2.
70 Letter to parents, n.d. [ca. 29 May 1937], RDP 40-9.
71 Pelham Edgar to R.D., partially dated letter, 1 July [1937], RDP 3-2.
72 Diary, 9 July 1937, RDP 11-15
73 Letter to parents, n.d. [ca. 9 July 1937], RDP 40-9.
74 Diary, 19 July 1937, RDP 11-15.
75 Ibid., 28 May 1937.
76 Ibid., 28 August 1937.
77 Letter to parents, n.d. [29 May 1937], RDP 40-9.

Chapter 10: 'This Winnipeg!'

1 Pelham Edgar to R.D., letter, 1 July 1937, RDP 3-2.
2 Arthur R.M. Lower, *My First Seventy-five Years*, 170.
3 Herbert Davis to R.D., letter, 12 August 1937, RDP 3-2.
4 Northrop Frye to R.D., partially dated letter, July 1937, RDP 3-2.
5 A.S.P. Woodhouse to R.D., letter, 15 August 1937, RDP 3-2.
6 Leith Ferguson to R.D., partially dated letter, 28 July [1937], RDP 3-2.
7 Garnett Sedgewick to R.D., letter, 19 July 1937, RDP 3-2.
8 W.L. Morton, *One University: A History of the University of Manitoba, 1877–1952*, 147–59.
9 Garnett Sedgewick to R.D., letter, 19 July 1937, RDP 3-2.
10 Doris Saunders, interview, 5 October 1994.
11 Lower, *My First Seventy-five Years*, 168.
12 Diary, 14 September 1937, RDP 11-15.
13 Mary Elizabeth Bayer, interview, 5 June 1995.
14 Letter to parents, n.d. [ca. 11 December 1937], RDP 40-9.
15 Ibid. [ca. 23 October 1937].
16 Ogden Turner, interview, 4 October 1994.

17 Mildred Gutkin, interview, 5 October 1994.

18 Ogden Turner, interview.

19 Diary, 20 September 1937, RDP 11-15.

20 Letter to parents, n.d. [ca. November 1937], RDP 40-9.

21 Diary, 16 September 1937, RDP 11-15.

22 Letter to parents, n.d. [16 October 1937], RDP 40-9.

23 Ibid. [ca. 28 August 1937].

24 Sidney Smith to R.D., letter, 22 October 1937, RDP 3-3.

25 Letter to parents, 10 October 1937, RDP 40-9.

26 George Ford, interview, 21 October 1994.

27 J. Max Patrick to the author, letter, 2 June 1995.

28 Letter to parents, 10 October 1937, RDP 40-9.

29 J.D. Robins to R.D., letter, 24 May 1938, RDP 3-8.

30 Gerald Riddell to R.D., letter, n.d. [ca. November 1937], RDP 3-3.

31 Desmond Pacey, to R.D., letter, n.d. [ca. spring 1938], RDP 3-7.

32 Henry Noyes to R.D., letter, 5 November 1937, RDP 3-3.

33 Ernest Sirluck, *First Generation: An Autobiography*, 47–8.

34 Letter to President Klinck, copy, 3 May 1940, RDP 3-16.

35 Alan Adamson to the author, letter, 16 January 1995.

36 Margaret (Bjornson) Elton to the author, letter, 30 November 1994.

37 Sirluck, *First Generation*, 47–8.

38 Ogden Turner, interview.

39 'Ferdinand and Others: A Note on Individualism,' *Manitoba Arts Review* 1, no. 3 (Spring 1939): 27–31.

40 Alan Adamson to the author, letter, 16 January 1995.

41 Diary, 9 December 1938, RDP 11-16.

42 Frances (Aikens) Riley, interview, 6 October 1994.

43 'Sundry Notes (for Novel),' RDP 11-45.

44 Gwladys Downes to the author, letter, 5 June 1996.

45 Ibid., 13 July 1997.

46 Diary, 9 August 1939, RDP 11-17.

47 Ibid., 1 September 1940, RDP 11-18.

48 Ibid., 22 August 1940, RDP 11-18.

49 Margaret (Bjornson) Elton to the author, letter, 30 November 1994.

50 Department of English, Report to the President's Report 1940–1941, University of Manitoba Special Collections.

51 J. Max Patrick to the author, letter, 1 June 1994.

52 Ibid.

53 Letter to Sidney Smith, 16 February 1942, RDP 3-15.

54 Letter to E.K. Brown, n.d. [ca. March 1940], RDP 3-16.

55 A.S.P. Woodhouse to R.D., letter, 17 February 1938, RDP 3-7.
56 E.K. Brown to R.D., partially dated letter, 31 May [1941], RDP 3-19.
57 A.S.P. Woodhouse to R.D., letter, 22 April 1944, RDP 4-12.
58 Kay Mark, interview, 5 March 1997.
59 Diary, 20 June 1941, RDP 11-19.
60 Carson Mark to R.D., letter, 15 August 1941, RDP 3-20.

Chapter 11: 'The End of an Era'

 1 Evelyn Smith to R.D., letter, 5 June 1941, RDP 3-20.
 2 Meredith Thompson to R.D., letter, 11 July 1939, RDP 3-12.
 3 *A Serious and Pathetical Contemplation of the Mercies of God, in Several Most Devout and Sublime Thanksgivings for the Same*, 4.
 4 As quoted in 'An Inquiry into Some Formal Problems in English Non-dramatic Literature of the Seventeenth Century,' 289.
 5 Malcolm Wallace to R.D., letter, 15 September 1939, RDP 3-13.
 6 Herbert Davis to R.D., letter, 25 December 1939, RDP 3-13.
 7 Diary, 17, 15, 18, 19 May 1940 respectively, RDP 11-18.
 8 Herbert Davis to R.D., letter, 18 February 1940, RDP 3-16.
 9 Margaret (Bjornson) Adamson to R.D., letter, May 1941, RDP 3-19.
10 Northrop Frye to R.D., letter, n.d. [ca. August 1940], RDP 3-17.
11 Northrop Frye, 'The Personal Legend,' in 'Ned Pratt: Two Recollections,' *Canadian Literature*, no. 21 (1964): 9.
12 Undated recommendations attached to letters from Albert Trueman, 14 August 1945, RDP 4-18.
13 Ruby Hootin to R.D., letter, 21 April 1943, RDP 4-7.
14 Diary, 21 January 1943, RDP 11-21.
15 Letter to parents, n.d. [ca. 14 March 1943], RDP 40-11.
16 Sidney Smith, in President's Report, 1942–3: 2, University of Manitoba Special Collections.
17 Department of English, in ibid., 36.
18 Chester Duncan to the author, letter, 8 May 1994.
19 Diary, 31 August 1942.
20 Letter to mother, 20 February 1943, RDP 40-15.
21 Sidney Smith, in President's Report, 1943–4: 7, University of Manitoba Special Collections.
22 Ruth (Schlass) Waldfogel to Perry Millar, interview, 23 February 1996.
23 Mildred (Shanas) Gutkin to the author, letter, 22 Feb. 1997; 5 Dec. 2000.
24 George Ford, interview, 21 October 1994.
25 Fredelle Bruser Maynard, *Raisins and Almonds*, 142–3.
26 Fredelle Bruser Maynard, *The Tree of Life*, 21, 65.

27 Ibid., 21.
28 George Ford, interview, 21 October 1994.
29 J. Max Patrick to R.D., letter, 30 January 1944, RDP 4-12.
30 A.S.P Woodhouse to R.D., letter, 15 February 1944, RDP 4-12.
31 Ibid., 22 April 1944, RDP 4-12.
32 Ibid., 4 February 1946, RDP 5-3.
33 George Ford, interview, 21 October 1994.
34 E.K. Brown to R.D., partially dated letter, 1 November [1941], RDP 4-1.
35 Letter to E.K. Brown, 8 January 1942, RDP 4-1.
36 Diary, 9 October 1941, RDP 11-19.
37 Ruth Schlass to R.D., letter, n.d. [ca. September 1941], RDP 4-1.
38 Letter to Ruth Schlass, copy, n.d. [ca. July 1942], RDP 4-4.
39 Ruth Schlass to R.D., letter, n.d., [24 July 1942], RDP 4-4.
40 Letter to Carson Mark, copy, 6 July 1942, RDP 4-4.
41 Carson Mark to R.D., letter, 10 July 1942, RDP 4-4.
42 Ruth Schlass to R.D., letter, 17 July 1942, RDP 4-4.
43 Constance Daniells to R.D., letter, n.d. [ca. mid-April 1931], RDP 1-4.
44 E.K. Brown to R.D., letter, 6 March 1942, RDP 4-3.
45 Department of English, in President's Report, 1938–9: 32, University of
    Manitoba Special Collections.
46 W.L. Morton, *One University: A History of the University of Manitoba, 1877–
    1952*, 170–1.
47 Sidney Smith, in President's Report, 1943–4: 5, University of Manitoba
    Special Collections.
48 Ibid., 6.
49 Morton, *One University*, 171.
50 Sidney Smith to R.D., letter, n.d. ['Sunday,' ca. 18 April 1943], RDP 4-18.
51 Letter to Sidney Smith, copy, 20 May 1943, RDP 4-18, University of Mani-
    toba Special Collections, UA 20, Box 41, Folder 3.
52 Ibid.
53 Sidney Smith to R.D., letter, 3 June 1943, RDP 4-8
54 Diary, 14 January 1944, RDP 11-22.
55 E.K. Brown to R.D., letter, 8 February 1944, RDP 4-12.
56 Sidney Smith to R.D., letter, 6 August 1944, RDP 4-13.
57 E.K. Brown to R.D., letter, 1 July 1944, RDP 4-13.
58 Doris Saunders to R.D., letter, 19 August 1944, RDP 4-13.

Chapter 12: 'O Canada'

1 Alan Hockin, interview, 20 February 1997.
2 Letter to President Klinck, UBC, copy, 3 May 1940, RDP 3-16.

3 George Ford told this to E.K. Brown, letter, 22 February 1941, University of Manitoba Special Collections.

4 Diary, 22 March 1939, RDP 11-17.

5 Paul Hiebert, *Sarah Binks*, 52.

6 Ibid., xv.

7 George Ford, interview, 21 October 1994.

8 Sinclair Ross, *As for Me and My House*, 5.

9 Letter to Sinclair Ross, n.d. [ca. 1941].

10 Sinclair Ross to R.D., letter, 27 April 1941, RDP 3-19.

11 Letter to Sinclair Ross, 25 May 1941, RDP 3-19. Margaret Laurence gives two dates for when she first read Ross's *As for Me and My House*: the first date was her last year in high school; the second was after she had become a student at the University of Manitoba. The second date is more likely because it is confirmed by a classmate, Lyall Powers. He recalls that *As for Me and My House* was on the upper-level honours curriculum at Manitoba. Laurence told him that she had just discovered this novel when Malcolm Ross, then teaching at Manitoba, drew her attention to it (Lyall Powers, interview, 24 October 1997).

12 Review of *As for Me and My House*, transcript, CBC broadcast, 25 November 1941, RDP 14-5.

13 'Sinclair Ross – Short Stories,' partially dated transcript, CBC broadcast, December 1941, RDP 14-5.

14 Discussion with the author after publication of her article '"No Other Way": Sinclair Ross's Stories and Novels,' *Canadian Literature*, no. 47 (1971): 49–66.

15 Sinclair Ross, interview, 18 March 1992.

16 George Ford, interview, 21 October 1994.

17 Wilfred Cude, 'Beyond Mrs. Bentley: A Study of *As for Me and My House*,' *Journal of Canadian Studies* 8, no. 1 (1973): 3–18.

18 E.J. Pratt to A. J. M. Smith, letter, 7 December 1942, unpublished 'Letters of E.J. Pratt,' in preparation by D.G. Pitt and Elizabeth Popham, AJMSP.

19 A.J.M. Smith to R.D., letter, 10 January 1943, RDP 4-7.

20 Ibid., 2 February 1943.

21 'Aquarius' [R.D.], 'To Sir O ... D ...,' *Canadian Forum* 17, no. 203 (Dec. 1937): 316.

22 Earle Birney to R.D., letter, 2 November 1937, RDP 3-3.

23 Northrop Frye, 'Canada and Its Poetry,' reprinted in *The Bush Garden: Essays on the Canadian Imagination*, 138.

24 Desmond Pacey to R.D., letter, 23 March 1943, RDP 4-7.

25 'The Future of Canadian Writing,' transcript, 18 November 1942, RDP 14-5.

26 'Editorial,' *The Manitoban Literary Supplement*, 18 February 1944.

27 Letter to Alan Creighton, 6 March 1944, RDP 4-12.

28 A.C. Hamilton, interview, 17 March 1997.

29 Harry and Mildred Gutkin, *The Worst of Times: The Best of Times*, 244.

30 Jack Ludwig to R.D., letter, 2 February 1953, RDP 6-16.

31 A.C. Hamilton, *Northrop Frye: Anatomy of His Criticism*, xiii.

32 Fredelle Bruser Maynard, *Raisins and Almonds*, 143.

33 Daniells itemized pages 178, 196, 200, 304, and 344 on an insert in his copy of Adele Wiseman's *The Sacrifice* – all pages with explicit biblical references.

34 Gwladys Downes, interview, 27 July 1997.

35 Patricia Blondal, *From Heaven with a Shout*. The epigraph is from 1 Thessalonians 4:16. The protagonist of this novel is an Englishwoman who, like Daniells, travels from London to Vancouver Island, but as the wife of one of twin brothers, known as 'The Doctor' and 'The Professor.' As her husband's English family lives up Island, she travels there by boat, thus retracing Daniells' travels in the early twenties. There she meets Oldham, an Anglican priest, who asks the quintessential Plymouth Brethren question: 'Are you a Christian?' The novel stresses religious themes. There is an extended meditation on the Canadian landscape, and the Vancouver Island family possesses a large collection of Canadian literature. Although the twin who is a doctor is a melancholiac who eventually commits suicide, the novel stresses the extraordinary closeness of the two brothers: the narrator reflects, 'I watched, fascinated, what often seemed duality in one man' (95).

36 Margaret Laurence to Adele Wiseman, letter, 21 July 1960, in John Lennox and Ruth Panofsky, eds, *Selected Letters of Margaret Laurence and Adele Wiseman*, 121–2.

37 Margaret Laurence, *Dance on the Earth: A Memoir*, 95–6.

38 'Milestones of Thought: Man Discovers Himself,' transcript, 22 March 1942, RDP 14-6.

39 'Classics of Tomorrow: *The Waste Land* by T.S. Eliot,' typescript, 13 October 1944, RDP 14-6.

40 Marshall McLuhan to R.D., letter, 3 October 1944, RDP 4-14. Laurence speaks of discovering her landscape in an essay on her literary beginnings, 'Where the World Began' (*Heart of a Stranger*, 213–19). Her 1944 classmate Alan Hockin recalled that members of their English honours class at United College invariably listened to Arthur Phelps when he broadcasted on literature on Winnipeg radio, and it is therefore likely that Laurence also heard Daniells (Hockin, interview, 20 February 1997).

41 Nathan Divinsky, later a professor at UBC, discussion, 15 September 1999.

42 Ogden Turner to R.D., letter, 11 January 1947, RDP 5-9.

43 'Farewell to Winnipeg,' in *Deeper into the Forest*, 64–5.

44 Alice Munro to the author, letter, 15 September 1997.

45 Margaret Laurence, *The Diviners*, 153.

46 Sandra Djwa, 'Roy Daniells and Margaret Laurence: Fiction and "So-Called Reality,"' paper presented at the conference 'Margaret Laurence and Her Times,' Winnipeg, 25 October 1997.

47 James King, *The Life of Margaret Laurence*, 327.

48 Margaret Laurence, 'A Fetish for Love,' in *The Tomorrow-Tamer*. This connection was brought to my attention by Suzanne James, an SFU graduate student.

49 Laurence, *The Diviners*, 278.

50 Ibid., 295.

51 Sinclair Ross's use of biblical myth can also be paralleled with T.S. Eliot's archetypes. See Sandra Djwa 'False Gods and the True Covenant: Thematic Continuity between Margaret Laurence and Sinclair Ross,' in *Margaret Laurence: The Writer and Her Critics*, 69, 72, 71.

52 Laurence, *The Diviners*, 155.

53 Laurence also borrows from Shakespeare's *The Tempest* to associate Morag with Miranda, Skelton with Prospero, and Jules, a Métis balladeer, with Caliban. See Barbara Godard, '*The Diviners* as Supplement: (M)Othering the Text,' *Open Letter* 7, no. 7 (1990): 26–73; and Neil ten Kortenaar, 'The Trick of Divining a Postcolonial Canadian Identity: Margaret Laurence between Race and Nation,' *Canadian Literature*, no. 149 (1996): 33.

54 Cited in Ildikó de Papp Carrington, '"Tales in the Telling": *The Diviners* as Fiction about Fiction,' *Essays on Canadian Writing*, nos. 9–10 (1977–8): 157.

55 Laurence wrote Purdy: '... he [Jack] didn't really think I was a novelist, and nothing much happened in *The Stone Angel* – so I packed my manuscript and took off' (Margaret Laurence to Al Purdy, letter, 5 February 1970, in John Lennox, ed., *Margaret Laurence – Al Purdy: A Friendship in Letters*, 168).

56 'You could make some shrewd guesses about the main character in this novel ... the division between fiction and so-called reality in my life seems an awfully uncertain one' (Margaret Laurence to Al Purdy, letter, 3 September 1971, in ibid., 230).

57 *The Diviners*, 206.

58 Margaret Laurence to Al Purdy, letter, 3 September 1971, in Lennox, ed., *Margaret Laurence – Al Purdy*, 230.

59 Letter to Kay Mark, 11 June 1946, RDP 4-3.

60 Letter to parents, n.d. [ca. summer 1933], RDP 40-5.

61 Letter to father, 13 March 1937, RDP 40-9

62 Diary, 24 May 1939, RDP 11-17.

63 'Sundry Notes (for Novel),' RDP 11-45.

64 Diary, 20 June 1942, RDP 11-20.

65 The several versions of the developing novel consist of approximately 106 pages placed together in file folders; some sections are dated, while others, undated, appear to be united by theme and style. It is clear that Daniells occasionally rewrote sections at a later date and inserted the revised passages. Furthermore, all of his literary papers were scattered during a break-in at the Daniellses' home and later reconstituted, which further complicated the dating process. Consequently, the following grouping is speculative, although the successive versions of the novel do show a developing writer and his emphasis on a Canadian context.

66 'Autobiographical Fragments – Fictionalized,' RDP 16-7.

67 'Autobiographical Fictionalized Fragments,' RDP 16-9.

68 All preceding quotations in this section are from 'Ms for Magnum Opus: Work in Progress' ['Oh Canada'], RDP 16-13.

69 'The Island: A Study in Insularity,' RDP 16-8.

70 'Overture,' *Here and Now* 1, no. 3 (1949): 5–8.

71 Letter to Laurenda Francis, n.d. [ca. September 1947].

Chapter 13: Casting Anchor

1 'In the Labyrinth: A Note on Franz Kafka,' *Manitoba Arts Review* 3, no. 1 (1942): 7.

2 Ibid., 6.

3 Ibid., 7.

4 Diary, 3 August 1935, RDP 11-13.

5 'Autobiographical Fragments – Fictionalized,' RDP 16-7.

6 T.S. Eliot, 'The Waste Land,' in *Collected Poems*, 69.

7 Diaries and Sundry Notes 1947, 1957, 1960, [ca. February 1946], in the possession of Laurenda Daniells; Horney, *The Neurotic Personality of Our Time*, 161.

8 Julian Huxley, 'Why I Am a Scientific Humanist?' *The Listener* 30, no. 78 (1943): 655–6.

9 Diaries and Sundry Notes, 1947, 1957, 1960, [March 1946].

10 Carson Mark to R.D., letter, 12 June 1943, RDP 4-8.

11 Diary, 17 May 1944, RDP 11-22.

12 Laurenda Daniells, 'Sally Ross,' in *Dictionary of Canadian Biography 1881–1890*, vol. xi, 775.

13 Laurenda Daniells, interview, 26 June 1998.

14 Diary, 2 July 1944, RDP 11-22.

15 Ibid., 26 November 1944.
16 Ibid., 2 December 1944.
17 Laurenda Daniells, discussion, 16 July 1998.
18 Diary, 13 December 1944.
19 Ibid., 25 December 1944.
20 Ibid., 9 January 1945, RDP 11-23.
21 Ibid., 30 January 1945.
22 Ibid., 2 February 1945.
23 Ibid., 9 February 1945.
24 Ibid., 8 March 1945.
25 Letter to parents, 24 October 1945, RDP 40-17.
26 Diary, 19 November 1945, RDP 11-23.
27 Ibid., 24 November 1945.
28 Ibid., 2 December 1945.
29 Ibid., 4, 16, and 19 December 1945.
30 Ibid., 25 December 1945.
31 'Baroque Form in English Literature,' *University of Toronto Quarterly* 14, no. 4 (1945): 393–407.
32 Diary, 1 January 1946, RDP 11-24.
33 Ibid., 13 May 1946.
34 Diaries and Sundry Notes, 1947, 1957, 1960, [ca. 1946].
35 W.H. Sheldon and S.S. Stevens, *The Varieties of Temperament*: *A Psychology of Constitutional Differences* (1944), 65–93.
36 Diaries and Sundry Notes, 1947, 1957, 1960, [ca. 1946].
37 Letter to President Klinck, copy, 3 May 1940, RDP 3-16.
38 Letter to Norman MacKenzie, copy, 9 March 1946, RDP 5-4.
39 Earle Birney to R.D., letter, 11 March 1946, RDP 5-4.
40 Letter to Garnett Sedgewick, copy, 10 March 1946, RDP 5-4.
41 Garnett Sedgewick to R.D., letter, 13 March 1946, RDP 5-4.
42 N.A.M. MacKenzie to R.D., letter, 13 March 1946, RDP 5-4.
43 Garnett Sedgewick to R.D., letter, 13 March 1946, RDP 5-4.
44 Earle Birney to R.D., letter, 20 March 1946, RDP 5-4.
45 N.A.M. MacKenzie to R.D., letter, 27 March 1946, RDP 5-4.
46 Letter to Laurenda Francis, partially dated [ca. March/April] 1946, RDP 9-4.
47 N.A.M. MacKenzie to R.D., letter, 4 April 1946, RDP 5-4.
48 Garnett Sedgewick to R.D., letter, 5 April 1946, RDP 5-4.
49 E.K. Brown to R.D., letter, 1 April 1946, RDP 5-4.
50 Earle Birney to R.D., letter, 18 April 1946, RDP 5-4.
51 George Brodersen, George H. Ford, M.S. Maynard, Malcolm Ross, Doris B.

Saunders, and J.B.C. Watkins to President Trueman, letter, 20 April 1946, RDP 5-4.

52 A[rthur] Lloyd Wheeler to R.D., letter, 24 April [1946], RDP 5-4.

53 William Robbins to R.D., letter, 23 April 1946, RDP 5-4.

54 Northrop Frye to R.D., letter, 30 May 1946, RDP 5-4.

55 President A.W. Trueman to A.J.M. Smith, letter, 20 June 1946, UA 20, 79-20, University of Manitoba Special Collections.

56 A.J.M. Smith to R.D., letter, 8 June 1946, UA 20, 79–20, University of Manitoba Special Collections.

57 Letter to A.J.M. Smith, 20 June 1946, UA 20, 79–20, University of Manitoba Special Collections.

58 A.J.M. Smith to R.D., letter, 17 August 1946, RDP 5-6.

59 Letter to A.W. Trueman, 11 July 1946, UA 20, 79–20, University of Manitoba Special Collections.

60 Letter to parents, n.d. [ca. June 1946], RDP 40-18.

Chapter 14: Anatomy of a Department

1 Earle Birney to Herman Singer, letter, 17 February 1947, EBP 18–26.

2 Although Sedgewick had published little, his dissertation had won an award at Harvard, his Alexander Lecture, *Of Irony, Especially in Drama* (1934), was recognized as a substantial piece of scholarship, and he was renowned for his teaching. Larsen, a Rhodes scholar from British Columbia, had attended Oxford and completed all the work for an edition of George Peele when he fell afoul of his supervisor. He returned to Canada without the degree, but his excellent work was incorporated in the Yale edition of *The Life and Works of George Peele* (1952), edited by Charles Tyler Prouty and dedicated to Larsen.

3 'Thorleif Larsen: 1887–1960,' obituary, *Transactions of the Royal Society of Canada*, ser. 3, 55 (1960–1): 127–8, RDP 29-1.

4 Geoffrey Andrew had earned an Oxford B.A. in history but was entitled to list himself as an M.A. because an Oxford graduate may obtain this degree upon payment of a fee.

5 Lee Stewart, *'It's Up to You': Women at UBC in the Early Years*, 76–7.

6 In the mid-fifties, the B.C. novelist Ethel Wilson told William Fredeman, then a new member of the English Department, that Sedgewick 'hated women' (William Fredeman, interview, 18 December 1997).

7 Jean Skelton MacLeod: '... once accepted, a woman became a person as far as he was concerned – there was no hostility or coldness' (quoted from G.P.V. Akrigg Papers, UBC, in Margery Fee, 'Puck's Green England and

the Professor of English: Post-Colonial Fantasies at the University of British Columbia,' *University of Toronto Quarterly* 64 [1990]: 406.

8 LS, letter L.

9 William Robbins to R.D., letter, 8 September 1947, RDP 5-11.

10 F.W. Watt to the author, letter, n.d. [ca. 15 May 2000].

11 David Williams, discussion, 7 May 1994.

12 'Profile of Garnett Sedgewick.'

13 F.W. Watt to the author, letter, n.d. [ca. 15 May 2000].

14 David Williams, discussion.

15 Garnett Sedgewick to Bob and Ruth apRoberts, letter, 19 September 1948, GGSP 5-3.

16 Craig Miller to the author, letter, 31 July 1993.

17 Edmund Morrison, interview, 9 August 1995.

18 Letter to Desmond Pacey, n.d., 'Thanksgiving' [ca. 13 October 1947], DPP 2-13.

19 F.W. Watt to the author, letter, n.d. [ca. 15 May 2000].

20 Jan de Bruyn, untitled tribute to Roy Daniells, *Acute News*, 25 May 1976 (reporting meeting in Quebec City at which R.D. was honoured), RDP 18-2.

21 Peter Howarth, interview, 19 March 1998.

22 Diary, 27 September 1946, RDP 11-24.

23 Ibid., 25, 27 October 1946.

24 Letter to Laurenda Francis, 31 January 1947, RDP 9-1.

25 Diary, 17 September 1947, RDP 11-24.

26 Laurenda Francis to R.D., letter, 21 September 1947, RDP 9-4.

27 Garnett Sedgewick to Bob and Ruth apRoberts, letter, 9 November 1947, GGSP 5-2.

28 Earle Birney to Lister Sinclair, letter, 2 November 1954, EBP 18-15.

29 Partially dated letter to Laurenda Francis, 24 May [1947], RDP 9-1.

30 Letter to Laurenda Francis, n.d. [1 May 1947].

31 Ibid., [ca. December 1947], RDP 9-4.

32 Ibid., mistakenly labelled 1947, [ca. 27 November 1946], RDP 9-1.

33 Diary, 8 July 1947, RDP 11-24.

34 Letter to Laurenda Francis, 23 February 1947, RDP 9-1.

35 George and Olga Volkoff, interview, 16 June 1992.

36 Eric P. Nicol to W.L. Mackenzie King, letter, 22 February 1947, RDP 5-9.

37 Diaries and Sundry Notes, 1 June 1947, in the possession of Laurenda Daniells.

38 Diaries and Sundry Notes, 1 January 1947.

39 Diaries and Sundry Notes, 13 January 1948, RDP 11-25.

40 Letter to Laurenda Francis, n.d. [ca. 4 February 1947], RDP 9-1.

41 Ibid., [ca. March 1947].

42 Laurenda Francis to R.D., partially dated letter, March 1947, RDP 9-4.

43 Ibid., May 1947.

44 Letter to Laurenda Francis, n.d. [ca. 1 June 1947], RDP 9-1.

45 Ibid., [ca. 6 January 1948].

46 Ibid., [ca. 24 March 1948], RDP 9-2.

47 Laurenda Francis to R.D., letter, 19 January 1947, RDP 9-4.

48 Letter to Laurenda Francis, 17 January 1947, RDP 9-1.

49 Diary, 16 August 1947, RDP 11-24.

50 Letter to Laurenda Francis, n.d. [9 December 1947], RDP 9-2.

51 Ibid., [ca. 29 January 1948].

52 Laurenda Francis to R.D., letter, 13 April 1948, RDP 9-4.

53 Letter to Laurenda Francis, n.d. [ca. May 1948], RDP 9-2.

54 Garnett Sedgewick to Robert and Ruth apRoberts, letter, 13 June 1948, GGSP 5-3.

55 Diary, 1 July 1948, RDP 11-25.

56 F.W. Watt to the author, letter, n.d. [ca. 15 May 2000].

57 Letter to Laurenda Francis, n.d. [ca. 11 February 1948], RDP 9-2.

58 Ogden Turner, interview, ca. April 1994. Turner recalled this incident with Maynard.

59 *Deeper into the Forest*, 19.

60 Fredelle Bruser Maynard, *The Tree of Life*, 65. Maynard's voice, like Shakespeare's Antony's, was 'propertied / As all the tuned spheres ... But when he meant to quail, and shake the Orb, / He was a rattling thunder.'

61 Max Maynard, 'Modern Enigma,' *Manitoba Arts Review* 4, no. 3 (Spring 1945): 32–3.

62 Garnett Sedgewick, typescript, CBC broadcast, 26 January 1949, 1–2, RDP 29-3.

63 Hugo McPherson, 'Roy Daniells: Humanist,' *British Columbia Library Quarterly* 24, no. 1 (July 1960): 30; W.G. Stobie, 'Two Volumes of Canadian Poetry,' *Winnipeg Free Press*, 12 February 1949, RDP 29-3.

64 James Reaney, 'Two Canadian Poets in Fine New Series,' *Toronto Telegram*, 2 April 1949, RDP 29-3.

65 Herbert Davis to R.D., letter, 4 January 1949, RDP 6-6.

66 Mabel Mackenzie to R.D., letter, 17 February 1949, RDP 6-6.

67 Desmond Pacey to R.D., letter, 24 January 1949, RDP 6-6.

68 James Reaney, interview, 9 April 1996; Eli Mandel to R.D., letter, n.d. [ca. 1963], RDP 7-19.

69 Phyllis Webb, inscription inside front cover, *Even Your Right Eye.*

70 Partially dated letter to mother, 26 December [1949], RDP 40-21.
71 Diary, 17 December 1949, RDP 11-25.

Chapter 15: The New Head

1 William Robbins, interview, 11 June 1992.
2 Edward Morrison, interview, 8 August 1995.
3 G.P.V. Akrigg, interview, 11 December 1997.
4 Garnett Sedgewick to Bob and Ruth apRoberts, letter, 6 April 1948, GGSP 5-2.
5 Letter to Laurenda Francis, n.d. [ca. 30 January 1948], RDP 9-1.
6 William Robbins, interview.
7 David Williams, discussion, 7 May 1994.
8 Esther Birney, interview, 16 August 1995.
9 F.W. Watt to the author, letter, n.d. [ca. 15 May 2000].
10 Daniells had been called in by the president to persuade the family not to take formal legal action against the professor. During this period, homosexuality was considered a crime, punishable by imprisonment.
11 Ira Dilworth to R.D., letter, 11 April 1948, RDP 6-2.
12 E.K. Brown to R.D., letter, 3 January 1948, RDP 6-1.
13 N.A.M. MacKenzie to R.D., letter, 6 February 1948, RDP 6-1.
14 Letter to Laurenda Francis, n.d. [ca. February 1948], RDP 9-2.
15 LS, letter L.
16 'Profile of Garnett Sedgewick.'
17 LS, letter L.
18 'Profile of Garnett Sedgewick.'
19 Jacob Zilber, interview, 27 January 1998.
20 Hilda Thomas, interview, 15 June 1995.
21 Earle Birney to R.D., letter, 16 April 1948, RDP 6-2.
22 Information from Hilda Thomas interview.
23 'Bad[minton] with Birney in eve. Beat him after grand struggle' (diary, 31 October 1932, RDP 11-10).
24 Gwladys Downes, interview, 27 July 1998.
25 Earle Birney to Lister Sinclair, letter, n.d. [1949], EBP 18-14.
26 Allan Pritchard, interview, 10 January 1996.
27 Edward Morrison, interview.
28 M.W. Steinberg, interview, 23 August 1995.
29 Elspeth Cameron, *Earle Birney*, 352.
30 Earle Birney to Stuart Kirby, letter, 23 April 1959, EBP 12-43.
31 Birney wrote to Elizabeth Campbell (7 August 1948) saying that he had

experimented with homosexuality: and his biographer, Elspeth Cameron, states that Birney had a brief affair with Frank Wilcox, an American professor in the English Department at UBC in the late twenties (Cameron, 50). Esther Birney believes that her husband had a brief affair with Garnett Sedgewick in the thirties, a relationship briefly suggested in *Down the Long Table* (interview, 16 August 1995).

32 M.W. Steinberg, interviews, 7 July 1992, 14 January 1998.
33 Earle Birney to Lister Sinclair, letter, 9 November 1948, EBP 18-14.
34 Peter Howarth, interview, 19 March 1998.
35 M.W. Steinberg, interview, 14 January 1998.
36 Ibid.
37 Letter to Laurenda Francis, n.d. [18 April 1947], RDP 9-1.
38 F.R. Scott, 'A Lass in Wonderland,' in *The Collected Poems*, 264.
39 Esther Birney, interview, 30 June 1995.
40 Edward Morrison, interview, 8 August 1995; Phyllis Webb, interview, 4 September 1996.
41 Earle Birney to Lister Sinclair, letter, 2 November 1954, EBP 18-15.
42 Earle Birney to Geoffrey Andrew, letter, 18 December 1951, EBP 8-9.
43 Letter to Earle Birney, 30 September 1952, EBP 8-10.
44 Earle Birney to N.A.M. MacKenzie, letter, 18 March 1955, EBP 13A-77a; 6 March 1961, EBP 13A-78.
45 'Geoff [Andrew] shocked me a bit with the fact that salary increases granted by the Board are Daniells $100, James $200, Soward $300, Birney $800. A jolt I must confess' (diary, 26 April 1955, RDP 11-30).
46 Diary, 30 September 1952, RDP 11-27.
47 Craig Miller, interview, 29 December 1993.
48 Earle Birney, interview, 6 October 1975.
49 Dean Sperrin Chant to R.D., letter, 18 February 1954, RDP 7-3.

Chapter 16: 'The Revolt of the Dukes'

1 M.W. Steinberg, interview, 8 July 1992.
2 Earle Birney to Herman Singer, letter, 'Good Friday,' [April] 1954, EBP, 18-31.
3 Ibid.
4 Notes beginning '1. Welcome meeting at last' [1954], EBP 8-10.
5 Earle Birney, partially dated interview, October 1980.
6 M.W. Steinberg, discussion, 1954, 23 August 1995.
7 Earle Birney to Herman Singer, 'Good Friday,' 1954, EBP 18-31; and to Pat and John Wardroper, 'Easter Friday,' 1954; and to Rosemary Baxter, 20 May 1954; as reported in Elspeth Cameron's *Earle Birney*, 352.

8 Earle Birney to Herman Singer, letter, 'Good Friday,' [April] 1954, EBP 18–31.

9 Ibid., 5 October 1954.

10 William Robbins to R.D., letter, 27 June 1954, RDP 6-18.

11 Diary, 6 August 1954, RDP 11-29.

12 Ibid., 18 August 1954.

13 G.P.V. Akrigg, interview, 11 December 1997.

14 Diary, 2 October 1954, RDP 11-29.

15 Ibid., 29 October 1954.

16 Ibid., 15 November 1954.

17 Edward Morrison, interview, 8 August 1995.

18 Diary, 30 October 1954, RDP 11-29.

19 M.W. Steinberg, interview, 23 August 1995.

20 Phyllis Hughes Ronimois, discussion, April 1998.

21 William Robbins, interview, 11 June 1992.

22 M.W. Steinberg, interview, 7 July 1992.

23 G.P.V. Akrigg, interview, 30 June 1992.

24 UBC Faculty of Arts Committee, 'Duties and Responsibilities of Heads of Departments,' draft, 22 October 1956, RDP 7-4.

25 E.J. Pratt to Earle Birney, 8 November 1955, EBP 15–45. This information also from Eve Whitaker, interview, August 1994.

26 Earle Birney, *Down the Long Table*, 153.

27 This connection may have been brought to Birney's attention by one of the then-contemporary Sather Classical Lectures by E.R. Dobbs, published as *The Greeks and the Irrational* (1951).

Chapter 17: Developing English

1 A.S.P. Woodhouse to R.D., letter, 15 March 1948, RDP 6-1.

2 Ibid., 24 January 1949, RDP 6-6.

3 Malcolm Ross to the author, letter, 5 May 1995.

4 M.W. Steinberg, interview, 14 January 1998.

5 Allan Pritchard to the author, letter, 11 June 1998.

6 Robin S. Harris, *English Studies at Toronto: A History*, 291.

7 York University, discussion with several faculty women, ca. 1971–2.

8 A.S.P. Woodhouse to Allan Pritchard, letter, 10 March 1958, RDP 7-14.

9 W.E. Fredeman, interview, 18 December 1997.

10 Fred Flahiff, interview, 29 October 1998.

11 The 1956 UBC calendar indicates that the English Department faculty included ten full professors: Daniells, Andrew, Birney, John Creighton,

Hunter Lewis, Mawdsley, Morrison, Read, Robbins, and Watters. All were Canadian with Ph.D.'s, except for Andrew, Lewis, and Read, whose highest degree was an M.A. There were five associate professors: four Canadians, G.P.V. Akrigg, R.C. Cragg, Dorothy Somerset, and M.W. Steinberg; and one American, J.G. Spaulding. All had Ph.D.'s except for Somerset, who had an M.A. The assistant professors were Edna Baxter, Jan de Bruyn, Ruth Humphrey, and Marion B. Smith. All were Canadian, but only Smith had a Ph.D. There were eight instructors (C.S. Burhans, Mabel Mackenzie, Hugo McPherson, C.W. Miller, A.E. Piloto, A.E. Sawyer, D.G. Stephens, and J. Waterhouse), and all but one, Burhans, were Canadian; most had an M.A. At the bottom of the heap were six lecturers, three with B.A.'s and three with M.A.'s: five were Canadian, among them Michael Booth and A.D. Pritchard; and one, poet M.W. La Follette, was American. R.J. Baker is not listed in the 1956–7 calendar, but he appears in the 1957–8 calendar as an instructor.

12 W.E. Fredeman, interview, 18 December 1997.
13 Ibid.
14 Elliot Gose to the author, letter, 8 June 1998.
15 G.P.V. Akrigg, interview, 11 December 1997.
16 William Robbins to R.D., letter, 9 June 1955, RDP 7-3.
17 W.E. Fredeman, interview.
18 Marjorie Garson, 'ACUTE, the First Twenty-Five Years 1957–1982,' ACUTE internal document, 1983, 2.
19 Letter to Desmond Pacey, 28 November 1956, DPP 2-14.
20 Garson, 'ACUTE, the First Twenty-Five Years 1957–1982,' 3–4.
21 Hugo McPherson, 'Roy Daniells: Humanist,' *British Columbia Library Quarterly* 24, no. 1 (July 1960): 34–5.
22 Diary, 16 June 1957, RDP 11-32.
23 Jean-Charles Falardeau, interview, 22 November 1979.
24 Earle Birney to 'Colleagues,' letter, 23 October 1957, EBP 8-13.
25 Earle Birney to Sperrin Chant, letter, 19 February 1957, EBP 8-13.
26 W.E. Fredeman, interview.
27 Allan Pritchard to the author, letter, 11 June 1998.
28 Laurenda Daniells to the author, letter, 21 July 1998.
29 Information from William Fredeman, interview, 18 December 1997.
30 M.W. Steinberg, interview, 14 January 1998.
31 Jean Mallinson, interview, 22 February 1998.
32 Jean Mallinson, 'Paradise Lost,' unpublished short story.
33 F.W. Watt to author, letter, n.d. [ca. 15 May 2000].
34 Hilda Thomas, interview, 15 June 1995.

35 Sheila Watson to R.D., letter, 19 September 1955, RDP 7-3.
36 Diary, 30 January 1956, RDP 11-31.
37 Information from Edmund Morrison, interview, 8 August 1995.
38 Marion Smith, typed verse attached by Birney to draft of undated letter to R.D., EBP 8–16.
39 A.S.P. Woodhouse to R.D., letter, 15 March 1948, RDP 6-1.
40 Mabel Mackenzie to R.D., letter, 3 November 1948, RDP 6-4.
41 Ibid., 17 February 1949, RDP 6-6.
42 Francis (Frazer) Baker, interview, 10 September 1993.
43 Mabel Mackenzie to Earle Birney, letter, n.d. [dated 'January or February 1949' by Birney], EBP 13A-72.
44 Laurenda Daniells overheard her husband's responses to A.S.P. Woodhouse's telephone call (Laurenda Daniells, interview, 10 September 1993).
45 Edmund Morrison, interview, 9 August 1995.
46 Diary, 12 May 1954, RDP 11-29.
47 Garson, 'ACUTE.'
48 Letter to A.S.P. Woodhouse, 17 March 1945, RDP 4-16.
49 *Milton, Mannerism and Baroque*, 167.
50 Diary, 22 June 1953, RDP 11-28.
51 Preceding information on HRC from [Viviane F. Launay,] *The Humanities Research Council of Canada / The Canadian Federation for the Humanities 1943– 1983: A Short History*, 1–11.
52 Letter to daughters, Susan and Sara, n.d. [November 1957], RDP 7-13.
53 Susan and Sara Daniells, interview, 1 April 1996.

Chapter 18: A Canadian Literature

1 Marshall McLuhan to R.D., letter, 3 October 1944, RDP 4-14.
2 Northrop Frye, 'Conclusion,' in Klinck et al., eds, *Literary History of Canada*, 824.
3 A.J.M. Smith, 'The Poet,' in *Writing in Canada: Proceedings of the Canadian Writers' Conference Held at Queen's University July 1955*, ed. George Whalley, 16.
4 Jay Macpherson to F.R. Scott, letter, 1 August 1955, FRSP.
5 Eli Mandel, interview, 5 January 1975.
6 Frank Scott, 'Introduction,' in Whalley, ed., *Writing in Canada*, 8–9; Malcolm Ross, interview, 25 May 1981. Ross had earlier contacted McClelland, who had been reluctant to proceed with a reprinting venture. The effect of the Kingston conference was thus persuasive.
7 F.R. Scott, 'The Canadian Writers' Conference,' *University of Toronto Quarterly* 25 (1955): 101–2.

8 George Woodcock, 'A View of Canadian Criticism,' *Dalhousie Review* 35 (1955): 223.

9 'Literature: Poetry and the Novel,' in Park, ed., *The Culture of Contemporary Canada*, 18, 5, 26.

10 Ibid., 44.

11 Kevin Brooks, 'Writing Instruction in Western Canadian Universities: A History of Nation-Building and Professionalism,' 172.

12 R.E. Watters to Carl F. Klinck, letter, quoted in *Giving Canada a Literary History*, 92.

13 Carl F. Klinck, Paper for graduate seminar at Leeds University, 3 March 1965, CFKP P704.

14 Carl F. Klinck to Marsh Jeanneret, letter, 17 October 1956, CFKP.

15 R.E. Watters to Carl F. Klinck, letter, 30 March 1959, CFKP 10–10J:4.

16 Letter to Carl F. Klinck, 30 June 1962, CFKP P716.

17 Ibid., 24 September 1962, CFKP 1A-5 D 4.

18 Ibid., 13 November 1962, CFKP 1A-4 D 6.

19 Ibid., 4 January 1963, CFKP Box 1A File 7 F 1.

20 Carl F. Klinck, Notes for a Proposed Essay on Roy Daniells, CFKP P716.

21 Letter to Carl F. Klinck, 2 January 1963, CFKP P716.

22 Ibid., 4 January 1963, 1A-7 F 1.

23 Carl F. Klinck, Notes for a Proposed Essay on Roy Daniells, CFKP P716.

24 Inglis Bell, interview, ca. 1973–4.

25 Koerner Foundation Application, in the possession of Laurenda Daniells; Laurenda Daniells, interview, June 1998.

26 George Woodcock, *Beyond the Blue Mountains: An Autobiography*, 65; 'The Tentative Confessions of a Prospective Editor,' *British Columbia Library Quarterly* 28, no. 1 (1959): 17–21.

27 Doug Fetherling, 'Literary Beaver,' *Canadian Forum*, March 1998, 23–6.

28 George Woodcock, 'Canadian Literature,' in *Beyond the Blue Mountains: An Autobiography*, 82–3. Woodcock explains that when he was invited to become editor of *Canadian Literature* by a committee headed by Roy Daniells, he felt that although he was an experienced editor, he did not have sufficient knowledge of the Canadian literary scene: accordingly, the committee agreed to advise him if needed in this area. Daniells, chair of this committee, appears to have fulfilled this function up to the seventies. His diary records that on 29 August 1967 he had lunch scheduled with 'Geo. Woodcock, Sandra Djwa, Don Stephens.' This lunch was called by Daniells at the UBC Faculty Club, where he asked me to write an article, 'Computers and Canadian Poetry,' published in *Canadian Literature*, no. 46 (Autumn 1970): 43–54.

Chapter 19: The Lions' Den

1 Introduction, *Milton, Mannerism and Baroque*, 3.
2 Letter to Desmond Pacey, 18 November 1959, DPP 2-4.
3 Diary, 10 and 13 December 1959, RDP 11-34.
4 Ibid., 25 December 1959, RDP 11-34.
5 Letter to Albert Trueman, draft, 6 August 1960, RDP 7-16.
6 *Milton, Mannerism, and Baroque*, 14.
7 Diary, 5 and 8 March 1960, RDP 11-35.
8 'An Inquiry into Some Formal Problems in English Non-dramatic Literature of the Seventeenth Century,' 20.
9 Sara (Daniells) Rilkoff, interview, 4 March 2000.
10 Diary, 17 March 1960, RDP 11-35.
11 Ibid., 20 October 1959, RDP 11-34
12 Diary, 2 January 1960, RDP 11-35.
13 Ibid., 4 and 8 January 1960, RDP 11-35.
14 Ibid., 19 January 1960, RDP 11-35.
15 Ibid., 2 March 1960.
16 Trip Diary, 9 May 1960, RDP 11–35
17 Ibid., 29 May 1960.
18 Ibid., 17 July 1960.
19 Letter to Carl F. Klinck, 14 September 1960; 30 June 1962, CFKP P716.
20 'Sonnet 8,' in *Deeper into the Forest*, 34.
21 Craig Miller, interview, 29 December 1993.
22 Diary, 6 December 1961, RDP 11-36.
23 Fred Stockholder to the author, letter, 3 January 2001.
24 Philip Pinkus, interview, 6 November 1994.
25 Ibid.
26 Unattributed verse, in 1961 correspondence file, RDP 7-17.
27 Diary, 1 January 1961, RDP 11-36.
28 Ibid., 3 January 1961.
29 Ibid., 29 May 1962, RDP 11-37.
30 Hilda Thomas, interview, 15 June 1995.
31 Earle Birney to R.D., letter, 22 October 1961, RDP 7-17.
32 Laurenda Daniells, interview, 19 July 1999.
33 'Psalm 37,' in *The Chequered Shade*, 41.
34 Louis Dudek, Review of *The Chequered Shade*, *Canadian Literature*, no. 16 (Spring 1963): 67.
35 The course was developed around the poetry text by Cleanth Brooks and Robert Penn Warren, *Understanding Poetry*.

36 Ellen Tallman, interview, 19 May 1998.
37 Jane Rule, interview, 22 January 1998.
38 Earle Birney, interview, ca. 1980.
39 Earle Birney to R.D., letter, 7 July 1962, RDP 7-18B.
40 Irving Layton to R.D., letter, 7 May 1962, Faculty of Arts, Dean's Office 7-28, UBC Special Collections.
41 Elspeth Cameron, *Earle Birney: A Life*, 427.
42 Letter to Dean Sperrin Chant, 17 May 1962, RDP 7-18B.
43 Earle Birney to R.D., letter, 7 July 1962, RDP 7-18B.
44 H.G. Files, copy of original letter, 17 May 1962, RDP 7-18B.
45 Irving Layton to R.D., letter, 14 June 1962, RDP 7-18B.
46 Frank Davey, 'Brief Review,' in *Tish 1–19*, 273.
47 Desmond Pacey to Irving Layton, letter, 18 June 1962, quoted in J.M.D. Pacey, 'An Unexpected Alliance' (Ph.D. diss., University of British Columbia, 1994).
48 Irving Layton to R.D., letter, 20 June 1962, RDP 7-18B.
49 Earle Birney to R.D., letter, 7 July 1962, RDP 7-18B.
50 Frank Davey, discussion, 7 June 1999.
51 Earle Birney, 'Testimony of a Canadian Educational Leader,' in *The Collected Poems of Earle Birney*, 2:58; Alan Adamson, interview, 16 March 1997. Adamson's first wife, Margaret Bjornson, confirmed that Daniells had told her of this incident relating to Sylvia Johnstone.
52 Letter to President Macdonald, 21 January 1964, RDP 7-20.
53 Earle Birney to President MacKenzie, letter, 11 Dec. 1961, EBP 13A-78.
54 Cameron, *Earl Birney*, 461.
55 Ibid., 462.
56 F.W. Watt to the author, letter, n.d. [ca. 15 May 2000].
57 Robert Harlow to R.D., letter, 29 December 1970, RDP 8-3.
58 Frank Davey, discussion, 7 June 1999.
59 Allan Pritchard, interview, 10 January 1996; Earle Birney, interview, ca. 1977.
60 LS, letter X.
61 Jane Rule, interview, 26 January 1998.
62 Frank Davey, discussion, 7 June 1999.
63 Jane Rule, interview, 26 January 1998.

Chapter 20: Academic Publishing

1 Draft of letter to Kaspar Naegle, 4 January 1964, RDP 18-41.
2 Letter to Murdo Mackinnon, 3 January 1964, RDP 7-20.

3 'An Inquiry into Some Formal Problems in English Non-dramatic Literature of the Seventeenth Century,' 32.

4 *Milton, Mannerism and Baroque*, 88.

5 Ibid., 166.

6 A.S.P. Woodhouse, 'The Argument of Milton's "Comus,"' *University of Toronto Quarterly* 11 (1941): 46–71.

7 *Milton, Mannerism and Baroque*, 7.

8 Ibid., 33.

9 Ibid., 69.

10 Ibid., 81.

11 Sid Warhaft, Review of *Milton, Mannerism and Baroque*, *Queen's Quarterly* 71 (1964): 137–8.

12 Marshall McLuhan and Harley Parker *Towards the Vanishing Point*, 17–19.

13 Paul Stanwood to the author, letter, 2 December 1993.

14 'The Mannerist Element in English Literature,' *University of Toronto Quarterly* 36 (1966): 1–11; 'Milton and Renaissance Art,' in *John Milton: Introductions*, ed. John Broadbent, 186–207.

15 Richard Levin to R.D., letter, 5 January 1969.

16 Northrop Frye, 'Preface to an Uncollected Anthology,' in *The Bush Garden: Essays on the Canadian Imagination*, 163.

17 Ibid., 164.

18 'Confederation to the First World War,' in *Literary History of Canada*, ed. Carl F. Klinck et al., 195.

19 Ibid., 195, 199.

20 *Literary History of Canada*, 398.

21 Ibid., 821, 846.

22 Ibid., 848–9.

23 Carl F. Klinck, Talk given to graduate students at Leeds University, 1965, CFKP P704; Carl F. Klink to R.D., letter, 3 July 1972, CFKP P716.

24 Carl F. Klinck, interview [ca. May 1981].

25 Letter to Carl F. Klinck, 25 October 1971, CFKP P716.

26 A.J.M. Smith, 'A Survey of English-Canadian Letters,' *University of Toronto Quarterly* 35 (1965): 107–16.

27 Lionel Stevenson, 'Literature in an Emerging Nation, *South Atlantic Quarterly* 64 (1965): 394–9.

28 'Emily Carr,' in *Our Living Tradition*, 4th ser., ed. Robert L. McDougall, 121, 126, 129.

29 Maria Tippett, *Emily Carr: A Biography*; Paula Blanchard, *The Life of Emily Carr*.

30 'The Special Quality,' in 'Ned Pratt: Two Recollections,' *Canadian Literature*, no. 21 (Summer 1964): 11.

31 'The Long-Enduring Spring,' *Canadian Literature*, no. 12 (Spring 1962): 6–14.

32 Diary, 2 June 1967, RDP 11-40.

33 'Literary Studies in Canada,' in *Scholarship in Canada, 1967: Achievement and Outlook*, ed. R.H. Hubbard, with an introduction by Watson Kirkconnell, 30, 33, 39.

34 'High Colonialism in Canada,' *Canadian Literature*, no. 40 (Spring 1969): 14.

35 'National Identity in English-Canadian Writing,' in *National Identity*, ed. K.L. Goodwin, 85.

36 Ibid., 87.

37 W.H. and Margaret New, interview, 23 January 2000.

38 *Alexander Mackenzie and the North West*, 13–14.

Chapter 21: University Professor

1 A.S.P. Woodhouse to R.D., letter, 14 October 1964.

2 Diary, 1 November 1964, RDP 11-38; draft of review of A.S.P. Woodhouse's *The Heavenly Muse: A Preface to Milton*, RDP 16-32.

3 '"He burnished ideas till they shone like revealed truth ...,"' *Varsity Graduate* (Spring 1961): 72.

4 F.W. Watt to author, n.d. [ca. 15 May 2000].

5 Diary, 28 December 1964, RDP 11-38.

6 Ibid., 19 February 1965, RDP 11-39.

7 Letter to Gordon Shrum, 23 October 1963, RDP 18-41.

8 Diary, 1 January 1965, RDP 11-39.

9 Edward Morrison, interview, 9 August 1995.

10 Diary, 11 May 1965, RDP 11-39.

11 Ibid., 30 June 1965.

12 Ibid., 19 October 1965.

13 Ibid., 21 and 22 November 1965.

14 Walter Koerner to R.D., letter, 17 November 1965, RDP 7-21.

15 Diary, 14 February 1966, RDP 11-40.

16 Ibid., 10 March 1966.

17 Ibid., 24 March 1996, RDP 11-40.

18 LS, letter K-2.

19 Ian Ross, interview, 10 February 2000.

20 See Wilfred Cude, 'Going Down into Death: A Reading of "Three lecture hours per week,"' in *Inside the Poem: Essays and Poems in Honour of Donald Stephens*, ed. W.H. New, 101–6.

21 Dorothy Somerset to R.D., letter, 14 June 1968, RDP 7-24.
22 Fredelle Bruser Maynard to R.D., letter, 20 January 1973, RDP 8-9.
23 Peter Howarth, interview, 19 March 1998.
24 Nancy L. Newsom to R.D., letter, 23 February 1961, RDP 7-17.
25 David Duerksen to R.D., letter, 11 June 1979, RDP 8-21.
26 Ibid., 13 December 1970, RDP 8-3.
27 Desmond Pacey, citation, RDP 10-7.
28 Diary, 14 October 1959, RDP 11-34 .
29 Ibid., 7 August 1971, RDP 11-41 .
30 Ibid., 3 October 1971, RDP 11-41.
31 Letter to Desmond Pacey, 1 January 1971, DPP 2-16.
32 'The Cultural History of Canada,' *Transactions of the Royal Society of Canada*, ser. 4, 10 (1972): 3–11.
33 Letter to Frances Halpenny, 14 January 1971, RDP 13-14.
34 Letter to Desmond Pacey, 11 February 1972, DPP 2-16.
35 Ibid.
36 Ibid.
37 P.D. Fleck, address, *ACUTE News*, 25 May 1976, RDP 18-2.
38 Rudolph Habenicht to R.D., letter, 10 February 1972, RDP 8-6.
39 Alexander Lectures, 5, 7, 8, 9 March 1972, RDP 13-13.
40 W.J. Keith, interview, 7 May 1994.
41 Diary, 11 March 1972, RDP 11-41.
42 Robert Finch to R.D., letter, 15 August 1972, RDP 8-8.
43 Letter to Desmond Pacey, 20 April 1972, DPP 2-16.
44 Diary, 24 May 1972, RDP 11-41.
45 Robert Finch to R.D., letter, 22 September 1972, RDP 8-8.
46 Contained in 'Carolingian Festival,' RDP 18-9.
47 Letter to Carl F. Klinck, 8 September 1972, CFKP P716.
48 Carl F. Klinck to R.D., drafted letter, n.d. [ca. Fall 1972], CFKP P716.
49 Letter to Carl F. Klinck, 22 September 1972, CFKP P716.
50 Letter to Carl F. Klinck, 6 February 1974, CFKP P716.
51 Letter to Carl F. Klinck, 5 August 1975, CFKP P716; notes for *Giving Canada a Literary History* and for Klinck's proposed essay on Roy Daniells, CFKP P716. When it became apparent to Klinck that he would not be able to undertake the latter essay, he passed on several files of his correspondence with Daniells for my future use. Some of these letters have provided the basis of this treatment of the *Literary History*. All Klinck's letters have now been archived at the University of Western Ontario.
52 Diary, 29 May 1973, RDP 11-41.

53 Ibid., 28 May 1973, RDP 11-41.
54 Vince Venables to R.D., letter, 24 March 1973, RDP 8-9.
55 Report on Simon Fraser University English Department [ca. February 1974], RDP 18-40.
56 Letter to Desmond Pacey, 20 April 1972, DPP 2-16.
57 Fredelle Bruser Maynard to R.D., letter, 20 January 1973, RDP 8-9.
58 Max Maynard to R.D., letter, 10 February 1973, RDP 8-9.
59 P.D. Fleck to R.D., letter, 9 February 1976, RDP 18-3.
60 Proceedings of ACUTE conference, 25 May 1976.

Chapter 22: The River of Time

1 Henry Vaughan, 'They are all gone into the world of light,' in *The Complete Poetry of Henry Vaughan*, ed. French Fogle, 270–1.
2 Diary, 6 and 9 December 1974, RDP 11-41.
3 R.D., dinner conversation, ca. 1971.
4 John Milton, *Paradise Lost*, Book iii, in *Complete Poems and Major Prose*, ed. Merritt Y. Hughes, lines 96–9.
5 Paul Stanwood, discussion, 11 December 1994.
6 David Duerksen to R.D., letter, 11 June 1979, RDP 8-21.
7 Letter to Jim Manly, 22 December 1973, RDP 8-12.
8 Northrop Frye to R.D., letter, 12 September 1973, RDP 8-10.
9 Ibid., copy of letter, 20 December 1973, NFP 13(9).
10 Diary, 6 December 1974, RDP 11-41.
11 Susan Daniells to parents, letter, 1 January 1975, RDP 8-13.
12 Letter to Desmond Pacey, 12 September 1965, DPP 2-15.
13 Ibid., 19 January 1975, DPP 2-16.
14 Desmond Pacey to R.D., letter, 21 January 1975, RDP [no box number].
15 Northrop Frye to R.D., letter, 19 March 1975, RDP 8-13; Hans Werner Bartsch, ed., *'Kerygma and Myth' by Rudolph Bultmann and Five Critics*, trans. Reginald H. Fuller, 12, 35.
16 Northrop Frye to R.D., letter, 1 April 1975, RDP 8-13.
17 Northrop Frye, Introduction, *The Great Code: The Bible and Literature*, xi.
18 Notes. Daniells had earlier recorded this view of Huxley in 'Diaries and Sundry Notes, 1947, 1957, 1960.'
19 'Readers' Confidential Reports,' n.d. [ca. March 1975], RDP 8-13.
20 Allan Pritchard to the author, letter, 11 June 1998.
21 Laurenda Daniells, interview, June 1998.
22 Convocation address, 29 May 1975.

23 Diary, 7 July 1975, RDP 11-42.
24 'Desmond Pacey,' *Canadian Literature*, no. 66 (Autumn 1975): 11–13.
25 Diary, 10 July 1975, RDP 11-42.
26 Ibid., 5 December 1975, RDP 11-42.
27 Ibid., 19 December 1975.
28 Ibid., 23 January 1976, RDP 11-43.
29 Robert Finch to R.D., letter, 25 February 1976, RDP 8-15.
30 Ibid., 17 March 1976.
31 Letter to Robert Finch, 4 February 1976, RDP 8-15.
32 Ibid., 4 March 1976.
33 Robert Finch to R.D., letter, 11 April 1976, RDP 8-15.
34 Letter to Robert Finch, 19 April 1976, RDP 8-15.
35 Robert Finch to R.D., letter, 24 July 1976, RDP 8-15.
36 Ibid., 20 August 1976, RDP 8-16.
37 Letter to Robert Finch, 23 September 1976, RDP 8-16.
38 Robert Finch to R.D., letter, 25 September 1976, RDP 8-16.
39 Letter to Robert Finch, 25 September 1976, RDP 8-16.
40 Robert Finch to R.D., letter, 13 October 1976, RDP 8-16.
41 Laurenda Daniells, interview, 7 August 1993.
42 Fredelle Bruser Maynard to R.D., letter, 23 December 1973, RDP 8-10.
43 Max Maynard to R.D., letter, n.d. [December 1979], RDP 8-21.
44 LS, letter O.
45 Ibid., letter X.
46 Ibid., letter R.
47 Ibid., letter V.
48 Ibid., letter W.
49 Letter to Carl F. Klinck, 21 May 1976, CFKP P716.
50 R.D., interview, 1 July 1979.
51 Jan Gorak, 'Northrop Frye and the Visionary Canon,' in *The Making of the Modern Canon: Genesis and Crisis of a Literary Idea*, 120–52.
52 Letter to Carl F. Klinck, 25 November 1977, CFKP P716.
53 Ibid., 8 June 1978, CFKP P716.
54 Letter to Carl F. Klinck, 21 June 1978, CFKP P716; Hans Werner Bartsch, ed., *'Kerygma and Myth' by Rudolph Bultmann and Five Critics*, trans. Reginald H. Fuller, 14–15.
55 Diary, 9 July 1979, 2 February 1979, RDP 11-44.
56 Ibid., 7 June 1978; 9 April 1979.
57 Laurenda Daniells, discussion, 29 April 1998.
58 Ibid.

59 *The Current of Time*, privately printed, 1981 (earlier title, 'Now I saw in my dream'), RDP 16-40.
60 Craig Miller, discussion, 6 April 1999.
61 'Plymouth Brother,' *Canadian Literature*, no. 90 (Autumn 1981): 35, 31.
62 Ibid., 31.
63 Ibid., 34–5.

Bibliography

Books, Critical Essays, Poems, and Reviews by Roy Daniells

'Acta Octobria.' *Acta Victoriana* 60, no. 2 (Nov. 1935): 4.

Alexander Mackenzie and the North West. London: Faber and Faber, 1969; Toronto: Oxford University Press, 1971.

'Baroque Form in English Literature.' *University of Toronto Quarterly* 14 (1945): 393–407.

'A Century and a Half of English Lyricism.' M.A. thesis, University of Toronto, 1931. RDP 16-5.

The Chequered Shade. Toronto: McClelland & Stewart, 1963.

'The Christian Drama of T.S. Eliot.' *Canadian Forum* 16, no. 187 (Aug. 1936): 20–1.

'Confederation to the First World War.' In *Literary History of Canada: Canadian Literature in English*. Ed. Carl F. Klinck et al. Toronto: University of Toronto Press, 1965. 191–207.

'Crawford, Carman and D.C. Scott.' In *Literary History of Canada: Canadian Literature in English*. Ed. Carl F. Klinck et al. Toronto: University of Toronto Press, 1965. 406–21.

'The Cultural History of Canada.' *Transactions of the Royal Society of Canada*, ser. 4, 10 (1972): 3–11.

The Current of Time. Privately printed, 1981.

Deeper into the Forest. Toronto: McClelland & Stewart, 1948.

'Desmond Pacey.' *Canadian Literature*, no. 66 (Autumn 1975): 11–13.

'Drifted Words.' Verse review of *The Geographical History of America or the Relation of Human Nature to the Human Mind*. By Gertrude Stein. *Canadian Forum* 16, no. 193 (Feb. 1937): 27. [Published under the pseudonym 'Aquarius']

'Emily Carr.' In *Our Living Tradition*. 4th ser. Ed. Robert L. McDougall.
   Toronto: University of Toronto Press, 1962. 119–34.
'Ferdinand and Others: A Note on Individualism.' *Manitoba Arts Review* 1, no.
   3 (Spring 1939): 27–31.
'He burnished ideas till they shone like revealed truth ...' *Varsity Graduate*
   [University of Toronto] (Spring 1961): 69–74.
'High Colonialism in Canada.' *Canadian Literature*, no. 40 (Spring 1969): 5–16.
'Human Values and the Evolution of Society.' In *Our Debt to the Future*. Ed. D.
   Murray. Studia Varia, no. 2. Toronto: University of Toronto Press, 1958. 117–19.
'In the Labyrinth: A Note on Franz Kafka.' *Manitoba Arts Review* 3, no. 1
   (Spring 1942): 3–13.
'An Inquiry into Some Formal Problems in English Non-dramatic Literature of
   the Seventeenth Century.' Ph.D. diss. University of Toronto, 1937.
Introduction. *As for Me and My House*. By Sinclair Ross. Toronto: New Cana-
   dian Library Series. Toronto: McClelland & Stewart, 1957. v–x.
'La Dollabella.' *Canadian Forum* 17, no. 195 (April 1937): 16. [Published under
   the pseudonym 'Aquarius']
'Lampman and Roberts.' In *Literary History of Canada: Canadian Literature in
   English*. Ed. Carl F. Klinck et al. Toronto: University of Toronto Press, 1965.
   389–405.
'Literary Studies in Canada.' In *Scholarship in Canada, 1967: Achievement and
   Outlook*. Ed. R.H. Hubbard. Introd. Watson Kirkconnell. Toronto: University
   of Toronto Press, 1968. 29–39.
'The Long-Enduring Spring.' *Canadian Literature*, no. 12 (Spring 1962): 6–14.
'Look Homeward Angel.' *Saturday Night* 51, no. 48 (3 Oct. 1936): 1. [Published
   as 'Anonymous']
'The Mannerist Element in English Literature.' *University of Toronto Quarterly*
   36 (1966): 5–11.
'Milton and Renaissance Art.' In *John Milton: Introductions*. Ed. John
   Broadbent. Cambridge: Cambridge University Press, 1973. 186–207.
Milton, Mannerism and Baroque. Toronto: University of Toronto Press, 1963.
'Minor Poets 1880–1920.' In *Literary History of Canada: Canadian Literature in
   English*. Ed. Carl F. Klinck et al. Toronto: University of Toronto Press, 1965.
   422–30.
'A Modern Marvell.' *Canadian Forum* 16, no. 187 (Aug. 1936): 18. [Published
   under the pseudonym 'Aquarius']
'The Muse in Chains.' Review of *A Study in Education*. By Stephen Potter.
   Canadian Forum 17, no. 198 (July 1937): 143.
'National Identity in English-Canadian Writing.' In *National Identity*. Ed. K.L.
   Goodwin. London: Heinemann Educational Books, 1970. 76–88.

'Outline of Canadian Literature in English.' In *The Culture of Contemporary Canada*. Ed. Julian Park. Ithaca, NY: Cornell University Press, 1957. 1–88.

'Overture.' *Here and Now* 1, no. 3 (Jan. 1949): 5–8.

'Plymouth Brother.' *Canadian Literature*, no. 90 (Autumn 1981): 25–37.

'A Quarter-Century of the Quarterly.' *University of Toronto Quarterly* 25 (1955): 4–5.

A Serious and Pathetical Contemplation of the Mercies of God, in Several Most Devout and Sublime Thanksgivings for the Same. By Thomas Traherne. Ed. Roy Daniells. Toronto: University of Toronto Press, 1941.

'The Special Quality.' In 'Ned Pratt: Two Recollections.' *Canadian Literature*, no. 21 (Summer 1964): 6–12.

'Thorleif Larsen: 1887–1960' [obituary]. *Transactions of the Royal Society of Canada*, ser. 3, 55 (1960–1): 127–8.

'To a Generation Unemployed.' *Canadian Forum* 17, no. 189 (16 Oct. 1936): 10. [Published under the pseudonym 'Aquarius']

'To Sir O... D...' *Canadian Forum* 17, no. 203 (Dec. 1937): 216. [Published under the pseudonym 'Aquarius']

'T.S. Eliot and His Relation to T.E. Hulme.' *University of Toronto Quarterly* 2 (1932–3): 380–96.

Works by Other Authors

Akrigg, G.P.V. 'Sedgewick: The Man and His Achievement.' Eleventh Garnett Sedgewick Memorial Lecture. UBC Department of English, Vancouver, 1980.

Anderson, Benedict. *Imagined Communities: Reflections on the Origin and Spread of Nationalism*. Rev. ed. London and New York: Verso, 1983, 1991.

Arnold, Matthew. *Literature and Dogma: An Essay towards a Better Apprehension of the Bible*. London: Smith Elder, 1886.

Ayre, John. *Northrop Frye: A Biography*. Toronto: First Vintage Books, 1989.

Babbitt, Irving. *Literature and the American College: Essays in Defense of the Humanities*. Boston and New York: Houghton Mifflin Co., 1908.

– *Rousseau and Romanticism*. Boston: Houghton Mifflin Co., [1919] 1957.

Betcherman, Lita-Rose. *The Little Band*. Ottawa: Deneau, 1982.

Birney, Earle. *Down the Long Table*. Toronto: McClelland & Stewart, [1955] 1975.

– *The Collected Poems of Earle Birney*. 2 vols. Toronto: McClelland & Stewart, 1975.

Bissell, Claude. *Halfway up Parnassus: A Personal Account of the University of Toronto 1932–1971*. Toronto: University of Toronto Press, 1974.

Blanchard, Paula. *The Life of Emily Carr.* Vancouver and Toronto: Douglas & McIntyre, [1987], 1988.

Blondal, Patricia. *From Heaven with a Shout.* Toronto: McClelland & Stewart, 1962.

Bottrall, Margaret. *Every Man a Phoenix: Studies in Seventeenth-Century Autobiography.* London: John Murray, 1958.

Brooks, Cleanth, and Robert Penn Warren. *Understanding Poetry.* New York: Holt, Rinehart and Winston, [1960].

Brooks, Kevin. 'Writing Instruction in Western Canadian Universities: A History of Nation-Building and Professionalism.' Ph.D. diss., Iowa State University, 1997.

Bunyan, John. *The Pilgrim's Progress.* New York: Holt, Rinehart and Winston, 1961.

Bush, Douglas. 'A.S.P. Woodhouse: Scholar, Critic, Humanist.' In *Essays in English Literature from the Renaissance to the Victorian Age.* Ed. Millar MacLure and F.W. Watt. Toronto: University of Toronto Press, 1964. 320–33.

C.J.B. 'The Coming of the Lord Draweth Nigh': An Examination of the Scriptures on the Length of the 'Times of the Gentiles.' Kansas City, 1914.

Cameron, Elspeth. *Earle Birney: A Life.* Toronto: Viking Penguin Books Canada, 1994.

Clifford, James. '"Hanging Up Looking Glasses at Odd Corners": Ethnobiographical Prospects.' In *Studies in Biography.* Ed. Daniel Aaron. Cambridge, MA: Harvard University Press, 1978. 41–56.

Cude, Wilfred. 'Beyond Mrs. Bentley: A Study of *As for Me and My House.' Journal of Canadian Studies* 8, no. 1 (Feb. 1973): 3–18.

– 'Going Down into Death: A Reading of "Three lecture hours per week."' In *Inside the Poem: Essays and Poems in Honour of Donald Stephens.* Ed. W.H. New. Toronto: Oxford University Press, 1992. 101–6.

Daniells, Laurenda. 'Sally Ross.' In *Dictionary of Canadian Biography.* Vol. XI. Toronto: University of Toronto Press, 775–6.

Davey, Frank. 'Brief Review.' *Tish* 13 (14 Sept. 1962). Reprinted in *Tish 1–19.* Ed. Frank Davey. Vancouver: Talonbooks, 1975. 273–4.

Davis, Herbert. 'John Milton.' *Dalhousie Review* 8 (1928): 299–315.

de Bruyn, Jan. 'Tribute to Roy Daniells.' *ACUTE News* [Quebec City] (25 May 1976): 1–11.

Denham, Robert D., ed. *The Correspondence of Northrop Frye and Helen Kemp, 1932–1939.* 2 vols. Toronto: University of Toronto Press, 1996.

de Papp Carrington, Ildikó. '"Tales in the Telling": *The Diviners* as Fiction about Fiction.' *Essays on Canadian Writing,* nos. 9–10 (Winter 1977–8): 154–69.

Djwa, Sandra. 'False Gods and the True Covenant: Thematic Continuity between Margaret Laurence and Sinclair Ross.' In *Margaret Laurence: The Writer and Her Critics*. Ed. W.H. New. Toronto: McGraw-Hill Ryerson, 1977. 66–84.

– 'Roy Daniells and Margaret Laurence: Fiction and "So-Called Reality."' Paper presented at the conference 'Margaret Laurence and Her Times.' Winnipeg, 25 October 1997.

Dudek, Louis. Review of *The Chequered Shade*. *Canadian Literature*, no. 16 (Spring 1963): 67–9.

Eliot, T.S. *Collected Poems 1909–1962*. New York: Harcourt Brace, [1963] 1968.

Fairley, Barker. 'Editorial.' *Canadian Forum* 1, no. 1 (Oct. 1920): 3.

– 'Open Letter to Professor Irving Babbitt.' *Canadian Forum* 11, no. 124 (Jan. 1931): 136–8.

Fee, Margery. 'Puck's Green England and the Professor of English: Post-Colonial Fantasies at the University of British Columbia.' *University of Toronto Quarterly* 64 (1995): 398–415.

Fetherling, Douglas. 'Literary Beaver: George Woodcock's Quiet Contribution to CanLit.' *Canadian Forum* 76, no. 867 (March 1998): 23–6.

Finch, Robert. Poems: 'I.' In 'A Letter: To Several Poets Addressed As One.' Unpublished typescript.

Fleck, P.D. 'Tribute to Roy Daniells.' *ACUTE News* (25 May 1976). RDP 18-2.

Fredeman, William E. 'Roy Daniells: 1902–1979.' *Proceedings of the Royal Society of Canada*, ser. 4, 17 (1979): ix–xi.

Frye, Northrop. 'Acta Locals.' *Acta Victoriana* 55, no. 5 (Feb.–March 1931): 38.

– 'The Case against Examinations.' *Acta Victoriana* 56, no. 6 (April 1932): 27–30.

– 'The Personal Legend.' In 'Ned Pratt: Two Recollections.' *Canadian Literature*, no. 21 (Summer 1964): 6–12.

– 'Conclusion.' In *Literary History of Canada*. Ed. Carl F. Klinck. Toronto: University of Toronto Press, 1965. 821–49.

– 'Canada and Its Poetry' and 'Preface to an Uncollected Anthology.' Reprinted in *The Bush Garden: Essays on the Canadian Imagination*. Toronto: Anansi, 1971. 129–43, 163–79.

– *The Great Code: The Bible and Literature*. New York and London: Harcourt Brace Jovanovich, 1981.

Garson, Marjorie. 'ACUTE, the First Twenty-Five Years 1957–1982: A Brief History of the Association of Canadian University Teachers of English.' ACUTE monograph, 1983.

Gill, Linda Wylie. 'Atrocities: The Hamilton Incident at the University of Manitoba, 1944.' Unpublished course paper, 12 March 1990.

Godard, Barbara. '*The Diviners* as Supplement: (M)Othering the Text.' *Open Letter* 7, no. 7 (1990): 26–73.

Gorak, Jan. 'Northrop Frye and the Visionary Canon.' In *The Making of the Modern Canon: Genesis and Crisis of a Literary Idea.* London and Atlantic Heights, NJ: Athlone Press, 1991. 120–52.

Graff, Gerald. *Professing Literature: An Institutional History.* Chicago: University of Chicago Press, 1987.

Groening, Laura Smyth. *E.K. Brown: A Study in Conflict.* Toronto: University of Toronto Press, 1993.

Gutkin, Harry, and Mildred Gutkin. *The Worst of Times: The Best of Times.* Markham, ON: Fitzhenry and Whiteside, 1987.

Hamilton, A.C. *Northrop Frye: Anatomy of His Criticism.* Toronto: University of Toronto Press, 1990.

Harris, Robin S. *English Studies at Toronto: A History.* Toronto: University of Toronto Press, 1988.

Haynal, André. *Depression and Creativity.* New York: International Universities Press, 1976.

Hiebert, Paul. *Sarah Binks.* Toronto: McClelland & Stewart, 1964.

Horney, Karen. *The Neurotic Personality of Our Time.* New York: Norton, 1937.

Hosek, Chaviva M. 'Women at Victoria.' In *From Cobourg to Toronto: Victoria University in Retrospect.* The Sesquicentennial Lectures, 1986. Ed. French S. Goldwin and Gordon L. McLennan. Toronto: Chartes Books, 1989. 58–62.

Huxley, Julian. 'Why I Am a Scientific Humanist?' *The Listener* 30, no. 78 (Dec. 1943): 655–6.

Jasen, Patricia. 'Arnoldian Humanism, English Studies and the Canadian University.' *Queen's Quarterly* 95 (1988): 550–66.

King, James. *The Life of Margaret Laurence.* New York: Alfred A. Knopf, 1997.

Klinck, Carl F., *Giving Canada a Literary History.* Ed. Sandra Djwa. Ottawa: Carleton University Press, 1991.

Klinck, Carl F., gen. ed., and Alfred G. Bailey, Claude Bissell, Roy Daniells, Northrop Frye, and Desmond Pacey, eds. *Literary History of Canada: Canadian Literature in English.* Toronto: University of Toronto Press, 1965.

Kortenaar, Neil ten. 'The Trick of Divining a Postcolonial Canadian Identity: Margaret Laurence between Race and Nation.' *Canadian Literature*, no. 149 (Summer 1996): 11–33.

[Launay, Viviane F.] *The Humanities Research Council of Canada / The Canadian Federation for the Humanities 1943–1983: A Short History.* Ottawa: Canadian Federation for the Humanities, 1983. 1–11.

Laurence, Margaret. 'A Fetish for Love.' In *The Tomorrow-Tamer.* Toronto: McClelland & Stewart, 1963. 78–104.

– *The Diviners.* Toronto: McClelland & Stewart, 1974.

– *Heart of a Stranger.* Toronto: McClelland & Stewart, 1976.

Lennox, John, ed. *Margaret Laurence – Al Purdy: A Friendship in Letters.* Toronto: McClelland & Stewart, 1993.

Lennox, John, and Ruth Panofsky, eds. *Selected Letters of Margaret Laurence and Adele Wiseman.* Toronto: University of Toronto Press. 1997.

Livesay, Dorothy. *Right Hand Left Hand.* Erin, ON: Press Porcépic, 1977.

– *Journey with My Selves: A Memoir 1909–1963.* Vancouver and Toronto: Douglas & McIntyre, 1991.

Lower, Arthur R.M. *My First Seventy-five Years.* Toronto: Macmillan, 1967.

Ludwig, Jack. 'Editorial.' *The Manitoban Literary Supplement,* 18 February 1944.

Mallinson, Jean. 'Paradise Lost.' Unpublished short story in the possession of the author.

Maynard, Fredelle Bruser. *Raisins and Almonds.* Don Mills, ON: PaperJacks, [1964] 1973.

– *The Tree of Life.* Toronto: Viking, 1988.

Maynard, Max. 'Modern Enigma.' *Manitoba Arts Review* 4, no. 3 (Spring 1945): 32–3.

McKillop, A.B. *Matters of Mind: The University in Ontario 1791–1951.* Toronto: University of Toronto Press, 1994.

McLuhan, Marshall, and Harley Parker. *Towards the Vanishing Point: Space in Poetry and Painting.* New York: Harper & Row, 1968.

McPherson, Hugo. 'Roy Daniells: Humanist.' *British Columbia Library Quarterly* 24, no. 1 (July 1960): 29–35.

Mee, Arthur, ed. *The Children's Encyclopaedia.* London: Carmelite House, n.d.

Milton, John. *Complete Poems and Major Prose.* Ed. Merritt Y. Hughes. New York: Odyssey Press, 1957.

Morton, W.L. *One University: A History of the University of Manitoba, 1877–1952.* Toronto: McClelland & Stewart, 1957.

Murray, Heather. *Working in English: History, Institution, Resources.* Toronto: University of Toronto Press. 1996.

Pacey, John Michael David. 'An Unexpected Alliance.' Ph.D. diss., University of British Columbia, 1994.

Pelmanism: The First Principles of Pelmanism. New York: The Pelman Institute of America, 1919/1924.

Prickett, Stephen. *Reading the Text: Biblical Criticism and Literary Theory.* London and Cambridge, MA: Basil Blackwell, 1991.

Reaney, James. 'Two Canadian Poets in Fine New Series.' *Toronto Telegram,* 2 April 1949.

Ross, Sinclair. *As for Me and My House*. Lincoln: University of Nebraska Press, [1941] 1978.

Scott, F.R. 'The Canadian Writers' Conference.' *University of Toronto Quarterly* 25 (1955): 101–2.

– *The Collected Poems*. Toronto: McClelland & Stewart, 1981.

Sedgewick, Eve Kosofsky. *Between Men: English Literature and Male Homosocial Desire*. New York: Columbia University Press, 1985.

Sheinin, Rose. 'The Changing Space for Women in Academe: The "En-gendering" of Knowledge.' In *The Illusion of Inclusion: Women in Post-Secondary Education*. Ed. Jacqueline Stalker and Susan Prentice. Halifax: Fernwood Publishing, 1998, 94–107.

Sheldon, W.H., and S.S. Stevens. *The Varieties of Temperament: A Psychology of Constitutional Differences*. New York: Harper & Brothers Publishers, 1944.

Sirluck, Ernest. *First Generation: An Autobiography*. Toronto: University of Toronto Press, 1996.

Smith, A.J.M. 'Poet.' In *Writing in Canada*. Ed. George Whalley. Toronto: Macmillan, 1956. 13–24.

– 'A Survey of English-Canadian Letters.' *University of Toronto Quarterly* 35 (1965): 107–16.

– *The Classic Shade: Selected Poems*. Introd. by M.L. Rosenthal. Toronto: McClelland & Stewart, 1978.

Smith, Sidney. 'President's Report.' 1942–3. University of Manitoba Special Collections.

– 'President's Report.' 1943–4. University of Manitoba Special Collections.

Spiller, Robert E., et al. *Literary History of the United States*. 4th rev. ed. New York: Macmillan, 1974.

Stevenson, Lionel. 'Literature in an Emerging Nation.' *South Atlantic Quarterly* 64 (1965): 394–9.

Stewart, Lee. *'It's Up to You': Women at UBC in the Early Years*. Vancouver: University of British Columbia Press, 1990.

Stobie, W.G. 'Two Volumes of Canadian Poetry.' *Winnipeg Free Press*, 12 February 1949.

Strouse, Jean. 'Semiprivate Lives.' In *Studies in Biography*. Ed. Daniel Aaron. Cambridge, MA: Harvard University Press, 1978. 113–29.

Styron, William. *Darkness Visible: A Memoir of Madness*. New York: Vintage Books, 1992.

Tippett, Maria. *Emily Carr: A Biography*. Toronto: Oxford University Press, 1979.

Vaughan, Henry. *The Complete Poetry of Henry Vaughan*. Ed. French Fogle. New York: Doubleday, 1964.

Waite, P.B. *Lord of Point Grey: Larry Mackenzie of U.B.C.* Vancouver: University of British Columbia Press, 1987.

Warhaft, Sid. Review of *Milton, Mannerism and Baroque. Queen's Quarterly* 71 (1964): 137–8.

Webb, Phyllis. *Even Your Right Eye.* Toronto: McClelland & Stewart, 1956.

Whalley, George. *Writing in Canada: Proceedings of the Canadian Writers' Conference Held at Queen's Univeristy July 1955.* Toronto: Macmillan, 1956. 8–9.

Will, J.S. 'In Defence of Professor Babbitt.' *Canadian Forum* 11, no. 125 (Feb. 1931): 177–8.

Wiseman, Adele. *The Sacrifice.* Toronto: Macmillan, 1956.

Woodcock, George. 'A View of Canadian Criticism.' *Dalhousie Review* 35 (1955): 216–23.

– 'The Tentative Confessions of a Prospective Editor.' *British Columbia Library Quarterly* 28, no. 1 (July 1959): 17–21.

– *The World of Canadian Writing: Critiques and Recollections.* Vancouver: Douglas & McIntyre, 1980.

– *Taking It to the Letter.* Dunvegan, ON: Quadrant Editions, 1981.

– *Beyond the Blue Mountains: An Autobiography.* Markham, ON: Fitzhenry and Whiteside, 1987.

Woodhouse, A.S.P. 'The Argument of Milton's "Comus."' *University of Toronto Quarterly* 11 (1941): 46–71.

– *The Heavenly Muse: A Preface to Milton.* Ed. Hugh MacCallum. Toronto: University of Toronto Press, 1972.

– ed. *Puritanism and Liberty: Being the Army Debates (1647–9) from the Clarke Manuscripts with Supplementary Documents.* Chicago: University of Chicago Press, [1938] 1968.

Illustration Credits

SPECIAL COLLECTIONS, UNIVERSITY OF BRITISH COLUMBIA: Daniells family, ca. 1914; Garnet Sedgewick, his mother, Bessie, Laurenda and Roy Daniells, 1948; Roy Daniells and Desmond Pacey, 1961

BRITISH COLUMBIA PROVINCIAL ARCHIVES: Jack Shadbolt, John McDonald, Roy Daniells, and Max Maynard, ca. 1926–7

LAURENDA DANIELLS, PRIVATE COLLECTION: Roy Daniells, graduation photo, 1930; Roy Daniells, Winnipeg, 1937; Laurenda Francis, Winnipeg, 1948; Roy Daniells, J.B. Priestley, and Earle Birney, 1956; Laurenda and Roy Daniells and their children on the *Homeric*, 1960

VICTORIA UNIVERSITY (UNIVERSITY OF TORONTO): Northrop Frye, graduation photo, 1933

Index